W9-AAH-181

Pat & Roy Blay
363-4569
19600 Pine Valley

A TIME FOR ASTROLOGY

A TIME FOR *Astrology*

by Jess Stearn

COWARD, McCANN & GEOGHEGAN, INC.

NEW YORK

PRINTED IN THE UNITED STATES OF AMERICA

This book was written for the young of all ages and is dedicated to my brother Sam, who will stay forever young.

"To everything there is a season, and a time to every purpose under the heaven:

"A time to be born, and a time to die; a time to plant, and a time to pluck up that which is planted;

"A time to kill, and a time to heal; a time to break down, and a time to build up;

"A time to weep, and a time to laugh; a time to mourn, and a time to dance;

"A time to cast away stones, and a time to gather stones together; a time to embrace, and a time to refrain from embracing.

"A time to get and a time to lose; a time to keep and a time to cast away;

"A time to rend, and a time to sew; a time to keep silence, and a time to speak;

"A time to love, and a time to hate, a time of war, and a time of peace."

—ECCLESIASTES

Contents

Appendices

THE HOROSCOPE

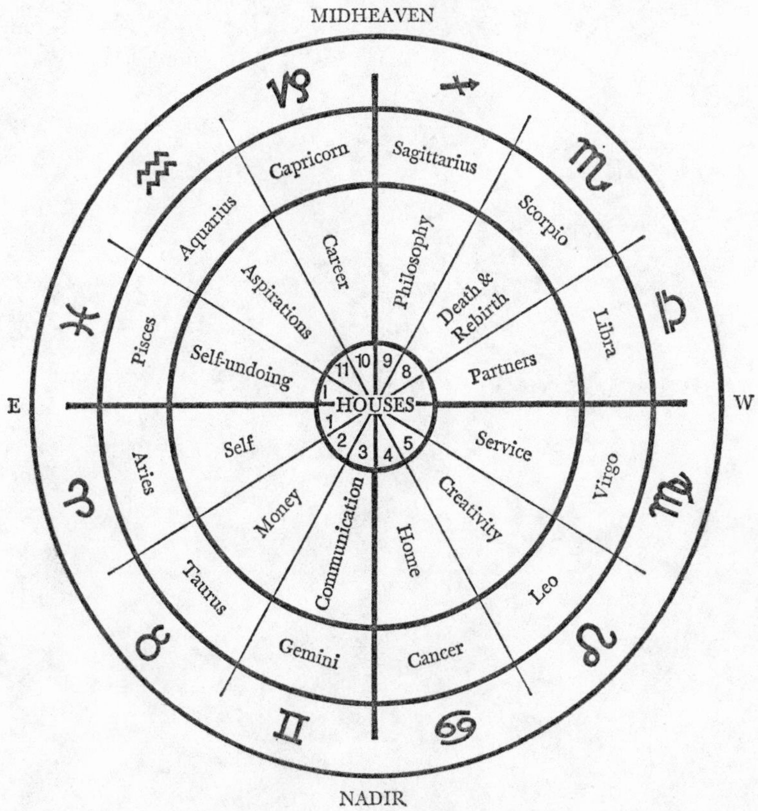

Aries—March 21 to April 19

Taurus—April 20 to May 20

Gemini—May 21 to June 20

Cancer—June 21 to July 22

Leo—July 23 to August 22

Virgo—August 23 to September 22

Libra—September 23 to October 22

Scorpio—October 23 to November 21

Sagittarius—November 22 to December 20

Capricorn—December 21 to January 19

Aquarius—January 20 to February 18

Pisces—February 19 to March 20

1

A Time to Investigate

It was a clear day in June 1970 in sunny California. Kate Lyman, sitting out in her patio and drinking in the heavenly sunshine, was idly scanning her personal horoscope when she suddenly sat up with a start.

In the chart, which she had progressed ahead in time, she saw coming up an aspect that she found unbelievable as she looked around the wooded serenity of her beloved Malibu hills.

There, inescapably, in the fourth house of her chart, the house of the home, in the sign of Pisces, the sign of sorrow and one's undoing —there the planets Mars, standing for fires and accidents, and Saturn, standing for restriction and loss, were in exact conjunction with one another, merging in the same degree to give added force to what they both stood for.

As a keen student of astrology, who gave lessons in its fundamentals because she believed in it so strongly, Kate Lyman had no question in her mind as to what Saturn and Mars together in the fourth house meant.

Having her own Sun in Sagittarius, which is a visionary sign, Kate Lyman immediately put aside her chart, walked into her house, reached for the telephone, and called her insurance agent.

"I want to increase my fire insurance," she said.

Three months later, as the flames, fanned by searing winds from the desert, raced through the Malibu hills, Mrs. Lyman grabbed up her six-year-old twins, her small menagerie of cats, and a few odds and ends, and beat the flames to Pacific Coast Highway on her way to safety.

As she had foreseen, the affliction was to her fourth house, and not to the first house of her person or the fifth of her children. Her home in Malibu's beautiful Sierra Retreat, overlooking the Pacific, had been leveled, and all its furnishings and her possessions destroyed. The only home spared on the street was that of a contractor, who had watched the approach of the flames, and then philosophically gone fishing, while the blaze raged up and down the Malibu hills, burning out scores of homes.

"His fourth house must have been favorably aspected," said astrologer Lyman, wiping away the suspicion of a tear as she surveyed the smoldering ruins of a home on which she had lavished much love and care.

Then she marched off, chin up, to gather the charred pieces of her life and plan for the new home she would need—and the extra insurance money that her devotion to astrology had ensured her.

Kate Lyman's prediction was by no means unusual. Astrologers are forever making uncanny predictions for themselves and others. Astrologer Sydney Omarr, when consulted by Hollywood star Kim Novak, advised her that she would not have to break a contract, and risk a suit, to get out of a picture she didn't want to make. Scanning a chart drawn up for the occasion, the astrologer foresaw:

"Something will happen to take you quite naturally out of the picture. So just go on location abroad, and plunge into your work as if nothing was wrong. And it will work out."

In England, Miss Novak inadvertently fell off a horse, injured herself, and the studio had no choice but to take her out of the picture.

As fascinating as they are, predictions are only a small part of astrology. There is hardly a phase of human activity astrology hasn't touched upon. Astrologers constantly advise people when to marry or separate, make a deal, or take a trip. There is a right time, they say, for every human endeavor. For, as the Bible says, there is a time to love and a time to hate, a time to live and a time to die.

My study of astrology, as the psychic, revolved about its relevance to life. What good was it if it didn't help people? As an abstract science, it was meaningless, but there was a whole school of astrologers, busy with their little esoteric charts, who strove to limit its scope to their own special interest and disdainfully looked down at what they called fortune telling.

And yet I have seen astrologers prepare their subjects for good events and bad—even to the deaths of loved ones—by not only foreseeing the future, but encouraging people's acceptance of it through this demonstration of the inevitability of human affairs. For in foreshadowing the destiny of man, astrology at the same time often provides the insight and self-knowledge that reconciles him to his place in the universe.

"All we can do is handle things," a wise old astrologer told me. "We can't stop the rain, but we can carry an umbrella—or stay indoors."

As my study continued, I discovered that there are many methods of working out charts—the Placidian or unequal house system, the sidereal, and the equal house system—but in every instance, it is still the planetary aspects, the positions of the planets in angular relationship to one another, that apparently give astrologers their message.

It was difficult at first to accept the concept that planets millions of miles away could influence our lives to a greater degree than our closest intimates—so much so that the ancients gave these distant affectors personalities as colorful today as before the time of Christ.

Saturn, I learned, is cold and restrictive, the teacher, and Saturn in one's Sun sign, as he had been in mine for two years or so, could be painfully impeding to one's aspirations, though I consoled myself with the astrological precept that I was growing through adversity.

Jupiter is expansive, the planet of plenty, a good friend, unless adversely aspected by heavy angular aspects that could make a pessimist even out of this natural optimist. And so it goes—Mercury, Venus, Mars, Pluto, Uranus, Neptune, and the Sun and the Moon. All mean something, separately, and collectively, and the sum total of their aspects—their oppositions, squares, conjunctions, trines and sextiles—speaks a language of its own.

While science, generally, frowns on astrology—not having explored it pragmatically—there have been scientists who conceded that the planets, like the Sun and the Moon, somehow affect human activity. And there has been some sign of scientific recognition. One of contemporary astrology's proudest hours came when ten members of the American Federation of Astrologers were invited to Cape Kennedy for the memorable moon shot of Apollo XII on November 14, 1969. And being astrologers, they naturally couldn't resist doing charts of the launching, based on its scheduled takeoff time. Two days before the actual launching, Frances Sakoian, a Boston astrologer, announced that the launch chart showed there would be trouble with the fuel. And just before the launch, to the great consternation of officials, one of the fuel tanks had to be replaced. "Mars," an astrologer explained casually, "was in the first house square Saturn in the third house of communications and short trips and Venus in the ninth of long trips." However, Mars was favorably aspected trine at a 120-degree angle to Uranus, the planet of the Space Age, and it was comfortably foreseen that the flight would be an epochal success.

The invitation to the astrologers was readily explained, if one considers the report by the French newspaper, *France Dimanche*, that the three moon men, Armstrong, Collins and Aldrin, were chosen for their mission only after their charts had shown they were the right men for the job. "The quality of the astrologer who cast these horoscopes cannot be doubted," the newspaper reported. "He was Professor Lester, an attaché to the service of science of the United Nations, who had been collaborating for many months with the directors of NASA [National Aeronautics and Space Administration]."

As in other fields, there have been frauds, charlatans and incompetents, but astrology, defended by such giants of astronomy as Kepler, Newton and Galileo, still has no better testimonial than its own workability.

The late Evangeline Adams, the foremost astrologer of her generation, and descendant of two Presidents, had no trouble confounding astrology's critics. Once a caller gave her the birth dates of two young people, and asked what she saw in their futures.

Miss Adams quickly worked out the charts, then pushed them aside.

"There's no use reading these horoscopes," she said.

"Why not?" asked the visitor.

"Because both of these children are dead—by drowning."

The caller's mouth fell open incredulously. She had given the astrologer the natal dates of the two children of the famous dancer Isadora Duncan. Both children had perished when their mother's car had plummeted out of control into a river.

But while the uninformed jeered, the New International Encyclopedia had this to report:

"The natural tendency of the ignorant and the credulous to seek for insight into the future has allowed a multitude of quacks to trade upon the name of astrology and to give the impression that it is beneath contempt. It is well to point out, however, that the predictions of the better class astrologers are not merely haphazard guesses, as is frequently supposed, but are based upon rigidly scientific determination from observed phenomena, according to definite rules of interpretation."

As well as presumably influencing individual affairs, the planets herald broad changes in the human drama. Saturn moving into Taurus, which rules the second house of money, in the spring of 1969 marked the beginning of a recession and a break in the stock market; Uranus, the planet of change, passing into the sign of Libra in the seventh house of partnerships, augured a new revolutionary conception of marriage; Neptune, the planet of movies and television, as well as illusion and deception, moving from the sensuous sign of Scorpio into spiritual Sagittarius in November 1970, presumably ushered in a fourteen-year renaissance of the spiritual.

Even the rising popularity of astrology itself was attributed to the planets. For when Uranus, the symbol of the Aquarian Age and astrology, in 1966 conjoined the planet Pluto, signifying the masses, in Virgo, the sign of service, astrology began its meteoric rise, staging a spectacular comeback after being stigmatized for centuries as a product of the Dark Ages.

The comeback was on a wide front. Astrology intruded even into politics. In 1966, during a heated California gubernatorial campaign, Governor Edmund (Pat) Brown accused Republican Ronald Reagan of using astrology to beat him, and Reagan, an Aquarian, merely smiled and kept blasting away as if victory was assured, and so it was. After his election, Governor Reagan was inaugurated at an unusual hour, just after midnight, but when astrology was mentioned, the former actor merely smiled.

With timing so important, astrology takes credit for the unprecedented success of the musical *Hair,* which not only saluted astrology with the hit song, "Aquarius (the Moon is in the Seventh House)," but had an astrologer, Marie Crummere, of New York, chart its various openings.

Nobody was surprised when the theatrical colony–Marlene Dietrich, Robert Cummings, Anne Francis, Ann Miller–consulted astrologers, as others would their psychiatrists. But the tycoons–the Morgans, Vanderbilts, the James J. Hills–and stockbrokers, doctors, and lawyers also found reassuring counsel in the stars.

In the realm of finance, astrology's timing has often spelled the difference between profit and loss, as so many Chicago businessmen knew from advisories from astrologer Katherine de Jersey. And the Indian astrologer, M. K. Gandhi, traveled three continents telling his clients when to duck in and out of the market.

Astrology, as Doris Chase Doane of Los Angeles has shown so often, can pick out a person's hidden talent and direct him into the proper career. In times of stress, it has encouraged many. In 1968, actress-dancer Ann Miller's career was at a standstill, but Hollywood astrologer Edith Randall predicted a new success cycle lasting seven years. Ann took heart, and shortly thereafter had her greatest success with the musical *Mame*. And she confidently looked forward through 1975. "After all," she explained, "everything she told me before had come true."

Large corporations, as well as individuals, have made use of astrology, though some call it astrophysics, astrodynamics, astral cycles. RCA Communications, concerned about its shortwave radio messages, employed technician John Nelson to plot charts anticipating disruptive magnetic storms, but wouldn't call it astrology, though his storm warnings all hinged on the influence of the planets. Electrical engineer David Williams, cable purchasing manager of the New York utility Consolidated Edison, turned astrologer to anticipate periodic slumps attributed to changing planetary aspects–and bought miles of costly cable at depressed prices, while unwitting superiors marveled at his business acumen.

Williams not only plotted the price trends of commodities and the stock market, but did birth charts for many companies. For Phillip Morris he correctly predicted a stock rise in a falling market in early 1970, and similarly advised officials of the New York Telephone Company they would get some of the rate increase they had applied for.

"The telephone company," Williams observed, "was a Gemini,

born on June 18, and it was ruled by Mercury, the planet of communication. How could it miss?"

I had no trouble relating to astrologers and this was readily explained by my own chart. Uranus, the symbol of astrology, was my rising planet, falling in my first house of Aquarius, where it properly belonged as the ruler of that sign. Moreover, it conjoined my Jupiter in Aquarius for an extra lift. My Mercury was in Aries in the third house of communication, and it was favorably aspected–sextile at 60 degrees–to Saturn in Gemini, which indicates a certain profundity not elsewhere apparent. Mercury was also sextile to Uranus, and so I obviously could be trusted to deal with this subject in an honorable manner.

The skeptics were not as kind.

As my study continued, with classes and consultations with the world's great astrologers, I naturally became aware of the amused reaction of friends to my growing interest, and I supposed the reaction would be no different among the uninformed generally.

Because of greater awareness perhaps, the famous and the successful often seemed more prone to accept the magic of the stars.

Evangeline Adams once asked a famous client, naturalist John Burroughs, why he believed in astrology.

His eyes turned toward the heavens.

"Why shouldn't I? Everything in the universe influences everything else, so naturally the stars must influence man."

Down through the ages, the unbelievers scoffed at Christ and his miracles, ridiculed Columbus and his claim that the world was round, flouted the concept that man would one day fly, or that, folly of follies, he would set foot upon the moon.

What did it matter that Christ came in fulfillment of a Jupiter-Saturn conjunction with Mars in Pisces, that he symbolized the new Piscean Age, the sign of compassion and martyrdom, and that his banner was that of Pisces the Fish?

Was it accident that He chose twelve apostles, one for each sign of the zodiac, to represent every shade and grade of human being there was?

Was it accident that the God of Moses made the heavens for signs and portents, and that the Bible was laden with astrology, even to the three Wise Men, who, in the most recent translation of the New Testament, became the three astrologers?

I was intrigued, with others, as Neil Armstrong, a Leo, and the first man to touch upon the Moon, addressed an uncertain Congress in astrological terms:

"We are in the Aquarian Age."

Was this Age not touched off, as some felt, on February 4, 1962, when the Sun and the Moon, and the five planets visible to the naked eye—Saturn, Jupiter, Mercury, Venus and Mars—were in one sign, the sign of Aquarius? Uranus was in opposition to all these heavenly bodies, and only Pluto and Neptune were uncritically aspected.

Was it not almost prophetic that an Aquarian President, Franklin Roosevelt, seeming intuitively to sense the shift from the Piscean to the Aquarian Age, changed the inaugural date of American presidents from March 4—Pisces—to January 20, the first day of Aquarius? And was not the Aquarian Age, with its symbol of the water-bearer, reflective of the recent trend to house gardening, organic foods, and ecology?

Just as man, through experience, through trial and error, had fastened upon the clock to signify the passage of time, so had he evolved the twelve signs of the zodiac, representing every type of person, and the twelve houses, representing every type of activity.

I soon knew enough about astrology not to judge people by their Sun signs alone. There were innumerable other factors, beginning with the rising sign—the position of the Sun in relation to the hour of birth—and the position of the natal Moon, which together with the Sun sign reflected that individual's personality and potential. And yet any one Sun sign did frequently express qualities more reflective of a certain personality than another did.

I had noticed certain similarities among individuals of the same sign, and these similarities enabled me at times to appear the magician. One day I met a Hollywood model named Edythe Girard, who in her dreamy blue-eyed beauty reminded me of another fashion model named Joan Scott—a Cancer, born on July 4.

Miss Girard asked if I could guess her sign.

Her smile, the tilt of her head, the heart-shaped, moonlike symmetry of her features, was again a striking reminder of Miss Scott.

"You are a Moon Child, a Cancer," I suggested.

She looked at me with surprise.

"Right."

I looked very wise.

"But you would never guess the date?" she ventured with a Joan Scott-like smile.

I had nothing to lose.

"July 4," I ventured.

Her jaw dropped.

"How did you ever get that?" she exclaimed.

On another occasion, after reading that property-loving Taureans, generally bull-like in appearance, gravitated to banking, I visited a bank in Malibu by the Pacific, and became engaged in conversation with the branch manager, Lauren Averill. Taking in his broad shoulders, bullish neck, solid mien, and his easy manner of being at home, I asked casually, "Are you a Taurus?"

"Yes," he said, "why do you ask?"

I mentioned that, astrologically, Taureans made good bankers.

"Do they procrastinate, too?" he asked.

Being a Taurus, I was an authority on the difficulty of getting down to things.

"Yes, but once started, there's no stopping them."

He sighed, looking at the golden sunshine bathing the beautiful hills outside his window.

"Well, I better get to it."

In the traditional conception of astrology, the Sun signs epitomize certain specialized qualities. Aries says, I am; Taurus, I have; Gemini, I think; Cancer, I feel; Leo, I command; Virgo, I dissect; Libra, I balance; Scorpio, I desire; Sagittarius, I see; Capricorn, I use; Aquarius, I know; Pisces, I believe.

Every sign has a good and bad side. Aries begins the wheel of the chart on the eastern horizon at the vernal equinox on March 21. Obviously a pioneering sign, it is enterprising and practical, but when crossed, impatient and insubordinate. Taurus is trustworthy and persevering, industrious, but bullheaded, domineering and indolent. Gemini is inquisitive, bright, facile, and also flighty, impulsive, unmotivated; Cancer, home-loving, maternal, sociable, and vain, acquisitive and moody. Leo is outspoken, magnetic and generous, and arrogant, overconfident, and promiscuous; Virgo, analytical, efficient, methodical and cold, calculating and hypercritical. Libra is judicious, refined, artistic, and deceitful, indecisive, loquacious; Scorpio, dauntless, penetrating, ambitious, and secretive, vengeful, sensual. Sagittarius is prophetic, cheerful, charitable, and haughty, brusque, extravagant; Capricorn, dignified, prudent and well organized, and bossy, glum and egotistical; Aquarius, humanitarian, inventive and sophisticated, and irrational, gullible and tyrannical; Pisces, idealistic, intuitive and inspired, and confused, indolent, and self-pitying.

The language of astrologers is pretty much what it has always been. In three or four thousand years, the zodiac, the twelve-sign circle forming the birth chart, has changed very little. The Roman versifier, Manilius, living at the time of Christ, drew on ancient lore as he traveled poetically through the signs, assigning to each its traditional rulership over a specific area of the body.

> "The Ram (Aries) defends the head; the neck the Bull (Taurus)
> "The Arms, bright Twins (Gemini), are subject to your rule.
> "The shoulder Leo, and the Crab's (Cancer) obeyed
> "In the breast, and in the guts the modest maid (Virgo).
> "In the buttocks Libra, Scorpio warms desires
> "In private parts, and spreads unruly fires.
> "The thighs the Centaur (Sagittarius),
> "And the Goat (Capricorn) commands the knees,
> "The parted legs in moist Aquarius meet,
> "And Pisces gives protection to the feet."

Just as the signs received these attributes through long observation, so were special qualities given the twelve houses. Each house had its own significance. The first was you, yourself; the second, money; the third, communication, the mind; the fourth, the home; the fifth, creativity; the sixth, public service; the seventh, partnerships; the eighth, death and regeneration; the ninth, philosophy; the tenth, career; the eleventh, friendships and aspirations; the twelfth, self-undoing, hidden things, the subconscious.

Intriguingly, the ancients knew more about the planetary rulers of these signs and houses than we do. Joseph, of the coat of many colors, that wise astrologer who correctly prophesied the seven fat years and the seven lean by an obvious Saturn quadrant for the Pharaoh of Egypt, spoke of twelve planets and lights, including Sun,

Moon and Earth. But to this day, with our powerful telescopes, we know only ten, and so double up Mars to rule Aries and to co-rule Scorpio with Pluto. Mercury rules both Gemini and Virgo, and Venus both Taurus and Libra. Eventually, as of old, the harmony of a ruling planet for every sign may be consummated with the discovery of Vulcan, a planet now only hinted at. With the assignment of Vulcan to Virgo, volatile Mercury would rule volatile Gemini, Pluto, the planet of regeneration, would single-rule Scorpio, the sign of death and regeneration, and planet Earth would be assigned to solid, stable Taurus. Venus, the planet of beauty, would apply only to Libra, the symbol of beauty.

While nobody to this day knows for sure how astrology works, there are plenty of theories.

"Astrology," postulated scientist-astrologer David Williams, "is an empiric science based upon the following fundamental principles. The Sun is the center of our solar system. From it emanate not only physical forces such as light, heat, magnetism, electricity, cosmic rays, but psychic, mental and spiritual forces. These forces impinge on and are modified by similar forces emanating from the planets, which, in their motions around the Sun, form aspects or configurations among themselves to the Sun and the Earth. These forces are further colored or modified by the actions of the zodiac, through which the heavenly bodies and the Earth move.

"In natal astrology a chart is prepared giving the position of the heavenly bodies at the instant of birth. This moment is considered to be the time the newborn infant takes its first breath, and its importance derives from the fact, scientifically demonstrated by Dr. G. R. Wait of the Department of Terrestrial Magnetism of the Carnegie Institution, Washington, D.C., that the air we breathe consists of electrically charged particles. It is believed that these particles are modified by the celestial rays effective at that instant of time and at that particular place, and hence have a profound effect upon the psychic, mental and physical bodies of the newborn infant.

"The basic heavenly pattern impressed upon these bodies at the time of birth is subject to modification by the subsequent movements of the heavenly bodies throughout the life of the individual."

There have been many other theories about how astrology works. Carl Jung, the distinguished humanist, advanced the concept of synchronicity, in which the movements of the celestial bodies correspond significantly with terrestrial events, without in any way being a causative agent. And Rudolf Tomaschek, professor of theoretical physics at the University of Munich in Germany, propounded:

1. That the planets, functioning as a macrocosm, influencing the earthly microcosm that is man, precipitate events ripe for manifestation, much as a lighted match precipitates a fire, without having much to say whether that fire will destroy a piece of paper or a city.

2. That the planets symbolize vital cosmic forces which harmonize with time and space in unfolding an animated universe, with a spiritual coherence that draws on the whole cosmos for its expression of unification of all things in that cosmos.

One thing was sure. The planets, including the Earth and the Sun and the Moon, were constantly interacting, and the resulting sunspot activity alone was sufficient to affect man. A. L. Tchijevsky, a Moscow professor of history, assembled a record in which he correlated solar activity from 500 B.C. to the year 1900 with changes that supposedly brought about wars, revolutions and migrations. Solar activity, apparent in showers of sunspots, caused great unrest, he held, encouraging the Jews of Russia to begin a period of migration, upsetting the conservative cabinets in England, and triggering the typhus and smallpox epidemics. The professor was sent to Siberia for his pains, since Stalin, then supreme dictator of Russia, decided that it was dangerous to make it appear as though sunspots–93 million miles away –had more impact on the Russian masses than a Capricorn Stalin.

In time, some astrologers believe, this art-science, through the endorsement of scientific research methods, may become the religion of the true sophisticates. It will not replace the conventional Christianity or Judaism, as it has not replaced Buddhism and Hinduism in areas where it is totally accepted, but it will modify these faiths and perhaps reinforce them in presenting a comprehensive picture of a limitless universe in which every person and event, regardless of how minuscule, is predictably a part of a universal order which clearly has a guiding intelligence.

"Acceptance of astrology," observed the Australian researcher L. Furze-Morrish, "would make it very difficult not to accept the existence of a Universal Mind–a Total Intelligence–behind all worlds. Such a pattern of order requires some kind of intelligence to explain it. In fact, this is the main argument against materialism, which is able to accept that an ordered, precise and time-setting universe originally came out of nothing by chance."

Though reluctant to emphasize prognostications for fear of being dismissed as fortune tellers, astrologers traditionally foretold changes in man and his environment through the symbolism of progressions, the movements of the transiting planets, and shrewd insight into the natal chart itself, as nothing happens to an individual, astrologically, unless its potential is clearly outlined at birth. This potential extends to everything under the Sun, including death.

Astrologer Carl Payne Tobey, writing about his Tucson neighbor, the great astrologer Grant Lewi, pointed out that Lewi, at 48, had seen his own imminent death in his chart, and since he didn't work with progressions—rating the planets ahead a day for a year—he had foreseen it in the transiting planets.

He was a Gemini, and transiting Saturn in Virgo on July 14, 1951, obversely squared his Sun in aspects to the fourth and eighth houses, both often related to death. Looking at his aspects, Grant Lewi changed the habits of a lifetime, and went out and bought some life insurance. It was quite providential, his foreshadowing of the destiny pattern he saw in his own chart. For, besides taking care of his widow and children, it made it philosophically possible for him to foresee his own end with equanimity. It was inevitable, as he saw it, and it rhymed with other events of a universal nature that were reflected as an orderly process through astrological symbols.

He died in the early morning hours of July 14, 1951, having refused first to make any appointments for the month of August. Death came peacefully, for there was no doubt in Grant Lewi's mind that life was a continuous, never-ending cycle.

He left many friends, and a practical legacy of his own skill:

"He didn't believe in paying for life insurance," said Tobey, "because he said he had no intention of dying right away. Right after his 49th birthday, he died suddenly of a cerebral hemorrhage. With astrology he saved himself 30 years of premiums. He paid one premium, and the insurance company did the rest."

And with astrology, working out a horoscope from an individual's time and place of birth, Tobey could do as well as his distinguished colleague. Scanning the chart he had just drawn up for the daughter of a prominent Tucson businessman, Tobey called the father in some alarm, and warned that the girl was a potential mental case on the verge of an imminent crackup.

A few days later, he received a grateful letter from the father, thanking him for enabling them to get her to a psychiatrist in time for the treatment they never suspected she needed. She had been living a life of quiet desperation in her inability to communicate an inner conflict that had brought her to the brink of suicide.

So often when an astrologer makes precise predictions skeptics are quick to claim it was not through astrology but by psychic powers. However, though many astrologers have some intuitive flair, as do some doctors, writers, engineers, there are aspects enough to justify any kind of a prediction. Some are based on the simplest conjunctions.

Years ago, Ted Thackrey Sr., a reporter on the New York *Post,* was considering leaving for a job in Shanghai. But it was a troubled period in China–April 1937–and a newsman friend, Ed Dolby, suggested Thackrey consult the astrologer, Ed Wagner, whose astrology column appeared in the *Post.*

Wagner, now editor of *Horoscope* Magazine, checked out Thackrey's birth date. It was November 17. He then produced a copy of the *Post,* which gave the Post's founding date as November 16, 1801.

The two Suns were practically conjunct, the nature of one synchronizing with the other.

"Since your birth date is practically that of the paper's," Wagner said, "it will be to your advantage to stay on. By November you should have a promotion, and you could become the top editor in time." He smiled. "But if you haven't been promoted by the end of November, pay no attention to my prediction."

Late that November, the two ran into each other in the hall, and Thackrey told the astrologer he had just been made feature editor.

In June 1939, new owners took over the *Post,* and Wagner's astrology column was dropped. But Thackrey stayed on, and eventually became editor-in-chief.

Without the psychic, Bombay-born M. K. Gandhi, who commutes between London, New York, and Los Angeles, has shown how precisely astrology pinpoints practical affairs. In London, before a professional doubter, P. G. Pendsay, secretary of the Commonwealth Correspondents' Association, Gandhi predicted Nixon's election by a hairline margin, and the ouster from power, on March 26, 1969, of the Pakistan premier Ayub Khan. The prediction, made two years before, was off by 24 hours, Ayub Khan being forced out on March 25.

Gandhi was a specialist in market trends, profiting with his principals when he predicted correctly. During the first week of May 1970, before a New York group including the publicist Roland Gammon, he forecast the market would reach a seven-year low in the Dow-Jones averages on May 26, but would rebound the next day, the 27th, and continue its surge for a week anyway.

His accuracy drew an accolade from Gammon:

"This prediction not only came true, but in the estimation of the professional witnesses amounts to a fantastically accurate projection of your astrological skills."

Quite often in the area of current events, astrologers turn to the planets rather than the newspapers or TV to learn what is happening and why. In August of 1968, astrologer Franka Moore of Los Angeles concluded that Richard Nixon would be elected President that November because of transiting Uranus stimulating his first house. For Uranus, the planet of change, she deduced, had been changing his personality and making him more outgoing. "Uranus is the awakener and the emancipator," she observed, "bringing new currents of thought, increasing the intuition and elevating the mind." And it was not only in his first house, which related to the President-to-be's personality, but activating a favorable Sun-Saturn trine in his natal chart, especially effective since Saturn ruled his Sun sign and, the Sun represents the deep, underlying core of the individual.

And when Uranus passed from Virgo into a seven-year transit of Libra in October 1968, it practically assured his election, since it stirred up his Capricorn Sun in coming to a square to that active cardinal sign. It also significantly trined his natal Uranus by exact degree at the time of the November election, suddenly reversing his fortune in dramatic Uranus fashion.

Astrologically, his nomination was assured on the first ballot. In a chart set for the Republican convention, the Moon on that day was in Capricorn, his Sun sign, and the ascendant of the chart was also his own, Virgo. "The individual whose chart fits the situation of the moment is usually the winner," observed astrologer Moore.

Spiro Agnew

Nov. 9, 1918

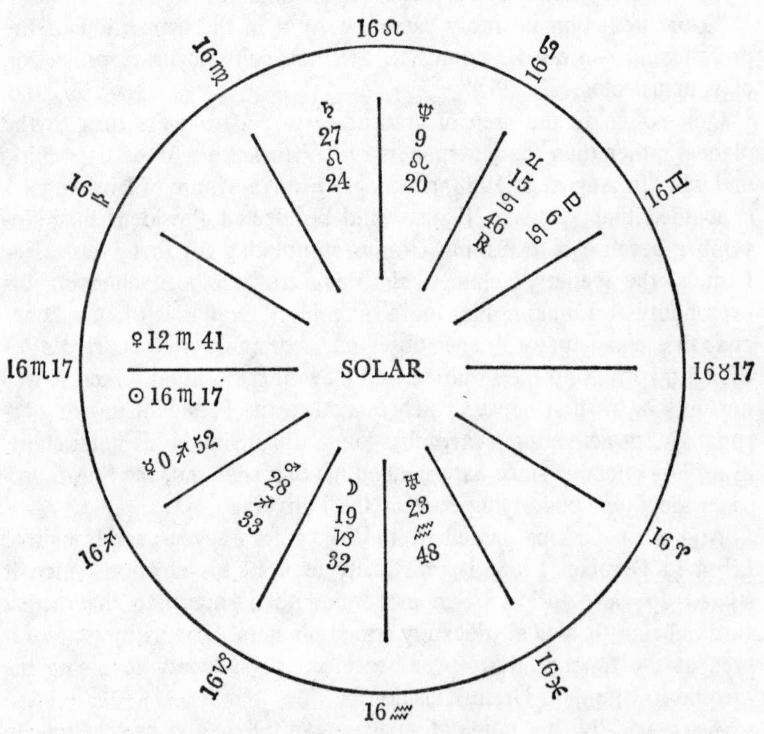

And Nixon, without realizing it, had made a very wise choice, astrologically speaking, in his running mate. For even before their election, Franka Moore decided they would have a remarkably harmonious relationship. "Spiro Agnew, born November 9, 1918, has a Scorpio Sun in favorable sextile (60 degree aspect) to Nixon's Sun. And his Moon in his solar chart is in the exact degree of Nixon's Sun —indicating a complete blending of personalities and aspirations.

"Any two people, in whatever relationship," she stressed, "who were fortunate enough to have this particular exchange of aspects would be blessed indeed."

Astrology has often thrown light on current events otherwise shrouded in mystery. After the murder in Los Angeles of actress Sharon Tate and four companions, astrologer Moore did what astrologers call a horary chart of the event, distributing the planets through the twelve houses of the zodiac as if the time of the question asked was the birth of a person. In this instance the question was:

"Who killed Sharon Tate?"

And the answer came back, correctly as it turned out: five people, under the influence of drugs, with the indication that they had scattered around the country, but would eventually be apprehended.

Miss Moore also did a birth chart or horoscope of the accused killer, Charles Manson, after he was apprehended, and of his alleged partner in murder, Susan Atkins.

Manson's birth had been recorded to the minute, November 12, 1934, at 4:40 P.M., in Cincinnati (Ohio) General Hospital. His birth name was Charles Milles Moddox. His mother was 18-year-old Kathleen Moddox; his natural father, William Manson, whose name he later took.

The chart showed Manson with a difficult childhood. His Moon in Aquarius, reflecting his home environment as the ruler of his fourth house, was square by degree to his natal Mercury in Scorpio, indicating that an irascible, eccentric personality would have developed out of this environment. As if this wasn't enough, his mind-ruling Mercury, accented by its rulership of the third house of the mind, negatively squared Pluto, in its afflicted state the planet of mobs and the underworld. Pluto also ruled his Scorpio Sun and governed the fourth house of his adult home—the Manson "family." And a Scorpio Sun, adversely aspected, was a clear reflection of Scorpio's role of avenger.

Charles Milles Moddox (Charles Manson)

Nov. 12, 1934

Cincinnati, Ohio

4:40 p.m.

Monday

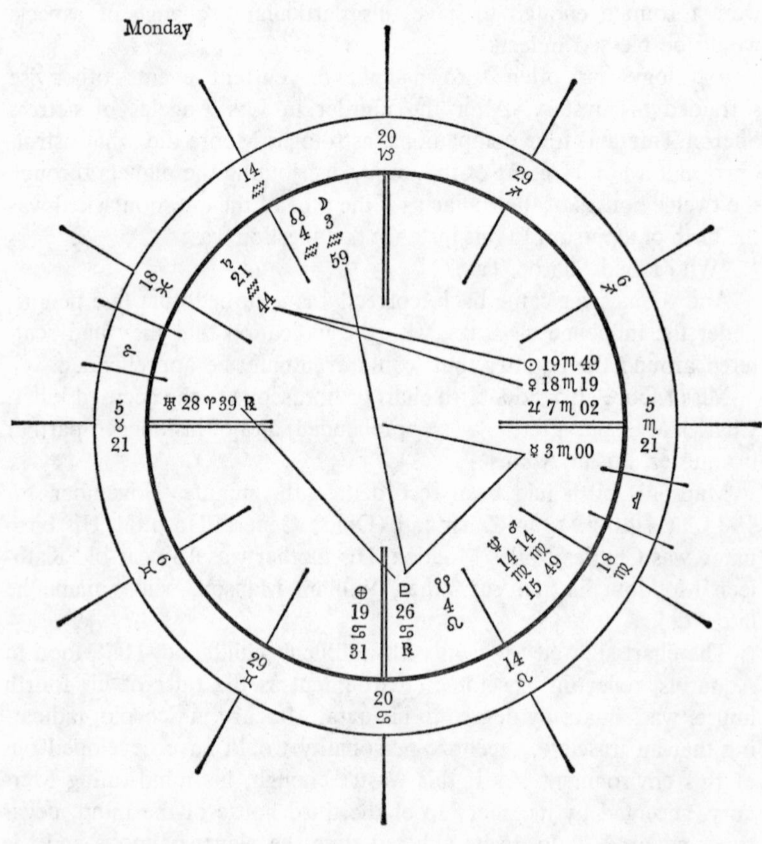

Susan Atkins

May 8, 1948

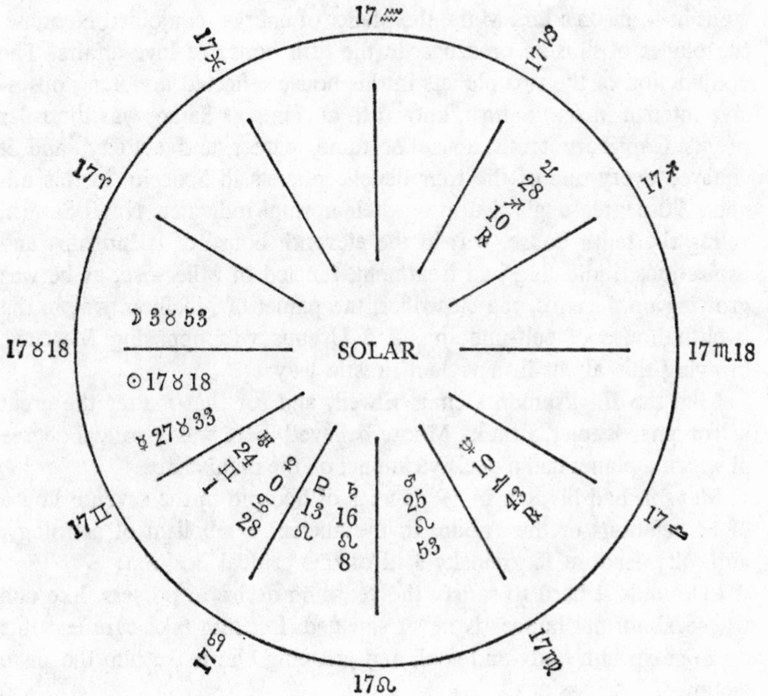

Susan Atkins, Manson's prime confederate in crime, was his opposite sign, a Taurus, the opposites complementing one another in this case. And since Manson had Taurus rising, this being the position of the Sun in relation to the hour of birth, the two were doubly complemented, the personality of one, the ascendant, blending with the Sun or deeper self of the other.

Manson was a strong Scorpio, with four planets, the Sun, Venus, Jupiter and Mercury all in this sign of sensuality and psychic power, presumably accounting for the magnetic sway this tiny bearded man had over his coterie of hippies.

Accenting the Scorpionic sexual motivation which seemed a constant in Manson's life, Mars, the planet of energy, conjoined Neptune, the planet of illusion or drugs, in the fifth house of love affairs. The conjunction of the two planets in this house reflected a violent, obsessive interest in sex. Saturn, known to ancients as Satan, was the ruler of his Capricorn tenth house of fame, career and activity, and it squared every one of the four benefic planets in Scorpio, in this adverse 90-degree angle distorting their normal influence. Natal Saturn, ruling the tenth house, was in the eleventh house of friendships and aspirations, indicating bad treatment, fancied or otherwise, as he was growing up. Uranus, the electrifier, the planet of rebellion, was in the twelfth house of self-undoing, and Uranus was opposing Mercury, bringing this about in a violent drastic way.

Like the Englishman Dennis Elwell, and for that matter the great astronomer Kepler, Franka Moore believed there was a critical degree at which a planet had a decisive impact on the natal chart.

Manson had his Sun in 19 degrees of Scorpio in the seventh house of associations or the public. In the ancient symbolism of astrology, authority Isadore Kozminsky said of this critical position:

"He finds it hard to satisfy the yearning desire to possess, like one whose abnormal hunger is never satisfied. Let him take care lest this craze grasp him body and soul, and grasping him make him the slave victim of his passions."

However trivial its expression, astrology is impressive as it works.

One day in June 1970, shortly before she had worked out her own progressed chart to her material advantage, astrology teacher Kate Lyman went about the job of purchasing a rug for her Malibu home in a smart shop in the Westwood section of Los Angeles.

The salesman was a tall, robust-appearing young man with a bull neck and hearty manner. After the usual skirmishing, a white shag rug was shown, and Kate decided to buy it if a six by nine section could be cut from a nine by eighteen.

The salesman said he would check and let her know. The next day on the telephone, she complained about the delay and the salesman said that he found it strange that a woman would walk into a shop and expect to buy a white shag rug to her specifications out of stock.

His brusqueness rubbed Kate the wrong way. "I suppose I'm naïve, but I don't go about buying rugs every day."

"That's all right," he relented. "I guess I'm headstrong."

"When were you born?" she asked.

"I'm a Taurus."

"That's obvious, but the day and year?" she said, reaching for her ephemeris, the astrologer's bible of planetary positions.

"May 18, 1936, in Denver, Colorado."

"Ah," she said, "you have the Moon in Aries."

"What does that mean?"

"That you're headstrong, as you say."

He grunted unhappily.

"And you also have Mercury in Gemini, the planet and sign of communication, so you should make a good salesman."

"That's nice of you," he purred.

"But then," she said with typical Sagittarian bluntness, "the Mercury is square to Neptune, the planet of deception and illusion, so you're probably also a pathological liar, so I probably won't get my rug when you promised it."

He groaned. "Lady, it's too much for me. I'm going across the street for a drink."

With the inquisitiveness of her Scorpio rising and Moon in Scorpio, astrologer Lyman thumbed through her ephemeris for the Jupiter in the salesman's chart. Jupiter represents excess, and it seemed to her that he was reacting excessively, and then she looked for Neptune, which represented escapism.

"Sure enough," she said, "I found Neptune in Virgo, the sign of work and service, square to Jupiter in Sagittarius, emphasizing this excess on the job."

But then she sighed in astrological satisfaction, reconciled to his behavior.

"What else would one expect from a poor Taurus with an afflicted Neptune?"

2

A Time for History

When the infinite Lord made the Sun, and the Sun gave off its first glow of light, warming that small planet we know as Earth, that was the beginning of astrology.

Before he could read or write, primitive man in his helpless nakedness scanned the skies, anxiously searching for signs of rain or snow, and in time he began to notice the cycles of the Sun in relationship to the seasons, and the phases of the Moon in terms of his moods and emotions. Long before the seven-day week or the 365-day year, the Moon and the Sun were his calendars, and he learned to count on the regularity of their appearance.

He learned to plant his seeds in the spring with the New Moon and to harvest with the Full Moon in the fall. There was a time, too, he found, to mate, and a time for children, a time to look for new hunting grounds, and a time to stay by the fire.

As the eons passed, man learned to tell the visible planets from the twinkling stars and, as he learned to write and make pictures, he gave these planets names and symbols that showed how much they meant to him. Jupiter brought the rain when he needed it, and Venus the Sun.

As he began to read the stars, man made them an important part of his everyday life, giving each of those he read by, its own day of the week. Sunday was the Sun's day; Monday the Moon's; Tuesday was the day of Tiw, the pagan God of War, akin to Mars; Wednesday was Woden's, the wise magician, or Mercury; Thursday was the day of the Norse god Thor, or Jupiter; and Friday belonged to the goddess Freya, the pagan Venus. Saturday, Saturn's day, was the solemn Jewish sabbath.

Long before recorded history, the resurrected artifacts of unexplained astrology clearly indicated a superior civilization that had once flourished in different parts of the world. In the dry mud at Tiahuanaco in Peru, seat of the unexplained Incan culture, were found the remains of a calendar tablet giving the positions of the Moon every hour, the movements adjusted to the rotation of the earth. With it were remnants of a giant block of red sandstone, whose astronomical symbols gave planetary positions corresponding with an accurate precession of the equinoxes of some 26,000 years.

Equally amazing was the fact that the ancient Mayans of Mexico, whose advanced culture has never been satisfactorily explained, revealed a knowledge of Venus' precise orbit around the Sun, knew of a terrestrial year of 364.242 days, and of the invisible planets Uranus and Neptune.

While the Middle East, the Tigris-Euphrates valley, has been considered the cradle of astrology and civilization, astrology was already in an advanced stage five thousand years ago, when the Sumerians became the first we know of to apply it empirically. Without instruments of any kind, perhaps relying on tradition, the Sumerians were remarkably aware that certain fixed stars were circled by planets invisible to the naked eye, planets which subsequent cultures attributed to mythology until Sir William Herschel, the English court astronomer, in 1781 became the first man to pick out a new planet—Uranus—with a telescope.

Although Fundamentalists might object to the use of the Holy Bible, our first continuous history, to show that astrology is a key to the human saga, the fact remains that this is fundamentally so. For in the "beginning," in the book called Genesis, it is clearly written:

"And God said, Let there be lights in the firmament of the heaven to divide the day from the night; and let them be for signs, and for seasons, and for days, and years."

In Genesis 37:9, Joseph, the son of Jacob, told his eleven brothers, who were selling him down to Egypt, of not eight but eleven planets, as he made a prediction:

"I have dreamed a dream more; and, behold, the sun and the moon and the eleven stars made obeisance to me."

In the recent Oxford version of the New Testament, the three Wise Men heralding the Christ child have now become astrologers, their quest touched off by the heavenly conjunction which traditionally fixed the time for the Messiah's birth.

As the apostle Matthew relates:

"Jesus was born at Bethlehem in Judea during the reign of Herod. After his birth astrologers from the east arrived in Jerusalem, asking:

" 'Where is the child who is born to be king of the Jews? We observed the rising of his star (the Star of Bethlehem) and we have come to pay him homage.' "

Just as Matthew tells of this portent, the apostle Luke (21:25) describes a Second Coming to be foretold above:

"Portents will appear in sun, moon and stars. On earth nations will stand helpless, not knowing which way to turn from the roar and surge of the sea; men will faint with terror at the thought of all that is coming upon the world; for the celestial powers will be shaken. And then they will see the Son of Man coming on a cloud with great power and glory. When all this begins to happen, stand upright and hold your heads high, because your liberation is near."

The symbolism is clear, for as Psalm 19 had instructed:

"The heavens declare the glory of God; and the firmament sheweth his handywork.

"Day unto day uttereth speech, and night unto night sheweth knowledge.

"There is no speech nor language, where their voice is not heard."

In challenging the faith of Job, the Lord speaks of astrology as if it were a privileged function:

"Canst thou bind the sweet influences of Pleiades, or loose the bands of Orion?

"Canst thou bring forth Mazzaroth in his season? Or canst thou guide Arcturus with his sons?

"Knowest thou the ordinances of heaven? Canst thou set the dominion thereof in the earth?"

There was a practical side to this astrology. The ancients began planting in the early spring, when the Pleiades showed themselves in the sky, and for forty days, while the Sun was in Aries and Taurus, the planting continued.

Even more than the Jews of Scripture, the contemporary Babylonians were into astrology–so much so that the prophet Isaiah could not resist the taunt:

"Thou art wearied in the multitude of thy counsels. Let now the astrologers, the stargazers, the monthly prognosticators, stand up and save thee from these things that shall come upon thee."

This didn't seem to bother the ancient Babylonians. They kept right on living by the astrological principles they had codified on tablet:

"If there's thunder in the month of Chabot there will be a plague of locusts.

"If a dark halo surrounds the Moon, the month will be cloudy and rainy."

Some of the astral code dealt with foreign affairs and the probability of war:

"If Mars is visible in the month of Tamoose (June and July, so obviously our Cancer), the warrior's bed will stay cold."

Mars was the god of War, and in Cancer brought out the impulse in the fighting man to protect home and hearth.

With Mercury (for trips) prominent, the battle would be at a distance:

"If Mercury is seen in the north there will be many corpses, and the King will invade a foreign country."

Some forecasts concerned the cost of living, a problem then as now, and the governing planet was the same used by modern astrologers to predict trends in the stock market and general economy.

"If Jupiter seems to enter into the Moon," one tablet said, "then prices will go down."

The Babylonians used the rising planet, the first-house planet nearest the ascendant, as well as the Sun and Moon, to foresee the individual's life. If a child was born with the Moon on the first house ascendant, he would have a bright, long life. With Jupiter on the ascendant, he would become rich as he grew old, and if Venus was rising, his life would be calm, and his days long and favorable.

Jupiter on the descendant, which was in the seventh house, as opposed to the ascendant, was especially bad for the king, since Jupiter was the king of planets. Other planets on the descendant had a correspondingly unfavorable effect, as they were manifestly opposed to the individual's personality.

Babylonian astrology was recorded on 70 clay tablets, the Illumination of Bel, found in the ruins of the library of King Ashurbanipal (669–633 B.C.) at Nineveh, Assyria, in 1851 A.D. According to Prof. A. H. Sayce, a student of this period, the Babylonian priests believed that predictable events were perfectly natural occurrences, determined by other natural occurrences, which could be correlated by a trained observer of the stars. "Hence, if a war with Elam had followed an eclipse of the Sun on a particular date, it was assumed that a recurrence of the eclipse on the same day would be followed by a recurrence of a war with Elam."

Astrology reached its zenith in Babylon between 625 and 538 B.C. Berossus, a priest, established a school of astrology on the Island of Cos about 280 B.C., from where it spread through Greece. It was carried to the west by the Arabs, after they destroyed the library of Alexandria centuries later.

To the Greeks, who personified everything, the planets were living things, likened to gods.

"We tend," said the Greek scholar Aristotle, "to think of the stars as mere bodies or items arranged in order, quite without soul or life. We ought rather to regard them as possessed of life and activity, for this world is inescapably linked to the motions of the world above. And all power in this world is ruled by these motions."

To Plato, greatest of the Greek philosophers and humanists, the planets were twelve gods—among them Pluto and Neptune, planets which we have only recently discovered. And these heavenly gods had essentially the same attributes that modern astrology assigned to the planets after centuries of pragmatic observation.

To Plato, Zeus, the Greek Jupiter, led the way in a heavenly procession reminiscent of the general precession of the planets. And like Joseph, Plato spoke of eleven planets—the twelfth being the Earth.

"Zeus, the mighty Lord holding the reins of a winged chariot, leads the way in heaven, ordering all and caring for all. And there follows him the heavenly array of gods and demigods, divided into *eleven* bands; for only Hestia (the Goddess of the Hearth—the earth-home) is left at home, but the rest of the twelve greater deities march in appointed order . . . each one fulfilling his own work."

The Roman Manilius, in his versifying, mentioned the planet Vulcan, which ruled Libra the Scales. Manilius assigned Mercury to the Crab, Cancer, and gave Mars to Scorpio, where it had been accepted until recently, when Pluto, on its discovery, was given to Scorpio and Mars retained rulership over Aries alone.

Apparently drawing on ancient lore, since there were no telescopes, Manilius spoke of the planet Neptune, not discovered until 1846, and incredibly gave it domain over Pisces the Fish, the sign assigned to it by astrologers on its discovery some 1,800 years later.

As for Pluto, discovered only in this generation, the ancients treated it as an old friend, and gave it rule over the underground, remarkably comparable to the underworld forces with which this planet was associated as soon as it was picked out of the sky in 1930.

The Greeks were ostensibly the first to use horoscopes with houses and signs allotted just as they are today. When Alexander the Great, a student of Aristotle's, invaded the Middle East and India, the Greek scholars traveling with him took over the Babylonian art, but their astrology, on a personal level, was beyond anything the Babylonians had done.

Again such development appears implausible unless one accepts Plato's account of a superior society of migrant Atlanteans, who, on being repulsed by the Athenians, were either absorbed with their customs, and/or wandered off to Cyprus, Egypt or Babylon, leaving traces of their culture.

In ancient Greece, the most civilized of contemporary cultures, nobody was in greater esteem than the astrologer. Hippocrates, the father of medicine, in whose name physicians swear the sacred Hippocratic oath, used astrology in his practice, and said that only a fool would treat a patient without first consulting his horoscope.

In medieval times, the leading physicians, including the French seer Nostradamus, were invariably also astrologers. Unaided by stethoscopes and cardiographs, they relied on planetary aspects in both diagnosis and treatment. Paracelsus, the most celebrated doctor of the 15th century, said no doctor should prescribe a remedy without checking the position of the Moon and the planets in his client's chart. He held that the five planets and two luminaries each governed a certain area of the body: Sun, the heart; Jupiter, the liver; Moon, the brain; Mars, the bile; Venus, the urogenital tract.

Like civilization generally, astrology gradually moved westward, from Babylon to Greece, and then to the greatest empire the world had ever seen—the Rome that lasted for twelve hundred years. It received great impetus because of the experience that Caesar Augustus, the first of the Roman emperors, had as a youth of 18.

The Roman historian, Suetonius, gives us the story:

"While in retirement at Apollonia (after adoptive father Julius Caesar's assassination, when he Augustus feared for his life) Augustus mounted with Agrippa (his boon companion) to the studio of the astrologer Theogenes. Agrippa was the first to try his fortune, and when a great and almost incredible career was predicted for him (he later became the first soldier of the Empire under Augustus), Augustus persisted in concealing the time of his birth and refusing to disclose it through diffidence and fear that he might be found to be less eminent. When at last he give it unwillingly and hesitatingly and only after many urgent requests, Theogenes sprang up and threw himself at his feet. From that time on, Augustus had such faith in his destiny that he made his horoscope public and issued a silver coin stamped with the sign of the constellation Capricorn under which he was born."

Curiously, indicating how important the ancients considered the Moon, Capricorn was Augustus' Moon sign. The Moon in Capricorn, known as the ruthless moon by astrologers, was prominent with other rulers with a similar singleminded sense of destiny—Adolf Hitler and Abraham Lincoln, who, from differing motives, still moved decisively to accomplish what they had to.

Moon in Capricorn puts a semblance of legality on everything it does, and Hitler had the Reichstag perfunctorily approve everything he did. Augustus' stress on legality was more substantial. Conditioned by a Libra Sun, the sign of the Scales, Augustus took a very real pride in his courts and the protection of the law for every Roman citizen, whether a Paul of Tarsus in Asia Minor or a lowly colonial in the Britain Agrippa had conquered for him.

Under Augustus' protection, astrology flourished in Rome, though there were periodic expulsions of Greek astrologers when their influence appeared to transcend that of the Emperor. Palace astrologers became prominent personages. Just as Augustus had Theogenes, his successor, Tiberius, had his favorite, Thrasyllus, a Greek, whom he had brought to Rome after Thrasyllus predicted that he would one day be master of the western world.

Thrasyllus was Tiberius' astrologer for 40 years. Without his assurances the Prince might have retired into oblivion after Augustus named several younger heirs ahead of him. But Thrasyllus counseled patience. Tiberius, he promised, would outlive them all.

Thrasyllus was probably the wisest of the ancient astrologers. Hitler's astrologers, discredited when they advised against his ill-starred Russian invasion, would have done well to have emulated his diplomacy.

With diabolical humor, the fickle Emperor said one day to the astrologer who knew all his secrets:

"And what of your own destiny, master astrologer?"

Thrasyllus softly replied:

"Sire, I stand at this moment in the most imminent peril."

At the cool rejoinder, the tyrant's whim passed, and Thrasyllus was spared to live to a ripe old age.

After Tiberius' death, many astrologers were banished as people began asking how long his successor, the mad Caligula, would rein, and whether, hopefully, he would meet a violent end. It also became illegal for an astrologer to pick death out of the Emperor's chart. Consequently, predictions of death have become unpopular, generally, and it is a rare astrologer, even now, who will intimately discuss the eighth house of death.

Ironically, with the decline of the Roman Empire, astrology, which gave the sign of the Fish to Christianity, suffered its greatest crisis because of Christianity.

After Constantine, in the fourth century, laid the groundwork for the Roman Catholic Church as the official state religion, this body, which had undergone terrible persecutions, turned on the astrologers. The Church objections were twofold: It opposed a rival to its own authority, as the Emperors had. And it objected to the idea that the future could be predicted, as astrology presupposed, because it felt this contradicted the doctrine that men were responsible for their actions and that they had a free will.

Over the centuries this rigid attitude posed quite a dilemma for churchmen who believed in astrology. Pierre Abélard, one of the great teachers of the Church, got around the conflict by concluding that it was possible to predict such natural phenomena as illness, weather, fertility, but not the ordinary run of human activities that seemed to reflect free will, choice of a mate, of a vocation, and of one's duties to State and Church.

In the Church attack on astrology, astrologers were posthumously blamed even for exposing the Christ child to Herod's wrath. In 400 A.D., St. John Chrysostom, patriarch of Constantinople, denounced the Magi for coming openly to Bethlehem in their quest of the infant. They should have known, he said, since they were astrologers, that their visit would bring the birth to the attention of Herod and other authorities. Despite this deep-rooted opposition, several Popes had their coronations set to the most propitious time, astrologically, and Pope Paul III used the astrologer Gauricus, who predicted that the Protestant heretic Martin Luther would go directly to Hell, not for conceiving the Reformation, but because he was a Scorpio, with heavy planets in that sign.

While astrology was officially tabooed by the Church, prominent churchmen continued their surreptitious study of the stars. During the reign of England's Henry I, the Archbishop of York died with a textbook of astrology under his pillow, and the dutifully outraged populace stoned his coffin.

And today, despite its official disapproval of the ancient science, the Vatican reportedly has the most voluminous library of astrology in the world.

Ironically, astrology had a rebirth with the Renaissance of the arts and sciences, particularly the upsurge in astronomy, on which its tables, giving the positions of the planets, are based. For while the modern astronomer may scoff, the giants of astronomy, the geniuses who tuned into the secrets of the solar system—the Copernicuses, Keplers, Galileos and Newtons—were all practicing astrologers and gloried in an art they considered the key to the universe.

At a time in the 17th century, when astrology was being taught in major European universities, Isaac Newton, famed for his principle of gravitation, attended Cambridge University just so he could study the celestial science. And when his contemporary Edmund Halley, discoverer of Halley's Comet, made a disparaging reference to astrology, Newton mildly protested:

"I have studied the subject, Mr. Halley; you have not."

As Newton knew, the ancients not only seemed to know more planets, but more about these planets than we do. They found them expansive, restrictive, dark, secretive, as the case might be. They were friends and neighbors, allies or adversaries. Jupiter or Jove was jovial, helpful, friendly; Saturn was often satanic, saturnine; Mars, martial or marvelous.

Only now are we beginning to examine seriously the olden belief which ascribed intrinsic action and motion, of their own special nature, to these heavenly bodies, which, as Aristotle observed, have so much bearing on our lives.

These planets, certain physicists have shown, are constantly giving off billions of cosmic particles, reflected in radiant energy, whose frequency is affected by the angles of confrontation with other planets millions or billions of miles away, for just as they are unconcerned with ephemerides, these planetary radiations are unconcerned with great distances, which have no diminishing effect on the nature or impulse of the rays they cast into space.

For every ray sent there was a receiver. "We all have certain electric and magnetic powers within us," said the humanist Goethe, "and ourselves exercise an attractive and repelling force, accordingly as we come into touch with something like or unlike."

The more gifted the mind, the more advanced its genius, the more closely in tune with the universe, the more immediate did the planets seem to it in their mysterious harmony with man. From Kepler's laws we learned that the planets move in an ellipse around the sun, with the line joining the center of each planet, including Earth, moving over equal areas of the ellipse in equal time. In keeping with a universal law that seemed translatable in universal mathematics, the square of the orbit period of each planet, the time for completion of its journey around the sun, was proportional to the cube of its mean distance from the sun.

Whether others understood the mathematical significance of this or not, it became apparent that the order of the planets, their size and their nature, were all interwoven in a mathematical equation as large as the universe itself.

Johannes Kepler like all great discoverers was a visionary. Kepler saw the planets as living, pulsating entities, whose effect on man was endless. And the most important planet of all to man—Earth—he saw as a living thing akin to man, with not only a body covered by grass and trees and nourished by the seas, but a soul, an *anima terra,* analogous to the human soul. This human soul, this microcosm, was in close conjunction with the planetary soul, the macrocosm—and just as everything else in nature was causatively produced, so were there tangible causal relationships between the planets and man, produced by the impact of a transmitter-like planetary source on an antenna-like receiver. "I speak here as do the astrologers," said this giant of astronomy. "If I should express my own opinion it would be that there is no evil star in the heavens, and this, among others, chiefly for the following reasons: It is the nature of man as such, dwelling as it does here on earth, that lends to the planetary radiations their effect on itself; just as the sense of hearing, endowed with the faculty of discerning chords, lends to music such power that it incites him who hears it to dance."

One planetary ray affected the others to the point of precipitating changes in weather, storms, earthquakes—all felt here on Earth through the agency of the anima terra, the very soul of the Earth responsive to the other planetary souls. And man, with his sensitivities to changes in atmospheric pressure, temperatures, and certain unmeasurable phenomena which are a product of this planetary interplay, is directly and decisively affected by the cosmic harmony.

"Nothing exists or happens in the visible heavens the significance of which is not extended further by way of some occult principle, to the Earth and the faculties of the natural things; and thus these animal faculties are affected here on earth exactly as the heavens themselves are affected."

Kepler's ideas on astrology were of course demolished by the same scientists who accepted Kepler's laws of planetary motions without question, the selfsame laws on which Newton based the theory of gravitation which has made it possible for man to soar to the Moon.

So far our probe of the Moon has revealed only that there is no life, as we know it, on its surface. In no way, however, does this diminish the influence of the Moon in our Earth lives. What woman doesn't know of the affect of the Moon cycle on her menstrual cycle, in keeping with what Kepler said about the planets having an effect on man in the precise manner that he is patterned to receive these effects?

But the founder of modern astronomy was by no means sold on the pat division of astrology into twelve signs and houses. Only the planetary aspects, the impact of one planet on another, impressed him. "The only part (of astrology) I kept are the aspects and I link astrology to the doctrine of the harmonies."

Heedless of Kepler, the twelve-sign zodiac has gone through changes over the centuries, as astrologers strove pragmatically to attribute to the signs, houses and planets the qualities they seemed to express best at the time. More than 2,000 years ago, Aristotle, the most erudite man of his time, told the boy Alexander that when he needed a laxative he should be careful that the Moon was in the water signs Scorpio or Pisces, or in Libra, which rules the kidneys.

Some authorities place the first recorded zodiacal year at 4699 B.C., with Taurus the Bull ruling the age. A system of twelve constellations was in existence by 1780 B.C., the year beginning at the Vernal Equinox, and the month beginning with the New Moon. The precession of the equinoxes, moving thirty degrees in the zodiac every 2,160 years, had moved into Aries. However, ancient astrology, about this time, stopped relating the signs of the zodiac to the precession of the constellations, moving from the sidereal system of astrology—precise star-sun time—to the tropical, which reflects the seasons of the year and the aspects of the planets beginning with an arbitrary 0 degrees Aries.

"The signs of the zodiac," relates astrologer Dave Williams, "were mapped out by the ancient priesthoods of Egypt and Mesopotamia in milestones corresponding to the twelve months of the year. Hence, the ecliptic circle or apparent path of the Sun is divided into 30-degree sections starting at the Vernal Equinox, the point of spring, where the Sun appeared to cross the equator on its northward journey. These sections were called signs, and were named after groups of stars whose rising and setting positions roughly corresponded to that of the Sun at a particular season."

The zodiac of the signs, he points out, was sometimes called the moving zodiac, since the first point of Aries was continually moving westward because of this precession of the equinoxes.

Differences in relating precession to the zodiac have produced varying opinions as to the time of the Aquarian Age. From his calculations, Dave Williams has it beginning in 1844 A.D. The Church of Light, which has engaged in extensive zodiacal research, begins it in 1881; astrologer Carroll Righter places it in 1904, when man first got into space. Others have mentioned 1781 and some, like esoteric astrologer Dane Rhudyar, say it is on its way in the next hundred years or so. However, the siderealists, those sticklers for a true equation of the constellations with the signs, say, with British astrologer Cyril Fagan, that the Piscean Age didn't begin until 213 A.D., and therefore the first point of Aquarius cannot occur before 2369 A.D.

As one looks about him, sensing the Uranian upheavals in social values, the flights into outer space, and the Uranian-generated electronic revolution which has made this possible, it is obvious that we are feeling the first twinges of an Aquarian Age whose ruling planet is Uranus.

"If it moos like a cow, gives milk like a cow, and looks like a cow," an astrologer friend observed, "it's a cow."

Just as astrologers have argued the signs, so have they debated the relevance of the houses. Carl Payne Tobey, the mathematically oriented astrologer, strikes a blow from his Tucson, Arizona, lair for equal houses, pointing out that in some areas of the globe, north of the Arctic Circle, for instance, it would be impossible to cast a chart for somebody born in that latitude by unequal house cusps, the Placidian system with its unequal house divisions taken from a table of houses, a system used by most Western astrologers for several centuries.

"Go far enough north," said this exponent of the equal house system, "and in the unequal house system all the signs would be squeezed into one house."

"Go far enough north," rejoined astrologer Franka Moore, an exponent of unequal houses, "and life is correspondingly limited—everybody is in their igloos doing the same thing."

Of the modern astrologers working with unequal houses, none did more to show how the system works in the tropical zones than the late Evangeline Adams. And though her professional adversaries insisted she was psychic, she pointed out that she tuned into aspects, not people, as she read for thousands she had never even seen.

To show that her astrology worked as a science, this exponent of the "ancient science" once dared the State of New York to put astrology on trial. Haled into court as a fortune teller, she secured the best counsel available and insisted on a hearing. She appeared in court with a stack of reference books, histories dating back to the Biblical era, and demanded in the interest of science that she be allowed to cast a horoscope of anybody chosen at random and give a reading of that person.

Trial Judge John J. Freschi looked up with interest. And then, entering into the spirit of the experiment, he gave her the birthday, hour and place of an individual unknown to her.

In a few minutes, with her trusty ephemeris, listing the position of the planets at the moment of birth, Evangeline Adams had set up the chart and begun her interpretation.

As she went into the person's life, discussing past occurrences, then elaborating on personality, aptitudes and character, the Judge's eyes widened.

"What you say about this person," he said, "is exactly right. I know because he is my son."

Judge Freschi's decision was history making, as it served to legalize astrology in New York and take it out of the dark ages to which its adversaries had consigned it for nearly two thousand years.

"The defendant," Freschi ruled, "raises astrology to the dignity of an exact science. In the reading of the horoscope, the defendant went through an absolutely mechanical, mathematical process to get at her conclusions. She claims that astrology never makes a mistake, though astrologers do, and that if the figures are correct, the information given is correct. She claims no faculty of foretelling by supernatural or magical means that which is future, or of discovering that which is hidden and obscure. But she does claim that Nature is to be interpreted by the influences that surround it."

And who is to deny that man is an integral part of that nature and has been ever since he first peered mutely into the skies and wondered what the future held in store for him?

3

A Time to Learn

In Yoga there is a saying that when the pupil is ready the teacher will arrive. And in astrology there is a time for every purpose, including study.

I had wondered how so many little old ladies with little or no education were able to do horoscopes, when I didn't seem to know where to begin. How could I get to know what it meant, or if it meant anything, when I couldn't tell whether the Moon was in Aquarius or Taurus, or whose ascendant was where?

I was told that astrology was a science, and maybe it is, and yet there was sharp disagreement on what the future held for me. Obviously, though the construction of the individual chart is mathematically precise, the delineation is an art, just as medicine is, with proper diagnosis hinging on the skill of the individual practitioner.

I wanted to read my own chart, to see the symbols suddenly come alive in reference to my own life, and that of persons close to me. And so I looked around for the right teacher.

Anybody with a few lessons in the methodology of astrology, I discovered, could, if properly instructed, learn to set up a chart, given the necessary birth data, and having a familiarity with an ephemeris listing the daily positions of the planets.

In Ralph Winters, a nonprofessional, I found a teacher who, because he was primarily a student, did not gloss over the fundamentals he had only recently acquired himself.

"I try to keep one lesson ahead of the class," said Winters with a smile.

Winters was a college man, a wartime pilot, and a motion picture executive. His genesis as an astrologer was intriguing.

Although friendly for years with the prominent Hollywood astrologer Carroll Righter, he had avoided astrology like the plague.

"Like others who know nothing about astrology, I thought there was nothing to it."

But about four years ago, Winters submitted tolerantly to a Righter horoscope, having through a process of gradual exposure begun to feel that even the Sun signs in some measure seemed to correspond to the personality of many people he knew.

"By that time," he said, "I had two ex-wives and four children, and now realized, knowing their signs, how these influenced our relationships."

His own chart was the convincer.

"In retrospect, I could understand my every move. My teenage love for music, earning my way through college playing in a band; my Libran interest in the arts, and my Leo-like preoccupation with the theatrical type of women I married."

Born October 19, 1917, at 1:30 A.M. in Ironton, Ohio, Winters was a Venus-ruled Libra, with dramatic Leo rising, and Moon in spiritually inclined Sagittarius.

Bemused by his own chart, he turned to those of his ex-wives. His first wife's was a solar chart, based on the day of birth, the exact hour not being known. This arbitrarily made her Sun or birth sign her rising sign, in 1 degree Virgo, since she was born August 24, and the onset of Virgo was August 23. Reviewing his own solar chart as a point of comparison, Winters made a belated discovery. "In my solar chart, the sign preceding my rising house of Libra was automatically in my twelfth house of secret enemies. That sign of course was Virgo, and my wife was a Virgo."

Winters then explored his second marriage.

With Leo rising in his own natal chart, he made a similar discovery. "My second wife's Sun sign was Cancer, and since it preceded my first house, Leo, in the twelfth house, she was also my secret enemy."

It seemed hardly fair to say that one's wife was a secret enemy merely because her Sun sign fell in her husband's twelfth house. But Winters recalled a recent incident for my benefit.

"Do you remember that psychic researcher who made your hackles rise?"

I almost felt them rising again.

"Well, he was an Aries, and in your solar chart Aries would be in your twelfth house of secret enemies preceding your first house of Taurus."

"There was nothing secret about it," I said.

"Now, in a natal chart, you have Capricorn rising in the first house, so your secret enemy there would be the preceding sign of Sagittarius."

My first wife was a Sagittarius.

"And what good does it do," I asked, "to know your wives were your secret enemies?"

"Understanding they couldn't help themselves, I lost my resentment, and that was good for me. Now if I had done their charts before marriage, I might never have married them, but it probably had to happen to help me grow."

Winters' second wife was more than his secret enemy. Astrologically-speaking, she presented an obstacle to be coped with and learned from. Since she was a Cancer or Moon Child, her Sun in Cancer was squared, at a ninety degree angle, to his Sun in Libra–a square being the most difficult aspect in astrology.

"There was nothing intrinsically wrong with either of them, or with me," he philosophically decided. "We had just married the wrong people. They were being themselves, and I myself, and it could never have worked: the charts showed that."

"Who should you have married?" I asked.

He frowned. "Sagittarius and Leo, both favorably aspected, both sextile (sixty degrees) to my Libra Sun would have been better, and Leo doubly so, since my rising sign was in Leo, and the opposite sign, aggressive Aries, might also have rounded out nonaggressive Libra. Of course, there are all kinds of aspects between the planets that modify a chart."

He had two children by each marriage. "My oldest daughter, Deborah, 17, is a Sagittarius, and that goes with Libra like ham with eggs. Rebecca, my second daughter, is an Aries, opposite my Libran seventh house of partners, and thus complements me!"

Robbie, his 12-year-old son, is a Taurus, Venus-ruled like Libra. This, together with Robbie's Sagittarius rising, favorably sextile both the Libra Sun and the Leo rising of the father, gave them instant rapport.

"We always like to do the same things together."

Daughter Laura, 10, is a Cancer or Moon Child.

"Cancer," I reminded him, "in your twelfth house is your secret enemy."

But there was a compensating factor. "Like myself, Laura has Leo rising, and the rising sign reflects the personality, so we have a great deal in common in our approach to life." (Before, of course, she betrayed him.)

"Being a Moon Child," he went on, oblivious of my parenthesis, "she is extremely sensitive. But knowing she is a Cancer, with the pride of Leo in her rising sign, I am extremely gentle with her. And since her Moon, her emotional nature, is in Aries, an aggressive sign, I know she can take the slings and arrows of fortune better in the long run than I can."

Laura's Taurus fell in the midheaven of the chart, the tenth house of profession, occupation, honor and fame. "Taurus is ruled by Venus, and Venus, the goddess of beauty, rules show business. Consequently, there is no doubt in my mind I have another actress in the house."

Deborah, at 17, was already embarked on a motion picture career, starring in a full-length feature, *The People Next Door,* and co-starring with Walter Matthau in *Kotch*. "Debbie has the mood-ruling Moon in Leo," Winters pointed out, "and that's the theatrical sign, almost guaranteeing a dramatic inclination."

With her Virgo rising, she was inclined, personality-wise, to be hypercritical, especially about her work, as Virgo was the work sign. "Consequently, I point out to her, when she is upset over studio conditions, that she will find it less wearing to adjust to the world, imperfect as it is, than to demand that it adapt to her finicky Virgo standards."

His knowing his son's chart had done wonders for their relationship. "Robbie had a great deal of trouble in school. Now if I hadn't seen his chart and known something of astrology, I don't think I could have had the same understanding of not only Robbie's problem but the school's."

"Did you take the teachers' charts?" I asked.

"Robbie's was enough. Robbie is a Taurus, and the average Taurean wants to know why. He isn't satisfied when the teacher tells him that two and two is four, he wants proof of it. On the other hand, though he is slow to accept facts, once he knows them, he knows them forever. Knowing this I tactfully suggested they let Robbie go at his own pace, and they agreed."

Robbie's rising sign, Sagittarius, explained his proficiency in sports. "Sagittarians are the athletes of the zodiac, and Robbie is a champion runner. He loves sports, fishing and hunting, and so I encourage these natural pursuits."

We finally got through the Winters family.

As so many others, I was particularly concerned how astrology related to my own affairs.

"One astrologer," I observed, "told me that with Neptune descendant and thereby an undermining influence in my seventh house of partners, I could expect deception from a wife or business associate."

"Neptune stands for deception or illusion, but it also stands for submarines, spiritualistic investigation, drugs, television and movies," Winters replied. "As I see it, you should have some activity in television and movies."

"What made you pick out that influence rather than the others?"

"It seems reasonable in view of the nature of your career."

"And when will that be?"

He consulted an ephemeris.

"June 19, 1971, when Saturn leaves your Sun sign."

It was now the spring of 1970.

"You mean I should forget television until then?"

"Not necessarily. Astrology never tells you that something can't be done, it merely points out the obstacles, and demands that you work harder to find your destiny."

Winters had several admonitions before class.

"Don't try to know it all at once," he said. "One of the major problems of astrology today is the number of students who, after studying a few months, present themselves as full-fledged astrologers, and even do charts for whoever will pay for them."

"I only want to know how it works," I said.

"As long as you're learning, why not profit enough to acquire self-knowledge through astrology? If it does no more than let you see yourself, it will have repaid all your time in class."

Winters' classes were held in an upstairs room in Righter's Hollywood home. The students came from every walk of life, acting, engineering, law, stenography, designing. They were of all ages, 18 to 70, and they had an interest in astrology as broad as life itself.

"I want to know," one student announced, "if astrology can help me know where I'm going and why."

He had come to the right place for introspection. For it soon became apparent that Winters' class was to be an adventure in self-realization. He was adept at it himself.

"Just like the Peggy Lee song," he told the class, "I was wondering 'Is this all there is?' I worked every day, went home at night, and every day was like the one before it, going nowhere. I felt it was time to get to know myself and know where I was going."

Two or three hands were promptly raised.

"What does astrology have to do with that?" a pretty girl inquired.

"Your chart will tell you about your natural aptitudes, and the kind of partners you should have in your personal life as well as in business. It will also tell you where you are going spiritually."

Another hand was raised.

"Suppose you don't like what the chart shows you?"

"Your chart is a road map, and you take the turn you want."

He chalked a circle on the blackboard, dividing it into twelve equal segments. "Each of these segments," he said, "is called a house. In these houses we place the signs of the zodiac, also twelve in number, and the ten planets that we presently know about, including the Sun and the Moon, which are really lights, but which possess sufficient powers, astrologically, to be dignified as planets."

He pointed to the first house, placed directly at the left under the horizontal line bisecting the circle, from East to West, and numbered counterclockwise from one to twelve. He wrote in the signs, using astrological symbols, beginning with Aries in the first house, commencing with March 21, the day of the Vernal Equinox, the first day of spring.

Winters marked an E for East, standing for the ascendant or eastern horizon, signifying the subject's rising sign. "One of the first functions is locating the rising sign, which is that apparent point on the Eastern horizon establishing the first house cusp."

The circle was divided into four equal quadrants, each containing the equivalent of three houses or ninety degrees; and each had its message. "As the planets enter the Eastern or first quadrant, it's time for preparation," Winters observed.

This seemed a rather striking statement.

"Preparation for what?" a student asked.

"Preparation for an event, or even your life's work."

"What planets?" another asked.

"Any planets, but Saturn particularly, which dominates the quadrant it is in for seven years."

He elaborated: "Saturn is a restrictive planet, and when Franklin D. Roosevelt had transiting Saturn in his first quadrant, he was struck down by polio, and through necessity had to take stock of himself. It was a period of quiet contemplation. Ironically, when Roosevelt's greatest adversary also had Saturn in his first quadrant, he was thrown in jail, and there marshaled his thoughts, and wrote the book, *Mein Kampf,* which was to become the Nazi bible. Both men used their time advantageously, for their own advancement, as Saturn slowly orbited through the quadrant of preparation, and both were ready, as Saturn moved into their second quadrants, to make their moves."

The second quarter was the building quadrant, promoting, socializing, getting one's work organized. In the third quadrant a rising Saturn makes it possible for the individual to realize the harvest from previous planning and action. "As Saturn crossed into the fourth quadrant, the individual turned his attention to his personal security, as he began to relax, enjoying the fruits of his labors."

The planets were no mere scratches on an astrologer's work pad. While they had no life on them, they were very much alive in their impact on one another and on the Earth. The Sun, though properly a luminary, was the most important of the heavenly bodies, its diameter of 840,000 miles helping to make up 99.9 percent of the planetary mass. Billions of its invisible rays, known as neutrinos, passed through man every day. The other planets, and the Moon, also had their influence, but the Sun was the life giver.

"Without it," said Winters, "plants and man could not grow or survive. As the source of all life it represents the real you, the self you are trying to know."

Its influence varied, depending on its position in the zodiac. "When the Sun is in Aries, the Ram, the person has the aggressive Aries characteristics. Aries want to be first, Aries are impatient, they can't stand to be idle. They're the ones you hear honking the horns in traffic. They are the pioneers, the innovators, honest, hopeful, straightforward. In the Old West they were the wagon masters, they helped open Alaska to the Gold Rush, and they ventured into outer space. With Aries in the first house, they are definitely inclined to head up or boss whatever job they're doing. However, they will work cheerfully for another, higher boss, provided this job superior doesn't tell them what to do."

Winters looked up from the blackboard with a smile.

"My daughter Rebecca is an Aries, and I have no trouble with Aries if I just stand aside and let her perform."

Winters likened the 360-degree zodiac to a wheel of progress, beginning with Aries, the essence of primitive individuality, and continuing counterclockwise through the twelfth house sign, Pisces. And though, he emphasized, the Sun sign was but one factor, it was still the strongest single influence in a chart.

Just as Aries was the pioneer or wagon master, Taurus the Bull, persevering and stubborn, was the home builder, who put down roots. Taureans are fond of money, not for hoarding, but for creative comforts with which they can adorn their homes and gratify the people they like, including themselves.

"They're always glad to pick up the check if they're having dinner or lunch with somebody they want to be with. They are especially good as bankers, either in handling their own business affairs or handling a bank, and they like their collateral in land, reflecting the fact that Taurus is the earthiest of the earth signs. Since Taurus is Venus-ruled, and Venus is the goddess of beauty, Taureans like to be surrounded by beauty, in the home and on their arm. They appreciate lovely paintings in their home; they love music, and either are good singers or have a deep feeling for it." Barbra Streisand, the reigning songstress, is a Taurus, as are Bing Crosby and Perry Como. Just as Aries stands for or ruled the head, through its ruling planet Mars, Taurus ruled the throat.

In view of all this Taurean love of property, how was it then that

Karl Marx, a Taurus, born May 5, 1818, in Germany, had propounded an un-Taurean philosophy opposed not only to bankers but to private property of any kind?

Winters smiled.

"That's the problem with Sun sign astrology, it doesn't begin to tell half the story. But we have to know what the various astrological symbols mean by themselves before we can get on with what they mean collectively."

"But how," I persisted, with Taurean perseverance, "was a man like Marx, with Sun, Moon and Venus in Taurus, the father of a Communist philosophy diametrically opposed to the bounty Taureans stand for?"

Winters' smile deepened, knowing that my own Sun, Moon and Venus were in Taurus.

"His Sun and Moon in Taurus, the sign of money, showed his liking for money, but both were square his humanitarian Aquarius ascendant, which made him money and property conscious and yet frustrated his quest for worldly goods for himself and others."

Looking at the total chart, one sees that the ruler of Marx's Aquarius ascendant, Uranus, in the philosophical sign of Sagittarius in the tenth house of career and fame, represented an unconventional or revolutionary approach to the earning of a livelihood. It squared not only the ascendant itself, but Pluto and Saturn in Neptune-ruled Pisces in the first house in his chart. "This signified that Saturn, the teacher, was imparting his revolutionary message, flavored by a certain Neptunean unreality, to the Pluto masses in the guise of Aquarian humanity."

Ironically, the leader of the revolution foreshadowed by Marx was another Taurean, Nicolai Lenin, born April 22, 1870, and his partner in revolution was his opposite sign, that military firebrand Leon Trotsky, a complementing Scorpio, born November 7, 1879.

All this was more than I had anticipated.

"Before the classes are over," Winters said, "all should be clear; meanwhile, we'll stick to fundamentals."

And so to the third house, and Gemini, the Twins, the house of brothers and sisters; of the flighty, often off in two directions at the same time. "Geminis," said Winters, "are perhaps not so much like children as they are childlike. Marry a Gemini and you are married to five different women, their moods and impulses varying so quickly they can't keep up with themselves. Like children, they are quick, alert, enthusiastic, but their attention soon wanders. Since Gemini is ruled by mental Mercury, Geminis are fitful and mercurial, in mind as well as body. The third house is the house of rapid communication—the telephone, telegraph, quick trips. They are fast-talking and glib, live by their wits, and have the wonderful party gift of thinking of what they should say at the time, not as an afterthought. They have a delightful sense of humor, a turn to the prankish, and a quick, roving eye. Even as they move down the aisle to the altar, they will look around the church to see what they may be missing."

John Kennedy was our first Gemini president, and he was a classic example of Gemini's ready charm and wit. But he had the Gemini tendency not to follow through, as witness the Bay of Pigs fiasco, and the lack of follow-up in on-the-site inspection of missile bases in Cuba.

As there are children, so are there parents, and Cancer, or Moon Child, representing the home, is the mother of the zodiac. She is the provider, the person most likely to say, "Would you like something to eat or drink?"

"Somebody," Winters told the class, "once said that Cancers had a deep-rooted fear of going hungry, and that's why they always seem to be storing food. Like the Crab, which is their symbol, Cancers like to hang onto things. Back in Ohio my family always had the cellar full of canned goods, and the icebox jammed.

"In the same way, Cancers like to keep their home. They may buy a new home, but they'll hang on to the old one. My parents own three houses."

I heard a chuckle. It was a neighboring student, Bill Corrado, the well-known psychic, who had bought a house in the San Fernando Valley section of Los Angeles, while still holding on to a house in Hollywood.

Bill was a Cancer, born July 5.

Cancer men, long after their majorities, are extremely attached to their mothers, and many a marriage to a Cancer husband has been periled by a wife's jealousy of a filial relationship she resented without understanding. Perhaps because they never throw anything away, Cancers love curios and antiques, and are a strong money sign, hoarding the wealth Taurus is so prone to spend.

Leo, fifth in the wheel, stands for the Sun, and, as such, is the king or queen of the zodiac. Like other royalty, whose whims are seldom questioned, pride is their weak suit. They express themselves boldly, theatrically, and can't brook contradiction. They have still another foible. "They consider themselves great lovers, and like to talk about their exploits," Winters said, "but usually they are spreading it on a bit."

Leo in the fifth house of children explains Leos' compatibility with children. "Leo's the one sign," Winters said, "that will be a child with children. They know exactly what children like, and think nothing of crawling on the floor or making faces with them. They'll bring home a puppy or a kitten, or a bird, anything to amuse their children. And the Leo might be critical of his offspring, but nobody else can be with impunity. However, they are not as tolerant of other people's children."

Leos are dramatically inclined, whatever their profession. Mae West in stage and screen, Alexandre Dumas, swashbuckling author of the *Three Musketeers,* and financier Bernard Baruch, who captured headlines sitting on a park bench and delivering himself of homilies.

With Virgo, the sixth house sign, the zodiac family circle broadended into a community, Virgo being the symbol of public service, work, labor. Virgo was the teacher, and therefore critical, meticulous, with an eye to detail and planning. "Their major problem," said Ralph, "is that they are hypercritical not only of others but themselves. Hence they are supersensitive to criticism leveled at themselves."

Mercury, which should logically be assigned to mercurial Gemini, was arbitrarily assigned to Virgo, as a mental sign of a certainly harder cast than Gemini. Virgo, cold, dry and melancholy, is also the sign of the Virgin. At the traditionally accepted time of Christ's birth, the constellation of Virgo rose at midnight, December 25, the date fixed by the Church for the Nativity.

Eventually, when the right time arrives for it, astrologically, Virgo might have another ruling planet. "Some astrologers feel that the Earth logically rules Taurus," Winters pointed out, "and others speculate that another planet, Vulcan, mythologically the consort of Venus, believed to be lurking behind Mercury, will eventually be discovered and assigned to Virgo, which is next door to Libra."

Winters didn't seem impressed by Virgo, whose most celebrated contemporary was a recent President, Lyndon Johnson. "They're lint pickers, great on detail, but painfully so. They make good musicians and composers, because they have the faculty of putting the notes in the right place."

I was especially interested to see how our Libran teacher would handle his sign.

"In Libra, the Sun is now in the seventh house. The adventurer has settled down, first in bands and groups, then the home and then the community, with its laws and civilization. Libra is the house of harmony and balance, and many judges and lawyers are Libras. Libras are especially upset by lack of harmony. They are the diplomats of the zodiac, often so tactful in their wish for harmony that their own views are subordinated and they may seem vacillating and deceptive, without really being so."

Dwight D. Eisenhower was the most prominent Libra of the day, and he illustrated the primary quality of the balancing Libra; first a diplomat, even though a soldier also. "It is unusual for Libra to be a General, but Eisenhower had strong planets in Scorpio (traditionally ruled by Mars). Also, anybody who knew him knew that his strong suit in World War II, when he commanded the Allied armies, was in weaving together a bunch of Scorpio prima donnas that included England's bumptious Field Marshal Bernard L. Montgomery, the impossible Frenchman, General Charles de Gaulle, and the temperamental General George Patton."

It took a Libra to know a Libra. "Behind this diplomacy," said Winters tactfully, "is a hidden need for approval, so true of so many Librans."

Like so many Librans, Eisenhower constantly put himself in the other person's place in assessing a situation. "Librans are not aggressive leaders," Winters observed, "and the country was run by committee when Ike was president. Libras keep saying, 'What do you think?' "

As the natural occupant of the seventh house, Libra was in the house of partners in its zodiacal opposition rounding out the first house representing the self. In astrology, as in life, opposites are often mutually attracting because one supplies what the other lacks. "Generally, people get along very well with their opposite sign, which is not so much opposite as complementary," Winters said. "Opposite Aries supplies the aggressiveness Libra needs, and passive Libra in turn gives impatient Aries balance. Taurus would get something from Scorpio, Gemini from Sagittarius, and Cancer from Capricorn."

Next was one of the most intriguing signs, Scorpio, which could be highly sensual or spiritual. Traditionally, Mars, the god of War, ruled Scorpio, but since the discovery of Pluto, many astrologers have assigned it to Scorpio, essentially a secretive sign, concerned with the best and worst of society. Pluto, associated with mysterious underground influences, is the planet of regeneration and it seemed to fit the eighth house influences of death, sex, and matters associated with the soul.

"Originally," said Winters, "Scorpio was assigned to the planet Mars because of Scorpio's warlike qualities. Scorpios on the positive side are government-conscious, with a passion for law and order. Where Libras are the judges and defense attorneys, Scorpios are the prosecutors. They like to set things right, and are often the policemen of the community, or the soldiers, surgeons and butchers. Often they become militant spiritual leaders. Evangelists like Billy Graham and Billy Sunday fight to save everybody, whether they like it or not."

There is a robustness about Scorpios, obviously necessary if, like Teddy Roosevelt, one of our more formidable Presidents, they are to "speak softly and carry a big stick."

As the community grows up, it builds churches and universities. The athletes of the zodiac are the Sagittarians, and they are also adventurers into spiritual matters as well as into the hunt. "They are the sign of lengthy communications, novels, tending to engage in studies in depth, rather than skimming the surface like Geminis. Geminis might start a local newspaper, collect all the gossip and publish it. Sagittarius is substantial, like its ruler, Jupiter, the largest of the planets. Gemini is as vapid as Mercury."

Every community must have its salesmen, and ninth-house Sagittarius, the sign of the traveler, makes a great salesman. Ruled by the planet of good fortune, Sagittarians are happy-go-lucky, optimistic, and generally honorable. "The Sagittarian salesman wouldn't sell anybody anything he wouldn't buy himself, whereas Gemini wouldn't think twice about it."

Capricorns, ruled by taskmaster Saturn, are the organizers of the community—the Howard Hugheses, the J. Paul Gettys, the Richard Nixons. "Well symbolized by the sign of the goat, they want to climb to the top of the mountain. Not happy without goals, they will circle the world to get to a point where they can ascend that mountain. They can be gloomy and forbidding at times, but in the main are serious, dedicated people with strong moral purpose as they drive to the top."

The eleventh house Aquarians are the community politicians, concerned in their gregariousness that they know best how people should live. "Aquarians are group conscious, and are rarely found alone. They like friends around, like the telephone to ring. They believe in their group mission, particularly for the downtrodden. 'If one person is a slave, nobody is free.' Abraham Lincoln, an Aquarius, freed the slaves. Franklin Roosevelt brought in group agencies to help the economically depressed, the wage slaves. Critics said he didn't care about the individual, only the masses—a demagogue."

Aquarius is the sign of the Aquarian Age, and Uranus, governing Aquarius, affects or controls electricity, space, social upheaval. "Thomas Edison, an Aquarian, invented electric lights and motion picture cameras; Lindberg was the first to fly the ocean; and John L. Lewis led the labor revolution."

Supposedly more famous people are Aquarians than any other sign, but this only seems so because, like Douglas MacArthur and Clark Gable, Aquarians are often involved with crowds and masses and consequently more publicized than other signs. However, they are seldom a part of the herd, but the shepherd who invariably walks a little apart from the flock. As the sign that feels it knows best, there is a tendency for Aquarians to become despotic, frequently grinding up their marriage partners, business associates, or the very masses they had undertaken to save through their superior knowledge.

Winters glumly shook his head as he consulted the blackboard. "Pisces, ruled by Neptune, is the dust bin of the zodiac. Everything not accounted for by the other signs has been swept into Pisces. It is a psychic house, the seat of enormous intuition. Edgar Cayce, the greatest of American psychics, was a Pisces. It is a dual sign, like

Gemini; Pisces can be either poetic or a screaming fishwife. And sometimes they can be both. They are devoted to the welfare of people. If you are in trouble, find a Pisces, he'll go right into the hospital and suffer with you, but he needs to be appreciated.

"When misunderstood, Pisces enjoy being martyrs. Materialism means nothing to them. Edgar Cayce walked around with holes in his shoes. They develop a veneer as they get older to protect their feelings. Rules and regulations are not for them; they can't be brainwashed. Their sensitive natures often don't permit them to stand up to unusual stress, and they turn for escape to drugs and alcohol. Pisces says, 'I believe,' but often isn't sure what he believes."

Piscean women are generally more attractive physically than other signs, as if to compensate for their emotional shortcomings. Piscean men—whose symbolic fish swim in opposite directions—are often torn by inner conflicts. But when, by application, they rise above their nature, as did President Andrew Jackson, they are as strong and steadfast as anybody could hope to be.

"You can generally tell a Pisces," said Winters, "but you can't tell him anything good."

4

A Time for the Moon

At different times, in different signs, the planets tell different things. Traditional astrology grouped these celestial bodies into malefics and benefics, and it was a commentary on our thinking that the malefics far outnumbered the benefics. Jupiter and Venus were the "good guys" of the skies, Uranus, Saturn and Mars the so-called bad guys, and the neutrals, Mercury, Neptune and Pluto, were traditionally bad when afflicted.

But to our teacher, there was no such thing as a bad planet, and even when badly aspected, squared at ninety degrees or in opposition at 180 degrees to other planets or signs, such as the ascendant, midheaven or house cusps, they serve to develop the individual who reacts boldly to the stress of events, bending a little perhaps, but never breaking.

"So Saturn delays, Uranus upsets, and Mars abrades," Winters said with a shrug. "Let them, and let us, be patient, adaptable and resolute, knowing that in time we can make the planets work for us by synchronizing fulfilling action or the pause that refreshes to a time when the position–or disposition–of the planets becomes personally more favorable."

As a Taurus, I had had transiting Saturn on my Sun for nearly two years, and I was almost beginning to imagine its cold clammy hand on me, there had been so many delays and restrictions in my life.

"Just do your work and be patient," Winters enjoined, "and when

Saturn finishes its two and a half year cycle in Taurus and moves into Gemini in June of 1971, you will feel as if a lid had been taken off your career, if you have met the challenges of this taskmaster by applying yourself vigorously to your labors during this period."

It was no time for marriage, while Saturn was over one's Sun, or for that matter, square to one's Sun sign, as, in a lesser degree, the Saturn-squared signs Leo and Aquarius were also under Saturn's restrictive influence at this time.

"This is the time for all good Taureans," said Winters, "to remain firm and hold the fort. For as the Bible promises of adversity, this, too, shall pass."

It seemed hardly fair to my Gemini friends that my gain, as Saturn moved out of Taurus, should be their loss. However, Geminis were forever jumping all over the lot, and a bit of Saturn for two and a half years might very well be just what they needed to pin them down.

"Saturn in Gemini," Winters confirmed, "is a very good position for this planet, as the two tend to balance each other out."

Moon, ascendant and planets—as the Sun—all flavored the signs they passed through with their unique personalities, and were in turn flavored by them. The transiting Moon, which moved the tides and obviously affected the fluids in the human body, was astrologically important because it ruled the emotions, and staying only two and a half days in each sign, in contrast to Uranus' seven years and Neptune's fourteen, subjected our subconscious to constant change. As they aspected one another, the Sun and the Moon together influenced love, marriage, birth, even birth control.

Although the Moon seemed inert to the step of our astronauts after their 225,000-mile flight into space, scientists, not astrologers, have shown how vitally it affects us earthlings. Not only has its gravitational force been proven to cause the tides, but scientists of the Bureau of Standards have reported a daily variation in the earth's magnetic field due to solar and lunar influences. Other scientists found a magnetic variation in the atmosphere 70 per cent greater a few days after the New and Full Moon than after the Moon's first and third quarters. An eight-year study of radio waves revealed them almost twice as strong before the Full Moon as the New Moon. People are directly affected, too. Professor Petersen, at the University of Illinois, confirming an old wives' tale, found male deaths to be numerous (presumably as they went berserk) and female deaths few during Full

Moon, the woman apparently better able to synchronize her cycles to those of the Moon, which, astrologically, stands for the female, as the Sun does for the male. The menstrual cycle in women is sharply activated at the New and Full Moon, and Surgeon Edson Andres of Tallahassee, Florida, finding a tendency to hemorrhage during Full Moon, avoids surgery at that time.

It is no wonder that the Moon, as Winters pointed out, is the planet of the female, the mother, the wife, the sweetheart, and that when it is afflicted to her own natal Sun, square or in opposition, the female often finds it hard to express her deepest feelings as she is in inner conflict with herself. This conflict is accentuated whenever the transiting moon hits such a natal Moon.

The natal Moon, to the degree of its influence, modifies the meaning of each sign it is in, beginning with the first house sign of Aries, a rather bleak place for the Moon, but still a beginning.

Moon in Aries

The Moon in Aries, said Winters, reflects a desire to be strong, independent and courageous. People ordinarily meek and mild, but with steel inside when the chips are down, often have Moon in Aries. They are interested in action and personal achievement, even when this secret desire is glossed over with a certain tenderness. In love they are ardent, but inclined to consider love a chase. Once they catch their quarry, they tend not to give him as much attention. It doesn't mean they aren't good husbands or wives, but that they feel the person is theirs, and that's it. They are faithful and loyal, but don't expect Moon in Aries to be affectionate, as they feel they've done all that during the romance, and it's done with. When they use their subconscious power to control and rule themselves, they're genuinely content. But all too often they try to control others, and that starts trouble.

Moon in Taurus

Taurus is the best place for the Moon, as it is unusually stable here. Though frequently accused of being money-minded, Taureans are actually driven by a subconscious desire for security, acquiring possessions, a home, land, a car, gilt-edged stocks. They are disposed to being affable, charming, gracious, and are extremely loyal, once sure their loyalty isn't misplaced. Slow to fall in love, once they have fallen, they love forever. Moon in Taurus would hardly ever think in terms of divorce, unless the other person committed the inexcusable sin of infidelity. Then they would tear themselves away, even if still in love. Loyal themselves, they can't brook disloyalty. Generally thinking well of themselves, they are driven by a desire to excel but often become overly complacent when success comes too easily. Or, reflecting the underlying indolence of the Taurus, they can sit back and not make a try, saying they could accomplish whatever it was if they wanted to. But the desire for security, when pinched for money, could prod their quest for aesthetic beauty. They like their comfort.

Moon in Gemini

Moon in Gemini wants to communicate their deepest feelings. They frequently have difficulty articulating what they are, but they never stop trying. They picture themselves as great intellects, discussing books, paintings, international affairs with fluency, though they may have read only the book reviews and the art critiques, and skimmed the front pages of the newspapers. A Gemini Moon is restless, constantly seeking, without quite knowing what he wants. The Gemini bride walking down the aisle would check all the men out of the corner of her eye to see what she was losing and the Gemini bridegroom would do as much with the women, then they would reassure themselves they had made the right choice. They collect a host of friends wherever they go, and they are always going. However, most of us would call such friends acquaintances. Moon in Gemini must be prevalent in Hollywood. For if you say to a person in Hollywood, "Do you know so and so?" he will invariably reply, even though he met the person only casually years before, "Oh, sure, he's a very good friend"—a typical Moon in Gemini answer.

Moon in Cancer

Moon in Cancer is extremely sensitive to their surroundings, both environmental and personal. They have strong feelings about their mothers, almost a psychic attunement at times. Their feelings are easily hurt when they're not listened to and respected, and they are incapable of masking their feelings. They are perfectly willing to give, provided they get back in proper measure what they've given out—a true Cancer attribute. When things don't go their way, they go into a shell and clam up. They have a marvelous intuition. Going right to the heart of a matter, they seem instinctively to know the need of the moment. There is some ability for sentimental poetry and music, as witness the Moon Child Anne Morrow Lindbergh, whose imagery was so fantastic that she could write a whole chapter about sea shells. Their major problem is that, being so sensitive, they not only worry themselves to distraction but others to the point of irritability. They should follow their own intuitions, and not listen to Mother.

Moon in Leo

Moon in Leo gives people a subconscious desire to rule or control. These individuals are not happy taking orders and have a need to be the attraction. Because of their underlying desire to exalt themselves, they are probably the most honorable sign of the zodiac. Moon in Leo would find it difficult to lie, cheat or steal, as it would disturb the royal conception they have of themselves. Hopeless romantics, they are married to their pride as well as to another person. They think of themselves as great lovers, and are inordinately generous to the loved one. But they require recognition, and are prone to discuss their own good points when nobody else will. They have an intense desire to rise and shine, to lift themselves to a position of trust and responsibility. They can't bear the thought of being second to anybody. Usually nobody begrudges them success, because they have achieved it honorably, and they let you know it.

Moon in Virgo

Moon in Virgo loves with mind rather than heart. It is cool and calculating, knows it, and equates this coolness with intellect. Individuals with this Virgo Moon are primarily interested in knowledge; quite a number become teachers or professional students. They make enormous demands on their own intelligence, while recognizing that the other person may not be as intelligent as they. They can be a bit patronizing, but, generally, they are reserved, don't like the limelight, and keep telling themselves they want knowledge to better serve others. And since they believe this, they very often make it happen. Not emotionally inclined, they normally wouldn't be attracted to a person who wasn't capable of conversing on an intellectual level. Since the sign is ruled by Mercury, they have a liking for change, travel, investigation. Because of a deep inner reserve, the person with Moon in Virgo is often in conflict with himself, but can be counted on to think his way out of it.

Moon in Libra

With the natal Moon in Libra, the individual is usually affected by others, as he essentially likes to please. He prefers to work in close association with others, and expresses his inner self with gentle courtesy. Because of his gentle instincts, affected by a love of elegance and beauty, and a passion for fairness, he frequently defends people under attack. He will readily do anything for anyone, as he finds it difficult to say no. However, because of his strong sense of justice, he will refuse to compromise his principles, and then the velvet glove becomes an iron fist. Moon in Libra sees both sides of a question and intuitively knows and understands each side. So their special genius is in the field of human relations. Their instincts are sound, and they do best when they follow them. They have a deep appreciation for the arts, but are so sensitive that they often can't sit through a sad motion picture without crying. While they make friends easily, they are particularly fond of young people. They are inclined to love and marriage, the Moon providing the emotional link to Libra's natural seventh house of partnerships.

Moon in Scorpio

Moon in Scorpio is the most difficult Moon position of all. Persons with Moon in Scorpio have an inclination to be spiritual, as they have a drive for perfection. However, they are extremely physical, and whoever said the spirit is willing but the flesh weak undoubtedly had Moon in Scorpio in mind. Consequently, with this inner God-like feeling they have for things to be proper and right, they feel ashamed a great deal of the time of the things they do sexually. They'll go along for weeks, months, not doing anything in this area that they feel wrong, and then they'll submit to their strong physical appetite. The key to this Moon position is self-control, and once they've learned this, the spiritual within them will come to the fore and they will find inner satisfaction. With this moon position, they can be militant evangelists, relentless detectives or great generals. They are tremendously intuitive, and when this is combined with their spiritual potential, they are on the highest plane in terms of morality and humanism—the Royal Eagle, not the stinging Scorpion.

Moon in Sagittarius

Mentally and inwardly they range the universe, and regardless of whatever mundane job they may have, they reach for the stars. In the same way, lofty aspirations cause them to set up unreachable goals that their conscious minds tell them they cannot achieve, and so this is frequently a device for getting out of attaining anything. When they do aim for a high but attainable goal, approaching it with all the spirituality and higher knowledge that Sagittarius can acquire, they can achieve enormously. However, it's generally difficult for them to settle on one thing because they're always looking for something better. One of their major problems is learning to accept life as it is, and people as they are. As Sagittarius is the sign of philosophy and higher learning, they have a potential for wisdom, or, conversely, a listless ennui that finds an excuse for not doing anything as there is no person or thing worth doing it for. What this Moon sign should do is learn to use the tools available, and adapt to the surroundings he is in. If he sits around and waits for the right surroundings, he might wait forever.

Moon in Capricorn

Moon in Capricorn thinks of himself as being practical and hard-headed, successfully competing with the world on its own terms, until he is strong enough to change the terms. Such apparently diverse types as Abraham Lincoln and Adolf Hitler had Moon in Capricorn, and as this is a ruthless Moon, they were ruthless in pursuit of their goals, and both fulfilled this sign's requirement of seizing power. The image of success plays constantly in the mind of people with this Moon position, and they will usually achieve success, in line with the idea that if you can get a mental picture of what you want out of life, you are on your way to getting it. Moon in Capricorn enjoys the contest, and the work that needs to be done to achieve a goal. However, these individuals are rarely satisfied with anything less than complete success, and so will not give up. Their security lies in the authority they have; they thrive on the respect of others. Not necessarily cold, they have control of their emotions. However, the danger comes in the event of failure, and then they become extremely bitter. They can't stand defeat, the world is over for them–and, like Hitler, they wipe out, one way or another.

Moon in Aquarius

A person with Moon in Aquarius feels that people need him, and therefore he is filled with the desire to make the world around him a better and happier place, whatever the cost to him–or them. Richard Nixon is one of the notable people with this position, and this tells you, if there is any doubt about it, that he means well. It is a marvelous Moon position, because its great purpose is to help people. Individuals with this Moon position don't even mind when they're imposed upon, since they'd rather be wrong nine times out of ten than take a chance on refusing the one who really deserves help. They often become a strong force for good, friends to humanity. This Moon position is disappointing to sweethearts or lovers because those with Moon in Aquarius usually don't zero in on one individual. They love everyone (even if they do seem aloof, like Nixon), and they would consider it enormously selfish if someone demanded their love at the expense of other people. They enjoy a gregarious social life, with themselves as the emotional center, though, physically, they may stand on the sidelines. If Moon in Aquarius can't get out, he'll live on the telephone, running up a mountainous phone bill in his endless efforts to run people's lives.

Moon in Pisces

Moon in Pisces is a spiritual position. Their desire is to achieve wisdom–not education, but the wisdom of the ages. They'd like to dwell in the misty perfection of Shangri-la and to know themselves, to be in tune, and not be troubled or have anything to do with security or trying to make a living. They just don't want to be bothered with anything mundane. If they can't get the material things of life, then they just develop a philosophy that makes these things unnecessary. They are great meditators and philosophers within themselves, and for themselves. Their greatest source of unhappiness is their violation of one of their own principles. You cannot brainwash Moon in Pisces because they develop their own code and their own laws. Your laws are not even considered, they're not necessary. Consequently, other people can be made very unhappy by a person with Moon in Pisces. We all like to have people operate in terms of our code, and the laws devised by Moon in Pisces have nothing to do with the reality of practical existence. Nevertheless, the person with Moon in Pisces probably has more chance to achieve self-realization than anyone else, because, if nothing else, he does get to know himself. And if he can stand himself, he's got it made.

To get the natal Moon sign, it is well, Winters stressed, to know the exact time of birth, since the Moon stays in a sign for less than two and a half days at a time.

It had been an interesting session, and yet I could see some puzzled looks in the class.

"Any questions?" Ralph Winters asked.

A young man looked up with a frown. "I know several people with Moon in Pisces, and they don't seem very spiritual. In fact, they're either drunk half the time or on drugs."

Winters stroked his chin. "You saw the negative side of this Pisces Moon. They probably felt they were not living up to their potential, and they would then develop along parallel lines with another water sign, Scorpio, which builds up a self-hate expressing itself in destruction (à la mass murderer Charles Manson) when it gets sidetracked to the physical. Out of lack of self-esteem, they would, like Scorpios, wallow in the mud, become alcoholics, drug addicts, suicides."

Sometimes, as in Manson's case, the feeling is inverted, and the hate turns outward. In reality, there is very little difference between suicide and homicide, the propelling drives being similar.

"The Moon position, next to the Sun sign, is the most important in a female chart," said Winters, "because women are moon-ruled, as witness their monthly cycle.

"Conversely, Mars is strongly indicative of the male drive. Where his Mars is at birth, in what house and sign, largely determines a man's level of action."

My Mars was in the seventh house in Cancer.

Winters smiled. "That proves the point. In the seventh house of associations it would be an expression of your energy force at work. You couldn't relax on a vacation if you wanted to. You'd soon become restless and want to get back into action, and the activity would be of a sensitive, even psychic nature, as Cancer is an intuitive water sign, and in the seventh house it would tend to color the quality of your work."

Astrology seemed to explain everything—seemed to, anyway.

"And where is your Mars?" I asked.

"In Leo, in the first house, of which Mars is the natural ruler, accenting its impact, and accounting, I suppose, for my robust, hearty nature."

Although we hadn't really gone into aspects, there was some class curiosity as to how the Moon and Sun flavored one another.

A middle-aged woman, a Libra, asked mildly:

"Would a person with both the Sun in Libra and the Moon in Pisces expressing badly be in a bad way?"

Winters had his own Sun well in mind.

"With his Libran sign of balance afflicted, he would consider the world out of balance, and Piscean-wise would contemplate getting it in balance. With an adverse Moon, making him think he had not lived up to expectations, he could go completely out of kilter. Kennedy's assassin, Lee Harvey Oswald, a Libra, was so out of balance that he thought if he killed Kennedy this might get things back in balance. And with an afflicted Moon in Capricorn, he was ruthless in expression."

Because of its rapid journey through the wheel of the horoscope, moving an average of twelve degrees a day, there is no better celestial timing device than the transiting Moon. "When it hits the fourth house," Winters said, "you can very well start something that will culminate successfully when it gets up to the tenth house. And if you were fortunate enough to have the new Moon cross the fourth house cusp at the same time your natal Moon was also in the fourth house," he added, "you would have an absolutely marvelous starting point for anything you wanted—with favorable aspects for at least two weeks—before it goes back down under the first cusp where it becomes inactive in terms of doing things."

As a reflection of the subconscious, the impressionable Moon stimulates the thought processes as it moves from sign to sign and house to house. "In your first house the transiting Moon has to do with yourself, what you want to accomplish for your own satisfaction. In the second house you plan ways and means of increasing your money, and in the third house you're thinking of communicating; the fourth house is the home and this is where you begin to take action. When it goes through the fourth house you will begin to gather your forces, and when it hits the fifth house off you go, on up to culmination at the top of the chart in the tenth house."

Since we were all pretty much creatures of mood, the transiting Moon, the one actually up in the skies, was of special importance.

As this Moon passed through a natal chart, picking up and coloring the quality of the houses and signs, it seemed to effectively foreshadow the nature of the subject's activity and the underlying emotion behind it.

"This Moon," said Winters, "can tell you why you're doing what you are."

Differently than the natal Moon, which kept its original influence throughout one's life, the transiting Moon was transitory in influence. But since it repeated its cycle every month, even its transitory nature could be counted on and anticipated if the individual knew his chart sufficiently well to keep track of the Moon as it moved through his twelve houses.

And of course any delineation began with the first house.

Transiting Moon—First House

You'll have a desire for change and be much less conservative during this two-day-and-seven-hour transit. It inclines you toward sociability and public affairs, or publicity—you want to push yourself forward, to get active. The first house being the natural home of Aries denotes enormous energy and impatience. You want to let people know that you're on the scene, and you'll be inclined to take the lead at this time.

Transiting Moon–Second House

You will turn your attention to matters of finance. It's a good time to plan increasing your personal income. It's also good for all matters of the second house, the house of your personal freedom, your money, your portable possessions. It's also good for vocal exercise, Taurus, the natural ruler of the second house, being the ruler of the throat. So practice your singing when the Moon is in the second house.

Transiting Moon–Third House

You have a very changeable flavor here, this being the natural house of Gemini and Mercury. If you made a decision when the Moon was transiting the third house, chances are that you'd change it, or, having done something, you'd do it over again. It's a good time for mental enlightenment, to find out more about various things you've been interested in.

Transiting Moon–Fourth House

Your living quarters or family and domestic affairs are highlighted. You might be interested in land or property, you might want to sell your house or redecorate it. You should not overindulge in food or drink, as there is a tendency to retain liquid. You would gain a pound or two during this two-day transit because of water retention. If your face is bloated at this time, don't worry about it. It's only the Moon.

Transiting Moon–Fifth House

Here the Moon may cause your interest to quicken regarding speculation or gambling, or just simply to take chances. It wouldn't necessarily have to be with money; it could also be in romance, with luck in love favored at this time. It gives you a sense of freedom and you are more affectionate at this time. When planning a party, have it while the Moon is transiting the fifth house for instant success. Actors would also find it a good time for interviews, because they'd be putting their best foot forward.

Transiting Moon–Sixth House

This is the house that has to do with employment or employees, and so interviews you went on during the two days when the Moon is in the fifth house bear fruit at this time in getting the job. You won't be at your best, physically, however, because as this is the house of health, you have to exercise a little more caution about overindulgence to maintain health. The intestinal tract, ruled by this house and its natural sign, Virgo, will be especially sensitive.

Transiting Moon–Seventh House

Law suits and all dealings with others–unions, partnerships, contractual arrangements–undertaken when the Moon is in this house are subject to changes. It's not a good time to get married or form a partnership or have anything to do with others in terms of permanence. Don't place confidence or reliability in others at this time.

Transiting Moon–Eighth House

In the eighth house, this transit inclines our attentions toward other people's money. If your interests are in other people, then it would intensify your interest in them. It also has a tendency to make you think of those who have passed on from this plane to the next. It's an excellent time for communing with the spirit world. You're vibrating here on an other-world frequency level. It should also be sexually interesting.

Transiting Moon–Ninth House

Your attention is turned to the higher channels of thought. You'll want to get away from ordinary workaday things, and if that Moon transited in the ninth house over a weekend, you may head for San Francisco, Miami, or Hawaii, anywhere just to put distance between yourself and the humdrum that bores you. The grass will look greener at this time in a distant field, and as this is the spiritual house, you might also have some dreams that are likely to be prophetic. So heed your dreams when the Moon is in the ninth house. There may be some surprises.

Transiting Moon–Tenth House

In this transit of the Moon, you certainly would be interested in your parents. In the fourth house, your parents were interested in you and you probably got a lot of advice. Now you may be giving them advice or getting in touch to find out how things are going with them. It also inclines you to business affairs or to an interest in professional people. As the Moon touches that tenth house, of midheaven activity, it might cause you to decide, "Well, I'm going to call my lawyer, I've been putting this off, and today I'm going to do it."

Transiting Moon–Eleventh House

You'll probably spend these two days or so contacting people you like, making new friends, or looking up old friends. You may be very inventive at this time, find new ways of doing things, since the eleventh house is ruled by Aquarius, and Uranus, the inventive planet, is its ruling body. When the Moon goes through its house you'll tend to find new approaches to old problems.

Transiting Moon–Twelfth House

The twelfth house transit awakens an interest in occult affairs or matters of secret or mysterious nature. You may also want to have that long-neglected physical checkup at this time, since the twelfth house has to do with institutions. You may be vulnerable to secret enemies, who will be more inclined to do little things behind your back, and you may be inclined to do the same. So watch out.

It had been a rather long time to spoon with the Moon. And with a sigh–a Moon sigh perhaps–Winters finished his classroom discourse.

"Next week," he said, "the planets."

5

A Time to Know Your Planets

With his first breath, before the anguished cry that announced his birth, the newborn child was stamped with the magnetic rays of the great cosmos. As a child of the universe, he became a reflection of the planetary aspects, a microcosm of the greater macrocosm above. And as these aspects changed with changing time, they constantly interacted with his magnetic field to affect the course of his life.

"There are," said Winters, "360 degrees in your wheel of life, and each one of these degrees has meaning, either by aspect to the various planets, the ascendant, the midheaven, the descendant, the nadir, or in solitude. This reflects the almost infinite number of different individuals. Even identical twins would be different if they were born as much as four minutes apart. Every four minutes your ascendant would change one degree and when your ascendant changes, your entire chart changes. If one twin was born in 29 degrees of Aries and the other twin took its first breath four minutes later, he would be in the first degree of Taurus rising. This could make an enormous difference in these two people. The Taurus person may be stocky and a little on the dark side, with brown or darker eyes, whereas the person born in Aries just four minutes before might have a light complexion and blond hair and be much taller than its so-called twin. So with these differences in degrees we find our infinite differences in people. So many people say astrology has no meaning because if it had meaning there'd only be twelve different kinds of people. And certainly it's obvious that there are more than that. That's an infinite number of people. In fact, there are no two people precisely alike, and there never have been. This will explain why that is. Obviously, a twenty minute difference in birth could result in as much as five degrees difference."

There were people practically alike, though, astro-twins, born at virtually the same moment in the same city, whose charts are almost identical. These astro-twins, though strangers, frequently lead parallel lives, marrying, having children, meeting success and failure, divorcing and dying, at the same time. Winters cited astro-twins born in nearby hamlets in New England, at the same sweep of the minute hand, on November 13, 1944. Unknown to each other, they entered the University of New Hampshire at the same time, then joined the same fraternity, became boon companions, and in their twentieth year perished together in a fraternity house fire in which they were the only fatalities. Everybody else escaped.

Their horoscopes were identical—and so was their destiny.

The rising sign, the face the individual shows to the world, changes every two hours, starting with the hour of birth. "The rising sign or ascendant," Winters explained, "is simply that sign that appeared to be rising over the eastern horizon at the time of the subject's birth."

If the Sun was in Libra when the individual was born, and he was born at sunrise or in the two hour segment of the zodiac thereafter, then he would be a double Libra and have Libra rising, on the cusp of his first house. The house cusps would then proceed counterclockwise, from Libra to Scorpio through all the signs to Virgo in the twelfth house.

The ascendant was considered an outer manifestation of the Sun sign it identified with, the individual presumably looking more like his rising sign than his Sun sign. A Scorpio rising, for instance, would tend to have dark hair, a little frizzy on the sides, a Roman nose and dark complexion. "All the things that have to do with the Scorpio Sun," Winters said, "would manifest with Scorpio rising, even though this wasn't what you were really like at all, but was only what you were presenting to the public, a reflection of your personality."

In his own case, as a Libra with Leo rising, Winters generally was taken for a Leo because he spoke with the dramatic flavor of a Leo, though he felt more a Libra, wanting to see the other fellow's side, deep down inside.

"When I answer that phone," Winters said, "I'm a Leo."

The individual is an activated composite of his planets and their aspects, of the interplay between Sun and Moon and rising sign, in the houses and signs which gives them their special expression. Venus is the emotional antenna, Mercury the messenger of the senses, Saturn, the delayer, the teacher, Uranus the rebel, Mars the energizer who makes things happen, Jupiter the optimistic ally, Neptune the hidden mind, the great deceiver, and Pluto the regenerator.

Saturn is inclined to keep the other planets in their place, and with his sobering influence, as a symbol of ultimate authority, he generally has the last word, and so that puts him first.

"We'll start our tour of the planets with Saturn," said he, "because Saturn runs your life, and don't forget it."

And so the excursion to our stars begins:

SATURN

Saturn is second only to Jupiter in size, 72,400 miles in diameter. Some 886 million miles from the Sun, it takes 28 to 30 years to complete its orbit around the Sun. "You can really guide your life with Saturn," Winters said. "Transmitting Saturn conjuncts its natal position at your 28th year, and at your 28th year you put away childish things and charge into life and settle down. This can result in marriage, a job start, or a beginning of a new life. When it comes around the second time and opposes its natal position, at 42, there's a change of life again, and this time with the ladies and probably the men, too, there's a little physical change. It's all controlled by Saturn and all on schedule. Saturn is the most important planet in your chart in terms of living in this world."

Saturn has been called the taskmaster, the teacher, the father, even likened to Satan. In one's Sun sign, Saturn tends to restrict and delay, but such restrictions could be good for the soul if the person grows within from the increased burdens he is called upon to shoulder.

In the same sign as Uranus, it could mean success in enterprises requiring a degree of planning, and in good aspect, sextile or trine, to the Sun or Moon, it indicates a long life and a vital one. Natal Saturn, unfavorably aspected to Uranus, in opposition, squared, or conjunct, indicates a heavy illness, or accident potential, in the individual charts; and in its transiting phase, similarly afflicted, it points to riots and insurrection, disregard for the rights of others, and disasters.

In favorable aspect to Neptune, it reflects a burst of inspiration, helpful in the creative arts and in investments. Unfavorably, it signifies losses through treachery or deception.

In the same sign as Mercury, Saturn keeps the emotions under control. "You'd be a darn good poker player with that position," Winters said. "And while you might not be lucky at love, you'd be very lucky in Las Vegas."

With Mars, Saturn tends to confusion.

"I have this position myself," said Winters, "so I've learned the hard way. I'd be on the defensive one minute, then suddenly overreact, until people weren't sure where I stood. And neither was I."

By knowing his Saturn, Winters came to know more about himself, and was more at peace for it.

"Knowing about it, I've overcome this Saturn-Mars thing, so now I'm off the defensive. I've learned the best defense is a good offense. You see, Mars wants to be the aggressor, to go out and do things, and Saturn wants to defend its position. So Mars would be the soldier that goes out to fight, and Saturn would stay in the fort and fight behind the embattlements. But if the Sun and the Moon are strongly placed and other planets are in favorable position, then you would have an admirable balance between defense and offense."

However dark the planets, there is usually a glimmer of Sun.

"If you have a very bad thing in a chart, it's been my experience there's always something to assist that. My Saturn and Mars together, for instance, are sextile to the Sun, so with this favorable aspect it has not been difficult to achieve a proper balance between those two conflicting forces."

Before that he had many anxious moments, turning for comfort to the Biblical injunction:

"I will never give you more than you can bear."

As other planets, Saturn flavors the sign it is in and is flavored by it. **Saturn in Aries** puts everything on an extremely personal basis. "It's reflected in a defensive tendency to think that the world is against you personally. Quite often these people have a chip on their shoulder. If an ordinance was passed saying that the public couldn't walk in a certain park, Saturn in Aries would say, 'Do you know they passed a law today saying *I* can't walk in the park?' They are always fighting City Hall."

Once **Saturn in Taurus** has achieved security, accumulating their share of retirement funds and gilt-edged government securities, then they are extremely generous to others in need because they recognize better than most the need for security. Until that time, however, they could stretch a dollar farther than anybody.

Like other students, I was interested in the positions that affected me, and when Winters said that **Saturn in Gemini** was one of the best positions for Saturn, the trip into class suddenly became worthwhile. Gemini's airiness made Saturn so extroverted that it became positive and outgoing. "Those with Saturn in Gemini attack life with vigor and speed," Winters said. "And they're so quick and elusive they can adapt to any situation. They are good in emergencies."

Saturn in Cancer clings to the mother in childhood, as they get older they turn to their husband or wife. They lack confidence and are looking for protectors, and frequently crawl into a shell. But once they know their problem, and work out of it, they can be pillars of society.

With **Saturn in Leo,** there is the tendency to lead the parade, as if almost instinctively knowing that being aggressive and outgoing was the way to cover up any feelings of insecurity. If such a person couldn't defend himself physically, he would claim he was sick, as he was never one to acknowledge a weakness. Or he would have some other dramatic excuse, never being one to miss a chance to dramatize.

Saturn in Virgo plunges into service and work for others. These people are sticklers for all the rules and regulations, so preoccupied with details that at times they spend so much time in a tree that they never notice the forest. "These people would be a lot happier if they drove their car more and polished it less. Their trouble is that they measure every little ingredient in a cake, and then some fire sign comes along and gobbles up the cake and leaves them the crumbs."

Saturn in Libra is well-balanced, knowing when to be aggressive and when defensive. In an air sign again, Saturn is again at its best. "Those with Saturn in Libra accept whatever life hands them, and they do what is necessary to be liked, without compromising their standards. Saturn in Libra could be a plus in any chart, making something out of a chart otherwise nondescript. It makes all the right moves. It's only when you are doing what you ought not to that you get in trouble with Saturn."

Saturn in Scorpio defend themselves by secrecy, by not letting the other person know their deeper thoughts and feelings. No matter how much they love, there is always one little corner of themselves that is their own. They might have a secret bank account, a private place to relax. "They have enormous strength, but just can't yield themselves completely."

Saturn in Sagittarius leads one to fall back on philosophy. These individuals face up to life with a wholesome attitude, feeling they'll always get what's coming to them because they know better than anyone else that they've done the right things. "Consequently," said Winters, "it's a position of great self-confidence."

Capricorn is ruled by Saturn, and Saturn has its greatest strength in that sign. "Unlike Saturn in Aries, which has to learn that the best defense is a good offense, those who have **Saturn in Capricorn** were born with this knowledge. They have to be careful of being hardheaded and hardhearted, since they will defend themselves against the world by conquering that world. Once they learn to control themselves and not others, they find that the greatest power comes from serving others."

Saturn in Aquarius is quite similar to Saturn in Capricorn with a major difference: They would not hurt anybody to achieve their goals of fame, fortune, authority. Again in an air sign, Saturn is at its best. There is no need to exercise the defensive side of Saturn's nature, as the aggressive side is working outwardly for humanity rather than inwardly for the self. "It is a marvelous position for statesmen, social workers, and others who try to better the world."

Saturn in Pisces has the usual Pisces problem. Life seems very hard for people in this position, and they are supersensitive to the woes and harshness of the world. Like the other water signs, Scorpio and Cancer, they look within themselves to learn what they are doing wrong. "This person gets into new kinds of spiritual and meditation groups in the search for self-realization, sublimating his own feelings of compassion for himself to others; he is capable of enormous sacrifices for his fellow man."

While comparatively few in our class had natal Saturn in Taurus, all were aware that transiting Saturn was presently in Taurus. It had a special effect on Taureans, Scorpios, whom it opposed, and Aquarians and Leos, whom it squared.

"They're all feeling it," Winters said, "Taureans more than anybody. It would cause them to be very much on the defensive, touchy, and subject to periods of depression and melancholy, without quite knowing why they felt that way."

It made those afflicted more security-conscious, and therefore more worried than usual when their security appeared threatened.

"Your chart," said Winters, "explains how the transiting planets affect you as it aspects your natal planets. For instance, Saturn in Taurus is approaching a square to my natal Saturn in Leo, and will stimulate my thinking in terms of security. I've been thinking of buying some land and building a home for retirement."

Winters, just past fifty, and looking younger, was hardly a case for retirement.

"That's what Saturn does for you," he said, "particularly when it's also approaching a square to my Leo ascendant."

Transiting Saturn was also approaching the midheaven or career point in Winters' career, and Saturn at that spot brought what one deserved: "If I get fired in the next few months, you'll know that somewhere along the line I dropped the ball. But if I get a promotion, it's because I earned it."

We all liked our teacher, and hoped that Saturn would be nice to him.

URANUS

Uranus is the planet of genius, creativity, explosiveness, revolution, infinite new horizons, the exciting ruler of Aquarius and the Aquarian Age, the planet that betokens astrology, electricity, aviation and boundless space. It was discovered in 1781 by William Herschel, the English court astronomer, the first planet to be picked out by a telescope, and was originally named Herschel for him, before it was given the name which foreshadowed the birth of the Uranian Age and the first uranium-generated atomic explosion. Some 1,782 million miles from the Sun, 31,000 miles in diameter, it takes 84 years to go around the Sun, staying seven years in each sign.

"Uranus," said Winters, "relates generally to our creativity, our originality and individuality. The position in each sign indicates the direction in which you will try to express this individuality." And, like other heavy planets, it also indicates broad trends in society.

Uranus was in Aries from 1928 to 1935, and individuals born in this period had the **Uranus in Aries** influence of a sharp mind, and the ability to make practical use of the many mechanical details that they grasped without apparent effort. "They think their own thoughts, and express them at the drop of a hat," Winters said. "They will talk for hours to make sure that you understand what they're thinking. They love action and are rarely idle. Aries being the pioneering sign, they come up with ideas that have never been thought of before."

Uranus in Taurus tends toward individualism in property matters. "It adds glamor to the nature," said our teacher, "and draws love to the warm-hearted Taurean who is illuminated by the brilliance of Uranus." In Taurus from 1935 to 1942, it ushered in the era of the charismatic dictators–Hitler, Mussolini, and Franklin Roosevelt, to a certain degree. "Uranus in Taurus brings revolutionary concepts to geographic boundaries, and people now reaching maturity with that position will clear away slums and make good housing for all."

Uranus in Gemini is a freedom-loving aspect. It was in Gemini when the Declaration of Independence was signed in 1776, again in 1863 when Lincoln's Emancipation Proclamation freed the slaves. This position (1942–1949) represented a new way of thinking. "A person with this position," said Winters, "would have a tendency to scatter his thinking and perhaps wind up not accomplishing much, but if he would concentrate on any one field he could create something marvelously new."

Uranus in Cancer (1949–56) is still very young, but is imbued with the urge to improve his living quarters. "My oldest daughters were born during this period," Winters said, "and in 17 years, they've changed residence twelve times–the older marrying at fifteen to accomplish the latest change. Usually, Cancer will buy a home and hang onto it, but Uranus, as the planet upsetting tradition, changes all that."

Uranus in Leo (1956–62) is impressed by greatness to the point of hero worship. "The last such generation was born between 1872 and

1878, and these people were the fiftyish newspaper editors and politicians who lionized Lindbergh when he flew the Atlantic in 1927, dramatized football's Four Horsemen of Notre Dame in the Golden Twenties that also produced such national idols in sports as football's Red Grange, baseball's Babe Ruth, and the ring's Jack Dempsey." There is only one drawback. "While it makes heroes of people, it likes nothing better than to be the hero—and that's why they take great pride in their heroes."

Uranus in Virgo (1962–68), now the youngsters running around from rompers up to the third-grader. While it seems doubtful, looking at them, nevertheless they could be efficiency experts when they reach maturity and they could change many things in terms of labor, education, hospitals, and other great institutions. "But of course all this has been happening with Uranus in Virgo in the realm of socialized medicine, free dental and eye clinics. The last previous time Uranus was in Virgo (1878–85), free education, public libraries, and labor unions came in."

The children born in the seven-year period starting in 1968 will have **Uranus in Libra.** There is hidden genius in this sign, said Winters, and the world can hardly wait its development. "There's a great leadership in that position. Between 1885 and 1891, many of the giants who influenced the modern world were born, subsequently bringing about the nuclear changes that ushered in the Aquarian Age. There are many eccentrics in this group, but when they learn to work in cooperative ventures there's no end to their organizational genius."

Uranus in Scorpio (1891–97) won't happen again until 1977–84, and it could be just as well. "Their genius," said Winters, "works through deep wells in the subconscious, making tremendous power for good or bad." The bad would be exemplified by gangster Al Capone, the good by Eisenhower, to cite the extremes. It is the position of the dictator. "They like to have people fear them; they want to be worshipped."

Uranus in Sagittarius (1897–1904) produced leaders with new concepts in philosophy and spirituality, who with their thinking led the unprecedented rebellion against the regimentation of organized religion. This was accented by **Uranus in Capricorn** (1904–12), where the conservative flavor of Capricorn was further upset, said Winters, by the Uranian planet of change. "Have you noticed the older judges, who you would think to be conservative, who have been condoning from the bench all this upsetting of tradition? Those of us who don't have Uranus in Capricorn look on in amazement and ask why they permit this."

The class was visibly impressed by Winters' observations.

"That must have been Chief Justice Warren's position," somebody said.

"No, he had Uranus in Sagittarius, he was an impractical visionary. He thought everything was wonderful from his ivory tower. But Uranus in Capricorn deliberately believes in rebellion, and thinks in conservative terms of something coming out of the debris of revolution."

I looked forward keenly to the next interpretation for a very personal reason.

Those with **Uranus in Aquarius** (1912–19) strive for a mass-oriented expression of their individual genius. They are for freedom of expression for everyone, and take for granted the dignity of the individual. Winters really was tuned in on this one. "They are the lamplighters of a new birth of freedom in an hour of darkness, also the acolytes of an Aquarian Age that is already on us."

After that, **Uranus in Pisces** (1919–27) was a bit of a letdown. They are in their forties, the mothers and fathers of the love generation they seem the last to understand. However, they did write the books and start the groups that dedicated themselves to Yoga, self-realization, and an interest in occult Eastern philosophies and religions. They were great mediators, meditating while Rome burned. "This position won't be around again until 2005–12," Winters said, "and by 2040, when those born under it achieve maturity, it won't be necessary to work if you don't want to. You can just sit around and meditate to your heart's desire."

MARS

Mars is the energy planet, conspicuous for its red brilliance, which makes it seem angry at times. It has two satellites, Phobos and Deimos, Fear and Panic, and this is about 50 million miles from Earth. Some 141 million miles from the Sun, it is 4,200 miles in diameter, not quite half the earth's size, and takes 687 days to move around the Sun, and through the zodiac.

Mars is the great aspecter, the catalyst that makes things happen. "The activities of your Sun sign and the inner desires of your Moon sign are expressed through Mars," Winters said. "The way you act is indicated by the sign that Mars is in. If it's in the same sign as the Sun this would give the individual a great abundance of energy, and at the same time a rather quick temper and a good deal of temperament."

Without aspects of some sort, good or bad, nothing seems to happen. When Mars is conjunct, in the same sign, with Venus, it quickens the emotions, resulting in a very ardent and passionate nature. Other aspects between the two planets channel the action in accordance with the nature of the aspect. "A natal trine of Mars-Venus would give the person an easy-going approach to love, and what he wanted would come to him. With a square, the appetite for romance would be there, but there would be irritation."

"Is a conjunction good or bad?" somebody asked.

"That depends on the planets. Uranus together with Venus would be an unconventional way of expressing the sexual desires, and that might be bad. Whereas Venus and Mars together would supply the energy Venus needs to express its affection, and that could be good. A natal conjunction heightens the influence of the planets involved, and whether this aspect is beneficial or detrimental depends on the nature of these planets. Mars-Saturn conjunct, for instance, would indicate an overvulnerability to other people."

On the other hand, a natal Jupiter conjunction with Saturn would tend to dispose the individual to a successful life due to a properly orthodox way of doing things.

It takes Mars an average of fifty-five days to go through each sign. In Aries, which it rules, Mars is energy personified, but it is often expressed in a contentious way. "Anybody who challenges a person with **Mars in Aries,"** said Winters, "had better be ready for a fight because he'll attack first and discuss it later." Positively, it is a strong position for activity requiring courage and aggressiveness—soldiers, policemen, prizefighters.

As Winters talked, I recalled a well-known actress with Mars in Aries, who was an Aries, to boot. A hippie had brushed against her car in a Hollywood street, and then scolded her for causing the accident. She jumped out of her car, yanked him from behind his wheel, and walloped him with her purse. "And don't let me see you again," she shouted, jumping back into her own car.

Mars in Taurus would channel that energy to building up an estate, and would also stimulate sexual activity. Taurus, ruled by the goddess of love, and symbolized by the Bull, is that kind of sign. Because of Taurus' stability, people with Mars in Taurus tend to passive resistance rather than violence. "Normally, they'll let you exhaust yourself, and then the battle is theirs."

Mars in Gemini are all over the place, not really getting much done, as the energy flows more through mind than body. "Because the energies dam up in the mind and often don't have an outlet, they incline to nervousness, and their health may be bad unless they exercise. They must discipline themselves to exercise, since mind control and bodily vigor are the things they must strive for."

I knew one person very well–or did I?–who had **Mars in Cancer.** "It is at a disadvantage here," said Winters, "because it's on the defensive. Instead of outer action, there's an anxious inner search for hazards, particularly around the home." Mars in Cancer make mountains out of mole hills, and the mountains could engulf them. "They need an outlet, work or family, and they are tremendous providers when positively aspected." But they should stop worrying about things that haven't happened. They would fight, if necessary, but only to protect loved ones.

Was this true of all Mars in Cancers?

"Pretty much so," said Winters, "and this deep-rooted feeling that they must defend themselves against the world is intensified when transiting Mars is passing over their natal Mars in Cancer."

"Can one do anything about it?" asked this Mars in Cancer.

"Just knowing about it is a help," Winters said, "since the person with this position can take its effects into consideration in talking himself out of largely imaginary fears. He can say, 'Oh, well, that's my Mars in Cancer,' and get on to something else. That's what astrology is all about–know thyself."

Mars in Leo people are willing servants of their ego. "It serves the main thrust of your nature," Winters said, "by insuring that you will always put your best foot forward." They know exactly what they are doing–fortunate ones–and what effect it will have. "They have an enormous animal magnetism and can literally get away with murder. Even when they get caught at something, everybody laughs and dismisses it as a lovable prank." In accordance with the inner you of their Sun sign, they like doing what makes them the center of attraction.

"If Sun Leo becomes an astrologer or mathematician," Winters observed with a smile, "he will change the accepted rules or regulations, the mathematician witth a new formula and the astrologer with a new system of houses or signs, so that he can say, 'That's the way I do astrology, you know.' "

Nobody I knew could crowd more "I's" into a sentence than a Leo with Mars or Mercury in Leo. "I am tired of talking about myself," one said once, "what do you have to say about me?"

Mars in Virgo is a respite from Leo. It is a great team position. "Leo or Sagittarius or Taurus thinks up a lot of wonderful ideas, and then Mars in Virgo comes along and attends to all the persnickety details that nobody else wants to bother with." From a very small beginning they could build an empire, if they left the trivia to others. "Virgo is Mercury-ruled and, with Mars there, is extremely intelligent, capable of great accomplishment if lint picking can be overcome."

Mars in Libra, the natural house of partners, touches off a great desire to be with others. "What they send out in the way of thoughts and feelings comes back to them magnetically charged." In love with love, constantly seeking perfection, when they don't find their ideal they are grievously disappointed. "Consequently," Winters observed, "they may become recluses and literally get out of the world." This is a weak position for Mars. No one on Earth can love like Mars in Libra, but only for a weekend."

I had understood that Libra was a homosexual sign, not that most Libras were homosexuals, but that more Libras were homosexuals than any other sign.

Winters nodded thoughtfully.

"Both Libra and Scorpio have homosexual tendencies. Since Libra is balance, in bad aspect it reflects an imbalance. And this could happen should Mars in Libra square the Moon, hidden desires, or Uranus, the great upsetter. Bad aspects to the Libra Sun may also do the trick, as with Oscar Wilde."

But Libra imbalanced is more bi-sexual. Badly aspected Scorpio is the out-and-out homosexual, with a tendency to perversion.

And that brought us to **Mars in Scorpio.**

"Its magnetism is extremely powerful, forcefully drawing others and holding them, and extracting from the world the maximum of material benefits. On the negative side those with this Mars position fear that the ends of their ego can not be achieved, and this results in timidity, vacillation, quarrelsomeness. They must learn to direct their energies away from themselves, to help people rather than to use them. Mars in Scorpio's intuitive powers are so strong that if they have an evil thought about another person, that person will know it. People actually cringe under the gaze of a person with Mars in Scorpio."

All I could think of, as Winters was talking, was Scorpionic Charles Manson, and those wild hypnotic eyes, which assertedly had compelled his entranced followers to kill Sharon Tate and her friends.

"Did Manson have Mars in Scorpio?"

Winters shook his head. "Mars in Virgo."

That is the team sign, and it was obvious that this Mars in Virgo had learned to leave the details to others. But Mars in Virgo was certainly no killer in itself.

"His Mars conjunct Neptune in the fifth house is an indication of mental disturbance and a scandal. And of course there were other things."

President Nixon had **Mars in Sagittarius.** This position spins off its excess energies into physical channels. They like to play games and are interested in sports. This seems to fit Nixon, who not only watches baseball or football games with relish, but goes into the team dressing rooms later to express his pleasure. Also mentally active, they would develop the ability to speak at great length, though not with the Gemini quickness of a John F. Kennedy. "Mars in Sagittarius is the kind of person," said Winters, "who would do his homework and have things well thought out with statistics."

Mars in Capricorn are born leaders, for they learn early in life that to give orders you must learn to take them. Their energies react in prudent, practical channels. "They are born wise," Winters said, "and make steady and sure progress in life. Self-control comes naturally, and they are solid administrators. They earn the respect of subordinates by never asking anybody to do anything they can't do themselves."

Mars in Aquarius would go out and ring doorbells to help people. But they often give parties for the sole purpose of having a lot of people around to satisfy their egos. Genuine humanitarianism is their best role, since this is the sign of the humanitarian, but there is a constant struggle within them between self and the group activity, resulting often in a high-strung individual, confused by the ambivalence of his own motivation. "If they devote their energies to the needs of others, like bread cast on the water it will come back manyfold."

Mars in Pisces, like so many planets colored by Pisces, tend to be introspective, brooding, and fearful of the unknown. They are great at storing ideas in the subconscious, then expressing them later. Often deep thinkers, they could give much to the world philosophically, once they learn the art of repose. "The world is full of woe, and they take it on their shoulders," Winters said. "They should give of themselves, but not all of themselves, and then they won't sit around later and feel sorry for themselves."

JUPITER

Somebody once said that with Jupiter on your side you didn't need anything else. "You can tell by its position in your chart," Winters said, "how and where your opportunities will come. So Jupiter indicates the type of work you ought to do, the vocational area where you will best succeed."

Jupiter, with a diameter of nearly 87,000 miles, is by far the largest planet, its mass exceeding that of all the others combined. Some 484 million miles from the Sun, it is colder than the Earth, with an outer sphere of ammonia, certainly an expansive substance, like Jupiter itself. Its orbit around the Sun takes twelve years, a year through each sign, and it is the one planet that reflects the joviality of a namesake, Jove or Jupiter. It is a good planet to have well-aspected, and even in a harsh sign–Capricorn or Scorpio–it is a harbinger of good.

Jupiter in Aries gives people the feeling, justified or not, that they can do anything they want to do. They have a tendency to overoptimism and, in not trying as hard as they should, are prone to failure. "They are good workers but don't like to take orders. That's why so many of them become bosses," Winters observed. "They're not trying so much to satisfy another person as themselves."

Jupiter in Taurus banks only on a sure thing, they aren't gamblers. "They wouldn't dream of going to the race track or Las Vegas, except for a day of pleasure. Jupiter is security-oriented in Taurus and wants something solid, like collecting works of art, which satisfies their Venus-Taurus hankering for luxury and beauty."

Jupiter in Gemini reflects an adventurous attitude; they like to roam the world, and might leave home early to try their luck. "They don't worry about money and have no regard for material things, but they're so lucky they would stumble over a pot of gold."

Jupiter in Cancer is an excellent money-making position. They aren't interested in salaried jobs, but look for the big opportunity to make a deal with a fancy commission. "They are pillars of society, for they not only make a lot of money, but are generous with it."

Jupiter in Leo, highlighting the Leo temperament, would like to be successful just to gain recognition. "They'd subordinate their incomes," said Winters, "if their associates would cover them with praise. They live for the opportunity to be appreciated and acclaimed."

Jupiter in Virgo is one of Jupiter's best positions. Those with this Jupiter position have the ability to start on a shoestring and build. "They'll take the little acorn every time and transform it into a mighty oak tree by their perseverance and attention to detail, doing everything properly to make it grow."

Jupiter in Libra can spot opportunity in almost anything, said Winters, but has difficulty deciding which venture to take. If possible, this position will try to get someone to go in with them, the old Libran partnership thing. "But they miss many opportunities because they are influenced so much by other people and vacillate accordingly."

Scorpio is a strong sign, Jupiter a bountiful planet, and so **Jupiter in Scorpio** has very little trouble finding opportunity, particularly since what they feel is needed is generally what the world thinks too. "They will never be a square peg in a round hole, because they know intuitively what is best for them and they do it. And they are so efficient they will bring in plenty of the green stuff."

It is hard to get a bad Jupiter, except when afflicted. "If it is squared or in opposition, especially to Saturn or Neptune, it will be negative, and everything it normally stands for alone in a sign will then be reversed," Winters pointed out.

Jupiter belongs in Sagittarius, and so **Jupiter in Sagittarius** is an extremely idealistic Jupiter. "Their greatest opportunity in life," said Winters, "is not in labor itself, but rather in knowledge, philosophy, adventure. They are tireless workers if the project suits their ideals. Otherwise they will quit abruptly and seek opportunity along non-material lines. They might go into the ministry or something that pays nothing but suits them."

Jupiter in Capricorn wants to be an authority, however small the area. "These individuals want to be looked up to and want people to feel they're important. Their goal is to get to the heights–to scale the mountain–where they will find power, fame and authority."

Offhand, I knew of one Jupiter in Capricorn.

His name: Richard Milhous Nixon.

"They are absolutely singleminded in their quest to attain their goal," Winters went on. "And I strongly urge you not to get in the way."

I looked forward to the next delineation for, again, a personal reason.

"Jupiter in Aquarius sees opportunity along broad social, artistic, political, humanitarian lines," Winters said. Often they take on jobs that seem impossible. "For instance, they'll set out to get the whole world to believe in astrology, and write a book about it."

Having also obsessed Mars in Cancer, I had a feeling I knew who Winters was talking about.

"They have a tendency," he continued, "to bite off more than they can chew, and so may wind up with nothing to show for what they've done."

He smiled. "Now, with a little Taurus in there, they'll be down to earth, and immediately realize they're not going to change the whole world, so they'll just try changing what's around them. It's a fabulous position provided the Earth's in there, too."

The power of suggestion was such that one student, with Jupiter in Aquarius and Sun, Moon, Venus in Taurus, sat back with a relaxed smile, almost as if he knew the world was waiting for the book he was doing, *A Time for Astrology*.

Jupiter in Pisces do their thing according to their own ethic. If their thing doesn't work out, they might then lapse into a self-indulgent martyrdom that could lead to excessive drinking, drugs, sex. "It could be a wonderful Jupiter position for humanity, if not thwarted to where they cut off the real world."

As far as we had gone, I had a pretty good idea of the meaning of each position as it stood alone, without being modified by other aspects. Venus in any particular sign, for instance, reacted emotionally like that sign. Venus in Sagittarius picks up the sign's freedom-loving quality, and would be upset if trapped into a romance that holds them down. Venus in Capricorn, on the other hand, would walk gladly into any relationship that would enhance their social status. Venus in Aquarius loves beauty for itself and humanity's sake, deemphasizing the physical; and a redblooded Venus in Taurus, squaring a partner with Venus in Aquarius, as it were, would have a good deal of trouble in the bedroom, provided they got there in the first place.

The classic way in which the sign colors the planet is reflected in the distinction between Venus in Pisces and in Sagittarius. In Pisces, Venus trusts over and over again, never recognizing whether the person they are emotional about is worthy of them. Quite differently, those with Venus in Sagittarius learn their lesson when they get burned, and never get singed again by the same fire.

Venus is the planet presumably most like the Earth. Some 67 million miles from the Sun, its 7,600-mile diameter is almost that of the earth's 7,900 miles, and its orbit around the Sun is 225 days. It is familiar to the eye, being the nearest planet to the Earth, and the brightest object in the sky next to the Sun and Moon. When ahead of the Sun, it is the Morning Star; behind the Sun it is visible in the western sky just after sunset as the Evening Star. Veiled in impenetrable cloud banks, its mysterious surface is truly symbolic of the eternal feminine.

VENUS

In orderly Libran fashion, Winters began his discussion of the love planet with the first house. Those with **Venus in Aries,** he said, react to love stimuli on a purely personal basis, and couldn't care less what happens to anybody, unless it is somebody they know and care about.

They are directly opposed to Venus in Aquarius, which gets excited about the multitude, but not the individual.

Venus in Taurus clarifies why Taurus is called the Bull. They are demonstrative, affectionate, sexy, doers not talkers, slow to give their love, wanting to be sure they are loved in return. But once assured, their loyalty is unquestioned, unless the partner proves disloyal first.

"Venus in Taurus," said Winters, "is a real lover."

Some in the class blushed, but others looked pleased. It was hard to tell who was more gratified—subject or object.

Winters wasn't partial to Geminis, and this feeling carried over to **Venus in Gemini.** "They kiss and tell," he said severely, judging as only a Libran would. "But there isn't any other Venus in the entire zodiac that it would be more fun to be with." He sighed. "You may think them fickle, but you can't help loving them if you don't mind sharing them."

Since Winters was admittedly partial to Cancer, he had doubtless known his share of Venus in Geminis, as this planet never got more than forty-eight degrees from the Sun, and Cancer Suns could have Venus in their own Sun sign, or in Gemini, or Leo.

Those with **Venus in Cancer** are interested in security on the home-front, and their affections, if they are a woman, are well-contained until they are sure that a suitor will be able to pay the bills and buy a home. A man with Venus in Cancer would assure his future before he took on the responsibility of a home.

"The superficial kiss or embrace won't work with them," said the cynical Winters. "They respond to the real thing, but can take it or leave it, if there's no tangible reward in sight."

As a Hollywood casting director, Winters was very much aware of **Venus in Leo,** and that position's flair for the dramatic. "If two people with Venus in Leo were smooching," he said, "both would be absolutely aware of how they looked." They are sincere, but in control of their emotions, while most of us aren't. "They belong on the stage, and if they aren't on the stage, then the world is their stage. The acting profession is a natural for them."

Venus in Virgo, like the Moon in Virgo, is too analytical to plunge headlong into a relationship. These individuals first have to satisfy their consciences through rationalization that it is proper eliciting pledges of undying devotion, and only then are ready for what other positions find unnecessary to justify. "They respond well to flowers and boxes of candy," said our teacher. "But they are the people at a cocktail party who take only one drink because they are afraid of what might happen later."

Venus in Libra never loses faith in love, no matter how many times they go to the well and find it dry. They have a host of friends because of their forgiving nature. "They're the darlings of social gatherings because they're affectionate without being importunate." But while it is an excellent natural position for Libra, its normal stable emotional balance could be wiped out by a Uranus, Mars or Saturn opposition. "So people with this position shouldn't get feeling smug," said Winters, "until they've seen the rest of the chart."

This brought up a delineation problem the class had not yet been confronted with.

"Why study what these positions mean, if they don't really mean that?" somebody asked.

"You have to know that two and two is four," Winters replied, "before you can subtract three from it. In other words, the position keeps its meaning, and is enhanced by favorable aspects, sextiles or trines, diminished or twisted around by oppositions, squares, or conjunctions, but always in accordance with the nature of the planet in that position."

"Saturn on Venus would hold it down," Winters explained. "Jupiter would give it verve, and Mars would give it enormous sex appeal."

I would have thought **Venus in Scorpio** a salty position, with the sky the limit sexually. But Venus in Scorpio was not to be confused with Moon in Scorpio or Scorpio rising, which was something else again. "Their emotions are profound," said Winters, "and they have a deep need for love of the highest spiritual type, and put their sex drive on that high level, refusing to compromise love for sex. They want to experience the highest emotions."

I could sense the confusion among the other tyros in the class.

"Venus softens Scorpio, and brings out its beautiful, high-minded side," said Winters.

I could see, looking around, that not everybody was convinced.

Winters laughed. "There's nothing like publicity, and Scorpio has had plenty of it."

"Neptune in Scorpio," I pointed out, "has apparently brought 14 years of pornography in pictures and print."

"But that," said Winters, "was Neptune, the dregs of the mind, not Venus, the goddess of love."

Venus in Sagittarius makes a sport of love, playing, as usual, to win. If they lose, they go out and try again. "It's hard to tie this position down," said our teacher, "for they're in love with freedom, which is like saying they're in love with love. And every planet in Sagittarius will want freedom in its own way."

I waited expectantly for the next interpretation. I had recently met a young lady with **Venus in Capricorn,** and I had noticed that all her male escorts, or the ones she spoke of, at least, were persons of some prominence. She had impressed me as being rather cold. "They are looking for the main chance," Winters began right off. "They mix solely in social circles that promise to improve their own station. While they won't marry for money alone, they wouldn't be interested in anybody that doesn't have it, or the prospect of getting it."

It explained the young lady perfectly.

Venus in Aquarius direct their emotions toward groups or humanity, and their personal love is related more to spiritual feelings than passions. They are sensual rather than sensuous, and are often content just taking in the beauty of their mate. It is a good sign for hippies and evangelists, as universal love is their vaunted goal.

Venus in Pisces, like any Piscean position, is nothing to trifle with. These individuals find it hard to express themselves, and as a result are overly responsive when somebody does them a small favor. They are constantly put upon by friends aware of their neurotic need for approval. But let this approval not be forthcoming, and they feel as if the world is against them. This is the sign of the Messiah complex, and of martyrdom, for few are the prophets recognized in their home country.

MERCURY

Mercury is the planet closest to the Sun, never more than 24 degrees away in the chart, and some 35 million miles distant in space. With Venus, it is the only other planet between the Earth and the Sun, which are 93 million miles apart. Its diameter is 3,100 miles, and because it is so close to the Sun, it takes only 88 days for its orbit. Astrologically, it is very similar to the antenna on the rooftop, bringing in the messages of the senses from the outer world. It controls the nervous system, and reflects the way we see, hear, taste, smell and touch, determining how the outer world appears to us.

Sound is extremely important to those with **Mercury in Aries,** and they are unhappy in a raucous atmosphere. Good music is soothing, unpleasant odors unpleasant, loud noises could result in a headache, and the sight of blood is often unnerving. But they stand pain well, as the sense of taste and touch are not highly activated, and Mars-ruled Aries is brave anyway.

Mercury in Taurus doesn't relate as well to the spoken word as to a book. People with this Mercury position are happy with a physically beautiful partner, not caring too much about the inner beauty which often escapes them. Being Venus-ruled, and yet under Mercury's Gemini influence, they are attracted to superficial beauty in art and landscapes. They are good observers, but don't listen well.

Mercury rules Gemini, and **Mercury in Gemini** gets the senses off to a flying start. The minds of people with this position are so active they seldom stop to think things through. Consequently, they know a little bit about everything but not a great deal about anything. "They are always thinking of what's going to happen next, too preoccupied to deal with what's going on. They're nearly always going through a phase of nervous exhaustion."

Mercury in Cancer are forever discussing their own feelings. Extremely impressionable, they could make a case out of a garbage truck rumbling noisily by in their street, or go into rhapsodies over the beauty of a rock in the desert. They take personally everything that affects their sense perception, thereby overreacting to beauty or ugliness.

With **Mercury in Leo,** people tend to change things around a bit, like a poem or a picture, and then claim credit for the whole production. "If someone with Mercury in Leo did a painting of you and took it home," Winters said, "he might be bold enough to add a few brush strokes and then say he had really perfected the picture. Such people have a tendency to hear conversations and then twist the words around so they can get credit for a bon mot. But they do have the grace to also see the other person's point of view."

Mercury in Virgo tend to intellectualize their sense impressions until they almost dissect them to death. By the time they get through weighing the vacation they are planning, they have taken the fun out of it, and there isn't much point to going. For girls with this position, Winters had words of advice. "They'll get a lot more enjoyment out of a kiss if they'll not analyze why they are getting it." As for the men: "They will enjoy a kiss a lot more if they'll stop thinking about the trouble it might lead to."

Mercury in Libra is concerned about proprieties. They like everything to be just right, in the home and out of it. "A woman with this position could visit your home and, annoyed that it wasn't spic and span, could interpret this as a lack of respect for her." For their part, they would rarely do anything to offend a friend, as they adhere to the conventional standards of good taste at the table or bed.

Mercury in Scorpio is intensely critical of anything found to be improper. "Many think them sharp-tongued, but they are merely expressing what their eagle eyes pick out. They take a dim view of someone parking in a red zone, as it's against the law, and they say so. And if they don't like the cut of somebody's suit, or the color of his shirt, they'll make their views known in no uncertain terms." They have an additional advantage. "They have a native sixth sense," said Winters, "and this picks up anything the other five miss. They see through a phony immediately."

Mercury in Sagittarius miss things under their noses because they have their eyes on the mountain. "They have a tendency to miss small talk as well as profound remarks because they are listening to the beat of their own inner drum. Their senses are sharp, but they must come down to earth to be effective."

Mercury in Capricorn doesn't miss a thing. It is the most observant Mercury position and sees everything exactly like it is. "They can hear their hair grow, smell a mouse a mile away. They really make excellent use of their senses. They can taste a pinch of salt in a gallon of soup. They can pick up flavor in foods, if there's garlic or nutmeg or oregano in something they can call it. And all of their senses are like that. Reality is what they're after. When somebody is saying something to them they are forever saying, 'Look, get to the point.' It's an excellent Mercury position for living on this Earth, and for material advancement."

Mercury in Aquarius, said Winters, gives a keen awareness of the needs of other people. "When people with this position see something, they see it in terms of the good it may do. A beautiful rose would make them think of a sick person, and they'd send it. On the downwind side of a pig sty, the odor wouldn't bother them, as they would think of the people profiting from the bacon that was being produced. They have a well-balanced concept of human values."

As usual, Pisces gives a highly subjective flavor to the planet in its sign. **Mercury in Pisces** sees and hears what he wants to. "If someone he dislikes paints a picture," Winters said, "he'd think it was awful, no matter how good it was; and if someone he liked sang like a frog, he'd say how good it sounded, and mean it. These individuals give a personal bias to all their sense perceptions, and it gets in the way of their judgment. You can't change a shovel into a violin because you hate digging. You have to see it as it is."

Mercury is constantly retrograding, otherwise it would get past the Sun. And when it is retrograding, in negative aspect, that is not the time to begin new projects or sign papers. That was Winters' definitive word on Mercury.

"Suppose one has a contract to sign for a new book or a motion picture?" I asked.

"I don't care if it's for a new porch or a vacuum cleaner," Winters replied. "You'll live to regret it. Wait till it goes direct."

We would be terminating the classes shortly, and several students asked when they would resume.

"After September 22," Winters said, "when Mercury goes direct."

Here at last was one teacher who practiced what he preached.

NEPTUNE

Neptune is as secretive as the subconscious it represents. Since it was first seen only 125 years ago, and its sidereal period around the Sun is 168 years, its complete orbit has not yet been observed. Some 33,000 miles in diameter, it is nearly three billion miles from the earth. Invisible to the naked eye, Neptune was picked out by powerful telescopes in 1846, though astrologers had been reporting its influence for some time before that, sensing the presence of an interacting planet making aspects they could see only in their charts.

If the Moon represents the desires of the subconscious, then Neptune is the subconscious. "It's what a person came into the world with from the subconscious point of view, and yet it still represents the quality of illusion." As much a part of the subconscious as memory or spiritual yearnings, it therefore stands for drugs, motion pictures, and the Freudian world which it foreshadowed by its own discovery.

Like other planets, it takes on the quality of the sign it is in, and passing through sensuous Scorpio for 14 years, it reflected the rise of the drug culture and of lascivious motion pictures. In 1971, it is well into Sagittarius, and hopefully the trend will be reversed, as witness already the response to the sentimental movie *Love Story,* and spirituality will be triumphant before it passes out of Sagittarius in 1984, into a transit through law-abiding Capricorn.

When discovered, Neptune was allotted to Pisces, an intuitive water sign, for besides being intuitive, Neptune rules the seas and the fish that swim in opposite directions. When Neptune is in the same sign as the Sun or Moon, the intuition dominates and people with this aspect act pretty much on hunches. Neptune blends well with the lighter planets, which it seems capable of enhancing. In good aspect to Venus, it is very idealistic and romantic; with Mercury it makes one keenly aware of the outer world and is especially helpful to stockbrokers and business people who make their living looking ahead. Having Neptune in the same sign with Mars, an individual would be so magnetically charged that he could open all doors, but they might be the wrong doors because Neptune can be so illusory.

The house position of course flavors the blend of planet and sign.

"What about Mars and Neptune in the seventh house?" asked a student with Mars and Neptune in the seventh.

"This conjunction would take effect quite naturally in that house," Winters replied with a smile. "You would instinctively pick out the wrong partner, in marriage or business."

On the other hand, bountiful Jupiter with Neptune together in the seventh is a wonderful aspect, the individual intuitively picking the right opportunity when it comes along, and the right girl or man, so well-endowed that he or she could laugh all the way to the church.

People with **Neptune in Aries** are almost nonexistent, as they would have to be over a hundred years old, and certainly Venus conjunct their Neptune, a love aspect, would be a meaningless aspect in this house. At any rate, those with Neptune in Aries were born with the conviction they were right, regardless of what experience said, so it could be just as well that they're not around in significant numbers.

Neptune in Taurus would be about eighty now, and they have an intuitive interest in people of property, and ways of gaining this type of security for themselves. With **Neptune in Gemini,** the zodiac is dealing with people in their late sixties, and they would be sitting on the U.S. Supreme Court now, accounting perhaps for some of the innovations and novel ideas from the subconscious of these oldsters. **Neptune in Cancer** was born between 1901 and 1915, and a person with this combination believes his home to be his castle. "Their early home environment made a strong impression on them," Winters observed. "And their instinctive reactions to life are more or less oriented to the home." Those with Neptune in Cancer depend on another person, and if they didn't have this person to lean on, they would go around with an empty feeling. The home is their strength.

With **Neptune in Leo,** the subconscious drive reflects a need for approval. "Their intuitions are highly creative and warm, but they must feel appreciated. If they're not loved, they feel as if their value is marked down. They came into the world with a good deal of wisdom, and they want you to be aware of it."

President Kennedy had **Neptune in Leo** (1915–1929) in his chart, and he handled himself well, publicly, though obviously on stage. But if Mercury, the mental planet, was squared—in afflicted aspect—to this position, the individual only thinks he was born wise, but is really engaged in self-deception. "This," said Winters, "is one example of how an aspect may counter or invert a planetary position."

Neptune in Virgo (1929–1943) has an instinct for work and service. "Unselfish service is the keynote to this position," Winters said. "They do best when their mind is on the other person; on themselves they get involved in a lot of little things that don't matter." **Neptune in Libra** (1943–1956) symbolizes the young adult group which has a broad and idealistic outlook, truly Neptunean. "These are the flower children who believe that loving one another is a beautiful thing." But if Neptune in Libra is in any way squared or badly aspected, it would account for the plastic hippies born with Libra out of balance.

Neptune in Scorpio, from 1956–1970, forms the present crop of subteeners, and when they become old enough to be an influence there could be a resurgence of drugs, because Neptune will then be out of spiritual Sagittarius (it stays there from 1970–1984). However, **Neptune in Capricorn,** beginning in 1984, would reflect a compensating subconscious instinct for self-preservation, and so they would still know how to survive and at the same time advance themselves, and build for the future.

Like others in the class, I was especially interested in **Neptune in Sagittarius,** as it was of the immediate present, and with movies being what they are, and the cries of those deluded by the Neptune in Scorpio years (1956–1970) for legalization of drugs, a spiritual renaissance could not come too soon. Astrologer Winters was optimistic, a Sagittarian quality brought out by his natal Moon and Venus conjuncting in natal Sagittarius. "Neptune in Sagittarius," he said, "is absolutely essential to undo the negative aspects of Neptune in Scorpio. Nudity and all that type of thing," added this born-wise Neptune in Leo, "won't be tolerated in this position and we will in a few years have a return to great artists and philosophies, and a spiritual upsurge." He added a word of caution. "We must watch out for the person who in his desire to be good becomes so fanatical that he causes enormous amounts of trouble."

It hardly seems necessary to bother with **Neptune in Aquarius,** which won't come along until the year 2000 and would then organize societies, groups and civil associations, presumably to save humanity from itself.

Neptune in Pisces, in its own sign a generation or so hence, might bring the ultimate period of self-realization which could result in a generation of idealists bringing peace to a turbulent world.

"Either that," said Winters, "or they'll be terribly confused, no novelty for Pisces."

PLUTO

Little is known about Pluto, since it was only discovered in 1930. It is more than three billion miles from the Earth, and its diameter, 3,600 miles, is less than half the Earth's. Yet it appears to have a strong magnetic effect not only on the Earth, where some think it touches off earthquakes, in sharp aspect to heavy planets like Uranus or Saturn. Its orbit is highly irregular in a regular pattern, and with its retrograding motion and its distance from the Sun, it takes 248 years to circle through the zodiac. It stays in signs for varying periods, generally from 15 to 30 years, and has been called the generation planet, the planet of revolution, evolution, regeneration or rebirth.

When it was discovered, many astrologers, who already thought astrology a definitive science, based on complete knowledge of the heavens, retired in embarrassment, feeling that everything they had done before with such assurance was now utterly inadequate because it had not been based on a total view of the planets.

But wiser heads were only too glad to add Pluto to their arsenal in the sky, and impute to it, ironically, the qualities of ancient mythology. It is the planet of the underworld, the hidden, the underground —the Hades of old—and it stands also for causes and the population mass. It was discovered, as were Uranus and Neptune, in time to foreshadow events it governed, in this case the surge of the gangster underworld, and the world-wide depression that wiped out millions. In time it promises to be a spiritually regenerating influence.

Pluto seems to affect the habit trends of whole generations. In the later degrees of Virgo, it touched off the astrology vogue in 1966, when it went conjunct to Uranus, the planet ruling astrology, opening up the masses to astrology for the first time in centuries. By fall of 1971 it will go into Libra, and in this sign of balance, the natural house of partners, it "promises," said Winters, to upset the balance of the whole marital system, abetted of course by Uranus, which is also in this sign, accenting the unconventional.

Only the very old had Pluto in Taurus, and there is virtually no one left who had **Pluto in Aries.** Most world leaders had Pluto in Gemini or Cancer. Nevertheless, as a trend setter, beginning with the first sign, Pluto made itself felt, constantly bringing new concepts as it changed signs. "When Pluto went into Aries, the sign of the pioneer," observed Winters, "the great trek began across the plains, and the Golden West was born."

Pluto in Taurus came in about 1853, and a few years later there was a war for freedom's cause over movable possessions called slaves. The Civil War came, and then the trailblazers and cattle barons fought over the range which was the fruit of their pioneering, and their bloody battles resulted unhappily in hundreds of western movies now on television's late, late shows.

As Pluto went into Gemini, an airy mental sign, in 1884, and stayed there until early 1914, men turned from violence, and debates around the potbellied stove were popular. Newspapers came into prominence, and the telephone, the Bell system being founded in the communicative sign of Gemini—on June 18. The mentally agile Joseph Kennedy was born when Pluto was in Gemini and so was Nixon. But this group is aging out, and Pluto in Cancer taking over. Consistently, when Pluto goes into a new sign great changes take place. In 1914, World War I broke out, and the world has never been the same. **Pluto in Cancer** puts emphasis on the homeland; the Fatherland, Deutschland über Alles, and patriotism were rampant. In this country, our boys marched off in 1917 to the accompaniment of universal flag waving. Big families were the rule, and the scientists dug up the past, in keeping with this Cancerian quality, opening the fabled tombs of the Egyptian pharaohs.

Pluto went into Leo in 1938, and national pride exerted itself, and there was another World War. Libran Japan, feeling its pride wounded, tried to get things back in balance for itself. But its Libra was badly aspected. "When Pluto went into Leo, Japanese pride became enormous and they wanted to get back into the eyes of the world as a great nation. And so they attacked. But they must not have known much about astrology," said Winters, "otherwise they never would have attacked a Cancer nation."

The American fighting men had Pluto in Cancer, and they were fighting for home and children. Even the nature of the victory was reflected by Pluto. "We won the war and everything we wanted, but with typical Leo generosity we gave it away. And being a Cancer country, once we beat them we immediately began to feed, clothe and shelter them to the point where Japan has become a very serious economic rival."

There would be another day of reckoning for a nation whose pride had been humbled. "Things are still out of balance as far as this Libra people is concerned," Winters stressed. "And one day they will rise up again, perhaps in an economic struggle that we might very well lose."

Pluto moved into Virgo in 1956, and the generation of children in this position were absolutely terrified, said Winters, of making a mistake. With Pluto in Virgo there was a large-scale revolution going on in the public service areas that Virgo ruled—strikes for the first time in the post office, school systems, and in labor generally. It boded a change in the whole concept of mass living, with a war if necessary, and the Vietnam War appeared to be doing just that, shaking the faith of many in the most venerable institutions, including government.

As a generation planet, Pluto in Virgo had brought in socialized medicine, free dental and eye clinics. The revolutions affecting the area of public service and health and labor that Virgo influenced would continue until 1971, though the children born in this period, from 1956 until 1971, would when they reached maturity, beginning in 1990 or so, start to reap the harvest of change whose seeds were sown at the time of their birth. "When they take their place in the world, it will be prepared for what they want to do," Winters said. "In terms of the enormous growth of intelligence, there will be a resulting growth in services. Letters will be a thing of the past, checks will disappear, banking will be on an entirely different basis, and the computers will take over. We've already started that transition through our credit cards, but when the Pluto-in-Virgo generation comes into leadership, they will put it all into effect, and that's how astrology works–the potential eventually realizing itself through self-knowledge."

When it moves into Libra in 1971, Pluto promises to bring about revolutionary alliances and partnerships, as well as with Uranus upsetting the marital convention and harbingering new outbreaks of violence before Pluto's ultimate regenerative influence restores the harmony natural to the sign of balance.

On the uncertain experience of Pluto's past, our teacher hazarded a bold prediction of the future. Out of the riots and demonstrations on our streets and campuses will come some very wonderful things. Pluto has a tendency to destroy the old, as a planet of regeneration and rebirth. "Hopefully, when Pluto changes to Libra, because of Libra's balance, it will not require another war to totally change the existing concepts of living, for Pluto does promise to bring a glorious new way of life out of the ashes of the old."

And who, eventually, would make it work?

"When the youngsters born with Pluto in Libra, from 1971 until roughly the turn of the century, come into power, then harmony will truly reign around the world. They will make it work."

And that–amen–is how astrology works.

6

A Time to Grow

Had Dr. Spock understood astrology, or perhaps even known about it, astrologers have said, he might better have understood what he was doing to the American child, its mother, and a society that had to put up with the product of permissiveness through early adolescence and beyond. There were cycles in each life from infancy, determinable by planetary aspects, and not all the Spocks, or all the baby books in the world, even the 22 million that told it like it wasn't, could explain these planetary influences.

In an age of growing disenchantment with psychiatry, it has become apparent through astrology that there are definite times of life when one is jovial or depressed, regardless of the passage of events.

From the age of three to 90, astrology offers an explanation of the critical periods in life that affect us all. These show themselves in the child beginning school at six, coming into adolescence at 14, and into maturity at 21. It is equally relevant at 30, when many women look searchingly for the first telltale wrinkles around the eyes and throat. It stamps our middle age at 40, and marks the advent of old age.

It tells us what to look for at each stage of our ripening age, and it points out the potential for growth, underlining that life can be beautiful at three-score-and-ten and more, provided the individual has met the challenge of the planets along the way, and thus prepared himself for new planetary challenges constantly forming with the advancing years.

It is a matter of harmonizing with the planets, as teacher Ralph Winters once pointed out. It is not fighting age at 40 with exterior applications of cosmetic surgery, but developing a compensating inner assurance, as Eleanor Roosevelt did, to the point that she became serenely beautiful with the years when she had been ugly in youth. As the Bible points out, it is futile to fight the stars, for the stars inevitably have the last word. *"They fought from heaven, the stars in their courses fought against Sisera."* And hapless Sisera, as the Book of Judges recounts, died from a hammer blow of which the human agency was the woman Jael.

For those who will heed the cycles of the stars, Jupiter has one message, Saturn another; Pluto tells its story, Uranus turns things around; even Neptune, the grand deceiver, can be counted on to delude if nothing else. Altogether, they tell us where it's at growthwise. Practically, it matters little whether the planets themselves produce these cycles, affecting our growth, or whether they are merely a reflection of this growth. In any case, they mirror the inevitability of human psychological changes, which in their inevitability, can be coped with instead of lamented, understood instead of shunned, and beneficially structured instead of stifled.

Almost any astrologer with an ephemeris to his name knows of the collusion of these heavenly bodies with the Earth bodies. But few studied its ramifications like Hollywood's Ruth Hale Oliver, a humanist very much aware of the social sciences and their limitations in the appraisal of man's place in the sun.

While she did not exclude any aspect of man's psychological growth, it was apparent to astrologer Oliver that the planets satisfactorily explained transition periods vaguely put down to "growing pains." How many mothers, divorced or widowed, struggling to bring up fatherless boys, have referred in despair to 14 and 15 as the impossible ages, not beginning to understand how the son so previously tractable and loving was suddenly so rebellious and unruly?

This was the period associated with puberty, traditionally a difficult age, with boys and girls experiencing the growing pains of acute sexual awareness, but it was more than that astrologically. It was Saturn time, adolescent time, actually, when Saturn, now opposing its birth position, became a critical factor in their lives, causing them to take a long appraising look at their elders.

Eventually, in adulthood, Saturn would take over, but not before Jupiter had expressed itself to the limit of its own influence, and the child whose growth it had marked had finally attained that psychological maturity so essential to healthy adjustment.

And it all began in infancy, as astrologer Oliver once told a forum of astrologers. "As we all know," she observed, "each person goes through certain psychological crises. We can look at a baby in his crib and say that when he is in his early teens, he will go through the crisis of adolescence. And when he is in his early forties he will go through the crisis of middle age."

The cycles themselves are as inexorable as the planets in their appointed rounds. They set a broad pattern, in which free will, as exemplified by the individual chart, has a certain wide area to roam and express itself. But the timing of the cycles, regardless of the variation in human reaction, is the same for all. And with the knowledge of their inevitability, and their rhyme and reason in the nature of things, comes hopefully a certain self-realization.

"We can time these crises through astrology," said Ruth Oliver, "and we can look more deeply into their nature and the way they affect people. All we have to know is the motion of the slow-moving planets: Jupiter, Saturn, Uranus, Neptune and Pluto. We have general rules that apply to everybody, but as each person is different, he will react differently. One person will go through the crisis gracefully, another will have a difficult time; to one it will be a short sharp experience, another's experience will be agonizingly drawn out."

Just as knowledge of astrological cycles can help one understand the child, so insight into the roles of the heavenly bodies opens up prospects of a fuller youth, middle age and old age, extending the span of usefulness to 84, the time it takes Uranus to complete its first cycle, or even to 89–90, the completion of Saturn's third cycle.

However, to attain this age productively, the person has to meet the challenges imposed by planetary restrictions on the way, and to adapt himself physically and emotionally. "Astrologically, 84 to 90 is the normal life span," said astrologer Oliver, "and we arbitrarily limit ourselves when we don't recognize that. We tend to live too much on a Saturn level. Every day people cut themselves off after one Saturn cycle and say life is over at 30. Other people cut themselves off at the second cycle, saying life is over at 60. If we lived more on the

Uranian level, responding to the electrifying challenges and upsets of Uranus, then we would not limit ourselves as we do, and we'd stay functioning and creative up to 85 or 90."

The planetary cycles are the same for people of roughly the same age. The fastest of the five slow planets, Jupiter, takes twelve years to swing through the zodiac, while Saturn makes it in 29–30 years; Uranus, 84 years; Neptune, twice that, or 168; and Pluto, with its irregular orbit, some 248 years.

These planets, so distant, yet giving off cosmic rays that affect the Sun, Earth, Moon and each other, have their own special message for earthlings as they cut their swath through the zodiac.

The critical aspects arrive at predictable intervals, when the transiting planets form certain angular aspects to their natal positions—a lower square, when the planet is 90 degrees from its natal spot; an opposition, 180 degrees from the birth point or halfway through the zodiac; an upper square, 270 degrees along the circle; and then a full return, conjoining its starting position.

Individual aspects modify the cyclical impact of the transits, but the basic pattern remains. "If a person has a well-aspected Jupiter," the astrologer said, "obviously during the first 24 years, Jupiter cycles will make him more confident and optimistic. On the other hand, a person with a badly aspected Jupiter but a strong Saturn (à la Nixon) may not do so well in those early years, but will develop a belated Saturn confidence in his own ability to overcome obstacles. So he may do better in adult life than a person off to Jupiter's flying start."

Youngsters with a particularly trying adolescence often have the critical Saturn opposition at 14 or 15 accented by a Saturn transit of special significance to them. "Suppose a person has Saturn at 0 degrees Aries and he comes to the critical turn of adolescence. If Saturn moves past this point and keeps moving, it would be a short crisis, but if Saturn should go forward, then retrograde, before it goes forward again, that would then prolong the adolescent crisis."

With Saturn at 0 Aries during a similar crisis, and the Sun at 15 Aries, the individual would no sooner get past Saturn opposing its own place, when he would be confronted with its opposition to his Sun. "That opposition is not too much unlike the opposition to its own place. Because the Sun is yourself, Saturn in opposition is other people, and they are being unsympathetic and restrictive, contributing to a prolonged and troublesome crisis."

An even more difficult adolescence results when the youth's natal Sun squares natal Saturn. "Thus every time transiting Saturn forms a critical aspect to his Saturn, it would form another to the Sun."

Like other astrologers, Ruth Oliver feels that adverse aspects, particularly Saturn squares and oppositions, push the individual into making something of himself. "Most astrologers agree that a chart with so-called good aspects, loaded with trines and sextiles, is a lazy chart. You have to have problems in your chart or you won't struggle, and if you don't struggle you won't accomplish. Demosthenes, the greatest orator of ancient Greece, was born with a stammer, but he put pebbles in his mouth and learned how to talk above the waves, getting rid of the stutter."

Closer at hand is an Aquarian with a difficult early chart so critically aspected that he left home at 13, determined, as true Aquarians usually are, to do his own thing. He was a true Aquarian. In the fourth house of the home, in Aquarius and Pisces, this young man had a stellium of five planets–Mercury, Sun, Saturn, Neptune, Venus. In Aquarius and Pisces, it was a strong aspect for an inventor, particularly in communication, film and electricity. But the young man didn't know this, as he didn't know anything about astrology. But he did know that he didn't want to be pushed into his father's feed and grain business. His mother, the fourth house influence, was sympathetic, and though he was too much a nonconformist to stay in school, she encouraged his study at home, taking on the Saturn role of teacher. The boy, interested in science and chemistry, wanted equipment for Aquarian Age type experiments, but got no support from his father.

The crisis of adolescence was clearly apparent in his chart. At 13, transiting Saturn had begun to oppose those five planets in the house of parents. "First it opposed Mercury, the mind, then his Sun, which indicates how one gets along with oneself, and then Saturn itself, the critical point of adolescence, then Neptune which could bring confusion about his goal, and Venus which could bring emotional discouragement. And while Saturn was opposing all these planets, it was moving through his tenth house of career."

These Saturnian aspects could signify lack of opportunities, obstacles, delay, or, if the individual reacted courageously, it could mean he would rise above his sphere in life by persevering. As the crisis of adolescence made itself felt, the surge for identity was so strong that the boy, turning from the Saturnian limitations in his home, went out into the world to make his own way. He got a job on a train as a candy butcher, put out his own newspaper by the time he was 15, and was on his way to ushering in the Aquarian Age with his inventions.

Neptune ruled the movies, and so that boy, Thomas A. Edison, was to invent the motion picture camera. Uranus ruled electricity, and this super-Aquarian with strong planets in Uranus-ruled Aquarius invented the light bulb. With his strongly activated Mercury, governing communication, he created the phonograph.

With a chart like young Edison's, astrologer Oliver observed, it would be foolhardy to put any curbs on this clear call to perform for the benefit of humanity.

So while the planetary cycles still fix the pattern of the person's growth, the individual chart shows how that person could best handle himself, or be handled, to get the most out of his potential. "If a child nowadays has that kind of configuration in his chart (all those Aquarian-flavored planets concentrated in one house and crying out for expression, and transiting Saturn in the tenth house of career opposed to both its natal place and the natal Sun), parents should let him do something more than just schoolwork. Such a child needs to make his mark in the world some way, to use this struggle to accomplish something, because if he does it at this age he will then have the strength and assurance to cope with a similar crisis, when it occurs again later in life. It doesn't mean that the child should quit school, but that everyone should be treated individually."

This means of course that every child should have his chart done, preferably from infancy. To astrologers this is no more unique than the practice of periodic medical examinations for Junior, except for the fact that the chart has to be done only once, and can then stand as a ready reference to the idiosyncrasies of Junior's growth.

However, even without an individual chart, periods of growth, common to man everywhere under the Sun, are apparent to well-schooled sky-watchers.

Jupiter, because of its relatively swift motion through the zodiac, forms its critical aspects before the slower-moving planets, thus becoming the planetary time clock of childhood.

"Jupiter," the astrologer pointed out, "forms four critical aspects in twelve years, or one every three years. When the child is three, the planet forms its first lower square to its natal position. The lower square is like a fourth house aspect, it is concerned with the child at home and relationship with parents, especially the mother. At three, the child has gotten past infancy, he knows how to talk and walk and learn, and he has self-assurance which he enjoys through the permissive, generous Jupiter environment in his family home. Jupiter forms the first opposition to its natal place at six. Now the opposition reflects the relationship to himself and his peers, so he has a feeling of generosity and outgoingness toward schoolmates, which gives him self-confidence as he starts school."

The next planet to affect Junior is Saturn. "Saturn is the planet that teaches you that when you put your finger on a hot stove you're going to get burned. So at age seven Saturn forms its first critical lower square to its natal position. And psychologists have noticed that children at this age undergo a brief but intense breakdown in personality. One moment they are overly self-confident, the next they cling to their parents and become crybabies. Psychologically, the child is trying to take the first step away, in a realistic Saturn way, from the permissiveness of his childhood home and from authority, which is also Saturn, but he isn't consciously aware of this.

"At the same time, the parents are, in a sense, pushing the child out at seven—they say to the little boy, 'You're too old to cry now, you're a big boy.' They say to the little girl, 'You're in school now, you're a big girl.' So the child wants to leave, is afraid to leave, is pushed off by the parents, and has this brief psychological breakdown in personality."

The next crisis develops at nine, when Jupiter forms the first upper square to its natal position. "An upper square is a tenth house square, so it's like the tenth house. It rules a culmination, a feat of success, an establishment of one's self in the Establishment, whatever one's Establishment is. And so, at nine the child has recovered his poise, and he's getting praise from the world, his tenth house, for what he has accomplished, and a lot of encouragement and permissiveness. We adults forget because we have been adults so long that, by the time a child has reached age nine, he has had a great deal of experience. He has learned to speak, to walk, to talk, to go to school, to make friends, to accept other people, to get along with his peers, to understand his adult world—a whole lifetime in his first nine years."

When Jupiter completes its first cycle, a new experience forms. "Adolescence begins at twelve, and the real crisis of adolescence comes at about 14–15. At twelve, with Jupiter again returning to its own place, this brings a fresh rush of assurance. Consequently a child at that age has the confidence and optimism to want to grow up into the adult world. Also, Jupiter is a religiously oriented planet and many children at twelve get intensely religious. At age 14–15 when Saturn opposes its own position, the child has to learn limitations in his relationship with his peers, to form relationships on a trial-and-error, give-and-take basis. Dating is difficult at this time, he is unsure of himself and self-conscious. One does not do things easily under Saturn, it makes for slow and tedious and sometimes painful action. All of this is understood, generally speaking, but what parents don't understand and astrology does, is that at 15 the child, for the first time, is seeing his parents through adult eyes. He is looking at his parents as if he were an adult. And his judgment is usually harsh. He sees all the Saturn-induced things in his parents: that they have made compromises with life, that they have gotten stuck in ruts, at least it seems so to him. Saturn again is the planet of reality—you see the flaws in people, and you understand that your parents are not perfect or all-powerful. This is difficult for a child to adjust to, and it makes the child difficult for the parents."

The parents naturally bridle at this judgment by a child whose obedience has been routine, until that point. And then begins the alienation of parent and child, with which this generation is all too familiar. While the parent is defending himself, defensively or aggressively, the 14- or 15-year-old begins to extend his judgment of his parents to what he imagines is his parents' world—Establishment materialism, the police, the laws, the school, authority wherever it shows its ugly head.

An understanding of astrology, observed Ruth Oliver, could help make this period of mutual judgments less personal, in the knowledge that much of human behavior is truly celestially oriented. Affecting a whole generation as it does, the first opposition of Saturn to its natal place is the harbinger of youthful revolt, and only in quality is it different each time from endless generations before. "At this age the youngster vows that he will not be held down or limited to custom, or give in to the Establishment as his parents have done. So there is a sort of triple effect here, with Saturn in its first opposition to its own natal position."

All is not lost, provided parents retain their cool and know their astrology. "Fortunately, when the child reaches age 15, Jupiter is forming a second lower square to its natal position; it's back in the fourth house, the home. Ideally, this means that the adolescent has the assurance of love and permissiveness in the home."

However, there are complications; the child has been torn between his struggle for achievement in the eyes of his peers and his efforts to reconcile his dwindling affinity for his parents with his own need for identity.

Ruth Oliver, not only an astrologer but a philosopher, as many astrologers are, recalled with a smile what Mark Twain said about adolescence:

"'When I was a boy of 14 my father was so ignorant I could hardly stand to have the Old Man around. But when I got to be 21, I was astonished at how much he had learned in seven years.'"

In some areas of cyclical growth, oppositions aren't as trying as squares. At 18, Jupiter again opposes its natal place, reflecting a Jupiterian permissiveness and self-assurance. Dating with the opposite sex, so difficult three years before, is now done quite comfortably.

At 21, perhaps the most significant milestone, three critical transits come together—that of Jupiter, Saturn and Uranus. "Jupiter reaches the upper square to its natal spot. The youth now attains his majority, his physical, psychological and legal responsibility, and is considered an adult.

"Generally, the world is generous with him at 21, helping him into the adult world it has helped him prepare for. At the same time Saturn also reaches the upper square to its natal position. So the young adult has not only the Jupiter tenth house influence of activity or career at this point, but the Saturn tenth house influence. With Saturn he knows he has earned his maturity. And because he knows he's proven himself, he feels able now to take hold of adult situations."

The third influence at this point is Uranus, which by age 21 forms a lower square to the position it occupied in one's natal chart. Uranus has a special quality, ruling each person's creative individuality, his unique creative genius. "He says to himself, 'I am I, and I am not anyone else, and this is my own divine will.'" And this will tells him to get out of the childhood home, abruptly and with finality. "Very often he does it himself with the liberating squared Sun-Uranian impact. He feels he is now on his own, out of the parents' shelter." And if he doesn't do this, the parents may do it for him. "Normally, when Uranus forms its first angular aspect in the life of the individual, he breaks out naturally into the life-style he wants as an adult. Usually, this break is easy, as so many are away at school at this point, and on graduating take their own jobs and apartments–or marry, making homes of their own."

Jupiter returns to its natal place for a second time, when a person reaches age 24. "Psychologists," Mrs. Oliver observed, "consider this a time of great self-assurance and poise; the struggles and uncertainties and pains of growing up have passed, and the world is the young person's oyster." Jupiter keeps aspecting every three years, but with diminishing importance from this point on, though each angular return does afford a certain poise and optimism during difficult times.

Anybody, particularly a woman, who has reached 30 knows its peculiar psychological impact. For the first time, the individual may realize that he is no longer a boy or girl, that like everybody else, his parents, his grandparents, his teachers and professors, he is subject to the passage of time, is getting older, and will one day be old. Saturn puts its chilling damper on him–Saturn, the taskmaster, which returns to its natal position at age 29–30, having completed its first trip through the zodiac.

"Many feel very old at this time, older than they have ever felt before and older than they will probably ever feel again. Some get very discouraged, feeling they have left their youth and the best of life behind and that ahead lies only a slow process of aging, and deterioration." Astrologically, psychologically and realistically this is a very shortsighted view. "Astrologically speaking, the time between 30 and 60, when Saturn completes its second cycle, is the time of greatest productivity. It's the time when the rich and the famous, the inventive and the creative, even the plodding, achieve that point in their careers where they discharge their obligations to society and themselves."

This first return of Saturn is often a time of great discontent and fault-finding. Youthful husbands keep picking at their wives, and wives at their husbands. To make matters worse, if they married at their majorities, or shortly thereafter, Saturn would be forming a lower square to the marriage event, adding the well known "seven-year-itch" to a period already fraught with friction.

Another Saturnian crisis arrives at ages 37–38 when Saturn forms a second lower square to its natal position. Unlike the 30-year period, this is not a favorite for psychological speculation. Astrologer Oliver nevertheless has counsel for people at this age, which she considers a particularly critical time psychologically. For this is the age period, on the parental level, when the seeds of the generation gap are generally sown. This is the time that misunderstandings develop from lack of parental rapport with children beginning to reach the teen-age level and doing some questioning of their own. It is the time, astrologer Oliver pointed out, that parents should discard viewpoints inherited from their parents and no longer applicable in managing their marriages or their children.

"The parents of this new breed of children must realize this is not their parents' home, or a reasonable facsimile, but one in which they should be establishing their own image in the mirror of the times. This will put family relationships on a sounder basis, making for more realistic communication, which will serve to draw the children closer to the home. Many of these children, with parents 37–38, will be at the critical 14–15 juncture themselves, and will have to be dealt with on a contemporary social basis, not in the atmosphere of a cultural lag equivalent to this parental generation being reared in a Victorian atmosphere."

There are other burdens at this Saturnian stage, which could be a great opportunity for learning, from one's children and from changing circumstances, or for sloughing things off. It is a period when the cost of raising a family is exemplified in that family's need for a house of its own, college planning, clothing and food. But while these are very real burdens, it is the Saturn lower square that makes them seem more burdensome at this time than they did before or would after.

So all Mom and Dad have to do is hang on and wait for forty to arrive. Middle age will bring new problems, taking the spotlight off the children for a while, as the parents come to the startling realization that they are no longer young. There is slight chance, in looking at the calendar—or the mirror—of the man or woman of forty deluding himself or herself about his travel-time through life. Neptune is forming its first lower square to its natal position, and no matter how a person might kid himself, the crisis of middle age is on him. As the planet of illusion, Neptune flavors this period with a moody nostalgia that brings a questioning of past values and builds up unrealistic images of the long-gone past.

It is a time for solemn introspection that often leads to barrooms or the psychiatrist's couch, as the individual suddenly feels his life has been to little purpose. "At this time people," observed Mrs. Oliver, "often have a feeling of nostalgia for their childhood, and with it a feeling that many values they have found sustaining have lost their relevance. They frequently become moody, and lapse into a world of their own, and because Neptune is intangible and illusory, the task of setting them straight is often harder to solve than a real problem."

The middle age crisis deepens as a new revolutionary planet takes hold. "Then, at 42, Uranus forms the opposition to its natal place, and the individual feels that he is in a rut and has to break out of it by any means possible. Many have a feeling of panic at this time, of being trapped, and with this Uranian impetus they are determined to change the mundane in their lives before it is too late. Quite frequently there is a last fling, the older man with a younger woman, or the reverse, and when this doesn't give the necessary freedom, there is separation and divorce.

"Possibly out of Uranian frustration, people have serious indispositions at this time. Men often have heart attacks at 42, with Uranus opposite its own place. If the desire to break out–in marriage or work –is strongly suppressed, there's a tremendous tension and a heart attack could result."

On the positive side, the Uranus opposition marks a breakthrough toward liberation of the personality. "If the 42-year-oldster has a job, he makes it freer, or he can get into some avocation providing a fresh outlet. If he's in a certain social standard he can break out of that and make a new standard. He gets back to where he had his first stirrings of identity, and he gets back to saying, 'I am I, and let me be.'"

It seems as if the planets are constantly forming new crises, for no sooner is the Neptunean-Uranian crisis on its way out than Saturn is back again, not as last time when the world seemed young and gay, or at 14 or 15 when there was the resilience of youth, buoyed by the optimism of a lower-square Jupiter. This time the individual is 45, in a critical Saturnian stage, when Saturn, the taskmaster, takes its toll of those who haven't come to grips with the planetary challenges of the past. As Saturn forms an opposition to its own natal place, as it did for the first time in adolescence, it ends the crisis of middle age begun by Neptune and Uranus. Middle age could be a rewarding period or a total loss. "If the Uranian rebellion has been abortive," said Mrs. Oliver, "and the person hasn't liberated himself, then Saturn causes new limits, and the person may feel doubly discouraged and closed in by custom and conformity. And so this time he may very well give up.

"On the other hand, if the Uranian experience was productive, the person will react well to the new limitations under which he finds himself. Fortunately, at this age, 45, Jupiter in the tenth house is forming the upper house square to its natal place, so that even with great personal turmoil, there are career opportunities, and the tenth house —the Establishment—is compensatingly tolerant of a middle-age rebellion that it recognized for what it is."

Increasingly, there is a tendency for Saturn to take over if the individual didn't profit with the years. But if he squarely faced Saturn's restrictions and worked around them, Saturn seems to turn benign after 50. "At age 52," Ruth Oliver said, "Saturn reaches its upper square, marking the time that the individual who had persevered really reaches his place in the Establishment. This is the time, if ever, that he should be known for what he is and what he's doing."

Old Man Saturn continues to dominate the succeeding crises. At age 59–60, it returns to its natal place for a second time, and the individual gets what he deserves out of life, good or bad. Many think of retiring from lifelong jobs at this time, to get into something else. But not until age 66, when Saturn forms its lower square in the fourth house of home and security, do they take retirement seriously—accounting for the accepted age of retirement at 65. But even so, life doesn't end there, unless the individual gives in to Saturn. "The fourth house is a time of endings and new beginnings; psychologically, it is a very good time to end one career and begin another."

The 60s are by no means the end of productive living. "When one is 63, Uranus forms the upper square to its natal place and this marks the climax of the individual's creative faculty. For this Uranian effect the individual doesn't have to be artistic. He could run a restaurant, be in politics, management, teaching. But whatever it is, his real creative power should just be coming into full flower at 63."

Looking around, this seems hard to accept, until one considers some of the people who never let age tell them what to do: indomitable Winston Churchill, in his sixties when he led embattled Britain to victory against Hitler; Charlie Chaplin, who at 63 took a wife three times younger than himself, had a slew of children, and produced some of his greatest pictures.

But 63 is still a lot of years, and many people that age appear to be openly deteriorating. "Astrologically speaking," said sixtyish Ruth Oliver, "age 63 is when the individual should be at his peak. There are many examples of people who got off to new things at this cycle of Uranus. One of the most interesting in history was Daniel Defoe. He lived a long life as a businessman, a political profiteer and a secret agent, and then in his early sixties he pioneered the novel–with *Moll Flanders* and *Robinson Crusoe*. He was one of the very first to do it, and he did it very well. Goethe, the German poet, playwright, and scientist, was most creative after 60, as were Victor Hugo, the French novelist, George Bernard Shaw, and others."

As did other astrologers, Ruth Oliver stressed free will in reacting to the planets. Pluto, for instance, is the planet of regeneration, and when it makes its critical angles, it would impose a set of entirely new standards, but only as one reacts, or adapts to these standards, does he find happiness or contentment–or the opposite.

"Pluto," observed Mrs. Oliver, "is very much like Scorpio (which it rules) in that it influences regeneration at the psychological level. So, as it forms a lower square to its own place, many of the childhood attitudes accepted without thought have to be ruthlessly rooted out and replaced with others more productive."

Pluto's impact is being felt very much now. People born between 1910 and 1914 are currently experiencing that lower square of Pluto to its natal place. In their late fifties and early sixties, they hold commanding positions in government, the courts, business and industry. They are products of the assembly age, introduced about the time of their birth by Henry Ford. They grew up with the idea that technology and progress were one and the same. And only now do they realize, with the growing crisis of pollution, that this isn't true, and they are going through a regeneration process. Regeneration, differing with each generation, is concerned at this stage of Pluto not only with the world-wide problem of urban pollution, which threatens to stifle the great cities of the world, but with the feelings of people for one another.

"Regeneration, like revolution," emphasized Mrs. Oliver, "can go one way or the other. The world could handle prejudice when everyone was a distance away. But we're all on top of each other now, so we've got to live together or go out together."

Pluto is speeding up now, and it will keep affecting people at continually younger ages for the next 35 years or so, bringing about a broader involvement in the necessary regeneration changes, physically and spiritually, if man, as we know him, is to survive beyond the turn of the century.

"With Pluto moving so much more rapidly now," said astrologer Oliver, "in five years people who were born in 1917 will feel its regenerative impact most acutely." They would be 58 then. "And the affected age will keep getting younger and younger, with the Pluto speedup, until people born in 1970–72 will experience this lower square transit at age 37."

Astrologer Oliver warned, just as President Nixon has, that the people of the world must meet the challenges of an ecology threatened by the mixed blessings of technology and a pride of nationality marred by hate and war. "Until the time this group gets to be 37," she said, "the world is going to have to watch itself to see that we use technology for its blessings and minimize dangerous side effects. After that, in the year 2007, with Pluto in 0 degrees Capricorn, the pressures will begin to ease and people can begin to enjoy the mechanical wonders they created for their own comfort and betterment."

7

A Time for the Subconscious

There was no psychiatry or psychology, as we know it, before Freud. Little was known of the secret mind, or of its ruler, Neptune, which was discovered in time to be equated astrologically with the mysterious subconscious.

Even to the initiated, the Neptunean mind was such that not even the most skilled could plumb its secrets with any assurance of success, and the wise therapist turned to any method he could for help in understanding the confused and stricken who came for help.

Because of astrology, Dr. Regis Riesenman, the well-known Washington, D.C., psychiatrist, was able to anticipate, as I recall, the suicide attempt of a patient who seemed anything but suicidal. It was all in her chart. I can also recall a distinguished physician at New York Hospital, a student of astrology, who professed to know more about his patients through analyzing their Sun, Moon and rising signs than he could have known in a dozen interviews.

In the affairs of the mind, there is often a reluctance to disclose those inner fears and insecurities which so often reflected a problem beyond the individual's own ken. But while the tongue, and the heart, might distract and block, baffling the therapist, there are few facets of personality, however hidden, that a clever astrologer cannot perceive.

I thought of this as I looked around the big room. Eight people were sitting in a loose semicircle, their eyes on the psychologist who, they hoped, might help them with problems that had many of them living lives of quiet desperation.

The scene recalled other group therapy sessions, with one distinction. In her approach to truth, the psychologist was invoking not only her own specialized skills, but her own considerable knowledge of astrology. She had worked out the eight horoscopes, examining their planetary aspects with the same concern she would a Rorschach or Binet test.

Her subjects were mostly middle-aged housewives, with the exception of an older man, who had a compelling urge to talk, and a young man, of twenty or so, who was sitting next to his mother. They were not classic housewife types, being slim, alert, with a common expression that I took to be one of searching. They were seekers who suspected that much of what they were searching for was muddled about inside. They were from one of the wealthiest suburban areas, California's Beverly Hills, so money, unless it was too much money, was not their problem.

In Dr. Zipporah Dobyns, a psychologist who was uniquely aware of astrology, they had a rare preceptor. Dr. Dobyns had other astrological workshops, including teaching sessions at the Experimental College of the University of California at Los Angeles (UCLA), and her primary efforts were devoted to the integration of psychological and astrological knowledge. Fourteen years with astrology had convinced her that it offered valuable insights into human personality, and she looked for the traditional psychological traits and categories in the complex patterns of the horoscope. But if the traditional formulas about human nature did not fit, she did not attempt to impose them. "I find much of the Freudian and behavioristic dogma too inadequate to do justice to human complexity. The recent development of humanistic psychology, some of the insights of the existentialists and phenomenologists, and especially the evidence of parapsychology all form a working hypothesis about the world and man. This includes a belief in some degree of 'free will,' however limited it may be in individual instances. If we accept life as essentially open-ended and creative, self-consciousness logically opens the way to some self-direction." And this astrology was supposed to do.

The workshop was starting, and my interest was centered in the mother and son, as this was classically a strong relationship which

NAME Mother

BIRTH: DAY **6** MONTH **3**

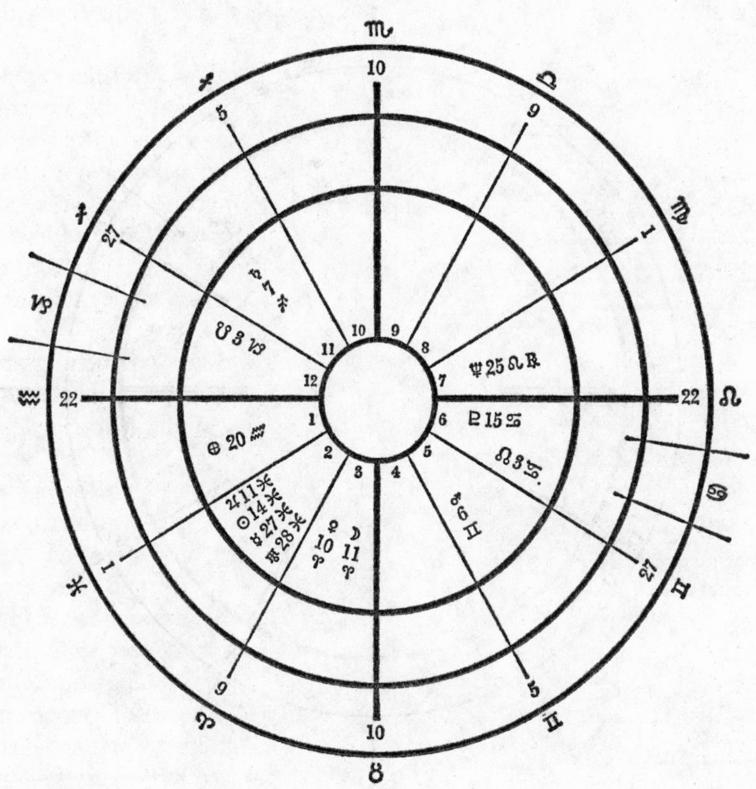

NAME Son

BIRTH: DAY 23 MONTH 2

Longitude: 76W

Latitude: 43N

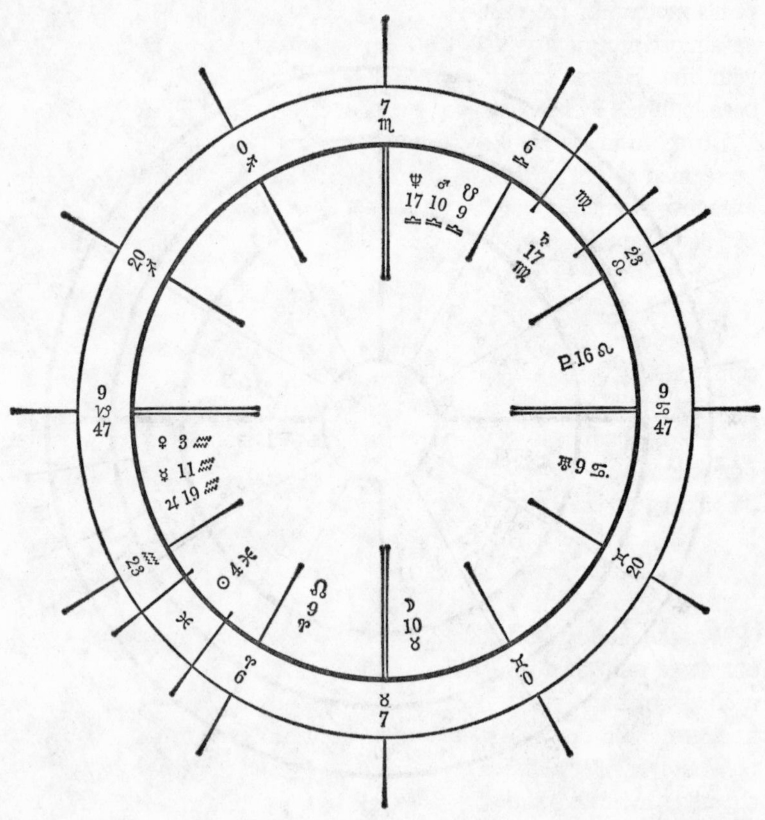

might offer powerful emotional reactions and interesting points of comparison. It was early in the analysis, and their charts had not yet been interpreted. Looking at the young man, who was tall and dark, stammering as he talked, I tried to imagine the relationship. Was it an Oedipus complex, the boy obsessed with an unhealthy love of his mother, or the converse? From the way she looked at him, with an almost proprietary air, I was convinced that her sun rose and set with him. He was spoiled rotten, of course, and since he had always been indulged by her, expected to be indulged at every turn.

I tried to guess his sign, deciding correctly that he was a Pisces—he seemed so out of things. I had more difficulty with the mother, an attractive woman in her forties. She seemed to have a close command of herself, speaking softly, and to the point. And yet, she, too, was a Pisces, which, as I recalled, was the sign of the martyr.

She was born on March 6, the son on February 23. His rising sign was Capricorn, and hers Aquarius, shifting the positions of their houses somewhat.

Since both were Pisces, they were under a Neptunean influence, and Pisces, badly aspected, presumably had more difficulties than any other sign in dealing with reality. This was a clue, but no more. I had no inkling of the boy's specific problems. But manifestly he was at loose ends. He had no academic qualifications for college; it was questionable that the armed services would take him, even on a limited basis; and he had no job training.

Was the mother fearful that he would be a drain on the family, aging but never quite maturing? Was she riddled with guilt over producing a child not quite up to normal? And what emotional factor, if any, had resulted in that stammer so often indicating underlying insecurity?

Whatever his apparent deficiencies, the chart, as Dr. Dobyns stressed, indicated the individual potential undeniably revealed in symbolic planetary aspects.

Peter's planets were evenly distributed, and he had a basically sunny disposition despite being a Pisces. Three positive planets in Aquarius in the first house—Mercury, Jupiter, Venus—implied that he liked people and had a bent for knowledge.

Although she had never seen Peter before, Dr. Dobyns seemed quite conversant with an appreciation of beauty not visible to the naked eye, but apparently tied in with his Moon in Taurus and Mars in Libra, both artistic signs as ruled by Venus.

"My feeling," observed the psychologist to the group at large, "is that there's some unexplored artistic potential here."

She sifted through the chart, as the youth kept his eyes glued on her. Uranus was in Cancer, in the sixth house, the sign of service to the public, and nobody with Uranus in this position could long be in a rut. "He needs variety in his job," she said, as he cheerfully nodded agreement. "He wouldn't be satisfied with the same routine all the time."

She turned to him directly. "There is natural teaching ability in this chart, the facility to explain to others, once you understand yourself. You could work very well with handicapped people in the arts or the handicrafts. You should explore various artistic expressions, discover what turns you on personally, then strive for an instructor's role."

From my own observation of the boy, who seemed young for his years, this was a rather unexpected conclusion. He would have been the last person in the room I would have picked out for a teacher. And it was obvious from her expression that the mother was thinking the same.

"The chart shows the potential, the rest is up to the individual," Dr. Dobyns explained. "The teaching signs are particularly the mental signs, Aquarius, above all, and Sagittarius. This influence is expressed by the prominence of Jupiter, the natural ruler of Sagittarius, in Aquarius, the first house, together with Mercury and Venus, representing communication, so there is the urge for knowledge and, with Aquarius-ruled Uranus in the sixth house of work, the urge to share the knowledge with others. It would be something he would find deeply satisfying."

Peter looked uncertainly at his mother and she gave him a reassuring smile.

As if anticipating this uncertainty, Dr. Dobyns said in returning to the chart: "There's a great deal of self-doubt, and at the same time of self-confidence, here. Capricorn rising always has a battle against self-doubt. Yet, Aquarius in the first house shows that you can accept yourself and be friendly and positive with people."

There was also a spiritual aspect, Neptune in Libra in the ninth house dealing with philosophic and religious thought, particularly as it was prominently aspected to the subconscious force of his Moon and the ascendant representing his outer expression. Neptune was also trine Jupiter, sextile Pluto in the seventh, and conjunct Mars and the south node. Neptune, ruling Pisces, stressed the potential for spiritual development, or confusion, depending on the native's own individual thrust. "The Piscean potential is for something quite idealistic, relating to beauty or altruistic service."

There were strong and weak points, and it became a matter of balancing one against another, Dr. Dobyns stressed.

"Your chart can show you what you have working for and against you. People would naturally like Peter, with Venus and Jupiter in the first house, and would tend to respond favorably. On the other hand, the north and south nodes of the Moon, in the third and ninth houses, in Aries and Libra, reflect a certain strain in forming permanent relationships."

As yet there had been little reaction from the group, but now one of the housewives stirred uneasily, raising a hand as she asked:

"Does Aquarius normally have trouble with authority?"

From her inflection, it would not have been difficult to pick out her own sign, as I had found not illogically that the astrology beginner's interest generally focused on his own Sun sign.

"They don't like to take orders, but they get along with equals as a rule," Dr. Dobyns replied.

The housewife gave a little satisfied smile and settled back.

Peter's chart was obviously not all sweetness or light, or he would not have been his stammering self. He was a strong Neptunean, and Neptune when it went sour, zodiacally, could really get in the way of a person seeing himself as he was or even as others saw him. Moreover, with Peter, the strong Aquarian influence was a disadvantage in dealing with older people at this stage of life, since, as a young man in the process of apprenticeship, he was constantly reminded of the imposition of authority.

"There is some conflict with authority here, with this much Uranus influence in the chart. Uranus (in Cancer) semi-square Pluto (in Leo) has a tendency to resist being told what to do while still being forced to do so."

The young man looked up with a frown. "My boss pushes a button and expects everybody to jump. He thinks I'm a robot."

The psychologist in Dr. Dobyns came to the fore.

"What is there about him you don't like?"

The boy looked off into space. "Oh, he's always saying to do it his way, as if there was no other way. Yet he keeps telling us to keep thinking for ourselves. How can we, when he's always breathing down our backs?"

He looked at his mother, and she looked back, gently reproving.

"You must remember that he has only one arm."

The boy grunted unintelligibly.

Again the psychologist in Dr. Dobyns was prominent.

"Think of the situation from his view," she said. "He's frustrated because of losing his arm and his physical strength, and he's taking out his frustrations in bossing you. You have to replace his arm and do exactly what it could do!"

She gave the chart another perusal, noting again the strong Aquarian and Piscean flavor.

"This chart is mostly air and water and neither of these like to work very hard. Venus, Jupiter and Mercury in the first house can be a little lazy, too. So part of your problem is just learning to work, to take orders, even if you don't like them."

Peter's mother permitted herself a sigh.

"Peter never picks up his clothes or makes his bed, or carries the dishes to the kitchen."

Peter smiled the assured smile of the son who has learned to make the most of an indulgent parent.

Noting the exchanges between mother and son, I was reminded of a conspicuous absence noted one weekend by a juvenile judge, who, looking around a courtroom of delinquent boys and their mothers, had growled, "Don't any of these boys have fathers?"

In this instance, without a father present, mother and son were clearly an example of togetherness, as Dr. Dobyns was quick to point out.

"There is a very close bond with the mother. His Moon in Taurus in the fourth house of the home shows a protective mother. The Moon, the key to the mother, also rules his seventh house of Cancer, the marriage house, so he's looking for a partner who can replace her. That may not be so easy."

She turned back to the youth. "With Pluto in the seventh, square to the Moon in the fourth, you have to make a pretty careful choice when it comes to a partner, marriage or business. There's a tendency to tension here."

The boy wore an incredulous look. "Pluto says all that?"

"Yes, it's shown by the T-square—the Moon in Taurus squaring not only Pluto but Jupiter and Mercury and Venus in the first, opposite Pluto. And then Uranus, the earth-shaker, in Cancer, is semi-square Pluto, so instability in close partnerships is suggested, even though the natural tendency, as seen in the chart, is to be very attached to things and to people."

Peter seemed to be enjoying his course in astrology, particularly, I suspected, with his first-house Jupiter in Aquarius, as the discussion centered about his favorite person—himself.

"What does Pluto in the seventh mean?" he asked.

"In this case, a strong parental pull. Your mother's Pluto is in Cancer, the sign of the mother, and it also rules the tenth house, which is the father. Because you have Scorpio, as ruled by Pluto, on the midheaven, there's a tendency to choose a partner who will play a parental role, overprotective, and basically domineering. But since the emotionally dependent Moon in Taurus in the fourth house of the home squares your Pluto in Leo in the marriage house, there is friction between the partner you choose for your dependency needs and the Aquarius side of you that wants personal freedom."

The boy and his mother exchanged fleeting smiles; both seemed well-satisfied with this interpretation.

Since leaving high school, Peter had worked at two jobs, one in a car wash, which he had considered beneath him, and one with a charitably oriented organization that repaired and sold old furniture, where he had had his boss trouble.

Dr. Dobyns, consulting the chart, saw him changing his work activity shortly, though not necessarily the job itself. "You're starting a whole new trip," said she in the vernacular of youth.

Transiting Uranus, the changer, had recently gone into Libra and was about to touch off his Libran Mars and Neptune, promising not only a switch in underlying thought patterns but in the work-energy forces affected by Mars.

Peter's dark, saturnine face, reflecting his Capricorn rising, brightened perceptibly.

"I thought about going into the armed services," he smiled.

There were expressions of incredulity among listening housewives.

Dr. Dobyns, normally a forthright Virgo, was the soul of tact. "I don't think you'd be very happy with that. Mars and Pluto, the two planets dealing with the military, have heavy aspects in your chart—the Moon in Taurus, reflecting your emotional dependence, squaring Pluto in the seventh house of associations, for one thing."

Peter did not look especially disappointed, and his mother's frown quickly disappeared.

"You'd find," Dr. Dobyns said, "that you'd get little freedom there."

There were differing opinions in the group. A trim woman, priding herself on her Yogic discipline, said, with the faintest tinge of disapproval, "Perhaps his wanting to join the armed forces is a way of expressing a secret desire to make peace with authority. He might really learn to take orders in the Army, and that,"—she glanced at the mother—"is what these kids need today, somebody to lay down the law to them."

There was a dissenting opinion. "Regardless of what he says, he really wants to escape authority," said another self-righteous middle-ager with an undoubted Jupiter in the first house.

Peter seemed quite relaxed. In his first brush with astrology, he was obviously impressed by his own significance.

Dr. Dobyns gave him an appraising glance. "You won't escape authority in the Marines or the Army. I wouldn't advise the service, especially considering the way your planets are aspected, and the trouble you had at the car wash and the furniture repair place."

Peter's head came up. "It wasn't my fault."

"Knowing what you like and don't like can be a big help. With Saturn in Virgo, in the eighth house, this shows a lesson to be learned in connection with service, and hard work and attention to detail and taking orders."

I had thought the eighth house dealt primarily with sex, death and legacies, a triumvirate that seemed oddly disjointed.

Dr. Dobyns demurred.

"I read the fifth as the house of romantic love and sex—the eighth is sometimes a sex house, but usually only when there are heavy aspects with the fifth. Here Mercury governs his fifth Gemini cusp and favorably trines his South Node and is conjunct Venus, which should symbolize a warm, comfortable and happy relationship with the opposite sex. The eighth, I believe, has more of a financial meaning, working with other people's money, government money or mutual funds."

Peter's Saturn was apparently well placed for a neophyte.

"Saturn in Virgo is well-aspected to Pluto in his house of partnerships, and to the Capricorn ascendant, governed by Saturn, indicating that he is capable of learning to do the Virgo thing–take orders, give service, handle detail, be a productive worker, even though it goes against his Aquarian urge for freedom."

Peter's interest, Neptunean because of his Pisces Sun, was of an ephemeral nature that didn't seem to grab onto anything for any length of time.

"How about travel?" he asked, with a glance at his mother.

"Potential travel is in your chart, Neptune is in the ninth house affecting long trips, but Neptune is often related to just dreaming about something, so it is never certain whether the person will actually do the thing or just think about it."

At this point, it wasn't plain what Peter was getting out of the analysis, aside from preening his Aquarian vanity. But it was self-evident that he was suffering from Neptunean delusions of grandeur that a doting mother had not seen fit to dispel. As others of his Neptune-in-Libra generation, his feelings about marriage and other traditional relationships, personal and professional, were somewhat nebulous. This was not helped any by Uranus in Cancer, tending to make the individual restless, impatient, and rather eccentric, as well as having the broader effect, shared by so many of this 1949–56 Uranian position, of breaking away from the authority of the home.

In a single session it was difficult to assess the basic accuracy of the astrological analysis. But it was apparent that the psychologist, through astrology, had established an enviable rapport with a complex subject in a matter of minutes, and was now about to tackle an equally difficult branch of this human equation.

The mother had been following the analysis with an expression of amusement. She was an exceptionally attractive woman, a mother several times over, with the well-schooled poise of the matron sure of her station in life.

As before, Dr. Dobyns seemed more involved in the chart than its flesh-and-blood subject.

Curiously, the mother was also a Pisces with Aquarius in the first house and Pisces in the second. And yet, looking at the two, sitting near one another, one would never have surmised that the dark youth with the restless features was related to the fair, elegant lady with the faintly detached air.

I supposed she was there out of curiosity or, more likely, because she had tried just about everything else with a son who obviously didn't relate to reality.

It struck others, too, as strange that mother and son should have so many astral points of similarity, and yet be so dissimilar.

"He has negative aspects to the third and ninth houses, which rule the mind, and to Mercury and Jupiter, the planets of communication and wisdom," the psychologist said in explanation.

She briefly compared the two charts. "There's much less in Aquarius for Mom, only the Part of Fortune, and much more in Pisces, but you" —she addressed the mother—"have an Aries grouping (the Moon and Venus) which fits in with Aquarius. Both Aries and Aquarius have this love of personal freedom, so you can understand Peter's problems readily and empathize with them."

The mother nodded perfunctorily. "That is correct."

The psychologist took in the fashionable figure at a glance. "You seem sure of yourself, but you have the same first house sign as Peter. This is accentuated with the south node square the Aries planets from the twelfth house of hidden things, a sign of deep inner misgivings."

The mother's eyes dropped.

"How do you know this?" I asked.

"The south node," Dr. Dobyns said briskly, "is reflected in heavy self-doubt, a tendency to guilt. It is well concealed in the twelfth house, and people don't see that, since Sagittarius in her eleventh house of friends presents an appearance of self-confidence and Aquarius in the first an open nature."

Dr. Dobyns studied the chart with a frown.

"Have you had any depressing problems recently, feelings of futility, of being blocked in? Transiting Saturn in Taurus has been square your Neptune in Leo for quite a while."

The woman shrugged. "No more so than anybody else."

"You have an unusually gifted mind, with that sharp Moon in Aries sextile mentally agile Mars in Gemini. Things come easy, too easy perhaps, and you hold back so that people, particularly those close to you, won't resent you."

The son regarded his mother fondly. "My Dad's the smart one in the family," he said. "He can do anything; but don't get in his way."

The mother's faint sneer had vanished and she was suddenly defensive.

"I've been very busy running a big house, and bringing up five children."

"Nobody with the mental aspects in your chart could be satisfied with that role alone–it's not challenge enough."

The rest were now eyeing the mother with frank curiosity. And one housewife asked with a trace of skepticism.

"Where is all this evident?"

The psychologist permitted herself a smile. "In the chart or the life?"

"The chart."

"All right, let's examine it. Her well-placed Neptune signifies qualities in the subconscious mind, tendencies which from the start of life seem to come to us without personal effort on our part, as if a karmic legacy from a past life.

"When strongly aspected, this may mean idealism and artistic talent, love of beauty, humanitarian instincts. In this chart Neptune strongly aspects Mercury and Uranus, so there is a good deal of psychological restlessness and psychic ability–none of which is being used.

"Venus rules the fourth house of home, and it's in the third, conjunct her Moon in Aries, which in the third house shows free, easy communication, the ability to talk comfortably with others with a certain amount of persuasive ability. Pisces doesn't often have this by itself, but must be supported by other signs which reflect language versatility and the ability to relax with and relax other people."

The power of suggestion was such that the mother, supported as she was by Aries and Gemini, began visibly to relax.

"I've thought of doing a number of things from time to time," she said. "But I wasn't quite sure what would suit me."

"It all depends on how serious you are about it."

The mother rested her chin in her hand. "Would I be good at real estate?"

Dr. Dobyns looked up with a smile.

"You'd really be good there, you have a good chart for a salesman, particularly with Mars in Gemini, in the fifth."

The woman's eyes crinkled in amusement.

"And what does Mars do?"

"In Gemini, a mental sign, it conveys the ability to communicate readily with some degree of personal skill and openness, force and persuasion, and sextile Venus in Aries to take initiative in interactions with people. And it's pretty favorable for real estate since Venus rules your Taurus fourth house of property."

There were also indications of trouble with children, but, as a good psychologist, Dr. Dobyns took a painless way of saying virtually the same thing. "Saturn in your eleventh house (Sagittarius) shows you have lessons to be gained in the area of knowledge through friends or children. It is an excellent teaching position."

The mother's face brightened.

"So, really, if I have the ability to communicate, I could communicate through teaching."

"You can do it through teaching or selling, public relations, advertising, and with Uranus in the second house of income, you could even get involved teaching astrology."

The mother's eyebrows went up the least bit.

"My husband makes a very large income, so I really don't think in terms of income so much as in achieving something, and I really don't know what that would be."

It struck me that she was a bit of a dilettante. Here she had been asking about real estate one moment ago, and now she was talking in diametrically opposite terms. She seemed, surprisingly, almost as much at loose ends as her son, without his excuse of youth.

"I have a feeling," she said, toying with a kerchief, "that there's more to life than making money."

The psychologist smiled. "It's the inner life that's important, particularly as we get older and assess our reasons for existence."

"I've raised a good family."

"That's often not enough, as our individuality, our craving for identity, can best be satisfied by responding to our inner urges to express our creative flair to the fullest."

"I've helped my husband; we were married when he was in college, and I helped him through."

She spoke matter-of-factly, as if she had only done what any wife would have done.

The boy, who had been listening quietly, perked up at the mention of his father.

"Nobody can top my Dad," he said with a stammer. "He's got an answer for everything."

The mother frowned.

"Now that the children are grown I'd really like to do something."

"You can do it," Dr. Dobyns said, "but you have your own inner doubts because your standards are so impossibly high."

This was presumably because of her strong Neptunean nature, the idealism that became so apparent with her Sun, Jupiter, Uranus and Mercury all in Neptunean-ruled Pisces. And Neptune, as we know, is the seat of the subconscious, and all the confusion–or inspiration–the subconscious is heir to.

With it all, I had the impression that she didn't have much stick-to-itiveness, and I supposed this was her Mars in Gemini, lending a volatile mercurial flavor to her Mars energy quotient. Or perhaps I was rationalizing, astrologically, what I already saw perceptively.

There was a bit of the Piscean martyr, expressed now as she asked, "Why do people always look to me to get a job done?"

"There's a natural leader in you, with that Jupiter and Mercury on your Sun."

"I come across like that, but I don't feel like it. I go to PTA meetings three times, and they want me to be president. Why?"

"Saturn is the most elevated planet in your chart and confers a natural affinity for authority."

She smiled. "I wish you could tell my husband that."

The boy again came to life. "Nobody tells my father anything," he stammered. "He tells them."

They had been married for nearly 25 years, and it would seem they would know one another by now.

"He doesn't want me to do anything but take care of the house." She moved her shapely shoulders. "And then he doesn't approve of anything I do." She seemed more and more defensive, more martyr-like.

The psychologist looked at her inquiringly. "For instance?"

She hesitated. "Oh, the other night, in front of guests, he went out of his way to point out that I didn't know how to serve cocktails properly."

Dr. Dobyns shrugged. "On the basis of the chart, you are capable of doing anything you want to do; that is provided you are willing to put forth the sustained effort. As we said of your son's chart, neither Aquarius nor Pisces likes to work very hard, and both are highly restless signs with a low threshold of boredom. But if you are not interested in a financial return from your own work, there is ample artistic ability indicated to suggest that you would enjoy an aesthetic hobby."

The boy, engrossed as he was in his Piscean-Aquarian self, didn't seem to have the slightest notion of his mother's problem. He looked at her fondly. "There's something for you, Mom."

She smiled perfunctorily in his direction. And again her interest in a career seemed to wander, and she took an entirely new tack.

"Do you see me going on a vacation soon?"

The change in emphasis didn't seem to faze the psychologist.

"The progressed Moon is forming aspects all through the summer, so you might go anytime. It will also be going through the ninth house of long-distance travel in the fall, with strong aspects to natal Mars and Moon."

"Is the Moon what you want to do?"

"In the progressed chart, the Moon is the one thing that moves month to month, ticking off activities. Also transiting Uranus in Libra is going into opposition to your natal Moon in the late summer, so travel is most likely at that time–since Uranus right now is affecting your life, indicating blocks."

The mother's attitude had changed sharply. Her patronizing tone had given way to frank interest, and some surprise, as the astrologer hit upon personality aspects and circumstances that the mother was familiar with. But now, suddenly, she seemed to be pulling in her traces, as if she had heard all she wanted.

The general discussion turned to other charts, but they held little interest for me, as the problem was obvious–the desperate moral bankruptcy of a surfeited suburbia.

But mother and son were much on my mind, and continued so for days. What, if anything, had been accomplished? Would there be a follow-up? Eventually, as I knew I would, I sought out Dr. Dobyns.

Many things had puzzled me. Yet, I had learned enough to at least ask the pertinent questions.

"Neither one," I ventured, "knew the first thing about astrology?"

Dr. Dobyns nodded. "Some of the people knew something, but they didn't."

"Then what brought her in?"

"Desperation, the kind of quiet desperation that is the yardstick of upper middle-class living today, expressing itself in sheer, unutterable boredom."

I shrugged. "She had five children, and a husband she helped make successful."

"That wasn't enough, not with her chart. She needed more than home and hearth. She was sensitive enough to have the feeling there was more to life than she was getting, but she didn't know how to go about it."

I had the feeling she wasn't going to do much about it.

"She has abilities she's not using, and people are always frustrated when they don't come up to their abilities. But she's indolent."

"Where do you see that?"

"That mass of planets in Pisces, Mars in Gemini, and her Aquarian ascendant, the air signs like things to come the easy way."

"But she's basically a water sign."

"True, but Pisces traditionally is the laziest sign of the zodiac. They want to do everything, in an illusory Neptunean way of course, but nothing that takes any effort."

My Uranus in Aquarius in the first house—the sign of independence—obviously framed my next question.

"How could a woman of intelligence put up with a marriage where she was constantly being demeaned?"

"I think she understands why he does it."

"That doesn't make it any easier."

"She's unhappy with her marriage, but not unhappy enough, with all those planets in the second house, to give up the financial comfort, so in the end she will do nothing."

"I suppose her confidence has been beaten down."

"Perhaps, but it was something she could have overcome by taking on challenges and besting them. Instead, she directs her energies to planning a vacation."

"Probably away from the husband," I said sourly.

Mother and son seemed under the same aspects, though he had none of her alertness.

"The boy seemed a little slow to me."

"Definitely slow," Dr. Dobyns concurred. "He's been tested as mentally retarded."

"How far did he go in school?"

"High school. He was in special classes for a while, but did manage to graduate."

I was puzzled by Dr. Dobyn's calm acceptance of Peter's slow mental condition, after having heard earlier about all his mental prowess, astrologically.

"I was talking about a potential," she explained. "It is all there. He can work it out, once he gets over a few of his hang-ups."

The stammer, of course, was the most obvious.

His Mars and Neptune (ruling the subconscious mentality of memory) were in Libra, the sign of balance, apparently unbalanced by the adverse square of Uranus in Cancer. But still there is no note of finality about squares, they only make one work harder.

"What was the point of stressing all this," Dr. Dobyns asked, "when it was accenting the positive that might be helpful?"

I looked at her doubtfully.

"Do you actually think he can teach?"

"At the level of his own knowledge, he can help others with similar problems. He's intelligent enough, just slow, and coddled a little by the mother. Once he gets away from home and fends for himself, he'll be all right."

"What caused that stammer?"

"Fear, or perhaps self-consciousness is a better phrase. Also there may be a self-conscious use of fear to control people, to keep them waiting and paying attention."

"And this fear was of whom?"

"Of anyone who would control and block his personal wishes."

"He seemed to get along with his mother."

"In a way. He had the idea that she, as well as his father, was riding him, but, of course, she would have been doing it protectively, to forestall the father's criticism. Uranus in Cancer, as this boy has it, can be a struggle between freedom and dependency. Uranus wants the freedom, Cancer the dependency.

"As we pointed out, he didn't like to take orders. With his Jupiter in Aquarius in the first house, he feels he has a right to what he wants when he wants it."

"Yet he showed a certain awe of his father."

"He was afraid of him," Dr. Dobyns corrected. "That showed in the tenth house rulers, Pluto and Mars, as keys to the father. Pluto opposed the Aquarian planets and squared the Moon, and Mars squared the ascendant and Uranus and was conjunct the South Node."

"That may have brought on the stammer?"

She shrugged. "Who can say?"

I was still dissatisfied, without quite knowing why, and then it dawned on me. So the son was slightly retarded, and dependent on a mother who was discontented with her lot without knowing what to do with it. But they were obviously only puppets, reacting to an agency we had no real insight into.

"We should have still another chart in the file," I said.

Dr. Dobyns understood instantly.

"Imagine that father coming down here to have his chart analyzed in front of all those people."

She smiled. "If he could do that, perhaps there might not be a problem."

It had ended on a very flat note, leaving me with a feeling of frustration.

"I could begin to understand the whole thing so much better if I knew what the father was like," I said to an astrologer friend later.

She smiled. "Well, you should be able to, from the horoscopes of the mother and the son—that's what astrology is all about, our relationships to the world around us."

I wasn't quite sure how this would work.

She examined the mother's chart. "The seventh house in the mother's horoscope is her husband, since this is the house of partnerships. In her chart this house is ruled by Leo, which is also the sign of the husband, and in this position gives the husband a commanding, imperious nature, kind at times, but always domineering, demanding respect at all times from those around him. And this would, conversely, give the tendency for others to feel inferior in his royal presence."

I was beginning to get a worm's-eye view of this absent father.

Her Sun–still the husband–square Saturn showed the head of the family to be shrewdly ambitious and selfish. "With the Sun square Mars in the sensitive, mutable signs of Pisces and Gemini, he shows an explosive temper, a great deal of nervous tension, and with this Mars in the mother's fifth house, representing children, the children could very easily be his major point of irritation."

In the boy's chart, the father, being obviously the dominant parent, was indicated by the tenth house. "Pluto, the ruler of the tenth, becomes the father here, and is in Leo (the husband) in the seventh house of partners and open enemies, and therefore he is a constant challenge to the son." Pluto in the seventh was exactly square mother Moon in the fourth house of the home.

The interpretation of this last aspect was Freudian in its depth.

"In the boy's subconscious," said my astrologer friend, "there is a growing feeling that the father is destructive to the mother."

I still didn't understand the boy's stammer.

"Mercury rules the mind and the speech," my astrologer friend said, "and it is opposite Pluto, the father in the boy's chart, and so is destructive to the son's mental and verbal expression."

And the mother was no help.

"The stammering would increase (and perhaps originated) when the boy was with mother and father at the same time, since his Mercury was also square the Moon, the mother, as well as being in opposition to the father."

Obviously, if he was protective towards his mother, he would be apprehensive of his father when the three were together.

"Since both mother and son are Pisces," the astrologer said, "there is a close psychic affinity between them, and the boy would be able to identify with his mother's secret fears."

I put the charts away. Maybe, I thought with a sigh, the boy knew what he was talking about when he said he'd like to be in the Army.

8

Time, Destiny and Free Will

There is a time to live and a time to die, a time to work and a time to idle, a time to love and a time to hate, and there is a time for doubt, and for questioning.

And the question, too, flung out of the human subconscious into the universal subconscious, has a time equation of its own to the astrologer. He answers questions of all kinds, dredged out of a subconscious need which prompted this question at this particular time, and he says that the question answers itself in the astrologer's chart erected for the precise moment the question was asked.

It is the purest form of astrology, the closest thing to divination that the astrologer knows, and it is called horary astrology. The horary astrologer claims that it is faultless, provided a question is basic enough to express itself at a time tied in with the destiny pattern. "Whatever is born or done this moment of time, has the qualities of this moment of time," said Jung. And every moment of time is different, with its own potential, and the question is part of that time.

"You must have a pressing problem, something that has been sitting on your mind, something that needs an answer," said astrologer Franka Moore. "For the answers, indirectly, come through a mind which asked the question at a time when the answer was already resolved in the subconscious but not yet articulated."

I had been sitting with Franka Moore in her pleasant San Fernando Valley home, occasionally rubbing the Southern California smog out of my eyes, as I puzzled over a time dimension that just made no sense in reference to whatever I knew of the nature of events.

"It must be a psychic thing," I said, not understanding how an astrological chart done for the hour could tell me whether I was going to take a trip, marry, or have some financial success or reverse.

Franka smiled and shook her head. "There's no extrasensory perception to it. It is something that you have wondered about, debated back and forth with yourself, often on both a conscious and subconscious level, and which has drawn more than you realize on the energies of your mind."

It was no clearer than before.

She elaborated.

"The question can't be off the top of your mind. It's deep and may not even be what you consciously think it is. The pattern is forming, the problem is there, the question is asked, and the answer lies within the person himself."

"But what has that to do with astrology?"

"Your aspects, the positions of the planets in the chart for the moment of the question, reflect the subconsciously forming pattern.

"In a gambling venture, for instance, the person already knows subconsciously that he's going to win, without realizing it consciously, and this accounts for his confidence."

I still did not grasp it.

"The question shows a predisposition to a problem in a certain area, and then something comes along and kicks it off, and the horary chart merely reflects what this is in terms of astrological symbols which pick up the pattern of the subconscious mind at that moment and its destiny."

As I thought about it, I recalled how astrologer Sydney Omarr had explained it. "A moment of time is frozen into eternity by capturing the positions of the planets at that moment."

"All right," I said now, looking at the clock. "Suppose I were to ask right now when I will be married again, now that would be something I've thought about."

"You aren't doing it with any great deal of emotion, are you?"

"I have it on my mind."

Franka looked at me doubtfully. "I'd say be careful."

"Well, that's not a horary."

"No, but I know your natal chart, and you have Neptune, the planet of deception and illusion, activated by Mars in the seventh house of partners, and in Cancer yet, ruling the home."

After two marriages this seemed rather academic.

"Neptune in the seventh house," she went on, "often marries out of pity, or to protect someone who has terrible weaknesses."

We seemed to have strayed from the question.

She made a few marks on a horoscope pad.

"Your question was framed at precisely 11:58 A.M."

"And you will do a chart from that?"

"Yes, this being March 28, the month being Aries, the rising sign for the day begins with Aries, and so figuring two hours for each sign, Cancer would be ascending at the time of the question. And so Cancer becomes your first house, and since Cancer rules your marriage house in the natal chart, this indicates what I didn't at first realize, that it was really a deep question."

She frowned. "Before I put in the transiting planets, and the Moon, which is the timer in a horary because it moves so fast, I take Saturn from your natal chart, as Evangeline Adams did so successfully, and put it in the horary. Saturn is the fear planet, the planet of restriction. It is concern, and the assumption is that if a person goes to an astrologer he's concerned about something.

"So your Saturn in Gemini would fall in the twelfth house of the horary, which is secret sorrow or self-undoing."

"Today," I said, quoting a line, "is the first day of the rest of my life. My question was, 'When will I be married?' "

"That is really not a valid question for a horary," said she. "The question should be, 'Will I marry Mary, or Jane, or somebody?' It should be personalized. Otherwise, it is obviously not very deep into the subconscious, and it is hard to have a subconscious pattern forming as regards marriage when there is no specific person to form it around."

"There may be somebody quite specific in my subconscious or hidden conscious," I said. "Or the question wouldn't have been asked. So, by your own definition, the aspects should pick up the answer to this evolving pattern."

She sighed.

"All right," she said, "I'll work it out, and get back to you."

The planets, houses and signs were placed in the chart as if it were a natal horoscope for the birth of a baby. The ascendant, representing my question, was 19 degrees of Cancer, and so the Moon, ruling Cancer, ruled my ascendant, becoming sole ruler of the chart.

The Moon is the thing to watch in a horary, and the Moon was in the fifth house of love affairs and children; the other fifth house influences of gambling and talent had no application to the question.

Franka was as matter-of-fact as a computer.

"You have the Moon in the fifth conjunct Neptune, the planet of illusion, and Neptune is retrograde, so there is some confusion about the question and the change it involves. However, the Moon is coming to a favorable trine (120-degree angular aspect) with Venus in the tenth house of activity, and Venus standing for love or marriage, it would indicate a favorable resolution to your question. But the final outcome of the chart rests with the fourth house, which stands for the end of the matter, and Jupiter and Uranus are sitting there, and both retrograde."

It sounded like double talk to me.

Franka laughed. "It is astrological double talk," she conceded, "and it means just that, there are two sides to the answer. You will eventually get married because of that Venus trine, but it will be delayed because of the fourth house retrograding planets."

"But if there is somebody to marry, subconscious or otherwise, why would it be deferred, if it's going to happen at all?"

Franka was never without an answer.

"The final aspect of the Moon qualifies the outcome. With the Moon in the fifth squaring transiting Pluto in Virgo, and Pluto being the ruler of the fifth, with Scorpio on its cusp, it confirms the confusion about love affairs and children, and a reluctance at this time, because of that square, to enter into a relationship that entertains this possibility of children."

I thought a moment.

"You have given an indeterminate answer to an indeterminate question."

"Exactly. The answer is yes, but the time is indeterminate because of your own subconscious vacillation."

Some time thereafter, I had a more immediate problem than marriage. This was now late April, and I had been invited to appear on the

Merv Griffin television show for May 14. From my astrology class I had learned that transiting Uranus, governing air travel and television, was retrograde, and this, astrologically, was no time to meet a commitment of this sort.

I phoned Franka Moore.

"Can you do a horary for me?"

"Is the question strongly motivated?"

"Shall I fly to New York to do the Griffin show?"

"Uranus won't go direct until June 2, and so I would advise a delay without even doing a horary. It's the wrong time to start this kind of project."

"Wouldn't the horary be more explicit?"

I could see her shrug over the phone.

"You asked your question at 10:22 A.M., so you have Cancer rising again, 21 degrees of Cancer actually on the first house cusp."

"How did you work that out so fast?"

"As you were talking, I checked the table of houses for the house cusps. However, it'll take a few minutes to chart the transiting planets for the day, so I'll call you back."

In an hour or so, the telephone rang.

"I've got news for you," Franka said. "You're not going to New York to do this show."

"Oh, yes I am," I said. "Since I spoke to you last, a production assitant from the Griffin show called and I put it off to May 28—they couldn't delay it any further."

Franka Moore laughed.

"I still don't see you going at this time. The chart's so obvious that any beginner would come up with this answer. Your third house is transportation, and Mercury rules it since Virgo, its sign, is on the third house cusp. The transiting Moon, the timer, which is you, the questioner, in a horary, is coming to an opposition of Mercury, and to cap things, you have two planets retrograde in the third house of travel, Pluto retrograde in Virgo, and Uranus retrograde in Libra."

Not being terribly knowledgeable, I was not terribly impressed.

"Pluto deals with the masses, right?" I said, for the sake of saying something.

"It deals also with television," she said. "And Uranus is electricity. Uranus, Neptune and Pluto, the last three planets discovered, all seem to have to do with television and radio."

Even the telephone call was opposing my journey. As communication, it fell into the third house of the horary chart with the two retrograde planets.

I was looking for a saver.

"Doesn't the third house rule only short trips?"

"Usually, we figure the ninth house for longer trips, out of the country or completely cross-country. But Neptune rules the ninth, and it is also retrograde. Wherever I looked you weren't going anywhere. So then I turned to the fourth house, the outcome of the matter. And what did I find? Jupiter in Scorpio, also retrograde, and Jupiter means it will come out all right in the end, but, retrograde, not as you planned. So I just wrote the whole thing off."

Two or three weeks passed, and I began making plans to leave California for New York. Then on May 26, two days before the show, the phone rang. It was the girl from the Griffin show again.

"I've got good news for you," she said, "the show is coming out to California the first week of June. So instead of bringing you to New York, we've got you down for June 8 in Los Angeles."

I could hardly restrain an exclamation.

"That's what the astrologer told me," I said.

"What astrologer?" She was immediately interested.

I explained what had happened, making light of it, and half-expecting her to do the same, when she suddenly asked:

"I wonder if she could tell me what's going to happen to me."

"That's not very specific," I said.

"I have to make a job decision, and don't know what to do."

"I don't know if she can do that, but give me your birth data."

Over the phone I could sense a moment of hesitation. And then she gave me the vital statistics that took her out of her twenties. She was born July 28, 1939, 4:00 A.M., in Youngstown, Ohio.

A few minutes later I phoned Franka Moore.

"I'll do the chart," she said, "but this girl has already made her decision."

Franka could no longer surprise me. "How do you know that?"

"I've done so many of these charts I can almost immediately visualize them. As a Leo with a 4 A.M. birth time, she obviously has Cancer rising. I checked her Moon while you were talking, and it's in Capricorn. And Mars, the planet of quick change, is in Cancer in the twelfth house opposing her natal Moon which also rules her Cancer ascendant. And the Moon, being in her sixth house, is in the kind of work she is doing, as the sixth relates to her job and co-workers. Also, her tenth house of activity with Aries on the cusp is ruled by Mars, and all this interaction between the first, the sixth and the tenth, involving the Moon and Mars, indicated a quick change."

"But how did you know the change had occurred?"

"Because the aspects were already there, and the twelfth house opposition (Mars to the Moon) indicated a certain impatience and irritability with co-workers that should have already triggered an impulsive change."

Her instant rundown of the aspects baffled me.

"How did you know Aries was in the tenth house of career?"

"That would be automatic, a ninety degree square from the Cancer ascendant."

Another puzzling thing was how a planet could rule one house and still be in another, influencing both.

"In astrology," Franka said, "the sign on the house cusp determines the ruling planet, and it affects that house as well as the one it's in natally. There is also the transiting planet. So one planet can have three different aspects in the individual's chart."

It was just another facet of astrology that could only be explained in the fact that it worked.

"I still don't see how you picked off the change," I said.

"The transiting Mars cycle (coming out of the twelfth house) touched off the Moon ascendant, which was opposed to her work, and the Mars ruler of the tenth was square her ascendant, which of course is the person herself, and so Mars would institute change involving her and her work."

"And how do you know it has already happened?"

"Transiting Mars in Cancer is already so close to her ascendant it must have produced sufficient energy to have prompted some action on the Moon ascendant's part. And Leos are spontaneous anyway, particularly with that twelfth house."

Franka was picking up steam. "And she's quite upset about the decision she made and will be for five or six weeks."

"And where did that come from?"

"When transiting Mars goes into a person's twelfth house, he or she starts reviewing the past two years—the period of Mars' complete cycle—and bugging himself or herself as to whether the right moves had been made. And Mars has been in the twelfth for more than a month."

The young producer called back before I could call her.

"Have you already left your job?" I asked.

"How did you know?"

"The astrologer told me you had acted impulsively and were now worried about it."

"I jumped without having a place to jump to, and I'm scared stiff."

"You'll get over that soon," I said authoritatively, "when Mars moves out of your twelfth house."

She could hardly wait for her chart, which Franka had ready in a few days.

By and large, it was an optimistic delineation.

"This girl has a strong career chart," Franka began. "But she's been having problems because transiting Saturn in Taurus squares her Leo Sun, squares the Pluto in Leo in her first house, blocking her for a while, until it moves out next April or May, which is when she should properly have made her move. Also Saturn is coming right to Uranus in her natal chart in the eleventh house, bringing a change of environment, friends, associations—a complete change in career or a move from coast to coast."

"And which is it?" I asked.

"It could be both, but since Saturn is coming to a square of Mercury in Leo, and Mercury in Virgo rules the fourth house of her home in her natal chart, I would assume that the change applied to her home, but with Virgo the work sign, her job may also be affected."

There was a pause, as she examined the chart for a few moments.

"I would say she'll be out here in Southern California—Los Angeles, specifically—by August."

"And you insist you're not psychic?"

"It's all in the chart. I suppose cross-country could also have meant Portland, Oregon, but Mercury in Virgo in the fourth reflects the change in home, and Los Angeles is a Virgo city, and besides, there has to be some common sense in an interpretation. You wouldn't tell a ninety-year-old man with Venus conjunct Uranus in Scorpio that he was going to have an unexpected affair, but that he would be making a new friend, unexpectedly. And since she is in television, and the television center is in Los Angeles, and the Virgo clue was there, I picked Los Angeles."

"How about the time?"

"With Libra also in the fourth house with Virgo, Venus ruling Libra becomes co-ruler of the home, and when transiting Mars hits that Venus in four or five weeks, she'll be more than ready for the cross-country change with transiting Uranus also in Libra helping Mars to activate things in that direction. Whenever you see a drastic residence change, the first house and the fourth must be involved, which they are in her chart—the first being the physical body, and the fourth the residence."

I passed the tidings on to the girl, stressing that she had a good career chart.

She had the natal planets, Saturn and Jupiter, in the tenth house of career, and since Pisces was on the house cusp, the ruler of the house was Neptune, which ruled over television and movies, and which was in the third house of the natal chart, the house of communication. Moreover, benevolent Jupiter rules the sixth house of work, which has Sagittarius for a house cusp, so she couldn't miss in the long run, and Saturn and Jupiter being elevated showed her reaching heights.

"Besides all that," I said, "you have six planets in angular houses, all aspecting one another, generating greater energy from being angular."

The girl seemed singularly unimpressed.

"I want to know about now," she said, with pardonable impatience as she hung up.

And so there it stayed for several weeks, until one day in August the telephone rang in my Pacific retreat. It was the girl again. She had moved to the West Coast, taken an apartment in the Hollywood district of Los Angeles, and was planning to work on the Coast.

Even without a horary, the astrologer had remarkably pinpointed the movements of a young lady she had never seen.

I had still another experience with one of Franka Moore's horary charts, so remarkable that I still can't believe it, no matter the aspects. I had lost or mislaid a pair of reading glasses, I knew not where, and on the slim chance that astrology might provide a clue, I had asked the astrologer: "Where are my glasses?"

She said she would try, but I must say she didn't sound too hopeful, and I really didn't blame her.

The next day she called.

"The horary," said she, almost as if disowning personal responsibility, "indicates that your glasses are in an area a little below the living-room of your home, and to the west of it a bit."

I sighed. "That would put it in the Pacific Ocean, since I look out on the beach below from my living-room."

Six months passed, and I chalked up another demerit for astrology, as there was no sight of the glasses.

One day, two young visitors from Los Angeles, Nancy Sparr and Grayce Rossnagel, were strolling the beach in front of my house. Spotting a dark object floating on the surf, Grayce reached down and picked it up. It was a pair of reading glasses.

"Do you know who these belong to?" she asked.

I took and examined them, not believing what I saw even in broad daylight.

They were my glasses, dredged out of the sea, a little bit below, and west of my living-room.

In essence, astrology, particularly horary astrology, points up the age-old dilemma of fate and free will. I had always assumed the two contradictory, but watching astrology—and life—at work, I saw that this was not the case. Major events occur without any volition or control on man's part. He finds himself in adverse situations—wars, storms, holocausts—in which his only choice is that of reaction, which is still free will.

Even as I wrote these lines, the flames were swirling about in the Malibu hills in Los Angeles and Southern California's worst fire disaster, leaving countless people prey to the elements. Some fled the fire scene, others stayed to cope with the blaze and saved their homes. Still others wept and said they wouldn't be back, and some swore they would rebuild on the ruins.

The event itself was clearly foreshadowed in the astrological aspects for the day, astrologers said, but the free will of the individual determined whether he would rise above that which he could not control.

On September 25, 1970, the day the fire broke out, Uranus, the planet of fire and explosion, was prominent in the Los Angeles chart. "Uranus," Franka Moore pointed out, "rules the fourth house of home and land in the city's chart, and transiting Uranus in Libra in the twelfth house is conjunct Venus, which rules the city's Libra ascendant, the people. This, together with Leo, a fire sign, in the midheaven of activity, plus activating angular Moon squares to Jupiter, Saturn and Venus, established the potential for an explosive fire. This was touched off on the 25th when the Moon went into Leo. Then as the Moon went into Virgo, an Earth sign, on the third day of the fire, the flames began to simmer down, and the danger was over."

The late Evangeline Adams was convinced that the individual carried his destiny around with him. She constantly stressed the rigidity of predicted events. But the astrologer could help. The chart was a road map of life, and he could guide the individual over the rough spots, and recognize the time to act for greater success.

Miss Adams did not pussyfoot about the role of death. She saw it plainly in most charts, and when she felt it relevant she allowed it quietly to affect her counseling.

The wife of a prominent merchant once asked if she should divorce him and marry another. Miss Adams compared the three charts. "The first thing I saw was that my client and her lover would never be happy together—that they might not even marry if they had the chance; and the second thing, which the stars indicated as clearly as the dawn indicates the coming day, was that her husband would not live beyond the following July."

Ethically, she could not discuss the foreseen death, but she strongly advised against the divorce, giving the lover's inadequacies as the reason.

That first week of July, the astrologer opened her newspaper one day, and there read the fulfillment of her prediction. The merchant had died on a fishing trip. The clandestine relationship, shorn of its intrigue, soon broke off.

On a rare occasion astrologer Adams felt it prudent to prepare a client for his passing. She had seen the death of a prominent Senator, very suddenly, away from home. From that point on, the Senator avoided leaving town. But being a public figure this was difficult. Two years later, on an unavoidable political mission, he suddenly dropped dead.

"Destiny," Miss Adams decided, "fulfills itself."

As Franka Moore saw it, there was a proper time to take a job, make a trip, enter into a marriage—and though the action itself might be inevitable, just as birth and death, the quality of the action could be influenced by the way one put his hand to it. And what was this way but a time equation of opportunity, readiness and ability?

It was in the stars that the girl from the Griffin show change her job and abode, but had she waited six months, until transiting Saturn was no longer square her Sun and first house planets in Leo, she could have spared herself needless fretting and concern, and then fallen into an opportunity just waiting for her.

Coincident with her own move, the Griffin show moved out to California, and so the change was there, whether she left her job or not.

I had had a previous experience with a horary without beginning to understand it. In a conversation with astrologer Sydney Omarr, I had mentioned that a former editor of mine, Floyd Barger of the New York *Daily News,* had asked me to rush a series of articles on Bishop James Pike's purported conversations with his dead son, Jim.

"Should I do it?" I asked Omarr, a specialist with horary charts.

"Why not?" said this former newsman.

"Is that a personal or professional opinion?"

"Personal, but why shouldn't you do it?"

"I'm not keen for it, and I don't know why. Would a horary be helpful?"

He shook his head. "I'll do it later today, but it looks pretty clear to me—a series of metaphysical articles in the country's largest circulation newspaper could only be beneficial."

He phoned hours later, and there was a certain speculative note in his voice which hadn't been there before.

"It seems hardly possible," he said, "but I did the horary, and it not only said you shouldn't do the articles, but that you wouldn't."

He explained.

"For one thing, the Moon was void of course, which is a technical way of saying it wouldn't aspect the Sun or any of the planets before leaving its current sign."

In 29 degrees of this sign, it only had one degree to go.

"For another thing, there are less than three degrees rising on the ascendant, and this shows the project is premature. But the rulers of the third and ninth houses, which stand for publishing, are favorably aspected, so you will eventually do the articles, to greater advantage than now."

Events proved Omarr the astrologer more knowledgeable than Omarr the individual.

For editor Barger changed the assignment from the Pike experience to one on psychic predictions I had already researched. I subsequently did the Pike story for a national magazine, which permitted considerably more time for a serious discussion of afterlife.

Omarr was impressed by his own horary.

"You wound up with two articles rather than one," he pointed out, "and had you done the Pike story in a hurry, it would undoubtedly have lacked the thought and care that eventually went into it."

He chuckled. "And you also made considerably more money by waiting."

Some events are obviously inevitable, and death is among these. But once foreseen in a chart indicating a subconscious pattern already formed, can it be delayed? On numerous occasions, Evangeline Adams dissuaded people from suicide attempts, pointing out that only the attempt was reflected in their chart, and since it was going to be unsuccessful, they should spare themselves—and others—the strain of this abortive effort. But these were still only attempts.

She tried closing her eyes to the death she saw, as nearly all astrologers do, and didn't impart what she saw to the individual. However, in the case of a personage, such as the ruler of a nation, she felt candor could help prepare that nation for a change.

Many considered her contemporary, Edward VII, a figurehead, but he was still the King of an England on the verge of a world war.

Asked to do the King's horoscope by Lady Paget, Evangeline Adams needed only to scan the aspects to the eighth house of death to know that Edward's end was near. "My first preliminary calculations," she wrote, "convinced me that I could draw no horoscope which would be a fit message to carry to a king."

But Lady Paget was importunate.

The astrologer was as euphemistic as the English language—and the stars—would permit.

"If he lives beyond next May," she told Lady Paget, "I'll either come to see him or send him his horoscope."

Neither was necessary. For on the sixth of May, the very time when Evangeline Adams saw the King's stars most grievously afflicted, Edward passed away.

Nobody loves the bearer of bad news, and Evangeline Adams was no exception. Consulting George V's chart soon after he succeeded Edward, she foresaw the reign would be a bloody one for the English people.

With a heavy heart, she confided what she had seen to English friends. Her private observations found their way to the London newspapers, and the resulting indignation compelled her to cancel a visit to the British Isles. She was persona non grata, until the Great War broke on England like a deluge.

Evangeline Adams was impressed by the inevitability of accidents. Scanning her own chart, and seeing that she was particularly vulnerable to accidents at this time, the astrologer stabled Jupiter, her high-spirited horse, and replaced him with a safer mount, a small, nondescript mare as lazy as she was fat. But the "safe" animal reared on its hind legs, and threw its distinguished rider to the ground, something the other horse had never done.

But the astrologer felt that astrology had been helpful. No serious injuries resulted, as might have from Jupiter's greater height and speed.

Could the accident have been avoided had she taken the precaution of not riding at all during this period? Evangeline Adams didn't think so. What the chart foreshadowed had to happen as foreshadowed, or astrology was a waste of time. One day she foresaw an accidental condition in her husband's chart, and brought it to his attention. "Being forewarned," she reported, "he protected himself in every conceivable way, and managed to come up to the last day of this period substantially intact."

As a special precaution that day, the Jordans (her married name) canceled plans to attend the theater with friends and entertained instead at their New York apartment. It was a happy occasion, and the host gaily opened a bottle of champagne. As he did so, the cork flew out with a loud report, struck him in the right eye, breaking his glasses, and inflicted a serious injury.

As the guests rushed to her husband's assistance, the astrologer dashed next door to her studio and quickly put together a horary chart, the question touching on the seriousness of the injury.

Scanning the result, she breathed easier, realizing what she would never have concluded from an inexpert diagnosis of the wound—"that no permanent injury would result from a mishap at that particular moment."

Evangeline Adams was no fatalist. She pointed out that there were forces at work in the universe affecting man, and that with the self-knowledge provided by astrology, man could make use of these forces for good or evil. "Mars may cause temper and inharmony, but its force can be transmuted into courage and the power to command opportunities. Venus may cause illicit love, but it can cause the poet to write beautiful verse or the humanitarian to build a beautiful city. Even Saturn in its most adverse aspects can be diverted, through knowledge, from greed and jealousy and fear to constructive activity on the physical, scientific or spiritual plane."

There were ways of imparting what she saw that could either encourage or distress the individual. "It would be easy to scare the poor man to death by stressing the evil influences, but it is just as easy and far more true to astrology to warn him against tendencies in the wrong direction and show him how, by cultivating and encouraging the good influences, he can ultimately drive out the bad."

Her charts helped the defeated and discouraged. "If they know that some situation bothering them will clear up as soon as their stars change, they are bound to take courage and fight on until more auspicious times."

The wife ready to break up her home held on when told the husband she loved would tire soon of the other woman; the businessman ready to close up shop took heart when told his *luck* was about to turn.

And what if the stars boded no favorable change? The astrologer could only point out the rough spots, and suggest an acceptance that would perhaps encourage greater inner growth and peace than would ordinarily flow out of an uninterrupted cycle of good fortune.

If a natal chart with all its foreshadowings was a valid one, the hour of birth, even when not precisely known, could be arrived at by checking back on certain major events in the life of the individual. And to some astrologers of an analytical turn, the very assumption of these events as a fixed pattern reflected their inevitability.

"Rectification of a chart would be impossible if there wasn't a fixed destiny pattern in a chart," said astrologer Maxine Bell. "The major events used in rectifying the chart for the birth hour includes events that cannot be repeated—the first marriage, the first child, the first long journey, the death of the parents, major accidents or surgery, first close brush with death through illness."

The astrologer's own father died in her 26th year. By rectifying her chart via progressions, a day or a degree per year, by using the rulers of the fourth and the tenth, the houses of parents, which made aspects to the eighth house of death, she made one step toward arriving at her rising sign.

Just as she could look backward to her father's death for a clue to her own uncertain birth time, Maxine Bell had been able to foreshadow his death from his natal chart. "He had Pisces on the eighth cusp, and there were heavy afflictions to the ruler Neptune at the time. Transiting Mars from the fourth house was also square an ascendant which had natal Saturn and Mars on it, indicating a quick accidental death."

As accurately as she could pinpoint it from the trigger action of the progressed Moon, death would come July 3 or 4, 1942, shortly before her 26th birthday.

Without telling her father what she saw, she advised him not to take any trips at that time, as he was planning to drive down from San Luis Obispo to Los Angeles to see her. She also tried to prepare her mother for the event, cushioning her against the shock.

On July 2, still trying to avert the pattern in the chart, she telephoned that she would be up to visit for the Fourth.

"We'll see," he said.

On the morning of the Fourth, as she was planning to leave for San Luis Obispo, the telephone rang. Her father, intending to surprise her, had started out for Los Angeles, driving with parking lights in the wartime blackout. He had crashed head-on with another car, and died at 7 A.M. that day. Several sailors, who had considered themselves fortunate to hitch a ride with him, also perished in the crash.

Maxine could only comfort herself with the realization that, given the destiny pattern in his chart, there was nothing she could have done.

News of her prediction brought one unexpected result. "I was approached by a man," she recalled, "who represented himself as an insurance agent. He wanted me to foretell when several clients would pass away, as he had figured out a way of taking out policies on their lives unknown to them." He had thought his plan out carefully. "He didn't want me to tell him exactly when they would die, but within three or four months, so it wouldn't look suspicious."

The experience made Maxine realize the risks of such predictions and she has made no similar predictions since.

The Bible says thy days are numbered like the hairs on thy head—and some astrologers saw proof positive of this in the charts of the Kennedy clan. Even before John F. Kennedy's election in 1960, astrologer David Williams had predicted that he would be elected and die in office, a victim of the Jupiter-Saturn conjunction that afflicted Presidents of the United States elected at 20-year intervals. To the chagrin of many, Olive Pryor, the forthright Long Island astrologer, not only confided to her class that the President would be assassinated, but virtually pinpointed the time.

Almost without exception, astrologers excitedly foresaw the event, but withheld pronouncements, because they felt this contrary to public policy.

"John Kennedy," Franka Moore observed, "had Uranus in the fourth house square Mars in the eighth, the classic assassination aspect. And his natal Uranus was square Mars, Mercury and Jupiter in the eighth, and Quincunx Saturn in his midheaven of career. All these afflictions were touched off by transiting Saturn in the fourth house opposing his career at the time he was murdered."

Like his brother, Robert Kennedy had a strong assassination aspect, his Mercury in Sagittarius in the eighth house of death squaring Uranus in Pisces in the twelfth, the house of the secret enemy, the assassin.

Curiously, the destiny patterns of Jack Kennedy and Lee Oswald, the assassin completely unknown to him, merged in their natal charts. Kennedy's had Uranus in the fourth, the end of the matter, squaring Mars in the eighth, showing a violent end by firearms. Oswald's pattern was the exact reverse, with Mars in the fourth violently squaring his Uranus. It was not only an indication of his complicity in Kennedy's assassination, but a foreshadowing of his own.

A similar destiny pattern for the two brothers was intriguingly re-

John F. Kennedy

May 29, 1917

3 p.m., Brookline, Mass.

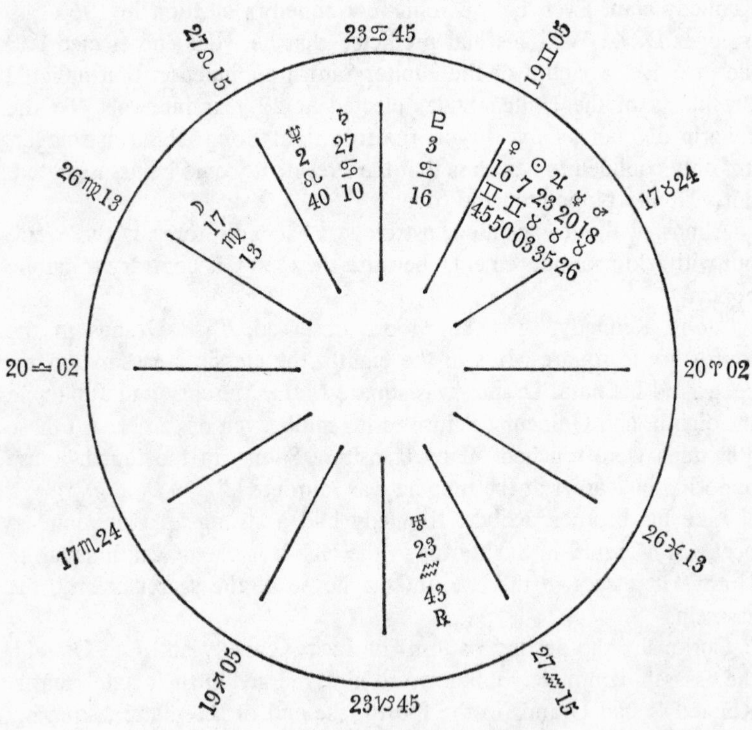

Robt. F. Kennedy

Nov. 20, 1925

Brookline, Mass.

3:10 P.M.

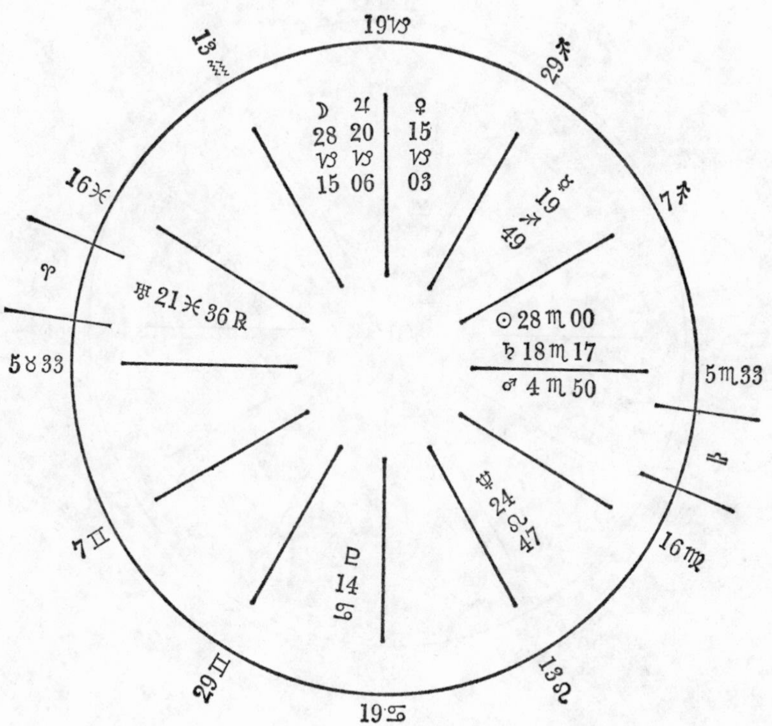

Lee Harvey Oswald

Oct. 18, 1939, New Orleans, La.

Longitude 90 W 04

Latitude 29 N 57

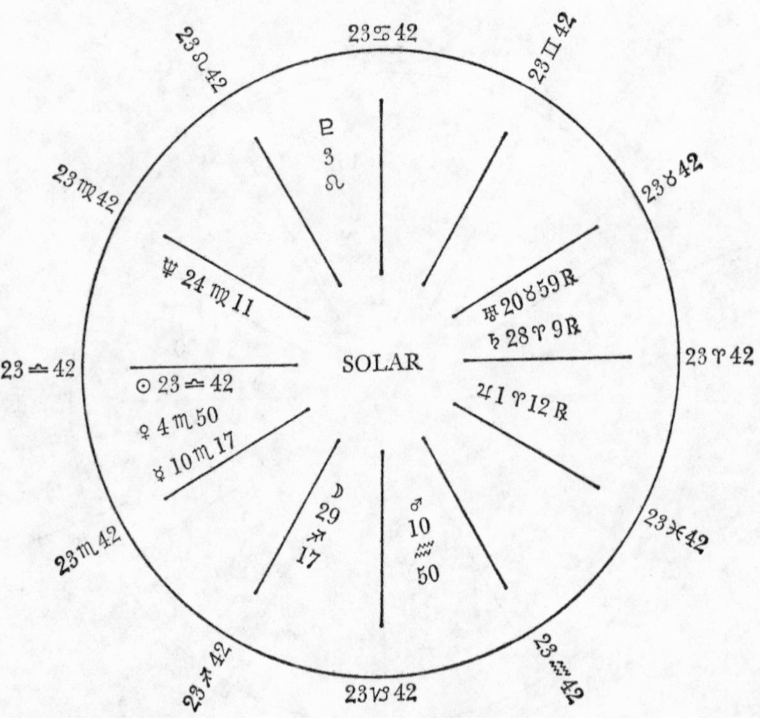

Joseph Kennedy

Sept. 6, 1888

Boston, Mass.

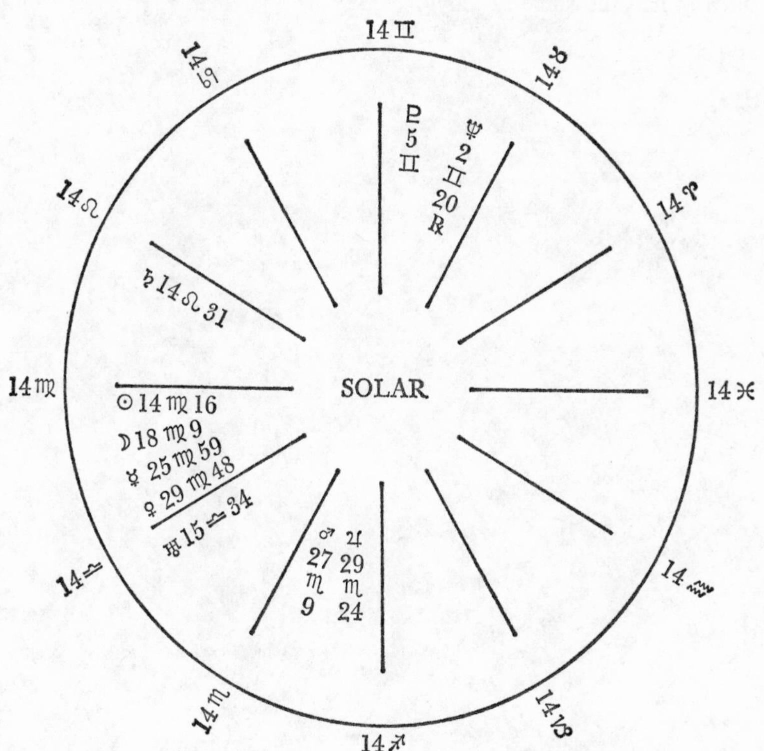

vealed in the chart of their father, the late Ambassador Joseph F. Kennedy. The elder Kennedy, born September 6, 1888, had Virgo on his first house cusp in his solar chart. His first son, Joseph, killed in World War II, belonged, astrologically, in his fifth house, the natural house of children. Franka Moore, who had made a study of the Kennedy's charts, pointed out that the children in a father's chart successively fell in alternating houses from the fifth.

"Consequently," said astrologer Moore, "Jack Kennedy who was the second child, and Robert, who was the eighth, were both represented by the seventh house of their father's chart, and both consequently had the same destiny."

9

A Time for Birth, Birth Control, Sickness and Health

On the basis of astrology the Astra Research Center for Planned Parenthood was founded in 1968 by the Czechoslovakian government. If the preliminary research of 13 years by gynecologist Dr. Eugen Jonas was confirmed, then parents everywhere would not only be able to predetermine the sex of their child, but to pick out the precise times they would be fertile—or infertile—and the best times, as well, to conceive for a healthy offspring.

Although the plan ostensibly pinpoints the certain time for pregnancy, the Jonas project is an obvious answer to the population explosion. In working with four thousand women volunteers, the Czech doctor, a practicing Catholic hoping for a natural rhythm that would obviate abortions, reported his method 99 per cent effective in regulating childbirth—the margin of error being a negligible statistical variation presumably due to erroneous information.

His research, questioned by many officials and scientists, was a blend of the old and the new. "We use astrological laws based on 5,000 years of experimentation and verified by computer techniques," he said. Starting positions for the doctor's calculations included, as any other natal chart, the hour, day, month, year and place the woman was born, together with the positions of the Moon, Sun, and planets at that time.

The method itself is quite simple. "For each patient," said Dr. Jonas, "I prepare a fertility calendar, by figuring the situation (the aspects) of the zodiac and then correlating the results with an electronic computer. In this way, I have succeeded in finding a relationship between the positions of the Moon, the Sun and the planets at the time of a woman's birth and her fertility cycle in maturity."

His research has excited the interest of medical specialists all over Europe, and the comment has been surprisingly favorable, with even the professional skeptics willing to check over his findings because the implications of what his discovery would mean for society.

In an objective summary of the Jonas program, the British medical journal, *GP,* designed as an information sheet for general practitioners, was quick to appraise its advantages.

"The method is natural, needing no special apparatus or drugs, and therefore posing no health problems. Most importantly, the method conflicts with no moral or ethical point of view on birth control."

GP was notably impressed by Jonas' statistics:

"The primary aim is to prevent conception, and numerical results so far indicate that reliability is more than 99 per cent."

Other benefits, the journal noted, included the ability to conceive with the Moon for a boy or girl, dispose of psychological sterility, and minimize the possibilities of miscarriages and birth defects.

Dr. Jonas' astrological formula for conception was readily understood by astrologers. For Jonas, unlike most doctors, considered that ancient doctors and astrologers, often one and the same, might have been right when they said that the Moon had a proven connection with the physical and psychological functions of the female, including the menstrual cycle. In the process of experimentation, he made the discovery that even supposedly infertile women were able to conceive at a time when the Moon and Sun were in the same angular relationship to one another in the heavens as they were in the natal chart of the particular woman.

He didn't know why this should be so, but it was so almost four thousand times, he claimed.

Still experimenting, he discovered, as ancient astrologers have claimed for centuries, that the sex of children could be regulated by the woman conceiving when the Moon was either in a masculine or feminine Sun sign—indicating very dramatically why these signs had been so classified by the ancients. In other words, by conceiving while the Moon was in Aries for two days or so, a mother would produce a male child, Aries being a masculine sign; a Taurus Moon would result in a girl, this alternation of sex holding true through the twelve signs of the zodiac.

In this fragile area of sexual predetermination, Jonas claimed only 87 per cent accuracy, his misses presumably belonging to miscalculations in conception time and the rapid movement of the Moon, which often placed it in two different signs on the same day.

Where imperfect children were born, Dr. Jonas discovered, as Evangeline Adams had long before, that the Sun and major planets, like Saturn and Jupiter, were often in opposition at the time of conception.

Consequently, by counseling against conception during these periods of opposition to the Sun, he was almost able to guarantee normal, healthy children.

"I can give each woman who wishes to have children," said Jonas, "the ideal dates for conceiving babies without any physical or psychological defects.

"The fact is simply that the stars regulate our lives—not because they are gods, as the ancients believed—but because they exercise a physical influence over human organisms."

Dr. Jonas' method may yet, as *GP* concludes, prove to be the answer to the population explosion. Meanwhile, other European physicians who have tested his Moon-Sun aspects and found that they work, are hopefully putting them to use where a child is wanted, or not wanted, as the case may be.

Because of the simplicity of the method, it didn't seem that one would have to be very scientific to prove it out. One needed only the proper time of conception—not always correct in retrospect—the natal chart of the mother, and the sex of her child.

And so, with the help of Los Angeles astrologer Vicky Monbarren, open to innovations with her pioneer Aries Sun sign, we undertook a little barnyard experiment of our own in the realm of both sexual predetermination and planned parenthood via the stars.

In all, seven cases of moonstruck maternity were analyzed, and in six of these cases, the Jonas method worked, to the last detail. In the seventh case, Vicky had not considered that the Moon had passed from the masculine sign of Libra to feminine Scorpio that same day, at about the hour that conception most reasonably could have occurred. This mistake was compounded by the unsureness of the prospective mother as to the precise moment of conception.

"Obviously," said Vicky, "she was thinking of other things at the time."

And so, the child, which figured to be a Libra boy from the mother's chart, was a girl instead, and most likely a Scorpio girl.

In the other cases, working backwards, four girls and two boys were correctly foreshadowed in the natal charts which pinpointed the time of conception and the sex of the child.

In every case but two, the birth data was obtained from a skeptical Los Angeles obstetrician, who refused to divulge the sex of the children beforehand. "Work it out yourself," he told Vicky, "and then call me and I'll tell you if you're right."

Confronted with the results, discounting the one discrepancy due to human error, he conceded magnanimously that it might be worth looking into by–naturally–scientists, which of course doctors were.

In five cases, only the date of the mother's birth, not the hour, was available. Nevertheless, the calculation still worked because the Moon staying two and a half days in the same sign did provide some margin for error.

In most prenatal astrology, where the precise birth hour is not known, a flat wheel, beginning with 0 degrees Aries, is set up, and the Moon and Sun positions for the day picked out of the ephemeris and put in, since it really didn't matter what house they were in, only the nearest possible degree and the sign. But Vicky thought that a solar chart, allowing a one degree variance for the Sun, which moved one degree a day along the zodiac, and 13 degrees for the Moon, its passage in one day, would provide all the easement that a woman determined to have a child–or equally determined not to have one–would require for peace of mind.

So it was that Vicky did solar birth charts for five of the Sun-Moon relationships, which brought the Moon within at least thirteen degrees of its natal aspect to the Sun, but which still offered this comparative aspect for the day.

The first mother studied was 29. Mary was born November 10, 1941, in Los Angeles. By solar chart, she had 17 degrees of Scorpio on the first house cusp, and her Moon, picked out of the ephemeris for that time, was in 21 degrees of Cancer—the distance between the Sun and the Moon, the formula worked out by Jonas, was 116 degrees of the 360-degree circle—with a traditional astrological variance of 17 degrees allowed for the influence of this Moon-Sun aspect.

"In other words," Vicky pointed out, "even though conception is essentially a one-day affair, to be on the safe side, not having the mother's birth hour, only the day, we would allow two to three days for conception, the time the Moon stays in one sign, to assure pregnancy, or by abstaining during this period, to avoid pregnancy."

This Scorpio mother's first child was conceived, as she was able to pinpoint from her diary, on November 4, 1965. On this day the Sun was in 11 degrees of Scorpio, and the Moon, in advance of the Sun, in 10 degrees Pisces—or 119 degrees apart.

"At one point during the day," Vicky observed, "with the Moon traveling about 13 degrees a day, the two would have been precisely 116 degrees apart—the Jonas aspect for conception."

And the Moon being in Pisces, a feminine sign, the subject of the comparison should have had a girl, and that's exactly what she had.

Jonas, of course, had precise birth dates to work with, thus providing a greater likelihood of accuracy. In the interest of our own experiment, I was anxious to pinpoint the exact Moon-Sun aspect at birth, thus, in its exactitude, narrowing the related Moon-Sun conception aspect down to the only day that the subject could possibly have become pregnant without any variance due to the use of a solar chart.

And so we looked into Margie's chart, since Margie not only knew her own precise time of birth, but by temperature readings to indicate ovulation had precisely fixed the hour of conception.

Margie was born November 13, 1940, at 12:24 A.M., in Los Angeles. Her Sun was in 20 degrees of Scorpio in the third house of her natal chart, or 76 degrees along the zodiac from her 4 degrees Virgo rising sign. And her Moon was in the first degree of Taurus in the ninth house, or 237 degrees, counterclockwise, on the arc of the zodiacal circle.

Hence her Sun and Moon, at birth, were 161 degrees apart.

On September 28, 1966, the day she conceived, the Sun was in 4 degrees Libra and the Moon was in 15 degrees Pisces. The angle between the two luminaries, which Jonas said fixed the period of fertility, was 165 degrees. And the Moon, being in Pisces, a feminine sign,

Conception Chart #1

NAME Mary Solar Chart

BIRTH: DAY 10 MONTH 11

YEAR 41

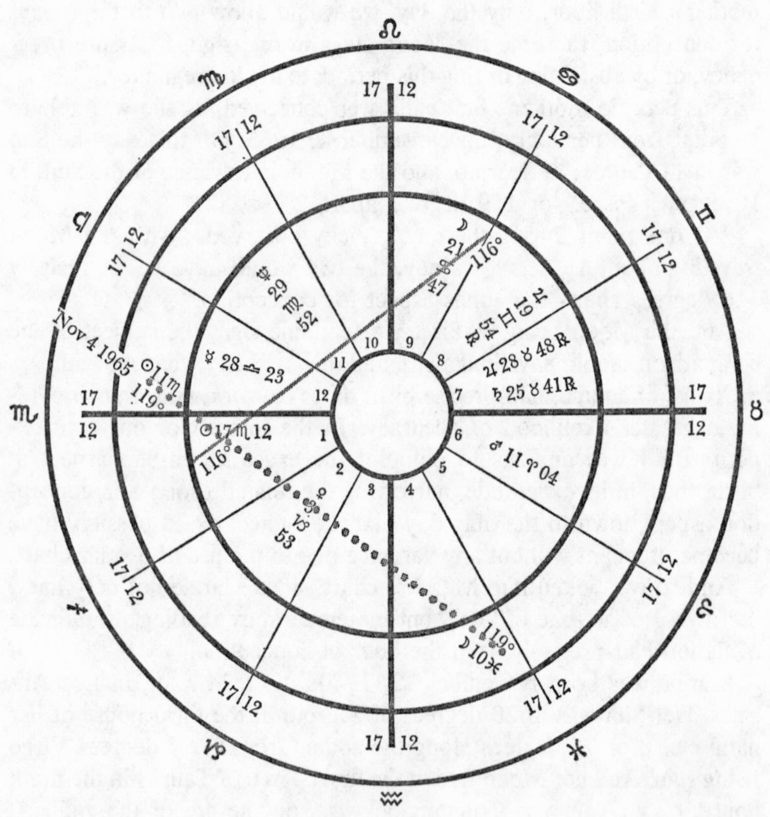

116° apart birth Sept

●●●●● first baby Nov 4–1965 119°

Conception Chart #2

NAME Margie

BIRTH: DAY 13 MONTH 11

YEAR 40 TIME 12:24 AM

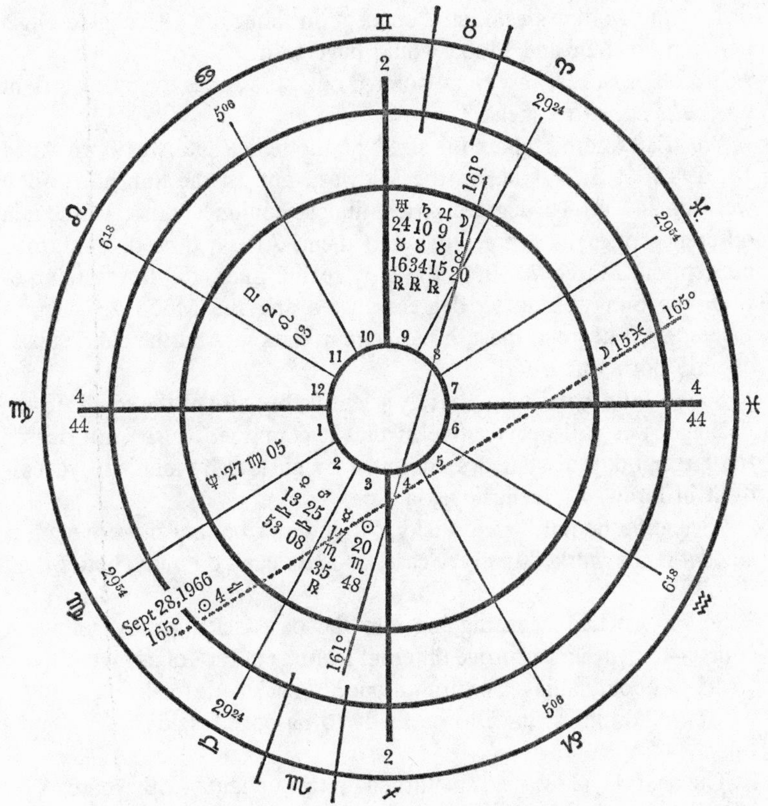

At birth the Sun and Moon were 160° apart which they had to be when conception took place. The moon has a 17° variance with which to work.

On Sept. 28, 1966, the Sun was in 4 Libra and the Moon in 15 Pisces 165° apart. Pisces is a feminine sign.

May 24–1967

a girl child was indicated. A female infant, born in due course, confirmed this part of the Jonas prospectus for birth control–in this instance, sex predetermination.

The variance between the 161 degree Moon-Sun aspect in Margie's natal chart, and the 165 degrees at the time of conception was inconsequential, as sometime during the night–actually only fifteen minutes or so from Margie's estimated conception time–the 161 degree angle between her Sun and Moon would have formed.

"In other words," as Vicky pointed out, "the Jonas formula hit right on the nose, so to speak."

We tried another chart for size; the mother, Edna, was born April 14, 1942, at 5:54 P.M., in the Midwest, and as the Sun and Moon were in 24 and 16 degrees Aries, almost conjunct, there was but a difference of eight degrees between them. At the time of confirmed conception, March 7, 1962, the only sexual interlude during this period, the Sun was at 15 degrees Pisces and the Moon 23 degrees Pisces, eight degrees apart, a perfect correlation. And the child subsequently born was a girl.

So our little experiment, hardly scientific because of the small survey package, was still provocative in that it confirmed to the nth degree the larger body of statistics compiled by an astrally-minded gynecologist in faraway Czechoslovakia.

"Scientific or not," said Vicky, "it couldn't be any more effective, since it really worked in every case, and you can't do much better than that."

So far we had been digging into the past–scientifically sound of course–to prove or disprove different features of the Jonas method.

"How about calling the turn on one?" I said.

"It would almost have to be ready to be born," said Vicky doubtfully.

The next day, however, she turned up triumphantly with a case.

The baby was due in a week.

The mother had been born August 23, 1947, and she had conceived, to the best of her knowledge, on January 13, 1970, when the Moon was in Aries, a masculine sign.

The prospective mother was a neighbor in the fertile San Fernando Valley.

Vicky, quickly scanning the Moon, had already predicted:

Conception Chart #3

NAME Edna

BIRTH: DAY 14 MONTH 4

YEAR 1942 TIME 5:54 PM

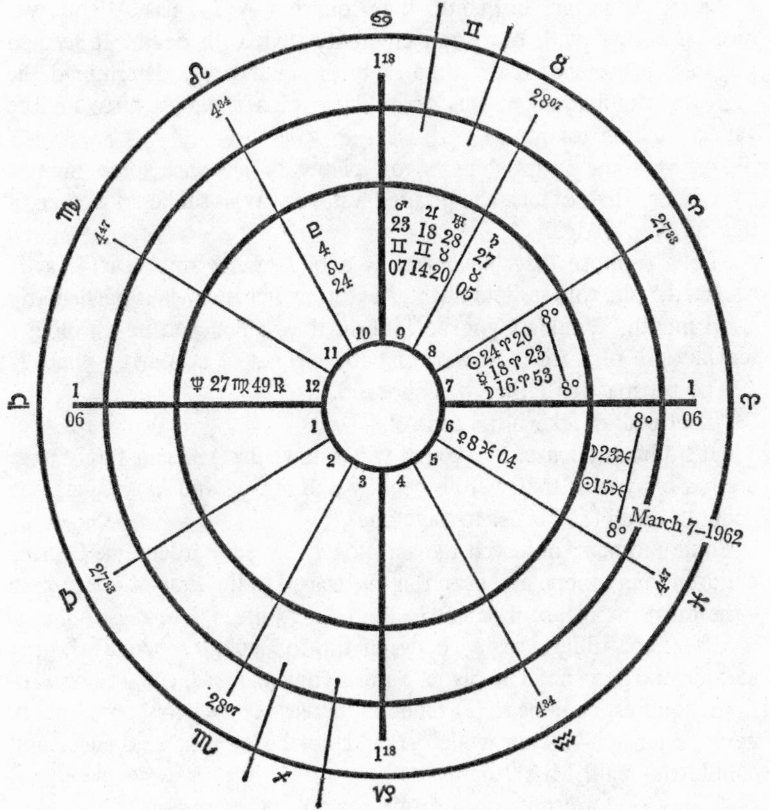

"You are going to have a boy."

"I want a girl," the mother replied.

"I'm afraid you're not going to get what you want."

The baby was born a few days later, on October 7—a boy.

Astrology had again triumphed.

What Jonas did with his fertility calendars and his computers, astrologer Evangeline Adams, who put no limitations on astrology—only on astrologers—had already done with her great flair for putting the science of the stars to practical use.

As an Aquarian, born into the Aquarian Age, Miss Adams was more absorbed with birth and creativity than with death. It seemed obvious to her that if the time of birth significantly determined the life of the individual, it was desirable to plan a baby's birth for the very best time for it.

During some years, hinging on planetary aspects, some months were better than others, she pointed out, so why not take advantage of this foreknowledge?

"Let's suppose that November is a bad month this year, heavily aspected," she told a male client, "and that February is a particularly good month. Wouldn't you be foolish, if you believed in astrology's teaching, to plan for a November baby instead of a February baby?"

The prospective father was shocked.

"That sounds like birth control."

"It's a birth release. If a young wife knows that she can surely have a good baby, one that will be healthy and strong and *lucky,* isn't she going to be all the keener to have one?"

Some mothers, observed the astrologer, have a harder time bearing children than others, and even this she traced to the time of conception—the most important moment in that child's life.

Often, the difference lay between the influence of benefic Jupiter and malefic Saturn. "The planet Saturn (adversely aspected in oppositions, squares, conjunctions) tends to increase congestion, contraction, nervous tension—factors which should not be present at a successful childbirth," said Miss Adams.

"If my sins are not forgiven me for any other reasons," this New England Puritan philosophized, "I expect they will be for the lives I have saved by telling mothers not to have babies while the influence of Saturn (opposing the Sun, for one) is in the ascendancy."

With the baby's chart, in the Adams venture into astrological eugenics, came a delineation of the best career for the newborn and a rundown on personality and aptitudes.

The astrologer considered each birth from the concept of the whole family. And if she was right, as well she could be, it could revolutionize the practice of grab-bag begetting, which may be responsible for so many children's being alien to their own parents. For the prospective child was to be scheduled under signs not only fortunate to himself, but in sympathy with the aspects of his parents in both their natal and progressed charts.

"Parents who would not stop to consider the prospects of their unborn children or even the advantages of an easy childbirth, might show some temporary restraint in the hope of benefiting their own fortunes," said this master of psychology.

While contemporary physicians, as a rule, sneered at astrology, there were some who have used it to advantage. Others were sufficiently sophisticated to recognize that it must have had some use or the ancient physicians would not have relied on it in their practices.

"In times past," wrote Dr. Lester King, senior editor of the journal of the American Medical Association, "people were just as intelligent as we are today. If what they did seems stupid, this does not mean that the people were stupid. It means only that we do not understand the context in which they operated."

The use of healing in the art of medicine, said Chicago's celebrated "doctor of broken hearts," Dr. Eugene Scheimann, is as old as medicine itself. "Astrological medicine," he said in the medically sponsored publication *Attitude,* "reigned supreme well into the Eighteenth Century. It has had the support of leading physicians throughout the ages. No lesser authorities than Hippocrates, the father of medicine, and Paracelsus, the father of therapeutics, accepted some of its doctrines."

The Chicago physician, a veteran of 40 years of medicine, quoted the physician whose name decorates the pledge of service that most doctors take:

"Attention," Hippocrates said, "must be paid to the rising of the stars, especially to those of Sirius and Arcturus, and further, to the setting of the Pleiades, for most diseases reach a crisis during such period."

And Paracelsus said even more emphatically:

"A physician without knowledge of the stars can neither understand the cause of, nor cure any diseases, not even so much as a toothache."

With the advance of science, physicians became more secure in their profession and discarded astrology; but, with a growing disenchantment with the current trend to impersonal medicine, the occultists, faith healers, and the medical astrologers have been staging a resurgence.

"Today, in this troubled world of ours," Dr. Scheimann reported, "we witness a strong revival of astrology, not by physicians, but by laymen. One of the reasons for the current fascination with astrology and other occult matters is, many observers believe, a trend to increasing dissatisfaction with depersonalized medicine and science, and frustration with what doctors and scientists cannot accomplish. Science can teach men how to master space or harness atomic energy, but very often it cannot teach men how to master their hostility or control their psychic energy—that mysterious force known variously as passion, love or libido. The modern doctor can transplant a human heart but often cannot teach his patient how to relax and sleep without drugs."

Aware that some modern doctors do invoke the ancient art, Dr. Scheimann posed the question:

"If so many patients believe in astrology, should the modern doctor, like his predecessors, use astrology to help some of his patients when the modern scientific method fails?"

There were physicians like Drs. F. Sims Pounds in Phoenix, Arizona, and James Stephenson in New York City who made use of astrology to some extent in treating their patients; and there were others, such as Dr. Edson Andrews of Tallahassee, who had found that hemorrhaging was commoner at the time of the full Moon, insignificant at the new Moon. He made his discovery empirically from observing hundreds of tonsillectomies after his nurse—as a woman more subject to Moon influences—suggested that the Moon might be responsible for some of the postoperative bleeding. She had ringed the dates of these emergencies on a calendar, and they were clustered around the full Moon.

At about the same time Dr. Jonas was beginning his experiments, Dr. Leonard J. Ravitz, formerly of the University of Pennsylvania School of Medicine, more recently a neurological consultant to the

Virginia Department of Health and Education, conducted experiments indicating that both birds and people might be affected by the Moon, with a resulting change in mood and activity. Apparently, the lunar changes affect the magnetic field of living organisms directly, or indirectly, through modifying effects on the earth's electrical field. In any case, Dr. Ravitz observed that the electrical output of birds and man fluctuates in certain definite rhythms which correspond to the phases of the Moon. These changes are marked in humans by fluctuations of mood and in birds by increased activity.

Obviously, in some way that we don't quite understand—though astrologers give the Moon rule of fluids and hormones—the heavenly bodies affect the state of our bodies and minds.

Just checking the planetary aspects in my chart, the well-known New York astrologer Isidor Oblo ten years earlier had told me to look out for trouble with my throat and my eyes. My throat problems, as a Taurus (sign ruler of the throat) with Uranus in the first house of body squared my Sun, had certainly verified his diagnosis. And I suppose he had gotten the eye problems out of Uranus in opposition to Mars, ruler of the eyes; even while writing this book, I am being treated for an eye condition.

Although he didn't practice medicine himself, Oblo worked closely with some openminded medical men in New York City, often making a diagnosis that precluded surgery.

Though few doctors would admit using his astrological knowledge, I was in his office on a number of occasions when doctors phoned in informal consultation.

One caller, a leading specialist, requested a diagnosis of his own disorder.

While I had no desire myself to be treated medically by an astrologer, I did find it interesting to check over the signs—and corresponding planets and houses—ruling each area of the body. Beginning with Aries, the first sign, which starts with the head, the Sun signs intriguingly work their way down the body, in the same order in which they move through the zodiac.

1. Aries (Mars)—rules the head, brain, eyes. Afflictions reflect in headaches, neuralgia, coma and trance.
2. Taurus (Venus)—rules the neck, throat, palate, larynx and ton-

sils, lower jaw, ears. Afflictions reflect in goiter, tonsillitis, quinsy.

3. Gemini (Mercury)–rules arms and hands, shoulders, lungs and the thymus gland, the upper ribs. Afflictions reflect in pneumonia, pleurisy, bronchitis, asthma.
4. Cancer (Moon)–rules esophagus, stomach, breast. Afflictions reflect in indigestion, hiccoughs, hypochondria, depression, cancer.
5. Leo (Sun)–rules heart, spine and spinal cord, aorta. Afflictions reflect in regurgitation, palpitations, fainting, aneurism, spinal meningitis, anemia.
6. Virgo (Mercury)–rules abdominal region, the large and small intestines, spleen. Afflictions reflect in tapeworms, malnutrition, appendicitis.
7. Libra (Venus)–rules kidneys, lumbar or lower back region, and the skin. Afflictions reflect in suppression of urine, inflammation of the ureter which connects to the bladder and kidneys.
8. Scorpio (Mars-Pluto)–rules the bladder, genital organs, prostate gland, descending colon. Afflictions reflect in diseases of the womb or ovaries, various venereal diseases, enlargement of prostate gland, problems with menses.
9. Sagittarius (Jupiter)–rules the hips and thighs, liver, sacral region of the spine, pancreas. Afflictions reflect in rheumatism, hip diseases.
10. Capricorn (Saturn)–rules skin and knees, and the bones. Afflictions reflect in eczema, other skin diseases, broken bones, arthritis.
11. Aquarius (Uranus)–rules from the knees to the ankles. Afflictions reflect in varicose veins, sprained ankles.
12. Pisces (Neptune)–rules the feet and toes. Afflictions reflect in troubles and deformities of the feet. Gives desire for drink and drugs which may cause delirium tremens.

Bred in a conventional atmosphere of immediate cause and effect, I found it hard to fathom how astrological symbols could reflect tangible illness. How could an afflicted Saturn, merely because it ruled the bones, indicate, with certain other afflicted aspects, a predisposition to arthritis? Or, for that matter, how could a badly aspected Jupiter reflect a blood problem–anemia, for instance?

I supposed that astrologer Sydney Omarr, a believer in synchronicity between the planets and human activity, would have suggested that they merely mirrored the illness and did not in any way influence it; when certain signs, houses or planets are afflicted, certain areas of the body are also afflicted.

It is a simple rule of astrology, for example, that where surgery is contemplated, the operation should take place in an unafflicted Moon sign–two signs from the part of the body under surgery.

"If the Moon were in Cancer," said the dean of medical astrologers, Edward Doane, "stomach or breast surgery would not be recommended until the Moon passed out of that sign." This held true for any afflicted planet in any sign governing the region of the body subject to surgery, and though it seemed far-fetched, it was hardly more fantastic than Dr. Andrews' correlation of the Moon and bleeding.

Edward Doane's name had become synonymous with medical astrology. He was then an old man, approaching 80, and confined to his home, but he had helped thousands over the years, some with diet and positive thinking, others by referring them to therapists after correctly diagnosing ailments that had eluded conventional approaches.

Aside from the fact that his subjects' problems were pinpointed by astrology, his remedies seemed basic enough, involving, as they did, deep breathing for better combustion of food, exercise for body tone and improved elimination to rid the body and blood of devitalizing toxics.

He was quite resigned about his own infirmities when I saw him, and pointed out that he had been living on borrowed time for several years, as he had already sustained a number of heart attacks.

In this case, Ed Doane should certainly have had an afflicted Sun or Leo, rulers of the heart.

"I had both," he said quietly.

As we sat together, in a cozy house overlooking Los Angeles, he seemed more disposed to talk about health and well being than illness, this being a reflection of his philosophy of positive thinking to stay well.

"What is the advantage," I asked, "in a person's knowing his weaknesses?"

Ed Doane had an instant reply. "He's able then to take precautionary action, diet and exercise, and to correct his thinking, introducing the mental antidotes that lift his spirits and give him a positive approach to life."

Calmness was an aid to health, and persons with an afflicted Moon or Neptune, particularly, should work at it. "When planets are in water signs (Cancer, Scorpio, Pisces) or the Moon receives afflictions of considerable strength, emotional elements tend to get the upper hand and cause disturbances to the health."

While everybody should breathe deeply or rhythmically for better health, with complete inhalations and exhalations, some have greater oxygen needs than others.

"With negative planets in Gemini, or Mercury similarly afflicted," Doane said, "the need to cultivate rhythmic breathing is especially great. When deliberate deep breathing has received sufficient attention, the subconscious mind will take over and keep it up without conscious attention."

It reminded me somewhat of Yogic breathing.

He nodded. "So many people sit long hours at desks without getting the oxygen they require. They should also get up occasionally, and flex the muscles, relieving body strain and giving the mind a rest."

Elimination is vital, and the chart should be scanned for weak points in this area. "Saturn," he said, "is the chief inhibitor of eliminative functions and applies particularly in colon elimination." Neptune is second because of the cluttering mental states it induces in its negative aspect.

"Attention should always be paid to body areas governed by Scorpio and Libra, and the planets ruling them, particularly Mars and Pluto, when looking to the kidneys."

It is essential to check out the Sun, for the Sun rules vitality through a presumed thyroid-pituitary relationship controlling the basal metabolism rate and the general tone of the system through the master gland, the anterior pituitary. "This gland," said Doane, "has a balancing function in counteracting imbalance in other glands."

The innate vitality of the system determines resistance to infection and rapidity of recovery.

"Aspects of Mars to the Sun, whether of the so-called good or bad type, are beneficial since great energy is added. Good aspects of Jupiter, which rules the liver, are excellent, but with squares and oppositions, there is a tendency to undermine the vitality with acid-forming foods, clogging the eliminative organs and helping to break down resistance."

Other planets have their zones of influence, and their aspects have to be watched, both natally and in progression, advancing a day for a year to find the significant aspect. "Venus, the ruler of Libra, ruling the skin, affects this organ because of its thyroid-gonad relationship, and consequently also affects the hair. Mars afflicts through overwork, the individual expending excessive energy without taking time to recharge."

I had read that Mars badly aspected is symptomatic of nervous problems.

Ed Doane shook his head. "Nervous breakdowns usually occur with Uranus afflicted to the ascendant or to Mercury, which is the nervous system. The ascendant stands for the person."

"And what would touch it off?"

"Almost any progression of the Moon forming an aspect to Uranus, conjoining, squaring or opposing."

As we were discussing symptoms, I brought up my own.

"I've always had throat trouble, I'm a Taurus with Taurus squaring Uranus in the first house."

"What is in Taurus?" he asked.

"Sun, Moon and Venus."

He frowned. "Sun and Venus square Uranus. That would be enough to give you a throat problem for the rest of your life."

"Suppose I do my breathing and think positively?"

He smiled. "It can't do any harm."

I had also had a bad case of acne in adolescence.

"Venus and Mars would have affected that," he said.

"Venus rules the skin, but why Mars?"

"Mars is the head, you probably had a square or opposition to Mars."

"Mars in the seventh opposed to Uranus and Jupiter in the first."

He nodded. "And Venus squares Uranus in the first house of the body."

Ed Doane usually acted only as a consultant, called in as a rule when the subject had no other place to turn.

A typical subject (or patient) was the young daughter of one of his astrology students. Upon becoming ill she had been taken to a doctor and her trouble diagnosed as tonsillitis. A blood count showed anemia so far advanced that physicians hesitated to operate. Thereupon the mother brought the child's chart to Ed Doane.

His astral-medical diagnosis confirmed what the doctors had said, but went farther and deeper.

"Neptune square to Venus and the Moon indicated tonsillitis, Venus, the ruler of Taurus, applying to the throat. Mercury, ruler of the girl's Virgo ascendant, was in the sixth house, opposing Jupiter by progression.

"The presence of Pluto in Cancer, plus the Neptune-Moon square, gave the individual an exceptionally sensitive stomach. The opposition of progressed Mercury to Jupiter, plus the natal inconjunct (150 degrees aspect) of Mars and Saturn had mapped impacted matter collecting on the intestinal tract. Saturn, in Virgo, ruling the intestines, was stronger in mapping an affliction in this area than was Jupiter in Virgo in its protecting role."

Depletion of the ability of the kidneys to eliminate toxins was signified by the progressed Venus (ruling Libra and the kidneys) squaring Neptune, ruler of a water sign, Pisces, and the afflicted natal Mars. "The toxics had collected in the system," he said, "and had literally backed up until the tonsils became affected."

The astral diagnosis embraced the whole system, on the theory that any bodily disorder is a product of total dis-ease. "While the tonsils can become infected for various reasons," Doane pointed out, "they usually indicate accumulated poisons in other parts of the organism."

Talking to the girl, he discovered her diet had been a nutritionist's nightmare. It featured sugars and starches, candies, soft drinks, white bread and potatoes, and had caused acidosis and bloating.

A series of colonic irrigations was recommended to clear out the intestinal tract. After the first colonic, the girl was placed for a month on a liquid diet of celery and carrot juice, including the tops, with some parsley juice, and fruit juice.

"Because of the afflicted Venus, there was a goiter problem," the astrologer pointed out, "and iodine was required. This was supplied in sea vegetation in tablet form. Vitamin E from lettuce juice was given to step up the internal secretion of the gonads."

After the liquid diet, wheat germ meal was given to provide minerals and vitamins. "Whole wheat and soy bean bread were added and some cottage cheese, which furnished complete protein. Meat was eliminated entirely from the diet, for as this chart (afflicted Saturn, Pork—and Neptune, Fish) indicated, she would never be able to handle meat successfully."

As the Doane therapy program unfolded, I was struck with a sense of familiarity. In its concept, in its utilization of natural remedies, the therapy was curiously akin to that of the psychic healer, Edgar Cayce.

"Since Jupiter was afflicted in the chart, the liver needed attention," Ed Doane went on, "and a rhubarb laxative was used and tomato juice (ten ounces at a time) with half a lemon squeezed in, taken three times a week on an empty stomach. Cucumber juice, without the seeds but with the peel, was used to flush out the kidneys more effectively than citrus juices alone would do."

The rest of this nutritional therapy followed:

"One egg yolk beaten in orange or grapefruit juice to supply sulphur for the pancreas (Jupiter-ruled). Cottage cheese (excellent where milk could not be handled successfully as with Neptune square Moon) supplied, along with the vegetable and fruit juices, an abundance of calcium."

In all, a quart of fruit juices was consumed daily, together with a pint of vegetable juices, and a variety of green leaf vegetables, cooked lightly with olive oil and very little water. Some fresh marrow broth, as a substitute for meat, was used to build back the red blood corpuscles.

The patient also required help in the sphere of the mind. Her physical condition was affected by a fear of death, mapped by a prominent Saturn near the ascendant and Neptune square the Moon in her eighth house of death. She was constantly encouraged to think strictly in terms of getting well, and her faith in a beneficent God was constantly shored up with spiritual discussions.

As the new diet began to work, and the toxics were eliminated, her symptoms, including the tonsillitis, disappeared, and her health progressed to where she had never felt better in her life.

Therapist Ed Doane was retired at this time, and his work being done by others on the basis of his experience. He had done what he had been sent to do, and now he sat waiting, his eyes far away.

As I left him, I had the feeling that he was looking past me to something beyond. Not many weeks elapsed before I learned that Ed Doane had passed on. I was reminded of a simple verse, from the pen of his late colleague Elbert Benjamine, one of the founders of astrology's Church of Light:

> "There is no death! What seems so is transition:
> This life of mortal breath
> Is but a suburb of the life elysian
> Whose portal we call death."

And so, looking back, I think I knew what Ed Doane had been waiting for. He had lived well, practicing what he preached, and now he had gone to his just reward, strong in the knowledge that he had done what he could for his God and fellow man.

10

A Time for Love and Marriage

There is a time for marriage, and for love, and the planets are more important than the color of his hair or the glow of her smile.

In the explosive activity of Uranus and Mars, many confuse sex with love, or marry without the least idea of what their partner is really like, finding out only too late that they should either have waited or married somebody else.

The late Evangeline Adams said that no couple should marry before having their charts compared, and astrologer Edith Randall suggested that perhaps no couple would marry after this comparison.

"Actually," she said once, "I'd be willing to bet that half the people who get married never would if they had their charts compared."

Aside from this comparison, easily managed by anybody familiarizing himself with the appendix material in this book, there were certain astrological clues that could be helpful in getting along with other signs.

Professional astrologers, as a rule, shied away from Sun sign astrology, the expediency of merely rating people by their birthdays, in the erroneous assumption that other Sun signs were mutually favorable merely because they were sextiled at sixty degrees.

In reality, adjoining Sun signs—Taurus and Gemini, for instance—could be more conducive to a love relationship. The probabilities are that one Sun or Venus would fall on the Sun or Venus of the other, as Venus is never more than 48 degrees from the Sun.

However, the Sun sign, being the real you, as Ralph Winters pointed out, still holds a certain correspondence with other planets, and the interested individual has some advantage in understanding the other person's sign.

To this purpose, astrologer Carol Peel, a Libra who had been teaching astrology in both Los Angeles and Palm Springs, California, prepared a zodiac tip sheet for would-be lovers, and, though designed for the ladies, it could also be applied by the male:

"So," said Carol, "starting with **Aries,** the first sign of the zodiac—because of their impulsive, daring nature you have to catch them on the spur of the moment when their fiery enthusiasm and passionate ardor are at a peak.

"In dealing with a **Taurus,** patience is the key word. It may take time to trigger emotions, but once you do, make certain you are ready for their intensely passionate nature.

"**Gemini**—first you must establish a mental rapport. If you succeed in appealing to their quick and alert mind, then all you have to do is catch them. Pinning down a Gemini is not easy.

"**Cancer**—this is not an easy catch. Their moodiness is so pronounced that timing is of the essence. Wining and dining in a romantic atmosphere, especially home cooking, is a quick way to light their fire. Once caught, they cling like the crab.

"**Leo**—subtle intrigue and the unique will capture their interest. For assured success, make certain Leo holds the spotlight and you will really make the lion purr.

"**Virgo**—this intellectual, analytical zodiac species finds it difficult to express emotion. Prove your integrity and loyalty and take your time. You have many tests to pass before Virgo gives in.

"**Libra**—avoid being harsh, coarse and blunt with the love children of the zodiac. Make them feel wanted and appeal to their sense of beauty and refinement. Theirs is a love worth winning if you understand them.

"**Scorpio**—whatever you do, don't play games, you'll be sorry if you do. Scorpio emotions are probably the most intense of the zodiac and are not to be tampered with. False pretense and phoniness is a taboo. It's not easy to turn on a Scorpio, but if you do, make sure you know what you're in for.

"**Sagittarius**—complete freedom is the keynote when dealing with this restless, fun-loving zodiac species. If you never question his actions and make him feel completely free, you have the secret formula.

"**Capricorn**—this is one sign you must impress by conforming to tradition. Emily Post is a good beginning. Be patient, interested in his accomplishments and always be ready to make the very best impression with his friends and business associates. If you can be an asset to his success, you are a sure winner.

"**Aquarius**—this is one sign who knows it all. Never try to prove him wrong if you want to appeal to his best interests. If you can adjust to his unpredictable, unconventional personality and help him fight the cause he believes in, you have won your way to his heart.

"**Pisces**—take it slow and easy, he is the incurable romantic. Sentiment and idealism are keys to his personality; always remember to maintain the illusion of constant beauty and romance."

Sun signs, reflecting the birth time, do pick up certain planetary aspects, fixing the positions of the heavier planets such as Pluto, Neptune, Uranus, Saturn and even Jupiter. And quite often, it was not the Sun sign that yielded the clue to the love temperament, but the combined planets as they aspected Venus, Sun, Moon, ascendant, midheaven, or themselves.

Venus, representing love, has its nature colored by its aspects to other planets. Venus square Saturn, for instance, would restrict a relationship, but Venus sextile or trine Saturn would indicate a long instructive friendship.

In a woman's chart, Venus and Sun in the same sign or Venus trine Mars, showed warmness for the opposite sex; the converse was true with the male who had Venus and Moon together.

As the love planet, Venus was of paramount importance in comparing lovers' charts. Venus in the same sign as the other's Sun, Moon or ascendant made for a strong relationship beyond mere physical expression. Venus together in the same signs was often love for love's sake, and Venus or Moon with another's Neptune reflected a shadowy love, based on illusions, which could still form an ideal relationship, as long as these illusions remained. If his Mars or Uranus were on her Venus, Sun or ascendant, there would be an instant attraction, quickly waning after the physical had been satiated—and so with this aspect it would be wise to wait before plunging into marriage.

For communication, the basis of most good relationships, Mercury in the same sign as the other's Sun and Venus makes for a spontaneous flow of ideas.

Jupiter on somebody's Sun is a provident aspect and, in this day of materialism, is often the best of aspects, particularly with the man older and wealthy, and the female young and pretty. At least one person is getting what she wanted.

Love and marriage are Number One on the astrologer's agenda, career, financial and health problems following closely after that. The subjects are of all ages and degrees, and often come together to have their charts compared as they wait.

As a Sagittarius herself, Los Angeles astrologer Edith Randall, who has charted hundreds of Hollywood personalities, has never been backward about expressing herself to her celebrated clientele.

"That's what they come for, the truth," she said once with typical candor, "and that's what they get." By and large, hers was a useful role. "I've saved many marriages, and I've broken up a lot, too. If they're sitting on a fence, and there's no chance of reconciliation, then they're better out of it. But if there is enough compatibility they can stay together through an adverse period. But they have to have elements in the chart showing the problem can be overcome."

Miss Randall appeared to be taking a lot on herself.

She shook her head.

"The individual makes the choice whether or not to accept what you tell her. As often as not, they go out and do it anyway. I told one man that if he married this woman, it would erupt in his face. 'Keep her as a friend,' I said. They got married, and it lasted a week."

"But at least," I interposed, "he got to run his own life."

She sniffed. "He could always have married somebody else and fulfilled the destiny pattern of his chart. That's where free will comes in, the way you handle things."

Edith Randall called them as she saw them. A client had come in years before with the chart of a man she wanted to marry.

The astrologer quickly scanned the two charts.

"You'd be foolish to marry him," she said. "It would never last. His Saturn on your Sun would stifle you; you'd be trying harder to get out than to get in."

As a Scorpio, Virgo rising, the girl flew into a temper, and stomped out of the office, saying, "To hell with astrology, I'll run my own life."

She was back in two years, profusely apologetic, with another man's chart.

"I'm glad you took my advice," Edith said.

The girl blushed.

"I didn't, but we're divorced now."

The aspects were better for a second marriage, Moon and Sun being in the same signs, with Venus on the other's ascendant. Mars and Uranus, adversely aspected to Mercury, gave the marriage added spice.

At the time, I was more interested in the aspects for Taurus and Leo than the guidance qualities of the astrologer.

"Nobody with transiting Saturn on his Sun, or Saturn square his Sun, as Taurus and Leo stand now, should marry anybody, until Saturn has gotten off their backs," she said. "They would only be putting their seed in barren soil, but if they wait until Saturn moves out of adverse aspect, after June of 1971, then their chances will be better, provided the other major aspects are favorable."

Saturn was a real damper. Only recently, a man who had been living with a woman without benefit of clergy checked about the prospects of marriage.

One glance at an afflicted Saturn decided the astrologer. "You'd be spoiling a beautiful friendship," she advised after poring over his chart. "You know, you really don't want to get married."

"I'm going to be married next week," he said.

Edith Randall recalled the incident vividly.

"I told him, 'You're crazy.' And he said, 'I don't know how to get out of it.'

"I said, 'What are you going to do, marry her and live with her for six months? All the marriage will do is end your friendship.'

"So he said to me, 'Would you tell her the same thing you're telling me?' I said absolutely. He said, 'She's your next appointment.' So when I saw her chart, I told her pretty much the same. I said, 'You don't want to marry this man,' and I told her why not. They'd had a big fight just the night before. So she got back to his office, and they sat down and talked, and they called the whole thing off. And just the other day, months later, I read for him, and he said, 'You certainly saved my life.'"

Like the police reporter who wanted the facts, I wanted the aspects in the case.

Edith Randall searched her memory.

"Saturn all over the place. Natal Saturn opposing his natal Venus and Moon. His aspects were bad for marriage. Saturn was afflicting him, and he had a heavy Uranian cycle, and Uranus in the seventh house of marriage. And he was a man who always got in with women 20 to 30 years younger than himself. He was in his sixties, and he hadn't been married for 40 years; but she was getting on, though 20 years younger than he, and had decided she wanted the security. But it wouldn't have lasted six months, and she would have had nothing. I convinced her of that. They really didn't have anything compatible for marriage, but for friendship it was great. Her Sun and four planets, Mercury and Venus included, fell in his eleventh house of friendship, so they had a great friendship until she started worrying about herself."

I wondered why a marriage knot should disrupt a relationship so like a marriage.

"Because it was a knot," Edith replied. "They'd been living together, but she could go her way—she had Aquarius rising, and they like to be detached."

"What were their Sun signs?"

"Libra and Virgo—he was the Libra. I don't recall all their planets, but it was not a marriage chart."

"What would you call the ideal marriage chart?"

"Venus conjunct the Moon, or the Sun, Venus trine or sextile the Sun or Moon—this gives compatibility. And if the two Mercurys are conjunct, sextile or trine, they'd have terrific communication. In most marriages people can't talk to each other. In this couple's charts, the Mercurys were out of aspect, having no relationship to one another, and essentially they didn't relate either, it was convenience. So you look at Mercury and at Venus, and you check the Moon and Sun. If the Moons square each other, there's a competitive drive, a clash of personality. If the Moon, Venus and the Mercurys are well-aspected, the marriage will work."

Like many laymen I had been intrigued by an astro-marital study made by the humanist-psychiatrist Dr. Carl Gustave Jung, one of the versatile minds of our time. Going through the zodiac, he found a greater chance of a successful marriage between two masculine or two feminine Sun signs sextile at 60 degree angles to each other.

Jung's study had been corroborated in part by a survey of divorced couples by Dr. John Finch, a professor of psychiatry at the Baylor Medical School in Texas.

Dr. Finch had gotten the names and birth times of some 400 divorced couples from the Houston courts, and divided them into two groups of six signs each. Under presumably a masculine influence, outgoing and aggressive, were Aries, Gemini, Leo, Libra, Sagittarius, Aquarius. And under feminine influence, presumably introspective and passive: Taurus, Cancer, Virgo, Scorpio, Capricorn, Pisces. Actually, Finch was reflecting the sextiles, the 60-degree aspects, which Jung thought the best Sun sign aspects for marital success. Finch's survey showed sixty percent of the divorced couples had incompatible birth signs, while only forty percent had been married to people with compatible signs. The difference was intriguing but hardly compelling.

Like so many other professional astrologers, Franka Moore didn't hold much with Sun signs.

"There's not enough to really go on," she said. Pisces and Capricorn are, for instance, both feminine, both sextile, and on the face of it they get along fine. But you cannot consider the Sun sign alone, because there are so many other overriding aspects. They could have Moon squared, and that would make them abrasive, and a Pisces person could have Saturn in Capricorn, and that wouldn't work.

"Take Leo and Aquarius, both masculine in influence, but they're air and fire, and air fans fire, and so you might get a disastrous fire, or a beautiful glow. With Scorpio and Taurus marrying–earth and water–you'd get mud, or the fertile blossoming of a lovely romance, depending on other aspects."

Despite everything I had heard about the Sun and the Moon and Venus and Mercury, and how great they are for love and marriage, I wondered why, even in the symbolism of astrology, this should be true.

"Any exchange between the Sun and the Moon is considered good," Miss Moore explained, "whether it's the man's Sun on her Moon, or her Moon on his Sun."

"And why is that?" I asked.

"The Sun is positive, the Moon negative or receptive, so it's a give and take—one gives the same way the other receives. Like the Sun in Taurus gives Taurean vibrations, the Moon in Taurus receives, understands the Taurus way of giving, whereas sometimes you can give to someone who doesn't understand your way of giving."

"How about Venus and Mercury in the same sign?"

"This is congenial mental exchange."

"Who would be the leader there?"

"Mercury leads and Venus just accepts or enlarges or softens or makes it easy for them."

I had a nutbreaker for Franka.

"In comparing two people for marriage, say one is 65 years old and the other 25 years old, how would you go about that?"

Franka didn't blink an eyelash.

"Now, most likely with a 25-year-old girl and a 65-year-old man, she wants a grandfather, or she wants money and security, waiting for him to kick over. In the beginning I wasn't that frank about it, but now you might as well be with some of the fluky things you see coming up for marriage and the attitudes with which people get married. In other words, what do you want from this marriage? There may be a lot of uncongenial aspects, but it'll show that this man will really give the money you want—a home, security and bank accounts, anything."

"You can tell that from his chart?"

"You can tell what his planets do to her second house. If she's marrying for money she doesn't want to marry somebody whose Saturn tenants her money house, she wants to marry someone whose Jupiter or Venus is there, or his Jupiter on her Sun, which is totally beneficent. And he doesn't want to marry someone whose Moon is there, because the Moon squanders her money."

"Are there many romances like that?"

"I've gotten to the point where I just ask them when I see quite a difference in age, what do they want from the marriage? If one's 25 and the other is 65, you know a mad roaring sex life isn't what they're looking for."

"Speaking of a mad sex life, isn't that the male Mars on the woman's Venus?"

"Mars is your animal energy. It's your physical drive. And it's how that Mars affects your Moon or your Venus or your ascendant. It's how one's animal energy affects the emotional nature of the other person."

"The ascendant is the individual's temperament?"

"It's the way they express. In other words, you're a Taurus, but you're transmitting your Taurus energy through your Capricorn ascendant."

I wondered how much she took on herself in advising couples. "Have you ever been so struck by the incompatibility of two people's charts that you advised them not to marry?"

"When I see, astrologically, that they can't effect a congenial marriage, I suggest that they take more time to see whether marriage is what they want. And so many times if they haven't worked it out over a period of time, then they won't marry. And they'll call me back and tell me and be glad. Now, I don't tell a girl anticipating her first marriage to go ahead and live with a man, but if it's someone who has been married, has children, and is thoroughly adult, then it's no longer a moral issue and I say give it more time."

Quite often people want different things of marriage.

"The man in this situation was ready to settle down and have a home. The girl had been married, had children, and was getting a divorce. So she was ready to cut loose after having been tied down for years. And he was ready to settle down, and these two concepts don't go together."

It all seemed more sociological than astrological. But the aspects were clear. "His chart showed he had had his fling and now he was reevaluating life and looking for different things."

"What indicated that?"

"Transiting Saturn was coming to his ascendant, meaning he was discarding the past, whereas Saturn was just coming over her descendant."

"It was a critical aspect."

"Seventh house, the house of partners, opposing the ascendant. So that indicated her divorce. Saturn in the marriage house often brings divorce. When Saturn starts to come up to that seventh house after 14 years in the lower chart, under the earth so to speak, the person usually has been tied down, and now wants to get out and become a part of the world again. Saturn was coming up for her, going down for him."

"But it was in her descendant?"

"It was, astrologically; in her seventh house, just above the horizon."

"Why is she considering marriage?" I asked.

"There was plenty of attraction between the charts—both mental and physical. There was a strong Uranus aspect, often love at first sight—Uranus to Venus or to the Moon or to the Sun, someone else's Uranus hitting your sign. Or it can be when the person's own Moon or Sun is hit by transiting Uranus, or their Venus is hit."

"So transiting Uranus was squaring her natal Moon and Venus?"

"Yes, and this can be very dynamic, but nine times out of ten under a Uranus aspect I suggest that people wait because it's over as fast as it starts, and that's just about what happened. And then their natal Marses squared each other. This can stir up a tremendous instinctual response, and they don't know till they've gotten involved that they aren't really compatible and they may still be sexually or physically challenged, but they can never really iron out all the problems."

As did many astrologers, Franka Moore based her appraisals of love's future on progressions in which the planets were progressed ahead in a chart a day for a year, or as the Bible (Ezekiel) said: "I have appointed thee each day for a year."

In this particular case, checking out the analysis she had already made, she progressed their natal charts using the rapidly moving Moon as a timer. And she clearly saw the outcome of the affair. Their progressed Moons, which theoretically stayed two and a half years in a sign, were in the same sign at this time, giving them added compatibility. "But her progressed Moon," the astrologer noted, "was to leave the sign six months ahead of his, altering her aspects and consequent response, thus causing her to reconsider the relationship before he would be ready for a change."

And so, in time, it happened as foreseen.

Franka Moore's astrological curiosity often prompted her to do charts of celebrated personalities, such as the Kennedys, Richard Nixon, and the Richard Burtons. With the Burtons her interest lay in the marital relationship of moviedom's tempestuous couple. Astrologically, they were a natural, both as a world-famed acting team, and as partners in real life.

In astrology, as nowhere else, the script begins with birth. The distaff partner, Eilzabeth Taylor, is a Pisces, with Libra rising, and Moon in Scorpio, born February 27, 1932, in London, England, at 7:56 P.M., Greenwich time. Burton's Sun was in Scorpio, blending with her Moon. He was born November 10, 1925, in Wales, and since Franka Moore had no exact hour of birth, she did a solar chart, using his Scorpio birth date to get the degree of his rising sign.

His Moon was in 7 degrees Virgo, a rather cold analytical position, but conjunct her Neptune in 6 degrees Virgo, which made for an idealistic attraction, which could last as long as "love's illusion" lasted. Moreover, his Neptune was conjunct her Jupiter, accenting an intuitive rapport to a point where one would know what the other was thinking without a word being said.

And this most benevolent conjunction for lovers, in her eleventh house of friendships, was trine, best aspect of all, to her Venus and Uranus in the seventh house of partnerships, indicating the marriage would last as long as they did. "For a lasting marriage, I always consider the aspects to the eleventh and seventh houses, on the theory that a couple must be friendly to stay together. Their Moon-Neptune also was conjunct in the eleventh house, activating that department of life in an idealistic way." Inevitably there was some discord. Their Mercurys were in square aspect, indicating some mental blocks or obstacles, but these were only irritations that added spice to the repast in view of all the favorable aspects.

From her natal chart, it was readily apparent why Elizabeth Taylor was the sex symbol she was. "She has Sun opposed Neptune, the same as Marlene Dietrich, which provides the magic charisma of mystery and allure. Her Venus in Aries is conjunct her Uranus in the seventh house, accounting for her sex appeal. Though it is hard for anybody with explosive Uranus in the seventh house to stay married, as witness her many marriages, she's found her Waterloo in Burton. He is colder than she emotionally, his Venus in Capricorn being the position of the status seeker. And of course the marriage boosted his career tremendously. Her Jupiter, greatest of the benefics, falls on his tenth house or midheaven of career, and to make the ham more binding, it's in Leo, the theatrical."

They would never have difficulty communicating. In fact, they may have communicated almost too well at the start, with her Mars, Sun and Mercury in his fourth house of the home. Undoubtedly, said

NAME Elizabeth Taylor

BIRTH: DAY 27 MONTH 2

YEAR 1932 TIME 7:56 PM

PLACE London,England

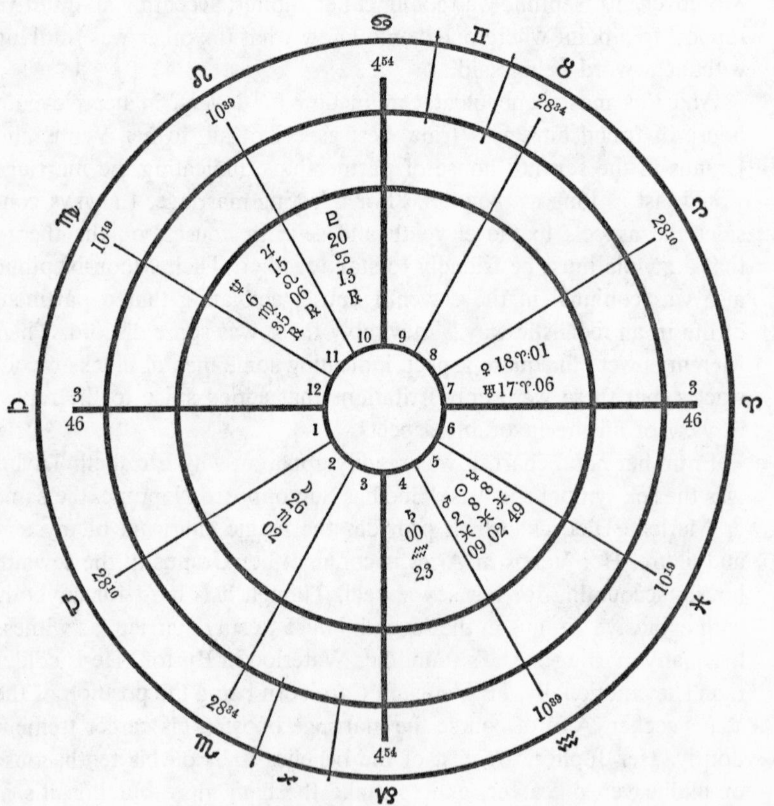

Richard Burton

Nov. 10, 1925

Pontrhydyfen, Wales

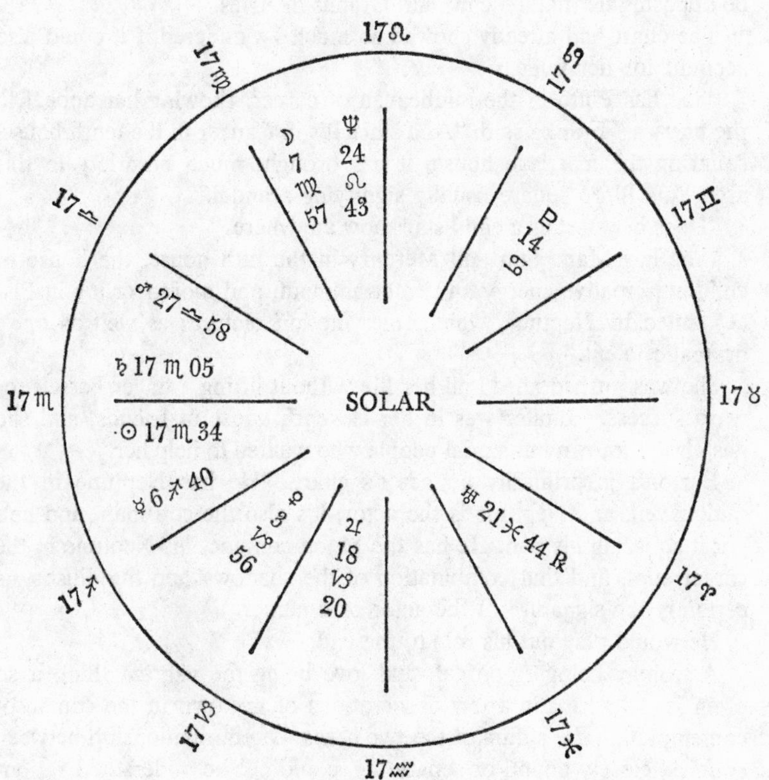

Franka, Mars in this position had a lot to do with breaking up his previous home and marriage.

The astrologer saw only one pitfall ahead, and that was the actress's health. Transiting Uranus was on her Libra ascendant, and transiting Saturn was in Taurus in her eighth house of sex, death and regeneration, until June, 1971. In the fourth house, the end of life, she had natal Saturn in Aquarius, and the ruler was Uranus, accenting its sudden action on her ascendant, or self. Mars stands for surgery, and it transited her fourth house in November, 1970, moving into her eighth house, of surgery and death, by 1972, when transiting Uranus would be opposing her natal Venus and Uranus in Aries.

The chart had already showed so much I wondered if it could also account for her fame.

"She has Pluto in the midheaven of career, showing her appeal to the masses," Franka said. "And since it's in Cancer in the tenth house, squaring the marriage house, it has brought much notoriety in this area, this Pluto square usually signifying scandal."

"Does her start as a child star show anywhere?"

"She has Mars, Sun and Mercury in the fifth house, the house of children, creative energy and entertainment, and moreover it's in Pisces, ruled by Neptune, which rules motion pictures as well as one's dramatic talent."

She was pushed ahead all her life without lifting a finger herself toward success. "Jupiter was in her eleventh house of friends, and she has always known influential people who wanted to help her."

Burton's is primarily an actor's chart. "He has Neptune in the midheaven, and Neptune is the actor, it's also the con man, and he's got it squaring his Sun. He has the Moon conjunct his Neptune in the career spot, and that combination of the shadowy and the illusory is certainly the signature of the actor or dreamer."

He would play out his role to the end.

Astrology being empirical, and love being the vagrant thing it so often is, I had made a few observations of my own in the course of contemplating the affairs of the two sexes. Often, relationship between couples, closely bound or separating, could not be understood rationally–until one compares their charts.

Astrologically–and practically–a relationship can endure beneficially only if there is little or no strain. I have seen couples apparently well matched in every respect head into the divorce court, and then I had found, comparing their charts, that his natal Saturn was on his bride's Sun, causing her to feel repressed and strained, even though he was not doing anything consciously to bring about this condition.

I had checked this aspect and been told by astrologers:

"Nobody should marry anybody—man or woman—who has natal Saturn on his or her natal ascendant, Sun, Venus or Mercury. They just wouldn't be able to communicate in a natural way, and would begin to get resentful, without even knowing why."

On the other hand, a man's Jupiter on a woman's Sun or ascendant —or the converse—would signify that he would give her anything she wanted.

The Sun of one in the eleventh house of the other indicates they would at least be friends, and as Ralph Winters pointed out, the Sun of one in the twelfth house of another indicates a secret enemy, even if this is not the intention.

In virtually every relationship but that between the two sexes, a mutual liking is the criterion of friendship. But in a romance, a magnetic attraction often draws together people who might otherwise have no deeper feeling for each other. Such relationships, inexplicable to others, are readily accounted for by the astrologer.

With both men and women, the excitement of Mars and Uranus, reacting to Venus, Moon, Sun, or ascendant, is so pleasurable that stimulated couples have no wish to be told their exciting relationship will soon wear thin, even if they have little else in common.

"If they really wanted to build an affair into something more," a friendly astrologer pointed out, "they would look for somebody with a Moon on their Sun, or the reverse, for complete rapport on both conscious and subconscious levels."

For mental stimulation there is nothing more activating than well-aspected natal Mercurys. For, as astrologer Vicky Monbarren pointed out, "If a couple can't communicate, they are lost."

The Mercury of one, well-aspected, could be trine, sextile or conjunct to the other's Mercury, or to Mars or Uranus, the Sun, Moon, or ascendant. There is really a wide range, so there is little excuse for not finding a sympathetic Mercury.

Very often, men and women find themselves head-over-heels in love, infatuated, fascinated, driven almost, without really understanding why, and frequently not even liking the other person.

At the height of this compulsion, they frequently get entangled in marriage, only to learn months later that the electric excitement of their relationship has run into a short circuit. And so often they reflect in dismay on their judgment and loyalties.

Astrologers say couples all too often meet when their progressed planets are in stimulating aspect, consummate the relationship under these aspects, and then, as with Franka Moore's twosome, find themselves hopelessly disenchanted when the progressed aspects run out.

"Had they good aspects together in their natal charts," astrologer Monbarren explained, "they would have then had something substantial to cling to, as the natal potential stays through life."

It is a mistake to assume that friendships and romances have a similar basis in astral aspects. For the demands are different on both the physical and psychic level. As a Taurus, I once came to the belated realization that three especially close male friends were Taureans, all older men, whose company and counsel I often enjoyed. Yet, though I respond to women of my sign, perhaps because of favorably aspected Mercurys and Venuses, as well as conjoining Suns, these relationships do not long endure, for the very reason that my male friendships mean so much: I just grow tired of the patronizing wisdom of Taurean women, whereas I think of Taurean men as being paternalistic.

As a rule, I find the opposite sign in ladies stimulating, presumably because opposites complement one another. In my case, the opposite is Scorpio, which has a sensuous charm of its own.

In no area is Sun sign astrology more prevalent than in that of love and marriage. The type of question most commonly asked of astrologers is: "How do Libra and Cancer go together?" or, "How about Virgo and Aquarius?"

I have known Aquarian wives who made mincemeat of Virgo husbands, and Virgo wives who similarly chopped up Aquarian husbands; and Librans who submitted passively to Cancers, and vice-versa. It is truly difficult to pair people purely on their Sun signs, though astrologer Carol Peel did highlight the distinctive qualities to be considered in evaluating each of the 12 signs.

Actually, if one is contemplating a lasting relationship with the other sex, specific planetary aspects have to be considered. Since affairs of the heart are a common problem, astrologers have elaborated on this subject *ad infinitum.* In surveying this field, Doris Chase Doane, of Professional Astrologers Incorporated, and Carol Peel collaborated in arriving at a marriage formula in which four factors are rated as staples.

The four factors cover partners, the opposite sex, affections, and love affairs. For the first factor, said this astrological pair, look to the seventh house, the department of life in the horoscope ruling partnerships and marriage. "From the planetary ruler of this house (governed by the sign on the house cusp)," said they, "you can gauge the general type of partners you will attract; and how the aspects made by this ruler indicate how partners will affect your life. For instance, if you find a harmonious trine (120 degree aspect) between the ruler of the seventh (partnership) and the ruler of the second (money) house, that partnership may help your financial status. But further, financial prosperity may contribute to success in your partnership. The ruler of the seventh house may fall in any other house, also applying the qualities of that house to the partnership."

While this seems hardly the romantic way, the astrologers maintain this is a marital factor more often than couples care to admit. To show how all these factors work, they produced a chart comparison of a very well-known couple, Prince Rainier and Princess Grace of Monaco who have lived, more or less, in a goldfish bowl.

Astrologically, they form an interesting comparison. Rainier is a Gemini, born May 31, 1923, at 6 A.M. Western Europe Time, in Monaco. He has a Cancer ascendant, and Moon in Sagittarius. The former Grace Kelly, an actress of note, is a Scorpio, born November 12, 1929, at 4:58 A.M., Eastern Standard Time, in Philadelphia. She has Libra rising, accounting for her beauty, and the Moon in Pisces, an intuitive position, which would also tend to make her sympathetic to the underprivileged.

In its examination of the marriage, our astrological team was concerned first about aspects to the seventh house. "Rainier," they pointed out, "has Capricorn on the seventh-house cusp, therefore Saturn would be the exclusive ruler of this partnership house, as there are no planets in the house. Saturn indicates serious-type partners or possibly good business partners, since Saturn is a business planet. Exalted (at its best influence) in Libra, Saturn makes a sextile aspect (60 degrees)

Natal and Progressed Chart

Princess Grace

November 12, 1929

4:58 A.M.

Philadelphia, Pa.

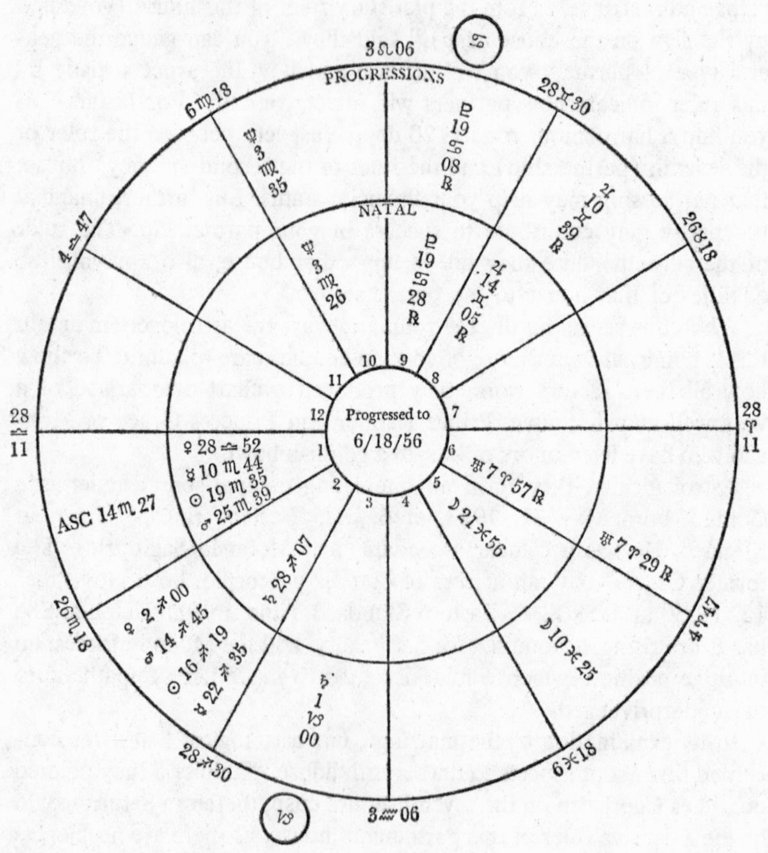

Natal and Progressed Chart

Prince Rainier

May 31, 1923—6 A.M.

Monte Carlo, Monaco

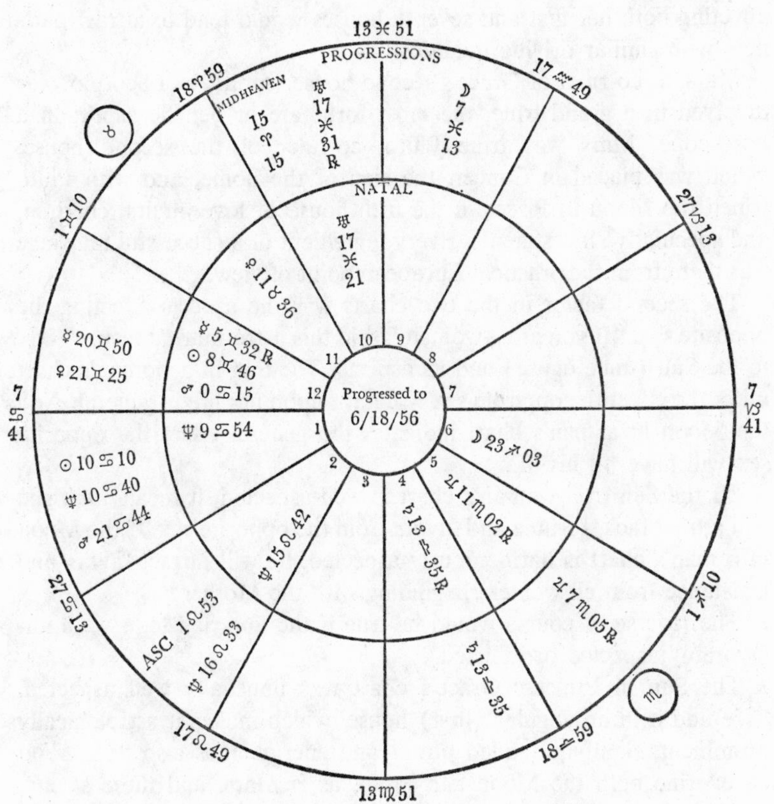

to Neptune, chief ruler of the second (money) house, and Neptune could very well indicate that the Prince's apparent financial splendor was a Neptunean illusion."

However, there was opportunity (sextile) for financial success—for Rainier—through this partnership.

In Princess Grace's chart, her seventh house, with Aries on the cusp, was ruled exclusively by a prominent, angular Mars, which was placed natally in the first house of self, accounting for her own energy and drive, particularly since it was in Scorpio, the sign it rules. Mars affecting both her first and seventh houses would tend to attract partners with similar driving qualities.

Mars, as co-ruler of Grace's second house (money) of Scorpio, was involved in a grand trine, the most fortunate or benefic aspect in a horoscope. Mars was trine Pluto, co-ruler of the second house, which was placed in Cancer, the sign of the home, and with Pluto trined the Moon in Pisces in the fifth house of love affairs, children, and speculative investments. Every ingredient of a successful marriage was there from the practical European point of view.

The second factor in the two charts was the aspects affecting the opposite sex. "If you are a woman," said this astro-marital team, "look to the Sun (male figure) and its aspects. The Sun in a woman's chart maps the effect the opposite sex will have upon her life in general. And the Moon in a man's chart indicates the general effect the opposite sex will have on his life.

"If the Sun in a woman's chart is well-aspected, it means that she will attract luck, fortune and favors from the opposite sex. If the Moon in a man's chart is harmoniously aspected, he will attract favors and assistance from all women, beginning with the Mother."

The reverse of course would be true if the Sun or Moon were unfavorably aspected or afflicted.

The Sun in Princess Grace's chart was unusually well aspected. "We find it in an angular (first) house, which makes it astrologically prominent, signifying added power and energy. It is also in a grand trine, trine both the Moon and Pluto, as is Mars, and these strong, harmonious aspects signify fortune and favor from men."

Curiously, the Moon in Rainier's chart was not as well aspected as his Princess' Sun. How, I wondered, could Grace be so favorably aspected for the opposite sex, and not her husband, considering the marriage had rocked along for 15 years now and been blessed with apparent serenity, and beautiful children, and that there was no such thing as one happy person in a marriage.

"His Moon," our team reported, "is square Uranus and the midheaven; it is in opposition to Mars, sesqui-square Venus [a relatively mild affliction] and semi-square Jupiter [again a modified affliction]." Astrologers Doane and Peel didn't beat around the bush. "Even though his Moon is strongly aspected, its Uranian-Mars discord is likely to attract to him misfortune from women. [But obviously not from Grace.] Nevertheless, women will play an important role in his life because of his active Moon."

Factor three, affections, was represented by the position of the love planet, Venus.

"Venus stands not only for the expression of your own affections, but for the affection you attract from others. If your Venus is prominent, affections are tremendously important in your life. Venus aspects show the tendency for success or lack of success in the expression of affections. The reasons why this is so can be gleaned from the house positions of the planets forming aspects to Venus. The things that conduce to or detract from affectional success, and the manner in which they do so, are mapped by the house that Venus actually occupies.

"In both charts we find Venus prominently situated. (On Grace's ascendant and in his eleventh house of friendships.) Therefore, affections have a strong bearing upon their happiness or lack of it. However, as Venus receives afflictions in both charts, from Jupiter (hers a sesqui-square and his an opposition), their affectional exchange may be less than affectionate at times."

In Grace's chart, Venus square Pluto indicates that obstacles (square) involving money matters (Pluto rules second) could lead to situations that would have a strong discordant impact upon her affections (Venus). "Since Venus also forms a sesqui-square (agitation) to Jupiter, not only her own money (second house) but her partner's money (eighth house) could provide another avenue of discord. However, since Venus is located within one degree of her ascendant in the first house (personal interest) she has the potential to control affection, thus determining success or lack of it."

This last analysis I found rather striking. As a newspaper reporter, interviewing the then 26-year-old actress when she was Hollywood's brightest star (and an astrology buff), I had wondered aloud that one with her beauty and charm had not yet been wed.

Grace Kelly, as she was then, replied quite matter-of-factly that she had put her career ahead of other considerations in her climb to success, and was now ready for the right man, were he to appear.

My only comment, as I recall, was that she had unusual control of her affections. And I remember her bridling at this, with all the fervor of Mars in Scorpio.

Factor four featured aspects to the fifth house, mapping the sexual part of marriage. "An estimate of the fifth house planetary rulers and their aspects determine whether or not actual love-making will benefit marriage. This holds true only if the couple marry for love. However, people do not always marry for love. If they do marry for love, the fifth house pictures energies which will add to or detract from marital happiness.

"Aside from love-making, the fifth house and the aspects made by its ruler(s) depict your relationship with children and how they affect your life. Furthermore, your chances of having children of your own are also shown. To determine this, check the sign of the Sun, Moon and ascendant, as well as the sign on the fifth house cusp. Children are indicated if these signs are fruitful–Cancer, Scorpio, Pisces, or moderately fruitful–Taurus, Gemini, Virgo, Libra, Sagittarius, Aquarius. Further testimony to children can be found if fruitful planets (Moon or Venus) also appear in the fifth house.

"In Princess Grace's chart, fruitful Moon is in the fruitful sign of Pisces in the fifth house. It is also in a grand water trine involving the Sun which is in the fruitful sign of Scorpio, and Pluto in the fruitful Cancer. Fruitful Pisces appears on her fifth house cusp. Moderately fruitful Libra rises on her ascendant.

"In the Prince's chart, the major benefic, Jupiter, is in the fifth house of children in fruitful Scorpio, and Jupiter is involved in a grand water trine with his ascendant in fruitful Cancer. Moderately fruitful Gemini is the location of his Sun. Not only is there a strong testimony for children in both charts, but the grand trines leading into both fifth houses map satisfaction where physical relations are concerned. These configurations indicate that luck, happiness and pleasure are associated with children."

And of course, as the world knows, they have a lovely family.

There is a time to love and to hate, and as many veterans of the matrimonial state are aware, marriage often draws on both emotions. And so likewise there is a right time—astrologically—to marry. There are three factors to consider in picking the time of the nuptials, and all have to do with progressed aspects, the astrologer progressing the charts of both principals a day for a year with these considerations in mind.

"First," said our two astrologers, "there should be harmonious progressed aspects, trine or sextile, strong enough to act as rallying forces, enabling the couple not only to come together but to overcome difficulties or differences sure to arise in any marriage. Secondly, there should be a harmonious progressed aspect involving the ruler of the seventh, marriage house, and, thirdly, Venus and the opposite sex planet, the Moon, should be unafflicted by progressions."

The marriage was analyzed from the outset of the romance to its culmination in marriage on April 18, 1956, at a time I found doubly interesting, considering the actress' interest in astrology.

Astrologers Doane and Peel drew a chart for the exact marriage time—11:10 A.M., Western Europe Time. The latitude was 43N45, the longitude 7E25 degrees. The Sun was elevated in the tenth house, near the midheaven, giving it strong expression, and exalted in Aries, where it best expresses its commanding influence. With the Sun thus doubly enhanced, the bridegroom would be the ruler of the household, but with her Moon practically on the Leo ascendant, she would know how to get around him to get what she wanted—this Moon position giving her the ability to maneuver flexibly. However, since the Moon was in the twelfth house of hidden things and seclusion, he would keep her out of the movies and behind the scenes pretty much.

Neptune in the fourth house showed that their home life was not all that it seemed to be, Neptune being the planet of illusion, and Saturn sitting in the fifth of the marriage chart indicated a loss or restriction in the area of children, speculation and entertainment—and certainly there was a loss when Grace Kelly, at the pinnacle of her career, left Hollywood. There was some loss of income, subsequently, from reduced revenue from the Monte Carlo gambling casinos, and the loss of a child through a miscarriage.

Venus in the eleventh house of friendships and aspirations was semi-sextile Mercury, indicating friendly communication with a wide circle

Marriage Chart—Princess Grace and Prince Rainier

April 18, 1956, 11:10 A.M.

Monte Carlo, Monaco

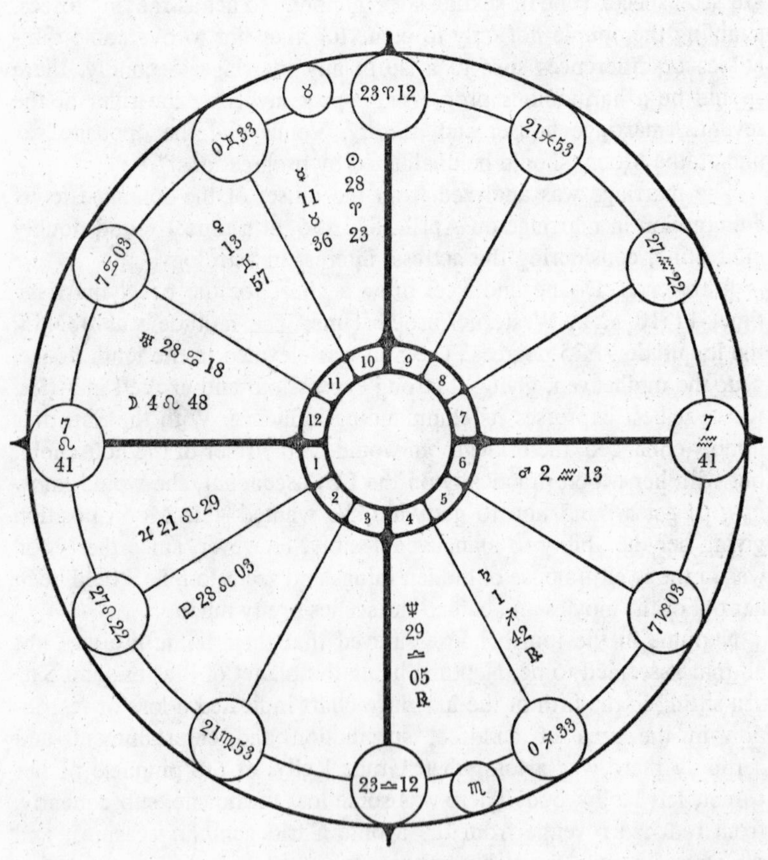

of influential friends—Mercury being in the tenth house of reputation and co-ruler of the eleventh house of friends.

Obviously, they could not have picked a better time for their marriage, had they been astrologers—or used one—if prominence and prestige was what they wanted together.

Our team now contemplated the progressions, reviewing the natal charts of both, progressed a day for a year from each birth to the date of the marriage.

"On the day they were married," our astrologers pointed out, "Prince Rainier's progressed Saturn, exclusive ruler of his seventh house, was inconjunct his natal midheaven, and conjunct natal Saturn. Their marriage was of great public (midheaven) interest.

"At that time, his progressed ascendant was sesqui-square natal and progressed Uranus, and there was no question but this affair was a sudden (Uranus) event for him (ascendant). It was in September of 1955 that Grace paid a courtesy call at the palace while she was in Monaco making a film. Very much aware of her presence, the Prince acted with the electrical swiftness of Uranus and asked a columnist to introduce him to Grace soon after. Their marriage captured international headlines (midheaven) just a few months later. It is interesting to note the always present human agency (the columnist) under Uranus progressions.

"Rainier's opposite sex planet, the progressed Moon in the ninth house, was trine his natal ascendant and sesqui-square progressed Mars in the first house. A still further indication of marriage is seen in his progressed Venus semi-sextile progressed Mars and conjunct progressed Mercury."

With his progressed Sun trine natal Jupiter in the fifth house, the subject of an heir occupied his mind.

"On the day of their marriage, Grace's exclusive seventh house ruler, Mars (Aries on the house cusp) was progressed to an opposition with natal Jupiter. However, the planet Mars in her natal chart was a member of a grand trine (to Moon in fifth and Pluto in the ninth), so this aspect added more energy to the trine, thus making the progressed opposition less discordant. Furthermore, progressed Jupiter was inconjunct natal Mercury (ruler of the ninth cusp) when she married, making a new beginning."

The marriage chart, as an event chart, was set up, and the planets distributed through the 12 signs of the zodiac, just as for the birth of a baby. Because of the hour chosen for the marriage, 11:10 A.M., and the date, April 18, Leo was on the ascendant in the marriage chart, becoming the cusp of the first house, and its ruler, the Sun, became the dominant planet. The Sun, representing the bridegroom, in its midheaven position was favorably trined to a Pluto-Jupiter conjunction beginning in the second house of money, and Rainier, at least, figured to do well financially through the marriage. With the ruler of the ascendant near the midheaven, moreover, the marriage was bound to bring great recognition and prestige.

However, astrologically, from the standpoint of a love match, it was not an ideal marriage. Restrictive Saturn, for one thing, was in the fifth house of sexual affairs, and square the Pluto-Jupiter conjunction in Leo, the ruling sign. Jupiter in the first house, adversely aspected, stood for a marriage affliction, which Uranus conjunct Moon in the twelfth house of secret matters would manage to keep from the public eye.

And, astrologers said, there was one seriously threatening aspect. In the marriage chart, the Sun (bridegroom) in the 10th squared the Moon (bride) and Uranus in the 12th of self-undoing and behind-the-scenes activity, and opposed shadowy Neptune in the fourth house of the home. The marriage, with its ups and downs, said the astrologers, would rock along comfortably for a couple of more years. Then in 1974, transiting Uranus—the upsetter—which is on the Princess' natal Libra ascendant, will square the Moon-Uranus conjunction, oppose the Sun in the marital midheaven, and conjunct illusory Neptune, making it more illusory than ever. At this time, there could be a serious crisis in the relationship.

However, the marriage is still better than most, and could have been even better had there been an effort to get Venus on the ascendant.

To appraise their marital chances, astrologically, other couples could apply the astrologers' four factors in choosing a lifetime partner, use similar progressions, and then cast the marriage chart for the most auspicious time. "In selecting your marriage chart, an event chart, which is cast for the moment the clergyman or justice says, 'I now pronounce you man and wife,' try," said astrologers Doane and Peel, "to get as good a seventh house as possible (by manipulating the time of the day to get the best placement of planets), principally the ruler of the first house (yourself) and the seventh house (your partner) being in good aspect."

And because a happy marriage is generally based on love and affection, Venus should be well aspected and making a harmonious aspect to the Moon.

"Venus, the goddess of Love," they said, "should reign over the planetary hour for which the marriage chart is set."

Venus, in the Rainiers' marriage chart, while not dominating, was in the eleventh house of friendship and aspirations—and fruitful marriage.

If children, prominence and prestige was what they wanted of marriage, they obviously had the right chart for it.

11

A Time for Homosexuality

Not since the time of the Roman decline has there been so much homosexuality. Ten years ago when I wrote *The Sixth Man,* there was criticism that the estimate of one out of every six adult American males being homosexual was high. Now, with rising female aggressiveness, there seems to be an ever greater rise in male passiveness and corresponding homosexuality.

In New York, San Francisco, Los Angeles, New Orleans, and other sophisticated cities, homosexuality is so blatant that homosexuals often capitalize on their homosexuality, openly giving preference to other homosexuals both socially and professionally.

While tolerance for homosexuality seemed to increase after World War II, it did not, as some astrologers suggested, become rampant until 1956 when Neptune, the planet of illusion, went into the sensuous, sometimes perverted sign of Scorpio for a 14-year stay.

In Hollywood, particularly, in the center for motion pictures, television, photography, some suggested that *The Sixth Man* could rightfully be retitled "The Third Man." And, as more homosexuals made no secret of their homosexuality, Hollywood became an excellent arena in which to appraise this social phenomenon astrologically.

I had known Hollywood's Maxine Bell as a counselor extraordinary for many years, without realizing how it was that she gained the insight for her counseling. She had no string of degrees, nor any pretension to specializing in the social studies. And yet she specialized in counseling people who had a problem that not only baffled the experts but was difficult to define, it had so many facets and complications.

This problem was homosexuality.

"How are you able to work with these people?" I asked one day.

She looked at me in surprise. "With astrology, of course."

"With astrology?" I repeated incredulously.

"Oh, yes. It's all revealed in the chart, and given this insight, I do what I can to pass self-knowledge on."

"I suppose if it's in the chart that justifies it."

"It's not purely a matter of destiny, but of predisposition." She smiled. "And if they're involved this way, they may as well enjoy it. None ever consult me because they want to change. They just want to be happy at what they're doing and, like other people, find the right mate to complete them."

"What can you tell them that they don't already know?"

"Mostly, as with people with other problems, you get them to take a good look at themselves, and assess their own faults and needs."

"Astrologically, how do you recognize their homosexuality?"

"It's a matter of aspects. Nearly all have an afflicted Venus, square to Uranus or Neptune or both, with Mars in bad aspect frequently intensifying the problem."

"Isn't there some particular sign that predisposes one to homosexuality?"

"Not really, though Libra, because of its delicate balance, appears to have more homosexuals than other signs once this balance is upset."

It did not mean that every Libra, or even most Libras, were predisposed to homosexuality—just that, by observation, there were more homosexuals born in Libra than in any other sign.

"This is particularly true," explained Maxine Bell, "when Mars is in Libra or badly aspected to it."

When homosexual, Libras are high-class homosexuals, because of the innate refinement and love of beauty (ruled by Venus) which makes so many of them artists, writers, interior decorators, beauticians, etc.

"Libras are aesthetic," Maxine pointed out. "They don't like tawdry relations. They like romance, soft lights, beautiful music, a lasting partner. They don't go for these overnight pickups that cause homosexuals so much trouble."

Aquarius, she found the most active sign for female homosexuals. "Lesbians predominate in this sign. They're so aggressive, and being such humanitarians, they love everybody."

Aquarians had struck me as being the truly fine humanitarians of the zodiac.

"That's true," she said, "but they're ruled by Uranus, and Uranus reflects a desire for the new and unusual, the unconventional."

Venus is the goddess of Love for very good reason. "Venus is the planet which shows the capability to express or accept affection. Mars shows capacity for passion, and so when you see the two together, in conjunction in the same sign, particularly the fire signs, Aries, Leo or Sagittarius, you have a good deal of fire which may or may not be well-directed, depending on the other aspects. If Saturn, Uranus or Neptune afflict Venus, we can look for sexual imbalance and frustration. Normal expression is blocked."

She thought a moment. "One of my clients, with a Venus squaring Uranus at an exact ninety degrees, couldn't have sex without artificial stimulation, and of course that sort of thing borders on degeneracy."

How was this expressed?

"A girl with Venus square Uranus, for example, would go for a hippie—he not only looked different, but would have to be different if he wanted to stay around."

There are other indications of a homosexual pattern: deceptive Neptune and Uranus conjunct in the fifth house, the house of love affairs.

But still there is no one aspect or sign that is definitive, but a combination of aspects. She took out the chart of a Leo, born July 31, 1932, at 9:30 A.M., in Michigan. His Uranus was in Aries in the eighth house of sex, indicating some sort of upheaval in his sex life. He also had Mars in the midheaven, giving energy to this activity, and Venus and Mercury badly aspected to Saturn, from the signs of the mother and the mind, Cancer and Virgo, and Saturn was in the fifth of love affairs. Additionally, he had Neptune in the twelfth house of deception in Virgo, which was also his rising sign, and so he just couldn't look at things straight.

His case was not as obvious as some with virtual stelliums, or blocs of planets, in one sign.

"The more planets there are in a house the more activity can be expected in that house. And the eighth house is definitely the natural house of Scorpio or sex. If you have three or four planets there you are overwhelmingly interested in the subject from the age of three on, so that when you're an adult you have to do something about it. Here we have a chart of a young man, we'll call him Ed—that's not his name, but this is what we'll use. A Libra, he has birth data of October 13, 1945, 2:00 P.M., in Tennessee, and he has four planets, the Sun, Jupiter, Mercury and Neptune, all in the sign of Libra in the eighth house. Now again, any large amount of planets in the eighth house will overstimulate the activity of sex. He has the unconventional sign of Aquarius rising, which means "Don't fence me in, I'll do as I please and I'm anti-establishment." He has Pluto in Leo, the sign of love affairs, in the seventh house which governs the world or people you come into contact with at close, intimate range. Then he has the discontented planet Mars in its worst sign of Cancer, conjunct Saturn, a sadistic influence. These are both malefics and they are both in the sixth house of health. He drinks himself to distraction constantly and doesn't take care of his health at all, and almost everyone he meets, thanks to Pluto on the seventh cusp, becomes his partner temporarily. He was well trained by an older man he lives with to become a commercial male prostitute."

"Does this turn up in the chart, this relationship with an older man?"

"Saturn represents an older man, and this was debilitated (in a weak sign for Saturn to be in, such as Cancer, and conjunct Mars in its worst sign). The partnership house is the seventh house and he had a close relationship from the time he was 18 to now when he's 27 with this older man, who is now dead, incidentally. Pluto is right on the cusp of the seventh and in this love sign of Leo he has quite a few relationships. Now the police constantly pick up this man in rest rooms taking on just anyone he might meet, so this will give you the caliber of his partnerships."

"Why did he come to you?"

"The older man came to me because he wanted me to keep a check on this young boy."

"What was his chart like?"

"He had Venus and Uranus square Neptune."

"What did you tell the older man when he came to see you?"

"Well, he brought me this young man's chart because he was so possessive and jealous of the young man that he wanted to engage me as sort of a psychic detective to see if the young man was having affairs, even when he was in jail."

"What indicated this excessive jealousy?"

"Scorpio."

"A lot of Scorpio?"

"Yes, he had Moon and Mercury both in Scorpio, and these people always have to keep a detective's finger on their lovers."

"What did you tell him?"

"I told him that I didn't traffic in that type of advice and if he wanted me to try to help the young man and talk to him I'd be glad to, which I did at a later date, but the young man had closed ears."

Maxine's files were bulging with homosexual charts. "Now we have another young man here, born June 18, 1925, at 2:04 A.M. in Oregon. This man is an ex-movie star who went very far in the movie world as an actor in the 40's and he's had quite a bit of success in other fields. He's a very fine writer and a great mimic and I've never seen anyone who can dance better, but he has his Venus in Cancer—which makes it hard for him to resist advances—with Pluto. Now Pluto is the natural ruler of Scorpio and it deals with having mass affairs rather than just one or two and this man is quite well known for that. Again we find Mars in Cancer and in the fourth house of the mother, and he clashed very badly with his mother, and this could have been the syndrome that later caused him to turn homosexual. I believe it was Mars and Jupiter in opposition to each other. He has Saturn in the sign of Scorpio in the sixth house of health and his many affairs with men finally led to prostate trouble—that area ruled by Scorpio. He also has Neptune in Leo, again the sign of love affairs, and in the fifth house, the natural house of Leo. And anyone who has Neptune in Leo is trying to find an ideal love situation that is superidealistic, and sometimes they will take devious paths, Neptune also being the planet of self-deception."

"Is that generally a homosexual situation?"

"Many times you find homosexuals with Neptune in the fifth house because they are looking for ideals."

"Don't you find that incongruous to have an ideal homosexual situation?"

"I'm not saying an ideal homosexual situation. I'm saying that these people are such idealists in finding any kind of love that, if they've had a couple of marriages that didn't work out, they're all too willing to try something else. Again, we have Neptune in the fiery sign of Leo in the fifth house of love affairs, we have the discontented Mars in the sign of the emotions and the home—so coming from an unhappy home he was perfectly willing with all of his good looks and available movie stars to shoot for a fancied ideal."

"Has he ever been married?"

"No. He was the lover of a very famous man, a surgeon and missionary who died. So this is very significant, but this boy is one of the most talented writers and actors I've ever known. He has Taurus rising, the Moon in Taurus in the first house which makes him a charmer, and I thought the world of him, and several times I rescued him from suicide attempts and drunken binges."

"Could you see the suicide in his chart? Evangeline Adams said she could look at a chart and see the suicide there."

"Yes, the ruler of the eighth house (death) in the seventh (open enemy) in opposition to the ascendant himself."

"What were the rulers of the eighth and seventh?"

"It depends on the chart. I'm just stating a rule. If they have the ruler of their eighth house in the house of the seventh or if they have the ruler of the first house in the twelfth which says 'I want to destroy myself, I'm self-destructive, I'm too much of an introvert, I can't face life.' Should both indications show up, they are definitely inclined to suicide."

"Is that in his chart?"

"No, he doesn't have the ruler of the first in the twelfth, just the other, and I don't think he'll ever actually commit suicide."

Many of the homosexuals lead ostensibly normal useful lives, their major problem being a homosexuality that would have been ruinous to reveal. This was particularly true of a strong Libra, born September 23, 1912, 7:30 A.M., in Southern California. Maxine was thoroughly familiar with his aspects. "A Libra with Libra rising, he has Sun, Mars and Venus all in Libra. And Venus is conjunct the ascendant so we know by this that he's a very nice looking person and we know that he's very compatible and leans toward having a mate, and as he is not a normal person, we wouldn't expect him to have a woman. Now, with all of this ascendant he has Neptune in Cancer square Venus, and

Venus square Uranus, with Uranus in opposition to Neptune, so he's just about as homosexual as anyone can get."

"Astrologically?"

"Yes. He's been with this man some 35 years now. To complicate the situation we have the Moon in Scorpio. This gives us quality of mind. So his quality of mind is centered in the sexual area and we also have the sign of the mind, Mercury, in Scorpio, so a great deal of thought is generated in that direction, and Jupiter in Scorpio which centers much attention in the sexual area."

"He should be a male prostitute almost, shouldn't he?"

"No, it happens that he's a minister, but he has this homosexual configuration and he has Uranus in the fourth house of the home. And he's invariably buying property, living in a house for three months and selling it. And you know Uranus is not a stable planet. Wherever it is, or the Moon, you can expect the greatest amount of change."

Believing in reincarnation as so many astrologers did, Maxine examined the chart for its particular karma, the unsolved problems presumably carried over from one life to another. "Now we find the karmic planet, Saturn, in the sign of Gemini retrograde in the eighth house. So with all this to-do about sex, we find the karma once again coming in the eighth house of the sex organs in the house of death. So, in his case his karma will be felt through abuse of sex. Now, with the Sun, Mars and Venus in Libra it shows that he is very artistic, and this is true, he is an artist."

He seemed unusually vulnerable, socially. "How did he happen to come to you?" I asked.

"He didn't come to me directly. He sent a nephew of his here to have a chart done. He was too embarrassed to come to me directly, not knowing if I was sympathetic or not. So he had me do his chart for a year ahead to see if he was going to take a trip to Europe. He has no interest in overcoming his problem. He's perfectly happy in his situation."

"What did the chart show?"

"He had a trip coming up, all right. Mercury is the symbol of travel, and he had the Sun and Mars going over it at the time he came to me."

And there was not much question what change he hoped traveling would bring him.

"He has 22 degrees of Libra ascending, and this ascendant makes him physically attractive. He's also a very highly sexed person with Venus conjunct Mars in the first house of Libra."

I wondered why he had become a minister.

"Many homosexuals are extremely idealistic and very much believers in God and they feel that their way of loving is far superior and purer."

"Where was his Neptune?"

"It was right up on the midheaven, in Cancer, 25 degrees. It means that he's a very sentimental person. He's wanted to break up with this man for some time but, with his great need for a partner and not having another one immediately to take the place, he has hesitated. They separate from time to time, but it seems to make their hearts grow fonder and they're still together."

"What vocation does the other man have?"

"This man keeps him. He gives him money to go to Europe and for other pleasures. He has a concentration of his own planets in Scorpio and three in Libra, the natural house of partners, so sex and marriage are very important to him."

In a homosexual pattern, the aspects work just as they do for heterosexuals, influencing the relationship between two men as they would that between a man and a woman, as witness a well-known studio makeup artist. He was a Leo, born July 31, 1932, at 9:30 A.M., in Wisconsin, and his problem was that he couldn't settle down to one partner, possibly because of a hypercritical attitude fostered by his Virgo rising sign. And, of course, regardless of bent, Leos pride themselves on being the greatest lovers of the zodiac, transcending even Scorpios and Taureans. "Leo," said Maxine, "is known for his preoccupation with many love affairs. He has Saturn in the fifth house in Aquarius retrograde. So this person has never had much luck with holding his lovers. Here again we find the unconventional planet Uranus in the eighth house retrograde, in Aries, and we have Venus again in Cancer and the Moon and Pluto in Cancer. Jupiter is in Leo, stressing this is a man of many affairs. He does seem to be very fickle toward his lovers because he's having countless affairs all the time, and his lovers often come to me to have charts done and to get advice. They're very disappointed with the fact that he will have two or three lovers in one night. The Moon in Cancer can sometimes be this fickle."

"How do you get that out of the Moon in Cancer?" I asked.

"They are more prone to affairs, as they are extremely discontented emotionally. But I put most of the blame in this chart on the unconventional planet of Uranus in the eighth house of sex and the perversion planet, Saturn, in the fifth of affairs, particularly unconventional because it is in Uranus' own sign of Aquarius."

I had never before heard Saturn spoken of so disrespectfully. "Why do you call Saturn the perversion planet?"

"Because he's the Satyr in mythology, the one with the horns and tail."

"I thought he was restrictive."

"He is, but the reason he's restrictive in the fifth house is that he has no feeling for anyone. Saturn in the fifth means, generally, that you don't really have any feeling or love for a person; it's cold. So these are just affairs for sexual release."

I wondered if anybody got helped.

"He didn't come to me for help, he came to me to find out when his next affair was due. He was just finishing up one and after two nights of being alone he was desperate, so he wondered what his prospects were for a new affair. I gave him the rundown on when the next affair would be likely. Whenever transiting Mars goes over the fifth house that starts things going."

For every male homosexual, there is presumably a female, a lesbian, though they function less openly and so seem less numerous.

"If you see two women kissing," Maxine said, "you put it down to natural affection. Now if two men are kissing . . ."

The women who consulted her were of all ages and degrees. And so she wasn't surprised when a professional counselor turned up one day for counsel. She was distinguished looking, middle-aged, a Scorpio, born November 2, 1918, at 2 A.M. in Michigan. "This lady has Virgo rising. She's very conservative. She has the Sun, Mercury and Venus in Scorpio, so again we have a great preoccupation with sex. With Neptune and Saturn, both malefic in the twelfth house, love affairs will bring her a great deal of sorrow. So she's tried to compensate by having a therapy workshop and by doing psychiatric nursing."

"Has she had affairs with males?" I asked.

"No, she has not. She came very close to that in 1966 when she fell hopelessly in love with a Yoga master on a nonsexual level; he was very ill at the time and incapable of anything."

Again, I wondered why a consultation had been sought.

"She came to me at a time when she was almost ready to have a complete nervous breakdown, and she didn't have a good philosophy, one that would hold her up, so I suggested that she go to this Yoga master whose philosophy was more of the Oriental. She took to this and she took to him and this was the first male influence in her life that was ever constructive. He was married and he was a homosexual, and his wife came to me for counseling because of that. And so he would not become involved. I've even seen her hug and kiss him, but it was on a nonsexual level, so she was just merely grateful."

"You weren't able to help her then?"

"Through him she was able to adopt the philosophy that she always should have had. She found a certain passive acceptance of herself, and it brought her peace."

"Did she live with a woman?"

"She had a young lady living with her, much younger as a matter of fact."

Just as heterosexuals do, so many older deviates seem to prefer the company of the young.

"Does a chart tell when a homosexual prefers a younger person?" I asked.

"Mercury in the fifth or eleventh house of friendships would show that. Mercury is younger people, Saturn older people."

As Maxine combed through her bulky file on homosexuals, it struck me that her work must be terribly depressing.

"Not particularly," she said. "They may be a little more volatile than other people, but at least they're consistent. In reviewing these charts, you'll notice a common pattern. In so many words, the malefic aspects with Venus and Uranus or Venus to Neptune, or Mars square Uranus, the unconventional, as Mars adds energy to the basic syndrome. And of course Neptune in the fifth house shows such a desperate search for idealism that they're not discriminating as to where they look for it."

I presented an age-old question.

"Do you think homosexuals are born, or made?"

And with her belief in reincarnation, Maxine replied: "Some are developed, some are born. It depends on past lives. If they were homosexuals as they closed their last life and had no desire to quit or reform, then they come back as a homosexual and they have their own karma they bring with them. The horoscope shows what that soul is and what it has learned through its past lives, and when people realize this and take astrology on that basis, there will be a great deal of progress made in psychiatry and medicine."

Even presupposing reincarnation, the fact remains that the only life that counts is the one being lived now. And the problem is quite real. In the search for a lasting relationship, the homosexual has even more difficulties than the average person (that is, if he isn't the average) because of the absence of normal social ties that serve to keep relationships together–family, children, home, legal involvements.

With homosexuals of substance, there is a tendency after a while to be chary of fly-by-night friends, and many turn to astrologers not only because they value their advice, but because there is no censure, as the astrologer recognizes that homosexuality is as much a part of that person's destiny pattern as birth or death.

"I have no wish to change, only to help," observed Edith Randall, the celebrated Hollywood astrologer, whose 60,000 astrological readings over the years include a sizable slice of the homosexual community. "A homosexual comes in, he's unhappy, not because he's a homosexual, he's unhappy usually because he doesn't have anybody to interest him at the moment."

We had been sitting around discussing love and marriage, when homosexuality unexpectedly reared its head.

It was a phenomenon that we both accepted as we did anything else in the passing scene, something to be dealt with because it was happening on all sides, in apparent ratio to the number of broken homes which spawned growing boys with no strong male identification.

"In time," I said, "it may take care of the population explosion."

"Not as long as people keep marrying," Miss Randall said.

"Are you in sympathy?" I inquired.

"Totally, as human beings. But of course the ones that come here need guidance, just as others do. The problems are usually the same—the other person, or the lack of another person."

"But the homosexual isn't coming to you because he's a homosexual," I reminded her.

"No. But I might still tell him that in a particular cycle or period of his life he shouldn't take anyone seriously. I might tell him that his emotional life has been bad because of his transiting aspects, but that this will change at a certain time, and this in itself is enough to quiet him down."

"Suppose they do not mention they are homosexuals?"

"I have a way of making them tell me. I read for a man the other night and I set his chart and saw what he was. Appearance isn't always signature for it because some of them are not obvious, so I said to him, 'You're a homosexual, aren't you?' and he said 'Yes.' And then, of course, I could pursue it. Sometimes I have to talk with a person for half an hour before I feel I am at a place where I can make him admit it."

"What is the advantage?"

"Then they talk more freely about their problems."

"What then do you do?"

"I can't do anything, nor do I do anything about getting them to change."

"What can you do if, say, he's broken off with somebody?"

"I have a way of talking to them so they feel a lot better after they've left here. I might point out it couldn't work out anyway because of somebody else in the picture. I read for a very prominent man in this town and a very attractive and wealthy one, and have for many years, and this man periodically gets in with all men younger than himself. He was married, and his marriage as far as he was concerned was a cover-up. But this man has gotten so if I say, 'You leave this birth date alone, it's no good for you,' he cuts it off right there. He's Scorpio and is able to face things better than others. Scorpio has the guts to do it, and he has learned the hard way that astrology's judgment is better than his."

12

A Time for Work

In time, with astrology, Ralph Winters had said, everybody would be happily doing the job for which he was best suited. It would be done with computers, sorting out the thousand and one aspects in a chart in relationship to the planetary aspects that seemed to apply best to a particular line of work. "One day," said Winters, "when a very advanced computer is finally programmed with all the various meanings and degrees and planets, their nodes, their parts of fortune, ascendant, midheaven, and all—when they have all that, then we'll have an exact provable science, and it will be taught in our universities and schools. And it won't be called astrology at that time, it will be astrophysics or some other name that will be acceptable to the public.

"Children's charts will be computed at birth, and they will be trained to do what they can do best and they will do those things that they came into the world to do. And they'll be perfectly happy, for example, laying bricks or being electricians or whatever it is—that's what they'll want to do and they won't be frustrated and driven to the psychiatrist's couch by parents forcing them to extend themselves into levels where they're not capable of being, or wouldn't be happy even if they were capable. At that point, painters or artists won't be made to labor long hours over algebra—they'll simply do what they want to do and they'll be encouraged and they'll be very happy doing it.

"The leaders of our government will be chosen that way, too. Those men with politically patterned charts will be instructed and guided in that way and will be put into positions of leadership. They'll be extremely happy to be there and we'll be extremely happy to have them there. Because they will then be functioning in a world that blends with their own personalities and that of the nation. And at that time we'll really have a government born of the people. It will be for us and will be run by us. Everyone will be doing with himself what he wants to do for the advancement of all."

To those knowing little about astrology, and that is virtually everybody but the astrologers, it seems that if there is anything to the science of the stars that certain Sun signs should have specific talents tending to certain professions. And it is true, to a limited extent, that where a person is a typical Sun sign, with strong aspects to his own Sun and ascendant, that the Sun sign seems to fit him and his work generally. The two greatest dancers of modern times were Nijinsky and Nureyev, both Pisces, and Pisces rules the feet. The three outstanding warriors of our time were Scorpios—Patton, Rommel and Montgomery; and Cancers and Taureans were usually the most successful bankers and financiers, Taurus being the second house of money, and Cancer the Crab being the acquisitive sign and ruling the fourth house of the home and land.

And of course there were our three Presidents who were Aquarians, the sign of the humanitarian who will save you whether you want to be saved or not, and all had led the country in wars against oppression—Lincoln (to free the slaves), McKinley (the Spanish-American War to liberate suffering Cuba) and Franklin Delano Roosevelt, who chose to save the world.

But how did one account for the fact that three of the greatest fighting men in the annals of pugilism were three different signs—Joe Louis (Taurus), Jack Dempsey (Cancer), and Gene Tunney (Gemini)?

The similarity was in the aspects, of course, in the prominence of Mars, which rules energy and vitality and gives courage and muscular coordination; prominent Mercurys which give the ability to size up a situation and make quick, almost instinctual decisions; strong Neptunes, which made them the showmen they were; and prominent Jupiters that provided the luck every leader needs to forge to the top.

To the master astrologer, Evangeline Adams, the elements of greatness were clearly apparent in the stars. "It was no accident," she wrote, "that John Burroughs became the greatest naturalist of his day. Mr. Burroughs couldn't have been anything else. He was born in April, in the pioneer sign, Aries, and under the influence of the earthy sign, Virgo, ruling nature study. The combination obviously and inevitably turned his pioneer spirit toward Nature. His Moon–the traveling planet–was in the sign Pisces, ruling the feet. This combination always means great activity in walking. Uranus was also in the sign Pisces, indicating that his best thinking would be done while walking."

Other planets revealed other important facets of his nature. "Jupiter was in his eleventh house of friends indicating that his greatest pleasures–as was indeed true–would come from his friends rather than from his family or close relatives; Venus was in mental Aries, showing that his pleasures would be intellectual rather than physical; Neptune (the subconscious) was in the house of children, foretelling that his keenest joy would be in the children of his imagination; and Uranus was in the house ruling animal life (the sixth house)." Since this was the planet of the inventor, and Burroughs was already an Aries innovator, it was clear what course his interests would take.

Had he been born a few days earlier, or a month later, with different aspects, he would have been an entirely different type of man, with a different career, as unbelievable as it may seem.

Since astrology is pragmatic, the meanings of the houses and signs have accrued slowly over the centuries, and the significance of Uranus, Neptune and Pluto, the last planets discovered, is constantly being enlarged by experience. Research into vocational astrology has been scant. So-called scientists have come up with planetary correlations with certain careers, while at the same time repudiating astrology to show how scientific they were. In his "The Cosmic Clocks," the French investigator, Michel Gauquelin, pointed out that 90 percent of the doctors in the French Academy of Medicine were born when Mars was rising on the subject's ascendant or culminating in his tenth house of career. He then denied astrology.

Actually, the only substantial astrological research into vocations has come with 30 years of painstaking appraisal of some 10,000 charts by Doris Chase Doane for the Church of Light in Los Angeles. The planetary aspects for diverse occupations, from stenographers and nurses to doctors and lawyers, were carefully analyzed only in charts where the precise birth time was available. And a number of planetary constants for various vocations were strikingly revealed.

The Doane study was not only concerned with the aspects for certain vocations, but with individual aptitudes that could be developed early, once recognized.

"It is not just a matter of finding a job," astral-researcher Doane observed, "but of somebody finding what is significant for them to do and then being able to tell how these aptitudes could be best expressed and at what time."

With her husband, the late Edward Doane, Doris Doane was among the few pioneers in modern research astrology, as befitted her Aries Sun sign. She was remarkably open in a field in which practitioners for years had husbanded their lore as if it were some secret alchemy, considering independent researchers poachers on a private preserve.

What Winters had suggested with computers, Doris Doane envisioned even now in the horse-and-buggy age of astrological research —a horoscopic appraisal of each and every child. "The first seven years of life are the formative years," she pointed out, "and during this period parents could find out the natural likes and dislikes of the child. If he has a strong Mars, they could get him interested in the type of things that would get him to do something with that Mars energy. You can't change Mars into Venus—Mars energy is going to remain Mars energy and it must express itself, but there are many different channels of expression."

A prominent (angular) Mars might signify a doctor, and a prominent Venus an interior decorator or even a beautician, but there was much more to it than that. Examining birth charts of a hundred medical men, Doris Doane had found that all but one had charts with Mars and Jupiter prominent, and all but one had active sixth and twelfth houses, the departments of public service and hospitals.

There is a simple formula for determining a planet's prominence, astrologically. "If a planet is in an angle (as Mars in the angular first, fourth, seventh or tenth houses) we consider it prominent because it expresses more powerfully in this angular position, or if it aspects the Sun, Moon or Mercury, or makes a lot of close aspects to other planets."

An appropriate energy pattern is required for a certain job, and the planets, however qualified by the houses and signs, are the sole source of this energy. "The more energy you have and the busier certain houses are, the more the attention is attracted to that department of life. Houses are important in certain vocations for this reason—you can have all of the aptitude and all of the training to develop the abilities, but if you don't have the right astrological environment, you have no place to express it. So the house is the environment. For instance, doctors, aside from having Mars and Jupiter powerful, must have an active sixth and twelfth houses (with aspects to their rulers, or planets in them)."

"How about an active second?" I asked, thinking of the fees exacted by so many doctors.

"If they become doctors to make a lot of money then the second house is important. If they become doctors to gain a lot of honor then the tenth house becomes prominent. But, primarily, it is the first and the sixth."

"Sixth being the department of life or house of service?"

"Yes, the house of service and the house of patients, inferiors, the sickroom, whereas the twelfth is the hospital, confinement."

Mars and Jupiter express themselves significantly in the doctors' charts. "Mars energy relates to surgical skill, administration of medicine and other methods of repairing the body. The prominent Jupiter maps the warmth, geniality, confidence and optimism communicated to the patient. Because of the power of suggestion, the personality of the doctor is a big factor in healing."

But suppose the patient doesn't heal?

"How about the eighth house (death), that would show, too, wouldn't it?"

"In terminal cases, but it would be the patient's chart that would show it, not the doctor's."

The importance of beginning vocational analysis with children was obvious.

"What do you tell a 50-year-old man who's a plumber, and yet from his chart shows a tremendous capacity for being a doctor?"

"You've got to give him a substitute that would adapt his particular abilities to his job. He might get into sanitary plumbing, or something like that." Mrs. Doane considered the case of a woman of 60 told by a vocational astrologer that she would have made a great physician. "She would be advised," astrologer Doane pointed out, "to get into something in the medical environment, as a dental aide or a pediatrician's assistant. She could find her satisfaction in the environment her energies crave. This is the secret of successful living, for each to find his own satisfaction in the quality of energies he expends."

Had she had this analysis at six rather than 60, her whole life—and that of others—might have been notably enriched.

Astrology works backwards and forwards, like a mathematical problem, and the constants in a doctor's chart are provable in retrospect. Astrologer Doane had studied the chart of the best known of American doctors. He was also a famous writer, whose books had sold more than 20 million copies, and he was very much in the news.

Dr. Benjamin Spock, the baby doctor, was born May 2, 1903, at 2 A.M. Eastern Standard Time, in New Haven, Connecticut. "He's a Taurus," Doris Doane observed, "with the Sun in the second house of money, and he has the friendly sign of Aquarius rising, the sign of Sagittarius, ruler of medicine, on the midheaven, his house of profession, and the ruler of that house is Jupiter in the compassionate sign of Pisces in the first house."

The direction of his energy flow is clearly shown. "The best aspect in his chart," said Doris, "is the natal Moon trine Jupiter and the Moon is in the fifth house of children. It's literally saying he should be a children's doctor."

His Moon in Cancer gave him the intuitive flair for diagnosis and made him seem like an old shoe around the house.

His natal Uranus in the tenth house or midheaven of activities gave him an unconventional approach that his conventional background would never have suggested.

"With his upbringing," Doris observed, "he was taught to control his Uranian urges. He came from a tightly knit family, and every time the kids would go away they would have to write two letters a week about everything that was happening around them. And if the parents didn't get a letter, the kids would get a telegram—write or come home."

They were a devoted, well-to-do family. "His mother gave up social activities to take care of her children. Mothers in that particular strata of society normally hired someone to take care of the children. But theirs was an affectionate family. He has Venus in the fourth house of the home. Venus rules the affections and it's trine Saturn in the

Dr. Benjamin Spock	Latitude: 41N18
May 2, 1903	Longitude: 72W55
New Haven, Connecticut	
2 a.m. EST	

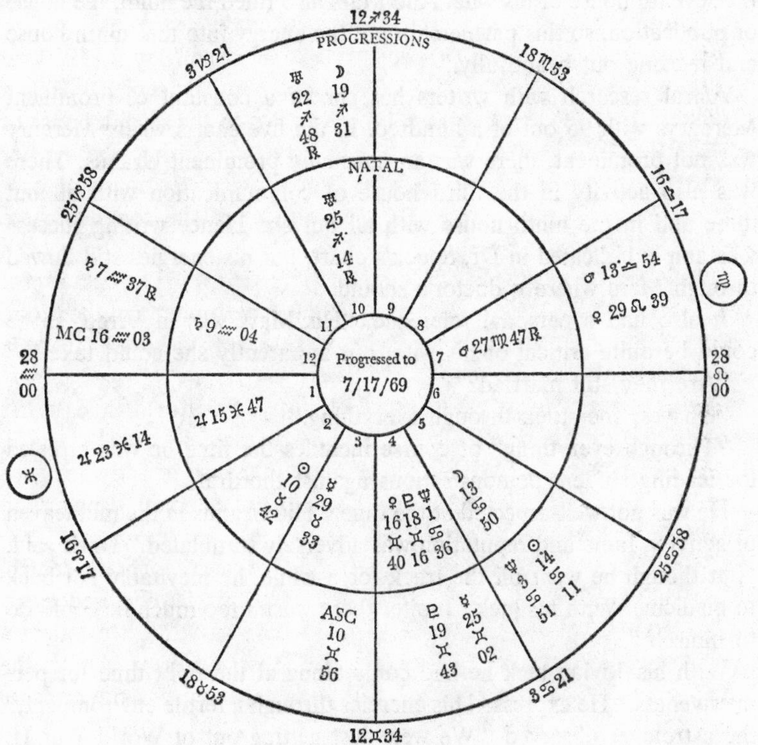

twelfth of hidden things, so he'd derive secret stimulation out of these affections. He had everything going for him—the professional, optimistic, affectionate support at home, rapport with women and children generally."

"How about his writing?"

"The aspects were tremendous. And furthermore, the chart showed it was his wife who helped him. Every evening from 9 P.M. until 1 A.M. the two of them sat down, and he dictated and she typed. And that is shown by Mercury in his third house of writing trine Mars in the seventh house of his wife. And Mars also ruled the ninth, the house of publication, so this partnership put the energy into that ninth house and it came out beautifully."

Astral research with writers has shown a constant of prominent Mercurys with 95 out of a hundred. In the five charts where Mercury was not prominent, there was an unusually prominent Uranus. There was also activity in the third house of communication with all but three and in the ninth house with all but six. Hence writing success was amply indicated in Dr. Spock's chart, but his energies still flowed through Mars where a doctor's should.

It also had a personal reference. "His Mars was in Virgo, so he could be quite critical of his wife, but apparently she could take it."

"Are they still married?"

"Oh yes, she stuck through everything."

"Through everything" of course includes the time he was arrested for leading student demonstrations against the draft.

He was not well-aspected at the time. "His Uranus in the midheaven of activity, fame and reputation was adversely stimulated," Doris said, "but though he went off the track for a while, he inevitably got back to medicine. With his lucky Jupiter there wasn't too much he could do to himself."

With his Jovian luck he had come along at the right time for permissiveness. "He expressed his energies through a fertile environment," the astrologer observed. "We were just getting out of World War II, people were tired, unsure of themselves, unconsciously looking for somebody to do their thinking for them. Discipline was lax, people were saying let your kids express themselves, and parents were afraid they'd wound the little kid's id."

In this atmosphere, Spock's books were a ray of sunshine.

"He was revered by all these mothers and the children," Doris said, "as is so plainly shown in his chart. Jupiter rules the midheaven which is his reputation. And the most fortunate aspect in his chart—the Moon (the mother) trine Jupiter—ties it together. The constants were there, and he had the right zodiacal environment to develop these potentials."

Without astrology, the father of permissiveness is clearly an enigma. Until he led the anti-draft, there had been no indication that he was anything but a benign coddler of "Spock-marked" children from the cradle to the grave.

But, astrologically, it is clearly foreshadowed. "Actually, his Pluto in the fourth house of the home opposed to Uranus in the tenth of career indicated that he would upset a great number of people with his activities. And Jupiter in the first house, the God complex, was a comforting position for a physician but, politically, revealed a demagogue who saw no side but his own. With Uranus in the tenth square his Jupiter in the first, he was bound to upset the applecart."

Astrologically, he still couldn't miss, though with Saturn in the twelfth house there was the tendency to be his own worst enemy. "In June, 1968, when convicted for abetting evasion of the draft, his progressed Moon had contacted natal Saturn in the twelfth house of confinement. But on July 11, 1969, when the conviction was overturned, his progressed midheaven, his reputation, was trine natal Venus. And the progressed Sun, in the most fortunate of progressed aspects, trined natal Jupiter in the first house."

We progressed naturally from medicine to the law and found a different constant. Lawyers, unlike doctors, don't require a powerful Mars. Of a hundred surveyed, all had a prominent Mercury or Uranus, and all but one had a prominent Saturn, accounting perhaps for their habitual pessimism and delays. "An active mind, alertness, ability to study and ease of expression are mapped by a prominent Mercury or Uranus," said Doris. "The ability to work hard at monotonous work, to evaluate systematic evidence, and to reason logically are mapped by Saturn. And in every one of the lawyers' charts there was an active ninth house, ruling legal activity and the courts."

As one examined these vocations, it was obvious how the influences assigned to the houses and the planets had developed over the years. In the dim past perhaps, some now-forgotten researcher had gone over similar ground, and passed on his observed correlations between activities on earth and the planets.

In much the same way, Doris Doane had established planetary correspondences between the planets and the so-called glamorous professions as well as the mundane–stenographers, store clerks, machinists, electricians.

Every one of one hundred stenographers she analyzed, for instance, had a chart with galvanizing Uranus aspecting the Sun, Moon, or Mercury, and Mercury or Uranus prominent or powerful. All had an active third house of communication. "Quickness in writing down thoughts, in grasping the ideas of others, and in placing the thoughts of others on paper is indicated by active Uranus-Mercury aspects. Things under Uranus-stimulus reflect human agency, and stenography has close contact with others. It is also the planet of short cuts and shorthand."

Third house activity was a necessity. "People who do not have the ruler of the third house powerfully aspected, or at least planets in the third, write very little."

Store clerks, who were primarily sales people, all had prominent Saturns, and all but one of the hundred studied had Pluto prominent; all but two Jupiter, all but three the Moon, and all but four Mercury. They were obviously a harmonious blend of outgoing energy. Ninety-five had active first houses, representing themselves, and 94 active seventh houses, essential in dealing with others. There were more clerks that were Libra, the diplomatic sign which rules the seventh house of the public, than any other Sun sign.

The syndrome or constant of the sales clerk was clearly shown. "Saturn, prominent in all hundred charts, maps the trade atmosphere in which a store clerk must feel at home, and the disciplined routine that is followed day after day. Jupiter is associated with salesmanship dependent upon good will. A prominent Moon indicates the people clerks contact daily. The practical intelligence mapped by Mercury is necessary to make out bills and keep a record of sales."

Curiously, Pluto, about which comparatively little is known, was prominent more often than Jupiter, Mercury and the Moon. And Doris Doane decided that Pluto ruled not only dealings with customers but with boss and co-workers as well. It was the people planet.

The seventh house was important, since the salesman's success depended on his impressing the public, and this was tied in with an active first house reflecting an outgoing personality which could flow through that seventh house.

With chart after chart, it was apparent how astrology had built up a body of equations between the departments of life in the twelve houses and the planets. What trail-blazing the Babylonians and the Greeks, and perhaps the Atlanteans had done with Jupiter, Saturn, Mars, Venus and Mercury, Doris Doane was doing with the more recent discoveries–Uranus, Neptune and Pluto. She was adding to their practical meaning by showing their impact on living.

So often planetary patterns vary with different careers. Artists have prominent Venuses and Mars, with Gemini their most frequent Sun sign. Electricians have Uranus prominent, and Pluto, which relates to hidden electromagnetic energies. Every engineer of the hundred reviewed had electric Uranus, mechanical Mars and disciplined Saturn prominent; every policeman, Saturn (restriction) and Mars (strife and crime), with active twelfth houses, the house of confinement and secret investigations. Actors, like athletes, had prominent Mars (drive and initiative) and Neptunes (glamor and drama), with active first and fifth houses. The athletes additionally featured prominent Mercurys, controlling the nervous reflexes; and the actors Uranus, the planet of magnetism and charm.

As she did with Dr. Spock, Doris had traced the evolution, astrologically, of a celebrated athlete. Like so many of my generation, I had been fascinated by the meteoric career of an Alabama farm boy who had become a glorious legend in his time, and was now having trouble adjusting to inglorious middle age.

In the beginning, I wondered, what aspects had contributed to making Joe Louis the most formidable fighting man of his time?

Astrologically, it was quite clear. Joe Louis had active first and fifth houses, and this was particularly good for a boxer.

"The first house," Doris explained, "represents the physical body, and the fifth amusement and also betting and public contests, as the house of hazards and speculation. These two houses provide the astrological environment a boxer needs. He could have all of the planetary constants for fighting, but without activity in those two houses he couldn't make it."

In Louis' chart, all of the required constants were prominent. "Mars

Joe Louis | Latitude: 32N54
May 13, 1914 | Longitude: 85W24
Lafayette, Alabama
8 a.m. CST

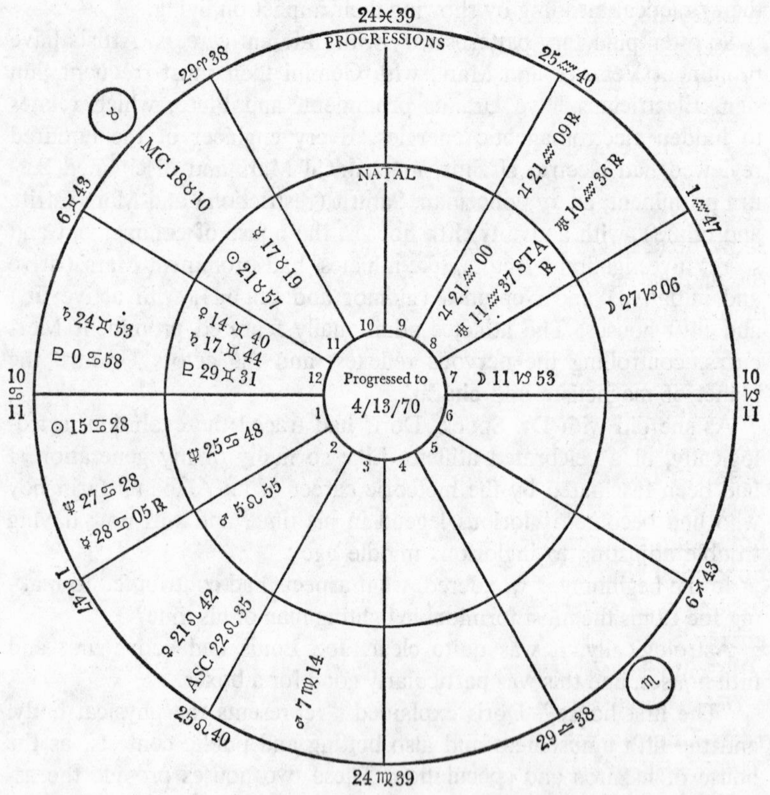

has five aspects, Jupiter six, Neptune six and Mercury six. An active house doesn't have to have a planet in it; the planet ruling the sign on the cusp can be very active and that links that house's department of life with the life pattern. In Joe Louis' chart, he had the first and fifth active, without one planet in his fifth house. However, Libra is on the cusp, so Venus, its ruler, is associated, and Scorpio is intercepted—so both Pluto and Mars are associated with this house. All three planets are active by aspect, and aspect shows strength."

Like Dr. Spock, Joe Louis is a Taurus. He was born May 13, 1914, in Lafayette, Alabama, at 8:00 A.M., Central Standard Time. He had Cancer rising and his Moon in Capricorn, practically opposed to that Cancer reflecting deep feelings that could be easily stirred.

The potential was all there. "He had Jupiter and Uranus in Aquarius," Doris pointed out, "trine Venus, Saturn and Pluto, all in Gemini, which rules the hands. And what always surprises me in an athlete, he had Neptune in the first house of Cancer. If he wanted to put on a show, he could do a good job of it. And that Neptune was closely trine the midheaven, which is his station and honor. His Mars was in Leo in the second house opposing Uranus in Aquarius, and this aspect could be explosive for a fighter."

His Sun was also rightly placed for a young man of humble origin seeking a place in the sun. It was in his eleventh house of aspirations, dreams, and the outcome of the matter. "Even the most retiring types," observed Doris Doane, "have a drive to significance, and we all have to satisfy it in some way. In Joe Louis' chart, in particular, his eleventh house Sun was conjunct Mercury and formed a square with that Mars opposition Uranus. That's a fixed square, a T-square by fixed signs, so fighting was a very good way for him to get rid of that dynamic energy."

"Could you tell by his chart that he would be a fighter?" I asked.

"You could say that he had pugilistic tendencies; anybody with a Mars-Uranus opposition would have that fighting instinct."

"How about his tenth house of career, his midheaven?"

"Neptune which rules the cusp of the tenth is in the first, the house of his personal interest, so this means he would more or less control this. But other discordant aspects gave him problems. This T-square involving five planets, and the Moon in Capricorn opposing the Cancer ascendant, would really give him moments when he would feel quite negative."

"He had trouble with managers and wives."

"With Neptune in Cancer in the first house, a person can't see things clearly. On top of that he has a very active twelfth house, things going on deviously behind the scenes, and Mercury which rules the cusp of the twelfth is in that fixed T-square, so he had quite a few mental complexes."

Only recently I had read where this magnificent fighting man, at 56, had entered a hospital to undergo psychiatric treatment for profound depression.

Mercury, the Moon and Uranus, the planetary constants for mental trouble, all afflicted, told the story.

In April of 1970, when he entered the hospital, all three were closely aspected in his chart. "The Moon (his mood) opposed his ascendant (self)," Doris pointed out, "and the Moon also ruled the ascendant. At this time he had the progressed Moon opposing progressed Mercury, the objective mind, and that progressed Mercury was in close orb to illusory Neptune, and whenever you have Mercury and Neptune in sharp aspect, the mind doesn't work as well."

At the time progressed Uranus aspected the Cancer ascendant, Uranus (the disrupter) added its tension. "Even under transiting Uranus aspects," observed Doris, "the individual has a hard time sleeping. If your Mercury is already afflicted and transiting Uranus comes along and hits it, you're uptight, you can't let down. So he already has this personal, emotional churn here, and then the high tension of progressed Uranus to the ascendant. But at the same time he had progressed Saturn, the Saturn of worry, despondency and fear, in the twelfth house square the natal midheaven. This meant that his fears were brought out before the public in announcements that he was having mental trouble, but there was a certain mystery surrounding these announcements because of this Neptunean influence in the first and tenth houses of person and activity."

The great champ was caught up in Saturn's second complete cycle in his life, and at a particularly trying time, astrologically, when transiting Saturn in Taurus was also passing over his Sun and his Mercury, traditional charger of the physical and nervous system.

"These Saturn cycles occur when one is between 27 and 29 years old and between 55 and 56 years old, possibly 57," said Doris. "These are the two times in a person's life, regardless of the chart, that he has to really assess what's going on in his life. Joe Louis once had all the public attention and now he didn't, and it would be harder for him to adjust to this Saturnian cycle than the average person. Also, he doesn't have a strong chart like Dr. Spock. He's only got two angular planets (planets in first, fourth, seventh or tenth houses) against Dr. Spock's six of high-energy flow, so he had to depend upon others for his strength rather than being his own master."

But yet, with his Gemini hands and his Mars in Leo opposite Uranus, and his Venus-Mars ruled fifth house, he was still pound for pound the greatest fighting man ever to draw on a laced glove.

Although plumbers can't be turned into doctors overnight, astrology has helped many people to new successes through changing their careers completely or getting them to change the emphasis of the old career. The dean of Sun sign astrology, Hollywood's Carroll Righter, has come up with beneficial advice for many of filmland's best-known stars. In the late fifties, checking comedian Bob Cummings' chart, he induced the actor to get out of television for a while, where he was growing stale, and turn to the stage.

"At the time," Cummings confirmed, "it was a great move."

Arlene Dahl, one of Righter's more beauteous clients, was in the screen doldrums ten years ago, and the astrologer, looking at her chart and its second-house money aspects, told her to switch from acting to business.

She laughed, but Righter persisted.

"You can't miss," he said. "You have a beautiful chart for business."

The star was sufficiently impressed to look about her for business opportunities. She started writing a beauty column, picked up by a national syndicate, then became a consultant to an advertising agency, and also got into cosmetics.

Righter's only complaint, as he reviewed her progress, was that she had never consulted him about her five marriages.

"I could have saved her a lot of heartaches by showing her that the charts were not favorable for these marriages," he said.

But then what kind of a vocation is marriage?

13

A Time for Nixon

There was a time for Washington and for Lincoln, for Jefferson, Jackson, Roosevelt and Truman, and there is a time for Richard Nixon, an unpopular figure, reminiscent of ancient Rome's Cicero, who, according to the stars, might very well become the "second father of his country."

Attacked by the press, lampooned by youth, ridiculed by the pseudo-intellectuals, he is still, the astrologers said, the right man at the right time.

Defeated for the Presidency in 1960, humiliated in his bid for the governorship of California in 1962, passed over by his own party in 1964, he had, with Capricornian resolution, traveled the world to successfully climb his particular mountain.

To many millions he is an enigma, but to astrologers, including Kiyo, the inscrutable Oriental who taught a class of hippies high in the Hollywood hills, there is no mystery about Richard Nixon and his rise to the Presidency.

"Whether you like it or not," she told her unsmiling students, "this is the most significant chart in the land, for as the President goes, so goes the country."

The class showed little interest in this symbol of a reactionary Establishment, but silently copied from the blackboard: Richard Milhous Nixon, January 9, 1913, 9:14 P.M., Yorba Linda, California. Sun sign Capricorn, Moon in Aquarius, Virgo rising.

Richard Nixon

Jan. 9, 1913

9:14 p.m.

Yorba Linda, Calif.

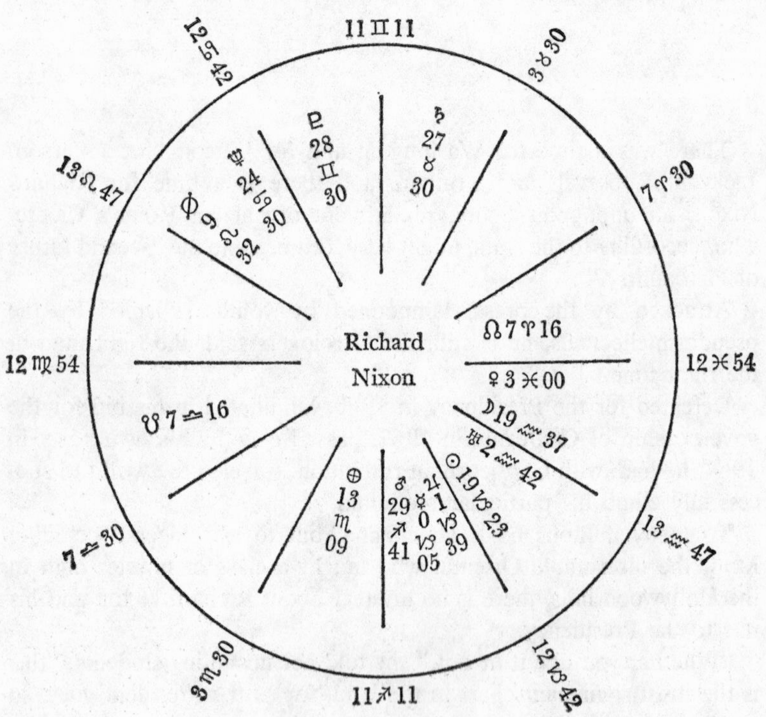

As Kiyo chalked in the positions of the planets in the President's birth chart, I looked around curiously. The students were all young, nobody older than 25, all from their dress and demeanor liberal if not hippie-minded. It was obvious from the rigid set of their mouths that they did not like Richard Milhous Nixon. But they were ready at least to listen to their teacher as she prepared not only to delineate the Nixon horoscope, but to progress his planets into the future.

As her eyes roamed over the group, she calmly pointed out: "Astrology should eliminate judgments that are purely subjective. Even so, it wasn't Nixon who took us into the Vietnam War, but John Kennedy, and Nixon is the first President to reduce the forces fighting a war he's trying to end."

Turning to the chart, she picked out the house of the zodiac in which the President's Sun sign stood at 19 degrees, then delivered her little bombshell.

"We see the Sun in Capricorn in the fifth house, conjunct Uranus. That makes him Uranian by nature, definitely of the Aquarian consciousness, definitely a humanitarian, definitely interested in the young. However, because of the Saturn ruling his Capricorn Sun, he has encountered delays in which he had necessary lessons to learn."

Before the class had a chance to react, she went on to explain that it was difficult to understand the Nixon who had begun to age with Aquarian grace, without some clue to a difficult childhood.

"A Capricorn child," Kiyo related, "has a hard time gaining confidence because he's out of step with children his own age. He's got an old head, and doesn't feel like frivolous games, and he's not overly strong as a child. Add to that the deprived aspect of the Moon's south node in the first house, and you get a very shy boy, who has to earn a position of poise by taking himself in hand the hard way. Children with this node position suffer in just not being able to look up, bashfully hanging their heads. Just the thought of appearing on a public platform would be a nightmare."

The South Node is a point in the heavens where the Moon crosses the path of the Sun, the ecliptic, from north latitude to south latitude. It is not a fortunate aspect. "It represents a remnant of early childhood, a shyness that never quite disappears. But with his Capricorn resolution, he has worked it out. He put an awful lot of work into himself, which few will ever know about, except his parents, himself, God, and the astrologers."

"I just don't see 'tricky Dicky' as a symbol of the great humanitarian age," said a youth with a beard and long flowing hair.

Kiyo was her imperturbable Oriental self.

"For the first time in this generation we have a Saturnine father image. It's not what we're accustomed to and it's not what youth has liked, but we were so shaken up with the terrible assassinations in high places that unconsciously, collectively, we have almost intuitively reached out for a safe, if not popular, leader."

Nixon's planets were pretty well scrambled. His South Node in the first house was in Libra, the Part of Fortune in Scorpio in the third, Mars in Sagittarius and Mercury and Jupiter in the fourth, the Sun in Capricorn and Uranus in Aquarius in the fifth, the Moon in Aquarius and Venus in Pisces in the sixth, the North Node in Aries in the seventh, Saturn in Taurus in the ninth, Pluto in Gemini in the tenth, and Neptune in Cancer in the eleventh.

His Venus in Pisces was an unlikely position for a cold, Saturnine personality.

"Venus in Pisces is an exalted position for Venus," said Kiyo. "It shows compassion for the underprivileged, and consideration for subordinates, in the sixth house of employees. It's how he relates to people beneath him, and he does assume that responsibility with more sensitivity than one would suppose from his obvious Saturn qualities. But even so, as a Capricorn, he insists on law and order as a prerequisite of justice. And our permissively trained youth don't like that."

The class again registered disagreement.

"Venus in Pisces," said one student, "is the mark of a Messiah complex, not true?"

Kiyo nodded. "That's one interpretation."

"He's trying to save everybody," the student went on, "whether they want it or not, and it has to be his way. He even kept Democrats in his Administration, to win them over. And in playing up to the young, he has ulterior motives."

"Yes, he wants to help them, and he wants them to help the nation, as he knows one day they will have to carry on."

Obviously, Nixon could only please this group by resigning.

Kiyo's eyes roved over the class. "The Sun in the fifth house means a great awareness of the youth of the nation. The young people tend to be hostile to the Saturnian figure, but we see astrologically that he has an awareness of both youth and education. With the Aquarius-Leo polarity, from the fifth to the eleventh houses, he understands the use of the dramatic appeal for education. And as the country verges more into the Aquarian Age he will increasingly incorporate Aquarian qualities, gradually discarding his prosaic Saturnian image."

The class was still skeptical.

"Why," asked a youth with long hair, "should a square like Nixon get with it?"

"Sun conjunct Uranus gives a brilliant, progressive intellect. The Capricorn quality has made him cautious and reserved and somewhat formal in his outer expression, but within he is very perceptive and much more liberal than his past positions would imply. Actually, with that Aquarian fifth house, he really relates more to youth than adults." She looked up with a smile that revealed her own Leonine flair for the dramatic. "Youth hasn't recognized these qualities in him yet because of the Capricorn-Saturn restrictions."

Some in the class cocked a jaundiced eye at the Presidential chart, others noncommittally chewed on pencils, completely unsold on the Nixon metamorphosis.

"Again," Kiyo went on imperturbably, "we have the Uranian influence, with the Moon in Aquarius in the sixth house of service. That certainly signifies a feeling of brotherhood, or humanitarianism, an unorthodox emotional makeup, with Sun, Moon and Uranus all together like that."

Hands flew up, and Kiyo nodded to a pretty girl with the colorful exterior of a flower child.

"His Sun is not really in significant aspect to Uranus," the girl protested.

"It's a wide conjunction, thirteen degrees," the teacher acknowledged, "but sixteen degrees still holds for the Sun, when the aspected planet is powerful, too."

Kiyo scanned the chart. "Not only is the Sun conjunct Uranus, but Uranus is conjunct the Moon. This indicates that both parents were strong and unique people, the Sun standing for the father, the Moon the mother, with Uranus in between coloring both in such a way that it makes for highly individualized parents." (Uranus–Moon was in 17-degree orb.)

Listening, I had to agree with the class that the prevailing image of Richard Nixon bore slight resemblance to the man emerging on Kiyo's blackboard.

"He's never had a very good press," she said in explanation. "Pluto rules his Scorpio-cusp third house of communication, and Pluto, retrograde, is in his tenth house of public image. So Pluto standing for the masses in Mercury-ruled Gemini would tend to bring misconceptions about him."

She elaborated:

"The press doesn't like him because he does work behind the scenes a lot. A prominent Pluto, Pluto being the planet of mystery, tends to give him a tremendous flair for backroom politics. He just doesn't show his hand, but mysteriously—and wisely—withholds his intentions."

"Doesn't he care about his popularity?" I asked.

"A man doesn't put out that much effort without caring. His is a well-planned life."

The class was still unimpressed. "He hasn't planned his image very well," a young dissident said.

"His publicity runs into disfavor intermittently with a Mars-Mercury opposition to Pluto, but with Pluto well-aspected, trine Venus, it's not as bad as it might be," Kiyo said. "Moreover, he has the Part of Fortune, an Arabic part, protecting his midheaven, his tenth house of career."

Ultimately, a new image, that of the liberating Aquarian, would emerge, and the American people would at last know they had a leader they had grievously underestimated.

Again the class disagreed.

"Mercury and Mars oppositions to Pluto, in the tenth house of reputation," said one youth severely, "could indicate continuing public antipathy."

Kiyo shook her head. "Mercury and Mars oppositions aren't anywhere as heavy as squares. And in this case, actually, they're helpful as they make him aware of his image, so he can work on it. Anyway, his Pluto, signifying how he strikes the public, isn't that bad. The Moon does trine Pluto beautifully, which means that the people will respect him. And regardless of the current turmoil on college campuses, his Saturn and Neptune, nicely sextiled, from the ninth house of higher education to the eleventh of friends, show a facility for appeasing traditional academic people, at the same time understanding the need for more interpersonal education."

A hand went up. "Doesn't that Pluto-Mercury aspect make him rather devious?"

"Yes, but only as a strategist. Pluto trine Venus is a very scrupulous aspect. And whether the press likes it or not, he is essentially a very moral man."

There was a general moan.

"Tricky Dicky highly moral?" somebody remonstrated.

Kiyo nodded emphatically. "The aspect for morality on a high level is Saturn in the ninth house of spiritual values in close trine to his Sun in the fifth house. Saturn there shows that he is ruled by religious fundamentals of the old style."

A student peered over at the chart.

"How about that Venus square Saturn, wouldn't that make him shifty in money matters?"

"It's not a very close square, six degrees. And a laxness in business could indicate more a lack of concern than any slackness in morality."

She gave her class a commanding look.

"You are judging Nixon over his early years, and he really isn't the same man. The chart definitely shows that.

"Along with other aspects, the ruler of his Virgo ascendant, Mercury, in the fourth house (and in wisely aging Capricorn, at that) was favorable to the removal of obstacles after middle age. And Saturn, Capricorn's ruling planet, was nearing completion of its second cycle through his zodiac, ending one learning process, and beginning another. Little by little he will take greater latitude, and the young people will help pave the way for his new direction."

This prospect seemed unlikely at the moment. "You mean this younger generation?" I asked.

"Oh, yes, that Sun in the young people's fifth house, they will accept him, I am sure."

"At what point?"

"That all depends on how many terms he has; we haven't researched that yet since we don't know the candidates for the 1972 election."

The classroom groaned.

"Four more years of Nixon," somebody said. "Ouch. He's got no style."

"Sure," Kiyo responded, "that's what makes him unpopular with people who want the flash of a Gemini Kennedy, who got himself killed. This Capricorn is more prudent, he won't get himself killed."

I wondered whether she was looking into Nixon's chart, or expressing an opinion.

"Progressing his chart, I found 1972, an election year, a very good year for him, so he obviously will be around and kicking."

There was another muffled groan. "Not as President again, not that."

"We shall see when we discuss the progressions, as that should also show, because of the close connection between President and nation, how the country will do."

Kiyo smiled benignly.

"Capricorns are never terribly popular, but they are useful restraints in times of chaotic change."

More and more, though, the Aquarian influence would take over. With the end of the second 28-year Saturn cycle when he became President, a deep inner searching opened up the 58-year-old Nixon's Aquarian potential, and gave a prod to his streak of Uranian unorthodoxy.

"The young, supposedly so open, don't want to admit they're wrong," Kiyo said, "and so don't recognize that Richard Nixon is not the man they thought he was." She smiled. "And one reason for that is that he isn't the man he was. From his Sun conjunct Uranus, in Aquarius, he's more and more metaphysically inclined, open to psychic phenomena, astrology, and all the various facets of the spiritual quest considered the exclusive bag of the young people. The overall chart shows that he will continually grow away from conventional ideologies." This was seen particularly in an inconjunct aspect, a 150-degree angular relationship of Mars and Mercury to Saturn, showing a state of transition away from what Saturn stands for. "The inconjunct aspect reflects movement and growth. Mercury is how one thinks, Mars energy and action, Saturn tradition. And he would be quick to move, once he was sure he was right. With Mars in Sagittarius, conjunct not only Mercury but Jupiter, the venturesome ruler of Sagittarius, he is quite adventurous for a Capricorn, with the courage of his convictions. He will risk a great deal for what he believes."

The class was not about to give the President points for courage.

"Where do you see him taking such risks?" a youthful skeptic demanded.

"Sun conjunct Uranus is a courageous indicator."

"But it's still a wide orb," the student reminded her.

"All I can give you is the astrology of it," Kiyo said. "He's more resourceful than any of you realize. His energizing Mars and communicative Mercury in Sagittarius, the sign of higher education and foreign affairs, give him the aspect of a well-rounded statesman. He's definitely aware of other cultures. He knows what's going on in other countries and has oriented himself to other philosophies."

As if to please the teacher with at least a neutral comment, a bearded student observed mildly.

"Pope Paul has Mars in Sagittarius."

"Is that right?" Kiyo responded. "Well, Mars in Sagittarius gives good musculature–a good tall body, athletic qualities, a lot of courage and energy."

"The Pope," the student added, "is tied in with the old way of doing things."

Kiyo shook her head. "Don't blame that on his Mars–that's something else."

Kiyo saw Nixon mellowing, becoming generous and merciful, because of expansive Jupiter in Capricorn conjunct his Sun. "It broadens the Capricorn outlook as he becomes more mature. Moreover, with years, Capricorns do get younger and more relaxed." (Jupiter–Sun was in 17-degree orb.)

To some degree this was also true of Moon in Capricorn and Capricorn rising.

"In Nixon's case," said Kiyo, "acceptance of adversity developed a sense of balance, and so, with the help of a benign Jupiter, he began to acquire a sense of humor."

I had attributed a new jocular Nixon to a carefully thought-out stance.

Kiyo shook her head. "No, this is the real Nixon, not only mellow, but primarily interested not in his own image but the country's."

The class shook their heads.

"Where do you see all that?" asked the young man with the beard.

"Venus trine Pluto reflects the ability to relate to people, and since Venus is in the sixth house of work and service and Pluto the tenth of activity, he dedicates his services to the masses."

"He doesn't seem that concerned about Negroes," somebody suggested.

"Pluto expresses the aggregate population, rather than select groups."

The road ahead was not to be easy for Nixon or the nation. Fixed stars, which some consider significant, were in stress position. "Saturn in Taurus, midpoint between the fixed stars of Pleiades and Caput Algol, at 29 and 25 degrees Taurus, form a heavy conjunction reflecting many sorrows."

"Will he knuckle under to these adverse aspects?" somebody asked hopefully.

"He will pass through numerous crises, gaining strength in the process. With that cluster of fixed stars, destiny brings what there is a capacity for, and the capacity is there. He lost two elections, and still came back."

Again a hand went up. "Aren't the fixed stars highly malefic on Saturn like that?"

"If one can weather the storm–and he's done it–it can bring fame and fortune and tremendous power. With Saturn in Taurus, trine his Sun, he has fantastic perseverance, as his adversaries are well aware."

Nixon had great inner resources with Jupiter and the Sun trine his Virgo ascendant, and Libra on the cusp of the second money house trine the midheaven, his professional status. He would never want for money, and the ruler of his ascendant, Mercury, placed in the fourth house of solid possessions, showed he would accumulate property (Key Biscayne, New York, San Clemente) in later life.

A hand went up.

"If his money house is so good, then why is the country in a recession?"

"It might have been worse with another President. With Capricornian prudence, he is trying to get the nation to tighten its belt, telling us not to be the wasteful children we've been."

She looked up at a sea of tight faces.

"That's a crock," one student said.

"No," Kiyo chided, "it's Saturn, the teacher, and it's a lesson we have needed. He's not bringing a depression, but forestalling one, by keeping inflation within bounds."

The stockmarket was down, and money tight at this time. But the riots in the cities that were fixtures of the Kennedy and Johnson administrations had faded out unnoticed, as if the rioters sensed a new strong hand that would brook no nonsense.

There was a question as to where Nixon stood even after the so-called Kent State massacre, where four students were killed during a riotous demonstration. The law-and-order Capricorn pointed out that death, however tragic, was always a contingency of violence.

After two years, Nixon was still feeling his way. But before his first term ran out, a Capricornian-Uranian Chief Executive would aggressively attack organized crime and civil violence, handle the pollution problem, and legislate for pure foods and the national health. That strong sixth house (with its Venus and Moon aspects) involving public service and national well-being would not be denied.

Kiyo talked as if Nixon would be President for a good many years.

"Progressed Jupiter is at twelve degrees of Capricorn, approaching a conjunction to his natal Sun, signifying an increase in popularity. Lady Luck is coming his way, his health and well-being will expand, and all good will be his."

"Does that include being President?" I asked.

She shook her head.

"You have to compare the candidates, not only to one another, but with the U.S. chart, and check the progressions and the transiting planets."

"Why not aspect him to the country's chart?"

Kiyo laughed. "That's the problem, what chart? Traditionally, astrologers equate the U.S. chart to the signing of the Declaration of Independence, July 4, 1776, in the wee hours of the morning—Cancer, with Gemini rising. But Manly Hall, the scholarly astrologer, claimed that after the document had been ratified some signers reported going out to supper, an evening meal. So he decided on Sagittarius rising. Sagittarius, as the opposite of Gemini, has many of its qualities, but expresses them differently."

She highlighted the distinctions.

"In a nation's chart, the first or rising house describes the collective

July 4, 1776

United States of America

Philadelphia, Pa.

Gemini Rising

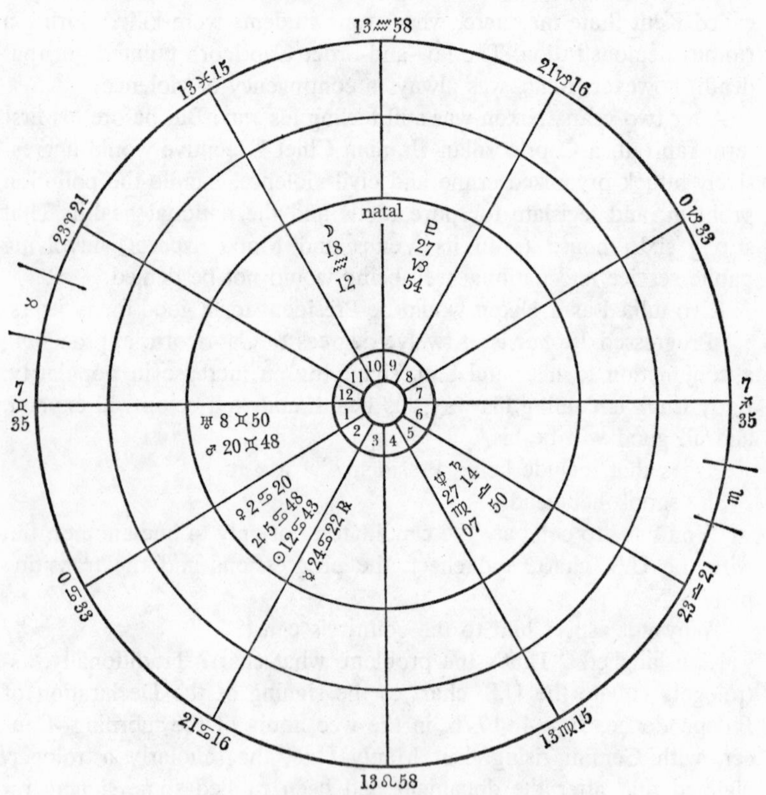

July 4, 1776 **United States of America**

Declaration of Independence

Philadelphia, Pa.

Sagittarius Rising

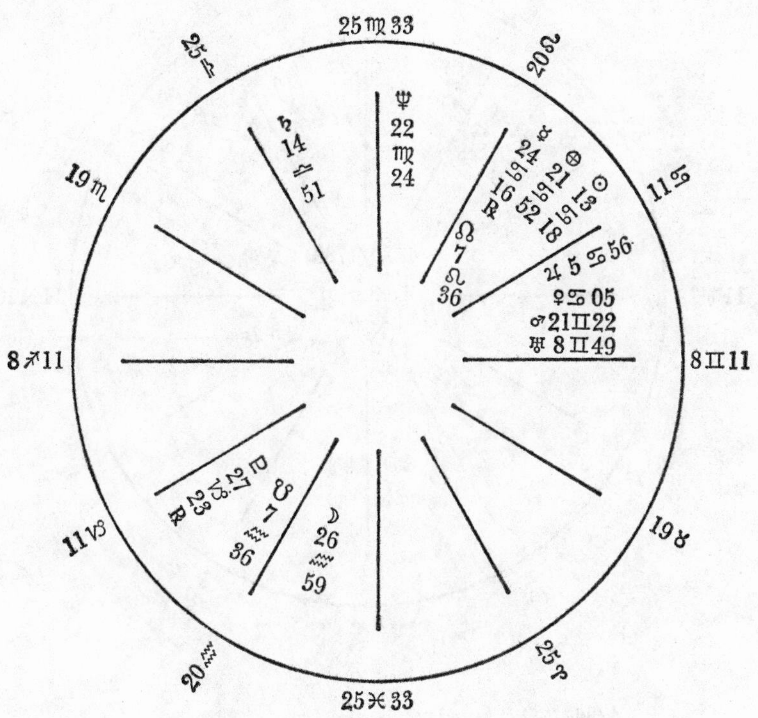

4:50 p.m. LMT, 4/4/1776 as per Manley Hall

True Horoscope of U.S.A.

Inauguration of George Washington

First President

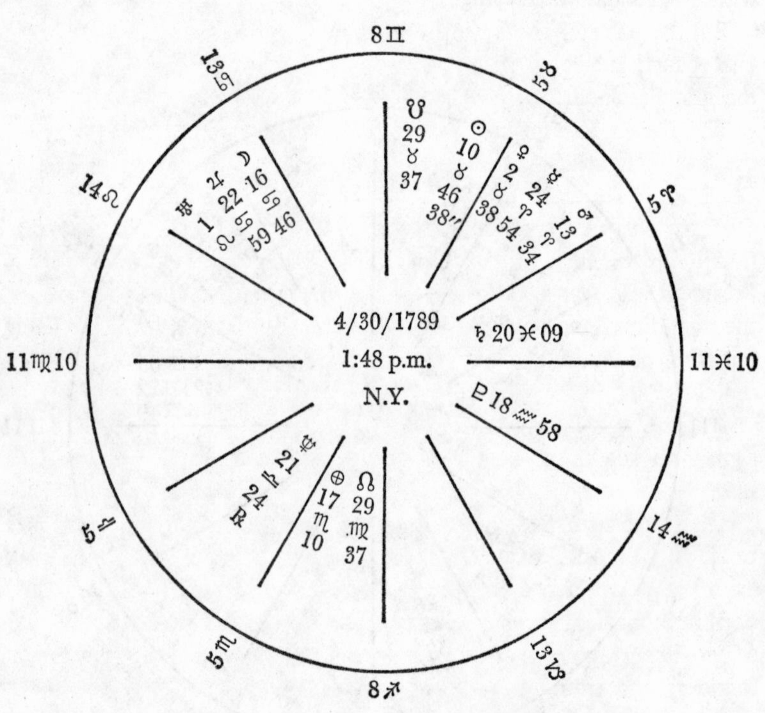

4/30/1789 Thursday

1:48:30 p.m. LMT. New York 40N43 74E00

as per Ralph Kraum

consciousness of the people. Gemini would be more childlike, Sagittarius more philosophic and expansive, more travel-conscious and prone to interests abroad. It would better explain our traditional generosity to other nations. Gemini rising doesn't fit the position of women in this country. It puts the nation's natal Moon in the tenth house of public image and career, instead of the fourth and the home, indicating a freedom for women not traditionally enjoyed in this country, as witness unequal wages for the same job."

But there is still another chart that some astrologers feel is the valid U.S. chart; it begins with the moment George Washington became the first President of the 13 United States.

The Ralph Kraum chart, named for the innovator, synchronized the first inaugural with the the affairs of the nation. It was set up for April 30, 1789, at 1:48:30 P.M., the precise moment the Father of his Country put his hand to the infant Ship of State. The country was then a nation, not a loose federation of states, and it was a time for a President. He was certainly the right man for that time—a Pisces in the dwindling Piscean Age, heading a Taurean nation with the determination of the bull, but which, like the bull, shattered everything in the china shop when it lost patience.

Originally, it had seemed odd that a country should have a birth sign. And yet, if the principle is sound, what affects one affects the mass. It is intriguing that ancient Rome, a militaristic state, was a Taurus, and so is modern Israel, which like Rome, had to become practically an armed camp to survive. England is an Aries, a pioneer explorer; Italy a fiery Leo; Red Russia a Scorpio, secretive, militaristic, born in bloodshed and war. La belle France of the Napoleonic era was a Leo like Napoleon; Germany an Aries like Bismarck, its modern founder; and present-day Egypt, born February 28, 1922, a paradoxical Pisces, submitting to the Russian yoke to liberate itself.

As for the U.S., Cancer or Taurus—both seem to fit. The United States, like the Cancerian Crab, fought only when concerned, and in their Taurean love of home, Americans rarely gave up their homeland. But while astrologers might argue which sign better suits the country, it seems obvious, astrologically, that the Kraum inaugural chart is the one to measure the Presidency with. It is clearly comparing birds of a feather.

14

. . . and the Nation

The Presidential chart said wonders.

In the midheaven of career, the Washington Inaugural chart stood at 8 degrees Gemini, and Nixon's at 11 Gemini. The Virgo ascendant, the personality, the Presidency, was virtually the same degree. Only one other President came nearly as close to the George Washington Inaugural chart, beginning with the Gemini midheaven and the Virgo ascendant, and there was no question where the country stood with him. That was Franklin D. Roosevelt, the only President to have four terms.

As Kiyo spread out the three charts, even a novice could see the transcending similarities in the natal cusps, which showed all three charts on fundamentally the same wave length. Beginning with the FDR ascendant, 14 degrees Virgo, against 11 Virgo for the Washington Inaugural chart and 13 Virgo for Nixon, the respective house cusps almost tripped over each other:

FDR		*Washington Inaugural*		*Nixon*	
8	Libra	5	Libra	7	Libra
8	Scorpio	5	Scorpio	3	Scorpio
11	Sagittarius	8	Sagittarius	11	Sagittarius
16	Capricorn	13	Capricorn	13	Capricorn

17	Aquarius	14	Aquarius	14	Aquarius
14	Pisces	11	Pisces	13	Pisces
8	Aries	5	Aries	7	Aries
8	Taurus	5	Taurus	3	Taurus
11	Gemini	8	Gemini	11	Gemini
16	Cancer	13	Cancer	13	Cancer
17	Leo	14	Leo	14	Leo

In the area of the professionally important midheaven, Nixon and FDR were equidistant from the Presidential chart, and Nixon one degree closer on the ascendant, and closer on most of the other cusps.

FDR had an instant romance with the country. Born January 30, 1882 (8:46 P.M.), he had Moon in Cancer, and his Sun in Aquarius, while in the nation's July 4 chart, the Sun was in Cancer and Moon in Aquarius. There could have been no better aspect for a long, happy union.

"If a man and a woman had these aspects," Kiyo said, "you could safely reserve a seat at their golden wedding anniversary."

At birth, Aquarian Roosevelt, like Lincoln, had the Aquarian broadness which made him sensitive to the mass welfare. Nixon, on the other hand, more like the last Capricorn President, austere-appearing Woodrow Wilson (December 28, 1856), had to develop this Aquarian potential.

Wilson, more so than Nixon, was never really understood by the country. Nevertheless, he had his Cancer on the midheaven of career, conjoining the country's Sun, and his Moon in Aquarius, where it had a friendly aspect to the nation's—enough to see him elected.

Only one President was actually born on July 4, with the nation, and that was Calvin Coolidge. Coolidge had perhaps the most tranquil administration of any President, in the seven boom years he served after the secretive death of Scorpionic Warren G. Harding. And, like Roosevelt and Nixon, Coolidge had Gemini in his midheaven, a few degrees from the Inaugural midheaven, and his ascendant at 7 degrees Virgo, only four degrees from the Washington Inaugural ascendant.

But neither Roosevelt nor Wilson nor Coolidge fit the Washington Inaugural or Presidential chart like Richard Milhous Nixon. "Not one chart in a million," said Kiyo, "and certainly no other politician's would match this U.S. chart as Nixon's does."

Franklin D. Roosevelt

Jan 30, 1882

8:46 p.m.

Hyde Park, N.Y.

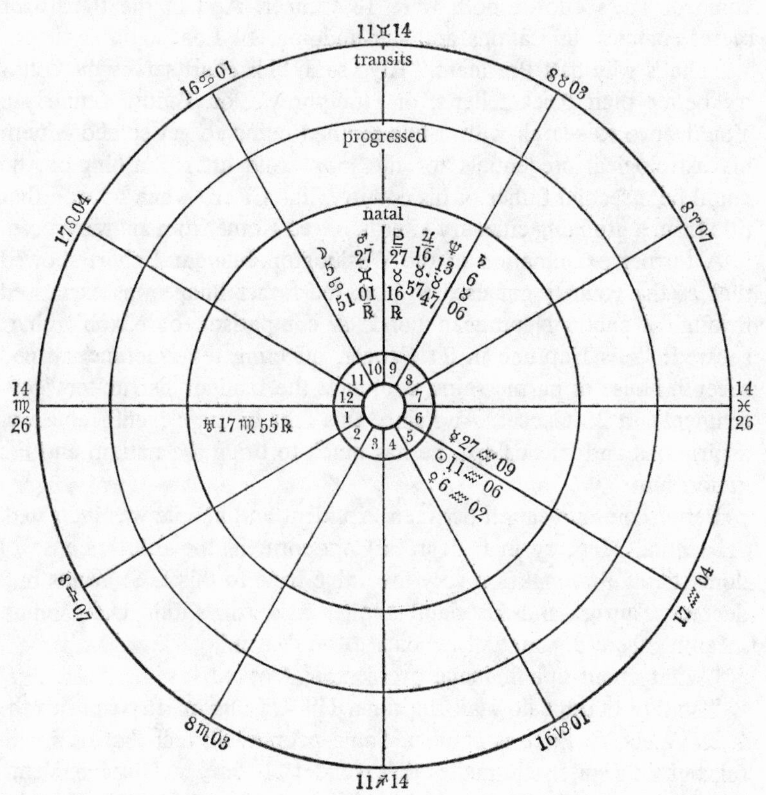

The fifth house cusp is particularly relevant, since it could confirm or disaffirm the affinity with the young that Kiyo had claimed. Remarkably, the fifth house cusps matched, both thirteen degrees Capricorn, in his own Sun sign, ruled by Saturn the teacher.

In the area of public service, health, labor, the sixth house cusps were also virtually identical at 14 degrees Aquarius, the sign of the humanitarian now coming to flower in the Aquarian Age.

The zodiacal polarities carried over to the eleventh and twelfth houses. In the eleventh house of friendship, aspirations and the outcome of one's efforts, both were 13 Cancer. And in the twelfth of secret enemies, limitations and self-undoing, 14 Leo.

"That's why he's President," Kiyo said, "his chart serves the country better than Rockefeller's, or Humphrey's, or Teddy Kennedy's. You'd have to search with a fine-toothed comb to get someone with his astrological credentials for the job." And after Washington, he could be a second father of his country, like Cicero when he won that title from a grudging citizenry after he saved Rome from anarchy.

A further examination of the Washington Inaugural chart showed that as the country got used to him, the father image was expressed through a subtle Neptunean bond. A comparison of Nixon's chart showed: "His Neptune in 24 Cancer, affecting the Neptunean-ruled seventh house of partnerships, conjuncts the Inaugural's Jupiter (government) in 23 Cancer. And since this falls in the eleventh house of aspirations and friendships, he has much to bring the nation, and the nation him."

Better communication between President and people was indicated. "His natal Mercury in 0 degrees Capricorn, in the fourth house of domestic affairs, makes a very favorable trine to this U.S. Venus in 2 degrees Taurus, and his natal Jupiter also trines this U.S. Venus, meaning there are mutual benefits to be drawn."

"What about our financial problems?" I asked.

"Bounty doesn't flow all the time. His Uranus exactly squares the U.S. Venus, so there is conflict. Some people will feel that he's willful, but his Jupiter still makes that wonderful trine, and Jupiter-Venus have the last word. Moreover, his Venus sextile the U.S. Venus helps smooth out a certain abrasive quality."

His Saturn on the south node was useful to the country, giving it a release from mounting pressures, and making him the scapegoat.

It seemed odd to hear a President so described.

Kiyo shrugged. "But isn't the goat–Capricorn–often the scapegoat? He's sacrificing himself, but he's strong enough to do it, knowing in the end he will successfully climb the mountain."

I did not share Kiyo's assurance that Nixon's image was to steadily improve. His "no-knock bill," designed to curb robbers, rapists and killers in the nation's capital, was under attack, and he was blamed for the war, inflation, unemployment. In view of all this carping, it was difficult to see how the President's image could do anything but dwindle along with his chances for re-election.

But Kiyo disagreed. "Regardless of the press, his popularity will grow, and at their expense, if necessary. He's definitely on the Aquarian upswing, definitely going to liberate himself, and he's bound to upset a few people doing it. I see Uranus as a freedom-bringing aspect, and transiting over his south node in Libra, reversing its restrictive influence, it's going to break him loose."

Kiyo turned to the progressions in the Nixon chart, the timing device by which astrologers foreshadow future events. "The progressed Moon approaching the progressed Sun starts a whole new phase, a whole new appraisal of his life. The Sun represents all the men in his life, the Moon all the women."

"And when does this happen?"

"It's already happening. The Sun conjunct the seventh house cusp really lights up this house of alliances, and his prestige will increase abroad as well as at home." The Cambodia adventure had already turned out well, and Nixon kept his promise to take out the troops.

"Regardless of the press," Kiyo said, "he's dedicated to keeping his word."

There was already evidence of a new Nixon image in the making. An article in *Show* magazine reported the conversion of liberal attorney Leonard Garment, who had voted against Nixon in 1960, and was now in his inner circle: "Garment, a Stevensonian Democrat, found his liberalism tested by Nixon's probity. Garment came to regard Nixon as a pragmatic liberal, a deep-seated Quaker, and a 'Victorian gentleman.' "

That, as Kiyo observed, was the Capricorn dully shining through.

"We should all be thankful for a Capricorn who will fight for an orderly society," she said.

But the President's Aquarian nature was featured in his progressions. "It shows Nixon's upswing in so many different ways. The progressed Venus in his natal chart is entering Taurus, a definite improvement from its fall in Aries, and will trine Jupiter, a marvelous aspect for making friends and influencing people."

In an ordinary man this aspect would normally affect his love life. But a President's love affair is with the country.

"Since he is President, you would say that his public would come to appreciate him more."

Not only was his progressed Venus in its element in Taurus, which it rules, balancing Capricorn's Saturnine quality, but it trined his natal Mercury, indicating that his appeal for the young would progress with his progressions. "Venus and Mercury represent the younger strata," Kiyo pointed out, "Jupiter and Saturn the older, which he relates to easily because of Saturn ruling Capricorn and his Jupiter in Capricorn. He sees increasingly the importance of relating to the young, and also to the women, with that transiting Uranus trine the Moon coming up. And that favorably progressed Venus-Mercury trine, improving his communication, will yet win these groups over."

In 1971, his progressed Jupiter would trine his ascendant Virgo, the sign of public service, and his public stature would increase. Jupiter meanwhile was favorably sextiled to his Part of Fortune, and his outlook would become more optimistic. Reflecting his own soaring Jovian spirits and his amiable good will, the public would begin to think of him as their leader and friend.

I regarded Kiyo doubtfully.

"He would have to end the war in Vietnam to cut into youth's ranks."

Kiyo examined the progressed chart.

"He could very well do that since he will be enjoying what is for him an unprecedented popularity."

But it will not all be smooth sailing. In crucial 1972, an election year, his progressed Venus, in two degrees Taurus, would square his natal Uranus, creating unexpected problems personally and otherwise. "Uranus rules his sixth house, so strong labor factions will show their displeasure at this time, and his own health won't be at its best. He may have nervous problems. Since Uranus, affecting the nervous system, is in the sixth house of health he's prone to nervousness anyway, and the Venus square, while not heavy, will bring additional complications."

While he might be annoyed with insubordination, even internal disloyalty, it would not upset his equilibrium.

"Progressed Venus conjunct the ninth house of communication spells out better publicity, broadening travel, and a good period for campaigning."

Kiyo was constantly going around the same mulberry bush.

"One way or another, you keep saying that he will be re-elected," I said.

She frowned. "1972 will be a year of crises. But progressed Mercury conjunct his north node will make communication solid with the country."

To check out her progressions she moved momentarily to transiting planets. "Transiting Uranus in Libra will soon trine his natal Moon and midheaven, and happily stay with him for another five years, and then in 1975 will trine his Pluto in the tenth house of repute, touching off a new unexpected wave of mass appeal."

Transiting Pluto was moving in Nixon's favor, too. Now in the last degrees of Virgo, it would have squared his natal Pluto in 28 degrees of Gemini in the tenth house by 1972, and also his natal Mars and Mercury.

"It's an activating factor," Kiyo said, "since a Capricorn can take squares, oppositions and conjunctions with far less crises than other signs because of his tough Saturnian nature."

Nixon's progressed Jupiter, moving closer to his Sun, would conjunct it in 1972, forming a harmonious aspect favorable to his fortunes.

Alarmists were already predicting so much street turmoil in 1972 that it might preclude the elections.

"There will be turmoil," Kiyo agreed, "but there will be an election, and Nixon's aspects will be better than when he was barely elected in 1968."

The transiting planets for 1972 clearly revealed civil disturbances. "Mars conjunct Uranus, a rather explosive aspect, at 20 degrees Libra, will upset the nation's balance. However, it will trine Saturn, so the discord will not get out of hand. Still this explosive conjunction will square the north node, which affects the emotional health of the nation, so people will be quite disturbed by November of 1972."

As a careful astrologer, Kiyo also used the Declaration of Independence Chart–July 4, 1776, Sagittarius rising–to check out Nixon's progress, the country's financial picture, and the general domestic and international situation.

Curiously, said Kiyo, this didn't alter things much, whether the July 4 chart was Gemini rising or its opposite, Sagittarius, as the President's life was inextricably interwoven with his opposite number, the country. "The country is not only his seventh house partner," Kiyo pointed out, "but his first house, for he represents the country. His second house is really the country's money, as is the eighth, which is other people's. The President of the United States, particularly in crisis, has no aspects not similarly shared by the country, and vice-versa."

In progressing the country's chart, a showdown between the old and the new was clearly in the offing in 1972. "Transiting Mars at 14 degrees Libra conjoining natal Saturn in the tenth house of the Establishment may bring the new and the older generations to a head-on clash," Kiyo said, "Mars representing the younger people, Saturn the older in this confrontation."

But Nixon, like Cicero of old, would act boldly and firmly. "The country's Mars aspect at 20 Libra will almost exactly square his natal Sun in 19:23 degrees Capricorn, uniting with the destiny pattern of his own Sun. In crisis, Capricorns have a way of showing unexpected strength, carrying a load which would break ordinary men. And with his Sun there, Nixon will have the vitality to handle the unexpected."

The progressions in the nation's chart, brought up to that date, July 1970, were soon successfully put to the test.

"The progressed Sun in 24 degrees Capricorn squaring the natal Mercury in the eighth house shows a breakdown in general communication," Kiyo had said. "Also, problems in the post office. The public is not long going to swallow the ridiculous cost and poor output of the mails."

Soon afterwards, in August 1970, the Nixon administration announced sweeping postal reforms, and Nixon, in an unprecedented move, set up an independent eleven-man board to supervise an agency long misused as a political plum.

While Nixon was making an effort to balance an economy partly thrown out of whack by de-escalation in Vietnam, there was no prospect of any real upturn in 1970, not with the nation's progressed Sun squaring the eighth house of other people's money.

But there was reason for cautious optimism. "The country's progressed Uranus retrogrades to 7 degrees of Gemini," said Kiyo, "and makes an exact sextile to the north node in that eighth money house so we won't go into a total depression."

The war in Vietnam would drag on through 1970, but in 1971 things would begin to happen, reflected by a change in the overseas image of the Ugly American. "Progressed Neptune on the U.S. midheaven shows our honor isn't quite as whistle clean as we'd like it to be. However, Neptune is approaching a nice trine to the progressed Pluto and the national image will improve abroad in 1971."

While Kiyo's contention that Nixon liked young people didn't sit well with the young, there was non-astrological evidence to support her view. Nixon's youth brigade featured a group of Washington advisers such as no President had ever had before. Their ages ranged from 22 to 29, and they were free to say whatever they thought. And their views often conflicted with the Administration's. But Nixon didn't seem to mind.

Always careful to distinguish between the majority of orderly open-minded students and a lawless minority, Nixon had tagged the current college-agers the brightest of generations, and he was obviously sympathetic to attacks on an impersonal, cookie-cutter type of education which unimaginative college administrators had foisted on students.

"There is a strong possibility," said Kiyo, "that the government will start subsidizing cultural improvement of the young. Mars rules the fifth house cusp of Aries in this Sagittarius-rising U.S. chart, specifically the school-going generation. And Mars, conjoining the teacher Saturn in Libra, which is influenced by Venus, affects the artistic and cultural.

"Saturn, on the other hand, rules the U.S. second house money cusp, Capricorn, so the White House, expressed by Saturn, will scrape together funds for these cultural improvements. The young people really want to be individuals, and Nixon knows this only too well from his own struggle to express himself."

In the end, as the nation's progressed chart showed, it would all turn out well, with special interest groups, the richly privileged and the clamoring minorities putting the unity of the nation first.

"The progressed Moon in Aries, the mood of people, will square the progressed Sun, bringing the Aries qualities of initiative and aggressiveness into sharp focus, with resulting release of strong energy forces. There will be such excesses that people will realize there must be a common responsibility toward the country if it is to be preserved."

"Where do you see this sudden awareness of responsibility?" I asked.

"Nixon will make people see it. That progressed Venus trine natal Jupiter in Nixon's chart shows he has the solution."

She had not yet flatly predicted Nixon's re-election or an end to Vietnam.

"I saw Nixon's popularity surging in 1971, our popular image improving abroad, and Nixon leading the country through a 1972 crisis, with his popularity peaking in 1975."

I would have liked her to be more definite.

"Not without the charts for candidates we don't know yet." She smiled. "However, it's reasonably sure. Even Mrs. Nixon's chart shows it."

"Mrs. Nixon's?"

"As Nixon goes, so goes Mrs. Nixon."

"And how does Mrs. Nixon go?"

The President's wife is a Pisces, born March 17, 1913, in Eli, Nevada. Without the precise birth hour Kiyo set up a solar chart, not as definitive as a natal chart, effective for progressions.

She promptly progressed Mrs. Nixon's planets to 1972. The progressed chart was loaded with benefics. Pat's progressed Jupiter in mid-Capricorn in her midheaven of reputation would then be in opposition to her natal Moon in Cancer. Progressed Venus would sextile her natal Sun, and progressed Mercury would trine her transiting Jupiter in November 1972–election time.

"Socially," said Kiyo, "she will be up there, stronger than ever, and in Washington nobody's so out of the swim as yesterday's First Lady –particularly a Nixon."

Mrs. Richard Nixon

March 17, 1913

Eli, Nevada

Solar Chart

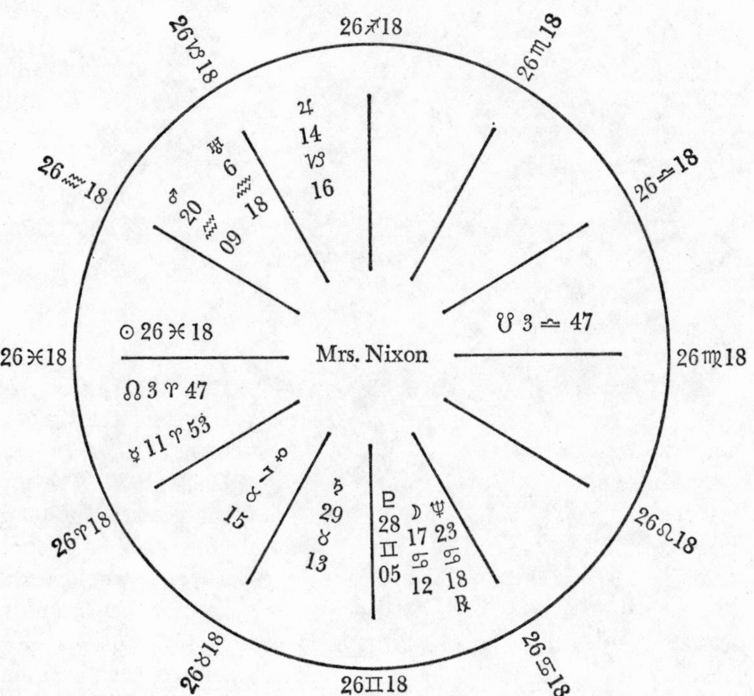

15

A Time to Invest—and to Gamble

Mrs. Estella Piffl, a motherly looking septuagenarian, looked at her husband across the breakfast table, and said quietly:

"Henry, you had better sell your stocks."

Henry Piffl, a practical man, laughed good-naturedly. "That's your astrology again."

His wife said mildly, "Saturn will be going into Taurus in a few weeks, in April of 1969, and Saturn represents restriction and loss. Taurus is the money sign, so the result is obvious, particularly with other aspects being what they are."

Henry Piffl protested, "You really don't expect me to sell because of Saturn, do you?"

"Not only that," his astrologer wife put in, "but in December of '69, Saturn in the second house will form an opposition to Jupiter, the planet of plenty, in the eighth house of other people's money, and the ensuing conflict between these planets will only serve to accelerate the decline."

That day Henry laughingly passed on his wife's forecast to his Los Angeles business associates, and they had a good laugh, too.

"Poor Henry," they said.

When the market began its decline in the Spring of 1969, after having touched the heights, ordinary investors could not believe it. And as the decline deepened, into the Fall and the Spring and Summer of

1970, the recession was on. Money became tight, interest rates went up, buying power slumped and the market was a pale shadow of its onetime self.

When, if ever, would it pick up?

Estella Piffl, peering into her charts, didn't see any real upturn until after 1972, and even then she saw a highly selective market. However, there was hope for an upturn before that, with restrictive Saturn moving out of Taurus in June of 1971. With the Saturn-Jupiter opposition ending even before that, in January 1971, when Jupiter moved from Scorpio into Sagittarius, the market did noticeably spurt, but new aspects, astrologer Piffl found, would serve to keep the market strength specialized through 1972.

Much as Kiyo had done for a projection of the political scene, Estella Piffl put the transiting planets in the U.S.'s chart to project the national economy.

Using the Gemini rising chart, she found Pluto hovering over Neptune, the planet of illusion, in the fifth house of speculation, and Neptune was square Mars, indicating a lot of activity without much happening.

Other astrologers were not as bearish. David Williams, the engineer turned astrologer, foresaw a market upturn in the last six months of 1971—Saturn having moved from Taurus into Gemini—with the advance extending into the first three months of 1972. That was as far as he had calculated ahead.

Williams had gone deeply into market cycles. As a specialist on economic trends, in a prediction of a Nixon victory and a recession published in *This Week* magazine just before the 1968 election, he pinpointed the decline for March-April 1969.

For Wall Streeters, Williams issues a quarterly market forecast, based on the Washington, D.C., chart, using the shorter planetary cycles of Mercury, Venus and Mars to reflect spasmodic movements in the market. The heavy planets seem to better reflect general business trends, as shown in Jupiter-Uranus aspects over the years. "There have been fifteen conjunctions of the two planets in the same degree of celestial longitude since 1761 and on thirteen occasions they coincided with a declining economy," Williams pointed out.

Ironically, Williams erred on a market forecast for the first quarter of 1970 by predicting an upturn in the face of the Jupiter-Saturn opposition in Taurus that he had originally called attention to.

But in his explanation of his miscue, others saw the validity of his major premise.

"The only other Jupiter-Saturn opposition in Taurus in this century occurred in 1911 and the Dow-Jones average dropped only 16 per cent, whereas in the current aspect (beginning in 1969), it dropped 21½ per cent."

Practicing what he preached, Williams showed a substantial profit over an eleven-year period, with 207 successful stock transactions out of 210.

"It was not done with mirrors, but with stars," he said.

Williams bases his confidence in the planets on the impact they appeared to have on earthlings. Or as *The Wall Street Journal* once summarized: "Mr. Williams believes that Jupiter, Saturn and Uranus, depending on their positions relative to the Sun and each other, exert either a stabilizing or an upsetting influence on interplanetary magnetic fields. When they are grouped around the sun in a roughly triangular configuration (trines), he says, their magnetic fields tend to create harmonious conditions. But when two or more planets line up in a straight line with the Sun (conjunctions or oppositions), inharmonious conditions result. These conditions affect the earth's magnetic field, says Mr. Williams, and in turn the magnetic fields which surround individuals. These magnetic disturbances, he claims, affect business confidence."

Why then, if astrology is a science, isn't it used more to make money with? The answer, of course, is that it is, when the astrologer reads the chart correctly. Such financial giants as the Morgans, Vanderbilts, and railroad builder James J. Hill profited enormously through Evangeline Adams' advice. The late J. P. Morgan not only had his chart done regularly, but subscribed to an Adams market service.

Crowed Miss Adams: "No further proof of his interest in the *science* is required beyond the fact that he renewed this service from year to year."

Evangeline Adams classified market speculation as a game of chance, pointing out that if the aspects were favorable the subject would as likely win at dice.

"When a man comes to me for advice on the stock market," she said, "I find out first of all whether the stars indicate that he's likely to be fortunate in speculative transactions. If he is, I tell him the periods that ought to be most propitious for such operations and the kinds of stock in which he is likely to be most successful."

Some astrologers evaluate not only trends but individual stocks. Peggy Reynolds, a New York City astrologer, is a Wall Street specialist, charting corporations from the day of inception to determine their market prospects. Her wide clientele includes brokers who occasionally use code names to cloak their identity.

Similarly, David Williams has appraised specific stocks, charting a company as if it were a person. At the request of a speculator, Williams recently plotted the chart of a popular favorite, the Fairchild Camera and Instrument Company, which specializes in aerial photography. This company was organized February 9, 1920, reorganized in Delaware on November 23, 1927, its astrological birth date.

"At the time this Company was incorporated, and thus became a living entity," he said, "the Sun, which represents the Company, its organization, management and aims, was in Sagittarius, ruled by the planet Jupiter. Jupiter therefore becomes the planetary ruler of the Company. Since the Sun was in a favorable relationship to Uranus—the planet of originality, new ideas, invention and big business—the indications were that the Company would be successful in a highly original and scientific field.

"The Company's ruling planet, Jupiter, which represents the money-making possibilities of the Company, was in a very favorable relationship with Mars, the planet of energy, and Uranus. This strengthened the indications that the Company would be successful in a scientific field, and also indicated that the Company's stock would be very active and increase in price.

"The Moon, which represents the public and the attitude of people toward the Company's products or services, although unfavorably related to Pluto, the planet of the masses, was favorably related to Mercury, the planet of communications, which also represents the mental, scientific and commercial ability of the Management. Mercury was also in favorable relationship to Pluto. Hence, the technically and scientifically oriented public would be favorably inclined toward the Company's products and services, while the masses would not."

Williams then summarized: "The planetary pattern at the time this Company was incorporated indicated that its growth would be slow and that the price of its stock would rise. The Company consequently became a leader in the manufacture of highly sophisticated precision instruments and optical products for specialized applications. But it did not do as well in the mass retail market with semiconductors, a relatively new product designed to replace electronic tubes."

Fairchild was traditionally a volatile stock. Around the $3–$4 level between 1948–58, it increased twenty-fold from 1958 to 1960, slipped to a low of 14 in 1964, then hit a high of 144 in 1966.

In 1969 the wild gyrations continued. The stock was 57 in July, and 102 in October.

"The 1969 low," explained Williams, "was due to the downward pull of the transiting Jupiter-Uranus conjunction (0 degrees) of July 20, 1969 (occurring once every twenty years), which opposed (180 degrees) the natal Jupiter-Uranus conjunction. The 1969 high was due to the upward pull of the Mars-Pluto trine (120 degrees) of October 30, 1969, which occurs only once every two years. This stimulated the trine (120 degrees) between natal Mars and natal Jupiter-Uranus."

Williams' 1970 forecast for Fairchild was already history. "There will be two major low spots," Williams predicted at the start of 1970. "One will occur on March 9, 1970, due to the Jupiter-Saturn opposition (the company ruled by Jupiter of course), but this should provide a favorable buying opportunity since transiting Jupiter would be 30 degrees from the Sun."

The second low spot was November 18, 1970. "This will be due," Williams said, "to a recurrence of the unfavorable Jupiter-Saturn opposition, but this will again provide a favorable buying opportunity, since transiting Jupiter will be conjunct natal Mercury-Mars."

On March 9, 1970 Fairchild traded at 76, down from the previous October high of 102. This could have been a favorable buying opportunity if one then sold promptly, for the stock hit 82 on March 31 then fell off rapidly until in November it was around the 20 mark.

As others who have played the market, I have found other speculation less painful. In an area that is frankly gambling, in the sports arena, astrologers confidently specialize in boxing, football, racing, and other contests. The late Llewellyn George prided himself on picking the winners of the annual Rose Bowl football games, always played on January 1, at the same hour, and in the same place, Pasadena. In his A to Z Horoscope Maker and Delineator, he observed, "The outcome of every game invariably concurs with the indications of the planets placed in this permanent (house) cusps chart."

Llewellyn also mapped the races successfully. One afternoon at Del Mar, near Los Angeles, the Sun was square Uranus, pointing to an upset. "The Moon was also sextile Venus within the hour of the race under consideration (the second), which suggested amorous connotations in the winner's name. Mars was on the descendant again, maturing a trine aspect to Jupiter in the tenth house. Such a circumstance implied that the longshot winner would have both Venusian and Martian characteristics in his name."

And sure enough: "A glance at the program revealed that Love's Arrow fitted the circumstances. Love's Arrow galloped to win with little effort, despite high odds."

Even more so than Llewellyn George, the contemporary astrologer Sydney Omarr, a former amateur boxer himself, has dramatically shown an uncanny ability to pick the winners in professional fights. As a youngster in Philadephia, Omarr, a self-schooled astrologer, picked 25 fights correctly before he went off on the 26th.

Philadelphia sportswriters joshed the teen-age astrologer but went along with his picks, and even the fighters were sufficiently impressed to be elated or deflated, as the prediction went. On one occasion lightweight champion Bob Montgomery, before a title bout with Beau Jack, cornered the stripling astrologer and demanded to know the outcome. Fortunately for Omarr, perhaps, the stars smiled on Montgomery, as one journalist humorously reported:

"Beau Jack's Aquarius will be rising, whatever that means, and Omarr says that ain't good. Montgomery will be ruled by Jupiter and the Moon and that is very copasetic. Mars also will rule Bob that night and that's the God of War, and with that gentleman on Montgomery's side, says Omarr, Beau Jack should have stood, instead of in the Garden ring, someplace else."

Subsequently, Omarr picked Montgomery to beat top contender

Fritzie Zivic of the fighting Pittsburgh Zivics. Zivic read about it in the papers, and told a Philadelphia sportswriter:

"Who is this Zombie they call Omarr who picks those fights by looking at the stars? They better lock that guy up. If I can find where he's sitting, I'll knock Montgomery right in his lap."

Zivic was justifiably indignant. "Imagine him saying I'm going to lose because I'm going into the fifth house. I don't have any fifth house, or even a fourth house. All I got is one house, and that one cost me thirty grand."

PS: Zivic lost the fight.

Joe Louis was probably the first fighter since the ancient gladiators of Rome to have his capabilities analyzed before a fight by a major astrologer.

"In his quiet, determined way," Omarr related, "as shown by the Sun-Mercury conjunction in Taurus in his solar chart, Joe has plodded on, meeting and overcoming obstacles. The Taurus emphasis can be seen in his thick neck and powerful shoulders. Joe takes a punch so well because of the development of his neck. Blows which would knock out an ordinary warrior resound off the Louis jaw, often failing even to jar him. His coordination and great will power are emphasized by the Sun-Mercury trine to his Moon in Capricorn (the ruthless Moon), in the eighth sector of his chart."

As a fight buff, Omarr was perhaps even more concerned than astrologer Doris Doane with the aspects governing the great champion's fighting equipment. "Venus, his ruling planet, is in Gemini in conjunction with Saturn in the first house. It is trine Jupiter and Uranus in Aquarius in the ninth. Gemini has rule over the hands and Joe's dynamite-laden fists were responsible for his sensational rise to the top of the boxing world."

There was no mystery about Omarr's early success as a seer. Actually, it was based on the planets, Sun, and the Moon, and his confidence in the elementary principles of astrology. As he seldom had a fighter's correct hour of birth, Omarr invariably set up a solar chart, the fighter's birth date becoming the degree of the ascendant, as the Sun sign represented the first house cusp. If, for instance, the fighter was born on August 5, he had 13 degrees of Leo on his ascendant, with each succeeding house cusp—Virgo, Libra, etc.—also having 13 degrees. The transiting planets for the day of the event, taken from the ephemeris, were then placed in the zodiacal wheel. Although all aspects were considered, the position of the transiting Moon in the chart was of paramount importance, as the Moon relates to public contests. "If the Moon apparently was going from the seventh house to the tenth," Omarr said, "then the fighter was in a strong position to win. If it was going from the first to the fourth, in the lower part of the chart, it seemed that he was not going to be utilizing the best of his abilities."

In his infancy as an astrologer, Omarr was content to work with a Moon which gave him 25 winners in a row. "I wanted results," he said, "and I found that when the Moon was heading for the tenth house, the Midheaven, the career house, that was it, while from the first to the fourth the fighter seemed subdued."

Later, as a famous astrologer, he subscribed to astrologer Carl Payne Tobey's concept of high and low lunar cycles.

Tobey, one of astrology's great innovators, had postulated that when the transiting Moon was in the subject's Sun sign, his cycle was high because judgment and intuition were at its peak. The Moon opposite the Sun conversely produced a low lunar cycle, a loser. Omarr found this worked out very well, but he still had winners whose lunar cycle was low. "The only way I could explain it, as I looked back," he said, "is that in public contests between boxers, when the winner had a low lunar cycle, the Moon was always in the seventh house of the public, which meant that he had the public favor. And as a youngster, it seemed to mean that public acclaim was generally synonymous with a winner."

In Los Angeles a few years ago, Omarr made his biggest betting coup before a crowded pressbox at the Santa Anita racetrack. Omarr, besides functioning as an astrologer, was a news editor for CBS radio in Los Angeles. Transferred at his own request to the station's sports desk, his Leo pride was wounded when his credentials as a sports reporter were challenged by superiors. With Leo assurance, he announced that he knew enough about the races to beat them.

His superiors laughed.

On a Saturday, an off-day from his job, Omarr attended the harness races. Carefully, he mapped a typical event chart for the first two races, the daily double, in which post time became the ascendant. Again, the Moon figured in Omarr's calculations. The Moon was in

Taurus at that time, and Taurus was ruled by Venus. From prominence of Venus, along with other factors in the chart, which he did not care to disclose, he concluded there would be a lush prize, the result of an upset. And so he selected the highest-priced longshots in each race.

The following Monday he marched into Station KNX (the CBS affiliate) and waved a ten dollar parimutuel ticket, as yet uncashed, under the nose of sports director Pat McGurk. It was worth $3,200, one of the largest payoffs in Santa Anita harness history.

A week later, to show it was no fluke, Omarr again visited Santa Anita, picking six out of eight races, with an associate from CBS at his elbow.

On this track record, I was anxious not only to test Omarr's methods, but, hopefully, to profit by them.

We had to wait for the most favorable auspices. Curiously, the Moon was at this time in Taurus, when Omarr had made his greatest triumph, but this wasn't a constant. He had discovered, through trial and error, that he had his best luck, speculatively, when the transiting Moon was in Aquarius, where he had natal Jupiter in his fifth house of speculation, in opposition to his Sun sign, Leo. And so we had to wait nearly three weeks for the Moon to get to Aquarius.

My astrology teacher Ralph Winters was not optimistic about my chances.

"It's good for him," he said, "but you'll lose."

"Why?" I asked.

"Because the Moon in Aquarius will be square your sign, Taurus."

"But suppose I pick the same horses."

"You won't."

"I am determined to."

Winters smiled. "Something will change your mind, transiting Saturn in Taurus square the Moon will have the last word."

Our long-delayed tour to Santa Anita took place on Wednesday, March 4, 1970. The Sun was in Pisces, and so at sunrise, the ascendant would be in Pisces, advancing into a new sign every two hours.

When I picked Omarr up in his Hollywood hills home, he wore a solemn expression.

"Did you pick up the racing forms?" I asked.

"The Moon," he said, "entered Aquarius at 6:36 A.M. today."

"Who do you like for the double?"

"At post time, it will be only five degrees in Aquarius."

It would be in Aquarius all day, staying, as it did, in the same sign for two and a half days.

He cast his eyes over the entries for the first race. "At 1 P.M., with Cancer coming up on the eastern horizon, the ascendant will be in approximately sixteen degrees of Cancer. The Moon is in the sign of the unusual (Aquarius is ruled by upsetting Uranus). We should have some reversal of form here."

"What does that mean?" I asked.

"There'll be an upset."

"Do the horses know about that?"

He gave me a patient look. "Obviously, you don't understand how it works."

"I thought the fastest horses, with the best jockey, usually won."

"But what makes him the fastest? That's the imponderable."

By this time we had arrived at the track and headed for a table at the rail, which Omarr had prudently reserved. Pluto, signifying crowds, was badly aspected.

Somehow out of the twelve-horse card, he managed to pick a nag with the unlikely monicker, Sonapanoma. It had finished tenth by eleven lengths the last time out, and sixth before that. It didn't seem a good bet to finish, let alone win.

"Where did you find him?" I asked.

"As I said, we must look for the unusual, an upset."

There was still time to bet the daily double, a winning combination of the first two races.

Omarr studied the second half of the double. "Wayne Harris, the jockey on Twelve Noon, is a Cancer, and Cancer will still be rising at post time."

This was readily computed from the fact that the sun rose in about twelve degrees of Pisces that day and that every two hours the ascendant progressed to the following sign.

"Suppose another jockey is also a Cancer, on a Cancer horse?" I asked.

Omarr nodded. "To do it properly, you'd need the chart of every trainer, jockey and horse. But that's impractical, so we do the best we can."

Sonapanoma I could not see and drifted to Lightning Sands, who at least reminded me I lived on the beach.

The first race, six furlongs, was close, with Lightning Sands helping to bring up the rear. The winner was an unlikely horse named Sonapanoma. It paid eight to one.

Omarr still needed the second race to collect his double. He had backed up his double with a place bet on Twelve Noon, at 12 to 1. I fastened on a horse named Gainsterne, an obvious choice.

Go-Annie-Go, completely ignored, romped home trailed by Twelve Noon and Gainsterne. Omarr was nosed out of the double, but had two winners in two races. Twelve Noon paid $11.40 to place.

The third race was off at 2:03 P.M., with 25 degrees Cancer on the ascendant. Omarr looked at the chart critically. "It's too bad we don't have the birth signs of all the jockeys, but we do know that the Moon which rules public contests is in the seventh house—the house of partnerships."

Omarr was undecided over two horses, Delightful Debut and Loyal Subject, both favorites, which, he said, had nothing to do with his selection.

"Are they sprinters?" I asked.

"That doesn't matter, either."

"Then what matters?"

He cocked a judicial eye at the racing form. "Loyalty is a Cancer quality. It also represents the parents, in the natural fourth house, who in this case—Delightful Debut—are trying to get their daughter off their hands, typical of the last degrees of Cancer."

He bet Delightful Debut, win and place, and took another ticket on Loyal Subject.

Unimpressed, I stayed out of this one.

Loyal Subject breezed home, with Delightful Debut second. Wayne Harris, the Cancer, brought in the third horse.

I gave Omarr a quizzical look. "Are you sure you didn't have this all figured out before you got out here?"

"I'm not doing that well," said this Leo, "I only have four out of four."

The ascendant or horizon of the chart was now beginning its ascent through the sign of Leo, and at 2:34, post time for the fourth race, was well along into this royal sign.

There were twelve horses in the race, but Omarr had eyes for two: Tall Duke and New Empire. "Tall Duke is a little more specific," he said.

"But Dukes aren't necessarily royal," I remonstrated.

"The Duke of Edinburgh is, and he's the only Duke I can think of."

The handicappers, picking off form, liked Where's the Action, and so did I.

Where's the Action finished fifth. Tall Duke won and paid five to one.

I shook my head. "Winters told me I'd lose with Aquarius squaring Taurus."

The ascendant was still in Leo in the fifth race. My eye ran down the chart and stopped at Very Noble.

"There's a winner, à la Omarr," I said.

He shook his head.

"I like Bold Delight."

"How do you figure that?"

"Leo is bold, enterprising. And have you noticed the jockey's name? Wellington. He was some kind of royalty."

"He was a Duke."

"There you are."

"But he wasn't royalty."

"But he ran things."

"Yes, he beat Napoleon at Waterloo."

"There you are," Omarr said triumphantly. "He's worth a ten spot."

As he ankled off to make his bet, I looked up to catch the eye of a middle-aged lady at a neighboring table.

"I couldn't help but overhear the conversation," she smiled. "Are you psychiatrists?"

"More like psychos," I said.

She nodded understandingly. "I had a husband like that. He finally disappeared."

Omarr returned with his ticket as the horses broke from the gate. Very Noble was the favorite, and I had gone to him, convinced that he was more royal than Bold Delight. It was hardly a contest. One horse took the lead and held it. But I didn't understand why Omarr was so pleased. Bold Delight only paid four to one.

The sixth race was for five year olds, a mile and a sixteenth. Leo was still on the ascendant. "Don't bet a favorite," Omarr said, "the winner won't be in the public favor." His eye traveled down the list of twelve horses. "With Leo, the sign of royalty, still rising, there is Royal Dude to consider."

"It is also the sign of the Sun," I said wisely.

"Yes," he nodded. "Sunny Corral would qualify."

Both were long shots.

"How about Honey Car?" I asked.

He frowned. "How does that figure?"

"He's got Shoemaker on him."

"Oh, that," he dismissed my suggestion with a wave of his hand.

"How about Leon's Alibi?" I countered. "That's close to Leo the Lion?"

His nose wrinkled in disgust. "That's the favorite, and the aspects are similar to the first race, where an upset was in order."

This race was giving the astrologer more trouble than any so far. He finally checked his watch nervously. "You better make the bets," he said, giving me $10 to bet on Royal Dude and $10 for Betty's Envoy, which had the advantage of being a long shot.

"I like Sunny Corral myself," I said.

"Why is that?"

"You got the Sun of Leo rising, and the confinement, the corral, with the Moon in the sixth house." (The Moon in Aquarius would now be dropping to oppose the Leo ascendant.)

"Wayne Harris is riding again," he said, "a horse named Pintore."

"So what's with him?"

"Well, the Moon's in the sixth house, and it rules Cancer, and Harris is a Cancer, and this is the sixth race."

"That's really stretching it. Now Sunny Corral answers all requirements."

He nodded, approving. "You're getting to be quite an astrologer."

I stood impotently at the end of a long line, inching toward the betting window, and just as the man ahead placed his bet, the buzzer ending the betting resounded. I had been shut out. With a sure winner, Sunny Corral, who fit all the astrological qualifications and was 22 to one besides, I had been unable to get my bet down.

I gave Omarr his money back.

He shrugged. "It's just as well," he said. "I felt funny not going to Harris."

It was the first race we didn't have a bet down, but it didn't seem to affect the horses. They took off in the usual manner.

Sunny Corral opened strong, but couldn't get up there. Royal Dude seemed to be carrying a staggering burden. Pintore took an early lead, and managed to nose out Shoemaker with Honey Car.

Omarr's reaction was the same as that of every horse player I had ever known. "I should have had him," he growled.

"Be content. Even when you pick the losers, you don't lose."

He smiled. "That's my Moon in Aquarius."

By this time I was disposed to leave. But Omarr prevailed on me to stay for one more race.

As I checked over the eight horses, Tralee Rose seemed to evoke hazy memories of happier days, but it was a favorite, and Omarr wasn't interested.

"Not in the last race," he protested. "We must be sporting."

I reminded him that I hadn't won a race.

"You don't use astrology," he said.

"You've been lucky," said I.

He sighed. "I've explained it astrologically every inch of the way."

"Well, explain again."

He had perused the list of selections briefly.

"Don't you ever check the past performances and times?" I asked.

He shrugged. "What for?" He cocked an eye at the big electric board. "Let's see, post time is 4:04 P.M., the last degrees of Leo, which rules the fifth house. This house, as you know, governs children, speculative matters, celebrations, and love affairs." His eye lit up.

"Now Belle Mere seems to fit the bill."

"Beautiful Mother."

"With Leo in its declining degrees, we no longer have a beautiful young girl, a child. She has grown up."

"That's really stretching it."

"I'm betting it across the board–win, show and place."

"I'm going to Tralee Rose."

He sniffed. "I never bet favorites," said he, making it seem like something unworthy.

"All right, I'll go to Shoemaker." This winningest jockey was aboard a nag named Sisal.

It was a stirring race, with Tralee Rose taking the lead, naturally, and not once relinquishing it. For place, the second spot, a photo finish was announced, between Belle Mere, who had closed fast at nine to one, and Center Balcony, the Duke of Wellington aboard. The Omarr luck had apparently failed for the first time that day. The numbers went up—Center Balcony, place, Belle Mere, show. Apparently the beautiful mother hadn't grown up fast enough.

But Omarr did some rapid calculating. He had bet fifty dollars across the board, getting back $6.20 for every two-dollar show ticket. Somehow, he managed to win on that race, too. And I of course lost again.

Omarr gave me a quizzical look. "The ascendant is no longer Leo, so we may as well leave—I've had it."

"You've had it?" I said. "I haven't had a winner all day."

Omarr smiled happily. "I guess Ralph Winters was right after all about your Taurus Sun squaring the Moon in Aquarius."

16

A Time Past and Future

In the late summer of 1970, as the planet Neptune hovered between sensuous Scorpio and spiritual Sagittarius, the era of incredible vulgarity appeared on the way out. In a spirit of revulsion, audiences throughout the country were finally walking out on filthy movies, sold out only a few months before, and a secret Hollywood survey revealed, incredibly, that salacious sex movies were everywhere losing money. For 14 long years, the planet ruling movies, television, drugs and the impressionable subconscious had been colored by the sign that so often reflected the depraved, and now its reign was hopefully at an end. But Neptune in Scorpio, marking the time of the ugly, the unkempt, the unwashed, the floaters, the drug-ridden, the lewd and the lascivious, was not to give up without a last gasp. In September 1970, newspapers were still full of ads for nude shows, stag shows, whip girls, anything pornographic that would draw a few dirty dollars through the turnstiles. "Myra Breckinridge" and "Beyond the Valley of the Dolls" were still making the motion picture circuit, television comedians were putting out sly innuendos on the late shows, and books frankly about sex were skimming the best-seller lists.

But if the astrologers were right in foreshadowing the spiritual trend starting in November 1970, when Neptune went firmly into Sagittarius to begin its 14-year passage through the sign of higher knowledge, then it was time at last for Harold Robbins, Jacqueline

Susann, producer Joe Levine, and the rest of the pornographers to get into something else.

It had been a painful cycle for many, beginning with the rise of the girlie magazines and a Supreme Court that drew no line on obscenity. Not since the French Revolution had there been such pandering to the crude, lewd and debased in the name of a free society. And the college professor who made this discovery after delving into the history of the obscene was blissfully unaware that this revolutionary period was that beginning in 1787, when Neptune had made its last trip through Scorpio.

It was all part of a pattern as broad as the universe, and man was a part of it, reacting individually or en masse to the impact of planets that triggered earthquakes, floods, wars and depressions.

We were by no means islands unto ourselves, and Neptune's behavior was more important at times than that of the man next door, for all life meshed with the rhythm of the universe. "Studies such as those begun by [Professor] Adrian and continued by [Professor] Burr," said Professor Ellsworth Huntington of Yale, "indicate that the human body has its own electrical field. If that is the case, variations in the external electrical field must inevitably influence the internal human field. It is likewise obvious that, if the electrical field of the Sun or of the solar system as a whole undergoes variation, there must be corresponding disturbances in the field of the Earth. Thus, there is a logical connection between solar activity, the Earth's atmosphere, a man's psychological reactions, prices on the stock market, and the ups and downs of business."

The late John J. O'Neill, a science editor who set out to disprove astrology and wound up supporting it, once observed that celestial elements are not contained within themselves but reach out to produce effects seemingly at a distance. "When a heavenly body extends its influence through space to produce an effect at a distance, that realm through which it reaches is just as much a part of the body as that portion contained within the material part of the body. But if anything we do not see produces an effect, we are very much inclined to think of that effect as having something mysterious connected with it."

Neptune, though a seeming eternity away, was actually in our backyard. "Each of the planets has a gravitational field around it," said

O'Neill, "and they all extend throughout the solar system and are most intimately and internally related."

And so it was that working together or separately, in conjunction or opposition, squared or sextiled, Saturn, Neptune, Jupiter, Venus, Pluto, Mars, Mercury and Uranus had an effect on the Earth, with the distance of the planets having not the slightest effect on the power of their rays, which were as strong on reaching Earth, as Einstein said, as they were on leaving their planetary home.

And they reflected a pattern assigned to them from experience over the centuries. And so with Neptune in Scorpio, as in the past, there was a concerted move by the young to denigrate the intellect, resulting in the onslaught on the campuses, and the underground drive to get everything down to the lowest common denominator of achievement. And so, in 1956, with the merger of the two, planet and sign, was born what astrologer Ruth Oliver called the Age of the Ugly.

It was a simple astrological deduction. "Neptune is drugs, Scorpio sex and realism," observed astrologer Oliver. "The Neptune influence in Scorpio fostered the illusion the young were telling it like it was. But really they were bent on showing how ugly the world was, and so made themselves ugly, while not proving anything but their own ugliness. They cultivated externals, long, matted hair, sordid friends, weird clothes, or no clothes at all, while smoking their pot, swallowing their LSD and 'speed,' and telling one another, as they dreamed through their ugly movies and life, that they were sharing something wonderful. Their minds were so distorted they didn't realize how distorted they were, as they tried to tear down the very institutions preparing them for useful living."

Now, hopefully, Sagittarius would change all that, with the introduction of a truly spiritual climate for the next fourteen years.

Along with the spiritual, of course, there was always the mundane. For the United States, particularly, the future was specifically foreshadowed, what with some astrologers foreseeing Nixon ending the war in Vietnam and winning re-election, a spurt in the stock market in the last half of 1971 and well into 1972, but with no real boom until 1975 or 1976.

Looking ahead to 1980, it seemed safe for the first time in 140 years for a man to run for President of the United States at 20-year intervals. In succession, without exception, seven Presidents, beginning with William Harrison in 1841, had died in office after being elected at the time of a Saturn-Jupiter conjunction in an Earth sign. In 1981, an inaugural year, the death cycle would presumably become inoperative because the conjunction of these two great planets, occurring every 20 years, would occur in Libra, an air sign. The series began with the 1842 conjunction in Capricorn, its converging influence already noticed when Harrison succumbed months before. Lincoln (1860) was elected with the conjunction in Virgo; with Garfield (1880) it was in Taurus; McKinley (1900) Capricorn; with Harding (1920) Virgo; with Roosevelt (1940) Taurus; and in 1960, with Kennedy, Capricorn.

By the time Kennedy ran for the Presidency, the apparent coincidence was sufficiently publicized to come to his attention. With Gemini humor, Kennedy retorted he would be the first to "break the jinx."

To astrology it was no jinx or coincidence, but could be explained through the influence of the Saturn-Jupiter conjunction on the U.S. chart for July 4, 1776. Saturn ruled the U.S. eighth house of death, and co-ruled with Uranus the tenth house of the Presidency. Moreover, Saturn, unfavorably aspected, was square (90 degrees) Jupiter and Mars, the planet of violence. These aspects, according to astrologer David Williams, who had right after Kennedy's nomination predicted his death in office, established a high degree of vulnerability to the Jupiter-Saturn cycle in the U.S. Presidency.

The conjunction had not operated in a fire sign, Aries, in Monroe's administration in 1821, and so Williams concluded it was malefic for Presidents only in its Earth cycle.

Time would tell how right he was.

As a rule, the astrologers have not been as foreboding as the psychics, who have generally seen only disaster, from the washing of California into the sea to an Armageddon that would leave the world a smoldering ruin.

The planets brought a reassuring message of orderliness even in disorder. Uranus passing into Libra in 1968 for seven years would bring its changes in the marriage scheme, since Uranus had the quality of changing, and certainly changing a state of affairs where so many marriages ended in divorce and so many others seemed shallow could hardly be a disaster.

In 1971, Pluto, the planet of the masses, would pass from Virgo in Libra. It would conjoin with Uranus in the sign of balance to bring harmonious change to a labor picture previously fraught with disharmony when the planet of labor was in the sign of labor, and the labor unions after a struggle began to open to blacks for the first time.

Neptune in Sagittarius would help restore sanity to the street and the campus long before the planet's 14-year transit was over, bringing with it a spiritual quest affecting collegians as well as the general population. Catholicism would, for a time, have a rebirth with a new idealism, as would Protestant persuasions that keyed their message to the love and compassion of Christ rather than narrow secularism and separation.

Sagittarius was not only the sign of higher philosophy but of adventure, and so the noncompetitors, the dropouts, the druggies would give way to a spirit of adventure among the young. "With Neptune in Sagittarius," observed Ruth Oliver, "people will feel adventurous, enthusiastic, idealistic, once more striving to accomplish. It will be fashionable to be square again, though we won't go back to the unrealistic Joe College days. There will be an undertone of seriousness on the campuses, and students will again be there to learn and teachers to teach, a most refreshing change."

But all was not to be sweetness and light. For corrupting Neptune in Scorpio had not only brought moral stagnation contaminating the spirit, but had extended its pollution to the physical environment, the air, water and earth. It was to get worse before it got better, and astrologer Oliver foresaw a tragic dilemma if man didn't face up to reality.

"Scorpio (a water sign)," she warned, "is stagnant water and pollution and Neptune is the proliferating planet, so Neptune in Scorpio has brought this proliferation of pollution. And then as Uranus goes into Scorpio in 1974 for seven years, we will either do something concrete about this pollution, or find that in half of our cities the population will become seriously ill."

In 1984, for those still around, Pluto, the planet of overpopulation and regeneration, would move into Scorpio, staying through 1995. "And that," warned astrologer Oliver, "is when the planet will die if we don't take care of it."

With three major planets—Neptune the deceiver, Uranus the

awakener and Pluto the regenerator–going through Scorpio one after another, the last 50 years of the twentieth century have a Scorpionic cast. The prospect depends on how things are handled, for Scorpio, the ruler of the eighth house, is not only the sign of death but also of regeneration.

"With Uranus in Scorpio," the astrologer observed, "we have a chance to do something positive about the atmosphere. And we'll also have to do something about the kids who got hooked on dope with Neptune in Scorpio, for if they are not salvaged they will tend to drag down our society."

Through astrology, the career of whole generations could be followed. The flower children, the hippie generation, broadly affecting the middle strata of society with their thought and appearance, were born when Neptune, the planet of idealism (and confusion) was in Libra, the sign of beauty, balance, art and marriage. They wanted their unions to be perfect, and grew up thinking marriage a stricture, and so they lived with one another freely, begat children, and told themselves they were preserving the beauty of love.

"Turn back one cycle of the zodiac," said Ruth Oliver, "and you will find the freedom-loving poets Shelley and Byron born with Neptune in Libra. Think of how idealistic they were about marriage. Shelley said he didn't believe in it, and that people could only stay together as long as they loved each other."

As I recalled it, Shelley's wife was married, but he wasn't. And when he ran off with another woman, his wife committed suicide. But that wouldn't deter Neptune in Libra.

Uranus ducking into Libra in 1968 for seven years, was to undo Neptune's hazy idealism. "Uranus," the astrologer noted, "upsets whatever is going on, and so it will turn around what Neptune in Libra started. The young people will find that all this free love doesn't work, not as they get older, and start thinking in terms of a family and making a living."

All these planets had been in Libra before, and nothing had destroyed the institution of marriage, though it had been bent a little. Now with Pluto also moving into Libra in 1972, adding a regenerative factor, it would bring about a rebirth of this institution among this group. "They will have learned by this time that children do not grow up properly unless they have a mother and a father who stay together responsibly."

With Pluto, the planet of the masses, in Libra, there would be more balance in the international situation. At home there would be a redress of wrongs in the interest of justice, and a reappraisal of the excesses which had marred the labor and college scene. "What we've had with Pluto in Virgo," said Ruth Oliver, "was the dispossessed, the Negro, the Puerto Rican, the American Indian, the Mexican-American, all wanting to be a part of the mainstream of society, and part of that society, including labor, not wanting to let them in." But in the sign of balance, rather than that of the hypercritical, there would be an end to students being pushed into college whether qualified or not, and of the riots that developed out of their inability to cope and their contempt of a society that gave them something for nothing.

"It was not what do I earn by being worthy," observed astrologer Oliver, "but rather having the advantages without the work–that is what Pluto in Virgo brought us."

In their orderly rhythm above, the planets reflect an orderly pattern below that is presumably the consequence of a perfectly plausible reaction to the constant ebb and flow of humanity's excesses and needs. For by the time a jaded society had passed through fourteen years of Neptune in Scorpio, it was certainly ready for whatever the passage through Sagittarius had to offer.

So again there was the question of synchronicity, the planets serving as a timepiece of human behavior, or of direct causal impact as planets pass into certain signs, or aspect one another in some significant manner.

As Ruth Oliver pointed out, the Victorian Age began with the conjunction of Uranus and Neptune in conservative, authoritarian Capricorn in 1821, and when Queen Victoria ascended the English throne in 1838, and lent her name to it, the cycle became equated with prudish morals and dress. Capricorn qualities dominated, with respect for the state, one's elders and parents prevailing. But the Victorian era ended shortly after the Queen's death in 1901. Uranus, moving half as fast as Neptune through the zodiac, returned to Capricorn in 1905 to form an opposition to Neptune in Cancer, the sign of woman and the home, and the tables were turned with the beginning of the women's suffrage movement, and the beginning of a Uranian revolt leading to the sweeping away of nearly all the crowned heads of Europe.

Now for 1993, there was the promise of a new Victorian Age, with the re-forming after 171 years of the Uranus-Neptune conjunction in Capricorn. And it promised, as before, a swing away from permissiveness to a fresh respect for authority. And, with the woman tired by now of being a slave to her own freedom, the man, in Capricorn fashion, would resume his Saturn-ruled role as the head of the family.

As well as being an escape valve for American Presidents, the Jupiter-Saturn conjunction in a Libra air sign in 1981 would promote a livelier rapport among peoples, with a greater sense of international fair play and a declining nationalism. With Neptune's influence in Sagittarius increasingly felt, higher learning would reach a point where people would look back just a few years and wonder how we were so limited intellectually and spiritually at this time.

Before it reflected the Aquarian Age in 1966, the conjunction of Pluto and Uranus last appeared in 1850 when it stirred the industrial revolution and, in forming, had influenced the social revolutions of 1848. It has now given impetus to violent insurrection around the world. Occurring in the earth sign of Virgo, the conjunction promises to bring about a renewed assault, not only on outmoded social structures, but on the destructive forces which have upset man's harmonious relationship with his Earth.

And just as the violence will give way to Saturnian order, so will the pollution of the air and water be neutralized to bring about a Uranian victory for the good earth, in keeping with the regenerative aspect of Pluto.

Astrology was a universal language, limited only by our own limitations. If we could but understand all its subtle shades and nuances, what mysteries of life it might reveal. As ever, I was intrigued by astrology's delicate balance between fate and free will. How much of life was ordered, and how much could we will? Were some things, as death, ordained at a certain time, and other things, the choice of wife, career, sickness or health, under human control? As I thought of the millions shunted off to war against their will, it seemed hardly likely that they had any choice except that of reaction.

If life, with all its gladness and tragedy, was not orderly, then it was accidental. And if it was accidental, then there was no guide to living, for death even could occur at any moment without meaning or warning. But this is not so. Life, reflected through the planets, is as orderly as they are. And so astrology, even in foreseeing the unfortunate, at the same time provides the assurance of an ordered future to which the knowledgeable individual can happily adjust.

Kate Lyman had foreseen a disastrous fire and had helped herself; Maxine Bell had seen her father's death, and prepared for it emotionally; Edith Randall had, by seeing a bright ray ahead, been able to hearten Ann Miller until the day that brightness materialized.

Could the foreseen event be avoided if seen clearly enough and precautions taken? I wondered, thinking of Evangeline Adams and her fall from a horse and the injury to her husband, and of Maxine Bell and her father.

Indicating a rather broad design, a foreshadowed event for any individual or group could turn up in almost any related chart, a friend's, a relative's, a head of state's, as well as that of the individual himself. The symbols are all in the horoscope, subject of course to proper interpretation. The revelation often comes without warning. The rational Zipporah Dobyns, psychologist as well as astrologer, looked into the chart of a newborn Arizona baby one day, and saw enough to realize there was a crisis in the offing for her connected with her parents.

From the baby's chart it could have been an accident, divorce, or death involving the parents, or all three, and it could be linked up with travel. Pluto, the planet of regeneration or death, squared the Moon, key to mother and home, and the South Node of the Moon was in the third house and Saturn in the ninth house—both houses of travel and both indicating difficulty or loss. Venus, a loved one, and key to the mother as ruler of the fourth house of the home, was in a precise square to Uranus, the planet of unexpected change, from the third house of short trips to the fifth house of children. And Mars, the planet of violence and accidents, was in the eighth house of death, and it squared the Moon, the mother. And with Uranus ruling the seventh house of partnerships, there was the strong possibility of divorce.

"I couldn't tell from the baby's chart which of these was more likely to happen," Zipporah acknowledged, "so I suggested that a chart be done on the parents."

The grandmother, who had requested the baby's chart, was sufficiently impressed, since her daughter and son-in-law had several times been on the verge of breaking up, to send on the birth data for them.

In their charts, the crisis potential appeared even more sharply: "Both parents had Uranus on the nadir or bottom of the chart in Gemini–Gemini being the sign of short trips and Uranus the key to accidents. Uranus was on the nadir, absolutely to the degree, on the fourth house cusp symbolizing the end of the matter, and it immediately showed the danger of a critical accident and fatality. The wife was in more imminent danger. For she, as a Gemini, had her Sun in the nadir, and with Uranus sitting there on the fourth cusp it signified an unexpected accident with a fatal outcome. The wife also had Mars in the first house of the self, indicating a tendency to accident proneness. And," said Zipporah, "she had the adverse South Node on her ascendant in Aquarius, which, as the sign associated with Uranus, heightened the potential for a fatality to the self."

The vulnerability of the marriage was reflected in Mars opposing Neptune in the seventh house of partnerships, and the husband's chart showed similar separative aspects between the first and the seventh houses.

The husband's chart also showed the potential for an automobile accident. His Mars conjunct Uranus reflected a violent temper and a streak of recklessness, and with Uranus retrograding in his third house of short trips, it was clear, together with other aspects, that the climate was ripe for a fatal car accident.

Zipporah sent the charts on to the grandmother, the wife's mother, and she promptly confirmed that the son-in-law was a reckless driver, that he did have a temper, that he had left his wife twice already but had come back, and they were now trying to make a go of it.

As tactfully as possible, the grandmother discussed the charts with her daughter and son-in-law, transmitting a warning of a car accident, without mentioning the possibility of a fatality.

That was the last word on the situation for a while. Two years later, Zipporah received a long-distance phone call from the grandmother. There had been an accident during a short trip, with her son-in-law at the wheel. Her daughter had been instantly killed. The husband and the child were unharmed.

The grandmother was philosophical. She believed in reincarnation, and believing astrology to be an expression of a never-ending cycle of life, she had been prepared for her daughter's transition.

Was this then the answer to life and its vicissitudes, the development of one's spiritual content, to a point where he felt at one with the universe? So much was in how one looked at things. One man saw a half-empty bottle; to another it was half-full. One in fear saw death in his horoscope as finality; for another it was the assurance of continuing life and opportunity until the time of transition.

The more one thinks about it, the more he is aware that astrological portents of the future are valid for very good reason. One person's destiny so often meshes with another's, to help each realize what destiny demands of them.

What seems accidental at times is so often part of a common destiny. Years ago, a young Evangeline Adams, with a few dollars in her purse and a strong sense of her own immediate destiny, descended on New York to make her fortune as an astrologer. The stars were at their best possible aspect for her, and she moved confidently into the strange city.

The first place she went to for a room, the Fifth Avenue Hotel, was happy to receive a blue-blooded Adams, but frowned on a red-blooded astrologer. And so she checked into the Windsor Hotel, where a more sophisticated owner, with a tolerant view of the occult, showed her through the hotel. The rooms on the fifth floor were cheaper and to her liking, but the impecunious Miss Adams chose a more expensive room on the ground floor where she could receive her trade.

The proprietor, a Mr. Leland, was quite taken with the young astrologer.

"Let me be the first to have a reading," he said.

As she calculated the position of his stars, the astrologer saw something that made her hesitate. Leland was under the worst possible aspects, with danger so imminent that it might overtake him at any moment.

As with Kate Lyman's chart, Saturn and Mars loomed in the fourth house to show loss in the home. Additionally, fiery Mars, the ruler of the fifth house of children, squared explosive Uranus-ruled Aquarius in the eighth house of death. And transiting Moon, the trigger, hitting the Saturn-Mars conjunction, could touch off the aspects at any time.

To Miss Adams' warning of impending disaster, Leland replied cheerfully:

"Oh, tomorrow's a holiday. Stocks can't go down."

Noticing that he had been under similar planetary conditions twice before, though not nearly as malefic, the astrologer asked if misfortune had struck at these times. Leland could only recall two fires, small ones, both at the hotel.

That night the Windsor Hotel went up in flames. Many lives were lost, including members of the Leland family. The fifth floor, which Miss Adams had avoided, was the first consumed by flames. Only the first floor was intact. With bodies dropping from the upper floors, Miss Adams gathered up her books and walked unharmed into the street.

The Windsor fire launched the astrologer's meteoric career. For Leland, though overwhelmed by the tragedy, told the newspapers that the disaster had been predicted by Evangeline Adams of Boston. The story appeared on the front pages, next to the story of the fire itself, and Evangeline Adams was an overnight celebrity, just as her own horoscope had foreseen.

Even in disaster, astrology clearly showed a well-defined order, of which man was an orderly part. There were no accidents, nothing happened by chance—not even fires.

"We are here," said astrologian Llewellyn George, "for certain natural purposes, each in his place, according to an orderly cosmic plan, with opportunities to produce certain results, but it remains for us to determine the quality of those results by refining our reactions to planetary influences."

The horoscope provides an inventory at birth of the individual's potential in tendencies, mental capacities, physical endowments. And it shows how and when he can best proceed to use what he has.

"Through astrology," said George, "we learn how to improve our fate by complying consciously with nature's laws instead of violating them."

Spiritually inclined themselves from their own ready grasp of astrology's link to a divinely-inspired universe, astrologers find it incongruous that formalized religions should oppose an astrology that makes this divine intelligence so clearly apparent. "One would imagine," said the Australian astrologian Furze-Moorish, "that anything which virtually demonstrates the existence of a Universal Intelligence would receive the open acclamation of churchmen. They complain of dwindling congregations and the lack of interest shown by modern youth in religion. And yet they refuse to take note of something which puts the existence of God beyond reasonable argument."

As Christ said, man is a creature of God's, his very child in fact, and his goal perfection, to be attained in a universe in which he lives in harmony only by understanding his relationship to the forces symbolized by the zodiac of life. For, as Furze-Morrish suggested, man and his universe of atoms, planets and solar systems are all similar infinities on different levels. "We are all," he summed up for astrology, "varying but related products of the Great Architect."

Appendices

The essentials of astrology for the beginner, including a short way to map accurately a natal chart–to find the Sun, Moon, Ascendant and planetary positions.

Complete Ascendant, Moon, Sun and planetary tables for birth dates from 1900 to 1975, plus a directory of leading astrologers in the United States and abroad.

APPENDIX I

Signs and Symbols

	Signs	Quality	Rulers		Area of Body
♈	Aries the Ram	Masculine–Fire	Mars	♂	Face & Head
♉	Taurus the Bull	Feminine–Earth	Venus-Earth	♀	Neck & Throat
♊	Gemini the Twins	Masculine–Air	Mercury	☿	Lungs & Arms
♋	Cancer the Crab	Feminine–Water	Moon	☽	Breast & Stomach
♌	Leo the Lion	Masculine–Fire	Sun	☉	Heart & Spine
♍	Virgo the Virgin	Feminine–Earth	Mercury	☿	Intestines
♎	Libra the Scales	Masculine–Air	Venus	♀	Kidneys
♏	Scorpio the Stinger	Feminine–Water	Mars-Pluto	♇	Sex Organs
♐	Sagittarius the Centaur	Masculine–Fire	Jupiter	♃	Thighs
♑	Capricorn the Goat	Feminine–Earth	Saturn	♄	Knees
♒	Aquarius the Water-Bearer	Masculine–Air	Uranus	♅	Ankles & Calves
♓	Pisces the Fish	Feminine–Water	Neptune	♆	Feet

Fire Signs–creative, active, aggressive
Earth Signs–dependable, practical, persevering
Air Signs–freedom-loving, versatile, alert
Water Signs–hypersensitive, emotional, introspective

Significant Orbs and Aspects Between Planets

Aspects may be good or bad depending on the degrees between planets. Trines, for instance, give ease and squares require effort to obtain desired ends.

Degrees	Aspects	Quality	Affects	
180 Degrees	Opposition	Major	Strain	☍
150 "	Quincunx	Minor	Change, Expansion	⊠
135 "	Sequi-quadrate	Minor	Agitation, Health	⚼
120 "	Trine	Major	Lucky, Easy, Beneficial	▷
90 "	Square	Major	Obstacles, Lessons	□
72 "	Quintile	Minor	Talent (Special)	Q
60 "	Sextile	Major	Favorable, Opportunity	✱
45 "	Semi-square	Minor	Friction	∠
30 "	Semi-sextile	Minor	Growth	⊻
0 "	Conjunction	Major	Power	☌

8 degrees before and after are generally accepted orbs of the major

aspects. Sun and Moon can be given 10 degrees on either side. Minor aspects give only 4 degrees on either side.

The fixed stars most generally used in horoscopes:

Zodiac Position		Influence
Caput Algol	25 ♉	Illness, Death, Violence
Pleiades (Weeping Sisters)	29 ♉	Tears
Asellus	6 ♌	Courage, Beneficence, Blindness
Antares	8 ♐	Rashness, Headstrongness, Eye affliction
Mirach	29 ♈	Beauty, Brilliance, Fortune
Fomalhaut	2 ♓	Fortune
Vindematrix	8 ♎	Widowhood
Procyon	24 ♋	Gifts, Legacies

Planets	Symbols	Days
Sun	☉	Sunday (Sun's Day)
Moon	☽	Monday (Moon's Day)
Mars	♂	Tuesday (Tiw's Day)
Mercury	☿	Wednesday (Woden's Day)
Jupiter	♃	Thursday (Thor's Day)
Venus	♀	Friday (Frey's Day)
Saturn	♄	Saturday (Saturn's Day)

APPENDIX II

Houses

Arabian Parts—Formula

Part of Fortune	= Asc. + ☽ − ☉
Part of Marriage	= Asc. + 7th − ♀
Part of Sickness	= Asc. + ♂ − ♄
Part of Surgery	= Asc. + ♄ − ♂
Part of Death	= Asc. + 8th − ☽
Part of Peril	= Asc. + Ruler of 8th − ♄

Matters of the Houses

1st House—The beginning, self-interest, the present, early environment

2nd House—Money, personal freedom, movable possessions, acquisitions

3rd House—Communications, short trips, the conscious mind

4th House—House and home, land, domestic affairs, end of life

5th House—Love affairs, children, talent, speculation, entertainment

6th House—Illness, employment, service and labor

7th House—Marriage, divorce, partnerships, the public

8th House—Other people's money, surgery, manner of death, regeneration

9th House—Long journeys, publishing, courts, philosophy, higher education

10th House—Career, reputation, activity, honors

11th House—Hopes and wishes, friends, groups

12th House—Institutions, escapism, self-undoing, subversion, subconscious

Persons of the Houses

1st House–You, the self, the body
2nd House–Bankers, investors
3rd House–Brothers, sisters, neighbors
4th House–Parent, provider, patron
5th House–Child, lover, entertainer, gambler
6th House–Workers, doctors, teachers, nurses, landlords
7th House–Partner, spouse, the public, adversaries
8th House–Investigators, grim reaper, generals
9th House–Strangers, publishers, clergymen, diplomats
10th House–Employer, parent, president, head man
11th House–Friends, advisers, social contacts
12th House–Widows and orphans, secret enemies

APPENDIX III

Kinds of Houses

1. *Angular*—Represents north, south, west, east. Planets have a greater scope of action than planets in other houses (1–4–7–10).
2. *Succedent Houses*—These houses succeed after the angular houses. Planets in these houses tend to give stability, willpower, fixity of purpose, no great activity (2–5–8–11).
3. *Cadent Houses*—Little activity, not much opportunity for action. They tend toward thought, communication of ideas, the ability to get along with people (3–6–9–12).

Houses of Function

1. *The Houses of Life*—1–5–9: These are houses of dynamic energy, enthusiasm, motivating power, religious conviction. One is self; five, children; nine, the philosophy of living.
2. *Houses of Endings*—4–8–12: The fourth house pictures the end of life or the end of a matter; the eighth house, death, regeneration; twelfth house, the subconscious, karma, what is brought into this life (the watery triplicity).
3. *Houses of Substances*—2–6–10: The second house depicts the accumulation of money, movable possessions; the sixth, the facility to work, or occupation; the tenth house relates to employer or profession, reputation and honors (earthy triplicity).
4. *Houses of Relationships*—3–6–11: Describe relationship in community. The third house, relatives, neighbors; the seventh, partners; the eleventh, friends and organizations (airy triplicity).

Angular Houses: The majority of planets in angular houses indicates a prominent position in the world. 1st: personal character; 4th: latter part of life; 7th: fortune of marriage; 10th: public recognition.

Succedent Houses: Majority of planets in succedent houses may make the subject stubborn and uncompromising.

Cadent Houses: Give little public recognition. Subject will probably complete a major part of any undertaking, but somebody else will get credit.

Cardinal Signs: Aries, Cancer, Libra, Capricorn—the creators.

Key Words: Ambitious, enthusiastic, ardent, independent, proud. They are most active when placed on the angles, their natural positions.

Fixed Signs: Taurus, Leo, Scorpio, Aquarius.

Key Words: Dogmatic, unyielding, determined, organizing, accumulative, egotistical, secretive, achieve slowly but surely.

Mutable Signs: Gemini, Virgo, Sagittarius, Pisces.

Key Words: Versatile, adaptable, responsive, changeable, scattered. They blend and sometimes bend.

Marilyn Monroe

June 1, 1926

Los Angeles, Calif.

9:30 a.m. P.S.T.

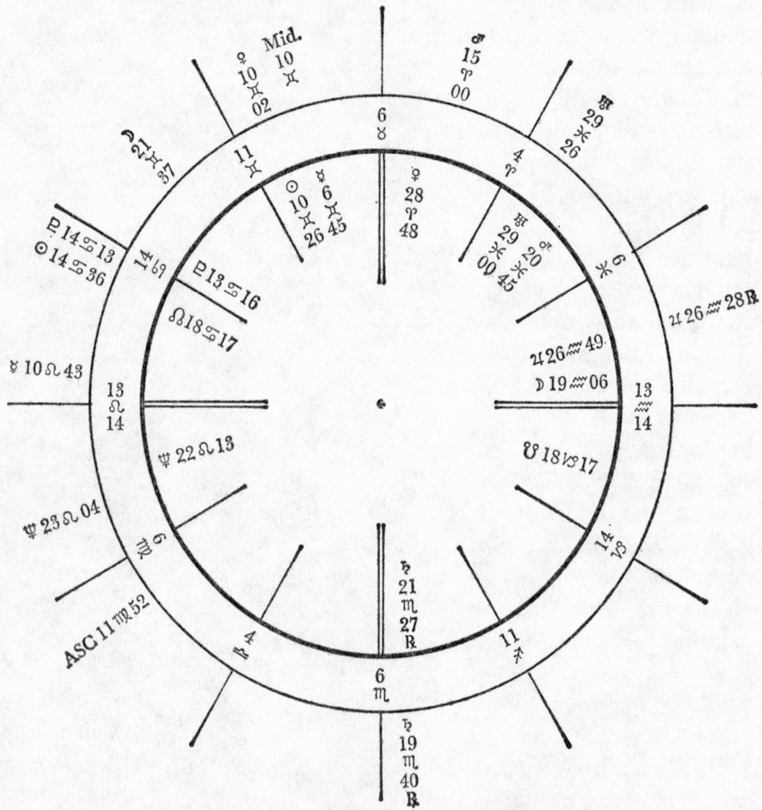

Progressed to Marilyn's death on August 5, 1962.
The natal chart is the inner circle. The progressed chart is the outer circle.

APPENDIX IV

How to Progress a Chart

(As shown in the progressed chart of Marilyn Monroe)

Marilyn Monroe was a Gemini, born June 1, 1926, 9:30 A.M., in Los Angeles, California. She died, a suicide, at the age of thirty six, on August 5, 1962. Her ascendant was in dramatic Leo, auspicious for an actress, and Neptune, the planet of motion pictures and self-undoing was in her first house, near the ascendant, governing herself and her self-motivation. This Neptune position also tended to put her in a fantasy world, and was related to indulgence in drink and drugs. Neptune's influence extended to the eighth house of death, since the sign it rules, Pisces, was on the cusp of this house, and the eighth house indicates the manner of death, which in this case was drugs–sleeping pills. Marilyn's eighth house not only harbored this strong Neptunean influence but also held an explosive conjunction of Mars and Uranus, traditionally the aspect of the unexpected or accidental. In an afflicted chart, the Sun, Moon and the ascendant usually have heavy aspects. The Sun ruled Marilyn's Leo ascendant, afflicted also by a first-house Neptune square to Saturn in the fourth house of the home and the end of life. Her Moon was in Aquarius in the seventh house (indicating her appeal to the public), but opposed Neptune, and was in turn square to that malignant Saturn. The cusp of Marilyn's fourth house was Scorpio, the natural tenant of the eighth, co-ruled, again, by accidental Mars and spooky Pluto, the planet of mystery, death and regeneration.

The day for a year method, mentioned in the Bible, was used by astrologer Franka Moore to progress Marilyn's chart to the date of death. Since Marilyn was born on June 1, 1926, progression-wise she would be one year old on June 2, 1926, one day being added for each year of her life, for the full 36 years. By this reckoning, her 36th year, again progression-wise, fell on July 7. The chart was mapped, as if a new chart, for July 7, 1926, 9:30 A.M. To find the ascendant first-house cusp for the progressed chart, Franka Moore consulted a table of houses. However, for a close approximation of the progressed rising sign, the ascendant tables in this Appendix could also be consulted.

From the planetary tables listed in the Appendix, as well as an ephemeris, the Sun, Moon and planets could be placed in the progressed chart, with its new ascendant of 11 degrees Virgo, progressed from the natal ascendant of 13 degrees Leo.

Normally, in a progressed chart, heavy afflictions from the natal chart, showing the individual's potential, are carried over and activated. At the time of Marilyn's death, as shown in the progressed chart, her progressed Midheaven was at ten degrees Gemini, conjunct her natal Sun, which was also ten degrees of Gemini. Her progressed Venus, which ruled her natal tenth house of activity, was conjunct her natal Sun and the progressed Midheaven. Since the two charts, natal and progressed, are considered together in setting the pattern for coming events, this indicated romantic publicity of an adverse nature at this time, as these three, progressed Venus, Midheaven and natal Sun, squared her progressed Virgo ascendant.

The tragic aspects were clearly apparent. Progressed Sun and progressed Pluto were exactly conjunct the 12th-house cusp of her natal chart, and the 12th house is the locale of self-undoing and suicide. These progressed planets squared progressed Mars, which ruled the fourth-house cusp of the end of life. The progressed Moon, ruler of the 12th natal house, exactly squared natal Mars in the eighth house of death. Her natal Moon, ruler of the tragic 12th, exactly squared progressed Saturn, doubly afflicted as it was retrograding at the time of her birth.

The seventh-house natal Moon-progressed Saturn square had been in effect the last ten years of her life, reflecting disappointment throughout this period in partnerships and marriages. And with Saturn retrograding, it set off the destructive suicidal pattern, which in the end became her destiny.

The Ascendant moves with the Sun, changing signs every two hours. Chart (facing) shows an average sunrise time of 6 a.m. on the Eastern horizon. Put your Sun (with its sign) in the time slot of your birth. If you are a Gemini, born at 11 a.m., put Gemini in the 10 to 12 a.m. time slot on the cusp of the tenth house, and then, counterclockwise, follow the wheel around, placing Cancer on the 11th house cusp, Leo on the 12th, and Virgo on the Ascendant, or first house cusp. You would then be a Gemini with Virgo rising, and Virgo in the first house.

SUN'S POSITION IN HOUSE AT YOUR BIRTH

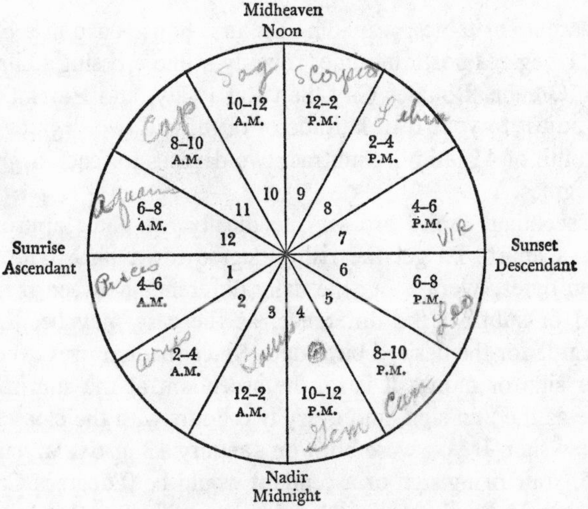

SUN'S POSITION IN SIGN OF YOUR BIRTH

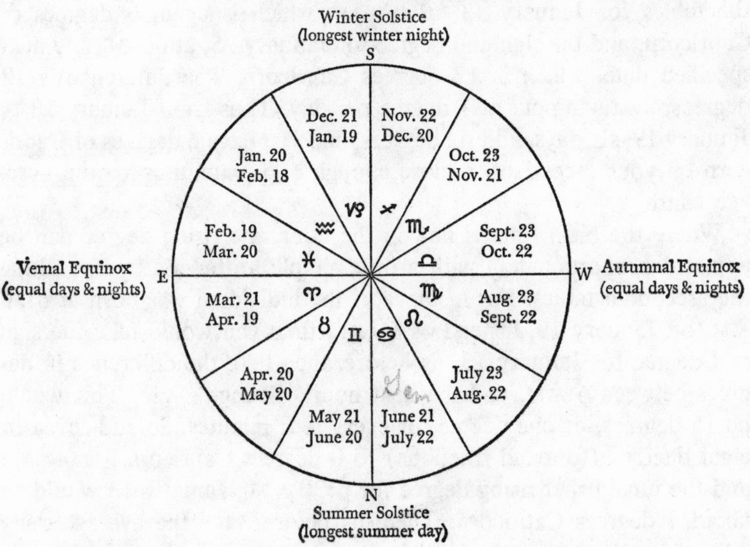

APPENDIX VI

How to Find Your Ascendant

The ascendant tables, providing the first house cusp in a chart, are set for 41 degrees north latitude, roughly a line crossing Philadelphia, Chicago, Omaha, Boulder City, Salt Lake City, and Eureka, California. To adjust to your own latitude of birth, add two degrees for each degree south of 41 latitude, subtract two degrees for each degree north of 41 degrees.

The ascendant tables are set specifically for dates approximately two weeks apart. To get the rising degree for a birth date between two given dates, average out the daily difference between these dates, then add or subtract the difference, as the case may be, to get the rising degree for the desired birth date. Since the Sun rises every day in whatever sign or month it is in, the ascendant at the sunrise hour is the same as the Sun sign, and every two hours with the clock it moves into a new sign. If you were born on January 13 at 6 A.M., sunrise on this date, your rising sign or ascendant would be 0 degrees Capricorn, and this would be shown in the tables, specifically. But if, say, you were born on January 19, at 6 A.M., take the sign and degree given in the tables for January 13, at 6 A.M., which is again 0 degrees of Capricorn, and the sign and degree for January 25, at 6 A.M., the next specified date, which is 12 degrees Capricorn. The difference is 12 degrees, averaging out at 1 degree per day. Thus from January 13 to January 19, six days, add six degrees, and you have 6 degrees of Capricorn on your ascendant, a close enough approximation for the average chart.

Where the birth time is not on the hour, the rising degree can be adjusted proportionately with a little simple arithmetic by consulting the ascendant tables. For instance, if the individual was born at 6:30 A.M. on January 19, instead of 6 A.M., then you would take the sign and degree for January 13, as before, then take the difference in degrees between 6 A.M. and the next hourly listing, 7 A.M. This would be 15 degrees, or one degree for every four minutes. So add seven or eight degrees (to avoid fractions) to 0 degrees Capricorn for 6 A.M., and the unadjusted rising degree for 6:30 A.M., January 13 would be about 7 degrees Capricorn. Then, as before, take the average daily difference of one degree in the ascendant at this time. Adding six degrees for six days, from January 13, you have 13 degrees of Capricorn on the ascendant for a 6:30 A.M. birth on January 19. (See Alice Zessin's Ascendant Chart, Appendix V.)

Once the ascendant or rising sign is determined, place it to that degree on the Eastern horizon of the 360-degree, twelve-house wheel to form the first house cusp. To avoid mathematical procedures confusing to the novice, use the simplified equal-house system for the placement of the succeeding house cusps, the same degree applying counterclockwise to each cusp. If the first house cusp, for instance, is 6 Capricorn, the second cusp would be 6 Aquarius, the third 6 Pisces, and so on around the wheel. Then consult the additional tables in this Appendix for moon and planetary positions at the time of birth, and place them in the various houses to the degree in which they belong. The position of the sun in this chart, appearing in the birth sign, is fixed by equating a degree for each day from the first day of that sign to the birthdate. In other words if you were born on January 15, your Sun would be about 25 degrees Capricorn, as the Sun generally goes into Capricorn on December 21. If you were born during daylight saving time or war time, subtract one hour, accordingly, from your birth time as a starter.

Normally, the ascendant changes every two hours, or thirty degrees. As a rule of thumb, to arrive at your ascendant quickly, fix the Eastern horizon for your Sun sign at 6 A.M. If you are, say, a Gemini, born between the approximate sunrise hour of 4 A.M. and 6 A.M., you would be a Gemini with Gemini rising. From 6 to 8 A.M. there would be a new ascendant on the Eastern horizon, and this, clockwise, would be in Cancer, and so if you were born in this two-hour period and are a Gemini, the likelihood would be that you had Cancer rising. From 8 to 10, the ascendant would be Leo, 10 to noon, Virgo, etc.

ASCENDANT TABLES

JANUARY –1–

A.M.			P.M.		
1 o'clock	20° of Libra	♎	1 o'clock	11° of Taurus	♉
2 "	1 " Scorpio	♏	2 "	1 " Gemini	♊
3 "	13 " Scorpio	♏	3 "	17 " Gemini	♊
4 "	25 " Scorpio	♏	4 "	2 " Cancer	♋
5 "	7 " Sagittarius	♐	5 "	15 " Cancer	♋
6 "	19 " Sagittarius	♐	6 "	27 " Cancer	♋
7 "	2 " Capricorn	♑	7 "	9 " Leo	♌
8 "	18 " Capricorn	♑	8 "	21 " Leo	♌
9 "	6 " Aquarius	♒	9 "	2 " Virgo	♍
10 "	27 " Aquarius	♒	10 "	14 " Virgo	♍
11 "	22 " Pisces	♓	11 "	26 " Virgo	♍
12 Noon	16 " Aries	♈	12 Midnight	8 " Libra	♎

JANUARY –13–

A.M.			P.M.		
1 o'clock	29° of Libra	♎	1 o'clock	27° of Taurus	♉
2 "	11 " Scorpio	♏	2 "	14 " Gemini	♊
3 "	23 " Scorpio	♏	3 "	29 " Gemini	♊
4 "	5 " Sagittarius	♐	4 "	12 " Cancer	♋
5 "	17 " Sagittarius	♐	5 "	24 " Cancer	♋
6 "	0 " Capricorn	♑	6 "	7 " Leo	♌
7 "	15 " Capricorn	♑	7 "	18 " Leo	♌
8 "	2 " Aquarius	♒	8 "	0 " Virgo	♍
9 "	22 " Aquarius	♒	9 "	12 " Virgo	♍
10 "	16 " Pisces	♓	10 "	24 " Virgo	♍
11 "	13 " Aries	♈	11 "	6 " Libra	♎
12 Noon	7 " Taurus	♉	12 Midnight	18 " Libra	♎

JANUARY –25–

A.M.			P.M.		
1 o'clock	8° of Scorpio	♏	1 o'clock	11° of Gemini	♊
2 "	20 " Scorpio	♏	2 "	26 " Gemini	♊
3 "	2 " Sagittarius	♐	3 "	9 " Cancer	♋
4 "	14 " Sagittarius	♐	4 "	22 " Cancer	♋
5 "	27 " Sagittarius	♐	5 "	4 " Leo	♌
6 "	12 " Capricorn	♑	6 "	16 " Leo	♌
7 "	28 " Capricorn	♑	7 "	27 " Leo	♌
8 "	17 " Aquarius	♒	8 "	9 " Virgo	♍
9 "	11 " Pisces	♓	9 "	21 " Virgo	♍
10 "	7 " Aries	♈	10 "	3 " Libra	♎
11 "	2 " Taurus	♉	11 "	15 " Libra	♎
12 Noon	23 " Taurus	♉	12 Midnight	27 " Libra	♎

FEBRUARY –6–

A.M.				P.M.			
1 o'clock	18°	of Scorpio	♏	1 o'clock	23°	of Gemini	♊
2 "	29	" Scorpio	♏	2 "	7	" Cancer	♋
3 "	12	" Sagittarius	♐	3 "	19	" Cancer	♋
4 "	24	" Sagittarius	♐	4 "	1	" Leo	♌
5 "	8	" Capricorn	♑	5 "	13	" Leo	♌
6 "	24	" Capricorn	♑	6 "	25	" Leo	♌
7 "	13	" Aquarius	♒	7 "	7	" Virgo	♍
8 "	5	" Pisces	♓	8 "	18	" Virgo	♍
9 "	1	" Aries	♈	9 "	0	" Libra	♎
10 "	27	" Aries	♈	10 "	12	" Libra	♎
11 "	19	" Taurus	♉	11 "	24	" Libra	♎
12 Noon	8	" Gemini	♊	12 Midnight	6	" Scorpio	♏

FEBRUARY –18–

A.M.				P.M.			
1 o'clock	27°	of Scorpio	♏	1 o'clock	4°	of Cancer	♋
2 "	9	" Sagittarius	♐	2 "	16	" Cancer	♋
3 "	21	" Sagittarius	♐	3 "	29	" Cancer	♋
4 "	5	" Capricorn	♑	4 "	11	" Leo	♌
5 "	20	" Capricorn	♑	5 "	22	" Leo	♌
6 "	9	" Aquarius	♒	6 "	4	" Virgo	♍
7 "	0	" Pisces	♓	7 "	16	" Virgo	♍
8 "	26	" Pisces	♓	8 "	28	" Virgo	♍
9 "	21	" Aries	♈	9 "	10	" Libra	♎
10 "	15	" Taurus	♉	10 "	22	" Libra	♎
11 "	3	" Gemini	♊	11 "	3	" Scorpio	♏
12 Noon	20	" Gemini	♊	12 Midnight	15	" Scorpio	♏

MARCH –2–

A.M.				P.M.			
1 o'clock	7°	of Sagittarius	♐	1 o'clock	15°	of Cancer	♋
2 "	20	" Sagittarius	♐	2 "	27	" Cancer	♋
3 "	3	" Capricorn	♑	3 "	9	" Leo	♌
4 "	18	" Capricorn	♑	4 "	21	" Leo	♌
5 "	6	" Aquarius	♒	5 "	2	" Virgo	♍
6 "	28	" Aquarius	♒	6 "	14	" Virgo	♍
7 "	22	" Pisces	♓	7 "	26	" Virgo	♍
8 "	18	" Aries	♈	8 "	8	" Libra	♎
9 "	12	" Taurus	♉	9 "	20	" Libra	♎
10 "	1	" Gemini	♊	10 "	1	" Scorpio	♏
11 "	18	" Gemini	♊	11 "	13	" Scorpio	♏
12 Noon	2	" Cancer	♋	12 Midnight	25	" Scorpio	♏

MARCH –14–

A.M.				P.M.			
1 o'clock	17° of	Sagittarius	♐	1 o'clock	25° of	Cancer	♋
2 "	1 "	Capricorn	♑	2 "	7 "	Leo	♌
3 "	15 "	Capricorn	♑	3 "	18 "	Leo	♌
4 "	2 "	Aquarius	♒	4 "	0 "	Virgo	♍
5 "	22 "	Aquarius	♒	5 "	12 "	Virgo	♍
6 "	16 "	Pisces	♓	6 "	23 "	Virgo	♍
7 "	13 "	Aries	♈	7 "	6 "	Libra	♎
8 "	7 "	Taurus	♉	8 "	18 "	Libra	♎
9 "	27 "	Taurus	♉	9 "	29 "	Libra	♎
10 "	14 "	Gemini	♊	10 "	11 "	Scorpio	♏
11 "	29 "	Gemini	♊	11 "	23 "	Scorpio	♏
12 Noon	12 "	Cancer	♋	12 Midnight	5 "	Sagittarius	♐

MARCH –26–

A.M.				P.M.			
1 o'clock	27° of	Sagittarius	♐	1 o'clock	4° of	Leo	♌
2 "	12 "	Capricorn	♑	2 "	16 "	Leo	♌
3 "	28 "	Capricorn	♑	3 "	28 "	Leo	♌
4 "	17 "	Aquarius	♒	4 "	9 "	Virgo	♍
5 "	11 "	Pisces	♓	5 "	21 "	Virgo	♍
6 "	7 "	Aries	♈	6 "	3 "	Libra	♎
7 "	2 "	Taurus	♉	7 "	15 "	Libra	♎
8 "	23 "	Taurus	♉	8 "	27 "	Libra	♎
9 "	11 "	Gemini	♊	9 "	9 "	Scorpio	♏
10 "	26 "	Gemini	♊	10 "	20 "	Scorpio	♏
11 "	10 "	Cancer	♋	11 "	2 "	Sagittarius	♐
12 Noon	22 "	Cancer	♋	12 Midnight	14 "	Sagittarius	♐

APRIL –7–

A.M.				P.M.			
1 o'clock	8° of	Capricorn	♑	1 o'clock	13° of	Leo	♌
2 "	24 "	Capricorn	♑	2 "	25 "	Leo	♌
3 "	13 "	Aquarius	♒	3 "	7 "	Virgo	♍
4 "	5 "	Pisces	♓	4 "	18 "	Virgo	♍
5 "	1 "	Aries	♈	5 "	0 "	Libra	♎
6 "	27 "	Aries	♈	6 "	12 "	Libra	♎
7 "	19 "	Taurus	♉	7 "	24 "	Libra	♎
8 "	8 "	Gemini	♊	8 "	6 "	Scorpio	♏
9 "	23 "	Gemini	♊	9 "	18 "	Scorpio	♏
10 "	7 "	Cancer	♋	10 "	29 "	Scorpio	♏
11 "	19 "	Cancer	♋	11 "	12 "	Sagittarius	♐
12 Noon	2 "	Leo	♌	12 Midnight	25 "	Sagittarius	♐

APRIL –18–

A.M.				P.M.			
1 o'clock	20° of	Capricorn	♑	1 o'clock	22° of	Leo	♌
2 "	7 "	Aquarius	♒	2 "	4 "	Virgo	♍
3 "	0 "	Pisces	♓	3 "	16 "	Virgo	♍
4 "	26 "	Pisces	♓	4 "	28 "	Virgo	♍
5 "	20 "	Aries	♈	5 "	9 "	Libra	♎
6 "	13 "	Taurus	♉	6 "	22 "	Libra	♎
7 "	3 "	Gemini	♊	7 "	3 "	Scorpio	♏
8 "	19 "	Gemini	♊	8 "	15 "	Scorpio	♏
9 "	3 "	Cancer	♋	9 "	27 "	Scorpio	♏
10 "	16 "	Cancer	♋	10 "	8 "	Sagittarius	♐
11 "	28 "	Cancer	♋	11 "	21 "	Sagittarius	♐
12 Noon	10 "	Leo	♌	12 Midnight	5 "	Capricorn	♑

APRIL –30–

A.M.				P.M.			
1 o'clock	3° of	Aquarius	♒	1 o'clock	1° of	Virgo	♍
2 "	25 "	Aquarius	♒	2 "	13 "	Virgo	♍
3 "	18 "	Pisces	♓	3 "	24 "	Virgo	♍
4 "	15 "	Aries	♈	4 "	7 "	Libra	♎
5 "	9 "	Taurus	♉	5 "	19 "	Libra	♎
6 "	29 "	Taurus	♉	6 "	1 "	Scorpio	♏
7 "	16 "	Gemini	♊	7 "	12 "	Scorpio	♏
8 "	0 "	Cancer	♋	8 "	24 "	Scorpio	♏
9 "	14 "	Cancer	♋	9 "	6 "	Sagittarius	♐
10 "	26 "	Cancer	♋	10 "	18 "	Sagittarius	♐
11 "	8 "	Leo	♌	11 "	2 "	Capricorn	♑
12 Noon	19 "	Leo	♌	12 Midnight	16 "	Capricorn	♑

MAY –16–

A.M.				P.M.			
1 o'clock	25° of	Aquarius	♒	1 o'clock	14° of	Virgo	♍
2 "	20 "	Pisces	♓	2 "	25 "	Virgo	♍
3 "	16 "	Aries	♈	3 "	7 "	Libra	♎
4 "	10 "	Taurus	♉	4 "	19 "	Libra	♎
5 "	1 "	Gemini	♊	5 "	1 "	Scorpio	♏
6 "	16 "	Gemini	♊	6 "	13 "	Scorpio	♏
7 "	1 "	Cancer	♋	7 "	24 "	Scorpio	♏
8 "	14 "	Cancer	♋	8 "	7 "	Sagittarius	♐
9 "	26 "	Cancer	♋	9 "	19 "	Sagittarius	♐
10 "	8 "	Leo	♌	10 "	2 "	Capricorn	♑
11 "	20 "	Leo	♌	11 "	17 "	Capricorn	♑
12 Noon	2 "	Virgo	♍	12 Midnight	5 "	Aquarius	♒

MAY –28–

A.M.				P.M.			
1 o'clock	14° of	Pisces	♓	1 o'clock	23° of	Virgo	♍
2 "	11 "	Aries	♈	2 "	5 "	Libra	♎
3 "	5 "	Taurus	♉	3 "	17 "	Libra	♎
4 "	26 "	Taurus	♉	4 "	28 "	Libra	♎
5 "	13 "	Gemini	♊	5 "	10 "	Scorpio	♏
6 "	28 "	Gemini	♊	6 "	22 "	Scorpio	♏
7 "	12 "	Cancer	♋	7 "	3 "	Sagittarius	♐
8 "	24 "	Cancer	♋	8 "	16 "	Sagittarius	♐
9 "	5 "	Leo	♌	9 "	29 "	Sagittarius	♐
10 "	17 "	Leo	♌	10 "	14 "	Capricorn	♑
11 "	29 "	Leo	♌	11 "	1 "	Aquarius	♒
12 Noon	11 "	Virgo	♍	12 Midnight	20 "	Aquarius	♒

JUNE –9–

A.M.				P.M.			
1 o'clock	3° of	Aries	♈	1 o'clock	2° of	Libra	♎
2 "	29 "	Aries	♈	2 "	14 "	Libra	♎
3 "	20 "	Taurus	♉	3 "	25 "	Libra	♎
4 "	9 "	Gemini	♊	4 "	7 "	Scorpio	♏
5 "	24 "	Gemini	♊	5 "	19 "	Scorpio	♏
6 "	8 "	Cancer	♋	6 "	1 "	Sagittarius	♐
7 "	20 "	Cancer	♋	7 "	13 "	Sagittarius	♐
8 "	2 "	Leo	♌	8 "	26 "	Sagittarius	♐
9 "	14 "	Leo	♌	9 "	10 "	Capricorn	♑
10 "	26 "	Leo	♌	10 "	26 "	Capricorn	♑
11 "	8 "	Virgo	♍	11 "	16 "	Aquarius	♒
12 Noon	20 "	Virgo	♍	12 Midnight	9 "	Pisces	♓

JUNE –21–

A.M.				P.M.			
1 o'clock	24° of	Aries	♈	1 o'clock	11° of	Libra	♎
2 "	16 "	Taurus	♉	2 "	23 "	Libra	♎
3 "	6 "	Gemini	♊	3 "	5 "	Scorpio	♏
4 "	21 "	Gemini	♊	4 "	16 "	Scorpio	♏
5 "	5 "	Cancer	♋	5 "	28 "	Scorpio	♏
6 "	18 "	Cancer	♋	6 "	10 "	Sagittarius	♐
7 "	0 "	Leo	♌	7 "	23 "	Sagittarius	♐
8 "	11 "	Leo	♌	8 "	6 "	Capricorn	♑
9 "	23 "	Leo	♌	9 "	22 "	Capricorn	♑
10 "	5 "	Virgo	♍	10 "	11 "	Aquarius	♒
11 "	17 "	Virgo	♍	11 "	4 "	Pisces	♓
12 Noon	29 "	Virgo	♍	12 Midnight	28 "	Pisces	♓

JULY –3–

A.M.					P.M.				
1 o'clock	12°	of	Taurus	♉	1 o'clock	20°	of	Libra	♎
2 "	2	"	Gemini	♊	2 "	2	"	Scorpio	♏
3 "	17	"	Gemini	♊	3 "	14	"	Scorpio	♏
4 "	2	"	Cancer	♋	4 "	25	"	Scorpio	♏
5 "	15	"	Cancer	♋	5 "	7	"	Sagittarius	♐
6 "	27	"	Cancer	♋	6 "	20	"	Sagittarius	♐
7 "	9	"	Leo	♌	7 "	3	"	Capricorn	♑
8 "	21	"	Leo	♌	8 "	18	"	Capricorn	♑
9 "	2	"	Virgo	♍	9 "	6	"	Aquarius	♒
10 "	14	"	Virgo	♍	10 "	27	"	Aquarius	♒
11 "	26	"	Virgo	♍	11 "	22	"	Pisces	♓
12 Noon	8	"	Libra	♎	12 Midnight	19	"	Aries	♈

JULY –14–

A.M.					P.M.				
1 o'clock	26°	of	Taurus	♉	1 o'clock	29°	of	Libra	♎
2 "	14	"	Gemini	♊	2 "	11	"	Scorpio	♏
3 "	28	"	Gemini	♊	3 "	22	"	Scorpio	♏
4 "	12	"	Cancer	♋	4 "	5	"	Sagittarius	♐
5 "	24	"	Cancer	♋	5 "	17	"	Sagittarius	♐
6 "	6	"	Leo	♌	6 "	0	"	Capricorn	♑
7 "	17	"	Leo	♌	7 "	15	"	Capricorn	♑
8 "	29	"	Leo	♌	8 "	2	"	Aquarius	♒
9 "	12	"	Virgo	♍	9 "	22	"	Aquarius	♒
10 "	23	"	Virgo	♍	10 "	6	"	Pisces	♓
11 "	5	"	Libra	♎	11 "	13	"	Aries	♈
12 Noon	17	"	Libra	♎	12 Midnight	6	"	Taurus	♉

JULY –26–

A.M.					P.M.				
1 o'clock	10°	of	Gemini	♊	1 o'clock	8°	of	Scorpio	♏
2 "	25	"	Gemini	♊	2 "	20	"	Scorpio	♏
3 "	9	"	Cancer	♋	3 "	2	"	Sagittarius	♐
4 "	21	"	Cancer	♋	4 "	14	"	Sagittarius	♐
5 "	3	"	Leo	♌	5 "	26	"	Sagittarius	♐
6 "	15	"	Leo	♌	6 "	11	"	Capricorn	♑
7 "	27	"	Leo	♌	7 "	27	"	Capricorn	♑
8 "	9	"	Virgo	♍	8 "	16	"	Aquarius	♒
9 "	20	"	Virgo	♍	9 "	10	"	Pisces	♓
10 "	2	"	Libra	♎	10 "	5	"	Aries	♈
11 "	14	"	Libra	♎	11 "	0	"	Taurus	♉
12 Noon	26	"	Libra	♎	12 Midnight	23	"	Taurus	♉

AUGUST –7–

A.M.				P.M.			
1 o'clock	22° of	Gemini	♊	1 o'clock	18° of	Scorpio	♏
2 "	6 "	Cancer	♋	2 "	29 "	Scorpio	♏
3 "	19 "	Cancer	♋	3 "	11 "	Sagittarius	♐
4 "	1 "	Leo	♌	4 "	25 "	Sagittarius	♐
5 "	13 "	Leo	♌	5 "	8 "	Capricorn	♑
6 "	24 "	Leo	♌	6 "	24 "	Capricorn	♑
7 "	7 "	Virgo	♍	7 "	13 "	Aquarius	♒
8 "	8 "	Virgo	♍	8 "	5 "	Pisces	♓
9 "	0 "	Libra	♎	9 "	1 "	Aries	♈
10 "	12 "	Libra	♎	10 "	27 "	Aries	♈
11 "	24 "	Libra	♎	11 "	19 "	Taurus	♉
12 Noon	6 "	Scorpio	♏	12 Midnight	8 "	Gemini	♊

AUGUST –19–

A.M.				P.M.			
1 o'clock	3° of	Cancer	♋	1 o'clock	27° of	Scorpio	♏
2 "	16 "	Cancer	♋	2 "	9 "	Sagittarius	♐
3 "	28 "	Cancer	♋	3 "	21 "	Sagittarius	♐
4 "	10 "	Leo	♌	4 "	5 "	Capricorn	♑
5 "	22 "	Leo	♌	5 "	20 "	Capricorn	♑
6 "	4 "	Virgo	♍	6 "	9 "	Aquarius	♒
7 "	16 "	Virgo	♍	7 "	0 "	Pisces	♓
8 "	28 "	Virgo	♍	8 "	26 "	Pisces	♓
9 "	9 "	Libra	♎	9 "	22 "	Aries	♈
10 "	22 "	Libra	♎	10 "	15 "	Taurus	♉
11 "	3 "	Scorpio	♏	11 "	4 "	Gemini	♊
12 Noon	15 "	Scorpio	♏	12 Midnight	20 "	Gemini	♊

AUGUST –31–

A.M.				P.M.			
1 o'clock	14° of	Cancer	♋	1 o'clock	6° of	Sagittarius	♐
2 "	26 "	Cancer	♋	2 "	19 "	Sagittarius	♐
3 "	8 "	Leo	♌	3 "	2 "	Capricorn	♑
4 "	19 "	Leo	♌	4 "	17 "	Capricorn	♑
5 "	1 "	Virgo	♍	5 "	5 "	Aquarius	♒
6 "	13 "	Virgo	♍	6 "	25 "	Aquarius	♒
7 "	25 "	Virgo	♍	7 "	20 "	Pisces	♓
8 "	7 "	Libra	♎	8 "	16 "	Aries	♈
9 "	19 "	Libra	♎	9 "	10 "	Taurus	♉
10 "	1 "	Scorpio	♏	10 "	0 "	Gemini	♊
11 "	12 "	Scorpio	♏	11 "	17 "	Gemini	♊
12 Noon	24 "	Scorpio	♏	12 Midnight	1 "	Cancer	♋

SEPTEMBER –12–

A.M.				P.M.			
1 o'clock	23° of	Cancer	♋	1 o'clock	15° of	Sagittarius	♐
2 "	5 "	Leo	♌	2 "	29 "	Sagittarius	♐
3 "	17 "	Leo	♌	3 "	14 "	Capricorn	♑
4 "	28 "	Leo	♌	4 "	1 "	Aquarius	♒
5 "	11 "	Virgo	♍	5 "	20 "	Aquarius	♒
6 "	22 "	Virgo	♍	6 "	15 "	Pisces	♓
7 "	4 "	Libra	♎	7 "	11 "	Aries	♈
8 "	16 "	Libra	♎	8 "	5 "	Taurus	♉
9 "	27 "	Libra	♎	9 "	26 "	Taurus	♉
10 "	10 "	Scorpio	♏	10 "	13 "	Gemini	♊
11 "	21 "	Scorpio	♏	11 "	28 "	Gemini	♊
12 Noon	3 "	Sagittarius	♐	12 Midnight	12 "	Cancer	♋

SEPTEMBER –24–

A.M.				P.M.			
1 o'clock	2° of	Leo	♌	1 o'clock	26° of	Sagittarius	♐
2 "	14 "	Leo	♌	2 "	11 "	Capricorn	♑
3 "	26 "	Leo	♌	3 "	27 "	Capricorn	♑
4 "	8 "	Virgo	♍	4 "	16 "	Aquarius	♒
5 "	20 "	Virgo	♍	5 "	9 "	Pisces	♓
6 "	2 "	Libra	♎	6 "	5 "	Aries	♈
7 "	14 "	Libra	♎	7 "	0 "	Taurus	♉
8 "	26 "	Libra	♎	8 "	22 "	Taurus	♉
9 "	8 "	Scorpio	♏	9 "	10 "	Gemini	♊
10 "	19 "	Scorpio	♏	10 "	25 "	Gemini	♊
11 "	1 "	Sagittarius	♐	11 "	9 "	Cancer	♋
12 Noon	13 "	Sagittarius	♐	12 Midnight	21 "	Cancer	♋

OCTOBER –6–

A.M.				P.M.			
1 o'clock	11° of	Leo	♌	1 o'clock	6° of	Capricorn	♑
2 "	23 "	Leo	♌	2 "	22 "	Capricorn	♑
3 "	5 "	Virgo	♍	3 "	10 "	Aquarius	♒
4 "	17 "	Virgo	♍	4 "	3 "	Pisces	♓
5 "	28 "	Virgo	♍	5 "	28 "	Pisces	♓
6 "	10 "	Libra	♎	6 "	24 "	Aries	♈
7 "	22 "	Libra	♎	7 "	17 "	Taurus	♉
8 "	4 "	Scorpio	♏	8 "	5 "	Gemini	♊
9 "	16 "	Scorpio	♏	9 "	21 "	Gemini	♊
10 "	28 "	Scorpio	♏	10 "	5 "	Cancer	♋
11 "	10 "	Sagittarius	♐	11 "	18 "	Cancer	♋
12 Noon	22 "	Sagittarius	♐	12 Midnight	0 "	Leo	♌

OCTOBER –18–

A.M.				P.M.			
1 o'clock	21° of	Leo	♌	1 o'clock	19° of	Capricorn	♑
2 "	3 "	Virgo	♍	2 "	7 "	Aquarius	♒
3 "	15 "	Virgo	♍	3 "	29 "	Aquarius	♒
4 "	27 "	Virgo	♍	4 "	24 "	Pisces	♓
5 "	9 "	Libra	♎	5 "	20 "	Aries	♈
6 "	20 "	Libra	♎	6 "	13 "	Taurus	♉
7 "	2 "	Scorpio	♏	7 "	3 "	Gemini	♊
8 "	14 "	Scorpio	♏	8 "	19 "	Gemini	♊
9 "	26 "	Scorpio	♏	9 "	3 "	Cancer	♋
10 "	8 "	Sagittarius	♐	10 "	16 "	Cancer	♋
11 "	21 "	Sagittarius	♐	11 "	28 "	Cancer	♋
12 Noon	4 "	Capricorn	♑	12 Midnight	10 "	Leo	♌

OCTOBER –30–

A.M.				P.M.			
1 o'clock	1° of	Virgo	♍	1 o'clock	3° of	Aquarius	♒
2 "	12 "	Virgo	♍	2 "	24 "	Aquarius	♒
3 "	24 "	Virgo	♍	3 "	19 "	Pisces	♓
4 "	6 "	Libra	♎	4 "	15 "	Aries.	♈
5 "	18 "	Libra	♎	5 "	9 "	Taurus	♉
6 "	0 "	Scorpio	♏	6 "	29 "	Taurus	♉
7 "	12 "	Scorpio	♏	7 "	16 "	Gemini	♊
8 "	23 "	Scorpio	♏	8 "	0 "	Cancer	♋
9 "	5 "	Sagittarius	♐	9 "	13 "	Cancer	♋
10 "	17 "	Sagittarius	♐	10 "	26 "	Cancer	♋
11 "	1 "	Capricorn	♑	11 "	8 "	Leo	♌
12 Noon	16 "	Capricorn	♑	12 Midnight	19 "	Leo	♌

NOVEMBER –11–

A.M.				P.M.			
1 o'clock	10° of	Virgo	♍	1 o'clock	20° of	Aquarius	♒
2 "	22 "	Virgo	♍	2 "	13 "	Pisces	♓
3 "	4 "	Libra	♎	3 "	9 "	Aries	♈
4 "	16 "	Libra	♎	4 "	4 "	Taurus	♉
5 "	27 "	Libra	♎	5 "	25 "	Taurus	♉
6 "	9 "	Scorpio	♏	6 "	12 "	Gemini	♊
7 "	21 "	Scorpio	♏	7 "	28 "	Gemini	♊
8 "	2 "	Sagittarius	♐	8 "	11 "	Cancer	♋
9 "	15 "	Sagittarius	♐	9 "	23 "	Cancer	♋
10 "	28 "	Sagittarius	♐	10 "	5 "	Leo	♌
11 "	12 "	Capricorn	♑	11 "	17 "	Leo	♌
12 Noon	29 "	Capricorn	♑	12 Midnight	28 "	Leo	♌

NOVEMBER –23–

A.M.				P.M.			
1 o'clock	19°	of Virgo	♍	1 o'clock	8°	of Pisces	♓
2 "	1	" Libra	♎	2 "	3	" Aries	♈
3 "	13	" Libra	♎	3 "	29	" Aries	♈
4 "	25	" Libra	♎	4 "	20	" Taurus	♉
5 "	7	" Scorpio	♏	5 "	9	" Gemini	♊
6 "	18	" Scorpio	♏	6 "	24	" Gemini	♊
7 "	0	" Sagittarius	♐	7 "	8	" Cancer	♋
8 "	12	" Sagittarius	♐	8 "	20	" Cancer	♋
9 "	25	" Sagittarius	♐	9 "	2	" Leo	♌
10 "	9	" Capricorn	♑	10 "	14	" Leo	♌
11 "	25	" Capricorn	♑	11 "	26	" Leo	♌
12 Noon	14	" Aquarius	♒	12 Midnight	7	" Virgo	♍

DECEMBER –5–

A.M.				P.M.			
1 o'clock	28°	of Virgo	♍	1 o'clock	26°	of Pisces	♓
2 "	10	" Libra	♎	2 "	22	" Aries	♈
3 "	21	" Libra	♎	3 "	15	" Taurus	♉
4 "	3	" Scorpio	♏	4 "	4	" Gemini	♊
5 "	15	" Scorpio	♏	5 "	20	" Gemini	♊
6 "	27	" Scorpio	♏	6 "	4	" Cancer	♋
7 "	9	" Sagittarius	♐	7 "	17	" Cancer	♋
8 "	21	" Sagittarius	♐	8 "	29	" Cancer	♋
9 "	5	" Capricorn	♑	9 "	11	" Leo	♌
10 "	20	" Capricorn	♑	10 "	22	" Leo	♌
11 "	9	" Aquarius	♒	11 "	4	" Virgo	♍
12 Noon	0	" Pisces	♓	12 Midnight	16	" Virgo	♍

DECEMBER –18–

A.M.				P.M.			
1 o'clock	9°	of Libra	♎	1 o'clock	20°	of Aries	♈
2 "	21	" Libra	♎	2 "	13	" Taurus	♉
3 "	2	" Scorpio	♏	3 "	3	" Gemini	♊
4 "	14	" Scorpio	♏	4 "	19	" Gemini	♊
5 "	26	" Scorpio	♏	5 "	3	" Cancer	♋
6 "	8	" Sagittarius	♐	6 "	16	" Cancer	♋
7 "	21	" Sagittarius	♐	7 "	28	" Cancer	♋
8 "	4	" Capricorn	♑	8 "	10	" Leo	♌
9 "	19	" Capricorn	♑	9 "	22	" Leo	♌
10 "	7	" Aquarius	♒	10 "	4	" Virgo	♍
11 "	29	" Aquarius	♒	11 "	16	" Virgo	♍
12 Noon	24	" Pisces	♓	12 Midnight	27	" Virgo	♍

APPENDIX VII

A Shortcut to the Moon

The Moon transits the zodiac every 30 days, and stays in each sign some 2½ days. Since the Moon represents the individual's emotional makeup, it is important astrologically to arrive at the correct Moon sign. The Moon moves approximately ½ degree per hour (33′ = 33 minutes), or 12 degrees for every 24-hour period. The Moon tables are calculated for zero hours or midnight Greenwich Mean Time. Because of the Moon's rapid motion, the Greenwich tables should first be adjusted to the time zone in which the individual was born. New York or Philadelphia, for instance, are in the Eastern Standard zone, 5 hours or 2½ zodiacal degrees west of the Greenwich meridian. To adjust to this time difference, add 2½ degrees (2 degrees to eliminate fractions) to the listed date immediately preceding the individual's birth date, and in the same way add 3 degrees for Central Time correction, 3½ (or 3) for Mountain Time, and 4 degrees for Pacific Standard, as in California. If, say, the individual was born in Kansas City, Missouri, on April 14, 1942, at 6:04 P.M., Central Standard Time, adjusted from 7:04 P.M. daylight time: an adjustment of 3 degrees would be made for Central Standard Time. This 3-degree difference would be added to the nearest preceding position in the Moon tables, midnight or zero hours April 13, 1942, or 22 degrees Pisces, to get the comparable zero hours Moon position for Kansas City on April 13, which would be 25 degrees Pisces. Since the subject was born at about 6 P.M., CST, on April 14, approximately one 24-hour day and 18 hours (a total of 42 hours) after the adjusted degree for zero hours or midnight April 13, 21 degrees (½ degree for each hour) would be added to the corrected degree of 25 Pisces. The resulting Moon position, since there are 30 degrees in each sign, would be 16 degrees Aries—close enough to get a significant aspect, and in this case the exact Moon position in this individual's precisely calculated natal chart.

MOON POSITIONS 1900–1975
Greenwich Mean Time
Midnight or Zero Hours

1900	Jan.	Feb.	Mar.	April	May	June	July	Aug.	Sept.	Oct.	Nov.	Dec.
1	2 ♑	25 ♒	3 ♓	27 ♈	4 ♊	22 ♋	25 ♌	9 ♎	23 ♏	27 ♐	16 ♒	25 ♓
3	2 ♒	25 ♓	4 ♈	26 ♉	1 ♋	17 ♌	19 ♍	2 ♏	18 ♐	23 ♑	15 ♓	24 ♈
5	1 ♓	24 ♈	3 ♉	23 ♊	26 ♋	11 ♍	12 ♎	27 ♏	14 ♑	21 ♒	15 ♈	23 ♉
7	0 ♈	22 ♉	1 ♊	18 ♋	21 ♌	4 ♎	7 ♏	23 ♐	13 ♒	21 ♓	15 ♉	22 ♊
9	28 ♈	13 ♊	27 ♊	12 ♌	15 ♍	29 ♎	2 ♐	20 ♑	13 ♓	22 ♈	14 ♊	19 ♋
11	25 ♉	12 ♋	22 ♋	6 ♍	8 ♎	24 ♏	28 ♐	19 ♒	13 ♈	22 ♉	12 ♋	15 ♌
13	21 ♊	7 ♌	16 ♌	0 ♎	3 ♏	20 ♐	26 ♑	19 ♓	13 ♉	20 ♊	8 ♌	10 ♍
15	15 ♋	1 ♍	9 ♍	24 ♎	28 ♏	17 ♑	25 ♒	19 ♈	11 ♊	16 ♋	2 ♍	4 ♎
17	10 ♌	24 ♍	3 ♎	19 ♏	24 ♐	15 ♒	24 ♓	17 ♉	7 ♋	11 ♌	26 ♍	28 ♎
19	4 ♍	18 ♎	27 ♎	14 ♐	21 ♑	13 ♓	23 ♈	14 ♊	2 ♌	6 ♍	20 ♎	22 ♏
21	27 ♍	12 ♏	22 ♏	10 ♑	18 ♒	12 ♈	21 ♉	10 ♋	27 ♌	29 ♍	14 ♏	17 ♐
23	21 ♎	8 ♐	17 ♐	7 ♒	17 ♓	10 ♉	17 ♊	5 ♌	20 ♍	23 ♎	8 ♐	13 ♑
25	16 ♏	4 ♑	14 ♑	6 ♓	15 ♈	7 ♊	13 ♋	0 ♍	14 ♎	17 ♏	4 ♑	10 ♒
27	12 ♐	3 ♒	12 ♒	6 ♈	14 ♉	4 ♋	8 ♌	23 ♍	8 ♏	11 ♐	0 ♒	8 ♓
29	10 ♑		11 ♓	5 ♉	12 ♊	0 ♌	3 ♍	17 ♎	2 ♐	6 ♑	27 ♒	6 ♈
31	10 ♒		12 ♈		9 ♋		27 ♍	11 ♏		3 ♒		4 ♉

1901	Jan.	Feb.	Mar.	April	May	June	July	Aug.	Sept.	Oct.	Nov.	Dec.
1	18 ♉	10 ♋	20 ♋	7 ♍	10 ♎	24 ♏	27 ♐	15 ♒	7 ♈	16 ♉	9 ♋	15 ♌
3	16 ♊	6 ♌	15 ♌	1 ♎	4 ♏	18 ♐	23 ♑	13 ♓	6 ♉	15 ♊	6 ♌	11 ♍
5	14 ♋	1 ♍	10 ♍	25 ♎	27 ♏	13 ♑	19 ♒	11 ♈	4 ♊	13 ♋	2 ♍	6 ♎
7	10 ♌	26 ♍	4 ♎	18 ♏	21 ♐	9 ♒	16 ♓	9 ♉	2 ♋	9 ♌	27 ♍	0 ♏
9	6 ♍	20 ♎	28 ♎	12 ♐	16 ♑	6 ♓	14 ♈	8 ♊	29 ♋	5 ♍	21 ♎	23 ♏
11	0 ♎	13 ♏	22 ♏	7 ♑	12 ♒	4 ♈	13 ♉	5 ♋	25 ♌	0 ♎	15 ♏	17 ♐
13	24 ♎	7 ♐	16 ♐	3 ♒	9 ♓	2 ♉	11 ♊	3 ♌	21 ♍	24 ♎	8 ♐	11 ♑
15	17 ♏	3 ♑	11 ♑	0 ♓	8 ♈	2 ♊	10 ♋	29 ♌	15 ♎	18 ♏	2 ♑	6 ♒
17	12 ♐	0 ♒	7 ♒	0 ♈	8 ♉	1 ♋	7 ♌	25 ♍	9 ♏	11 ♐	26 ♑	2 ♓
19	8 ♑	28 ♒	6 ♓	0 ♉	8 ♊	29 ♋	4 ♍	19 ♎	3 ♐	5 ♑	22 ♒	28 ♓
21	5 ♒	28 ♓	6 ♈	0 ♊	7 ♋	26 ♌	29 ♍	13 ♏	27 ♐	0 ♒	19 ♓	26 ♈
23	4 ♓	27 ♈	6 ♉	29 ♊	5 ♌	21 ♍	23 ♎	7 ♐	22 ♑	26 ♒	17 ♈	25 ♉
25	3 ♈	26 ♉	6 ♊	26 ♋	0 ♍	15 ♎	17 ♏	1 ♑	18 ♒	24 ♓	17 ♉	25 ♊
27	1 ♉	23 ♊	3 ♋	22 ♌	25 ♍	9 ♏	11 ♐	27 ♑	16 ♓	24 ♈	17 ♊	25 ♋
29	29 ♉		29 ♋	16 ♍	19 ♎	3 ♐	6 ♑	24 ♒	16 ♈	24 ♉	17 ♋	23 ♌
31	26 ♊		25 ♌		12 ♏		2 ♒	22 ♓		24 ♊		20 ♍

1902	Jan.	Feb.	Mar.	April	May	June	July	Aug.	Sept.	Oct.	Nov.	Dec.
1	2♎	16♏	24♏	7♑	10♒	28♓	5♉	28♊	22♌	28♍	15♏	18♐
3	26♎	10♐	18♐	2♒	6♓	26♈	4♊	28♋	20♍	24♎	9♐	12♑
5	20♏	4♑	12♑	28♒	3♈	25♉	4♋	27♌	16♎	19♏	3♑	5♒
7	14♐	29♑	7♒	25♓	2♉	26♊	4♌	25♍	11♏	13♐	27♑	29♒
9	8♑	25♒	3♓	24♈	2♊	26♋	3♍	21♎	5♐	7♑	21♒	25♓
11	3♒	22♓	1♈	28♉	2♋	24♌	0♎	15♏	29♐	1♒	16♓	21♈
13	29♒	19♈	29♈	23♊	1♌	21♍	25♎	9♐	23♑	26♒	13♈	20♉
15	25♓	17♉	28♉	21♋	29♌	16♎	19♏	3♑	18♒	22♓	12♉	20♊
17	22♈	15♊	26♊	18♌	24♍	10♏	13♐	27♑	14♓	19♈	12♊	20♋
19	21♉	14♋	24♋	15♍	19♎	4♐	6♑	22♒	11♈	18♉	12♋	20♌
21	19♊	12♌	22♌	10♎	13♏	28♐	1♒	18♓	8♉	17♊	11♌	18♍
23	19♋	9♍	18♍	4♏	7♐	22♑	26♌	15♈	7♊	16♋	8♍	14♎
25	17♌	5♎	13♎	23♏	1♑	16♒	21♓	12♉	5♋	14♌	4♎	9♏
27	14♍	0♏	8♏	22♐	25♑	11♓	18♈	10♊	3♌	11♍	29♎	3♐
29	10♎		2♐	16♑	19♒	7♈	15♉	9♋	1♍	7♎	24♏	27♐
31	4♏		25♐		15♓		14♊	7♌		3♏		20♑

1903	Jan.	Feb.	Mar.	April	May	June	July	Aug.	Sept.	Oct.	Nov.	Dec.
1	2♒	18♓	27♓	17♉	25♊	19♌	27♍	16♏	1♑	3♒	17♓	20♈
3	26♒	13♈	23♈	15♊	24♋	17♍	23♎	11♐	25♑	27♒	12♈	17♉
5	21♓	10♉	20♉	13♋	22♌	14♎	19♏	5♑	19♒	22♓	9♉	15♊
7	17♈	7♊	18♊	11♌	20♍	9♏	13♐	28♑	13♓	17♈	6♊	14♋
9	14♉	7♋	16♋	10♍	17♎	4♐	8♑	22♒	8♈	13♉	4♋	13♌
11	13♊	7♌	16♌	7♎	13♏	29♐	1♒	16♓	3♉	10♊	3♌	12♍
13	13♋	6♍	15♍	4♏	8♐	23♑	25♒	11♈	29♉	8♋	1♍	9♎
15	14♌	5♎	12♎	0♐	2♑	16♒	19♓	6♉	27♊	6♌	29♍	6♏
17	13♍	1♏	9♏	24♐	26♑	10♓	14♈	3♊	25♋	5♍	26♎	2♐
19	10♎	26♏	4♐	18♑	20♒	5♈	10♉	1♋	25♌	3♎	23♏	27♐
21	6♏	20♐	28♐	12♒	14♓	1♉	7♊	1♌	24♍	1♏	19♐	22♑
23	0♐	14♑	22♑	6♓	10♈	29♉	7♋	1♍	23♎	28♏	13♑	15♒
25	24♐	8♒	16♒	2♈	7♉	29♊	8♌	1♎	20♏	23♐	7♒	9♓
27	17♑	2♓	11♓	28♈	5♊	29♋	8♍	28♎	15♐	18♑	1♓	3♈
29	11♒		6♈	26♉	5♋	29♌	6♎	25♏	10♑	11♒	25♓	28♈
31	6♓		3♉		4♌		3♏	19♐		5♓		24♉

1904	Jan.	Feb.	Mar.	April	May	June	July	Aug.	Sept.	Oct.	Nov.	Dec.
1	9 ♊	1 ♌	24 ♌	17 ♎	24 ♏	12 ♑	15 ♒	29 ♓	13 ♉	18 ♊	9 ♌	17 ♍
3	8 ♋	1 ♍	24 ♍	16 ♏	21 ♐	6 ♒	8 ♓	22 ♈	9 ♊	15 ♋	7 ♍	16 ♎
5	8 ♌	1 ♎	24 ♎	13 ♐	16 ♑	0 ♓	2 ♈	17 ♉	5 ♋	13 ♌	6 ♎	14 ♏
7	8 ♍	29 ♎	22 ♏	8 ♑	11 ♒	24 ♓	26 ♈	13 ♊	4 ♌	12 ♍	5 ♏	12 ♐
9	6 ♎	26 ♏	18 ♐	3 ♒	4 ♓	8 ♈	21 ♉	11 ♋	4 ♍	12 ♎	4 ♐	10 ♑
11	3 ♏	21 ♐	12 ♑	26 ♒	28 ♓	13 ♉	18 ♊	10 ♌	4 ♎	12 ♏	2 ♑	5 ♒
13	29 ♏	15 ♑	6 ♒	20 ♓	23 ♈	10 ♊	17 ♋	10 ♍	4 ♏	10 ♐	26 ♑	0 ♓
15	24 ♐	9 ♒	0 ♓	14 ♈	18 ♉	8 ♋	17 ♌	10 ♎	2 ♐	7 ♑	22 ♒	23 ♓
17	18 ♑	3 ♓	23 ♓	9 ♉	15 ♊	7 ♌	16 ♍	9 ♏	28 ♐	2 ♒	16 ♓	17 ♈
19	12 ♒	26 ♓	18 ♈	5 ♊	13 ♋	6 ♍	15 ♎	6 ♐	23 ♑	26 ♒	9 ♈	12 ♉
21	6 ♓	21 ♈	12 ♉	2 ♋	11 ♌	4 ♎	12 ♏	1 ♑	17 ♒	19 ♓	4 ♉	7 ♊
23	29 ♓	15 ♉	8 ♊	0 ♌	9 ♍	2 ♏	9 ♐	26 ♑	11 ♓	13 ♈	29 ♉	4 ♋
25	24 ♈	12 ♊	5 ♋	28 ♌	7 ♎	29 ♏	4 ♑	20 ♒	4 ♈	7 ♉	25 ♊	2 ♌
27	19 ♉	9 ♋	3 ♌	27 ♍	5 ♏	25 ♐	29 ♑	14 ♓	28 ♈	2 ♊	22 ♋	0 ♍
29	17 ♊	9 ♌	3 ♍	26 ♎	3 ♐	20 ♑	23 ♒	7 ♈	23 ♉	28 ♊	19 ♌	28 ♍
31	16 ♋		3 ♎		29 ♐		17 ♓	1 ♉		25 ♋		26 ♎

1905	Jan.	Feb.	Mar.	April	May	June	July	Aug.	Sept.	Oct.	Nov.	Dec.
1	10 ♏	1 ♑	11 ♑	27 ♒	0 ♈	14 ♉	18 ♊	6 ♌	28 ♍	7 ♏	0 ♑	6 ♒
3	8 ♐	27 ♑	6 ♒	21 ♓	24 ♈	9 ♊	14 ♋	4 ♍	27 ♎	6 ♐	27 ♑	1 ♓
5	5 ♑	22 ♒	0 ♓	15 ♈	18 ♉	4 ♋	11 ♌	3 ♎	26 ♏	4 ♑	23 ♒	26 ♓
7	1 ♒	16 ♓	24 ♓	9 ♉	12 ♊	1 ♌	8 ♍	2 ♏	24 ♐	1 ♒	17 ♓	20 ♈
9	25 ♒	9 ♈	18 ♈	3 ♊	7 ♋	28 ♌	6 ♎	0 ♐	21 ♑	26 ♒	11 ♈	13 ♉
11	19 ♓	3 ♉	12 ♉	28 ♊	4 ♌	25 ♍	5 ♏	27 ♐	16 ♒	20 ♓	5 ♉	7 ♊
13	13 ♈	27 ♉	6 ♊	24 ♋	1 ♍	24 ♎	3 ♐	24 ♑	11 ♓	14 ♈	28 ♉	2 ♋
15	7 ♉	23 ♊	1 ♋	21 ♌	29 ♍	23 ♏	1 ♑	20 ♒	5 ♈	8 ♉	23 ♊	27 ♋
17	2 ♊	20 ♋	28 ♋	20 ♍	29 ♎	22 ♐	28 ♑	15 ♓	29 ♈	2 ♊	17 ♋	23 ♌
19	28 ♊	19 ♌	27 ♌	20 ♎	29 ♏	20 ♑	24 ♒	9 ♈	23 ♉	26 ♊	13 ♌	20 ♍
21	26 ♋	19 ♍	27 ♍	20 ♏	28 ♐	16 ♒	19 ♓	2 ♉	17 ♊	21 ♋	10 ♍	18 ♎
23	25 ♌	19 ♎	27 ♎	20 ♐	25 ♑	11 ♓	13 ♈	26 ♉	12 ♋	17 ♌	8 ♎	17 ♏
25	24 ♍	18 ♏	27 ♏	17 ♑	21 ♒	5 ♈	6 ♉	21 ♊	8 ♌	15 ♍	8 ♏	17 ♐
27	23 ♎	15 ♐	25 ♐	12 ♒	15 ♓	28 ♈	1 ♊	17 ♋	7 ♍	14 ♎	8 ♐	16 ♑
29	21 ♏		21 ♑	6 ♓	8 ♈	23 ♉	26 ♊	14 ♌	6 ♎	15 ♏	8 ♑	13 ♒
31	18 ♐		15 ♒		2 ♉		22 ♋	13 ♍		15 ♐		9 ♓

1906	Jan.	Feb.	Mar.	April	May	June	July	Aug.	Sept.	Oct.	Nov.	Dec.
1	22 ♓	6 ♉	13 ♉	27 ♊	0 ♌	19 ♍	27 ♎	20 ♐	13 ♒	19 ♓	5 ♉	8 ♊
3	16 ♈	29 ♉	7 ♊	22 ♋	26 ♌	17 ♎	26 ♏	19 ♑	10 ♓	14 ♈	0 ♊	2 ♋
5	10 ♉	24 ♊	1 ♋	18 ♌	24 ♍	17 ♏	26 ♐	18 ♒	6 ♈	9 ♉	23 ♊	26 ♋
7	4 ♊	19 ♋	27 ♋	15 ♍	23 ♎	17 ♐	25 ♑	15 ♓	1 ♉	3 ♊	17 ♋	20 ♌
9	28 ♊	15 ♌	23 ♌	15 ♎	23 ♏	17 ♑	23 ♒	11 ♈	25 ♉	27 ♊	11 ♌	15 ♍
11	24 ♋	13 ♍	22 ♍	15 ♏	24 ♐	15 ♒	20 ♓	5 ♉	19 ♊	21 ♋	6 ♍	12 ♎
13	20 ♌	11 ♎	21 ♎	15 ♐	23 ♑	12 ♓	15 ♈	29 ♉	13 ♋	15 ♌	4 ♎	11 ♏
15	17 ♍	10 ♏	20 ♏	13 ♑	20 ♒	6 ♈	9 ♉	23 ♊	8 ♌	12 ♍	3 ♏	11 ♐
17	15 ♎	8 ♐	19 ♐	10 ♒	15 ♓	1 ♉	3 ♊	17 ♋	4 ♍	10 ♎	3 ♐	11 ♑
19	13 ♏	6 ♑	17 ♑	6 ♓	10 ♈	24 ♉	27 ♊	12 ♌	1 ♎	9 ♏	3 ♑	11 ♒
21	12 ♐	3 ♒	13 ♒	0 ♈	4 ♉	18 ♊	21 ♋	9 ♍	0 ♏	9 ♐	2 ♒	9 ♓
23	10 ♑	0 ♓	9 ♓	25 ♈	27 ♉	12 ♋	16 ♌	6 ♎	29 ♏	3 ♑	29 ♒	5 ♈
25	8 ♒	25 ♓	4 ♈	18 ♉	21 ♊	7 ♌	12 ♍	4 ♏	28 ♐	6 ♒	25 ♓	29 ♈
27	4 ♓	20 ♈	28 ♈	12 ♊	15 ♋	2 ♍	9 ♎	2 ♐	25 ♑	3 ♓	20 ♈	23 ♉
29	29 ♓		22 ♉	6 ♋	10 ♌	29 ♍	7 ♏	1 ♑	23 ♒	28 ♓	14 ♉	17 ♊
31	24 ♈		15 ♊		5 ♍		6 ♐	29 ♑		23 ♈		11 ♋

1907	Jan.	Feb.	Mar.	April	May	June	July	Aug.	Sept.	Oct.	Nov.	Dec.
1	23 ♋	9 ♍	18 ♍	9 ♏	17 ♐	11 ♒	18 ♓	6 ♉	21 ♊	23 ♋	7 ♍	10 ♎
3	17 ♌	5 ♎	15 ♎	7 ♐	16 ♑	8 ♓	15 ♈	1 ♊	15 ♋	17 ♌	2 ♎	7 ♏
5	12 ♍	2 ♏	12 ♏	6 ♑	14 ♒	5 ♈	10 ♉	25 ♊	9 ♌	12 ♍	29 ♎	6 ♐
7	8 ♎	0 ♐	11 ♐	4 ♒	12 ♓	0 ♉	4 ♊	18 ♋	3 ♍	7 ♎	27 ♏	5 ♑
9	5 ♏	28 ♐	9 ♑	1 ♓	8 ♈	25 ♉	28 ♊	12 ♌	28 ♍	4 ♏	26 ♐	5 ♒
11	4 ♐	28 ♑	7 ♒	28 ♓	3 ♉	19 ♊	21 ♋	7 ♍	24 ♎	2 ♐	25 ♑	4 ♓
13	4 ♑	27 ♒	5 ♓	24 ♈	28 ♉	13 ♋	15 ♌	1 ♎	21 ♏	0 ♑	23 ♒	1 ♈
15	4 ♒	25 ♓	3 ♈	20 ♉	22 ♊	6 ♌	9 ♍	27 ♎	19 ♐	28 ♑	21 ♓	28 ♈
17	3 ♓	21 ♈	29 ♈	14 ♊	16 ♋	0 ♍	4 ♎	25 ♏	17 ♑	26 ♒	18 ♈	23 ♉
19	0 ♈	16 ♉	24 ♉	8 ♋	9 ♌	25 ♍	1 ♏	23 ♐	16 ♒	24 ♓	14 ♉	18 ♊
21	26 ♈	10 ♊	18 ♊	1 ♌	4 ♍	22 ♎	19 ♏	22 ♑	15 ♓	22 ♈	9 ♊	12 ♋
23	20 ♉	4 ♋	12 ♋	26 ♌	0 ♎	20 ♏	28 ♐	22 ♒	13 ♈	18 ♉	3 ♋	5 ♌
25	14 ♊	28 ♋	6 ♌	21 ♍	27 ♎	20 ♐	28 ♑	21 ♓	10 ♉	13 ♊	27 ♋	29 ♌
27	7 ♋	22 ♌	0 ♍	19 ♎	26 ♏	20 ♑	28 ♒	19 ♈	5 ♊	7 ♋	21 ♌	23 ♍
29	2 ♌		27 ♍	18 ♏	26 ♐	20 ♒	27 ♓	15 ♉	29 ♊	1 ♌	15 ♍	18 ♎
31	26 ♌		24 ♎		26 ♑		24 ♈	9 ♊		25 ♌		15 ♏

1908	Jan.	Feb.	Mar.	April	May	June	July	Aug.	Sept.	Oct.	Nov.	Dec.
1	29 ♏	21 ♑	15 ♒	8 ♈	15 ♉	2 ♋	4 ♌	19 ♍	4 ♏	9 ♐	0 ♒	10 ♓
3	28 ♐	22 ♒	15 ♓	6 ♉	11 ♊	26 ♋	28 ♌	13 ♎	0 ♐	6 ♑	29 ♒	8 ♈
5	29 ♑	22 ♓	14 ♈	3 ♊	6 ♋	20 ♌	22 ♍	7 ♏	26 ♐	4 ♒	28 ♓	6 ♉
7	29 ♒	20 ♈	12 ♉	28 ♊	0 ♌	14 ♍	16 ♎	3 ♐	24 ♑	3 ♓	27 ♈	3 ♊
9	27 ♓	17 ♉	8 ♊	22 ♋	24 ♌	8 ♎	12 ♏	1 ♑	24 ♒	3 ♈	25 ♉	0 ♋
11	25 ♈	12 ♊	2 ♋	16 ♌	18 ♍	4 ♏	9 ♐	1 ♒	25 ♓	3 ♉	22 ♊	25 ♋
13	20 ♉	6 ♋	26 ♋	10 ♍	13 ♎	1 ♐	8 ♑	1 ♓	24 ♈	1 ♊	17 ♋	19 ♌
15	15 ♊	29 ♋	19 ♌	4 ♎	9 ♏	29 ♐	7 ♒	1 ♈	23 ♉	27 ♊	11 ♌	13 ♍
17	9 ♋	23 ♌	14 ♍	0 ♏	6 ♐	28 ♑	7 ♓	0 ♉	19 ♊	22 ♋	5 ♍	7 ♎
19	2 ♌	17 ♍	8 ♎	27 ♏	4 ♑	28 ♒	7 ♈	27 ♉	13 ♋	15 ♌	29 ♍	1 ♏
21	26 ♌	11 ♎	4 ♏	24 ♐	3 ♒	26 ♓	4 ♉	22 ♊	7 ♌	9 ♍	24 ♎	27 ♏
23	20 ♍	7 ♏	0 ♐	22 ♑	1 ♓	24 ♈	0 ♊	16 ♋	1 ♍	3 ♎	19 ♏	24 ♐
25	14 ♎	3 ♐	27 ♐	20 ♒	29 ♓	20 ♉	25 ♊	10 ♌	25 ♍	28 ♎	16 ♐	23 ♑
27	10 ♏	1 ♑	25 ♑	19 ♓	27 ♈	16 ♊	19 ♋	4 ♍	19 ♎	23 ♏	13 ♑	22 ♒
29	7 ♐	0 ♒	24 ♒	17 ♈	24 ♉	10 ♋	13 ♌	28 ♍	14 ♏	20 ♐	11 ♒	21 ♓
31	6 ♑		24 ♓		19 ♊		7 ♍	22 ♎		17 ♑		19 ♈

1909	Jan.	Feb.	Mar.	April	May	June	July	Aug.	Sept.	Oct.	Nov.	Dec.
1	3 ♉	22 ♊	2 ♋	18 ♌	20 ♍	4 ♏	7 ♐	26 ♑	19 ♓	28 ♈	20 ♊	25 ♋
3	0 ♊	17 ♋	27 ♋	11 ♍	14 ♎	29 ♏	4 ♑	25 ♒	19 ♈	28 ♉	17 ♋	21 ♌
5	26 ♊	12 ♌	21 ♌	5 ♎	8 ♏	25 ♐	2 ♒	25 ♓	18 ♉	25 ♊	13 ♌	16 ♍
7	21 ♋	6 ♍	14 ♍	29 ♎	3 ♐	22 ♑	0 ♓	24 ♈	16 ♊	22 ♋	8 ♍	10 ♎
9	15 ♌	29 ♍	8 ♎	24 ♏	29 ♐	20 ♒	29 ♓	22 ♉	12 ♋	17 ♌	1 ♎	3 ♏
11	9 ♍	23 ♎	2 ♏	19 ♐	25 ♑	18 ♓	27 ♈	19 ♊	7 ♌	11 ♍	25 ♎	27 ♏
13	3 ♎	18 ♏	27 ♏	15 ♑	23 ♒	16 ♈	25 ♉	15 ♋	2 ♍	4 ♎	19 ♏	22 ♐
15	27 ♎	13 ♐	22 ♐	12 ♒	21 ♓	15 ♉	22 ♊	10 ♌	26 ♍	28 ♎	13 ♐	18 ♑
17	22 ♏	10 ♑	19 ♑	11 ♓	21 ♈	13 ♊	18 ♋	5 ♍	19 ♎	22 ♏	8 ♑	15 ♒
19	18 ♐	9 ♒	17 ♒	11 ♈	20 ♉	10 ♋	14 ♌	29 ♍	13 ♏	16 ♐	4 ♒	12 ♓
21	17 ♑	10 ♓	18 ♓	11 ♉	18 ♊	6 ♌	8 ♍	22 ♎	7 ♐	11 ♑	2 ♓	10 ♈
23	16 ♒	10 ♈	18 ♈	10 ♊	15 ♋	0 ♍	2 ♎	16 ♏	2 ♑	8 ♒	0 ♈	9 ♉
25	16 ♓	9 ♉	18 ♉	7 ♋	10 ♌	24 ♍	26 ♎	11 ♐	29 ♑	6 ♓	29 ♈	8 ♊
27	15 ♈	6 ♊	15 ♊	2 ♌	4 ♍	18 ♎	20 ♏	7 ♑	27 ♒	6 ♈	29 ♉	6 ♋
29	13 ♉		11 ♋	26 ♌	28 ♍	12 ♏	15 ♐	4 ♒	27 ♓	6 ♉	28 ♊	3 ♌
31	10 ♊		6 ♌		22 ♎		12 ♑	4 ♓		6 ♊		29 ♌

1910	Jan.	Feb.	Mar.	April	May	June	July	Aug.	Sept.	Oct.	Nov.	Dec.
1	12 ♍	25 ♎	3 ♏	17 ♐	21 ♑	10 ♓	19 ♈	12 ♊	4 ♌	10 ♍	26 ♎	28 ♏
3	6 ♎	19 ♏	27 ♏	12 ♑	17 ♒	9 ♈	18 ♉	10 ♋	1 ♍	5 ♎	20 ♏	22 ♐
5	29 ♎	13 ♐	21 ♐	8 ♒	15 ♓	8 ♉	17 ♊	8 ♌	26 ♍	29 ♎	13 ♐	16 ♑
7	23 ♏	9 ♑	16 ♑	6 ♓	14 ♈	8 ♊	15 ♋	5 ♍	21 ♎	23 ♏	7 ♑	11 ♒
9	18 ♐	6 ♒	14 ♒	6 ♈	14 ♉	7 ♋	13 ♌	0 ♎	15 ♏	16 ♐	1 ♒	6 ♓
11	14 ♑	4 ♓	13 ♓	6 ♉	14 ♊	5 ♌	10 ♍	25 ♎	8 ♐	10 ♑	27 ♒	3 ♈
13	11 ♒	3 ♈	12 ♈	6 ♊	13 ♋	2 ♍	5 ♎	18 ♏	2 ♑	5 ♒	24 ♓	2 ♉
15	9 ♓	2 ♉	12 ♉	4 ♋	10 ♌	27 ♍	29 ♎	12 ♐	27 ♑	2 ♓	23 ♈	1 ♊
17	7 ♈	0 ♊	11 ♊	1 ♌	6 ♍	21 ♎	22 ♏	7 ♑	24 ♒	1 ♈	24 ♉	2 ♋
19	6 ♉	28 ♊	8 ♋	27 ♌	0 ♎	14 ♏	16 ♐	2 ♒	22 ♓	0 ♉	24 ♊	1 ♌
21	4 ♊	24 ♋	4 ♌	21 ♍	24 ♎	8 ♐	11 ♑	0 ♓	22 ♈	0 ♊	23 ♋	29 ♌
23	1 ♋	20 ♌	0 ♍	15 ♎	17 ♏	2 ♑	7 ♒	28 ♓	21 ♉	0 ♋	21 ♌	25 ♍
25	28 ♋	15 ♍	24 ♍	9 ♏	11 ♐	28 ♑	4 ♓	26 ♈	20 ♊	28 ♋	16 ♍	20 ♎
27	24 ♌	10 ♎	18 ♎	2 ♐	6 ♑	24 ♒	2 ♈	25 ♉	17 ♋	24 ♌	11 ♎	13 ♏
29	19 ♍		12 ♏	26 ♐	1 ♒	21 ♓	0 ♉	23 ♊	14 ♌	19 ♍	5 ♏	7 ♐
31	13 ♎		5 ♐		27 ♒		28 ♉	20 ♋		14 ♎		1 ♑

1911	Jan.	Feb.	Mar.	April	May	June	July	Aug.	Sept.	Oct.	Nov.	Dec.
1	13 ♑	0 ♓	9 ♓	0 ♉	8 ♊	2 ♌	9 ♍	27 ♎	11 ♐	13 ♑	27 ♒	0 ♈
3	8 ♒	27 ♓	6 ♈	29 ♉	8 ♋	0 ♍	5 ♎	21 ♏	5 ♑	7 ♒	22 ♓	27 ♈
5	3 ♓	24 ♈	4 ♉	28 ♊	6 ♌	26 ♍	0 ♏	15 ♐	29 ♑	2 ♓	19 ♈	26 ♉
7	0 ♈	22 ♉	3 ♊	26 ♋	3 ♍	21 ♎	24 ♏	8 ♑	24 ♒	28 ♓	18 ♉	26 ♊
9	27 ♈	20 ♊	1 ♋	23 ♌	29 ♍	15 ♏	18 ♐	3 ♒	19 ♓	25 ♈	18 ♊	27 ♋
11	26 ♉	19 ♋	29 ♋	19 ♍	24 ♎	9 ♐	12 ♑	27 ♒	16 ♈	24 ♉	17 ♋	26 ♌
13	25 ♊	17 ♌	27 ♌	15 ♎	18 ♏	3 ♑	6 ♒	23 ♓	13 ♉	22 ♊	16 ♌	23 ♍
15	25 ♋	15 ♍	23 ♍	10 ♏	12 ♐	27 ♑	0 ♓	19 ♈	11 ♊	21 ♋	13 ♍	19 ♎
17	23 ♌	11 ♎	19 ♎	4 ♐	6 ♑	21 ♒	26 ♓	16 ♉	10 ♋	19 ♌	9 ♎	14 ♏
19	20 ♍	6 ♏	14 ♏	27 ♐	0 ♒	16 ♓	22 ♈	15 ♊	8 ♌	16 ♍	4 ♏	8 ♐
21	16 ♎	0 ♐	7 ♐	21 ♑	24 ♒	13 ♈	20 ♉	14 ♋	6 ♍	13 ♎	29 ♏	2 ♑
23	10 ♏	23 ♐	1 ♑	16 ♒	20 ♓	11 ♉	19 ♊	13 ♌	4 ♎	8 ♏	23 ♐	26 ♑
25	3 ♐	17 ♑	25 ♑	12 ♓	18 ♈	10 ♊	19 ♋	12 ♍	0 ♏	3 ♐	17 ♑	19 ♒
27	27 ♐	13 ♒	21 ♒	9 ♈	17 ♉	11 ♋	19 ♌	9 ♎	25 ♏	27 ♐	11 ♒	14 ♓
29	22 ♑		17 ♓	8 ♉	17 ♊	11 ♌	17 ♍	5 ♏	19 ♐	20 ♑	5 ♓	9 ♈
31	17 ♒		15 ♈		17 ♋		14 ♎	29 ♏		14 ♒		5 ♉

1912	Jan.	Feb.	Mar.	April	May	June	July	Aug.	Sept.	Oct.	Nov.	Dec.
1	19 ♉	12 ♋	6 ♌	29 ♍	5 ♏	22 ♐	25 ♑	9 ♉	25 ♈	1 ♊	23 ♋	2 ♍
3	19 ♊	13 ♌	6 ♍	27 ♎	1 ♐	16 ♑	18 ♒	3 ♈	21 ♉	28 ♊	21 ♌	0 ♎
5	20 ♋	13 ♍	5 ♎	23 ♏	26 ♐	10 ♒	12 ♓	28 ♈	18 ♊	26 ♋	20 ♍	28 ♎
7	20 ♌	11 ♎	2 ♏	18 ♐	20 ♑	4 ♓	6 ♈	24 ♉	16 ♋	25 ♌	18 ♎	24 ♏
9	19 ♍	7 ♏	28 ♏	12 ♑	13 ♒	28 ♓	2 ♉	22 ♊	16 ♌	24 ♍	15 ♏	20 ♐
11	16 ♎	2 ♐	22 ♐	6 ♒	8 ♓	23 ♈	29 ♉	22 ♋	16 ♍	23 ♎	12 ♐	15 ♑
13	11 ♏	26 ♐	16 ♑	0 ♓	2 ♈	21 ♉	28 ♊	22 ♌	15 ♎	20 ♏	7 ♑	9 ♒
15	5 ♐	19 ♑	10 ♒	25 ♓	29 ♈	20 ♊	29 ♋	22 ♍	13 ♏	16 ♐	1 ♒	3 ♓
17	29 ♐	13 ♋	4 ♓	21 ♈	27 ♉	20 ♋	29 ♌	21 ♎	9 ♐	11 ♑	25 ♒	26 ♓
19	23 ♑	8 ♓	29 ♓	18 ♉	26 ♊	20 ♌	28 ♍	17 ♏	3 ♑	5 ♒	19 ♓	21 ♈
21	16 ♒	2 ♈	25 ♈	16 ♊	25 ♋	18 ♍	25 ♎	12 ♐	27 ♑	29 ♒	13 ♈	17 ♉
23	11 ♓	28 ♈	22 ♉	14 ♋	24 ♌	15 ♎	21 ♏	7 ♑	21 ♒	23 ♓	9 ♉	15 ♊
25	5 ♈	25 ♉	19 ♊	13 ♌	22 ♍	11 ♏	16 ♐	0 ♒	15 ♓	18 ♈	7 ♊	14 ♋
27	1 ♉	23 ♊	18 ♋	11 ♍	18 ♎	6 ♐	10 ♑	24 ♒	9 ♈	14 ♉	5 ♋	14 ♌
29	28 ♉	22 ♋	16 ♌	8 ♎	14 ♏	1 ♑	3 ♒	18 ♓	5 ♉	11 ♊	4 ♌	13 ♍
31	27 ♊		15 ♍		9 ♐		27 ♒	13 ♈		9 ♋		11 ♎

1913	Jan.	Feb.	Mar.	April	May	June	July	Aug.	Sept.	Oct.	Nov.	Dec.
1	25 ♎	13 ♐	22 ♐	8 ♒	10 ♓	24 ♈	27 ♉	17 ♋	10 ♍	18 ♎	10 ♐	16 ♑
3	21 ♏	8 ♑	17 ♑	2 ♓	4 ♈	19 ♉	24 ♊	16 ♌	10 ♎	18 ♏	8 ♑	11 ♒
5	16 ♐	2 ♒	11 ♒	25 ♓	28 ♈	16 ♊	23 ♋	16 ♍	9 ♏	16 ♐	3 ♒	5 ♓
7	11 ♑	26 ♒	5 ♓	19 ♈	24 ♉	14 ♋	22 ♌	16 ♎	7 ♐	12 ♑	28 ♒	29 ♓
9	5 ♒	20 ♓	29 ♓	14 ♉	20 ♊	12 ♌	21 ♍	14 ♏	3 ♑	7 ♒	21 ♓	23 ♈
11	29 ♒	13 ♈	23 ♈	10 ♊	17 ♋	10 ♍	19 ♎	10 ♐	28 ♑	1 ♓	15 ♈	17 ♉
13	23 ♓	8 ♉	17 ♉	7 ♋	15 ♌	9 ♎	17 ♏	6 ♑	22 ♒	25 ♓	9 ♉	13 ♊
15	17 ♈	4 ♊	13 ♊	4 ♌	14 ♍	6 ♏	13 ♐	1 ♒	16 ♓	18 ♈	4 ♊	9 ♋
17	12 ♉	1 ♋	10 ♋	3 ♍	12 ♎	4 ♐	9 ♑	25 ♒	9 ♈	12 ♉	0 ♋	7 ♌
19	9 ♊	0 ♌	9 ♌	2 ♎	10 ♏	0 ♑	4 ♒	19 ♓	3 ♉	7 ♊	26 ♋	5 ♍
21	7 ♋	1 ♍	9 ♍	2 ♏	8 ♐	26 ♑	28 ♒	12 ♈	28 ♉	3 ♋	24 ♌	3 ♎
23	7 ♌	1 ♎	9 ♎	0 ♐	5 ♑	20 ♒	22 ♓	6 ♉	23 ♊	0 ♌	22 ♍	1 ♏
25	8 ♍	0 ♏	8 ♏	27 ♐	0 ♒	14 ♓	16 ♈	1 ♊	20 ♋	28 ♌	21 ♎	29 ♏
27	7 ♎	27 ♏	6 ♐	22 ♑	24 ♒	8 ♈	10 ♉	27 ♊	18 ♌	27 ♍	20 ♏	27 ♐
29	5 ♏		2 ♑	16 ♒	18 ♓	2 ♉	5 ♊	25 ♋	18 ♍	27 ♎	18 ♐	24 ♑
31	1 ♐		26 ♑		12 ♈		3 ♋	25 ♌		26 ♏		19 ♒

1914	Jan.	Feb.	Mar.	April	May	June	July	Aug.	Sept.	Oct.	Nov.	Dec.
1	1 ♓	15 ♈	23 ♈	8 ♊	12 ♋	2 ♍	11 ♎	4 ♐	26 ♑	1 ♓	16 ♈	19 ♉
3	25 ♓	9 ♉	17 ♉	3 ♋	8 ♌	0 ♎	9 ♏	2 ♑	21 ♒	25 ♒	10 ♉	13 ♊
5	19 ♈	3 ♊	11 ♊	29 ♋	6 ♍	29 ♎	8 ♐	29 ♑	16 ♓	19 ♈	4 ♊	7 ♋
7	13 ♉	29 ♊	7 ♋	27 ♌	5 ♎	29 ♏	6 ♑	25 ♒	11 ♈	13 ♉	28 ♊	2 ♌
9	8 ♊	26 ♋	4 ♌	26 ♍	5 ♏	28 ♐	4 ♊	20 ♓	4 ♉	7 ♊	22 ♋	28 ♌
11	4 ♋	25 ♌	3 ♍	27 ♎	5 ♐	26 ♑	0 ♓	14 ♈	28 ♉	1 ♋	18 ♌	25 ♍
13	2 ♌	25 ♍	3 ♎	27 ♏	4 ♑	22 ♒	24 ♓	8 ♉	22 ♊	26 ♋	15 ♍	23 ♎
15	1 ♍	24 ♎	3 ♏	25 ♐	1 ♒	16 ♓	18 ♈	2 ♊	18 ♋	22 ♌	14 ♎	23 ♏
17	29 ♍	22 ♏	2 ♐	22 ♑	26 ♒	10 ♈	12 ♉	27 ♊	14 ♌	21 ♍	14 ♏	23 ♐
19	28 ♎	20 ♐	0 ♑	17 ♒	20 ♓	4 ♉	6 ♊	22 ♋	13 ♍	21 ♎	15 ♐	22 ♑
21	26 ♏	16 ♑	26 ♑	12 ♓	14 ♈	28 ♉	2 ♋	20 ♌	13 ♎	21 ♏	14 ♑	19 ♒
23	23 ♐	11 ♒	20 ♒	5 ♈	8 ♉	23 ♊	28 ♋	19 ♍	13 ♏	21 ♐	11 ♒	15 ♓
25	19 ♑	6 ♓	14 ♓	29 ♈	2 ♊	19 ♋	25 ♌	18 ♎	12 ♐	19 ♑	7 ♓	10 ♈
27	15 ♒	29 ♓	8 ♈	23 ♉	27 ♊	16 ♌	23 ♍	17 ♏	9 ♑	15 ♒	1 ♈	3 ♉
29	9 ♓		2 ♉	17 ♊	22 ♋	13 ♍	22 ♎	15 ♐	6 ♒	10 ♓	25 ♈	27 ♉
31	3 ♈		26 ♉		19 ♌		20 ♏	12 ♑		4 ♈		21 ♊

1915	Jan.	Feb.	Mar.	April	May	June	July	Aug.	Sept.	Oct.	Nov.	Dec.
1	4 ♋	21 ♌	29 ♌	21 ♎	0 ♐	23 ♑	29 ♒	16 ♈	1 ♊	2 ♋	17 ♌	20 ♍
3	29 ♋	18 ♍	27 ♍	21 ♏	0 ♑	21 ♒	26 ♓	11 ♉	24 ♊	26 ♋	12 ♍	18 ♎
5	25 ♌	16 ♎	26 ♎	20 ♐	28 ♑	17 ♓	20 ♈	5 ♊	18 ♋	21 ♌	10 ♎	17 ♏
7	22 ♍	14 ♏	25 ♏	18 ♑	25 ♒	12 ♈	14 ♉	28 ♊	13 ♌	18 ♍	9 ♏	17 ♐
9	19 ♎	13 ♐	24 ♐	15 ♒	20 ♓	6 ♉	8 ♊	23 ♋	10 ♍	16 ♎	9 ♐	18 ♑
11	18 ♏	11 ♑	21 ♑	11 ♓	15 ♈	29 ♉	2 ♋	18 ♌	7 ♎	15 ♏	9 ♑	17 ♒
13	17 ♐	8 ♒	18 ♒	5 ♈	9 ♉	23 ♊	26 ♋	14 ♍	5 ♏	14 ♐	7 ♒	14 ♓
15	16 ♑	5 ♓	14 ♓	0 ♉	2 ♊	17 ♋	21 ♌	11 ♎	7 ♐	13 ♑	4 ♓	10 ♈
17	14 ♒	1 ♈	9 ♈	24 ♉	26 ♊	12 ♌	17 ♍	9 ♏	2 ♑	11 ♒	0 ♈	4 ♉
19	10 ♓	25 ♈	3 ♉	17 ♊	20 ♋	7 ♍	14 ♎	4 ♐	0 ♒	7 ♓	25 ♈	28 ♉
21	5 ♈	19 ♉	27 ♉	11 ♋	15 ♌	4 ♎	12 ♏	6 ♑	27 ♒	3 ♈	20 ♉	22 ♊
23	29 ♈	13 ♊	21 ♊	6 ♌	11 ♍	2 ♏	11 ♐	4 ♒	24 ♓	28 ♈	13 ♊	16 ♋
25	23 ♉	7 ♋	15 ♋	2 ♍	8 ♎	1 ♐	10 ♑	2 ♓	20 ♈	23 ♉	7 ♋	10 ♌
27	17 ♊	3 ♌	10 ♌	0 ♎	7 ♏	2 ♑	9 ♒	29 ♓	15 ♉	17 ♊	1 ♌	4 ♍
29	12 ♋		7 ♍	29 ♎	8 ♐	1 ♒	7 ♓	24 ♈	9 ♊	10 ♋	25 ♌	0 ♎
31	8 ♌		6 ♎		8 ♑		4 ♈	19 ♉		4 ♌		27 ♎

1916	Jan.	Feb.	Mar.	April	May	June	July	Aug.	Sept.	Oct.	Nov.	Dec.
1	11 ♏	4 ♑	28 ♑	20 ♓	26 ♈	12 ♊	15 ♋	29 ♌	16 ♎	23 ♏	15 ♑	24 ♒
3	10 ♐	4 ♒	27 ♒	17 ♈	21 ♉	6 ♋	8 ♌	24 ♍	12 ♏	20 ♐	14 ♒	22 ♓
5	11 ♑	3 ♓	25 ♓	13 ♉	16 ♊	0 ♌	2 ♍	19 ♎	10 ♐	19 ♑	12 ♓	19 ♈
7	11 ♒	1 ♈	22 ♈	7 ♊	9 ♋	23 ♌	27 ♍	16 ♏	8 ♑	17 ♒	9 ♈	15 ♉
9	9 ♓	27 ♈	17 ♉	1 ♋	3 ♌	18 ♍	23 ♎	14 ♐	7 ♒	15 ♓	6 ♉	11 ♊
11	6 ♈	22 ♉	12 ♊	25 ♋	27 ♌	14 ♎	20 ♏	13 ♑	6 ♓	14 ♈	2 ♊	5 ♋
13	1 ♉	16 ♊	5 ♋	19 ♌	22 ♍	11 ♏	19 ♐	13 ♒	5 ♈	11 ♉	27 ♊	29 ♋
15	25 ♉	9 ♋	29 ♋	14 ♍	19 ♎	11 ♐	19 ♑	13 ♓	3 ♉	7 ♊	21 ♋	22 ♌
17	19 ♊	3 ♌	24 ♌	11 ♎	18 ♏	11 ♑	20 ♒	11 ♈	29 ♉	1 ♋	14 ♌	16 ♍
19	13 ♋	28 ♌	19 ♍	9 ♏	17 ♐	11 ♒	19 ♓	8 ♉	23 ♊	25 ♋	8 ♍	11 ♎
21	7 ♌	23 ♍	16 ♎	8 ♐	17 ♑	10 ♓	16 ♈	3 ♊	17 ♋	18 ♌	3 ♎	7 ♏
23	1 ♍	20 ♎	14 ♏	7 ♑	16 ♒	7 ♈	12 ♉	27 ♊	11 ♌	13 ♍	0 ♏	5 ♐
25	27 ♍	17 ♏	12 ♐	5 ♒	13 ♓	2 ♉	6 ♊	20 ♋	5 ♍	8 ♎	27 ♏	5 ♑
27	23 ♎	15 ♐	10 ♑	3 ♓	10 ♈	27 ♉	0 ♋	14 ♌	0 ♎	3 ♏	26 ♐	5 ♒
29	20 ♏	14 ♑	8 ♒	0 ♈	5 ♉	21 ♊	24 ♋	8 ♍	26 ♎	3 ♐	26 ♑	4 ♓
31	19 ♐		6 ♓		0 ♊		17 ♌	3 ♎		1 ♑		3 ♈

1917	Jan.	Feb.	Mar.	April	May	June	July	Aug.	Sept.	Oct.	Nov.	Dec.
1	16 ♈	4 ♊	13 ♊	28 ♋	29 ♌	14 ♎	18 ♏	7 ♑	1 ♓	9 ♈	1 ♊	6 ♋
3	12 ♉	29 ♊	8 ♋	21 ♌	23 ♍	10 ♏	15 ♐	7 ♒	1 ♈	9 ♉	28 ♊	1 ♌
5	7 ♊	22 ♋	1 ♌	15 ♍	18 ♎	7 ♐	14 ♑	7 ♓	1 ♉	7 ♊	23 ♋	25 ♌
7	2 ♋	16 ♌	25 ♌	10 ♎	14 ♏	5 ♑	13 ♒	7 ♈	28 ♉	3 ♋	17 ♌	19 ♍
9	26 ♋	10 ♍	19 ♍	5 ♏	12 ♐	4 ♒	13 ♓	5 ♉	24 ♊	27 ♋	11 ♍	13 ♎
11	19 ♌	4 ♎	13 ♎	2 ♐	9 ♑	3 ♓	12 ♈	2 ♊	18 ♋	21 ♌	5 ♎	7 ♏
13	13 ♍	29 ♎	9 ♏	29 ♐	7 ♒	1 ♈	9 ♉	27 ♊	12 ♌	15 ♍	29 ♎	3 ♐
15	7 ♎	24 ♏	5 ♐	27 ♑	6 ♓	28 ♈	5 ♊	21 ♋	6 ♍	9 ♎	25 ♏	0 ♑
17	2 ♏	22 ♐	2 ♑	25 ♒	4 ♈	25 ♉	0 ♋	15 ♌	0 ♎	3 ♏	21 ♐	28 ♑
19	29 ♏	21 ♑	0 ♒	24 ♓	2 ♉	21 ♊	24 ♋	9 ♍	24 ♎	28 ♏	18 ♑	27 ♒
21	28 ♐	21 ♒	0 ♓	23 ♈	29 ♉	16 ♋	18 ♌	3 ♎	19 ♏	24 ♐	16 ♒	25 ♓
23	28 ♑	21 ♓	29 ♓	20 ♉	25 ♊	10 ♌	12 ♍	27 ♎	14 ♐	21 ♑	0 ♓	23 ♈
25	28 ♒	20 ♈	28 ♈	17 ♊	20 ♋	3 ♍	6 ♎	22 ♏	11 ♑	19 ♒	28 ♓	21 ♉
27	28 ♓	18 ♉	26 ♉	12 ♋	14 ♌	27 ♍	0 ♏	18 ♐	9 ♒	18 ♓	27 ♈	18 ♊
29	26 ♈		22 ♊	6 ♌	7 ♍	22 ♎	26 ♏	16 ♑	9 ♓	18 ♈	25 ♉	14 ♋
31	22 ♉		16 ♋		1 ♎		23 ♐	15 ♒		17 ♉	22 ♊	9 ♌

1918	Jan.	Feb.	Mar.	April	May	June	July	Aug.	Sept.	Oct.	Nov.	Dec.
1	21 ♌	5 ♎	13 ♎	29 ♏	3 ♑	24 ♒	4 ♈	27 ♉	17 ♋	21 ♌	7 ♎	9 ♏
3	15 ♍	29 ♎	7 ♏	24 ♐	0 ♒	22 ♓	2 ♉	24 ♊	12 ♌	16 ♍	0 ♏	3 ♐
5	8 ♎	23 ♏	2 ♐	20 ♑	28 ♒	21 ♈	0 ♊	20 ♋	7 ♍	10 ♎	24 ♏	28 ♐
7	3 ♏	19 ♐	27 ♐	18 ♒	27 ♓	20 ♉	27 ♊	15 ♌	1 ♎	3 ♏	18 ♐	23 ♑
9	28 ♏	16 ♑	24 ♑	17 ♓	26 ♈	18 ♊	24 ♋	10 ♍	24 ♎	27 ♏	13 ♑	19 ♒
11	25 ♐	16 ♒	24 ♒	18 ♈	26 ♉	16 ♋	19 ♌	4 ♎	18 ♏	21 ♐	9 ♒	17 ♓
13	23 ♑	16 ♓	24 ♓	18 ♉	24 ♊	11 ♌	14 ♍	28 ♎	12 ♐	16 ♑	6 ♓	15 ♈
15	22 ♒	16 ♈	25 ♈	16 ♊	21 ♋	6 ♍	8 ♎	22 ♏	7 ♑	13 ♒	5 ♈	14 ♉
17	21 ♓	14 ♉	24 ♉	13 ♋	16 ♌	0 ♎	2 ♏	16 ♐	4 ♒	12 ♓	5 ♉	13 ♊
19	20 ♈	11 ♊	21 ♊	8 ♌	10 ♍	24 ♎	26 ♏	13 ♑	3 ♓	12 ♈	5 ♊	12 ♋
21	18 ♉	7 ♋	16 ♋	2 ♍	4 ♎	18 ♏	21 ♐	11 ♒	4 ♈	12 ♉	4 ♋	9 ♌
23	14 ♊	2 ♌	11 ♌	25 ♍	28 ♎	13 ♐	18 ♑	10 ♓	4 ♉	12 ♊	1 ♌	5 ♍
25	10 ♋	26 ♌	5 ♍	19 ♎	22 ♏	11 ♑	16 ♒	10 ♈	3 ♊	10 ♋	27 ♌	29 ♍
27	5 ♌	20 ♍	28 ♍	13 ♏	17 ♐	7 ♒	15 ♓	9 ♉	1 ♋	6 ♌	21 ♍	23 ♎
29	29 ♌		22 ♎	8 ♐	13 ♑	5 ♓	14 ♈	7 ♊	27 ♋	1 ♍	15 ♎	17 ♏
31	23 ♍		16 ♏		10 ♒		13 ♉	4 ♋		25 ♍		11 ♐

1919	Jan.	Feb.	Mar.	April	May	June	July	Aug.	Sept.	Oct.	Nov.	Dec.
1	24 ♐	12 ♒	20 ♒	12 ♈	21 ♉	13 ♋	19 ♌	6 ♎	20 ♏	22 ♐	7 ♒	11 ♓
3	19 ♑	10 ♓	19 ♓	12 ♉	20 ♊	11 ♌	16 ♍	0 ♏	14 ♐	16 ♑	3 ♓	9 ♈
5	16 ♒	8 ♈	18 ♈	12 ♊	19 ♋	7 ♍	10 ♎	24 ♏	8 ♑	11 ♒	0 ♈	8 ♉
7	14 ♓	7 ♉	17 ♉	10 ♋	16 ♌	2 ♎	4 ♏	18 ♐	3 ♒	8 ♓	0 ♉	8 ♊
9	12 ♈	5 ♊	16 ♊	6 ♌	11 ♍	26 ♎	28 ♏	12 ♑	0 ♓	7 ♈	0 ♊	8 ♋
11	10 ♉	2 ♋	13 ♋	1 ♍	5 ♎	20 ♏	22 ♐	8 ♒	28 ♓	6 ♉	0 ♋	7 ♌
13	8 ♊	29 ♋	9 ♌	26 ♍	29 ♎	13 ♐	17 ♑	5 ♓	27 ♈	6 ♊	29 ♋	5 ♍
15	7 ♋	25 ♌	4 ♍	20 ♎	23 ♏	8 ♑	12 ♒	3 ♈	26 ♉	5 ♋	26 ♌	1 ♎
17	4 ♌	21 ♍	29 ♍	14 ♏	16 ♐	3 ♒	9 ♓	1 ♉	24 ♊	3 ♌	21 ♍	25 ♎
19	0 ♍	15 ♎	23 ♎	7 ♐	11 ♑	29 ♒	6 ♈	29 ♉	22 ♋	29 ♌	16 ♎	19 ♏
21	25 ♍	9 ♏	17 ♏	1 ♑	6 ♒	26 ♓	4 ♉	28 ♊	19 ♌	24 ♍	10 ♏	12 ♐
23	19 ♎	3 ♐	11 ♐	26 ♑	2 ♓	24 ♈	3 ♊	25 ♋	15 ♍	19 ♎	4 ♐	6 ♑
25	13 ♏	27 ♐	5 ♑	22 ♒	0 ♈	23 ♉	2 ♋	23 ♌	10 ♎	13 ♏	27 ♐	0 ♒
27	7 ♐	22 ♑	0 ♒	20 ♓	29 ♈	22 ♊	0 ♌	19 ♍	5 ♏	7 ♐	21 ♑	25 ♒
29	2 ♑		28 ♒	20 ♈	29 ♉	21 ♋	28 ♌	14 ♎	28 ♏	0 ♑	16 ♒	21 ♓
31	28 ♑		27 ♓		29 ♊		24 ♍	8 ♏		24 ♑		18 ♈

1920	Jan.	Feb.	Mar.	April	May	June	July	Aug.	Sept.	Oct.	Nov.	Dec.
1	2 ♉	25 ♊	20 ♋	11 ♍	17 ♎	2 ♐	5 ♑	20 ♒	8 ♈	15 ♉	7 ♋	17 ♌
3	1 ♊	24 ♋	18 ♌	8 ♎	11 ♏	26 ♐	29 ♑	15 ♓	4 ♉	13 ♊	6 ♌	14 ♍
5	1 ♋	23 ♌	16 ♍	3 ♏	5 ♐	20 ♑	23 ♒	11 ♈	2 ♊	11 ♋	4 ♍	11 ♎
7	1 ♌	21 ♍	12 ♎	27 ♏	29 ♑	14 ♒	18 ♓	7 ♉	0 ♋	9 ♌	1 ♎	6 ♏
9	0 ♍	17 ♎	7 ♏	21 ♐	23 ♑	9 ♓	14 ♈	5 ♊	29 ♋	7 ♍	27 ♎	1 ♐
11	26 ♍	11 ♏	1 ♐	15 ♑	17 ♒	4 ♈	11 ♉	4 ♋	28 ♌	5 ♎	22 ♏	25 ♐
13	21 ♎	5 ♐	25 ♐	9 ♒	13 ♓	2 ♉	10 ♊	4 ♌	26 ♍	1 ♏	16 ♐	19 ♑
15	15 ♏	29 ♐	19 ♑	4 ♓	10 ♈	1 ♊	10 ♋	3 ♍	23 ♎	26 ♏	10 ♑	13 ♒
17	9 ♐	23 ♑	14 ♒	1 ♈	8 ♉	2 ♋	10 ♌	1 ♎	18 ♏	20 ♐	4 ♒	7 ♓
19	3 ♑	18 ♒	10 ♓	0 ♉	8 ♊	2 ♌	9 ♍	28 ♎	13 ♐	14 ♑	28 ♒	1 ♈
21	27 ♑	15 ♓	7 ♈	29 ♉	8 ♋	1 ♍	7 ♎	23 ♏	6 ♑	8 ♒	23 ♓	28 ♈
23	22 ♒	12 ♈	5 ♉	29 ♊	7 ♌	28 ♍	2 ♏	17 ♐	0 ♒	3 ♓	20 ♈	26 ♉
25	18 ♓	9 ♉	4 ♊	27 ♋	5 ♍	23 ♎	26 ♏	10 ♑	25 ♒	28 ♓	18 ♉	25 ♊
27	15 ♈	7 ♊	2 ♋	25 ♌	1 ♎	17 ♏	20 ♐	4 ♒	20 ♓	26 ♈	17 ♊	26 ♋
29	12 ♉	6 ♋	0 ♌	21 ♍	26 ♎	11 ♐	14 ♑	29 ♒	17 ♈	24 ♉	17 ♋	26 ♌
31	11 ♊		28 ♌		20 ♏		8 ♒	25 ♓		23 ♊		24 ♍

1921	Jan.	Feb.	Mar.	April	May	June	July	Aug.	Sept.	Oct.	Nov.	Dec.
1	8 ♎	25 ♏	3 ♐	17 ♑	19 ♒	4 ♈	8 ♉	28 ♊	22 ♌	0 ♎	21 ♏	25 ♐
3	3 ♏	19 ♐	27 ♐	11 ♒	13 ♓	29 ♈	5 ♊	28 ♋	22 ♍	29 ♎	17 ♐	21 ♑
5	28 ♏	13 ♑	21 ♑	5 ♓	8 ♈	27 ♉	4 ♋	29 ♌	21 ♎	26 ♏	13 ♑	15 ♒
7	22 ♐	6 ♒	15 ♒	0 ♈	5 ♉	26 ♊	5 ♌	28 ♍	18 ♏	22 ♐	7 ♒	8 ♓
9	16 ♑	0 ♓	9 ♓	26 ♈	2 ♊	25 ♋	5 ♍	26 ♎	14 ♐	17 ♑	1 ♓	2 ♈
11	9 ♒	25 ♓	4 ♈	23 ♉	1 ♋	25 ♌	3 ♎	23 ♏	9 ♑	11 ♒	24 ♓	27 ♈
13	3 ♓	20 ♈	0 ♉	21 ♊	0 ♌	23 ♍	0 ♏	18 ♐	2 ♒	5 ♓	19 ♈	23 ♉
15	28 ♓	16 ♉	26 ♉	19 ♋	28 ♌	20 ♎	26 ♏	12 ♑	26 ♒	29 ♓	15 ♉	21 ♊
17	23 ♈	13 ♊	24 ♊	17 ♌	26 ♍	16 ♏	21 ♐	6 ♒	20 ♓	24 ♈	12 ♊	20 ♋
19	20 ♉	12 ♋	22 ♋	16 ♍	23 ♎	11 ♐	15 ♑	29 ♒	15 ♈	19 ♉	10 ♋	19 ♌
21	18 ♊	12 ♌	21 ♌	14 ♎	19 ♏	6 ♑	9 ♒	23 ♓	10 ♉	16 ♊	9 ♌	18 ♍
23	19 ♋	12 ♍	21 ♍	11 ♏	15 ♐	0 ♒	2 ♓	18 ♈	6 ♊	14 ♋	7 ♍	16 ♎
25	19 ♌	11 ♎	19 ♎	6 ♐	9 ♑	24 ♒	26 ♓	13 ♉	3 ♋	12 ♌	5 ♎	12 ♏
27	19 ♍	8 ♏	16 ♏	1 ♑	3 ♒	17 ♓	21 ♈	9 ♊	1 ♌	10 ♍	2 ♏	9 ♐
29	17 ♎		11 ♐	25 ♑	27 ♒	12 ♈	16 ♉	7 ♋	1 ♍	9 ♎	29 ♏	4 ♑
31	12 ♏		6 ♑		21 ♓		14 ♊	7 ♌		7 ♏		29 ♑

1922	Jan.	Feb.	Mar.	April	May	June	July	Aug.	Sept.	Oct.	Nov.	Dec.
1	11 ♒	25 ♓	4 ♈	19 ♉	25 ♊	17 ♌	26 ♍	18 ♏	8 ♑	12 ♒	27 ♓	28 ♈
3	5 ♓	19 ♈	28 ♈	15 ♊	22 ♋	15 ♍	24 ♎	15 ♐	3 ♒	6 ♓	20 ♈	23 ♉
5	28 ♓	13 ♉	22 ♉	11 ♋	20 ♌	13 ♎	21 ♏	11 ♑	27 ♒	0 ♈	14 ♉	18 ♊
7	22 ♈	9 ♊	18 ♊	9 ♌	18 ♍	11 ♏	18 ♐	6 ♒	21 ♓	23 ♈	9 ♊	15 ♋
9	18 ♉	7 ♋	15 ♋	9 ♍	17 ♎	9 ♐	14 ♑	0 ♓	14 ♈	17 ♉	5 ♋	12 ♌
11	15 ♊	7 ♌	15 ♌	8 ♎	16 ♏	6 ♑	10 ♒	24 ♓	8 ♉	12 ♊	1 ♌	9 ♍
13	14 ♋	7 ♍	15 ♍	8 ♏	14 ♐	1 ♒	4 ♓	18 ♈	3 ♊	8 ♋	28 ♌	7 ♎
15	14 ♌	7 ♎	15 ♎	6 ♐	11 ♑	26 ♒	28 ♓	12 ♉	28 ♊	5 ♌	27 ♍	6 ♏
17	13 ♍	6 ♏	14 ♏	3 ♑	6 ♒	20 ♓	21 ♈	7 ♊	25 ♋	3 ♍	26 ♎	4 ♐
19	12 ♎	2 ♐	11 ♐	28 ♑	0 ♓	13 ♈	16 ♉	3 ♋	24 ♌	3 ♎	26 ♏	3 ♑
21	9 ♏	28 ♐	7 ♑	22 ♒	23 ♓	8 ♉	11 ♊	1 ♌	24 ♍	3 ♏	24 ♐	29 ♑
23	6 ♐	22 ♑	1 ♒	15 ♓	17 ♈	3 ♊	9 ♋	1 ♍	25 ♎	2 ♐	22 ♑	25 ♒
25	1 ♑	16 ♒	25 ♒	9 ♈	12 ♉	0 ♋	8 ♌	1 ♎	24 ♏	0 ♑	17 ♒	19 ♓
27	25 ♑	10 ♓	19 ♓	4 ♉	8 ♊	29 ♋	7 ♍	1 ♏	22 ♐	26 ♑	11 ♓	13 ♈
29	19 ♒		13 ♈	29 ♉	5 ♋	27 ♌	6 ♎	29 ♏	18 ♑	21 ♒	5 ♈	6 ♉
31	13 ♓		7 ♉		3 ♌		5 ♏	25 ♐		15 ♓		1 ♊

1923	Jan.	Feb.	Mar.	April	May	June	July	Aug.	Sept.	Oct.	Nov.	Dec.
1	14 ♊	2 ♌	10 ♌	2 ♎	11 ♏	4 ♑	10 ♒	26 ♓	10 ♉	12 ♊	27 ♋	3 ♍
3	10 ♋	1 ♍	9 ♍	3 ♏	11 ♐	2 ♒	6 ♓	20 ♈	4 ♊	6 ♋	23 ♌	0 ♎
5	8 ♌	0 ♎	9 ♎	3 ♐	10 ♑	28 ♒	0 ♈	14 ♉	28 ♊	1 ♌	21 ♍	29 ♎
7	6 ♍	28 ♎	9 ♏	1 ♑	6 ♒	22 ♓	24 ♈	8 ♊	23 ♋	28 ♌	20 ♎	29 ♏
9	4 ♎	27 ♏	8 ♐	27 ♑	1 ♓	16 ♈	18 ♉	3 ♋	20 ♌	27 ♍	21 ♏	29 ♐
11	2 ♏	24 ♐	5 ♑	22 ♒	25 ♓	9 ♉	12 ♊	29 ♋	19 ♍	27 ♎	21 ♐	28 ♑
13	0 ♐	21 ♑	1 ♒	17 ♓	19 ♈	4 ♊	7 ♋	26 ♌	18 ♎	27 ♏	20 ♑	25 ♒
15	28 ♐	16 ♒	25 ♒	10 ♈	13 ♉	28 ♊	3 ♌	24 ♍	18 ♏	27 ♐	17 ♒	21 ♓
17	25 ♑	11 ♓	20 ♓	4 ♉	7 ♊	23 ♋	0 ♍	23 ♎	17 ♐	24 ♑	12 ♓	15 ♈
19	20 ♒	5 ♈	13 ♈	28 ♉	2 ♋	20 ♌	28 ♍	22 ♏	14 ♑	20 ♒	6 ♈	9 ♉
21	15 ♓	28 ♈	7 ♉	22 ♊	27 ♋	17 ♍	26 ♎	20 ♐	10 ♒	15 ♓	0 ♉	2 ♊
23	9 ♈	22 ♉	1 ♊	17 ♋	23 ♌	15 ♎	25 ♏	17 ♑	6 ♓	9 ♈	24 ♈	27 ♊
25	2 ♉	17 ♊	25 ♊	13 ♌	21 ♍	14 ♏	23 ♐	14 ♒	0 ♈	3 ♉	18 ♊	21 ♋
27	26 ♉	13 ♋	21 ♋	11 ♍	20 ♎	14 ♐	21 ♑	9 ♓	24 ♈	27 ♉	12 ♋	17 ♌
29	22 ♊		18 ♌	11 ♎	20 ♏	12 ♑	18 ♒	4 ♈	18 ♉	21 ♊	7 ♌	13 ♍
31	18 ♋		17 ♍		19 ♐		13 ♓	28 ♈		15 ♋		10 ♎

1924	Jan.	Feb.	Mar.	April	May	June	July	Aug.	Sept.	Oct.	Nov.	Dec.
1	24 ♎	17 ♐	12 ♑	3 ♓	7 ♈	23 ♉	25 ♊	11 ♌	29 ♍	6 ♏	0 ♑	8 ♒
3	23 ♏	16 ♑	10 ♒	28 ♓	2 ♉	16 ♊	19 ♋	6 ♍	26 ♎	5 ♐	28 ♑	6 ♓
5	22 ♐	14 ♒	6 ♓	23 ♈	26 ♉	10 ♋	14 ♌	2 ♎	24 ♏	4 ♑	26 ♒	2 ♈
7	21 ♑	11 ♓	2 ♈	17 ♉	19 ♊	4 ♌	9 ♍	29 ♎	22 ♐	2 ♒	22 ♓	27 ♈
9	20 ♒	6 ♈	27 ♈	11 ♊	12 ♋	29 ♌	5 ♎	27 ♏	21 ♑	29 ♒	18 ♈	22 ♉
11	16 ♓	1 ♉	21 ♉	5 ♋	7 ♌	25 ♍	3 ♏	26 ♐	19 ♒	25 ♓	12 ♉	15 ♊
13	11 ♈	25 ♉	14 ♊	29 ♋	3 ♍	23 ♎	2 ♐	25 ♑	16 ♓	21 ♈	7 ♊	9 ♋
15	5 ♉	19 ♊	9 ♋	24 ♌	0 ♎	22 ♏	1 ♑	24 ♒	13 ♈	16 ♉	1 ♋	3 ♌
17	29 ♉	13 ♋	3 ♌	21 ♍	29 ♎	23 ♐	1 ♒	21 ♓	8 ♉	10 ♊	24 ♋	27 ♌
19	23 ♊	9 ♌	0 ♍	20 ♎	29 ♏	23 ♑	0 ♓	17 ♈	2 ♊	4 ♋	18 ♌	22 ♍
21	18 ♋	5 ♍	28 ♍	21 ♏	29 ♐	22 ♒	27 ♓	12 ♉	26 ♊	28 ♋	13 ♍	18 ♎
23	13 ♌	3 ♎	27 ♎	21 ♐	29 ♑	18 ♓	22 ♈	6 ♊	20 ♋	22 ♌	10 ♎	16 ♏
25	10 ♍	1 ♏	26 ♏	19 ♑	26 ♒	14 ♈	16 ♉	0 ♋	15 ♌	18 ♍	8 ♏	16 ♐
27	7 ♎	0 ♐	25 ♐	17 ♒	22 ♓	8 ♉	10 ♊	24 ♋	10 ♍	16 ♎	8 ♐	17 ♑
29	5 ♏	28 ♐	23 ♑	12 ♓	17 ♈	2 ♊	4 ♋	19 ♌	8 ♎	15 ♏	9 ♑	17 ♒
31	3 ♐		20 ♒		11 ♉		28 ♋	15 ♍		15 ♐		15 ♓

1925	Jan.	Feb.	Mar.	April	May	June	July	Aug.	Sept.	Oct.	Nov.	Dec.
1	28 ♓	15 ♉	23 ♉	7 ♋	9 ♌	23 ♍	28 ♎	19 ♐	13 ♒	21 ♓	12 ♉	16 ♊
3	24 ♈	9 ♊	17 ♊	1 ♌	3 ♍	20 ♎	26 ♏	19 ♑	12 ♓	19 ♈	8 ♊	10 ♋
5	19 ♉	3 ♋	11 ♋	25 ♌	28 ♍	18 ♏	25 ♐	19 ♒	11 ♈	17 ♉	2 ♋	4 ♌
7	12 ♊	27 ♋	5 ♌	20 ♍	25 ♎	17 ♐	26 ♑	19 ♓	9 ♉	12 ♊	26 ♋	28 ♌
9	6 ♋	21 ♌	29 ♌	17 ♎	24 ♏	17 ♑	26 ♒	17 ♈	4 ♊	7 ♋	20 ♌	22 ♍
11	0 ♌	16 ♍	25 ♍	15 ♏	23 ♐	17 ♒	24 ♓	13 ♉	29 ♊	0 ♌	14 ♍	17 ♎
13	24 ♌	11 ♎	21 ♎	13 ♐	22 ♑	15 ♓	21 ♈	8 ♊	22 ♋	24 ♌	9 ♎	13 ♏
15	19 ♍	8 ♏	19 ♏	12 ♑	21 ♒	12 ♈	17 ♉	2 ♋	16 ♌	19 ♍	6 ♏	12 ♐
17	14 ♎	6 ♐	16 ♐	10 ♒	18 ♓	7 ♉	11 ♊	26 ♋	10 ♍	14 ♎	3 ♐	11 ♑
19	11 ♏	4 ♑	15 ♑	7 ♓	15 ♈	2 ♊	5 ♋	19 ♌	5 ♎	11 ♏	2 ♑	11 ♒
21	10 ♐	3 ♒	13 ♒	5 ♈	10 ♉	26 ♊	29 ♋	14 ♍	1 ♏	8 ♐	1 ♒	10 ♓
23	10 ♑	3 ♓	11 ♓	1 ♉	5 ♊	20 ♋	22 ♌	8 ♎	28 ♏	6 ♑	29 ♒	7 ♈
25	10 ♒	1 ♈	9 ♈	27 ♉	29 ♊	13 ♌	16 ♍	4 ♏	25 ♐	4 ♒	27 ♓	4 ♉
27	9 ♓	28 ♈	6 ♉	21 ♊	23 ♋	7 ♍	11 ♎	1 ♐	23 ♑	2 ♓	24 ♈	0 ♊
29	7 ♈		1 ♊	15 ♋	17 ♌	2 ♎	7 ♏	29 ♐	22 ♒	0 ♈	20 ♉	25 ♊
31	3 ♉		25 ♊		11 ♍		5 ♐	28 ♑		28 ♈		19 ♋

1926	Jan.	Feb.	Mar.	April	May	June	July	Aug.	Sept.	Oct.	Nov.	Dec.
1	1 ♌	15 ♍	24 ♍	10 ♏	17 ♐	9 ♒	18 ♓	10 ♉	29 ♊	2 ♌	16 ♍	18 ♎
3	24 ♌	9 ♎	18 ♎	7 ♐	14 ♑	7 ♓	16 ♈	7 ♊	23 ♋	26 ♌	10 ♎	13 ♏
5	18 ♍	4 ♏	13 ♏	3 ♑	12 ♒	5 ♈	14 ♉	2 ♋	17 ♌	20 ♍	5 ♏	9 ♐
7	12 ♎	0 ♐	9 ♐	1 ♒	10 ♓	3 ♉	10 ♊	26 ♋	11 ♍	14 ♎	0 ♐	6 ♑
9	8 ♏	28 ♐	7 ♑	0 ♓	9 ♈	0 ♊	5 ♋	20 ♌	5 ♎	8 ♏	26 ♐	3 ♒
11	5 ♐	27 ♑	6 ♒	29 ♓	7 ♉	26 ♊	0 ♌	14 ♍	29 ♎	3 ♐	23 ♑	1 ♓
13	4 ♑	27 ♒	6 ♓	28 ♈	5 ♊	21 ♋	24 ♌	8 ♎	24 ♏	29 ♐	20 ♒	0 ♈
15	4 ♒	28 ♓	6 ♈	26 ♉	1 ♋	15 ♌	17 ♍	2 ♏	19 ♐	26 ♑	19 ♓	28 ♈
17	4 ♓	27 ♈	5 ♉	23 ♊	25 ♋	9 ♍	11 ♎	27 ♏	16 ♑	24 ♒	18 ♈	26 ♉
19	4 ♈	23 ♉	2 ♊	17 ♋	19 ♌	3 ♎	6 ♏	23 ♐	15 ♒	24 ♓	17 ♉	23 ♊
21	1 ♉	19 ♊	27 ♊	11 ♌	13 ♍	28 ♎	2 ♐	22 ♑	15 ♓	24 ♈	15 ♊	19 ♋
23	27 ♉	13 ♋	21 ♋	5 ♍	7 ♎	24 ♏	29 ♐	22 ♒	16 ♈	23 ♉	11 ♋	14 ♌
25	22 ♊	6 ♌	15 ♌	29 ♍	2 ♏	21 ♐	28 ♑	22 ♓	15 ♉	21 ♊	7 ♌	8 ♍
27	16 ♋	0 ♍	9 ♍	24 ♎	29 ♏	20 ♑	22 ♒	22 ♈	12 ♊	16 ♋	1 ♍	2 ♎
29	9 ♌		3 ♎	20 ♏	26 ♐	19 ♒	28 ♓	20 ♉	8 ♋	11 ♌	24 ♍	26 ♎
31	3 ♍		28 ♎		24 ♑		27 ♈	16 ♊		5 ♍		21 ♏

1927	Jan.	Feb.	Mar.	April	May	June	July	Aug.	Sept.	Oct.	Nov.	Dec.
1	4 ♐	23 ♑	0 ♒	23 ♓	2 ♉	24 ♊	0 ♌	16 ♍	0 ♏	2 ♐	18 ♑	24 ♒
3	1 ♑	22 ♒	0 ♓	24 ♈	2 ♊	21 ♋	25 ♌	10 ♎	23 ♏	26 ♐	14 ♒	22 ♓
5	29 ♑	22 ♓	0 ♈	24 ♉	0 ♋	17 ♌	20 ♍	3 ♏	18 ♐	22 ♑	12 ♓	20 ♈
7	28 ♒	21 ♈	1 ♉	22 ♊	26 ♋	12 ♍	13 ♎	27 ♏	13 ♑	19 ♒	11 ♈	20 ♉
9	26 ♓	19 ♉	29 ♉	18 ♋	21 ♌	6 ♎	7 ♏	22 ♐	11 ♒	18 ♓	12 ♉	20 ♊
11	25 ♈	16 ♊	26 ♊	13 ♌	15 ♍	29 ♎	2 ♐	19 ♑	10 ♓	18 ♈	12 ♊	18 ♋
13	22 ♉	12 ♋	21 ♋	7 ♍	9 ♎	24 ♏	27 ♐	17 ♒	10 ♈	19 ♉	10 ♋	15 ♌
15	19 ♊	7 ♌	16 ♌	1 ♎	3 ♏	19 ♐	24 ♑	16 ♓	10 ♉	18 ♊	7 ♌	11 ♍
17	15 ♋	1 ♍	10 ♍	24 ♎	27 ♏	15 ♑	22 ♒	15 ♈	9 ♊	15 ♋	2 ♍	5 ♎
19	10 ♌	25 ♍	4 ♎	18 ♏	22 ♐	12 ♒	20 ♓	14 ♉	6 ♋	11 ♌	27 ♍	29 ♎
21	4 ♍	19 ♎	27 ♎	13 ♐	18 ♑	10 ♓	19 ♈	12 ♊	1 ♌	6 ♍	20 ♎	23 ♏
23	28 ♍	12 ♏	21 ♏	8 ♑	15 ♒	8 ♈	17 ♉	9 ♋	26 ♌	0 ♎	14 ♏	17 ♐
25	22 ♎	7 ♐	16 ♐	5 ♒	13 ♓	7 ♉	15 ♊	4 ♌	21 ♍	24 ♎	8 ♐	12 ♑
27	16 ♏	3 ♑	12 ♑	3 ♓	12 ♈	5 ♊	12 ♋	0 ♍	15 ♎	17 ♏	3 ♑	8 ♒
29	12 ♐		9 ♒	2 ♈	11 ♉	3 ♋	8 ♌	24 ♍	8 ♏	11 ♐	28 ♑	5 ♓
31	8 ♑		8 ♓		10 ♊		3 ♍	18 ♎		5 ♑		2 ♈

1928	Jan.	Feb.	Mar.	April	May	June	July	Aug.	Sept.	Oct.	Nov.	Dec.
1	16 ♈	9 ♊	4 ♋	24 ♌	28 ♍	13 ♏	15 ♐	1 ♒	20 ♓	28 ♈	21 ♊	29 ♋
3	15 ♉	7 ♋	1 ♌	19 ♍	22 ♎	7 ♐	9 ♑	27 ♒	18 ♈	27 ♉	20 ♋	27 ♌
5	14 ♊	5 ♌	27 ♌	13 ♎	16 ♏	1 ♑	4 ♒	24 ♓	17 ♉	26 ♊	17 ♌	23 ♍
7	12 ♋	1 ♍	22 ♍	7 ♏	10 ♐	25 ♑	0 ♓	22 ♈	15 ♊	24 ♋	14 ♍	18 ♎
9	10 ♌	26 ♍	17 ♎	1 ♐	3 ♑	20 ♒	27 ♓	20 ♉	13 ♋	21 ♌	9 ♎	12 ♏
11	6 ♍	21 ♎	11 ♏	25 ♐	28 ♑	17 ♓	25 ♈	18 ♊	10 ♌	17 ♍	3 ♏	6 ♐
13	1 ♎	14 ♏	4 ♐	19 ♑	24 ♒	15 ♈	23 ♉	17 ♋	7 ♍	12 ♎	27 ♏	29 ♐
15	25 ♎	8 ♐	28 ♐	15 ♒	21 ♓	14 ♉	22 ♊	15 ♌	3 ♎	6 ♏	20 ♐	23 ♑
17	19 ♏	3 ♑	23 ♑	12 ♓	20 ♈	13 ♊	22 ♋	12 ♍	28 ♎	0 ♐	14 ♑	18 ♒
19	13 ♐	28 ♑	20 ♒	11 ♈	20 ♉	13 ♋	20 ♈	7 ♎	22 ♏	24 ♐	8 ♒	13 ♓
21	7 ♑	26 ♒	18 ♓	12 ♉	20 ♊	12 ♌	17 ♍	2 ♏	16 ♐	18 ♑	4 ♓	9 ♈
23	4 ♒	24 ♓	18 ♈	12 ♊	19 ♋	9 ♍	12 ♎	26 ♏	9 ♑	12 ♒	0 ♈	8 ♉
25	1 ♓	24 ♈	18 ♉	10 ♋	17 ♌	4 ♎	6 ♏	20 ♐	4 ♒	8 ♓	29 ♈	7 ♊
27	29 ♓	22 ♉	17 ♊	8 ♌	13 ♍	28 ♎	0 ♐	14 ♑	1 ♓	7 ♈	29 ♉	7 ♋
29	27 ♈	20 ♊	14 ♋	3 ♍	7 ♎	22 ♏	24 ♐	9 ♒	28 ♓	6 ♉	0 ♋	7 ♌
31	25 ♉		11 ♌		1 ♏		18 ♑	6 ♓		6 ♊		6 ♍

1929	Jan.	Feb.	Mar.	April	May	June	July	Aug.	Sept.	Oct.	Nov.	Dec.
1	19 ♍	5 ♏	13 ♏	27 ♐	28 ♑	14 ♓	19 ♈	10 ♊	4 ♌	12 ♍	2 ♏	6 ♐
3	15 ♎	29 ♏	7 ♐	20 ♑	23 ♒	10 ♈	17 ♉	10 ♋	3 ♍	10 ♎	28 ♏	0 ♑
5	9 ♏	23 ♐	1 ♑	15 ♒	18 ♓	8 ♉	16 ♊	10 ♌	2 ♎	7 ♏	22 ♐	24 ♑
7	3 ♐	16 ♑	25 ♑	10 ♓	16 ♈	8 ♊	16 ♋	9 ♍	29 ♎	2 ♐	16 ♑	18 ♒
9	26 ♐	11 ♒	19 ♒	7 ♈	14 ♉	8 ♋	16 ♌	7 ♎	24 ♏	26 ♐	10 ♒	12 ♓
11	20 ♑	7 ♓	15 ♓	6 ♉	14 ♊	8 ♌	15 ♍	4 ♏	18 ♐	20 ♑	4 ♓	7 ♈
13	15 ♒	3 ♈	13 ♈	5 ♊	14 ♋	6 ♍	12 ♎	28 ♏	12 ♑	14 ♒	29 ♓	4 ♉
15	10 ♓	0 ♉	10 ♉	4 ♋	12 ♌	3 ♎	7 ♏	22 ♐	6 ♒	9 ♓	26 ♈	2 ♊
17	6 ♈	28 ♉	9 ♊	2 ♌	10 ♍	28 ♎	1 ♐	16 ♑	0 ♓	4 ♈	24 ♉	2 ♋
19	3 ♉	26 ♊	7 ♋	29 ♌	6 ♎	22 ♍	25 ♐	10 ♒	26 ♓	1 ♉	23 ♊	2 ♌
21	1 ♊	25 ♋	5 ♌	26 ♍	1 ♏	16 ♐	19 ♑	4 ♓	22 ♈	29 ♉	23 ♋	2 ♍
23	1 ♋	24 ♌	3 ♍	22 ♎	25 ♏	10 ♑	13 ♒	0 ♈	19 ♉	28 ♊	22 ♌	29 ♍
25	0 ♌	21 ♍	0 ♎	17 ♏	19 ♐	4 ♒	7 ♓	26 ♈	17 ♊	27 ♋	19 ♍	26 ♎
27	0 ♍	10 ♎	26 ♎	11 ♐	13 ♑	28 ♒	3 ♈	23 ♉	15 ♋	25 ♌	16 ♎	21 ♏
29	27 ♍		21 ♏	5 ♑	7 ♒	23 ♓	29 ♈	20 ♊	14 ♌	22 ♍	11 ♏	15 ♐
31	23 ♎		15 ♐		1 ♓		26 ♉	19 ♋		19 ♎		9 ♑

1930	Jan.	Feb.	Mar.	April	May	June	July	Aug.	Sept.	Oct.	Nov.	Dec.
1	21 ♑	6 ♓	15 ♓	1 ♉	8 ♊	1 ♌	10 ♍	2 ♏	19 ♐	22 ♑	6 ♓	8 ♈
3	15 ♒	0 ♈	9 ♈	28 ♉	6 ♋	0 ♍	8 ♎	28 ♏	14 ♑	16 ♒	0 ♈	3 ♉
5	8 ♓	25 ♈	5 ♉	25 ♊	4 ♌	28 ♍	5 ♏	23 ♐	8 ♒	10 ♓	25 ♈	29 ♉
7	3 ♈	21 ♉	1 ♊	23 ♋	3 ♍	25 ♎	1 ♐	17 ♑	1 ♓	4 ♈	21 ♉	27 ♊
9	28 ♈	19 ♊	28 ♊	22 ♌	1 ♎	21 ♏	25 ♐	11 ♒	25 ♓	29 ♈	17 ♊	25 ♋
11	26 ♉	18 ♋	27 ♋	21 ♍	28 ♎	16 ♐	20 ♑	4 ♓	20 ♈	24 ♉	15 ♋	24 ♌
13	25 ♊	18 ♌	27 ♌	19 ♎	25 ♏	11 ♑	14 ♒	28 ♓	14 ♉	21 ♊	13 ♌	22 ♍
15	25 ♋	19 ♍	27 ♍	16 ♏	20 ♐	5 ♒	7 ♓	22 ♈	10 ♊	18 ♋	11 ♍	20 ♎
17	26 ♌	17 ♎	25 ♎	12 ♐	15 ♑	29 ♒	1 ♈	18 ♉	8 ♋	16 ♌	10 ♎	17 ♏
19	25 ♍	14 ♏	22 ♏	7 ♑	9 ♒	23 ♓	26 ♈	14 ♊	7 ♌	16 ♍	8 ♏	14 ♐
21	22 ♎	9 ♐	17 ♐	1 ♒	3 ♓	17 ♈	22 ♉	13 ♋	6 ♍	15 ♎	5 ♐	9 ♑
23	18 ♏	3 ♑	11 ♑	25 ♒	27 ♓	13 ♉	19 ♊	13 ♌	6 ♎	13 ♏	1 ♑	4 ♒
25	12 ♐	27 ♑	5 ♒	19 ♓	22 ♈	11 ♊	19 ♋	13 ♍	5 ♏	10 ♐	26 ♑	28 ♒
27	6 ♑	20 ♒	29 ♒	14 ♈	19 ♉	11 ♋	20 ♌	13 ♎	2 ♐	6 ♑	20 ♒	22 ♓
29	0 ♒		23 ♓	10 ♉	17 ♊	11 ♌	20 ♍	11 ♏	28 ♐	1 ♒	14 ♓	16 ♈
31	24 ♒		18 ♈		16 ♋		18 ♎	7 ♐		24 ♒		11 ♉

1931	Jan.	Feb.	Mar.	April	May	June	July	Aug.	Sept.	Oct.	Nov.	Dec.
1	24 ♉	13 ♋	21 ♋	14 ♍	23 ♎	15 ♐	20 ♑	6 ♓	20 ♈	22 ♉	9 ♋	16 ♌
3	21 ♊	13 ♌	21 ♌	15 ♎	22 ♏	12 ♑	15 ♒	29 ♓	13 ♉	17 ♊	6 ♌	14 ♍
5	20 ♋	13 ♍	21 ♍	14 ♏	20 ♐	7 ♒	9 ♓	23 ♈	8 ♊	13 ♋	3 ♍	12 ♎
7	19 ♌	13 ♎	21 ♎	12 ♐	17 ♑	1 ♓	3 ♈	17 ♉	4 ♋	10 ♌	2 ♎	11 ♏
9	19 ♍	11 ♏	20 ♏	8 ♑	11 ♒	25 ♓	27 ♈	12 ♊	1 ♌	9 ♍	2 ♏	10 ♐
11	17 ♎	7 ♐	17 ♐	3 ♒	5 ♓	19 ♈	21 ♉	9 ♋	1 ♍	9 ♎	2 ♐	9 ♑
13	14 ♏	3 ♑	12 ♑	27 ♒	29 ♓	13 ♉	17 ♊	8 ♌	1 ♎	9 ♏	1 ♑	5 ♒
15	10 ♐	27 ♑	6 ♒	21 ♓	23 ♈	9 ♊	15 ♋	7 ♍	1 ♏	8 ♐	27 ♑	1 ♓
17	6 ♑	21 ♒	0 ♓	14 ♈	18 ♉	6 ♋	13 ♌	7 ♎	0 ♐	6 ♑	23 ♒	25 ♓
19	0 ♒	15 ♓	24 ♓	9 ♉	13 ♊	4 ♌	13 ♍	6 ♏	27 ♐	2 ♒	17 ♓	18 ♈
21	25 ♒	9 ♈	18 ♈	4 ♊	10 ♋	2 ♍	11 ♎	4 ♐	23 ♑	26 ♒	10 ♈	12 ♉
23	18 ♓	3 ♉	12 ♉	0 ♋	7 ♌	0 ♎	9 ♏	0 ♑	17 ♒	20 ♓	4 ♉	7 ♊
25	12 ♈	27 ♉	7 ♊	27 ♋	5 ♍	28 ♎	7 ♐	26 ♑	11 ♓	14 ♈	28 ♉	3 ♋
27	6 ♉	23 ♊	3 ♋	25 ♌	4 ♎	26 ♏	3 ♑	20 ♒	5 ♈	7 ♉	24 ♊	29 ♋
29	1 ♊		0 ♌	24 ♍	2 ♏	24 ♐	29 ♑	14 ♓	28 ♈	2 ♊	19 ♋	27 ♌
31	29 ♊		29 ♌		1 ♐		24 ♒	8 ♈		27 ♊		25 ♍

1932	Jan.	Feb.	Mar.	April	May	June	July	Aug.	Sept.	Oct.	Nov.	Dec.
1	9 ♎	2 ♐	26 ♐	15 ♒	19 ♓	3 ♉	5 ♊	21 ♋	11 ♍	18 ♎	12 ♐	20 ♑
3	7 ♏	29 ♐	22 ♑	10 ♓	12 ♈	27 ♉	0 ♋	18 ♌	9 ♎	18 ♏	11 ♑	18 ♒
5	5 ♐	26 ♑	18 ♒	4 ♈	6 ♉	21 ♊	26 ♋	15 ♍	8 ♏	18 ♐	9 ♒	14 ♓
7	3 ♑	22 ♒	12 ♓	27 ♈	0 ♊	16 ♋	22 ♌	14 ♎	7 ♐	16 ♑	5 ♓	8 ♈
9	0 ♒	16 ♓	7 ♈	21 ♉	24 ♊	12 ♌	19 ♍	12 ♏	5 ♑	12 ♒	29 ♓	2 ♉
11	26 ♒	10 ♈	0 ♉	15 ♊	19 ♋	8 ♍	17 ♎	10 ♐	2 ♒	8 ♓	23 ♈	26 ♉
13	20 ♓	4 ♉	24 ♉	9 ♋	15 ♌	6 ♎	15 ♏	8 ♑	28 ♒	2 ♈	17 ♉	20 ♊
15	14 ♈	28 ♉	18 ♊	5 ♌	12 ♍	5 ♏	14 ♐	6 ♒	23 ♓	26 ♈	11 ♊	14 ♋
17	8 ♉	23 ♊	13 ♋	3 ♍	11 ♎	4 ♐	13 ♑	2 ♓	18 ♈	20 ♉	5 ♋	9 ♌
19	2 ♊	19 ♋	10 ♌	2 ♎	11 ♏	4 ♑	10 ♒	27 ♓	12 ♉	14 ♊	29 ♋	4 ♍
21	28 ♊	17 ♌	9 ♍	2 ♏	11 ♐	2 ♒	7 ♓	22 ♈	5 ♊	8 ♋	24 ♌	1 ♎
23	24 ♋	16 ♍	9 ♎	3 ♐	10 ♑	29 ♒	2 ♈	15 ♉	29 ♊	3 ♌	21 ♍	29 ♎
25	22 ♌	15 ♎	9 ♏	2 ♑	8 ♒	24 ♓	26 ♈	9 ♊	24 ♋	29 ♌	20 ♎	28 ♏
27	21 ♍	14 ♏	8 ♐	29 ♑	3 ♓	18 ♈	19 ♉	4 ♋	21 ♌	27 ♍	20 ♏	28 ♐
29	20 ♎	12 ♐	6 ♑	24 ♒	27 ♓	11 ♉	13 ♊	29 ♋	19 ♍	27 ♎	20 ♐	28 ♑
31	18 ♏		2 ♒		21 ♈		8 ♋	27 ♌		27 ♏		26 ♒

1933	Jan.	Feb.	Mar.	April	May	June	July	Aug.	Sept.	Oct.	Nov.	Dec.
1	9 ♓	25 ♈	2 ♉	16 ♊	18 ♋	4 ♍	10 ♎	2 ♐	26 ♑	4 ♓	23 ♈	27 ♉
3	5 ♈	19 ♉	26 ♉	10 ♋	13 ♌	0 ♎	8 ♏	1 ♑	24 ♒	1 ♈	18 ♉	21 ♊
5	29 ♈	12 ♊	20 ♊	5 ♌	8 ♍	29 ♎	7 ♐	1 ♒	22 ♓	27 ♈	12 ♊	14 ♋
7	22 ♉	7 ♋	14 ♋	0 ♍	6 ♎	28 ♏	7 ♑	0 ♓	19 ♈	22 ♉	6 ♋	8 ♌
9	16 ♊	1 ♌	9 ♌	28 ♍	5 ♏	29 ♐	7 ♒	27 ♓	14 ♉	16 ♊	0 ♌	2 ♍
11	11 ♋	27 ♌	6 ♍	27 ♎	5 ♐	29 ♑	6 ♓	23 ♈	8 ♊	10 ♋	24 ♌	27 ♍
13	6 ♌	24 ♍	3 ♎	26 ♏	5 ♑	27 ♒	2 ♈	18 ♉	2 ♋	4 ♌	19 ♍	24 ♎
15	1 ♍	22 ♎	2 ♏	26 ♐	4 ♒	24 ♓	28 ♈	12 ♊	26 ♋	28 ♌	16 ♎	23 ♏
17	28 ♍	20 ♏	1 ♐	24 ♑	1 ♓	19 ♈	22 ♉	6 ♋	20 ♌	24 ♍	15 ♏	23 ♐
19	25 ♎	19 ♐	0 ♑	21 ♒	27 ♓	13 ♉	16 ♊	0 ♌	16 ♍	22 ♎	15 ♐	23 ♑
21	23 ♏	17 ♑	27 ♑	17 ♓	22 ♈	7 ♊	9 ♋	25 ♌	13 ♎	21 ♏	15 ♑	23 ♒
23	23 ♐	15 ♒	24 ♒	12 ♈	16 ♉	0 ♋	3 ♌	20 ♍	11 ♏	20 ♐	13 ♒	21 ♓
25	22 ♑	12 ♓	20 ♓	7 ♉	10 ♊	24 ♋	28 ♌	17 ♎	10 ♐	19 ♑	11 ♓	17 ♈
27	20 ♒	8 ♈	16 ♈	1 ♊	3 ♋	18 ♌	24 ♍	15 ♏	8 ♑	17 ♒	7 ♈	11 ♉
29	17 ♓		10 ♉	25 ♊	27 ♋	14 ♍	20 ♎	13 ♐	6 ♒	14 ♓	2 ♉	6 ♊
31	12 ♈		4 ♊		22 ♌		18 ♏	11 ♑		10 ♈		29 ♊

1934	Jan.	Feb.	Mar.	April	May	June	July	Aug.	Sept.	Oct.	Nov.	Dec.
1	11 ♋	26 ♌	5 ♍	22 ♎	29 ♏	23 ♑	1 ♓	23 ♈	10 ♊	12 ♋	26 ♌	28 ♍
3	5 ♌	21 ♍	0 ♎	20 ♏	28 ♐	22 ♒	0 ♈	19 ♉	4 ♋	6 ♌	20 ♍	23 ♎
5	29 ♌	16 ♎	26 ♎	18 ♐	27 ♑	20 ♓	26 ♈	13 ♊	28 ♋	0 ♍	15 ♎	20 ♏
7	24 ♍	13 ♏	23 ♏	16 ♑	25 ♒	16 ♈	22 ♉	7 ♋	21 ♌	24 ♍	11 ♏	18 ♐
9	19 ♎	10 ♐	21 ♐	14 ♒	23 ♓	12 ♉	16 ♊	1 ♌	15 ♍	19 ♎	9 ♐	17 ♑
11	17 ♏	10 ♑	19 ♑	12 ♓	19 ♈	7 ♊	10 ♋	25 ♌	10 ♎	16 ♏	7 ♑	16 ♒
13	16 ♐	9 ♒	18 ♒	10 ♈	15 ♉	1 ♋	4 ♌	19 ♍	6 ♏	13 ♐	5 ♒	14 ♓
15	16 ♑	9 ♓	17 ♓	7 ♉	11 ♊	25 ♋	27 ♌	13 ♎	2 ♐	10 ♑	4 ♓	12 ♈
17	16 ♒	7 ♈	15 ♈	2 ♊	5 ♋	19 ♌	21 ♍	9 ♏	0 ♑	9 ♒	1 ♈	9 ♉
19	15 ♓	4 ♉	12 ♉	27 ♊	29 ♈	12 ♍	16 ♎	6 ♐	28 ♑	7 ♓	29 ♈	5 ♊
21	13 ♈	29 ♉	7 ♊	21 ♋	22 ♌	7 ♎	12 ♏	4 ♑	27 ♒	6 ♈	26 ♉	0 ♋
23	8 ♉	23 ♊	1 ♋	14 ♌	16 ♍	4 ♏	10 ♐	4 ♒	27 ♓	4 ♉	21 ♊	24 ♋
25	3 ♊	17 ♋	25 ♋	9 ♍	12 ♎	2 ♐	10 ♑	4 ♓	25 ♈	1 ♊	16 ♋	18 ♌
27	26 ♊	10 ♌	18 ♌	4 ♎	9 ♏	2 ♑	10 ♒	3 ♈	23 ♉	26 ♊	10 ♌	12 ♍
29	20 ♋		13 ♍	1 ♏	8 ♐	2 ♒	10 ♉	1 ♉	18 ♊	20 ♋	4 ♍	6 ♎
31	14 ♌		9 ♎		8 ♑		9 ♈	27 ♉		14 ♌		1 ♏

1935	Jan.	Feb.	Mar.	April	May	June	July	Aug.	Sept.	Oct.	Nov.	Dec.
1	14 ♏	4 ♑	12 ♑	5 ♓	14 ♈	6 ♊	10 ♋	25 ♌	10 ♎	13 ♏	1 ♑	8 ♒
3	11 ♐	4 ♒	12 ♒	5 ♈	13 ♉	2 ♋	5 ♌	19 ♍	4 ♏	8 ♐	27 ♑	6 ♓
5	11 ♑	4 ♓	12 ♓	5 ♉	10 ♊	27 ♋	29 ♌	13 ♎	29 ♏	4 ♑	25 ♒	4 ♈
7	11 ♒	4 ♈	12 ♈	2 ♊	6 ♋	21 ♌	23 ♍	7 ♏	24 ♐	1 ♒	24 ♓	3 ♉
9	10 ♓	2 ♉	11 ♉	29 ♊	1 ♌	15 ♍	17 ♎	2 ♐	22 ♑	0 ♓	24 ♈	1 ♊
11	9 ♈	29 ♉	8 ♊	23 ♋	25 ♌	9 ♎	11 ♏	29 ♐	21 ♒	0 ♈	23 ♉	29 ♊
13	6 ♉	24 ♊	3 ♋	17 ♌	19 ♍	3 ♏	8 ♐	28 ♑	21 ♓	0 ♉	21 ♊	25 ♋
15	2 ♊	18 ♋	27 ♋	10 ♍	13 ♎	29 ♏	5 ♑	28 ♒	22 ♈	29 ♉	17 ♋	20 ♌
17	27 ♊	12 ♌	20 ♌	5 ♎	8 ♏	27 ♐	4 ♒	28 ♓	21 ♉	27 ♊	12 ♌	14 ♍
19	21 ♋	5 ♍	14 ♍	29 ♎	4 ♐	25 ♑	4 ♓	28 ♈	18 ♊	22 ♋	6 ♍	8 ♎
21	15 ♌	29 ♍	8 ♎	25 ♏	2 ♑	24 ♒	3 ♈	25 ♉	13 ♋	16 ♌	0 ♎	2 ♏
23	8 ♍	23 ♎	3 ♏	21 ♐	29 ♑	23 ♓	2 ♉	21 ♊	8 ♌	10 ♍	24 ♎	27 ♏
25	2 ♎	18 ♏	28 ♏	19 ♑	28 ♒	21 ♈	29 ♉	16 ♋	1 ♍	4 ♎	19 ♏	23 ♐
27	26 ♎	15 ♐	24 ♐	17 ♒	26 ♓	18 ♉	24 ♊	10 ♌	25 ♍	28 ♎	14 ♐	20 ♑
29	22 ♏		22 ♑	15 ♓	24 ♈	15 ♊	19 ♋	4 ♍	19 ♎	23 ♏	11 ♑	18 ♒
31	19 ♐		21 ♒		22 ♉		14 ♌	28 ♍		18 ♐		17 ♓

1936	Jan.	Feb.	Mar.	April	May	June	July	Aug.	Sept.	Oct.	Nov.	Dec.
1	1 ♈	24 ♉	18 ♊	6 ♌	9 ♍	23 ♎	25 ♏	11 ♑	1 ♓	9 ♈	3 ♊	10 ♋
3	29 ♈	21 ♊	14 ♋	0 ♍	3 ♎	17 ♏	20 ♐	8 ♒	1 ♈	10 ♉	2 ♋	8 ♌
5	27 ♉	17 ♋	9 ♌	24 ♍	26 ♎	12 ♐	16 ♑	7 ♓	1 ♉	9 ♊	0 ♌	4 ♍
7	24 ♊	12 ♌	3 ♍	18 ♎	20 ♏	7 ♑	13 ♒	6 ♈	29 ♉	7 ♋	25 ♌	29 ♍
9	20 ♋	6 ♍	27 ♍	11 ♏	15 ♐	3 ♒	11 ♓	5 ♉	27 ♊	3 ♌	20 ♍	22 ♎
11	16 ♌	0 ♎	21 ♎	6 ♐	10 ♑	0 ♓	9 ♈	3 ♊	23 ♋	28 ♌	14 ♎	16 ♏
13	10 ♍	24 ♎	14 ♏	0 ♑	6 ♒	28 ♓	8 ♉	0 ♋	19 ♌	23 ♍	7 ♏	10 ♐
15	4 ♎	18 ♏	9 ♐	26 ♑	4 ♓	27 ♈	6 ♊	27 ♋	14 ♍	17 ♎	1 ♐	4 ♑
17	28 ♎	13 ♐	4 ♑	24 ♒	2 ♈	26 ♉	4 ♋	22 ♌	8 ♎	10 ♏	25 ♐	0 ♒
19	22 ♏	9 ♑	1 ♒	23 ♓	2 ♉	25 ♊	1 ♌	17 ♍	2 ♏	4 ♐	20 ♑	26 ♒
21	18 ♐	7 ♒	29 ♒	23 ♈	2 ♊	22 ♋	26 ♌	11 ♎	25 ♏	28 ♐	16 ♒	23 ♓
23	15 ♑	6 ♓	0 ♈	23 ♉	0 ♋	18 ♌	21 ♍	5 ♏	19 ♐	23 ♑	13 ♓	21 ♈
25	13 ♒	7 ♈	0 ♉	22 ♊	27 ♋	13 ♍	15 ♎	29 ♏	14 ♑	19 ♒	11 ♈	20 ♉
27	13 ♓	6 ♉	0 ♊	19 ♋	23 ♌	7 ♊	9 ♏	23 ♐	11 ♒	18 ♓	11 ♉	19 ♊
29	12 ♈	4 ♊	27 ♊	15 ♌	17 ♍	1 ♏	3 ♐	19 ♑	9 ♓	18 ♈	11 ♊	18 ♋
31	10 ♉		23 ♋		11 ♎		28 ♐	17 ♒		18 ♉		16 ♌

1937	Jan.	Feb.	Mar.	April	May	June	July	Aug.	Sept.	Oct.	Nov.	Dec.
1	29 ♌	14 ♎	22 ♎	6 ♐	9 ♑	25 ♒	2 ♈	24 ♉	18 ♋	25 ♌	14 ♎	17 ♏
3	24 ♍	8 ♏	16 ♏	0 ♑	3 ♒	22 ♓	0 ♉	23 ♊	15 ♌	22 ♍	8 ♏	11 ♐
5	19 ♎	2 ♐	10 ♐	24 ♑	29 ♒	20 ♈	29 ♉	22 ♋	13 ♍	17 ♎	2 ♐	4 ♑
7	12 ♏	26 ♐	4 ♑	20 ♒	27 ♓	19 ♉	28 ♊	20 ♌	9 ♎	12 ♏	26 ♐	28 ♑
9	6 ♐	21 ♑	29 ♑	18 ♓	26 ♈	20 ♊	28 ♋	17 ♍	4 ♏	6 ♐	19 ♑	23 ♒
11	1 ♑	18 ♒	26 ♒	18 ♈	26 ♉	19 ♋	26 ♌	13 ♎	28 ♏	29 ♐	14 ♒	18 ♓
13	26 ♑	16 ♓	25 ♓	18 ♉	26 ♊	18 ♌	23 ♍	8 ♏	21 ♐	23 ♑	9 ♓	15 ♈
15	22 ♒	14 ♈	24 ♈	17 ♊	25 ♋	14 ♍	18 ♎	1 ♐	15 ♑	18 ♒	6 ♈	13 ♉
17	20 ♓	13 ♉	23 ♉	16 ♋	22 ♌	9 ♎	12 ♏	25 ♐	10 ♒	15 ♓	5 ♉	13 ♊
19	18 ♈	11 ♊	22 ♊	13 ♌	18 ♍	3 ♏	5 ♐	20 ♑	7 ♓	13 ♈	6 ♊	14 ♋
21	16 ♉	9 ♋	19 ♋	8 ♍	12 ♎	27 ♏	29 ♐	15 ♒	4 ♈	12 ♉	6 ♋	14 ♌
23	14 ♊	6 ♌	16 ♌	3 ♎	6 ♏	21 ♐	24 ♑	12 ♓	3 ♉	12 ♊	5 ♌	11 ♍
25	13 ♋	2 ♍	11 ♍	27 ♎	0 ♐	15 ♑	19 ♒	9 ♈	2 ♊	11 ♋	2 ♍	7 ♎
27	10 ♌	28 ♍	6 ♎	21 ♏	24 ♐	9 ♒	15 ♓	7 ♉	0 ♋	9 ♌	28 ♍	2 ♏
29	7 ♍		1 ♏	15 ♐	18 ♑	5 ♓	12 ♈	5 ♊	28 ♋	5 ♍	23 ♎	26 ♏
31	2 ♎		24 ♏		12 ♒		10 ♉	3 ♋		1 ♎		20 ♐

1938	Jan.	Feb.	Mar.	April	May	June	July	Aug.	Sept.	Oct.	Nov.	Dec.
1	1 ♑	16 ♒	25 ♒	13 ♈	20 ♉	14 ♋	23 ♌	13 ♎	0 ♐	2 ♑	15 ♒	17 ♓
3	25 ♑	12 ♓	21 ♓	11 ♉	20 ♊	13 ♌	21 ♍	9 ♏	24 ♐	26 ♑	10 ♓	13 ♈
5	20 ♒	8 ♈	18 ♈	10 ♊	19 ♋	14 ♍	17 ♎	3 ♐	18 ♑	20 ♒	5 ♈	10 ♉
7	15 ♓	5 ♉	15 ♉	8 ♋	17 ♌	8 ♎	12 ♏	27 ♐	11 ♒	14 ♓	2 ♉	8 ♊
9	11 ♈	2 ♊	13 ♊	6 ♌	15 ♍	3 ♏	7 ♐	21 ♑	6 ♓	10 ♈	0 ♊	8 ♋
11	8 ♉	1 ♋	11 ♋	4 ♍	11 ♎	28 ♏	0 ♑	15 ♒	1 ♈	7 ♉	29 ♊	8 ♌
13	7 ♊	0 ♌	10 ♌	1 ♎	6 ♏	21 ♐	24 ♑	9 ♓	27 ♈	5 ♊	28 ♋	7 ♍
15	7 ♋	29 ♌	8 ♍	27 ♎	1 ♐	15 ♑	18 ♒	4 ♈	24 ♉	3 ♋	26 ♌	4 ♎
17	7 ♌	27 ♍	6 ♎	22 ♏	25 ♐	9 ♒	12 ♓	0 ♉	22 ♊	1 ♌	24 ♍	0 ♏
19	6 ♍	24 ♎	2 ♏	16 ♐	18 ♑	3 ♓	7 ♈	27 ♉	20 ♋	29 ♌	21 ♎	26 ♏
21	3 ♎	19 ♏	26 ♏	10 ♑	12 ♒	28 ♓	4 ♉	25 ♊	19 ♌	27 ♍	16 ♏	20 ♐
23	29 ♎	13 ♐	20 ♐	4 ♒	7 ♓	24 ♈	1 ♊	25 ♋	18 ♍	24 ♎	11 ♐	14 ♑
25	23 ♏	6 ♑	14 ♑	28 ♒	2 ♈	22 ♉	1 ♋	25 ♌	16 ♎	21 ♏	6 ♑	8 ♒
27	16 ♐	0 ♒	8 ♒	24 ♓	0 ♉	22 ♊	1 ♌	24 ♍	12 ♏	16 ♐	0 ♒	2 ♓
29	10 ♑		3 ♓	22 ♈	29 ♉	23 ♋	1 ♍	21 ♎	8 ♐	10 ♑	23 ♒	26 ♓
31	4 ♒		0 ♈		29 ♊		0 ♎	17 ♏		3 ♒		21 ♈

1939	Jan.	Feb.	Mar.	April	May	June	July	Aug.	Sept.	Oct.	Nov.	Dec.
1	4 ♉	24 ♊	3 ♋	27 ♌	6 ♎	26 ♏	1 ♑	16 ♒	0 ♈	4 ♉	22 ♊	0 ♌
3	2 ♊	24 ♋	3 ♌	26 ♍	4 ♏	22 ♐	25 ♑	10 ♓	24 ♈	29 ♉	20 ♋	29 ♌
5	1 ♋	25 ♌	3 ♍	25 ♎	0 ♐	17 ♑	19 ♒	3 ♈	19 ♉	25 ♊	18 ♌	27 ♍
7	2 ♌	25 ♍	3 ♎	22 ♏	26 ♐	11 ♒	13 ♓	28 ♈	15 ♊	23 ♋	16 ♍	25 ♎
9	2 ♍	23 ♎	1 ♏	18 ♐	21 ♑	4 ♓	7 ♈	23 ♉	13 ♋	22 ♌	15 ♎	22 ♏
11	0 ♎	19 ♏	28 ♏	13 ♑	15 ♒	28 ♓	1 ♉	20 ♊	12 ♌	21 ♍	13 ♏	19 ♐
13	27 ♎	14 ♐	23 ♐	7 ♒	8 ♓	23 ♈	28 ♉	19 ♋	13 ♍	21 ♎	11 ♐	15 ♑
15	23 ♏	8 ♑	17 ♑	0 ♓	3 ♈	19 ♉	26 ♊	19 ♌	13 ♎	19 ♏	7 ♑	10 ♒
17	17 ♐	2 ♒	10 ♒	25 ♓	28 ♈	17 ♊	25 ♋	19 ♍	11 ♏	16 ♐	2 ♒	4 ♓
19	11 ♑	26 ♒	4 ♓	20 ♈	25 ♉	16 ♋	26 ♌	19 ♎	8 ♐	12 ♑	26 ♒	28 ♓
21	5 ♒	20 ♓	29 ♓	16 ♉	23 ♊	16 ♌	25 ♍	16 ♏	4 ♑	6 ♒	20 ♓	22 ♈
23	29 ♒	14 ♈	24 ♈	13 ♊	21 ♋	15 ♍	23 ♎	12 ♐	28 ♑	0 ♓	14 ♈	17 ♉
25	23 ♓	9 ♉	19 ♊	11 ♋	20 ♌	13 ♎	20 ♏	7 ♑	22 ♒	24 ♓	9 ♉	13 ♊
27	17 ♈	6 ♊	16 ♋	9 ♌	18 ♍	10 ♏	15 ♐	1 ♒	15 ♓	18 ♈	5 ♊	11 ♋
29	13 ♉		14 ♌	7 ♍	16 ♎	6 ♐	10 ♑	25 ♒	9 ♈	13 ♉	2 ♋	10 ♌
31	10 ♊		13 ♍		13 ♏		4 ♒	18 ♓		9 ♊		9 ♍

1940	Jan.	Feb.	Mar.	April	May	June	July	Aug.	Sept.	Oct.	Nov.	Dec.
1	24 ♍	16 ♏	9 ♐	26 ♑	29 ♒	13 ♈	15 ♉	1 ♋	22 ♌	0 ♎	24 ♏	1 ♑
3	22 ♎	12 ♐	5 ♑	21 ♒	23 ♓	7 ♉	10 ♊	29 ♋	22 ♍	1 ♏	23 ♐	28 ♑
5	19 ♏	8 ♑	29 ♑	14 ♓	16 ♈	2 ♊	7 ♋	28 ♌	22 ♎	0 ♐	20 ♑	24 ♒
7	15 ♐	2 ♒	23 ♒	8 ♈	11 ♉	28 ♊	5 ♌	28 ♍	21 ♏	28 ♐	16 ♒	18 ♓
9	11 ♑	27 ♒	17 ♓	2 ♉	5 ♊	25 ♋	3 ♍	27 ♎	18 ♐	24 ♑	10 ♓	12 ♈
11	6 ♒	20 ♓	11 ♈	26 ♉	1 ♋	23 ♌	2 ♎	25 ♏	15 ♑	19 ♒	4 ♈	6 ♉
13	0 ♓	14 ♈	5 ♉	21 ♊	28 ♋	21 ♍	0 ♏	22 ♐	10 ♒	13 ♓	27 ♈	0 ♊
15	24 ♓	8 ♉	29 ♉	18 ♋	26 ♌	19 ♎	28 ♏	18 ♑	4 ♓	7 ♈	21 ♉	25 ♊
17	17 ♈	3 ♊	25 ♊	15 ♌	24 ♍	17 ♏	25 ♐	13 ♒	28 ♓	1 ♉	16 ♊	21 ♋
19	12 ♉	29 ♊	22 ♋	14 ♍	23 ♎	15 ♐	21 ♑	7 ♓	22 ♈	24 ♉	11 ♋	18 ♌
21	7 ♊	27 ♋	20 ♌	14 ♎	22 ♏	12 ♑	17 ♒	1 ♈	15 ♉	19 ♊	7 ♌	15 ♍
23	5 ♋	27 ♌	21 ♍	14 ♏	21 ♐	8 ♒	11 ♓	25 ♈	10 ♊	14 ♋	4 ♍	13 ♎
25	4 ♌	28 ♍	21 ♎	12 ♐	17 ♑	3 ♓	5 ♈	19 ♉	5 ♋	11 ♌	3 ♎	12 ♏
27	4 ♍	27 ♎	20 ♏	9 ♑	13 ♒	27 ♓	29 ♈	13 ♊	2 ♌	9 ♍	2 ♏	10 ♐
29	4 ♎	26 ♏	18 ♐	5 ♒	7 ♓	21 ♈	23 ♉	10 ♋	0 ♍	8 ♎	2 ♐	9 ♑
31	2 ♏		14 ♑		1 ♈		18 ♊	7 ♌		9 ♏		6 ♒

1941	Jan.	Feb.	Mar.	April	May	June	July	Aug.	Sept.	Oct.	Nov.	Dec.
1	19 ♒	4 ♈	12 ♈	26 ♉	29 ♊	16 ♌	24 ♍	16 ♏	10 ♑	17 ♒	4 ♈	7 ♉
3	14 ♓	28 ♈	6 ♉	20 ♊	24 ♋	13 ♍	21 ♎	15 ♐	7 ♒	13 ♓	28 ♈	1 ♊
5	8 ♈	21 ♉	29 ♉	15 ♋	20 ♌	11 ♎	20 ♏	13 ♑	3 ♓	7 ♈	22 ♉	25 ♊
7	2 ♉	16 ♊	24 ♊	11 ♌	17 ♍	10 ♏	19 ♐	11 ♒	29 ♓	2 ♉	16 ♊	19 ♋
9	26 ♉	11 ♋	19 ♋	9 ♍	16 ♎	10 ♐	18 ♑	8 ♓	23 ♈	25 ♉	10 ♋	14 ♌
11	21 ♊	9 ♌	16 ♌	8 ♎	17 ♏	10 ♑	16 ♒	3 ♈	17 ♉	19 ♊	4 ♌	9 ♍
13	17 ♋	7 ♍	15 ♍	9 ♏	17 ♐	8 ♒	13 ♓	27 ♈	11 ♊	13 ♋	0 ♍	6 ♎
15	14 ♌	6 ♎	15 ♎	9 ♐	16 ♑	4 ♓	7 ♈	21 ♉	5 ♋	8 ♌	27 ♍	4 ♏
17	12 ♍	5 ♏	15 ♏	7 ♑	13 ♒	29 ♓	1 ♉	15 ♊	0 ♌	5 ♍	26 ♎	4 ♐
19	10 ♎	3 ♐	14 ♐	4 ♒	9 ♓	23 ♈	25 ♉	10 ♋	27 ♌	3 ♎	26 ♏	5 ♑
21	8 ♏	1 ♑	11 ♑	29 ♒	3 ♈	17 ♉	19 ♊	5 ♌	25 ♍	3 ♏	27 ♐	4 ♒
23	6 ♐	27 ♑	7 ♒	24 ♓	26 ♈	11 ♊	14 ♋	2 ♍	24 ♎	3 ♐	26 ♑	2 ♓
25	4 ♑	23 ♒	2 ♓	18 ♈	20 ♉	5 ♋	10 ♌	0 ♎	24 ♏	3 ♑	23 ♒	28 ♓
27	1 ♒	18 ♓	27 ♓	11 ♉	14 ♊	1 ♌	7 ♍	29 ♎	23 ♐	1 ♒	19 ♓	22 ♈
29	27 ♒		21 ♈	5 ♊	8 ♋	27 ♌	4 ♎	28 ♏	20 ♑	27 ♒	13 ♑	16 ♉
31	22 ♓		14 ♉		4 ♌		2 ♏	26 ♐		22 ♓		10 ♊

1942	Jan.	Feb.	Mar.	April	May	June	July	Aug.	Sept.	Oct.	Nov.	Dec.
1	22 ♊	7 ♌	15 ♌	4 ♎	11 ♏	5 ♑	13 ♒	3 ♈	20 ♉	22 ♊	5 ♌	7 ♍
3	16 ♋	3 ♍	12 ♍	2 ♏	11 ♐	5 ♒	12 ♓	29 ♈	14 ♊	15 ♋	29 ♌	3 ♎
5	11 ♌	29 ♍	9 ♎	2 ♐	11 ♑	3 ♓	7 ♈	24 ♉	7 ♋	9 ♌	25 ♍	0 ♏
7	6 ♍	27 ♎	7 ♏	1 ♑	9 ♒	29 ♓	3 ♉	17 ♊	1 ♌	4 ♍	22 ♎	29 ♏
9	2 ♎	25 ♏	6 ♐	29 ♑	6 ♓	24 ♈	27 ♉	11 ♋	26 ♌	0 ♎	21 ♏	29 ♐
11	0 ♏	23 ♐	4 ♑	26 ♒	2 ♈	18 ♉	21 ♊	5 ♌	22 ♍	28 ♎	21 ♐	29 ♑
13	28 ♏	22 ♑	2 ♒	22 ♓	27 ♈	12 ♊	14 ♋	0 ♍	18 ♎	26 ♏	20 ♑	28 ♒
15	28 ♐	20 ♒	29 ♒	17 ♈	21 ♉	6 ♋	8 ♌	25 ♍	16 ♏	25 ♐	18 ♒	26 ♓
17	28 ♑	18 ♓	26 ♓	12 ♉	15 ♊	29 ♋	3 ♍	22 ♎	14 ♐	24 ♑	15 ♓	21 ♈
19	26 ♒	13 ♈	21 ♈	6 ♊	8 ♋	24 ♌	28 ♍	19 ♏	13 ♑	21 ♒	12 ♈	16 ♉
21	23 ♓	8 ♉	16 ♉	0 ♋	2 ♌	19 ♍	25 ♎	17 ♐	11 ♒	19 ♓	7 ♉	11 ♊
23	18 ♈	2 ♊	10 ♊	24 ♋	27 ♌	15 ♎	23 ♏	17 ♑	9 ♓	15 ♈	2 ♊	5 ♋
25	12 ♉	26 ♊	4 ♋	18 ♌	23 ♍	13 ♏	22 ♐	16 ♒	6 ♈	11 ♉	26 ♊	28 ♋
27	6 ♊	20 ♋	28 ♋	14 ♍	20 ♎	13 ♐	22 ♑	14 ♓	2 ♉	5 ♊	20 ♋	22 ♌
29	0 ♋		23 ♌	12 ♎	19 ♏	14 ♑	22 ♒	11 ♈	27 ♉	0 ♋	13 ♌	16 ♍
31	24 ♋		20 ♍		20 ♐		20 ♓	7 ♉		23 ♋		11 ♎

1943	Jan.	Feb.	Mar.	April	May	June	July	Aug.	Sept.	Oct.	Nov.	Dec.
1	25 ♎	16 ♐	26 ♐	19 ♒	27 ♓	17 ♉	21 ♊	6 ♌	21 ♍	25 ♎	14 ♐	22 ♑
3	22 ♏	15 ♑	25 ♑	18 ♓	24 ♈	12 ♊	15 ♋	20 ♌	15 ♎	21 ♏	12 ♑	21 ♒
5	22 ♐	16 ♒	24 ♒	15 ♈	21 ♉	7 ♋	9 ♌	24 ♍	11 ♏	17 ♐	10 ♒	19 ♓
7	23 ♑	15 ♓	23 ♓	12 ♉	16 ♊	0 ♌	3 ♍	18 ♎	7 ♐	15 ♑	8 ♓	17 ♈
9	23 ♒	13 ♈	21 ♈	8 ♊	10 ♋	24 ♌	27 ♍	14 ♏	5 ♑	13 ♒	6 ♈	14 ♉
11	21 ♓	10 ♉	18 ♉	2 ♋	4 ♌	18 ♍	22 ♎	11 ♐	3 ♒	12 ♓	4 ♉	10 ♊
13	18 ♈	4 ♊	13 ♊	26 ♋	28 ♌	13 ♎	18 ♏	10 ♑	3 ♓	11 ♈	1 ♊	5 ♋
15	13 ♉	28 ♊	7 ♋	20 ♌	22 ♍	10 ♏	16 ♐	10 ♒	3 ♈	10 ♉	27 ♊	0 ♌
17	8 ♊	22 ♋	0 ♌	14 ♍	18 ♎	8 ♐	16 ♑	9 ♓	2 ♉	7 ♊	22 ♋	23 ♌
19	2 ♋	16 ♌	24 ♌	10 ♎	15 ♏	8 ♑	17 ♒	9 ♈	29 ♉	2 ♋	16 ♌	17 ♍
21	25 ♋	10 ♍	19 ♍	7 ♏	14 ♐	8 ♒	16 ♓	7 ♉	24 ♊	26 ♋	9 ♍	11 ♎
23	19 ♌	5 ♎	14 ♎	5 ♐	13 ♑	7 ♓	14 ♈	3 ♊	18 ♋	20 ♌	3 ♎	7 ♏
25	13 ♍	1 ♏	11 ♏	3 ♑	12 ♒	5 ♈	11 ♉	27 ♊	12 ♌	13 ♍	29 ♎	4 ♐
27	8 ♎	28 ♏	8 ♐	2 ♒	10 ♓	1 ♉	6 ♊	21 ♋	5 ♍	8 ♎	26 ♏	2 ♑
29	4 ♏		6 ♑	0 ♓	8 ♈	27 ♉	0 ♋	15 ♌	0 ♎	4 ♏	24 ♐	2 ♒
31	1 ♐		5 ♒		4 ♉		24 ♋	9 ♍		0 ♐		1 ♓

1944	Jan.	Feb.	Mar.	April	May	June	July	Aug.	Sept.	Oct.	Nov.	Dec.
1	15 ♓	7 ♉	0 ♊	17 ♋	19 ♌	2 ♎	5 ♏	22 ♐	12 ♒	21 ♓	14 ♉	21 ♊
3	14 ♈	4 ♊	26 ♊	10 ♌	12 ♍	27 ♎	0 ♐	20 ♑	13 ♓	21 ♈	13 ♊	18 ♋
5	11 ♉	29 ♊	20 ♋	4 ♍	6 ♎	22 ♏	27 ♐	19 ♒	13 ♈	21 ♉	10 ♋	14 ♌
7	7 ♊	23 ♋	14 ♌	28 ♍	1 ♏	19 ♐	26 ♑	19 ♓	12 ♉	19 ♊	6 ♌	8 ♍
9	2 ♋	17 ♌	7 ♍	22 ♎	27 ♏	16 ♑	25 ♒	18 ♈	10 ♊	15 ♋	0 ♍	2 ♎
11	26 ♋	10 ♍	1 ♎	17 ♏	23 ♐	15 ♒	24 ♓	17 ♉	6 ♋	10 ♌	24 ♍	26 ♎
13	20 ♌	4 ♎	25 ♎	13 ♐	20 ♑	13 ♓	22 ♈	13 ♊	1 ♌	3 ♍	18 ♎	20 ♏
15	13 ♍	28 ♎	20 ♏	10 ♑	18 ♒	11 ♈	20 ♉	9 ♋	25 ♌	27 ♍	12 ♏	16 ♐
17	7 ♎	23 ♏	16 ♐	7 ♒	16 ♓	9 ♉	16 ♊	3 ♌	18 ♍	21 ♎	7 ♐	12 ♑
19	2 ♏	20 ♐	13 ♑	6 ♓	15 ♈	7 ♊	12 ♋	28 ♌	12 ♎	15 ♏	3 ♑	9 ♒
21	28 ♏	18 ♑	12 ♒	5 ♈	13 ♉	3 ♋	7 ♌	21 ♍	6 ♏	10 ♐	29 ♑	7 ♓
23	26 ♐	18 ♒	11 ♓	5 ♉	11 ♊	28 ♋	1 ♍	15 ♎	10 ♐	6 ♑	26 ♒	5 ♈
25	25 ♑	18 ♓	11 ♈	3 ♊	8 ♋	23 ♌	25 ♍	9 ♏	26 ♐	2 ♒	25 ♓	4 ♉
27	25 ♒	18 ♈	11 ♉	0 ♋	3 ♌	16 ♍	18 ♎	4 ♐	22 ♑	0 ♓	24 ♈	2 ♊
29	25 ♓	17 ♉	8 ♊	25 ♋	27 ♌	10 ♎	13 ♏	0 ♑	21 ♒	29 ♓	23 ♉	0 ♋
31	24 ♈		4 ♋		20 ♍		8 ♐	28 ♑		0 ♉		26 ♋

1945	Jan.	Feb.	Mar.	April	May	June	July	Aug.	Sept.	Oct.	Nov.	Dec.
1	9 ♌	24 ♍	2 ♎	16 ♏	20 ♐	8 ♒	16 ♓	9 ♉	2 ♋	8 ♌	25 ♍	28 ♎
3	4 ♍	17 ♎	26 ♎	11 ♐	15 ♑	5 ♓	14 ♈	7 ♊	28 ♋	3 ♍	19 ♎	21 ♏
5	28 ♍	11 ♏	20 ♏	5 ♑	11 ♒	3 ♈	12 ♉	5 ♋	24 ♌	28 ♍	13 ♏	15 ♐
7	21 ♎	6 ♐	14 ♐	1 ♒	9 ♓	2 ♉	11 ♊	2 ♌	19 ♍	22 ♎	6 ♐	9 ♑
9	16 ♏	1 ♑	9 ♑	29 ♒	8 ♈	2 ♊	9 ♋	28 ♌	13 ♎	16 ♏	0 ♑	4 ♒
11	11 ♐	29 ♑	7 ♒	29 ♓	8 ♉	1 ♋	6 ♌	23 ♍	7 ♏	9 ♐	25 ♑	0 ♓
13	7 ♑	28 ♒	6 ♓	0 ♉	8 ♊	28 ♋	2 ♍	17 ♎	1 ♐	3 ♑	20 ♒	28 ♓
15	5 ♒	27 ♓	6 ♈	0 ♊	6 ♋	24 ♌	27 ♍	11 ♏	25 ♐	28 ♑	18 ♓	26 ♈
17	3 ♓	27 ♈	6 ♉	28 ♊	3 ♌	19 ♍	21 ♎	5 ♐	20 ♑	25 ♒	17 ♈	26 ♉
19	2 ♈	25 ♉	5 ♊	25 ♋	28 ♌	13 ♎	15 ♏	29 ♐	17 ♒	24 ♓	17 ♉	25 ♊
21	1 ♉	22 ♊	2 ♋	20 ♌	23 ♍	7 ♏	9 ♐	25 ♑	16 ♓	24 ♈	18 ♊	24 ♋
23	29 ♉	18 ♋	28 ♋	14 ♍	16 ♎	1 ♐	4 ♑	23 ♒	16 ♈	24 ♉	17 ♋	22 ♌
25	26 ♊	14 ♌	23 ♌	8 ♎	10 ♏	26 ♐	0 ♒	22 ♓	16 ♉	24 ♊	14 ♌	18 ♍
27	22 ♋	8 ♍	17 ♍	2 ♏	4 ♐	21 ♑	28 ♒	21 ♈	15 ♊	22 ♋	9 ♍	12 ♎
29	17 ♌		11 ♎	26 ♏	29 ♐	18 ♒	26 ♓	20 ♉	12 ♋	18 ♌	4 ♎	6 ♏
31	12 ♍		5 ♏		25 ♑		25 ♈	18 ♊		13 ♍		0 ♐

1946	Jan.	Feb.	Mar.	April	May	June	July	Aug.	Sept.	Oct.	Nov.	Dec.
1	12 ♐	27 ♑	5 ♒	24 ♓	2 ♉	26 ♊	4 ♌	23 ♍	9 ♏	11 ♐	25 ♑	28 ♒
3	6 ♑	23 ♒	2 ♓	24 ♈	2 ♊	25 ♋	2 ♍	19 ♎	3 ♐	5 ♑	19 ♒	23 ♓
5	1 ♒	21 ♓	0 ♈	24 ♉	2 ♋	23 ♌	28 ♍	13 ♏	27 ♐	29 ♑	15 ♓	21 ♈
7	27 ♒	19 ♈	29 ♈	23 ♊	1 ♌	20 ♍	23 ♎	7 ♐	21 ♑	24 ♒	13 ♈	20 ♉
9	24 ♓	17 ♉	28 ♉	21 ♋	27 ♌	14 ♎	17 ♏	1 ♑	16 ♒	21 ♓	12 ♉	20 ♊
11	22 ♈	15 ♊	26 ♊	17 ♌	23 ♍	8 ♏	11 ♐	25 ♑	12 ♓	19 ♈	12 ♊	20 ♋
13	21 ♉	13 ♋	24 ♋	13 ♍	17 ♎	2 ♐	4 ♑	20 ♒	10 ♈	18 ♉	11 ♋	19 ♌
15	19 ♊	11 ♌	20 ♌	8 ♎	11 ♏	26 ♐	29 ♑	17 ♓	8 ♉	17 ♊	10 ♌	17 ♍
17	18 ♋	8 ♍	16 ♍	2 ♏	5 ♐	20 ♑	24 ♒	14 ♈	7 ♊	16 ♋	7 ♍	13 ♎
19	16 ♌	3 ♎	12 ♎	26 ♏	29 ♐	14 ♒	20 ♓	12 ♉	5 ♋	13 ♌	3 ♎	7 ♏
21	13 ♍	28 ♎	6 ♏	20 ♐	23 ♑	10 ♓	17 ♈	10 ♊	1 ♌	10 ♍	28 ♎	1 ♐
23	8 ♎	22 ♏	0 ♐	14 ♑	17 ♒	7 ♈	15 ♉	8 ♋	0 ♍	6 ♎	22 ♏	25 ♐
25	2 ♏	15 ♐	23 ♐	8 ♒	13 ♓	5 ♉	14 ♊	7 ♌	27 ♍	1 ♏	16 ♐	18 ♑
27	26 ♏	10 ♑	18 ♑	5 ♓	11 ♈	4 ♊	13 ♋	5 ♍	23 ♎	25 ♏	9 ♑	12 ♒
29	20 ♐		13 ♒	3 ♈	11 ♉	4 ♋	12 ♌	2 ♎	17 ♏	19 ♐	3 ♒	7 ♓
31	14 ♑		10 ♓		11 ♊		10 ♍	27 ♎		13 ♑		2 ♈

1947	Jan.	Feb.	Mar.	April	May	June	July	Aug.	Sept.	Oct.	Nov.	Dec.
1	16 ♈	7 ♊	18 ♊	11 ♌	19 ♍	8 ♏	12 ♐	26 ♑	11 ♓	16 ♈	5 ♊	14 ♋
3	13 ♉	6 ♋	16 ♋	9 ♍	16 ♎	3 ♐	5 ♑	20 ♒	6 ♈	12 ♉	4 ♋	13 ♌
5	13 ♊	6 ♌	15 ♌	6 ♎	11 ♏	27 ♐	29 ♑	14 ♓	2 ♉	9 ♊	2 ♌	12 ♍
7	13 ♋	6 ♍	14 ♍	3 ♏	6 ♐	20 ♑	23 ♒	9 ♈	29 ♉	7 ♋	1 ♍	9 ♎
9	13 ♌	4 ♎	11 ♎	28 ♏	0 ♑	14 ♒	17 ♓	5 ♉	26 ♊	6 ♌	28 ♍	5 ♏
11	12 ♍	0 ♏	8 ♏	22 ♐	24 ♑	8 ♓	12 ♈	2 ♊	25 ♋	4 ♍	26 ♎	1 ♐
13	9 ♎	24 ♏	2 ♐	16 ♑	18 ♒	3 ♈	9 ♉	1 ♋	25 ♌	3 ♎	22 ♏	25 ♐
15	4 ♏	18 ♐	26 ♐	10 ♒	12 ♓	0 ♉	7 ♊	1 ♌	24 ♍	0 ♏	17 ♐	19 ♑
17	28 ♏	12 ♑	20 ♑	4 ♓	8 ♈	29 ♉	7 ♋	1 ♍	22 ♎	26 ♏	11 ♑	13 ♒
19	22 ♐	6 ♒	14 ♒	0 ♈	6 ♉	28 ♊	7 ♌	0 ♎	18 ♏	21 ♐	5 ♒	7 ♓
21	15 ♑	1 ♓	9 ♓	28 ♈	5 ♊	29 ♋	7 ♍	27 ♎	13 ♐	15 ♑	29 ♒	1 ♈
23	9 ♒	26 ♓	5 ♈	26 ♉	5 ♋	28 ♌	5 ♎	23 ♏	7 ♑	9 ♒	23 ♓	27 ♈
25	4 ♓	23 ♈	3 ♉	25 ♊	4 ♌	26 ♍	2 ♏	17 ♐	1 ♒	3 ♓	19 ♈	24 ♉
27	29 ♓	20 ♉	0 ♊	24 ♋	2 ♍	22 ♎	27 ♏	11 ♑	25 ♒	28 ♓	16 ♉	23 ♊
29	26 ♈		29 ♊	22 ♌	0 ♎	17 ♏	21 ♐	5 ♒	20 ♓	24 ♈	14 ♊	23 ♋
31	23 ♉		27 ♋		25 ♎		14 ♑	29 ♒		22 ♉		23 ♌

1948	Jan.	Feb.	Mar.	April	May	June	July	Aug.	Sept.	Oct.	Nov.	Dec.
1	7 ♍	29 ♎	20 ♏	6 ♑	8 ♒	22 ♓	24 ♈	12 ♊	3 ♌	12 ♍	5 ♏	11 ♐
3	6 ♎	25 ♏	16 ♐	0 ♒	2 ♓	16 ♈	20 ♉	10 ♋	4 ♍	12 ♎	3 ♐	8 ♑
5	2 ♏	19 ♐	10 ♑	24 ♒	26 ♓	12 ♉	17 ♊	10 ♌	4 ♎	11 ♏	0 ♑	3 ♒
7	28 ♏	13 ♑	4 ♒	18 ♓	21 ♈	9 ♊	16 ♋	10 ♍	3 ♏	9 ♐	26 ♑	28 ♒
9	22 ♐	7 ♒	28 ♒	13 ♈	17 ♉	8 ♋	16 ♌	10 ♎	1 ♐	5 ♑	20 ♒	21 ♓
11	16 ♑	1 ♓	22 ♓	8 ♉	14 ♊	7 ♌	16 ♍	8 ♏	26 ♐	0 ♒	14 ♓	15 ♈
13	10 ♒	25 ♓	16 ♈	4 ♊	12 ♋	6 ♍	14 ♎	4 ♐	21 ♑	24 ♒	7 ♈	10 ♉
15	4 ♓	19 ♈	11 ♉	1 ♋	10 ♌	4 ♎	11 ♏	0 ♑	15 ♒	17 ♓	2 ♉	6 ♊
17	28 ♓	14 ♉	7 ♊	29 ♋	9 ♍	1 ♏	7 ♐	24 ♑	9 ♓	11 ♈	27 ♉	3 ♋
19	22 ♈	11 ♊	5 ♋	28 ♌	7 ♎	28 ♏	2 ♑	18 ♒	2 ♈	6 ♉	24 ♊	1 ♌
21	18 ♉	9 ♋	3 ♌	27 ♍	5 ♏	23 ♐	27 ♑	12 ♓	27 ♈	1 ♊	21 ♋	0 ♍
23	16 ♊	9 ♌	3 ♍	25 ♎	1 ♐	18 ♑	21 ♒	5 ♈	21 ♉	27 ♊	19 ♌	28 ♍
25	15 ♋	9 ♍	2 ♎	23 ♏	27 ♐	12 ♒	15 ♓	29 ♈	17 ♊	24 ♋	17 ♍	26 ♎
27	16 ♌	9 ♎	1 ♏	19 ♐	22 ♑	6 ♓	8 ♈	24 ♉	14 ♋	22 ♌	16 ♎	24 ♏
29	16 ♍	7 ♏	28 ♏	14 ♑	16 ♒	0 ♈	3 ♉	21 ♊	12 ♌	21 ♍	14 ♏	20 ♐
31	15 ♎		24 ♐		10 ♓		28 ♉	19 ♋		21 ♎		16 ♑

1949	Jan.	Feb.	Mar.	April	May	June	July	Aug.	Sept.	Oct.	Nov.	Dec.
1	29 ♑	14 ♓	22 ♓	7 ♉	11 ♊	0 ♌	8 ♍	1 ♏	23 ♐	29 ♑	15 ♓	18 ♈
3	23 ♒	7 ♈	16 ♈	1 ♊	6 ♋	27 ♌	6 ♎	29 ♏	20 ♑	24 ♒	9 ♈	11 ♉
5	17 ♓	1 ♉	10 ♉	26 ♊	3 ♌	25 ♍	4 ♏	26 ♐	15 ♒	18 ♓	3 ♉	5 ♊
7	11 ♈	25 ♉	4 ♊	23 ♋	0 ♍	24 ♎	2 ♐	23 ♑	9 ♓	12 ♈	27 ♉	0 ♋
9	5 ♉	21 ♊	0 ♋	21 ♌	29 ♍	23 ♏	0 ♑	18 ♒	3 ♈	6 ♉	21 ♊	26 ♋
11	0 ♊	19 ♋	27 ♋	20 ♍	29 ♎	21 ♐	27 ♑	13 ♓	27 ♈	29 ♉	16 ♋	22 ♌
13	27 ♊	19 ♌	27 ♌	20 ♎	28 ♏	18 ♑	22 ♒	7 ♈	21 ♉	24 ♊	12 ♌	20 ♍
15	26 ♋	19 ♍	27 ♍	20 ♏	27 ♐	14 ♒	17 ♓	0 ♉	15 ♊	19 ♋	9 ♍	18 ♎
17	25 ♌	19 ♎	27 ♎	19 ♐	23 ♑	9 ♓	10 ♈	24 ♉	10 ♋	16 ♌	8 ♎	17 ♏
19	25 ♍	17 ♏	26 ♏	15 ♑	19 ♒	3 ♈	4 ♉	19 ♊	7 ♌	15 ♍	8 ♏	16 ♐
21	23 ♎	14 ♐	23 ♐	10 ♒	13 ♓	26 ♈	28 ♉	15 ♋	6 ♍	15 ♎	8 ♐	15 ♑
23	20 ♏	10 ♑	19 ♑	4 ♓	6 ♈	20 ♉	24 ♊	14 ♌	7 ♎	15 ♏	7 ♑	12 ♒
25	17 ♐	4 ♒	14 ♒	28 ♓	0 ♉	16 ♊	21 ♋	13 ♍	7 ♏	15 ♐	4 ♒	8 ♓
27	13 ♑	29 ♒	8 ♓	22 ♈	25 ♉	12 ♋	19 ♌	13 ♎	6 ♐	12 ♑	0 ♓	2 ♈
29	7 ♒		1 ♈	16 ♉	20 ♊	10 ♌	18 ♍	12 ♏	3 ♑	9 ♒	24 ♓	26 ♈
31	2 ♓		25 ♈		16 ♋		17 ♎	10 ♐		3 ♓		19 ♉

1950	Jan.	Feb.	Mar.	April	May	June	July	Aug.	Sept.	Oct.	Nov.	Dec.
1	1 ♊	17 ♋	25 ♋	15 ♍	23 ♎	17 ♐	24 ♑	14 ♓	29 ♈	1 ♊	15 ♋	18 ♌
3	26 ♊	15 ♌	23 ♌	15 ♎	23 ♏	16 ♑	22 ♒	9 ♈	23 ♉	25 ♊	10 ♌	14 ♍
5	22 ♋	13 ♍	21 ♍	15 ♏	23 ♐	14 ♒	18 ♓	3 ♉	16 ♊	19 ♋	5 ♍	11 ♎
7	19 ♌	11 ♎	21 ♎	14 ♐	22 ♑	10 ♓	13 ♈	27 ♉	11 ♋	14 ♌	3 ♎	10 ♏
9	17 ♍	10 ♏	20 ♏	12 ♑	19 ♒	5 ♈	7 ♉	21 ♊	6 ♌	11 ♍	2 ♏	11 ♐
11	14 ♎	8 ♐	18 ♐	9 ♒	14 ♓	28 ♈	0 ♊	15 ♋	3 ♍	9 ♎	3 ♐	11 ♑
13	13 ♏	5 ♑	16 ♑	4 ♓	8 ♈	22 ♉	25 ♊	11 ♌	1 ♎	9 ♏	3 ♑	10 ♒
15	11 ♐	2 ♒	12 ♒	29 ♓	1 ♉	16 ♊	19 ♋	8 ♍	0 ♏	9 ♐	2 ♒	8 ♓
17	9 ♑	28 ♒	7 ♓	23 ♈	25 ♉	10 ♋	15 ♌	6 ♎	29 ♏	8 ♑	29 ♒	3 ♈
19	7 ♒	23 ♓	2 ♈	16 ♉	19 ♊	5 ♌	12 ♍	4 ♏	27 ♐	5 ♒	24 ♓	27 ♈
21	3 ♓	18 ♈	26 ♈	10 ♊	13 ♋	1 ♍	9 ♎	2 ♐	25 ♑	2 ♓	18 ♈	21 ♉
23	28 ♓	11 ♉	19 ♉	4 ♋	8 ♌	28 ♍	7 ♏	0 ♑	22 ♒	27 ♓	12 ♉	15 ♊
25	22 ♈	5 ♊	13 ♊	29 ♋	5 ♍	26 ♎	5 ♐	28 ♑	18 ♓	21 ♈	6 ♊	9 ♋
27	15 ♉	29 ♊	8 ♋	25 ♌	2 ♎	25 ♏	4 ♑	26 ♒	13 ♈	15 ♉	0 ♋	3 ♌
29	9 ♊		3 ♌	23 ♍	1 ♏	25 ♐	3 ♒	22 ♓	7 ♉	9 ♊	24 ♋	28 ♌
31	4 ♋		1 ♍		1 ♐		0 ♓	17 ♈		3 ♋		24 ♍

1951	Jan.	Feb.	Mar.	April	May	June	July	Aug.	Sept.	Oct.	Nov.	Dec.
1	7 ♎	29 ♏	10 ♐	3 ♒	11 ♓	29 ♈	2 ♊	16 ♋	2 ♍	6 ♎	27 ♏	5 ♑
3	5 ♏	28 ♐	9 ♑	1 ♓	7 ♌	23 ♉	26 ♊	10 ♌	27 ♍	3 ♏	26 ♐	5 ♒
5	4 ♐	28 ♑	7 ♒	27 ♓	2 ♉	17 ♊	20 ♋	5 ♍	23 ♎	1 ♐	25 ♑	3 ♓
7	4 ♑	26 ♒	5 ♓	23 ♈	26 ♉	11 ♋	13 ♌	0 ♎	21 ♏	0 ♑	23 ♒	0 ♈
9	4 ♒	24 ♓	1 ♈	18 ♉	20 ♊	4 ♌	8 ♍	26 ♎	19 ♐	28 ♑	20 ♓	26 ♈
11	2 ♓	19 ♈	27 ♈	12 ♊	14 ♋	29 ♌	3 ♎	24 ♏	17 ♋	26 ♒	16 ♈	21 ♉
13	29 ♓	14 ♉	22 ♉	5 ♋	8 ♌	24 ♍	0 ♏	22 ♐	16 ♒	24 ♓	12 ♉	16 ♊
15	24 ♈	8 ♊	16 ♊	29 ♋	2 ♍	20 ♎	28 ♏	22 ♑	15 ♓	20 ♈	7 ♊	10 ♋
17	18 ♉	2 ♋	9 ♋	24 ♌	28 ♍	19 ♏	28 ♐	22 ♒	12 ♈	16 ♉	1 ♋	3 ♌
19	12 ♊	26 ♋	4 ♌	20 ♍	26 ♎	19 ♐	28 ♑	20 ♓	8 ♉	11 ♊	25 ♋	27 ♌
21	5 ♋	21 ♌	29 ♌	18 ♎	26 ♏	20 ♑	28 ♒	17 ♈	3 ♊	5 ♋	19 ♌	21 ♍
23	0 ♌	17 ♍	26 ♍	17 ♏	26 ♐	19 ♒	26 ♓	13 ♉	27 ♊	29 ♋	13 ♍	17 ♎
25	25 ♌	14 ♎	24 ♎	17 ♐	26 ♑	17 ♓	22 ♈	7 ♊	21 ♋	23 ♌	9 ♎	14 ♏
27	21 ♍	12 ♏	22 ♏	16 ♑	24 ♒	13 ♈	17 ♉	1 ♋	15 ♌	18 ♍	6 ♏	13 ♐
29	17 ♎		21 ♐	14 ♒	21 ♓	8 ♉	11 ♊	25 ♋	10 ♍	14 ♎	5 ♐	14 ♑
31	15 ♏		20 ♑		16 ♈		5 ♋	19 ♌		12 ♏		14 ♒

1952	Jan.	Feb.	Mar.	April	May	June	July	Aug.	Sept.	Oct.	Nov.	Dec.
1	29 ♒	19 ♈	10 ♉	26 ♊	28 ♋	11 ♍	14 ♎	3 ♐	24 ♑	3 ♓	26 ♈	2 ♊
3	27 ♓	15 ♉	6 ♊	20 ♋	22 ♌	6 ♎	10 ♏	1 ♑	24 ♒	3 ♈	24 ♉	28 ♊
5	23 ♈	10 ♊	0 ♋	14 ♌	16 ♍	2 ♏	8 ♐	1 ♒	24 ♓	2 ♉	20 ♊	23 ♋
7	18 ♉	4 ♋	24 ♋	8 ♍	11 ♎	0 ♐	7 ♑	1 ♓	24 ♈	29 ♉	15 ♋	17 ♌
9	13 ♊	27 ♋	18 ♌	3 ♎	7 ♏	29 ♐	8 ♒	1 ♈	21 ♉	25 ♊	9 ♌	11 ♍
11	7 ♋	21 ♌	12 ♍	29 ♎	5 ♐	29 ♑	7 ♓	29 ♈	17 ♊	20 ♋	3 ♍	5 ♎
13	0 ♌	15 ♍	7 ♎	26 ♏	4 ♑	28 ♒	6 ♈	25 ♉	11 ♋	13 ♌	27 ♍	0 ♏
15	24 ♌	10 ♎	3 ♏	24 ♐	3 ♒	26 ♓	3 ♉	20 ♊	5 ♌	7 ♍	22 ♎	26 ♏
17	18 ♍	6 ♏	29 ♏	22 ♑	1 ♓	23 ♈	29 ♉	14 ♋	29 ♌	1 ♎	18 ♏	24 ♐
19	13 ♎	2 ♐	27 ♐	20 ♒	29 ♓	19 ♉	23 ♊	8 ♌	23 ♍	26 ♎	15 ♐	23 ♑
21	9 ♏	1 ♑	25 ♑	18 ♓	26 ♈	14 ♊	17 ♋	2 ♍	17 ♎	22 ♏	13 ♑	22 ♒
23	7 ♐	0 ♒	24 ♒	16 ♈	22 ♉	9 ♋	11 ♌	26 ♍	12 ♏	19 ♐	11 ♒	20 ♓
25	6 ♑	0 ♓	23 ♓	13 ♉	18 ♊	2 ♌	5 ♍	20 ♎	9 ♐	16 ♑	9 ♓	18 ♈
27	7 ♒	29 ♓	21 ♈	9 ♊	12 ♋	26 ♌	29 ♍	15 ♏	6 ♑	14 ♒	7 ♈	15 ♉
29	7 ♓	27 ♈	18 ♉	4 ♋	6 ♌	20 ♍	23 ♎	12 ♐	4 ♒	13 ♓	6 ♉	11 ♊
31	5 ♈		14 ♊		0 ♍		19 ♏	10 ♑		12 ♈		7 ♋

1953	Jan.	Feb.	Mar.	April	May	June	July	Aug.	Sept.	Oct.	Nov.	Dec.
1	19 ♋	4 ♍	12 ♍	27 ♎	2 ♐	21 ♑	0 ♓	24 ♈	15 ♊	20 ♋	5 ♍	7 ♎
3	13 ♌	27 ♍	6 ♎	22 ♏	28 ♐	19 ♒	29 ♓	21 ♉	11 ♋	15 ♌	29 ♍	1 ♏
5	7 ♍	21 ♎	0 ♏	18 ♐	25 ♑	18 ♓	27 ♈	18 ♊	6 ♌	9 ♍	23 ♎	26 ♏
7	1 ♎	16 ♏	25 ♏	14 ♑	22 ♒	16 ♈	25 ♉	14 ♋	0 ♍	2 ♎	17 ♏	21 ♐
9	25 ♎	12 ♐	21 ♐	12 ♒	21 ♓	14 ♉	21 ♊	9 ♌	23 ♍	26 ♎	12 ♐	17 ♌
11	20 ♏	10 ♑	18 ♑	11 ♓	20 ♈	12 ♊	17 ♋	3 ♍	17 ♎	20 ♏	7 ♑	14 ♒
13	18 ♐	9 ♒	17 ♒	11 ♈	19 ♉	9 ♋	12 ♌	26 ♍	11 ♏	15 ♐	4 ♒	12 ♓
15	16 ♑	10 ♓	18 ♓	11 ♉	17 ♊	4 ♌	6 ♍	20 ♎	5 ♐	10 ♑	1 ♓	10 ♈
17	16 ♒	10 ♈	18 ♈	9 ♊	13 ♋	28 ♌	0 ♎	14 ♏	1 ♑	7 ♒	0 ♈	9 ♉
19	16 ♓	8 ♉	17 ♉	5 ♋	8 ♌	22 ♍	24 ♎	9 ♐	28 ♑	6 ♓	29 ♈	7 ♊
21	15 ♈	5 ♊	14 ♊	0 ♌	2 ♍	16 ♎	18 ♏	6 ♑	27 ♒	5 ♈	29 ♉	5 ♋
23	12 ♉	1 ♋	10 ♋	24 ♌	26 ♍	10 ♏	14 ♐	4 ♒	27 ♓	6 ♉	27 ♊	2 ♌
25	8 ♊	25 ♋	4 ♌	18 ♍	20 ♎	6 ♐	12 ♑	4 ♓	28 ♈	5 ♊	24 ♋	27 ♌
27	4 ♋	19 ♌	28 ♌	12 ♎	15 ♏	3 ♑	10 ♒	4 ♈	27 ♉	3 ♋	20 ♌	21 ♍
29	28 ♋		21 ♍	6 ♏	11 ♐	1 ♒	10 ♓	4 ♉	25 ♊	29 ♋	14 ♍	15 ♎
31	22 ♌		15 ♎		8 ♑		9 ♈	2 ♊		23 ♌		9 ♏

1954	Jan.	Feb.	Mar.	April	May	June	July	Aug.	Sept.	Oct.	Nov.	Dec.
1	21 ♏	7 ♑	15 ♑	5 ♓	14 ♈	8 ♊	15 ♋	3 ♍	19 ♎	21 ♏	5 ♑	9 ♒
3	17 ♐	5 ♒	13 ♒	5 ♈	14 ♉	7 ♋	12 ♌	28 ♍	12 ♏	14 ♐	0 ♒	5 ♓
5	13 ♑	4 ♓	12 ♓	6 ♉	14 ♊	4 ♌	8 ♍	23 ♎	6 ♐	9 ♑	26 ♒	3 ♈
7	10 ♒	3 ♈	12 ♈	6 ♊	12 ♋	0 ♍	3 ♎	16 ♏	0 ♑	4 ♒	24 ♓	2 ♉
9	8 ♓	2 ♉	12 ♉	4 ♋	9 ♌	24 ♍	27 ♎	10 ♐	26 ♑	1 ♓	23 ♈	2 ♊
11	7 ♈	0 ♊	10 ♊	0 ♌	4 ♍	18 ♎	20 ♏	5 ♑	23 ♒	0 ♈	24 ♉	2 ♋
13	5 ♉	27 ♊	7 ♋	25 ♌	28 ♍	12 ♏	15 ♐	1 ♒	22 ♓	0 ♉	24 ♊	1 ♌
15	3 ♊	23 ♋	3 ♌	19 ♍	22 ♎	6 ♐	10 ♑	29 ♒	21 ♈	1 ♊	23 ♋	28 ♌
17	1 ♋	19 ♌	28 ♌	13 ♎	16 ♏	1 ♑	6 ♒	27 ♓	21 ♉	0 ♋	19 ♌	23 ♍
19	27 ♋	13 ♍	22 ♍	7 ♏	10 ♐	27 ♑	3 ♓	26 ♈	20 ♊	27 ♋	15 ♍	18 ♎
21	23 ♌	7 ♎	16 ♎	1 ♐	4 ♑	23 ♒	1 ♈	25 ♉	17 ♋	23 ♌	9 ♎	11 ♏
23	17 ♍	1 ♏	10 ♏	25 ♐	0 ♒	20 ♓	29 ♈	23 ♊	13 ♌	18 ♍	3 ♏	5 ♐
25	11 ♎	25 ♏	4 ♐	20 ♑	26 ♒	19 ♈	28 ♉	20 ♋	8 ♍	12 ♎	27 ♏	29 ♐
27	5 ♏	19 ♐	28 ♐	16 ♒	24 ♓	17 ♉	26 ♊	16 ♌	3 ♎	6 ♏	20 ♐	24 ♑
29	29 ♏		24 ♑	14 ♓	23 ♈	17 ♊	24 ♋	12 ♍	27 ♎	0 ♐	14 ♑	19 ♒
31	24 ♐		21 ♒		23 ♉		20 ♌	7 ♎		23 ♐		15 ♓

1955	Jan.	Feb.	Mar.	April	May	June	July	Aug.	Sept.	Oct.	Nov.	Dec.
1	29 ♓	22 ♉	3 ♊	25 ♋	2 ♍	19 ♎	22 ♏	6 ♑	22 ♒	27 ♓	18 ♉	26 ♊
3	27 ♈	20 ♊	1 ♋	22 ♌	28 ♍	14 ♏	16 ♐	1 ♒	18 ♓	25 ♈	18 ♊	26 ♋
5	26 ♉	19 ♋	28 ♋	18 ♍	22 ♎	7 ♐	10 ♑	26 ♒	15 ♈	23 ♉	17 ♋	25 ♌
7	25 ♊	17 ♌	25 ♌	13 ♎	16 ♏	1 ♑	4 ♒	22 ♓	13 ♉	22 ♊	15 ♌	22 ♍
9	24 ♋	13 ♍	22 ♍	8 ♏	10 ♐	25 ♑	29 ♒	19 ♈	11 ♊	20 ♋	12 ♍	18 ♎
11	22 ♌	9 ♎	17 ♎	2 ♐	4 ♑	19 ♒	25 ♓	16 ♉	9 ♋	18 ♌	8 ♎	12 ♏
13	19 ♍	4 ♏	12 ♏	25 ♐	28 ♑	15 ♓	22 ♈	15 ♊	8 ♌	15 ♍	3 ♏	6 ♐
15	14 ♎	27 ♏	5 ♐	19 ♑	23 ♒	12 ♈	20 ♉	13 ♋	5 ♍	11 ♎	27 ♏	0 ♑
17	8 ♏	21 ♐	29 ♐	14 ♒	19 ♓	10 ♉	19 ♊	12 ♌	2 ♎	7 ♏	21 ♐	23 ♑
19	1 ♐	16 ♑	23 ♑	10 ♓	17 ♈	10 ♊	19 ♋	10 ♍	28 ♎	1 ♐	15 ♑	17 ♒
21	25 ♐	11 ♒	19 ♒	9 ♈	17 ♉	11 ♋	18 ♌	7 ♎	23 ♏	25 ♐	8 ♒	12 ♓
23	20 ♑	8 ♓	16 ♓	8 ♉	17 ♊	10 ♌	16 ♍	3 ♏	17 ♐	18 ♑	3 ♓	8 ♈
25	16 ♒	6 ♈	15 ♈	8 ♊	17 ♋	8 ♍	12 ♎	27 ♏	10 ♑	12 ♒	29 ♓	5 ♉
27	12 ♓	4 ♉	14 ♉	8 ♋	15 ♌	4 ♎	7 ♏	21 ♐	5 ♒	8 ♓	27 ♈	4 ♊
29	10 ♈		13 ♊	6 ♌	12 ♍	28 ♎	1 ♐	14 ♑	0 ♓	5 ♈	26 ♉	4 ♋
31	8 ♉		12 ♋		7 ♎		24 ♐	9 ♒		3 ♉		5 ♌

1956	Jan.	Feb.	Mar.	April	May	June	July	Aug.	Sept.	Oct.	Nov.	Dec.
1	19 ♌	10 ♎	1 ♏	16 ♐	17 ♑	1 ♓	5 ♈	24 ♉	16 ♋	25 ♌	17 ♎	23 ♏
3	18 ♍	5 ♏	26 ♏	10 ♑	11 ♒	26 ♓	1 ♉	22 ♊	15 ♌	24 ♍	14 ♏	18 ♐
5	14 ♎	0 ♐	20 ♐	3 ♒	6 ♓	22 ♈	29 ♉	21 ♋	15 ♍	22 ♎	10 ♐	13 ♑
7	9 ♏	24 ♐	13 ♑	28 ♒	1 ♈	20 ♉	28 ♊	22 ♌	14 ♎	19 ♏	5 ♑	7 ♒
9	3 ♐	17 ♑	7 ♒	23 ♓	28 ♈	20 ♊	28 ♋	22 ♍	11 ♏	15 ♐	29 ♑	1 ♓
11	27 ♐	11 ♒	2 ♓	20 ♈	26 ♉	20 ♋	28 ♌	20 ♎	7 ♐	9 ♑	23 ♒	25 ♓
13	20 ♑	6 ♓	28 ♓	17 ♉	26 ♊	19 ♌	27 ♍	16 ♏	1 ♑	3 ♒	17 ♓	20 ♈
15	14 ♒	1 ♈	24 ♈	16 ♊	25 ♋	18 ♍	24 ♎	11 ♐	25 ♑	27 ♒	12 ♈	16 ♉
17	9 ♓	27 ♈	21 ♉	14 ♋	23 ♌	14 ♎	19 ♏	5 ♑	19 ♒	21 ♓	8 ♉	14 ♊
19	4 ♈	24 ♉	19 ♊	12 ♌	21 ♍	10 ♏	14 ♐	28 ♑	13 ♓	17 ♈	6 ♊	14 ♋
21	0 ♉	22 ♊	17 ♋	10 ♍	17 ♎	5 ♐	8 ♑	22 ♒	8 ♈	13 ♉	5 ♋	14 ♌
23	28 ♉	21 ♋	16 ♌	8 ♎	13 ♏	29 ♐	1 ♒	16 ♓	4 ♉	11 ♊	4 ♌	13 ♍
25	27 ♊	21 ♌	14 ♍	4 ♏	8 ♐	22 ♑	25 ♒	11 ♈	0 ♊	9 ♋	2 ♍	10 ♎
27	27 ♋	20 ♍	12 ♎	29 ♏	2 ♑	16 ♒	19 ♓	7 ♉	28 ♊	7 ♌	0 ♎	7 ♏
29	27 ♌	17 ♎	9 ♏	24 ♐	26 ♑	10 ♓	14 ♈	3 ♊	26 ♋	5 ♍	27 ♎	2 ♐
31	26 ♍		4 ♐		19 ♒		10 ♉	1 ♋		3 ♎		27 ♐

1957	Jan.	Feb.	Mar.	April	May	June	July	Aug.	Sept.	Oct.	Nov.	Dec.
1	9 ♑	24 ♒	3 ♓	18 ♈	22 ♉	13 ♋	22 ♌	15 ♎	6 ♐	11 ♑	25 ♒	27 ♓
3	3 ♒	18 ♓	27 ♓	13 ♉	19 ♊	12 ♌	21 ♍	13 ♏	2 ♑	5 ♒	19 ♓	21 ♈
5	27 ♒	12 ♈	21 ♈	9 ♊	17 ♋	10 ♍	19 ♎	9 ♐	26 ♑	29 ♒	13 ♈	16 ♉
7	21 ♓	6 ♉	16 ♉	6 ♋	15 ♌	8 ♎	16 ♏	4 ♑	20 ♒	23 ♓	7 ♉	11 ♊
9	15 ♈	2 ♊	12 ♊	4 ♌	13 ♍	6 ♏	12 ♐	29 ♑	14 ♓	16 ♈	3 ♊	8 ♋
11	11 ♉	0 ♋	9 ♋	3 ♍	12 ♎	3 ♐	8 ♑	23 ♒	8 ♈	11 ♉	29 ♊	6 ♌
13	8 ♊	0 ♌	9 ♌	2 ♎	10 ♏	29 ♐	2 ♒	17 ♓	2 ♉	6 ♊	26 ♋	4 ♍
15	7 ♋	0 ♍	9 ♍	1 ♏	7 ♐	24 ♑	26 ♒	11 ♈	26 ♉	2 ♋	23 ♌	3 ♎
17	7 ♌	1 ♎	9 ♎	29 ♏	3 ♑	18 ♒	20 ♓	5 ♉	22 ♊	29 ♋	22 ♍	1 ♏
19	7 ♍	29 ♎	7 ♏	25 ♐	28 ♑	12 ♓	14 ♈	0 ♊	19 ♋	27 ♌	21 ♎	29 ♏
21	7 ♎	26 ♏	4 ♐	20 ♑	22 ♒	6 ♈	8 ♉	26 ♊	18 ♌	27 ♍	20 ♏	26 ♐
23	4 ♏	21 ♐	0 ♑	14 ♒	16 ♓	0 ♉	4 ♊	25 ♋	18 ♍	27 ♎	17 ♐	22 ♑
25	0 ♐	15 ♑	24 ♑	8 ♓	10 ♈	26 ♉	2 ♋	25 ♌	19 ♎	26 ♏	14 ♑	17 ♒
27	24 ♐	9 ♒	18 ♒	2 ♈	5 ♉	23 ♊	1 ♌	25 ♍	18 ♏	23 ♐	9 ♒	11 ♓
29	18 ♑		11 ♓	27 ♈	1 ♊	22 ♋	1 ♍	25 ♎	15 ♐	19 ♑	3 ♓	5 ♈
31	12 ♒		6 ♈		29 ♊		1 ♎	23 ♏		13 ♒		29 ♈

1958	Jan.	Feb.	Mar.	April	May	June	July	Aug.	Sept.	Oct.	Nov.	Dec.
1	11 ♉	27 ♊	5 ♋	26 ♌	5 ♎	28 ♏	5 ♑	24 ♒	9 ♈	11 ♉	26 ♊	1 ♌
3	6 ♊	25 ♋	3 ♌	26 ♍	5 ♏	27 ♐	2 ♒	18 ♓	2 ♉	5 ♊	21 ♋	27 ♌
5	3 ♋	25 ♌	3 ♍	27 ♎	4 ♐	24 ♑	28 ♒	12 ♈	26 ♉	29 ♊	17 ♌	24 ♍
7	2 ♌	25 ♍	3 ♎	26 ♏	3 ♑	20 ♒	22 ♓	6 ♉	20 ♊	25 ♋	15 ♍	23 ♎
9	1 ♍	24 ♎	3 ♏	24 ♐	29 ♑	14 ♓	16 ♈	0 ♊	16 ♋	22 ♌	14 ♎	23 ♏
11	29 ♍	22 ♏	2 ♐	21 ♑	24 ♒	8 ♈	10 ♉	25 ♊	14 ♌	21 ♍	14 ♏	22 ♐
13	28 ♎	19 ♐	29 ♐	16 ♒	18 ♓	2 ♉	4 ♊	22 ♋	13 ♍	21 ♎	14 ♐	21 ♑
15	25 ♏	14 ♑	24 ♑	10 ♓	12 ♈	26 ♉	0 ♋	20 ♌	13 ♎	21 ♏	13 ♑	18 ♒
17	22 ♐	9 ♒	19 ♒	3 ♈	6 ♉	21 ♊	27 ♋	19 ♍	12 ♏	20 ♐	20 ♒	13 ♓
19	18 ♑	4 ♓	13 ♓	27 ♈	0 ♊	18 ♋	25 ♌	18 ♎	11 ♐	18 ♑	5 ♓	8 ♈
21	13 ♒	28 ♓	6 ♈	21 ♉	25 ♊	15 ♌	23 ♍	17 ♏	8 ♑	14 ♒	29 ♓	1 ♉
23	7 ♓	21 ♈	0 ♉	15 ♊	21 ♋	13 ♍	22 ♎	14 ♐	4 ♒	8 ♓	23 ♈	25 ♉
25	1 ♈	15 ♉	24 ♉	11 ♋	18 ♌	11 ♎	20 ♏	11 ♑	29 ♒	2 ♈	17 ♉	19 ♊
27	25 ♈	9 ♊	18 ♊	8 ♌	16 ♍	9 ♏	18 ♐	7 ♒	23 ♓	26 ♈	11 ♊	15 ♋
29	19 ♉		14 ♋	6 ♍	14 ♎	8 ♐	15 ♑	2 ♓	17 ♈	20 ♉	5 ♋	11 ♌
31	14 ♊		12 ♌		14 ♏		11 ♒	27 ♓		14 ♊		8 ♍

1959	Jan.	Feb.	Mar.	April	May	June	July	Aug.	Sept.	Oct.	Nov.	Dec.
1	21 ♍	14 ♏	25 ♏	17 ♑	24 ♒	10 ♈	12 ♉	26 ♊	12 ♌	17 ♍	9 ♏	17 ♐
3	19 ♎	12 ♐	23 ♐	14 ♒	19 ♓	4 ♉	6 ♊	21 ♋	9 ♍	15 ♎	9 ♐	17 ♑
5	17 ♏	10 ♑	20 ♑	9 ♓	13 ♈	27 ♉	0 ♋	17 ♌	6 ♎	15 ♏	9 ♑	16 ♒
7	16 ♐	8 ♒	17 ♒	4 ♈	7 ♉	21 ♊	25 ♋	13 ♍	5 ♏	14 ♐	7 ♒	13 ♓
9	15 ♑	4 ♓	12 ♓	28 ♈	0 ♊	15 ♋	20 ♌	10 ♎	3 ♐	13 ♑	3 ♓	8 ♈
11	13 ♒	29 ♓	7 ♈	21 ♉	24 ♊	10 ♌	16 ♍	8 ♏	2 ♑	10 ♒	29 ♓	3 ♉
13	9 ♓	23 ♈	1 ♉	15 ♊	18 ♋	6 ♍	13 ♎	7 ♐	0 ♒	6 ♓	23 ♈	26 ♉
15	3 ♈	17 ♉	25 ♉	9 ♋	13 ♌	3 ♎	12 ♏	5 ♑	27 ♒	2 ♈	17 ♉	20 ♊
17	27 ♈	11 ♊	19 ♊	4 ♌	10 ♍	1 ♏	11 ♐	4 ♒	23 ♓	27 ♈	11 ♊	14 ♋
19	21 ♉	5 ♋	13 ♋	1 ♍	8 ♎	1 ♐	10 ♑	1 ♓	18 ♈	21 ♉	5 ♋	8 ♌
21	15 ♊	1 ♌	9 ♌	29 ♍	7 ♏	1 ♑	9 ♒	27 ♓	12 ♉	15 ♊	29 ♋	3 ♍
23	10 ♋	29 ♌	7 ♍	29 ♎	8 ♐	1 ♒	6 ♓	22 ♈	6 ♊	8 ♋	24 ♌	29 ♍
25	7 ♌	27 ♍	6 ♎	29 ♏	8 ♑	28 ♒	2 ♈	17 ♉	0 ♋	3 ♌	19 ♍	26 ♎
27	4 ♍	26 ♎	6 ♏	29 ♐	6 ♒	24 ♓	27 ♈	10 ♊	24 ♋	28 ♌	17 ♎	25 ♏
29	2 ♎		5 ♐	27 ♑	3 ♓	19 ♈	20 ♉	4 ♋	20 ♌	25 ♍	17 ♏	25 ♐
31	0 ♏		4 ♑		28 ♓		14 ♊	29 ♋		24 ♎		26 ♑

1960	Jan.	Feb.	Mar.	April	May	June	July	Aug.	Sept.	Oct.	Nov.	Dec.
1	10 ♒	0 ♈	20 ♈	5 ♊	7 ♋	22 ♌	25 ♍	15 ♏	8 ♑	17 ♒	8 ♈	14 ♉
3	8 ♓	25 ♈	15 ♉	29 ♊	1 ♌	16 ♍	21 ♎	13 ♐	7 ♒	15 ♓	5 ♉	9 ♊
5	5 ♈	20 ♉	9 ♊	23 ♋	25 ♌	12 ♎	19 ♏	13 ♑	6 ♓	13 ♈	0 ♊	3 ♋
7	29 ♈	13 ♊	3 ♋	17 ♌	21 ♍	11 ♏	19 ♐	13 ♒	4 ♈	9 ♉	25 ♊	27 ♋
9	23 ♉	7 ♋	27 ♋	13 ♍	18 ♎	10 ♐	19 ♑	12 ♓	1 ♉	5 ♊	19 ♋	20 ♌
11	17 ♊	1 ♌	22 ♌	10 ♎	17 ♏	11 ♑	19 ♒	10 ♈	27 ♉	29 ♊	12 ♌	14 ♍
13	11 ♋	27 ♌	18 ♍	8 ♏	17 ♐	11 ♒	18 ♓	6 ♉	21 ♊	23 ♋	6 ♍	9 ♎
15	5 ♌	22 ♍	15 ♎	8 ♐	17 ♑	9 ♓	15 ♈	1 ♊	15 ♋	16 ♌	2 ♎	6 ♏
17	0 ♍	19 ♎	13 ♏	7 ♑	15 ♒	6 ♈	10 ♉	25 ♊	9 ♌	11 ♍	28 ♎	5 ♐
19	26 ♍	16 ♏	11 ♐	5 ♒	13 ♓	1 ♉	4 ♊	18 ♋	3 ♍	7 ♎	27 ♏	5 ♑
21	22 ♎	15 ♐	10 ♑	2 ♓	9 ♈	25 ♉	28 ♊	12 ♌	28 ♍	4 ♏	26 ♐	5 ♒
23	20 ♏	13 ♑	8 ♒	29 ♓	4 ♉	19 ♊	22 ♋	7 ♍	25 ♎	2 ♐	26 ♑	4 ♓
25	19 ♐	12 ♒	6 ♓	24 ♋	28 ♉	13 ♋	16 ♌	2 ♎	22 ♏	1 ♑	24 ♒	2 ♈
27	19 ♑	10 ♓	2 ♈	19 ♉	22 ♊	7 ♌	10 ♍	28 ♎	20 ♐	29 ♑	22 ♓	28 ♈
29	18 ♒	7 ♈	28 ♈	13 ♊	16 ♋	1 ♍	5 ♎	25 ♏	18 ♑	27 ♒	18 ♈	23 ♉
31	16 ♓		23 ♉		10 ♌		1 ♏	23 ♐		25 ♓		18 ♊

1961	Jan.	Feb.	Mar.	April	May	June	July	Aug.	Sept.	Oct.	Nov.	Dec.
1	29 ♊	14 ♌	22 ♌	8 ♎	13 ♏	4 ♑	13 ♒	6 ♈	26 ♉	0 ♋	15 ♌	16 ♍
3	23 ♋	8 ♍	17 ♍	4 ♏	10 ♐	3 ♒	12 ♓	4 ♉	22 ♊	25 ♋	8 ♍	10 ♎
5	17 ♌	2 ♎	11 ♎	0 ♐	9 ♑	2 ♓	10 ♈	0 ♊	16 ♋	18 ♌	2 ♎	5 ♏
7	11 ♍	27 ♎	7 ♏	28 ♐	7 ♒	0 ♈	7 ♉	25 ♊	10 ♌	12 ♍	27 ♎	2 ♐
9	5 ♎	23 ♏	3 ♐	26 ♑	5 ♓	27 ♈	3 ♊	19 ♋	3 ♍	6 ♎	23 ♏	29 ♐
11	1 ♏	21 ♐	1 ♑	24 ♒	3 ♈	23 ♉	28 ♊	13 ♌	27 ♍	1 ♏	20 ♐	28 ♑
13	28 ♏	21 ♑	0 ♒	23 ♓	0 ♉	19 ♊	22 ♋	6 ♍	22 ♎	27 ♏	17 ♑	26 ♒
15	27 ♐	21 ♒	29 ♒	21 ♈	27 ♉	13 ♋	16 ♌	0 ♎	17 ♏	23 ♐	15 ♒	24 ♓
17	28 ♑	21 ♓	29 ♓	19 ♉	23 ♊	7 ♌	9 ♍	24 ♎	13 ♐	20 ♑	13 ♓	22 ♈
19	28 ♒	19 ♈	27 ♈	15 ♊	17 ♋	1 ♍	3 ♎	20 ♏	10 ♑	19 ♒	12 ♈	20 ♉
21	27 ♓	16 ♉	24 ♉	9 ♋	11 ♌	25 ♍	28 ♎	17 ♐	9 ♒	18 ♓	10 ♉	16 ♊
23	24 ♈	11 ♊	19 ♊	3 ♌	5 ♍	19 ♎	24 ♏	15 ♑	8 ♓	17 ♈	7 ♊	12 ♋
25	20 ♉	5 ♋	13 ♋	27 ♌	29 ♍	16 ♏	22 ♐	15 ♒	8 ♈	15 ♉	4 ♋	6 ♌
27	14 ♊	29 ♋	7 ♌	21 ♍	24 ♎	14 ♐	22 ♑	15 ♓	7 ♉	13 ♊	28 ♋	0 ♍
29	8 ♋		1 ♍	16 ♎	21 ♏	13 ♑	22 ♒	15 ♈	5 ♊	8 ♋	22 ♌	24 ♍
31	2 ♌		25 ♍		20 ♐		22 ♓	13 ♉		3 ♌		18 ♎

1962	Jan.	Feb.	Mar.	April	May	June	July	Aug.	Sept.	Oct.	Nov.	Dec.
1	0 ♏	17 ♐	26 ♐	17 ♒	26 ♓	19 ♉	26 ♊	13 ♌	28 ♍	1 ♏	16 ♐	22 ♑
3	26 ♏	15 ♑	24 ♑	16 ♓	25 ♈	17 ♊	22 ♋	8 ♍	22 ♎	25 ♏	12 ♑	18 ♒
5	23 ♐	15 ♒	23 ♒	17 ♈	25 ♉	14 ♋	17 ♌	1 ♎	16 ♏	19 ♐	8 ♒	16 ♓
7	22 ♑	15 ♓	23 ♓	16 ♉	23 ♊	9 ♌	11 ♍	25 ♎	10 ♐	15 ♑	5 ♓	14 ♈
9	22 ♒	15 ♈	24 ♈	14 ♊	19 ♋	3 ♍	5 ♎	19 ♏	6 ♑	12 ♒	5 ♈	14 ♉
11	21 ♓	13 ♉	22 ♉	11 ♋	13 ♌	27 ♍	29 ♎	14 ♐	3 ♒	11 ♓	5 ♉	13 ♊
13	19 ♈	10 ♊	19 ♊	5 ♌	7 ♍	21 ♎	24 ♏	11 ♑	3 ♓	11 ♈	5 ♊	11 ♋
15	16 ♉	5 ♋	14 ♋	29 ♌	1 ♎	16 ♏	20 ♐	10 ♒	3 ♈	12 ♉	3 ♋	7 ♌
17	13 ♊	29 ♋	9 ♌	23 ♍	25 ♎	11 ♐	17 ♑	9 ♓	3 ♉	11 ♊	0 ♌	3 ♍
19	8 ♋	23 ♌	2 ♍	17 ♎	20 ♏	8 ♑	16 ♒	9 ♈	2 ♊	8 ♋	25 ♌	27 ♍
21	3 ♌	17 ♍	26 ♍	11 ♏	16 ♐	6 ♒	15 ♓	8 ♉	29 ♊	4 ♌	19 ♍	20 ♎
23	27 ♌	11 ♎	20 ♎	6 ♐	12 ♉	4 ♓	14 ♈	6 ♊	25 ♋	28 ♌	12 ♎	14 ♏
25	20 ♍	5 ♏	14 ♏	2 ♑	10 ♒	3 ♈	12 ♉	2 ♋	19 ♌	22 ♍	6 ♏	9 ♐
27	14 ♎	0 ♐	9 ♐	29 ♑	7 ♓	1 ♉	9 ♊	28 ♋	13 ♍	16 ♎	1 ♐	5 ♑
29	8 ♏		5 ♑	27 ♒	6 ♈	29 ♉	5 ♋	22 ♌	7 ♎	10 ♏	26 ♐	1 ♒
31	4 ♐		3 ♒		5 ♉		1 ♌	16 ♍		4 ♐		29 ♒

1963	Jan.	Feb.	Mar.	April	May	June	July	Aug.	Sept.	Oct.	Nov.	Dec.
1	13 ♓	6 ♉	17 ♉	8 ♋	14 ♌	29 ♍	2 ♏	16 ♐	1 ♒	7 ♓	29 ♈	8 ♊
3	11 ♈	4 ♊	15 ♊	4 ♌	9 ♍	23 ♎	25 ♏	10 ♑	29 ♒	6 ♈	0 ♊	8 ♋
5	9 ♉	1 ♋	12 ♋	29 ♌	3 ♎	17 ♏	20 ♐	6 ♒	27 ♓	6 ♉	29 ♊	6 ♌
7	8 ♊	28 ♋	7 ♌	24 ♍	26 ♎	11 ♐	15 ♑	4 ♓	26 ♈	6 ♊	28 ♋	3 ♍
9	5 ♋	23 ♌	2 ♍	18 ♎	20 ♏	6 ♑	11 ♒	2 ♈	25 ♉	4 ♋	24 ♌	28 ♍
11	2 ♌	18 ♍	27 ♍	11 ♏	14 ♐	1 ♒	8 ♓	0 ♉	24 ♊	1 ♌	19 ♍	23 ♎
13	28 ♌	12 ♎	21 ♎	5 ♐	9 ♑	27 ♒	5 ♈	29 ♉	21 ♋	27 ♌	14 ♎	16 ♏
15	22 ♍	6 ♏	14 ♏	29 ♐	4 ♒	24 ♓	4 ♉	27 ♊	17 ♌	22 ♍	7 ♏	10 ♐
17	16 ♎	0 ♐	8 ♐	24 ♑	0 ♓	23 ♈	2 ♊	24 ♋	13 ♍	17 ♎	1 ♐	4 ♑
19	10 ♏	25 ♐	3 ♑	21 ♒	28 ♓	22 ♉	1 ♋	21 ♌	8 ♎	11 ♏	25 ♐	28 ♑
21	4 ♐	21 ♑	29 ♑	19 ♓	28 ♈	22 ♊	29 ♋	17 ♍	2 ♏	4 ♐	19 ♑	23 ♒
23	0 ♑	19 ♒	26 ♒	19 ♈	28 ♉	20 ♋	26 ♌	12 ♎	26 ♏	28 ♐	14 ♒	20 ♓
25	27 ♑	18 ♓	26 ♓	20 ♉	28 ♊	18 ♌	21 ♍	6 ♏	19 ♐	22 ♑	10 ♓	17 ♈
27	24 ♒	17 ♈	26 ♈	20 ♊	26 ♋	13 ♍	16 ♎	29 ♏	14 ♑	18 ♒	8 ♈	16 ♉
29	23 ♓		26 ♉	18 ♋	22 ♌	8 ♎	10 ♏	23 ♐	9 ♒	15 ♓	7 ♉	16 ♊
31	22 ♈		25 ♊		17 ♍		3 ♐	18 ♑		14 ♈		15 ♋

1964	Jan.	Feb.	Mar.	April	May	June	July	Aug.	Sept.	Oct.	Nov.	Dec.
1	0 ♌	19 ♍	10 ♎	25 ♏	27 ♐	11 ♒	16 ♓	6 ♉	29 ♊	8 ♌	29 ♍	4 ♏
3	28 ♌	15 ♎	5 ♏	18 ♐	20 ♑	6 ♓	12 ♈	5 ♊	28 ♋	6 ♍	25 ♎	29 ♏
5	24 ♍	9 ♏	29 ♏	12 ♑	15 ♒	3 ♈	10 ♉	4 ♋	26 ♌	3 ♎	20 ♏	23 ♐
7	19 ♎	3 ♐	22 ♐	7 ♒	11 ♓	1 ♉	10 ♊	3 ♌	24 ♍	29 ♎	14 ♐	16 ♑
9	13 ♏	26 ♐	16 ♑	2 ♓	8 ♈	1 ♊	10 ♋	2 ♍	21 ♎	24 ♏	8 ♑	10 ♒
11	7 ♐	21 ♑	11 ♒	0 ♈	7 ♉	1 ♋	9 ♌	0 ♎	16 ♏	18 ♐	1 ♒	4 ♓
13	0 ♑	16 ♒	8 ♓	29 ♈	8 ♊	1 ♌	8 ♍	26 ♎	10 ♐	12 ♑	26 ♒	29 ♓
15	25 ♑	13 ♓	6 ♈	29 ♉	8 ♋	29 ♌	5 ♎	20 ♏	4 ♑	5 ♒	21 ♓	26 ♈
17	20 ♒	10 ♈	5 ♉	28 ♊	6 ♌	26 ♍	0 ♏	14 ♐	28 ♑	0 ♓	18 ♈	25 ♉
19	17 ♓	8 ♉	3 ♊	26 ♋	3 ♍	21 ♎	24 ♏	8 ♑	22 ♒	27 ♓	17 ♉	25 ♊
21	14 ♈	7 ♊	2 ♋	23 ♌	29 ♍	15 ♏	17 ♐	2 ♒	18 ♓	25 ♈	17 ♊	25 ♋
23	12 ♉	5 ♋	29 ♋	19 ♍	24 ♎	9 ♐	11 ♑	27 ♒	16 ♈	23 ♉	17 ♋	25 ♌
25	10 ♊	3 ♌	26 ♌	15 ♎	18 ♏	2 ♑	5 ♒	23 ♓	14 ♉	23 ♊	16 ♌	23 ♍
27	9 ♋	0 ♍	23 ♍	9 ♏	12 ♐	26 ♑	0 ♓	20 ♈	12 ♊	21 ♋	13 ♍	19 ♎
29	8 ♌	27 ♍	18 ♎	3 ♐	5 ♑	21 ♒	26 ♓	17 ♉	10 ♋	19 ♌	9 ♎	14 ♏
31	6 ♍		13 ♏		29 ♑		23 ♈	15 ♊		16 ♍		8 ♐

1965	Jan.	Feb.	Mar.	April	May	June	July	Aug.	Sept.	Oct.	Nov.	Dec.
1	20 ♐	4 ♒	12 ♒	28 ♓	3 ♉	25 ♊	4 ♌	27 ♍	17 ♏	20 ♐	4 ♒	6 ♓
3	13 ♑	28 ♒	7 ♓	25 ♈	2 ♊	25 ♋	4 ♍	25 ♎	12 ♐	14 ♑	28 ♒	0 ♈
5	7 ♒	23 ♓	2 ♈	22 ♉	0 ♋	24 ♌	2 ♎	21 ♏	6 ♑	8 ♒	22 ♓	25 ♈
7	1 ♓	18 ♈	29 ♈	20 ♊	29 ♋	22 ♍	29 ♎	15 ♐	0 ♒	2 ♓	17 ♈	22 ♉
9	26 ♓	15 ♉	25 ♉	18 ♋	27 ♌	19 ♎	24 ♏	9 ♑	24 ♒	26 ♓	14 ♉	20 ♊
11	22 ♈	13 ♊	23 ♊	16 ♌	25 ♍	14 ♏	18 ♐	3 ♒	18 ♓	22 ♈	11 ♊	19 ♋
13	19 ♉	12 ♋	21 ♋	15 ♍	22 ♎	9 ♐	12 ♑	27 ♒	13 ♈	18 ♉	9 ♋	18 ♌
15	18 ♊	11 ♌	20 ♌	12 ♎	18 ♏	3 ♑	6 ♒	21 ♓	8 ♉	15 ♊	8 ♌	17 ♍
17	18 ♋	11 ♍	19 ♍	9 ♏	13 ♐	27 ♑	0 ♓	16 ♈	4 ♊	13 ♋	6 ♍	15 ♎
19	18 ♌	10 ♎	17 ♎	4 ♐	7 ♑	21 ♒	24 ♓	11 ♉	2 ♋	11 ♌	4 ♎	11 ♏
21	18 ♍	6 ♏	14 ♏	29 ♐	1 ♒	15 ♓	19 ♈	8 ♊	0 ♌	10 ♍	1 ♏	7 ♐
23	15 ♎	1 ♐	9 ♐	23 ♑	24 ♒	10 ♈	15 ♉	6 ♋	0 ♍	8 ♎	28 ♏	2 ♑
25	10 ♏	25 ♐	3 ♑	16 ♒	19 ♓	6 ♉	13 ♊	6 ♌	29 ♍	6 ♏	23 ♐	26 ♑
27	5 ♐	19 ♑	27 ♑	11 ♓	14 ♈	4 ♊	12 ♋	6 ♍	28 ♎	3 ♐	18 ♑	20 ♒
29	28 ♐		21 ♒	6 ♈	12 ♉	4 ♋	12 ♌	6 ♎	25 ♏	28 ♐	12 ♒	14 ♓
31	22 ♑		15 ♓		10 ♊		13 ♍	4 ♏		22 ♑		8 ♈

1966	Jan.	Feb.	Mar.	April	May	June	July	Aug.	Sept.	Oct.	Nov.	Dec.
1	20 ♈	8 ♊	17 ♊	8 ♌	18 ♍	10 ♏	17 ♐	4 ♒	18 ♓	21 ♈	7 ♊	13 ♋
3	16 ♉	6 ♋	14 ♋	8 ♍	17 ♎	8 ♐	12 ♑	28 ♒	12 ♈	15 ♉	3 ♋	10 ♌
5	13 ♊	6 ♌	14 ♌	8 ♎	15 ♏	4 ♑	7 ♒	22 ♓	6 ♉	10 ♊	0 ♌	8 ♍
7	13 ♋	6 ♍	14 ♍	7 ♏	13 ♐	29 ♑	1 ♓	15 ♈	1 ♊	6 ♋	28 ♌	7 ♎
9	13 ♌	6 ♎	15 ♎	5 ♐	8 ♑	23 ♒	25 ♓	9 ♉	26 ♊	3 ♌	27 ♍	5 ♏
11	13 ♍	5 ♏	13 ♏	1 ♑	3 ♒	17 ♓	19 ♈	5 ♊	24 ♋	2 ♍	26 ♎	3 ♐
13	11 ♎	1 ♐	10 ♐	25 ♑	27 ♒	11 ♈	13 ♉	1 ♋	24 ♌	2 ♎	25 ♏	1 ♑
15	8 ♏	26 ♐	5 ♑	19 ♒	21 ♓	6 ♉	10 ♊	0 ♌	24 ♍	2 ♏	23 ♐	27 ♑
17	4 ♐	20 ♑	29 ♑	13 ♓	15 ♈	1 ♊	7 ♋	0 ♍	24 ♎	1 ♐	19 ♑	22 ♒
19	29 ♐	14 ♒	22 ♒	7 ♈	10 ♉	29 ♊	7 ♌	1 ♎	23 ♏	28 ♐	14 ♒	16 ♓
21	23 ♑	7 ♓	16 ♓	2 ♉	6 ♊	27 ♋	6 ♍	0 ♏	20 ♐	24 ♑	9 ♓	10 ♈
23	17 ♒	1 ♈	10 ♈	27 ♉	4 ♋	26 ♌	6 ♎	27 ♏	15 ♑	18 ♒	2 ♈	4 ♉
25	10 ♓	25 ♈	5 ♉	23 ♊	2 ♌	25 ♍	4 ♏	23 ♐	10 ♒	12 ♓	26 ♈	29 ♉
27	4 ♈	20 ♉	0 ♊	21 ♋	0 ♍	23 ♎	1 ♐	18 ♑	4 ♓	6 ♈	21 ♉	25 ♊
29	29 ♈		26 ♊	19 ♌	28 ♍	20 ♏	26 ♐	13 ♒	27 ♓	0 ♉	16 ♊	23 ♋
31	24 ♉		24 ♋		27 ♎		21 ♑	7 ♓		25 ♉		21 ♌

1967	Jan.	Feb.	Mar.	April	May	June	July	Aug.	Sept.	Oct.	Nov.	Dec.
1	5 ♍	28 ♎	8 ♏	29 ♐	4 ♒	20 ♓	21 ♈	5 ♊	22 ♋	27 ♌	20 ♎	28 ♏
3	4 ♎	26 ♏	6 ♐	25 ♑	29 ♒	13 ♈	15 ♉	0 ♋	19 ♌	27 ♍	20 ♏	28 ♐
5	2 ♏	23 ♐	3 ♑	20 ♒	23 ♓	7 ♉	9 ♊	27 ♋	18 ♍	27 ♎	20 ♐	27 ♑
7	29 ♏	19 ♑	28 ♑	14 ♓	17 ♈	1 ♊	5 ♋	25 ♌	18 ♎	27 ♏	18 ♑	23 ♒
9	26 ♐	14 ♒	23 ♒	8 ♈	10 ♉	26 ♊	2 ♌	24 ♍	17 ♏	25 ♐	15 ♒	19 ♓
11	23 ♑	8 ♓	17 ♓	2 ♉	5 ♊	22 ♋	29 ♌	23 ♎	15 ♐	23 ♑	10 ♓	13 ♈
13	18 ♒	2 ♈	11 ♈	25 ♉	29 ♊	19 ♌	28 ♍	21 ♏	13 ♑	18 ♒	4 ♈	6 ♉
15	12 ♓	26 ♈	4 ♉	20 ♊	25 ♋	17 ♍	26 ♎	19 ♐	9 ♒	13 ♓	28 ♈	0 ♊
17	6 ♈	20 ♉	28 ♉	15 ♋	22 ♌	15 ♎	24 ♏	16 ♑	4 ♓	7 ♈	21 ♉	24 ♊
19	0 ♉	14 ♊	23 ♊	12 ♌	20 ♍	14 ♏	22 ♐	12 ♒	28 ♓	1 ♉	15 ♊	19 ♋
21	24 ♉	11 ♋	10 ♋	11 ♍	19 ♎	12 ♐	19 ♑	7 ♓	22 ♈	24 ♉	10 ♋	15 ♌
23	20 ♊	9 ♌	17 ♌	10 ♎	19 ♏	11 ♑	16 ♒	2 ♈	16 ♉	18 ♊	5 ♌	12 ♍
25	17 ♋	9 ♍	17 ♍	11 ♏	18 ♐	8 ♒	11 ♓	25 ♈	9 ♊	13 ♋	1 ♍	9 ♎
27	16 ♌	9 ♎	17 ♎	10 ♐	16 ♑	3 ♓	6 ♈	19 ♉	4 ♋	8 ♌	29 ♍	8 ♏
29	5 ♍		17 ♏	8 ♑	13 ♒	28 ♓	29 ♈	13 ♊	0 ♌	6 ♍	28 ♎	7 ♐
31	14 ♎		16 ♐		8 ♓		23 ♉	8 ♋		5 ♎		6 ♑

1968	Jan.	Feb.	Mar.	April	May	June	July	Aug.	Sept.	Oct.	Nov.	Dec.
1	20 ♑	9 ♓	0 ♈	14 ♉	17 ♊	2 ♌	7 ♍	28 ♎	22 ♐	1 ♒	21 ♓	25 ♈
3	18 ♒	4 ♈	24 ♈	8 ♊	11 ♋	27 ♌	4 ♎	26 ♏	20 ♑	28 ♒	16 ♈	19 ♉
5	14 ♓	28 ♈	18 ♉	2 ♋	5 ♌	24 ♍	2 ♏	25 ♐	18 ♒	24 ♓	10 ♉	13 ♊
7	9 ♈	22 ♉	12 ♊	27 ♋	1 ♍	22 ♎	1 ♐	24 ♑	15 ♓	19 ♈	4 ♊	7 ♋
9	2 ♉	16 ♊	6 ♋	23 ♌	29 ♍	21 ♏	1 ♑	23 ♒	11 ♈	14 ♉	28 ♊	0 ♌
11	26 ♉	11 ♋	1 ♌	20 ♍	28 ♎	22 ♐	0 ♒	20 ♓	6 ♉	8 ♊	22 ♋	25 ♌
13	20 ♊	7 ♌	28 ♌	20 ♎	28 ♏	22 ♑	28 ♒	15 ♈	0 ♊	1 ♋	16 ♌	20 ♍
15	15 ♋	4 ♍	27 ♍	20 ♏	29 ♐	20 ♒	25 ♓	10 ♉	23 ♊	25 ♋	11 ♍	17 ♎
17	12 ♌	2 ♎	26 ♎	20 ♐	28 ♑	17 ♓	20 ♈	4 ♊	17 ♋	20 ♌	9 ♎	16 ♏
19	8 ♍	1 ♏	25 ♏	18 ♑	25 ♒	11 ♈	14 ♉	27 ♊	12 ♌	17 ♍	7 ♏	16 ♐
21	6 ♎	29 ♏	24 ♐	15 ♒	20 ♓	5 ♉	7 ♊	22 ♋	9 ♍	15 ♎	8 ♐	16 ♑
23	4 ♏	27 ♐	22 ♑	11 ♓	15 ♈	29 ♉	1 ♋	17 ♌	7 ♎	14 ♏	8 ♑	16 ♒
25	2 ♐	25 ♑	18 ♒	5 ♈	8 ♉	23 ♊	26 ♋	14 ♍	2 ♏	14 ♐	7 ♒	14 ♓
27	1 ♑	21 ♒	14 ♓	29 ♈	2 ♊	17 ♋	21 ♌	11 ♎	4 ♐	13 ♑	5 ♓	10 ♈
29	29 ♑	17 ♓	8 ♈	23 ♉	26 ♊	12 ♌	18 ♍	9 ♏	3 ♑	11 ♒	0 ♈	4 ♉
31	26 ♒		3 ♉		20 ♋		14 ♎	7 ♐		8 ♓		28 ♉

1969	Jan.	Feb.	Mar.	April	May	June	July	Aug.	Sept.	Oct.	Nov.	Dec.
1	10 ♊	24 ♋	2 ♌	18 ♍	24 ♎	16 ♐	25 ♑	18 ♓	7 ♉	10 ♊	24 ♋	25 ♌
3	4 ♋	19 ♌	27 ♌	15 ♎	23 ♏	16 ♑	25 ♒	15 ♈	2 ♊	4 ♋	18 ♌	20 ♍
5	28 ♋	14 ♍	23 ♍	13 ♏	22 ♐	16 ♒	23 ♓	11 ♉	26 ♊	28 ♋	12 ♍	15 ♎
7	22 ♌	10 ♎	20 ♎	12 ♐	21 ♑	14 ♓	20 ♈	6 ♊	20 ♋	22 ♌	7 ♎	2 ♏
9	17 ♍	7 ♏	17 ♏	11 ♑	20 ♒	10 ♈	15 ♉	0 ♋	14 ♌	16 ♍	4 ♏	11 ♐
11	13 ♎	5 ♐	16 ♐	9 ♒	17 ♓	5 ♉	9 ♊	23 ♋	8 ♍	12 ♎	2 ♐	11 ♑
13	10 ♏	3 ♑	14 ♑	7 ♓	13 ♈	0 ♊	3 ♋	17 ♌	3 ♎	9 ♏	1 ♑	10 ♒
15	9 ♐	3 ♒	12 ♒	3 ♈	8 ♉	24 ♊	26 ♋	11 ♍	29 ♎	7 ♐	0 ♒	9 ♓
17	9 ♑	2 ♓	10 ♓	29 ♈	3 ♊	17 ♋	20 ♌	6 ♎	26 ♏	5 ♑	28 ♒	6 ♈
19	9 ♒	0 ♈	8 ♈	24 ♉	27 ♊	11 ♌	14 ♍	2 ♏	24 ♐	3 ♒	26 ♓	2 ♉
21	8 ♓	26 ♈	4 ♉	18 ♊	21 ♋	5 ♍	9 ♎	29 ♏	23 ♑	2 ♓	22 ♈	28 ♉
23	5 ♈	21 ♉	28 ♉	12 ♋	14 ♌	0 ♎	6 ♏	28 ♐	21 ♒	29 ♓	18 ♉	22 ♊
25	0 ♉	15 ♊	22 ♊	6 ♌	9 ♍	26 ♎	4 ♐	27 ♑	20 ♓	26 ♈	14 ♊	16 ♋
27	25 ♉	8 ♋	16 ♋	1 ♍	4 ♎	25 ♏	3 ♑	27 ♒	18 ♈	23 ♉	8 ♋	10 ♌
29	18 ♊		10 ♌	26 ♍	2 ♏	25 ♐	4 ♒	26 ♓	15 ♉	18 ♊	2 ♌	4 ♍
31	12 ♋		5 ♍		1 ♐		3 ♓	24 ♈		12 ♋		28 ♍

1970	Jan.	Feb.	Mar.	April	May	June	July	Aug.	Sept.	Oct.	Nov.	Dec.
1	10 ♎	28 ♏	8 ♐	1 ♒	10 ♓	2 ♉	8 ♊	24 ♋	9 ♍	11 ♎	28 ♏	5 ♑
3	6 ♏	27 ♐	6 ♑	0 ♓	8 ♈	28 ♉	3 ♋	18 ♌	2 ♎	6 ♏	25 ♐	3 ♒
5	4 ♐	27 ♑	5 ♒	29 ♓	6 ♉	24 ♊	27 ♋	11 ♍	26 ♎	1 ♐	22 ♑	1 ♓
7	4 ♑	27 ♒	5 ♓	27 ♈	3 ♊	19 ♋	21 ♌	5 ♎	21 ♏	28 ♐	20 ♒	29 ♓
9	4 ♒	27 ♓	5 ♈	25 ♉	28 ♊	13 ♌	15 ♍	0 ♏	18 ♐	25 ♑	18 ♓	27 ♈
11	4 ♓	25 ♈	3 ♉	20 ♊	23 ♋	6 ♍	9 ♎	25 ♏	15 ♑	24 ♒	17 ♈	25 ♉
13	3 ♈	21 ♉	0 ♊	15 ♋	17 ♌	0 ♎	3 ♏	22 ♐	15 ♒	23 ♓	16 ♉	22 ♊
15	29 ♈	16 ♊	25 ♊	9 ♌	10 ♍	25 ♎	0 ♐	21 ♑	15 ♓	23 ♈	13 ♊	17 ♋
17	25 ♉	10 ♋	19 ♋	2 ♍	5 ♎	22 ♏	28 ♐	21 ♒	15 ♈	22 ♉	9 ♋	12 ♌
19	19 ♊	4 ♌	12 ♌	27 ♍	0 ♏	20 ♐	28 ♑	22 ♓	14 ♉	19 ♊	4 ♌	16 ♍
21	13 ♋	28 ♌	6 ♍	22 ♎	27 ♏	19 ♑	28 ♒	21 ♈	11 ♊	14 ♋	28 ♌	0 ♎
23	7 ♌	22 ♍	1 ♎	18 ♏	25 ♐	18 ♒	27 ♓	18 ♉	6 ♋	8 ♌	22 ♍	24 ♎
25	1 ♍	16 ♎	22 ♎	15 ♐	24 ♑	17 ♓	25 ♈	14 ♊	0 ♌	2 ♍	16 ♎	19 ♏
27	25 ♍	12 ♏	22 ♏	13 ♑	22 ♒	15 ♈	22 ♉	9 ♋	24 ♌	26 ♍	11 ♏	16 ♐
29	19 ♎		19 ♐	11 ♒	21 ♓	12 ♉	18 ♊	3 ♌	17 ♍	20 ♎	7 ♐	14 ♑
31	15 ♏		16 ♑		18 ♈		12 ♋	27 ♌		15 ♏		13 ♒

1971	Jan.	Feb.	Mar.	April	May	June	July	Aug.	Sept.	Oct.	Nov.	Dec.
1	27 ♒	20 ♈	0 ♉	20 ♊	25 ♋	9 ♍	11 ♎	25 ♏	12 ♑	18 ♒	11 ♈	19 ♉
3	26 ♓	18 ♉	28 ♉	16 ♋	19 ♌	3 ♎	5 ♏	20 ♐	10 ♒	17 ♓	11 ♉	19 ♊
5	24 ♈	14 ♊	24 ♊	11 ♌	13 ♍	27 ♎	0 ♐	17 ♑	9 ♓	18 ♈	11 ♊	17 ♋
7	21 ♉	10 ♋	19 ♋	4 ♍	6 ♎	21 ♏	26 ♐	16 ♒	9 ♈	18 ♉	9 ♋	13 ♌
9	18 ♊	5 ♌	14 ♌	28 ♍	0 ♏	17 ♐	23 ♑	15 ♓	9 ♉	17 ♊	5 ♌	8 ♍
11	13 ♋	29 ♌	7 ♍	22 ♎	25 ♏	14 ♑	21 ♒	14 ♈	7 ♊	14 ♋	0 ♍	2 ♎
13	8 ♌	22 ♍	1 ♎	16 ♏	21 ♐	11 ♒	20 ♓	13 ♉	4 ♋	9 ♌	24 ♍	26 ♎
15	2 ♍	16 ♎	25 ♎	11 ♐	17 ♑	9 ♓	18 ♈	11 ♊	0 ♌	3 ♍	18 ♎	20 ♏
17	26 ♍	10 ♏	19 ♏	7 ♑	14 ♒	7 ♈	16 ♉	7 ♋	24 ♌	27 ♍	12 ♏	15 ♐
19	19 ♎	5 ♐	14 ♐	4 ♒	12 ♓	6 ♉	14 ♊	3 ♌	18 ♍	21 ♎	6 ♐	10 ♑
21	14 ♏	1 ♑	10 ♑	2 ♓	11 ♈	4 ♊	11 ♋	27 ♌	12 ♎	15 ♏	1 ♑	6 ♒
23	10 ♐	0 ♒	8 ♒	1 ♈	10 ♉	1 ♋	6 ♌	21 ♍	6 ♏	9 ♐	26 ♑	3 ♓
25	7 ♑	29 ♒	8 ♓	1 ♉	9 ♊	28 ♋	1 ♍	15 ♎	0 ♐	4 ♑	23 ♒	1 ♈
27	7 ♒	0 ♈	8 ♈	1 ♊	7 ♋	23 ♌	25 ♍	9 ♏	24 ♐	29 ♑	21 ♓	0 ♉
29	6 ♓		8 ♉	29 ♊	3 ♌	17 ♍	19 ♎	3 ♐	20 ♑	27 ♒	20 ♈	29 ♉
31	6 ♈		7 ♊		27 ♌		13 ♏	28 ♐		26 ♓		27 ♊

1972	Jan.	Feb.	Mar.	April	May	June	July	Aug.	Sept.	Oct.	Nov.	Dec.
1	11 ♋	29 ♌	20 ♍	5 ♏	7 ♐	23 ♑	29 ♒	21 ♈	14 ♊	23 ♋	12 ♍	16 ♎
3	8 ♌	24 ♍	14 ♎	28 ♏	1 ♑	19 ♒	26 ♓	19 ♉	12 ♋	19 ♌	6 ♎	10 ♏
5	4 ♍	18 ♎	8 ♏	22 ♐	26 ♑	15 ♓	24 ♈	18 ♊	9 ♌	15 ♍	1 ♏	3 ♐
7	28 ♍	12 ♏	2 ♐	17 ♑	22 ♒	14 ♈	23 ♉	16 ♋	5 ♍	10 ♎	24 ♏	27 ♐
9	22 ♎	6 ♐	26 ♐	13 ♒	20 ♓	13 ♉	22 ♊	13 ♌	1 ♎	4 ♏	18 ♐	21 ♑
11	16 ♏	1 ♑	21 ♑	11 ♓	19 ♈	13 ♊	21 ♋	10 ♍	25 ♎	28 ♏	12 ♑	16 ♒
13	10 ♐	27 ♑	18 ♒	10 ♈	19 ♉	12 ♋	18 ♌	5 ♎	19 ♏	21 ♐	6 ♒	11 ♓
15	6 ♑	25 ♒	17 ♓	11 ♉	20 ♊	10 ♌	14 ♍	29 ♎	13 ♐	15 ♑	2 ♓	8 ♈
17	2 ♒	24 ♓	17 ♈	11 ♊	18 ♋	6 ♍	9 ♎	23 ♏	7 ♑	10 ♒	29 ♓	7 ♉
19	0 ♓	23 ♈	17 ♉	9 ♋	15 ♌	1 ♎	3 ♏	17 ♐	2 ♒	7 ♓	28 ♈	7 ♊
21	28 ♓	22 ♉	16 ♊	6 ♌	10 ♍	25 ♎	27 ♏	12 ♑	29 ♒	5 ♈	29 ♉	7 ♋
23	26 ♈	19 ♊	13 ♋	1 ♍	5 ♎	19 ♏	21 ♐	7 ♒	27 ♓	5 ♉	29 ♊	6 ♌
25	25 ♉	16 ♋	9 ♌	26 ♍	29 ♎	13 ♐	16 ♑	4 ♓	27 ♈	6 ♊	28 ♋	4 ♍
27	23 ♊	12 ♌	4 ♍	20 ♎	22 ♏	7 ♑	12 ♒	3 ♈	26 ♉	5 ♋	25 ♌	0 ♎
29	20 ♋	7 ♍	29 ♍	13 ♏	16 ♐	3 ♒	9 ♓	1 ♉	25 ♊	3 ♌	21 ♍	24 ♎
31	16 ♌		23 ♎		11 ♑		7 ♈	0 ♊		29 ♌		18 ♏

1973	Jan.	Feb.	Mar.	April	May	June	July	Aug.	Sept.	Oct.	Nov.	Dec.
1	0 ♐	14 ♑	22 ♑	8 ♓	14 ♈	7 ♊	16 ♋	8 ♍	28 ♎	0 ♐	13 ♑	15 ♒
3	24 ♐	2 ♒	17 ♒	6 ♈	14 ♉	7 ♋	15 ♌	6 ♎	22 ♏	24 ♐	7 ♒	9 ♓
5	18 ♑	5 ♓	14 ♓	5 ♉	14 ♊	7 ♌	14 ♍	1 ♏	16 ♐	17 ♑	1 ♓	5 ♈
7	13 ♒	1 ♈	11 ♈	4 ♊	13 ♋	5 ♍	10 ♎	26 ♏	9 ♑	11 ♒	27 ♓	2 ♉
9	8 ♓	29 ♈	10 ♉	3 ♋	11 ♌	1 ♎	5 ♏	19 ♐	3 ♒	6 ♓	25 ♈	1 ♊
11	5 ♈	27 ♉	8 ♊	1 ♌	8 ♍	26 ♎	29 ♏	13 ♑	28 ♒	3 ♈	23 ♉	1 ♋
13	2 ♉	25 ♊	6 ♋	28 ♌	4 ♎	20 ♏	23 ♐	7 ♒	24 ♓	0 ♉	23 ♊	2 ♌
15	1 ♊	24 ♋	4 ♌	24 ♍	29 ♎	14 ♐	16 ♑	2 ♓	21 ♈	29 ♉	22 ♋	0 ♍
17	0 ♋	22 ♌	1 ♍	20 ♎	23 ♏	8 ♑	10 ♒	28 ♓	19 ♉	27 ♊	20 ♌	28 ♍
19	0 ♌	20 ♍	28 ♍	14 ♏	17 ♐	1 ♒	5 ♓	24 ♈	17 ♊	26 ♋	18 ♍	24 ♎
21	28 ♌	16 ♎	24 ♎	8 ♐	11 ♑	26 ♒	1 ♈	22 ♉	15 ♋	24 ♌	14 ♎	19 ♏
23	25 ♍	10 ♏	18 ♏	2 ♌	4 ♒	21 ♓	27 ♈	20 ♊	13 ♌	21 ♍	9 ♏	13 ♐
25	20 ♎	4 ♐	12 ♐	26 ♑	29 ♒	18 ♈	25 ♉	19 ♋	11 ♍	17 ♎	4 ♐	7 ♑
27	15 ♏	28 ♐	6 ♑	20 ♒	25 ♓	16 ♉	24 ♊	18 ♌	9 ♎	13 ♏	28 ♐	0 ♒
29	8 ♐		0 ♒	16 ♓	23 ♈	6 ♊	24 ♋	16 ♍	5 ♏	8 ♐	22 ♑	24 ♒
31	2 ♑		25 ♒		22 ♉		24 ♌	14 ♎		1 ♑		18 ♓

1974	Jan.	Feb.	Mar.	April	May	June	July	Aug.	Sept.	Oct.	Nov.	Dec.
1	1 ♈	20 ♉	0 ♊	23 ♋	2 ♍	23 ♎	29 ♏	14 ♑	29 ♒	2 ♈	19 ♉	26 ♊
3	27 ♈	18 ♊	28 ♊	21 ♌	0 ♎	19 ♏	23 ♐	8 ♒	23 ♓	27 ♈	16 ♊	24 ♋
5	25 ♉	17 ♋	27 ♋	20 ♍	27 ♎	14 ♐	17 ♑	2 ♓	18 ♈	23 ♉	14 ♋	23 ♌
7	24 ♊	18 ♌	26 ♌	18 ♎	23 ♏	9 ♑	11 ♒	26 ♓	13 ♉	20 ♊	12 ♌	22 ♍
9	25 ♋	17 ♍	25 ♍	15 ♏	18 ♐	2 ♒	5 ♓	20 ♈	9 ♊	17 ♋	11 ♍	19 ♎
11	25 ♌	16 ♎	23 ♎	10 ♐	12 ♑	26 ♒	29 ♓	16 ♉	7 ♋	16 ♌	9 ♎	16 ♏
13	24 ♍	12 ♏	20 ♏	5 ♑	6 ♒	20 ♓	24 ♈	13 ♊	6 ♌	15 ♍	7 ♏	12 ♐
15	20 ♎	7 ♐	15 ♐	28 ♑	0 ♓	15 ♈	20 ♉	12 ♋	6 ♍	14 ♎	4 ♐	7 ♑
17	16 ♏	0 ♑	9 ♑	22 ♒	25 ♓	12 ♉	19 ♊	12 ♌	5 ♎	12 ♏	29 ♐	2 ♒
19	10 ♐	24 ♑	2 ♒	17 ♓	20 ♈	10 ♊	18 ♋	12 ♍	4 ♏	9 ♐	24 ♑	25 ♒
21	4 ♑	18 ♒	26 ♒	12 ♈	18 ♉	10 ♋	19 ♌	12 ♎	1 ♐	4 ♑	18 ♒	19 ♓
23	27 ♉	12 ♓	21 ♓	9 ♉	16 ♊	10 ♌	19 ♍	9 ♏	26 ♐	28 ♑	11 ♓	13 ♈
25	21 ♒	7 ♈	17 ♈	7 ♊	15 ♋	9 ♍	17 ♎	5 ♐	20 ♑	22 ♒	6 ♈	9 ♉
27	15 ♓	3 ♉	13 ♉	5 ♋	14 ♌	7 ♎	13 ♏	29 ♐	13 ♒	16 ♓	1 ♉	6 ♊
29	10 ♈		11 ♊	4 ♌	13 ♍	3 ♏	8 ♐	23 ♑	7 ♓	10 ♈	28 ♉	4 ♋
31	6 ♉		8 ♋		10 ♎		2 ♑	17 ♒		6 ♉		4 ♌

1975	Jan.	Feb.	Mar.	April	May	June	July	Aug.	Sept.	Oct.	Nov.	Dec.
1	19 ♌	12 ♎	21 ♎	11 ♐	14 ♑	29 ♒	0 ♈	15 ♉	2 ♋	9 ♌	2 ♎	11 ♏
3	18 ♍	10 ♏	19 ♏	6 ♑	9 ♒	23 ♓	24 ♈	10 ♊	0 ♌	8 ♍	2 ♏	9 ♐
5	16 ♎	6 ♐	15 ♐	1 ♒	3 ♓	17 ♈	19 ♉	7 ♋	0 ♍	9 ♎	1 ♐	7 ♑
7	13 ♏	1 ♑	10 ♑	24 ♒	26 ♓	11 ♉	16 ♊	6 ♌	0 ♎	9 ♏	29 ♐	3 ♒
9	9 ♐	25 ♑	4 ♒	18 ♓	21 ♈	7 ♊	13 ♋	6 ♍	0 ♏	7 ♐	25 ♑	28 ♒
11	4 ♑	19 ♒	28 ♒	12 ♈	16 ♉	4 ♋	12 ♌	6 ♎	29 ♏	4 ♑	20 ♒	22 ♓
13	28 ♑	12 ♓	21 ♓	7 ♉	12 ♊	3 ♌	12 ♍	5 ♏	25 ♐	20 ♑	14 ♓	16 ♈
15	22 ♒	6 ♈	15 ♈	2 ♊	8 ♋	1 ♍	11 ♎	2 ♐	20 ♑	24 ♒	8 ♈	10 ♉
17	16 ♓	0 ♉	10 ♉	28 ♊	6 ♌	0 ♎	8 ♏	28 ♐	15 ♒	17 ♓	2 ♉	5 ♊
19	9 ♈	25 ♉	5 ♊	25 ♋	4 ♍	28 ♎	5 ♐	23 ♑	9 ♓	11 ♈	26 ♉	1 ♋
21	4 ♉	22 ♊	1 ♋	24 ♌	3 ♎	25 ♏	1 ♑	18 ♒	2 ♈	5 ♉	22 ♊	28 ♋
23	0 ♊	20 ♋	29 ♋	23 ♍	2 ♏	22 ♐	26 ♑	12 ♓	26 ♈	0 ♊	18 ♋	26 ♌
25	28 ♊	20 ♌	29 ♌	22 ♎	0 ♐	18 ♑	21 ♒	5 ♈	20 ♉	25 ♊	15 ♌	24 ♍
27	27 ♋	21 ♍	29 ♍	21 ♏	26 ♐	13 ♒	15 ♓	29 ♈	15 ♊	21 ♋	13 ♍	22 ♎
29	27 ♌		29 ♎	19 ♐	22 ♑	7 ♓	9 ♈	23 ♉	11 ♋	18 ♌	12 ♎	20 ♏
31	28 ♍		27 ♏		17 ♒		3 ♉	19 ♊		17 ♍		18 ♐

APPENDIX VIII

A Shortcut to the Sun and the Planets

In the case of the heavier planets–Pluto, Neptune, Uranus, Saturn, Jupiter–the daily rate of motion is so slight, considerably less than a degree a month in some cases, that no time correction is significant in placing the planets in their proper sign in the do-it-yourself chart. The daily position of the faster planets and the Sun can be easily adjusted to the individual's birth date by calculating their average daily movement from the positions listed at the first of each month. Mars moves daily an average of 45 minutes or ¾ degree, the Sun 59 minutes, just short of a degree, Venus an average 1 degree and 12 minutes, and Mercury 1 degree and 24 minutes. Multiply daily movement by the number of days from the first of the month to the birth date to get a more accurate position of these planets in the chart. Or, more quickly but less accurately, add one degree for every day after the first of the given month until the subject's birth date. Using the rising degree on the Eastern Horizon, or the ascendant, as the starting point, the planetary positions, together with those of the Moon and the Sun, can then each be placed in their proper house and sign in the equal house chart as described in finding the ascendant. The significance of these planetary positions and the aspects they make can then be clarified by reviewing the instructive material in Chapters 3, 4 and 5.

Tables show by date and degree when planets are retrograde and direct. In the heavier planets, the movement is so slight that the change is insignificant in mapping a chart. However, retrograding planets reflect a negative period for undertaking any activity that these planets govern. For instance, it would be inadvisable, astrologically, to undertake a new venture or sign a contract when the planet Mercury, ruling communication and things of the mind, was retrograde. Saturn retrograde indicates additional delays and losses, etc.

PLANETARY POSITIONS FOR THE FIRST OF EACH MONTH
NOON GREENWICH MEAN TIME

1900

MONTH	♇	♆	♅	♄	♃	♂	☉	♀	☿
JAN.	15 ♊	25 ♊	10 ♐	28 ♐	1 ♐	14 ♑	11 ♑	7 ♒	20 ♐
FEB.	15	25	12	1 ♑	7	8 ♒	12 ♒	15 ♓	6 ♒
MAR. ...	15	24	12	4	10	0 ♓	10 ♓	19 ♈	26 ♓
APR.	15	24	12	5	11	25	11 ♈	25 ♉	28 ♓
MAY	15	25	12	5	9	18 ♈	11 ♉	26 ♊	15 ♈
JUNE ...	16	26	10	3	5	11 ♉	11 ♊	20 ♋	13 ♊
JULY ...	17	27	9	1	2	3 ♊	9 ♋	20 ♋	5 ♌
AUG. ...	17	28	9	29 ♐	1	24	9 ♌	8 ♋	8 ♌
SEPT. ...	18	29	9	28	3	15 ♋	9 ♍	24 ♋	27 ♌
OCT. ...	18	29	9	29	7	3 ♌	8 ♎	22 ♌	21 ♎
NOV. ...	17	29	11	1 ♑	13	20	9 ♏	27 ♍	2 ♐
DEC. ...	17	28	12	4	19	3 ♍	9 ♐	3 ♏	20 ♏

1901

MONTH	♇	♆	♅	♄	♃	♂	☉	♀	☿
JAN.	16 ♊	28 ♊	14 ♐	8 ♑	26 ♐	12 ♍	10 ♑	11 ♐	28 ♐
FEB.	16	27	16	11	3 ♑	10	12 ♒	20 ♑	19 ♒
MAR. ...	16	26	17	14	8	0	10 ♓	25 ♒	21 ♓
APR.	16	27	17	16	12	23 ♌	11 ♈	3 ♈	13 ♓
MAY	16	27	16	16	13	27	10 ♉	11 ♉	26 ♈
JUNE ...	17	28	15	15	12	8 ♍	10 ♊	19 ♊	29 ♊
JULY ...	18	29	14	13	8	23	9 ♋	25 ♋	26 ♋
AUG. ...	18	0 ♋	13	11	5	11 ♎	9 ♌	3 ♍	19 ♋
SEPT. ...	19	1	13	10	3	0 ♏	8 ♍	11 ♎	13 ♍
OCT. ...	19	1	14	10	5	21	8 ♎	17 ♏	0 ♏
NOV. ...	18	1	15	12	9	13 ♐	8 ♏	23 ♐	16 ♏
DEC. ...	18	1	17	14	15	6 ♑	9 ♐	26 ♑	22 ♏

1902

MONTH	♇	♆	♅	♄	♃	♂	☉	♀	☿
JAN.	17 ♊	0 ♋	18 ♐	18 ♑	22 ♑	0 ♒	10 ♑	24 ♒	10 ♑
FEB.	17	29 ♊	20	21	29	24	12 ♒	2 ♓	0 ♓
MAR. ...	17	29	21	24	5 ♒	16 ♓	10 ♓	18 ♒	21 ♒
APR.	17	29	21	27	11	10 ♈	11 ♈	28 ♒	17 ♓
MAY	17	29	21	28	15	3 ♉	10 ♉	24 ♓	13 ♉
JUNE ...	18	0 ♋	20	27	17	26	10 ♊	27 ♈	3 ♋
JULY ...	19	1	18	26	16	17 ♊	9 ♋	1 ♊	28 ♊
AUG. ...	19	3	18	23	13	8 ♋	8 ♌	8 ♋	27 ♋
SEPT. ...	20	3	17	22	9	28	8 ♍	16 ♌	26 ♍
OCT. ...	20	4	18	21	7	17 ♌	7 ♎	23 ♍	2 ♏
NOV. ...	19	4	19	22	9	5 ♍	8 ♏	1 ♏	20 ♎
DEC. ...	19	3	21	25	13	21	8 ♐	9 ♐	2 ♐

1903

MONTH	♇	♆	♅	♄	♃	♂	☉	♀	☿
JAN.	18 ♊	2 ♋	23 ♐	28 ♑	18 ♒	5 ♎	10 ♑	18 ♑	21 ♑
FEB.	18	1	24	2 ♒	25	15	11 ♒	27 ♒	14 ♒
MAR. ...	18	1	25	5	2 ♓	16	10 ♓	2 ♈	13 ♒
APR.	18	1	26	7	9	6	11 ♈	10 ♉	29 ♓
MAY	18	2	25	9	16	28 ♍	10 ♉	16 ♊	28 ♉
JUNE ...	19	3	24	9	21	0 ♎	10 ♊	22 ♋	13 ♊
JULY ...	20	4	23	8	23	11	8 ♋	24 ♌	17 ♊
AUG. ...	20	5	22	6	23	27	8 ♌	21 ♍	14 ♌
SEPT. ...	21	6	22	4	20	16 ♏	8 ♍	1 ♎	4 ♎
OCT. ...	21	6	22	3	16	6 ♐	7 ♎	17 ♍	12 ♎
NOV. ...	20	6	23	3	14	29	8 ♏	25 ♍	26 ♎
DEC. ...	20	5	25	5	14	22 ♑	8 ♐	21 ♎	14 ♐

1904

MONTH	♇	♆	♅	♄	♃	♂	☉	♀	☿
JAN.	19 ♊	4 ♋	27 ♐	8 ♒	18 ♓	16 ♒	10 ♑	26 ♏	29 ♑
FEB.	19	4	28	12	24	10 ♓	11 ♒	3 ♑	18 ♑
MAR. ...	19	3	29	15	0 ♈	3 ♈	10 ♓	8 ♒	21 ♒
APR.	19	3	0 ♑	18	8	26	11 ♈	16 ♓	17 ♈
MAY	19	4	0	20	15	18 ♉	11 ♉	23 ♈	26 ♉
JUNE ...	20	5	29 ♐	21	21	10 ♊	11 ♊	1 ♊	19 ♉
JULY ...	21	6	28	20	26	1 ♋	9 ♋	7 ♋	29 ♊
AUG. ...	21	7	26	18	0 ♉	21	9 ♌	15 ♌	0 ♍
SEPT. ...	22	8	26	16	0	11 ♌	9 ♍	24 ♍	1 ♎
OCT. ...	22	8	26	15	27 ♈	0 ♍	8 ♎	1 ♏	20 ♍
NOV. ...	21	8	27	15	23	19	9 ♏	9 ♐	9 ♏
DEC. ...	21	8	29	16	21	7 ♎	9 ♐	16 ♑	26 ♐

1905

MONTH	♇	♆	♅	♄	♃	♂	☉	♀	☿
JAN.	20 ♊	7 ♋	1 ♑	19 ♒	21 ♈	24 ♎	10 ♑	23 ♒	8 ♑
FEB.	20	6	2	22	24	9 ♏	12 ♒	28 ♓	19 ♑
MAR. ...	20	5	4	25	29	20	10 ♓	26 ♈	3 ♓
APR.	20	5	4	29	5 ♉	25	11 ♈	14 ♉	0 ♉
MAY	20	6	4	1 ♓	12	20	10 ♉	4 ♉	28 ♈
JUNE ...	21	7	3	3	20	10	10 ♊	2 ♉	18 ♉
JULY ...	22	8	2	3	26	10	9 ♋	23 ♉	17 ♋
AUG. ...	22	9	1	1	2 ♊	20	9 ♌	25 ♊	6 ♍
SEPT. ...	23	10	0	29 ♒	6	6 ♐	8 ♍	0 ♌	4 ♍
OCT. ...	23	10	0	27	6	26	8 ♎	5 ♍	29 ♍
NOV. ...	22	10	1	26	4	18 ♑	8 ♏	13 ♎	21 ♏
DEC. ...	22	10	3	27	0	10 ♒	9 ♐	21 ♏	0 ♑

1906

MONTH	♇	♆	♅	♄	♃	♂	☉	♀	☿
JAN.	21 ♊	9 ♋	5 ♑	29 ♒	27 ♉	4 ♓	10 ♑	0 ♑	18 ♐
FEB.	21	8	6	3 ♓	27	27	12 ♒	9 ♒	28 ♑
MAR. ...	21	8	8	6	29	18 ♈	10 ♓	14 ♓	18 ♓
APR.	21	8	8	10	4 ♊	11 ♉	11 ♈	22 ♈	17 ♈
MAY	21	8	8	13	10	2 ♊	10 ♉	29 ♉	14 ♈
JUNE ...	22	9	8	15	17	23	10 ♊	8 ♋	1 ♊
JULY ...	23	10	6	15	24	13 ♋	9 ♋	13 ♌	1 ♌
AUG. ...	23	11	5	14	0 ♋	3 ♌	8 ♌	19 ♍	26 ♌
SEPT. ...	24	12	5	12	6	23	8 ♍	24 ♎	20 ♌
OCT. ...	24	13	5	10	10	12 ♍	7 ♎	23 ♏	13 ♎
NOV. ...	23	13	5	8	11	1 ♎	8 ♏	14 ♐	0 ♐
DEC. ...	23	12	7	9	9	20	8 ♐	6 ♐	5 ♐

1907

MONTH	♇	♆	♅	♄	♃	♂	☉	♀	☿
JAN.	22 ♊	11 ♋	9 ♑	10 ♓	5 ♋	9 ♏	10 ♑	2 ♐	22 ♐
FEB.	22	10	10	13	2	28	11 ♒	25 ♐	11 ♒
MAR. ...	22	10	12	17	1	14 ♐	10 ♓	24 ♑	28 ♓
APR.	22	10	13	20	3	0 ♑	11 ♈	29 ♒	19 ♓
MAY	22	10	13	24	7	12	10 ♉	5 ♈	18 ♈
JUNE ...	23	11	12	26	13	19	10 ♊	12 ♉	20 ♊
JULY ...	24	12	11	27	19	15	8 ♋	18 ♊	4 ♌
AUG. ...	24	13	10	27	26	7	8 ♌	26 ♋	27 ♋
SEPT. ...	25	14	9	25	3 ♌	11	8 ♍	4 ♍	2 ♍
OCT. ...	25	15	9	23	8	23	7 ♎	12 ♎	25 ♎
NOV. ...	24	15	10	21	12	12 ♒	8 ♏	20 ♏	29 ♏
DEC. ...	24	14	11	21	14	2 ♓	8 ♐	28 ♐	18 ♏

1908

MONTH	♇	♆	♅	♄	♃	♂	☉	♀	☿
JAN.	23 ♊	14 ♋	13 ♑	22 ♓	12 ♌	23 ♓	10 ♑	6 ♒	2 ♑
FEB.	23	13	14	25	8	15 ♈	11 ♒	15 ♓	24 ♒
MAR. ...	23	12	16	28	5	5 ♉	11 ♓	20 ♈	8 ♓
APR.	23	12	17	2 ♈	4	26	11 ♈	25 ♉	14 ♓
MAY	23	13	17	5	5	16 ♊	11 ♉	26 ♊	3 ♉
JUNE ...	24	13	16	8	9	6 ♋	11 ♊	19 ♋	3 ♋
JULY ...	25	14	15	10	14	26	9 ♋	16 ♋	15 ♋
AUG. ...	25	16	14	10	21	16 ♌	9 ♌	6 ♋	21 ♋
SEPT. ...	26	16	13	9	28	5 ♍	9 ♍	23 ♋	19 ♍
OCT. ...	26	17	13	7	4 ♍	24	8 ♎	23 ♌	3 ♏
NOV. ...	26	17	14	4	9	14 ♎	9 ♏	28 ♍	0 ♏
DEC. ...	25	17	15	3	13	4 ♏	9 ♐	4 ♏	27 ♏

1909

MONTH	♇	♆	♅	♄	♃	♂	☉	♀	☿
JAN.	24 ♊	16 ♋	17 ♑	4 ♈	15 ♍	24 ♏	10 ♑	12 ♐	15 ♑
FEB.	24	15	18	6	13	15 ♐	12 ♒	21 ♑	28 ♒
MAR. ...	24	14	20	9	9	4 ♑	10 ♓	26 ♒	15 ♒
APR.	24	14	21	13	6	24	11 ♈	4 ♈	22 ♓
MAY	24	15	21	17	5	14 ♒	10 ♉	11 ♉	21 ♉
JUNE ...	25	15	21	20	6	4 ♓	10 ♊	19 ♊	28 ♊
JULY ...	26	17	20	22	10	21	9 ♋	26 ♋	20 ♊
AUG. ...	26	18	18	23	15	4 ♈	9 ♌	4 ♍	5 ♌
SEPT. ...	27	19	17	23	21	6	8 ♍	11 ♎	1 ♎
OCT. ...	27	19	17	21	28	29 ♓	8 ♎	17 ♏	27 ♎
NOV. ...	27	19	18	18	4 ♎	26	8 ♏	23 ♐	21 ♎
DEC. ...	26	19	19	17	10	4 ♈	9 ♐	26 ♑	8 ♐

1910

MONTH	♇	♆	♅	♄	♃	♂	☉	♀	☿
JAN.	26 ♊	18 ♋	21 ♑	17 ♈	13 ♎	18 ♈	10 ♑	23 ♒	26 ♑
FEB.	25	17	22	18	15	5 ♉	12 ♒	29 ♒	29 ♑
MAR. ...	25	17	24	21	13	22	10 ♓	15 ♒	15 ♒
APR.	25	17	25	24	10	11 ♊	11 ♈	27 ♒	6 ♈
MAY	25	17	25	28	6	0 ♋	10 ♉	24 ♓	1 ♊
JUNE ...	26	18	25	2 ♉	5	19	10 ♊	28 ♈	0 ♊
JULY ...	27	19	24	5	6	8 ♌	9 ♋	2 ♊	20 ♊
AUG. ...	27	20	23	6	10	27	8 ♌	9 ♋	22 ♌
SEPT. ...	28	21	22	6	15	17 ♍	8 ♍	16 ♌	5 ♎
OCT. ...	28	21	21	5	21	6 ♎	7 ♎	23 ♍	28 ♍
NOV. ...	28	22	22	3	28	27	8 ♏	2 ♏	1 ♏
DEC. ...	27	21	23	1	4 ♏	17 ♏	8 ♐	10 ♐	19 ♐

1911

MONTH	♇	♆	♅	♄	♃	♂	☉	♀	☿
JAN.	27 ♊	20 ♋	24 ♑	0 ♉	10 ♏	8 ♐	10 ♑	19 ♑	26 ♑
FEB.	26	20	26	1	13	0 ♑	12 ♒	28 ♒	16 ♑
MAR. ...	26	19	28	3	15	21	10 ♓	2 ♈	24 ♒
APR.	26	19	29	6	13	14 ♒	11 ♈	10 ♉	23 ♈
MAY	26	19	29	10	10	6 ♓	10 ♉	16 ♊	17 ♉
JUNE ...	27	20	29	14	6	29	10 ♊	22 ♋	16 ♉
JULY ...	28	21	28	17	5	20 ♈	9 ♋	24 ♌	5 ♋
AUG. ...	28	22	27	19	6	11 ♉	8 ♌	21 ♍	3 ♍
SEPT. ...	29	23	26	20	10	28	8 ♍	28 ♍	23 ♍
OCT. ...	29	24	25	20	15	9 ♊	7 ♎	14 ♍	21 ♍
NOV. ...	29	24	26	17	21	9	8 ♏	24 ♍	13 ♏
DEC. ...	28	23	27	15	28	0	8 ♐	22 ♎	28 ♐

1912

MONTH	♇	♆	♅	♄	♃	♂	☉	♀	☿
JAN.	28 ♊	23 ♋	28 ♑	14 ♉	5 ♐	24 ♉	10 ♑	26 ♏	25 ♐
FEB.	27	22	0 ♒	14	10	1 ♊	11 ♒	3 ♑	22 ♑
MAR. ...	27	21	2	15	14	12	11 ♓	8 ♒	10 ♓
APR.	27	21	3	18	15	28	11 ♈	16 ♓	29 ♈
MAY	27	21	3	22	14	14 ♋	11 ♉	23 ♈	19 ♈
JUNE ...	28	22	3	26	11	2 ♌	12 ♊	1 ♊	23 ♉
JULY ...	29	23	2	29	7	20	9 ♋	8 ♋	25 ♋
AUG. ...	29	24	1	2 ♊	6	10 ♍	9 ♌	16 ♌	5 ♍
SEPT. ...	0 ♋	25	0	4	7	29	9 ♍	24 ♍	24 ♌
OCT. ...	0	26	0	4	11	19 ♎	8 ♎	1 ♏	6 ♎
NOV. ...	0	26	0	2	16	10 ♏	9 ♏	10 ♐	26 ♏
DEC. ...	29 ♊	26	1	0	23	2 ♐	9 ♐	16 ♑	24 ♐

1913

MONTH	♇	♆	♅	♄	♃	♂	☉	♀	☿
JAN.	29 ♊	25 ♋	2 ♒	28 ♉	0 ♑	23 ♐	10 ♑	23 ♒	19 ♐
FEB.	28	24	4	27	7	16 ♑	12 ♒	28 ♓	4 ♒
MAR. ...	28	24	6	28	12	8 ♒	10 ♓	26 ♈	24 ♓
APR.	28	23	7	1 ♊	16	2 ♓	11 ♈	12 ♉	3 ♈
MAY	28	23	8	4	18	25	10 ♉	0 ♉	14 ♈
JUNE ...	29	24	7	8	17	18 ♈	10 ♊	1 ♉	10 ♊
JULY ...	0 ♋	25	7	12	13	11 ♉	9 ♋	23 ♉	4 ♌
AUG. ...	0	26	5	15	10	2 ♊	9 ♌	25 ♊	14 ♌
SEPT. ...	1	27	4	17	8	22	8 ♍	0 ♌	25 ♌
OCT. ...	1	28	4	18	9	8 ♋	8 ♎	6 ♍	19 ♎
NOV. ...	1	28	4	17	13	21	9 ♏	14 ♎	2 ♐
DEC. ...	0	28	5	15	18	24	9 ♐	21 ♏	23 ♏

1914

MONTH	♇	♆	♅	♄	♃	♂	☉	♀	☿
JAN.	0 ♋	27 ♋	6 ♒	13 ♊	25 ♑	16 ♋	10 ♑	0 ♑	27 ♐
FEB.	29 ♊	26	8	11	3 ♒	7	12 ♒	9 ♒	17 ♒
MAR. ...	29	26	9	12	9	7	10 ♓	14 ♓	25 ♓
APR.	29	25	11	13	15	16	11 ♈	23 ♈	14 ♓
MAY	29	26	12	16	20	0 ♌	10 ♉	0 ♊	23 ♈
JUNE ...	0 ♋	26	12	20	22	16	10 ♊	8 ♋	27 ♊
JULY ...	1	27	11	24	22	3 ♍	9 ♋	13 ♌	29 ♋
AUG. ...	1	28	10	28	19	22	8 ♌	20 ♍	20 ♋
SEPT. ...	2	29	9	1 ♋	15	11 ♎	8 ♍	24 ♎	10 ♍
OCT. ...	2	0 ♌	8	2	13	1 ♏	7 ♎	23 ♏	29 ♎
NOV. ...	2	0	8	2	13	23	8 ♏	12 ♐	21 ♏
DEC. ...	2	0	9	0	17	15 ♐	8 ♐	2 ♐	20 ♏

1915

MONTH	♇	♆	♅	♄	♃	♂	☉	♀	☿
JAN.	1 ♋	0 ♌	10 ♒	28 ♊	22 ♒	8 ♑	10 ♑	1 ♐	8 ♑
FEB.	0	29 ♋	12	26	29	2 ♒	12 ♒	25 ♐	29 ♒
MAR. ...	0	28	13	25	6 ♓	24	10 ♓	24 ♑	25 ♒
APR.	0	28	15	26	13	18 ♓	11 ♈	0 ♓	16 ♓
MAY	1	28	16	29	20	11 ♈	10 ♉	5 ♈	10 ♉
JUNE ...	1	28	16	2 ♋	25	5 ♉	10 ♊	12 ♉	3 ♋
JULY ...	2	29	15	6	28	27	9 ♋	19 ♊	2 ♋
AUG. ...	3	0 ♌	14	10	28	18 ♊	8 ♌	27 ♋	24 ♋
SEPT. ...	3	2	13	14	26	8 ♋	8 ♍	5 ♍	24 ♍
OCT. ...	3	2	12	15	22	26	7 ♎	12 ♎	3 ♏
NOV. ...	3	3	12	17	19	13 ♌	8 ♏	21 ♏	21 ♎
DEC. ...	3	3	12	16	19	25	8 ♐	28 ♐	0 ♐

1916

MONTH	♇	♆	♅	♄	♃	♂	☉	♀	☿
JAN.	2 ♋	2 ♌	14 ♒	13 ♋	22 ♓	0 ♍	10 ♑	7 ♒	19 ♑
FEB.	2	1	15	11	28	23 ♌	11 ♒	15 ♓	19 ♒
MAR. ...	1	0	17	10	4 ♈	13	11 ♓	20 ♈	13 ♒
APR.	1	0	19	10	12	11	11 ♈	26 ♉	28 ♓
MAY	2	0	19	12	19	19	11 ♉	26 ♊	28 ♉
JUNE ...	2	1	20	15	25	2 ♍	11 ♊	18 ♋	17 ♊
JULY ...	3	2	19	19	1 ♉	17	9 ♋	13 ♋	18 ♊
AUG. ...	4	3	18	23	4	6 ♎	9 ♌	4 ♋	13 ♌
SEPT. ...	4	4	17	26	5	25	9 ♍	23 ♋	4 ♎
OCT. ...	4	5	16	29	3	15 ♏	8 ♎	23 ♌	16 ♎
NOV. ...	4	5	16	1 ♌	29 ♈	8 ♐	9 ♏	28 ♍	25 ♎
DEC. ...	4	5	16	0	26	0 ♑	9 ♐	4 ♏	13 ♐

1917

MONTH	♇	♆	♅	♄	♃	♂	☉	♀	☿
JAN.	3 ♋	4 ♌	18 ♒	28 ♋	26 ♈	24 ♑	11 ♑	13 ♐	0 ♒
FEB.	3	3	19	26	28	18 ♒	12 ♒	21 ♑	20 ♑
MAR. ...	2	3	21	24	3 ♉	10 ♓	11 ♓	26 ♒	19 ♒
APR.	2	2	22	24	9	4 ♈	11 ♈	5 ♈	14 ♈
MAY	3	2	23	25	16	27	11 ♉	12 ♉	29 ♉
JUNE ...	3	3	24	27	24	20 ♉	10 ♊	20 ♊	21 ♉
JULY ...	4	4	23	1 ♌	0 ♊	12 ♊	9 ♋	27 ♋	26 ♊
AUG. ...	5	5	22	5	6	3 ♋	9 ♌	5 ♍	28 ♌
SEPT. ...	5	6	21	9	10	23	8 ♍	12 ♎	3 ♎
OCT. ...	5	7	20	12	12	12 ♌	8 ♎	18 ♏	20 ♍
NOV. ...	5	7	20	14	10	29	8 ♏	24 ♐	7 ♏
DEC. ...	5	7	20	15	6	15 ♍	9 ♐	26 ♑	24 ♐

1918

MONTH	♇	♆	♅	♄	♃	♂	☉	♀	☿
JAN.	4♋	6♌	21♒	13♌	3♊	27♍	10♑	22♒	15♑
FEB.	4	6	23	11	2	3♎	12♒	25♒	18♑
MAR. ...	3	5	25	9	3	29♍	10♓	13♒	0♓
APR.	3	4	26	8	8	18	11♈	26♒	28♈
MAY	4	4	27	8	14	14	10♉	24♓	3♉
JUNE ...	4	5	28	10	20	21	10♊	28♈	17♉
JULY ...	5	6	27	13	27	4♎	9♋	3♊	14♋
AUG. ...	6	7	26	17	4♋	21	8♌	9♋	5♍
SEPT. ...	6	8	25	21	10	10♏	8♍	17♌	9♍
OCT. ...	7	9	24	24	14	0♐	7♎	24♍	27♍
NOV. ...	6	9	24	27	16	23	8♏	3♏	19♏
DEC. ...	6	9	24	28	15	15♑	8♐	10♐	0♑

1919

MONTH	♇	♆	♅	♄	♃	♂	☉	♀	☿
JAN.	5♋	9♌	25♒	28♌	11♋	10♒	10♑	19♑	18♐
FEB.	5	8	27	26	7	4♓	12♒	28♒	26♑
MAR. ...	5	7	28	24	6	26	10♓	3♈	15♓
APR.	5	7	0♓	22	7	20♈	11♈	11♉	22♈
MAY	5	7	1	21	11	12♉	10♉	17♊	14♈
JUNE ...	5	7	2	23	17	4♊	10♊	22♋	28♉
JULY ...	6	8	1	25	23	25	9♋	24♌	29♋
AUG. ...	7	9	1	29	0♌	16♋	8♌	20♍	29♌
SEPT. ...	7	10	29♒	3♍	6	6♌	8♍	25♍	20♌
OCT. ...	8	11	28	6	12	25	7♎	11♍	11♎
NOV. ...	8	12	28	9	16	13♍	8♏	24♍	28♏
DEC. ...	7	11	28	11	18	1♎	8♐	22♎	12♐

1920

MONTH	♇	♆	♅	♄	♃	♂	☉	♀	☿
JAN.	7♋	11♌	29♒	12♍	17♌	17♎	10♑	27♏	20♐
FEB.	6	10	1♓	10	13	0♏	11♒	4♑	8♒
MAR. ...	6	9	2	8	10	8	11♓	9♒	28♓
APR.	6	9	4	6	8	7	11♈	17♓	22♓
MAY	6	9	5	5	9	27♎	11♉	24♈	18♈
JUNE ...	7	9	6	5	13	21	11♊	2♊	19♊
JULY ...	7	10	6	7	18	27	9♋	9♋	5♌
AUG. ...	8	11	5	10	24	10♏	9♌	17♌	1♌
SEPT. ...	9	12	3	14	1♍	28	9♍	28♏	1♍
OCT. ...	9	13	2	18	7	18♐	8♎	2♏	24♎
NOV. ...	9	14	2	21	13	10♑	9♏	10♐	1♐
DEC. ...	8	14	2	24	17	3♒	9♐	17♑	19♏

1921

MONTH	♇	♆	♅	♄	♃	♂	☉	♀	☿
JAN.	8 ♋	13 ♌	3 ♓	25 ♍	19 ♍	27 ♒	11 ♑	24 ♒	2 ♑
FEB.	7	12	4	24	18	21 ♓	12 ♒	29 ♓	23 ♒
MAR. ...	7	12	6	22	14	12 ♈	10 ♓	25 ♈	14 ♓
APR.	7	11	8	20	11	5 ♉	11 ♈	10 ♉	14 ♓
MAY	7	11	9	18	9	27	11 ♉	27 ♈	0 ♉
JUNE ...	8	11	10	18	10	18 ♊	10 ♊	0 ♉	2 ♋
JULY ...	8	12	10	19	13	8 ♋	9 ♋	23 ♉	19 ♋
AUG. ...	9	13	9	22	19	29	9 ♌	25 ♊	20 ♋
SEPT. ...	10	14	8	26	25	19 ♌	8 ♍	1 ♌	17 ♍
OCT. ...	10	15	7	29	1 ♎	8 ♍	8 ♎	6 ♍	2 ♏
NOV. ...	10	16	6	3 ♎	8	27	9 ♏	15 ♎	6 ♏
DEC. ...	10	16	6	6	13	15 ♎	9 ♐	22 ♏	25 ♏

1922

MONTH	♇	♆	♅	♄	♃	♂	☉	♀	☿
JAN.	9 ♋	15 ♌	7 ♓	7 ♎	17 ♎	4 ♏	10 ♑	1 ♑	13 ♑
FEB.	8	15	8	7	19	21	12 ♒	10 ♒	0 ♓
MAR. ...	8	14	10	6	18	5 ♐	10 ♓	15 ♓	16 ♒
APR.	8	13	11	4	14	18	11 ♈	24 ♈	20 ♓
MAY	8	13	13	2	11	25	10 ♉	1 ♊	18 ♉
JUNE ...	9	14	13	1	9	22	10 ♊	8 ♋	0 ♋
JULY ...	10	14	14	1	10	13	9 ♋	14 ♌	22 ♊
AUG. ...	10	15	13	4	13	13	8 ♌	20 ♍	2 ♌
SEPT. ...	11	17	12	7	18	24	8 ♍	24 ♎	29 ♍
OCT. ...	11	17	11	10	25	11 ♑	8 ♎	23 ♏	0 ♏
NOV. ...	11	18	10	14	1 ♏	1 ♒	8 ♏	10 ♐	20 ♎
DEC. ...	11	18	10	17	8	23	9 ♐	29 ♏	6 ♐

1923

MONTH	♇	♆	♅	♄	♃	♂	☉	♀	☿
JAN.	10 ♋	18 ♌	10 ♓	19 ♎	13 ♏	15 ♓	10 ♑	0 ♐	25 ♑
FEB.	10	17	12	20	17	8 ♈	12 ♒	25 ♐	4 ♒
MAR. ...	9	16	13	19	19	28	10 ♓	25 ♑	14 ♒
APR.	9	16	15	17	18	20 ♉	11 ♈	0 ♓	3 ♈
MAY	9	15	16	15	15	10 ♊	10 ♉	6 ♈	0 ♊
JUNE ...	10	16	17	14	11	1 ♋	10 ♊	13 ♉	5 ♊
JULY ...	11	16	18	14	9	21	9 ♋	19 ♊	18 ♊
AUG. ...	11	18	17	15	10	11 ♌	8 ♌	27 ♋	19 ♌
SEPT. ...	12	19	16	18	13	0 ♍	8 ♍	6 ♍	5 ♎
OCT. ...	12	20	15	21	19	20	7 ♎	13 ♎	3 ♎
NOV. ...	12	20	14	25	25	9 ♎	8 ♏	22 ♏	29 ♎
DEC. ...	11	20	14	28	2 ♐	28	8 ♐	29 ♐	17 ♐

1924

MONTH	♇	♆	♅	♄	♃	♂	☉	♀	☿
JAN.	11 ♋	20 ♌	14 ♓	1 ♏	8 ♐	18 ♏	10 ♑	8 ♒	28 ♑
FEB.	11	19	16	2	14	8 ♐	11 ♒	16 ♓	16 ♑
MAR. ...	10	18	17	2	18	27	11 ♓	21 ♈	24 ♒
APR.	10	18	19	0	20	16 ♑	11 ♈	26 ♉	22 ♈
MAY	11	18	20	28 ♎	19	4 ♒	11 ♉	26 ♊	21 ♉
JUNE ...	11	18	21	26	16	20	11 ♊	16 ♋	17 ♉
JULY ...	12	19	22	26	12	2 ♓	9 ♋	9 ♋	4 ♋
AUG. ...	13	20	21	27	10	5	9 ♌	3 ♋	3 ♍
SEPT. ...	13	21	20	29	11	28 ♒	9 ♍	23 ♋	26 ♍
OCT. ...	13	22	19	2 ♏	14	26	8 ♎	23 ♌	21 ♍
NOV. ...	13	22	18	6	20	5 ♓	9 ♏	29 ♍	13 ♏
DEC. ...	13	23	18	9	26	20	9 ♐	5 ♏	28 ♐

1925

MONTH	♇	♆	♅	♄	♃	♂	☉	♀	☿
JAN.	13 ♋	22 ♌	18 ♓	12 ♏	3 ♑	8 ♈	11 ♑	13 ♐	29 ♐
FEB.	12	21	19	14	10	27	12 ♒	22 ♑	22 ♑
MAR. ...	12	21	21	14	16	16 ♉	10 ♓	27 ♒	7 ♓
APR.	11	20	23	13	20	5 ♊	11 ♈	5 ♈	0 ♉
MAY	12	20	24	11	22	25	11 ♉	13 ♉	22 ♈
JUNE ...	12	20	25	9	22	14 ♋	10 ♊	21 ♊	21 ♉
JULY ...	13	21	25	8	19	3 ♌	9 ♋	27 ♋	23 ♋
AUG. ...	14	22	25	8	15	23	9 ♌	5 ♍	5 ♍
SEPT. ...	14	23	24	10	13	12 ♍	9 ♍	13 ♎	27 ♌
OCT. ...	15	24	23	12	13	2 ♎	8 ♎	18 ♏	3 ♎
NOV. ...	15	25	22	16	17	22	9 ♏	24 ♐	24 ♏
DEC. ...	14	25	22	20	22	12 ♏	9 ♐	26 ♑	27 ♐

1926

MONTH	♇	♆	♅	♄	♃	♂	☉	♀	☿
JAN.	14 ♋	24 ♌	22 ♓	23 ♏	29 ♑	3 ♐	10 ♑	21 ♒	18 ♐
FEB.	13	24	23	25	6 ♒	25	12 ♒	22 ♒	2 ♒
MAR.	13	23	25	26	13	14 ♉	10 ♓	10 ♒	22 ♓
APR.	13	22	26	26	19	7 ♒	11 ♈	29 ♒	9 ♈
MAY	13	22	28	24	24	28	10 ♉	25 ♓	14 ♈
JUNE ...	13	22	29	21	27	21 ♓	10 ♊	29 ♈	6 ♊
JULY ...	14	23	29	20	27	11 ♈	9 ♋	3 ♊	3 ♌
AUG. ...	15	24	29	19	24	0 ♉	8 ♌	10 ♋	19 ♌
SEPT. ...	16	25	28	21	20	14	8 ♍	17 ♌	22 ♌
OCT. ...	16	26	27	23	18	19	8 ♎	25 ♍	17 ♎
NOV. ...	16	27	26	26	18	12	8 ♏	3 ♏	1 ♐
DEC. ...	16	27	26	0 ♐	21	5	9 ♐	11 ♐	27 ♏

1927

MONTH	♇	♆	♅	♄	♃	♂	☉	♀	☿
JAN.	15 ♋	27 ♌	26 ♓	3 ♐	26 ♒	8 ♉	10 ♑	20 ♑	25 ♐
FEB.	14	26	27	6	3 ♓	20	12 ♒	29 ♒	14 ♒
MAR. ...	14	25	28	7	10	4 ♊	10 ♓	4 ♈	27 ♓
APR.	14	25	0 ♈	8	17	21	11 ♈	12 ♉	15 ♓
MAY	14	24	2	6	24	8 ♋	10 ♉	17 ♊	21 ♈
JUNE ...	15	24	3	4	29	27	10 ♊	23 ♋	24 ♊
JULY ...	15	25	3	2	3 ♈	15 ♌	9 ♋	24 ♌	1 ♌
AUG. ...	16	26	3	1	3	5 ♍	8 ♌	19 ♍	22 ♋
SEPT. ...	17	27	2	2	1	24	8 ♍	22 ♍	7 ♍
OCT. ...	17	28	1	4	27 ♓	14 ♎	7 ♎	9 ♍	27 ♎
NOV. ...	17	29	0	7	24	4 ♏	8 ♏	23 ♍	25 ♏
DEC. ...	17	29	0	10	23	25	8 ♐	22 ♎	19 ♏

1928

MONTH	♇	♆	♅	♄	♃	♂	☉	♀	☿
JAN.	16 ♋	29 ♌	0 ♈	14 ♐	27 ♓	17 ♐	10 ♑	27 ♏	5 ♑
FEB.	16	28	2	17	2 ♈	10 ♑	11 ♒	4 ♑	27 ♒
MAR. ...	15	27	2	19	8	2 ♒	11 ♓	10 ♒	29 ♒
APR.	15	27	4	19	15	25	12 ♈	18 ♓	16 ♓
MAY	15	26	5	18	23	18 ♓	11 ♉	24 ♈	9 ♉
JUNE ...	16	27	7	16	29	12 ♈	11 ♊	3 ♊	4 ♋
JULY ...	17	27	7	14	5 ♉	4 ♉	9 ♋	9 ♋	6 ♋
AUG. ...	17	28	7	13	9	25	9 ♌	18 ♌	24 ♋
SEPT. ...	18	29	6	13	10	14 ♊	9 ♍	26 ♍	23 ♍
OCT. ...	18	0 ♍	5	14	9	29	8 ♎	3 ♏	4 ♏
NOV. ...	18	1	4	17	5	9 ♋	10 ♏	11 ♐	24 ♎
DEC. ...	18	1	4	20	1	7	9 ♐	17 ♑	0 ♐

1929

MONTH	♇	♆	♅	♄	♃	♂	☉	♀	☿
JAN.	17 ♋	1 ♍	4 ♈	24 ♐	1 ♉	25 ♊	11 ♑	24 ♒	19 ♑
FEB.	17	0	5	27	3	21	12 ♒	29 ♓	23 ♒
MAR. ...	16	0	6	29	7	27	10 ♓	25 ♈	13 ♒
APR.	16	29 ♌	8	0 ♑	13	9 ♋	11 ♈	8 ♉	26 ♓
MAY	16	29	9	0	20	24	11 ♉	24 ♈	26 ♉
JUNE ...	17	29	11	28 ♐	27	11 ♌	10 ♊	29 ♈	22 ♊
JULY ...	18	29	11	26	4 ♊	28	9 ♋	24 ♉	18 ♊
AUG. ...	18	0 ♍	11	24	10	17 ♍	9 ♌	26 ♊	10 ♌
SEPT. ...	19	1	11	24	15	7 ♎	9 ♍	1 ♌	3 ♎
OCT. ...	20	2	9	25	16	27	8 ♎	7 ♍	21 ♎
NOV. ...	20	3	8	27	15	18 ♏	9 ♏	15 ♎	23 ♎
DEC. ...	19	4	8	0 ♑	12	9 ♐	9 ♐	23 ♏	11 ♐

1930

MONTH	♇	♆	♅	♄	♃	♂	☉	♀	☿
JAN.	19 ♋	3 ♍	8 ♈	4 ♑	8 ♊	2 ♑	10 ♑	2 ♑	29 ♑
FEB.	18	3	8	7	6	26	12 ♒	11 ♒	22 ♑
MAR. ...	18	2	10	10	8	18 ♒	10 ♓	16 ♓	17 ♒
APR.	17	1	11	12	12	12 ♓	11 ♈	24 ♈	11 ♈
MAY	18	1	13	12	17	5 ♈	10 ♉	1 ♊	0 ♊
JUNE ...	18	1	14	11	24	29	10 ♊	9 ♋	24 ♉
JULY ...	19	1	15	9	1 ♋	21 ♉	9 ♋	15 ♌	23 ♊
AUG. ...	20	2	15	6	8	12 ♊	8 ♌	20 ♍	26 ♌
SEPT. ...	20	4	15	5	14	3 ♋	8 ♍	24 ♎	4 ♎
OCT. ...	21	5	14	6	18	20	8 ♎	22 ♏	22 ♍
NOV. ...	21	5	12	7	20	5 ♌	8 ♏	7 ♐	5 ♏
DEC. ...	21	6	12	10	20	15	9 ♐	25 ♏	22 ♐

1931

MONTH	♇	♆	♅	♄	♃	♂	☉	♀	☿
JAN.	20 ♋	6 ♍	12 ♈	14 ♑	16 ♋	16 ♌	10 ♑	29 ♏	20 ♑
FEB.	19	5	12	17	12	5	12 ♒	25 ♐	17 ♑
MAR. ...	19	4	13	20	11	28 ♋	10 ♓	25 ♑	28 ♒
APR.	19	3	15	22	11	1 ♌	11 ♈	1 ♓	27 ♈
MAY	19	3	17	23	15	11	10 ♉	6 ♈	8 ♉
JUNE ...	19	3	18	23	20	25	10 ♊	14 ♉	16 ♉
JULY ...	20	4	19	21	27	12 ♍	9 ♋	20 ♊	10 ♋
AUG. ...	21	5	19	19	3 ♌	0 ♎	8 ♌	28 ♋	4 ♍
SEPT. ...	22	6	19	17	10	20	8 ♍	6 ♍	15 ♍
OCT. ...	22	7	18	17	16	10 ♏	7 ♎	14 ♎	24 ♍
NOV. ...	22	8	17	18	20	1 ♐	8 ♏	22 ♏	17 ♏
DEC. ...	22	8	16	20	23	24	8 ♐	0 ♑	29 ♐

1932

MONTH	♇	♆	♅	♄	♃	♂	☉	♀	☿
JAN.	21 ♋	8 ♍	15 ♈	24 ♑	22 ♌	17 ♑	10 ♑	8 ♒	20 ♐
FEB.	21	7	16	27	18	11 ♒	11 ♒	16 ♓	25 ♑
MAR. ...	20	7	17	1 ♒	15	4 ♓	11 ♓	21 ♈	14 ♓
APR.	20	6	19	3	13	29	12 ♈	26 ♉	25 ♈
MAY	20	5	21	5	13	22 ♈	11 ♉	26 ♊	16 ♈
JUNE ...	21	5	22	5	17	15 ♉	11 ♊	15 ♋	27 ♉
JULY ...	21	6	23	3	22	6 ♊	9 ♋	6 ♋	29 ♋
AUG. ...	22	7	23	1	28	28	9 ♌	1 ♋	2 ♍
SEPT. ...	23	8	23	29 ♑	5 ♍	18 ♋	10 ♍	23 ♋	21 ♌
OCT. ...	23	9	22	28	11	6 ♌	8 ♎	24 ♌	10 ♎
NOV. ...	23	10	21	29	17	24	9 ♏	29 ♍	28 ♏
DEC. ...	23	10	20	1 ♒	21	8 ♍	9 ♐	6 ♏	17 ♐

1933

MONTH	♇	♆	♅	♄	♃	♂	☉	♀	☿
JAN.	23 ♋	10 ♍	19 ♈	4 ♒	23 ♍	18 ♍	11 ♑	14 ♐	20 ♐
FEB.	22	10	20	8	22	19	12 ♒	23 ♑	8 ♒
MAR. ...	21	9	21	11	19	11	10 ♓	28 ♒	27 ♓
APR.	21	8	23	14	16	2	11 ♈	6 ♈	26 ♓
MAY	21	7	24	16	13	3	11 ♉	13 ♉	16 ♈
JUNE ...	22	7	26	16	14	13	11 ♊	21 ♊	15 ♊
JULY ...	23	8	27	15	17	27	9 ♋	28 ♋	5 ♌
AUG. ...	23	9	27	13	22	15 ♎	9 ♌	6 ♍	5 ♌
SEPT. ...	24	10	27	11	28	4 ♏	9 ♍	13 ♎	29 ♌
OCT. ...	24	11	26	10	5 ♎	24	8 ♎	19 ♏	22 ♎
NOV. ...	25	12	25	10	11	17 ♐	9 ♏	24 ♐	2 ♐
DEC. ...	24	12	24	12	17	9 ♑	9 ♐	26 ♑	19 ♏

1934

MONTH	♇	♆	♅	♄	♃	♂	☉	♀	☿
JAN.	24 ♋	12 ♍	23 ♈	14 ♒	21 ♎	3 ♒	10 ♑	20 ♒	0 ♑
FEB.	23	12	24	18	23	28	12 ♒	18 ♒	21 ♒
MAR. ...	23	11	25	21	22	20 ♓	10 ♓	8 ♒	19 ♓
APR.	23	10	26	25	19	14 ♈	11 ♈	26 ♒	13 ♓
MAY	23	10	28	27	16	7 ♉	10 ♉	25 ♓	28 ♈
JUNE ...	23	10	0 ♉	28	13	29	10 ♊	29 ♈	0 ♋
JULY ...	24	10	1	28	14	20 ♊	9 ♋	4 ♊	24 ♋
AUG. ...	25	11	1	26	17	11 ♋	9 ♌	10 ♋	19 ♋
SEPT. ...	25	12	1	24	22	1 ♌	8 ♍	18 ♌	14 ♍
OCT. ...	26	13	0	22	28	20	8 ♎	25 ♍	1 ♏
NOV. ...	26	14	29 ♈	22	5 ♏	8 ♍	8 ♏	4 ♏	12 ♏
DEC. ...	26	15	28	23	11	25	9 ♐	12 ♐	23 ♏

1935

MONTH	♇	♆	♅	♄	♃	♂	☉	♀	☿
JAN.	25 ♋	15 ♍	28 ♈	25 ♒	17 ♏	10 ♎	10 ♑	21 ♑	11 ♑
FEB.	25	14	28	28	21	21	12 ♒	0 ♓	0 ♓
MAR. ...	24	13	29	2 ♓	23	25	10 ♓	4 ♈	19 ♒
APR.	24	12	0 ♉	5	23	18	11 ♈	12 ♉	18 ♓
MAY	24	12	2	8	20	8	10 ♉	18 ♊	15 ♉
JUNE ...	24	12	4	10	16	7	10 ♊	23 ♋	2 ♋
JULY ...	25	12	5	10	14	16	9 ♋	24 ♌	25 ♊
AUG. ...	26	13	5	9	14	2 ♏	8 ♌	18 ♍	29 ♋
SEPT. ...	27	14	5	7	17	20	8 ♍	19 ♍	27 ♍
OCT. ...	27	15	5	5	22	10 ♐	7 ♎	7 ♍	2 ♏
NOV. ...	27	16	3	4	28	3 ♑	8 ♏	23 ♍	20 ♎
DEC. ...	27	17	2	4	5 ♐	26	8 ♐	22 ♎	3 ♐

1936

MONTH	♇	♆	♅	♄	♃	♂	☉	♀	☿
JAN.	27 ♋	17 ♍	2 ♉	6 ♓	12 ♐	20 ♒	10 ♑	28 ♏	23 ♑
FEB.	26	16	2	9	18	14 ♓	11 ♒	5 ♑	10 ♒
MAR. ...	25	16	3	13	22	6 ♈	11 ♓	10 ♒	14 ♒
APR.	25	15	4	16	24	0 ♉	12 ♈	18 ♓	2 ♈
MAY	25	14	6	19	24	22	11 ♉	25 ♈	1 ♊
JUNE ...	26	14	8	22	21	13 ♊	11 ♊	3 ♊	9 ♊
JULY ...	26	14	9	23	17	4 ♋	9 ♋	10 ♋	19 ♊
AUG. ...	27	15.	10	22	15	24	9 ♌	18 ♌	18 ♌
SEPT. ...	28	16	9	20	15	14 ♌	9 ♍	26 ♍	6 ♎
OCT. ...	29	17	9	18	18	3 ♍	8 ♎	3 ♏	7 ♎
NOV. ...	29	18	8	16	24	22	9 ♏	11 ♐	28 ♎
DEC. ...	29	19	6	16	0 ♑	10 ♎	8 ♐	18 ♑	16 ♐

1937

MONTH	♇	♆	♅	♄	♃	♂	☉	♀	☿
JAN.	28 ♋	19 ♍	6 ♉	17 ♓	7 ♑	28 ♎	11 ♑	22 ♒	0 ♒
FEB.	27	18	6	20	14	14 ♏	12 ♒	29 ♓	18 ♑
MAR. ...	27	18	7	23	20	26	11 ♓	25 ♈	22 ♒
APR.	26	17	8	27	24	5 ♐	11 ♈	5 ♉	19 ♈
MAY	27	16	10	1 ♈	27	4	11 ♉	21 ♈	24 ♉
JUNE ...	27	16	11	3	27	24 ♏	11 ♊	28 ♈	18 ♉
JULY ...	28	17	13	5	24	20	9 ♋	24 ♉	1 ♋
AUG. ...	29	17	14	5	20	27	9 ♌	26 ♊	1 ♍
SEPT. ...	29	18	14	3	18	12 ♐	9 ♍	2 ♌	0 ♎
OCT. ...	0 ♌	19	13	1	18	1 ♑	8 ♎	8 ♍	20 ♍
NOV. ...	0	20	12	29 ♓	21	22	9 ♏	16 ♎	11 ♏
DEC. ...	0	21	11	28	26	15 ♒	9 ♐	23 ♏	27 ♐

1938

MONTH	♇	♆	♅	♄	♃	♂	☉	♀	☿
JAN.	29 ♋	21 ♍	10 ♉	29 ♓	3 ♒	8 ♓	10 ♑	2 ♑	5 ♑
FEB.	29	21	10	2 ♈	10	1 ♈	12 ♒	11 ♒	20 ♑
MAR. ...	28	20	10	5	17	22	10 ♓	16 ♓	4 ♓
APR.	28	19	12	8	23	14 ♉	11 ♈	25 ♈	0 ♉
MAY	28	19	14	12	28	5 ♊	10 ♉	2 ♊	26 ♈
JUNE ...	28	18	15	15	2 ♓	26	10 ♊	9 ♋	19 ♑
JULY ...	29	19	17	17	2	16 ♋	9 ♋	15 ♌	19 ♋
AUG. ...	0 ♌	19	18	18	0	6 ♌	9 ♌	21 ♍	6 ♍
SEPT. ...	1	20	18	17	26 ♒	26	8 ♍	24 ♎	1 ♍
OCT. ...	1	22	18	15	23	15 ♍	8 ♎	22 ♏	1 ♎
NOV. ...	2	23	16	13	23	5 ♎	8 ♏	5 ♐	22 ♏
DEC. ...	1	23	15	11	25	23	9 ♐	21 ♏	29 ♐

1939

MONTH	♇	♆	♅	♄	♃	♂	☉	♀	☿
JAN.	1 ♌	23 ♍	14 ♉	12 ♈	1 ♓	13 ♏	10 ♑	28 ♏	18 ♐
FEB.	0	23	14	13	7	2 ♐	12 ♒	25 ♐	0 ♒
MAR.	0	22	14	16	14	19	10 ♓	25 ♑	19 ♓
APR.	29 ♋	21	16	20	21	6 ♑	11 ♈	1 ♓	14 ♈
MAY	29	21	17	23	28	21	10 ♉	7 ♈	13 ♈
JUNE ...	0 ♌	21	19	27	4 ♈	2 ♒	10 ♊	14 ♉	3 ♊
JULY ...	0	21	21	0 ♉	8	4	9 ♋	21 ♊	2 ♌
AUG. ...	1	21	22	1	9	27 ♑	8 ♌	29 ♋	23 ♌
SEPT. ...	2	23	22	1	7	24	8 ♍	7 ♍	21 ♌
OCT. ...	3	24	22	29 ♈	3	3 ♒	7 ♎	14 ♎	14 ♎
NOV. ...	3	25	20	27	0	19	8 ♏	23 ♏	0 ♐
DEC. ...	3	25	19	25	29 ♓	8 ♓	8 ♐	0 ♑	2 ♐

1940

MONTH	♇	♆	♅	♄	♃	♂	☉	♀	☿
JAN.	2 ♌	26 ♍	18 ♉	24 ♈	1 ♈	28 ♓	10 ♑	9 ♒	23 ♐
FEB.	2	25	18	26	6	19 ♈	11 ♒	17 ♓	12 ♒
MAR. ...	1	25	19	28	12	9 ♉	11 ♓	22 ♈	29 ♓
APR.	1	24	20	1 ♉	19	0 ♊	12 ♈	27 ♉	17 ♓
MAY	1	23	21	5	27	20	11 ♉	26 ♊	21 ♈
JUNE ...	1	23	23	9	4 ♉	10 ♋	11 ♊	13 ♋	23 ♊
JULY ...	2	23	25	12	9	29	9 ♋	2 ♋	3 ♌
AUG. ...	3	24	26	14	14	18 ♌	9 ♌	0 ♋	25 ♋
SEPT. ...	4	25	26	15	15	8 ♍	9 ♍	23 ♋	6 ♍
OCT. ...	4	26	26	14	14	27	8 ♎	24 ♌	27 ♎
NOV. ...	4	27	25	11	11	17 ♎	9 ♏	0 ♎	28 ♏
DEC. ...	4	27	24	9	7	7 ♏	9 ♐	6 ♏	19 ♏

1941

MONTH	♇	♆	♅	♄	♃	♂	☉	♀	☿
JAN.	4 ♌	28 ♍	23 ♉	8 ♉	6 ♉	28 ♏	11 ♑	15 ♐	5 ♑
FEB.	3	27	22	8	7	19 ♐	12 ♒	23 ♑	27 ♒
MAR. ...	2	27	23	10	11	8 ♑	11 ♓	28 ♒	4 ♓
APR.	2	26	24	13	17	29	11 ♈	7 ♈	15 ♓
MAY	2	25	25	17	24	20 ♒	11 ♉	14 ♉	5 ♉
JUNE ...	3	25	27	21	1 ♊	11 ♓	11 ♊	22 ♊	4 ♋
JULY ...	3	25	29	24	8	0 ♈	9 ♋	29 ♋	11 ♋
AUG. ...	4	26	0 ♊	27	14	15	9 ♌	6 ♍	22 ♋
SEPT. ...	5	27	0	28	19	24	9 ♍	14 ♎	21 ♍
OCT. ...	6	28	0	28	21	20	8 ♎	19 ♏	3 ♏
NOV. ...	6	29	29 ♉	26	21	12	9 ♏	25 ♐	28 ♎
DEC. ...	6	0 ♎	28	24	17	14	9 ♐	26 ♑	28 ♏

1942

MONTH	♇	♆	♅	♄	♃	♂	☉	♀	☿
JAN.	5 ♌	0 ♎	27 ♉	22 ♉	13 ♊	25 ♈	10 ♑	19 ♒	17 ♑
FEB.	4	0	26	22	11	11 ♉	12 ♒	14 ♒	27 ♒
MAR. ...	4	29 ♍	27	23	12	27	10 ♓	6 ♒	14 ♒
APR.	4	28	28	26	16	15 ♊	11 ♈	25 ♒	23 ♓
MAY	4	27	29	29	21	3 ♋	10 ♉	25 ♓	23 ♉
JUNE ...	4	27	1 ♊	3 ♊	28	22	10 ♊	29 ♈	26 ♊
JULY ...	5	27	3	7	5 ♋	11 ♌	9 ♋	4 ♊	19 ♊
AUG. ...	5	28	4	10	12	0 ♍	9 ♌	11 ♋	7 ♌
SEPT. ...	6	29	5	12	18	20	8 ♍	19 ♌	2 ♎
OCT. ...	7	0 ♎	4	12	23	9 ♎	8 ♎	26 ♍	26 ♎
NOV. ...	7	1	4	11	25	0 ♏	8 ♏	5 ♏	22 ♎
DEC. ...	7	2	2	9	25	20	9 ♐	12 ♐	9 ♐

1943

MONTH	♇	♆	♅	♄	♃	♂	☉	♀	☿
JAN.	7 ♌	2 ♎	1 ♊	7 ♊	22 ♋	12 ♐	10 ♑	21 ♑	27 ♑
FEB.	6	2	1	6	18	4 ♑	12 ♒	0 ♓	26 ♑
MAR. ...	5	1	1	6	15	25	10 ♓	5 ♈	16 ♒
APR.	5	0	2	8	16	18 ♒	11 ♈	13 ♉	8 ♈
MAY	5	0	3	11	19	11 ♓	10 ♉	18 ♊	1 ♊
JUNE ...	5	29 ♍	5	15	24	4 ♈	10 ♊	24 ♋	27 ♉
JULY ...	6	29	7	19	0 ♌	25	9 ♋	24 ♌	21 ♊
AUG. ...	7	0 ♎	8	23	7	16 ♉	8 ♌	17 ♍	23 ♌
SEPT. ...	8	1	9	25	14	5 ♊	8 ♍	15 ♍	5 ♎
OCT. ...	8	2	9	27	20	18	7 ♎	5 ♍	25 ♍
NOV. ...	9	3	8	26	24	22	8 ♏	22 ♍	3 ♏
DEC. ...	9	4	7	24	27	14	8 ♐	22 ♎	20 ♐

1944

MONTH	♇	♆	♅	♄	♃	♂	☉	♀	☿
JAN.	8 ♌	4 ♎	6 ♊	22 ♊	27 ♌	5 ♊	10 ♑	28 ♏	25 ♑
FEB.	8	4	5	20	23	8	12 ♒	5 ♑	16 ♑
MAR.	7	3	5	20	20	18	11 ♓	11 ♒	27 ♒
APR.	6	3	6	21	17	2 ♋	12 ♈	19 ♓	26 ♈
MAY	6	2	7	24	18	18	11 ♉	26 ♈	13 ♉
JUNE ...	7	2	9	28	21	6 ♌	11 ♊	4 ♊	17 ♉
JULY ...	7	2	11	1 ♋	25	24	9 ♋	11 ♋	9 ♋
AUG. ...	8	2	12	5	1 ♍	13 ♍	9 ♌	19 ♌	5 ♍
SEPT. ...	9	3	13	8	8	2 ♎	9 ♍	27 ♍	19 ♍
OCT. ...	10	4	13	10	14	22	8 ♎	4 ♏	24 ♍
NOV. ...	10	5	12	11	20	13 ♏	9 ♏	12 ♐	16 ♏
DEC. ...	10	6	11	9	25	4 ♐	9 ♐	18 ♑	0 ♑

1945

MONTH	♇	♆	♅	♄	♃	♂	☉	♀	☿
JAN.	10 ♌	6 ♎	10 ♊	7 ♋	27 ♍	27 ♐	11 ♑	25 ♒	23 ♐
FEB.	9	6	9	5	27	20 ♑	12 ♒	29 ♓	24 ♑
MAR. ...	8	6	9	4	24	12 ♒	11 ♓	24 ♈	11 ♓
APR.	8	5	10	4	20	6 ♓	11 ♈	3 ♉	28 ♈
MAY	8	4	11	7	18	29	11 ♉	18 ♈	18 ♈
JUNE ...	8	4	13	10	18	23 ♈	11 ♊	27 ♈	24 ♉
JULY ...	9	4	15	14	21	14 ♉	9 ♋	24 ♉	26 ♋
AUG. ...	10	4	16	18	25	6 ♊	9 ♌	27 ♊	4 ♍
SEPT. ...	11	5	17	21	1 ♎	26	9 ♍	2 ♌	22 ♌
OCT. ...	11	6	17	24	8	13 ♋	8 ♎	8 ♍	7 ♎
NOV. ...	12	7	17	25	14	27	9 ♏	17 ♎	27 ♏
DEC. ...	12	8	16	24	20	3 ♌	9 ♐	24 ♏	22 ♐

1946

MONTH	♇	♆	♅	♄	♃	♂	☉	♀	☿
JAN.	11 ♌	9 ♎	14 ♊	22 ♋	25 ♎	28 ♋	10 ♑	3 ♑	19 ♐
FEB.	11	8	14	20	27	17	12 ♒	12 ♒	5 ♒
MAR. ...	10	8	13	18	27	14	10 ♓	17 ♓	25 ♓
APR.	10	7	14	18	24	22	11 ♈	26 ♈	0 ♈
MAY	9	6	15	20	20	4 ♌	11 ♉	3 ♊	15 ♈
JUNE ...	10	6	17	20	18	20	10 ♊	10 ♋	12 ♊
JULY ...	10	6	19	26	18	6 ♍	9 ♋	16 ♌	5 ♌
AUG. ...	11	6	20	0 ♌	21	25	9 ♌	21 ♍	11 ♌
SEPT. ...	12	7	22	4	25	15 ♎	8 ♍	25 ♎	26 ♌
OCT. ...	13	8	22	7	1 ♏	5 ♏	8 ♎	21 ♏	20 ♎
NOV. ...	13	9	21	9	8	26	8 ♏	2 ♐	2 ♐
DEC. ...	13	10	20	9	14	18 ♐	9 ♐	18 ♏	21 ♏

1947

MONTH	♇	♆	♅	♄	♃	♂	☉	♀	☿
JAN.	13 ♌	11 ♎	19 ♊	7 ♌	20 ♏	11 ♑	10 ♑	27 ♏	28 ♐
FEB.	12	11	18	4	25	5 ♒	12 ♒	25 ♐	18 ♒
MAR. ...	12	10	18	3	27	27	10 ♓	26 ♑	23 ♓
APR.	11	9	18	2	27	22 ♓	11 ♈	2 ♓	14 ♓
MAY	11	9	20	3	24	15 ♈	10 ♉	8 ♈	25 ♈
JUNE ...	11	8	21	5	20	8 ♉	10 ♊	15 ♉	28 ♊
JULY ...	12	8	23	8	18	0 ♊	9 ♋	21 ♊	27 ♋
AUG. ...	13	9	25	12	18	22	8 ♌	29 ♋	19 ♋
SEPT. ...	14	9	26	16	21	12 ♋	8 ♍	8 ♍	11 ♍
OCT. ...	14	10	26	19	26	0 ♌	7 ♎	15 ♎	0 ♏
NOV. ...	15	12	26	22	2 ♐	17	8 ♏	24 ♏	18 ♏
DEC. ...	15	12	25	23	8	0 ♍	8 ♐	1 ♑	21 ♏

1948

MONTH	♇	♆	♅	♄	♃	♂	☉	♀	☿
JAN.	14 ♌	13 ♎	23 ♊	22 ♌	15 ♐	7 ♍	10 ♑	10 ♒	9 ♑
FEB.	14	13	22	20	21	4	12 ♒	18 ♓	29 ♒
MAR. ...	13	12	22	18	26	23 ♌	11 ♓	22 ♈	22 ♒
APR.	13	12	23	16	29	18	12 ♈	27 ♉	18 ♓
MAY	13	11	24	16	29	24	11 ♉	26 ♊	14 ♉
JUNE ...	13	10	25	18	26	6 ♍	11 ♊	11 ♋	4 ♋
JULY ...	14	10	27	20	22	21	10 ♋	29 ♊	29 ♊
AUG. ...	14	11	29	24	19	9 ♎	9 ♌	29 ♊	28 ♋
SEPT. ...	15	12	0 ♋	28	20	29	9 ♍	23 ♋	27 ♍
OCT. ...	16	13	1	1 ♍	22	19 ♏	8 ♎	24 ♌	3 ♏
NOV. ...	16	14	0	4	27	11 ♐	9 ♏	0 ♎	21 ♎
DEC. ...	16	15	29 ♊	6	3 ♑	4 ♑	9 ♐	7 ♏	3 ♐

1949

MONTH	♇	♆	♅	♄	♃	♂	☉	♀	☿
JAN.	16 ♌	15 ♎	28 ♊	6 ♍	11 ♑	27 ♑	11 ♑	15 ♐	22 ♑
FEB.	15	15	27	4	18	22 ♒	12 ♒	24 ♑	15 ♒
MAR. ...	15	15	27	2	23	14 ♓	11 ♓	29 ♒	14 ♒
APR.	14	14	27	0	29	8 ♈	11 ♈	8 ♈	0 ♈
MAY	14	13	28	29 ♌	2 ♒	1 ♉	11 ♉	15 ♉	29 ♉
JUNE ...	14	13	0 ♋	0 ♍	2	24	11 ♊	23 ♊	14 ♊
JULY ...	15	12	1 ♋	2	0	15 ♊	9 ♋	29 ♋	18 ♊
AUG. ...	16	13	3	6	26 ♑	6 ♋	9 ♌	7 ♍	15 ♌
SEPT. ...	17	14	4	9	23	27	9 ♍	14 ♎	5 ♎
OCT. ...	18	15	5	13	23	15 ♌	8 ♎	20 ♏	13 ♎
NOV. ...	18	16	5	17	25	3 ♍	9 ♏	25 ♐	26 ♎
DEC. ...	18	17	4	19	0 ♒	19	9 ♐	26 ♑	14 ♐

1950

MONTH	♇	♆	♅	♄	♃	♂	☉	♀	☿
JAN.	18 ♌	17 ♎	3 ♋	19 ♍	7 ♒	2 ♎	11 ♑	17 ♒	0 ♒
FEB.	17	17	2	18	14	10	12 ♒	10 ♒	19 ♑
MAR. ...	16	17	1	17	21	9	11 ♓	5 ♒	20 ♒
APR.	16	16	1	14	27	28 ♍	11 ♈	25 ♒	15 ♈
MAY	16	15	2	13	3 ♓	22	11 ♉	25 ♓	27 ♉
JUNE ...	16	15	4	13	6	27	10 ♊	0 ♉	19 ♉
JULY ...	17	15	5	14	7	8 ♎	9 ♋	5 ♊	28 ♊
AUG. ...	18	15	7	17	6	25	9 ♌	12 ♋	29 ♌
SEPT. ...	19	16	9	21	2	14 ♏	8 ♍	19 ♌	2 ♎
OCT. ...	19	17	9	25	28 ♒	4 ♐	8 ♎	27 ♍	20 ♍
NOV. ...	20	18	9	28	28	26	9 ♏	5 ♏	8 ♏
DEC. ...	20	19	9	1 ♎	0 ♓	19 ♑	9 ♐	13 ♐	25 ♐

1951

MONTH	♇	♆	♅	♄	♃	♂	☉	♀	☿
JAN.	20 ♌	19 ♎	7 ♋	3 ♎	5 ♓	14 ♒	10 ♑	22 ♑	12 ♑
FEB.	19	20	6	2	11	8 ♓	12 ♒	1 ♓	19 ♑
MAR. ...	18	19	5	1	18	0 ♈	10 ♓	6 ♈	2 ♓
APR.	18	18	6	28 ♍	26	23	11 ♈	14 ♉	29 ♈
MAY	17	17	6	26	2 ♈	16 ♉	10 ♉	19 ♊	27 ♈
JUNE ...	17	17	8	26	8	8 ♊	10 ♊	24 ♋	17 ♉
JULY ...	18	17	10	27	13	28	9 ♋	24 ♌	16 ♋
AUG. ...	19	17	11	29	14	19 ♋	9 ♌	16 ♍	6 ♍
SEPT. ...	20	18	13	2 ♎	13	9 ♌	8 ♍	12 ♍	6 ♍
OCT. ...	21	19	14	6	9	28	8 ♎	3 ♍	28 ♍
NOV. ...	22	20	14	10	6	17 ♍	8 ♏	23 ♍	20 ♏
DEC. ...	22	21	13	13	4	4 ♎	9 ♐	23 ♎	0 ♑

1952

MONTH	♇	♆	♅	♄	♃	♂	☉	♀	☿
JAN.	21 ♌	22 ♎	12 ♋	15 ♎	6 ♈	21 ♎	10 ♑	28 ♏	18 ♐
FEB.	21	22	11	15	11	6 ♏	12 ♒	6 ♑	28 ♑
MAR. ...	20	21	10	14	16	15	11 ♓	12 ♒	18 ♓
APR.	19	21	10	12	23	18	12 ♈	20 ♓	19 ♈
MAY	19	20	11	10	1 ♉	10	11 ♉	27 ♈	14 ♈
JUNE ...	19	19	12	9	8	1	11 ♊	5 ♊	2 ♊
JULY ...	20	19	14	9	14	4	10 ♋	12 ♋	2 ♌
AUG. ...	21	19	16	10	19	16	9 ♌	20 ♌	27 ♌
SEPT. ...	22	20	17	13	21	3 ♐	9 ♍	28 ♍	21 ♌
OCT. ...	23	21	18	17	20	23	8 ♎	5 ♏	14 ♎
NOV. ...	23	22	19	21	17	15 ♑	9 ♏	13 ♐	0 ♐
DEC. ...	23	23	18	24	13	8 ♒	9 ♐	19 ♑	7 ♐

1953

MONTH	♇	♆	♅	♄	♃	♂	☉	♀	☿
JAN.	23 ♌	24 ♎	17 ♋	27 ♎	11 ♉	1 ♓	11 ♑	25 ♒	23 ♐
FEB.	22	24	16	27	12	25	12 ♒	29 ♓	12 ♒
MAR. ...	22	24	15	27	16	16 ♈	11 ♓	24 ♈	29 ♓
APR.	21	23	15	25	22	9 ♉	12 ♈	0 ♉	20 ♓
MAY	21	22	15	23	28	0 ♊	11 ♉	15 ♈	19 ♈
JUNE ...	21	21	17	21	5 ♊	22	11 ♊	27 ♈	20 ♊
JULY ...	22	21	18	21	12	11 ♋	9 ♋	24 ♉	4 ♌
AUG. ...	23	21	20	22	19	2 ♌	9 ♌	27 ♊	28 ♋
SEPT. ...	24	22	22	24	24	22	9 ♍	3 ♌	3 ♍
OCT. ...	24	23	23	28	26	11 ♍	8 ♎	9 ♍	26 ♎
NOV. ...	25	24	23	1 ♏	26	1 ♎	9 ♏	17 ♎	1 ♐
DEC. ...	25	25	23	5	23	19	9 ♐	25 ♏	19 ♏

1954

MONTH	♇	♆	♅	♄	♃	♂	☉	♀	☿
JAN.	25 ♌	26 ♎	22 ♋	8 ♏	19 ♊	7 ♏	11 ♑	4 ♑	3 ♑
FEB.	24	26	20	9	17	25	12 ♒	13 ♒	25 ♒
MAR. ...	23	26	19	10	17	11 ♐	10 ♓	18 ♓	11 ♓
APR.	23	25	19	8	20	26	11 ♈	26 ♈	14 ♓
MAY	23	24	20	6	25	6 ♑	11 ♉	3 ♊	2 ♉
JUNE ...	23	24	21	4	2 ♋	8	10 ♊	11 ♋	3 ♋
JULY ...	23	23	23	3	9	1	9 ♋	16 ♌	16 ♋
AUG. ...	24	24	24	3	15	25 ♐	9 ♌	22 ♍	20 ♋
SEPT. ...	25	24	26	4	22	3 ♑	9 ♍	26 ♎	18 ♍
OCT. ...	26	25	27	8	27	19	8 ♎	21 ♏	3 ♏
NOV. ...	27	26	28	12	0 ♌	7 ♒	9 ♏	29 ♏	3 ♏
DEC. ...	27	27	27	15	0	28	9 ♐	15 ♏	26 ♏

1955

MONTH	♇	♆	♅	♄	♃	♂	☉	♀	☿
JAN.	27 ♌	28 ♎	26 ♋	19 ♏	27 ♋	20 ♓	10 ♑	26 ♏	15 ♑
FEB.	26	28	25	21	23	12 ♈	12 ♒	25 ♐	29 ♒
MAR. ...	25	28	24	21	20	2 ♉	10 ♓	26 ♑	15 ♒
APR.	25	27	24	20	20	24	11 ♈	2 ♓	21 ♓
MAY	24	26	24	18	23	14 ♊	10 ♉	8 ♈	21 ♉
JUNE ...	24	26	25	16	28	4 ♋	10 ♊	16 ♉	29 ♊
JULY ...	25	26	27	15	4 ♌	24	9 ♋	22 ♊	20 ♊
AUG. ...	26	26	29	15	11	14 ♌	9 ♌	0 ♌	4 ♌
SEPT. ...	27	26	1 ♌	16	17	4 ♍	8 ♍	8 ♍	0 ♎
OCT. ...	28	27	2	19	23	23	8 ♎	16 ♎	29 ♎
NOV. ...	29	28	3	22	28	13 ♎	8 ♏	24 ♏	20 ♎
DEC. ...	29	29	2	26	1 ♍	2 ♏	9 ♐	2 ♑	7 ♐

1956

MONTH	♇	♆	♅	♄	♃	♂	☉	♀	☿
JAN.	28 ♌	0 ♏	1 ♌	29 ♏	1 ♍	22 ♏	10 ♑	10 ♒	26 ♑
FEB.	28	1	0	2 ♐	28 ♌	12 ♐	12 ♒	18 ♓	1 ♒
MAR. ...	27	0	29 ♋	3	25	2 ♑	11 ♓	23 ♈	16 ♒
APR.	26	0	28	2	22	22	12 ♈	27 ♉	7 ♈
MAY	26	29 ♎	29	1	22	11 ♒	11 ♉	25 ♊	2 ♊
JUNE ...	26	28	0 ♌	29 ♏	25	29	11 ♊	9 ♋	1 ♊
JULY ...	27	28	1	27	29	13 ♓	10 ♋	26 ♊	21 ♊
AUG. ...	28	28	3	26	5 ♍	23	9 ♌	29 ♊	22 ♌
SEPT. ...	29	29	5	27	11	21	9 ♍	23 ♋	6 ♎
OCT. ...	0 ♍	29	6	29	18	13	8 ♎	25 ♌	29 ♍
NOV. ...	0	1 ♏	7	2 ♐	24	16	9 ♏	1 ♎	2 ♏
DEC. ...	0	2	7	6	29	27	9 ♐	7 ♏	20 ♐

1957

MONTH	♇	♆	♅	♄	♃	♂	☉	♀	☿
JAN.	0 ♍	2 ♏	6 ♌	9 ♐	1 ♎	14 ♈	11 ♑	16 ♐	28 ♑
FEB.	0	3	5	12	1	2 ♉	12 ♒	25 ♑	17 ♑
MAR. ...	29 ♌	2	4	14	29 ♍	19	11 ♓	0 ♓	25 ♒
APR.	28	2	3	14	25	9 ♊	12 ♈	8 ♈	23 ♈
MAY	28	1	3	13	22	28	11 ♉	15 ♉	18 ♉
JUNE ...	28	0	4	11	22	18 ♋	11 ♊	23 ♊	16 ♉
JULY ...	29	0	6	9	25	6 ♌	9 ♋	0 ♌	6 ♋
AUG. ...	29	0	8	8	29	26	9 ♌	8 ♍	3 ♍
SEPT. ...	1 ♍	1	9	8	5 ♎	16 ♍	9 ♍	15 ♎	24 ♍
OCT. ...	2	1	11	10	11	5 ♎	8 ♎	20 ♏	22 ♍
NOV. ...	2	3	12	13	18	25	9 ♏	25 ♐	14 ♏
DEC. ...	2	4	12	16	24	15 ♏	9 ♐	26 ♑	29 ♐

1958

MONTH	♇	♆	♅	♄	♃	♂	☉	♀	☿
JAN.	2 ♍	4 ♏	11 ♌	20 ♐	29 ♎	7 ♐	11 ♑	15 ♒	27 ♐
FEB.	1	5	10	23	1 ♏	28	12 ♒	6 ♒	23 ♑
MAR. ...	1	5	8	25	1	19 ♑	11 ♓	3 ♒	9 ♓
APR.	0	4	8	26	29 ♎	10 ♒	11 ♈	25 ♒	0 ♉
MAY	0	3	8	25	25	4 ♓	11 ♉	26 ♓	20 ♈
JUNE ...	0	2	9	23	22	26	11 ♊	0 ♉	22 ♉
JULY ...	0	2	10	21	22	17 ♈	9 ♋	5 ♊	24 ♋
AUG. ...	1	2	12	19	25	7 ♉	9 ♌	13 ♋	5 ♍
SEPT. ...	2	3	14	19	29	23	9 ♍	20 ♌	25 ♌
OCT. ...	3	4	15	20	5 ♏	2 ♊	8 ♎	27 ♍	5 ♎
NOV. ...	4	5	16	23	12	27 ♉	9 ♏	6 ♏	25 ♏
DEC. ...	4	6	17	26	18	18	9 ♐	11 ♐	26 ♐

1959

MONTH	♇	♆	♅	♄	♃	♂	☉	♀	☿
JAN.	4 ♍	7 ♏	16 ♌	0 ♑	24 ♏	17 ♉	10 ♑	23 ♑	18 ♐
FEB.	4	7	15	3	29	26	12 ♒	2 ♓	3 ♒
MAR. ...	3	7	13	6	2 ♐	9 ♊	10 ♓	6 ♈	23 ♓
APR.	2	6	13	7	2	25	11 ♈	14 ♉	6 ♈
MAY	2	5	12	7	29 ♏	12 ♋	10 ♉	20 ♊	14 ♈
JUNE ...	2	5	13	6	26	0 ♌	10 ♊	24 ♋	8 ♊
JULY ...	2	4	14	4	23	18	9 ♋	24 ♌	4 ♌
AUG. ...	3	4	16	1	23	8 ♍	9 ♌	14 ♍	16 ♌
SEPT. ...	4	5	18	0	25	27	8 ♍	8 ♍	23 ♌
OCT. ...	5	6	20	1	29	17 ♎	8 ♎	2 ♍	18 ♎
NOV. ...	6	7	21	3	5 ♐	8 ♏	8 ♏	22 ♍	2 ♐
DEC. ...	6	8	21	6	12	29	9 ♐	23 ♎	24 ♏

1960

MONTH	♇	♆	♅	♄	♃	♂	☉	♀	☿
JAN.	6 ♍	9 ♏	21 ♌	10 ♑	19 ♐	21 ♐	10 ♑	29 ♏	26 ♐
FEB.	6	9	20	13	25	14 ♑	12 ♒	7 ♑	16 ♒
MAR. ...	5	9	18	16	0 ♑	6 ♒	11 ♓	12 ♒	26 ♓
APR.	4	9	17	18	3	29	12 ♈	20 ♓	15 ♓
MAY	4	8	17	18	4	23 ♓	11 ♉	27 ♈	24 ♈
JUNE ...	4	7	18	17	1	16 ♈	11 ♊	5 ♊	28 ♊
JULY ...	4	7	19	15	27 ♐	8 ♉	10 ♋	12 ♋	0 ♌
AUG. ...	5	7	21	13	24	0 ♊	9 ♌	20 ♌	21 ♋
SEPT. ...	6	7	23	12	24	19	9 ♍	28 ♍	10 ♍
OCT. ...	7	8	24	12	26	5 ♋	8 ♎	5 ♏	0 ♏
NOV. ...	8	9	26	13	2 ♑	16	9 ♏	13 ♐	23 ♏
DEC. ...	8	10	26	16	7	17	9 ♐	20 ♑	21 ♏

1961

MONTH	♇	♆	♅	♄	♃	♂	☉	♀	☿
JAN.	8 ♍	11 ♏	26 ♌	20 ♑	14 ♑	8 ♋	11 ♑	26 ♒	8 ♑
FEB.	7	11	24	23	22	0	12 ♒	0 ♈	0 ♓
MAR. ...	7	11	23	26	27	3	11 ♓	23 ♈	26 ♒
APR.	6	11	22	28	3 ♒	14	12 ♈	26 ♈	17 ♓
MAY	6	10	22	0 ♒	6	28	11 ♉	13 ♈	10 ♉
JUNE ...	6	9	22	29 ♑	7	14 ♌	11 ♊	26 ♈	4 ♋
JULY ...	6	9	23	28	5	2 ♍	9 ♋	24 ♉	3 ♋
AUG. ...	7	9	25	26	1	20	9 ♌	28 ♊	25 ♋
SEPT. ...	8	9	27	24	28 ♑	10 ♎	9 ♍	3 ♌	24 ♍
OCT. ...	9	10	29	23	27	0 ♏	8 ♎	10 ♍	4 ♏
NOV. ...	10	11	0 ♍	24	0 ♒	21	9 ♏	18 ♎	22 ♎
DEC. ...	10	12	1	26	4	13 ♐	9 ♐	25 ♏	1 ♐

1962

MONTH	♇	♆	♅	♄	♃	♂	☉	♀	☿
JAN.	10 ♍	13 ♏	0 ♍	0 ♒	11 ♒	6 ♑	11 ♑	5 ♑	20 ♑
FEB.	10	14	29 ♌	3	18	0 ♒	12 ♒	14 ♒	21 ♒
MAR. ...	9	14	28	7	25	22	11 ♓	19 ♓	14 ♒
APR.	8	13	27	9	1 ♓	16 ♓	11 ♈	27 ♈	27 ♓
MAY	7	12	26	11	7	9 ♈	11 ♉	4 ♊	27 ♉
JUNE ...	7	11	27	11	11	3 ♉	11 ♊	11 ♋	19 ♊
JULY ...	8	11	28	10	13	25	9 ♋	17 ♌	17 ♊
AUG. ...	9	11	0 ♍	8	11	16 ♊	9 ♌	22 ♍	12 ♌
SEPT. ...	10	11	2	6	8	6 ♋	9 ♍	25 ♎	4 ♎
OCT. ...	11	12	3	5	4	24	8 ♎	20 ♏	19 ♎
NOV. ...	12	13	5	5	3	10 ♌	9 ♏	26 ♏	24 ♎
DEC. ...	12	14	5	7	5	21	9 ♐	12 ♏	12 ♐

1963

MONTH	♇	♆	♅	♄	♃	♂	☉	♀	☿
JAN.	12 ♍	15 ♏	5 ♍	10 ♒	9 ♓	24 ♌	10 ♑	26 ♏	29 ♑
FEB.	11	16	4	13	15	16	12 ♒	25 ♐	21 ♑
MAR. ...	11	16	3	17	22	7	10 ♓	27 ♑	19 ♒
APR.	10	15	2	20	29	8	11 ♈	3 ♓	12 ♈
MAY	10	14	1	22	6 ♈	16	11 ♉	9 ♈	0 ♊
JUNE ...	10	14	2	23	13	29	10 ♊	16 ♉	21 ♉
JULY ...	10	13	2	22	17	15 ♍	9 ♋	23 ♊	25 ♊
AUG. ...	11	13	4	21	19	3 ♎	9 ♌	1 ♌	27 ♌
SEPT. ...	12	13	6	18	19	23	9 ♍	9 ♍	6 ♎
OCT. ...	13	14	8	17	15	13 ♏	8 ♎	16 ♎	21 ♍
NOV. ...	14	15	9	17	11	5 ♐	8 ♏	25 ♏	6 ♏
DEC. ...	14	16	10	18	10	27	9 ♐	2 ♑	23 ♐

1964

MONTH	♇	♆	♅	♄	♃	♂	☉	♀	☿
JAN.	14 ♍	17 ♏	10 ♍	20 ♒	11 ♈	21 ♑	10 ♑	11 ♒	18 ♑
FEB.	14	18	9	24	15	15 ♒	12 ♒	19 ♓	18 ♑
MAR. ...	13	18	8	27	20	9 ♓	11 ♓	23 ♈	1 ♓
APR.	12	17	7	1 ♓	28	3 ♈	12 ♈	28 ♉	29 ♈
MAY	12	17	6	3	5 ♉	25	11 ♉	25 ♊	4 ♉
JUNE ...	12	16	6	5	12	19 ♉	11 ♊	7 ♋	17 ♉
JULY ...	12	15	7	4	18	10 ♊	10 ♋	23 ♊	14 ♋
AUG. ...	13	15	9	3	23	1 ♋	9 ♌	28 ♊	6 ♍
SEPT. ...	14	15	10	1	26	21	9 ♍	23 ♋	10 ♍
OCT. ...	15	16	12	29 ♒	26	10 ♌	8 ♎	25 ♌	27 ♍
NOV. ...	16	17	14	28	22	27	9 ♏	1 ♎	20 ♏
DEC. ...	16	18	15	29	19	12 ♍	9 ♐	8 ♏	1 ♑

1965

MONTH	♇	♆	♅	♄	♃	♂	☉	♀	☿
JAN.	16 ♍	19 ♏	15 ♍	1 ♓	16 ♉	24 ♍	11 ♑	17 ♐	20 ♐
FEB.	16	20	14	5	17	28	13 ♒	25 ♑	27 ♑
MAR. ...	15	20	13	8	20	21	11 ♓	0 ♓	16 ♓
APR.	15	20	12	12	26	11	12 ♈	9 ♈	23 ♈
MAY	14	19	11	14	2 ♊	9	11 ♉	16 ♉	15 ♈
JUNE ...	14	18	11	17	9	18	11 ♊	24 ♊	29 ♉
JULY ...	14	17	12	17	16	2 ♒	10 ♋	1 ♌	0 ♌
AUG. ...	15	17	13	16	23	18	9 ♌	8 ♍	0 ♍
SEPT. ...	16	18	15	14	28	8 ♏	9 ♍	16 ♎	21 ♌
OCT. ...	17	18	17	12	1 ♋	28	8 ♎	21 ♏	11 ♎
NOV. ...	18	19	18	11	1	21 ♐	9 ♏	25 ♐	29 ♏
DEC. ...	19	20	19	11	29 ♊	13 ♑	9 ♐	25 ♑	14 ♐

1966

MONTH	♇	♆	♅	♄	♃	♂	☉	♀	☿
JAN.	19 ♍	21 ♏	20 ♍	12 ♓	24 ♊	7 ♒	11 ♑	13 ♒	21 ♐
FEB.	18	22	19	15	23	2 ♓	12 ♒	2 ♒	9 ♒
MAR. ...	18	22	18	19	21	24	11 ♓	4 ♒	28 ♓
APR.	17	22	17	23	25	18 ♈	11 ♈	25 ♒	23 ♓
MAY	16	21	16	26	29	10 ♉	11 ♉	26 ♓	17 ♈
JUNE ...	16	20	16	28	6 ♋	3 ♊	11 ♊	1 ♉	17 ♊
JULY ...	17	20	16	0 ♈	12	24	9 ♋	6 ♊	5 ♌
AUG. ...	17	19	18	29 ♓	19	14 ♋	9 ♌	13 ♋	2 ♌
SEPT. ...	18	20	19	28	26	5 ♌	9 ♍	22 ♌	0 ♍
OCT. ...	19	20	21	25	1 ♌	23	8 ♎	28 ♍	24 ♎
NOV. ...	20	21	23	23	4	12 ♍	9 ♏	7 ♏	2 ♐
DEC. ...	21	23	24	23	5	29	9 ♐	14 ♐	19 ♏

1967

MONTH	♇	♆	♅	♄	♃	♂	☉	♀	☿
JAN.	21 ♍	24 ♏	25 ♍	24 ♓	2 ♌	14 ♎	10 ♑	23 ♑	1 ♑
FEB.	20	24	24	26	28 ♋	27	12 ♒	2 ♓	22 ♒
MAR. ...	20	24	23	0 ♈	25	3 ♏	10 ♓	7 ♈	16 ♓
APR.	19	24	22	3	25	29 ♎	11 ♈	15 ♉	13 ♓
MAY	19	23	21	7	27	19	11 ♉	21 ♊	29 ♈
JUNE ...	18	22	20	10	2 ♌	16	10 ♊	25 ♋	1 ♋
JULY ...	19	22	21	12	7	22	9 ♋	24 ♌	21 ♋
AUG. ...	19	22	22	12	14	7 ♏	9 ♌	13 ♍	19 ♋
SEPT. ...	20	22	24	11	21	25	9 ♍	5 ♍	16 ♍
OCT. ...	21	22	26	9	27	14 ♐	8 ♎	0 ♍	2 ♏
NOV. ...	22	23	28	7	2 ♍	7 ♑	8 ♏	22 ♍	9 ♏
DEC. ...	23	25	29	6	5	0 ♒	9 ♐	22 ♎	24 ♏

1968

MONTH	♇	♆	♅	♄	♃	♂	☉	♀	☿
JAN.	23 ♍	26 ♏	29 ♍	6 ♈	6 ♍	24 ♒	10 ♑	29 ♏	12 ♑
FEB.	23	26	29	8	3	18 ♓	12 ♒	7 ♑	0 ♓
MAR. ...	22	27	28	11	0	10 ♈	11 ♓	13 ♒	18 ♒
APR.	21	26	27	15	27 ♌	3 ♉	12 ♈	21 ♓	21 ♓
MAY	21	26	26	19	26	25	11 ♉	28 ♈	19 ♉
JUNE ...	20	25	25	22	28	17 ♊	11 ♊	6 ♊	1 ♋
JULY ...	20	24	26	24	3 ♍	7 ♋	10 ♋	13 ♋	23 ♊
AUG. ...	21	24	27	26	8	27	9 ♌	21 ♌	2 ♌
SEPT. ...	22	24	29	25	15	17 ♌	9 ♍	29 ♍	0 ♎
OCT. ...	23	25	0 ♎	23	21	6 ♍	8 ♎	6 ♏	1 ♏
NOV. ...	24	26	2	21	28	25	9 ♏	14 ♐	21 ♎
DEC. ...	25	27	4	19	3 ♎	13 ♎	9 ♐	20 ♑	7 ♐

1969

MONTH	♇	♆	♅	♄	♃	♂	☉	♀	☿
JAN.	25 ♍	28 ♏	4 ♎	19 ♈	6 ♎	1 ♏	11 ♑	26 ♒	26 ♑
FEB.	25	29	4	20	6	18	13 ♒	0 ♈	6 ♒
MAR. ...	24	29	3	23	4	2 ♐	11 ♓	22 ♈	15 ♒
APR.	23	28	2	26	0	13	12 ♈	23 ♈	4 ♈
MAY	23	28	1	0 ♉	27 ♍	17	11 ♉	11 ♈	1 ♊
JUNE ...	23	27	0	4	26	10	11 ♊	26 ♈	6 ♊
JULY ...	23	26	0	7	28	3	10 ♋	25 ♉	19 ♊
AUG. ...	24	26	1	9	3 ♎	6	9 ♌	28 ♊	20 ♌
SEPT. ...	24	26	3	9	8	19	9 ♍	4 ♌	7 ♎
OCT. ...	25	27	5	7	15	6 ♑	8 ♎	10 ♍	4 ♎
NOV. ...	26	28	7	5	22	28	9 ♏	18 ♎	0 ♏
DEC. ...	26	29	8	3	27	20 ♒	9 ♐	26 ♏	18 ♐

1970

MONTH	♇	♆	♅	♄	♃	♂	☉	♀	☿
JAN.	27 ♍	0 ♐	9 ♎	2 ♉	3 ♏	13 ♓	11 ♑	5 ♑	29 ♑
FEB.	27	1	9	3	6	6 ♈	12 ♒	14 ♒	18 ♑
MAR. ...	27	1	8	5	6	26	11 ♓	19 ♓	23 ♒
APR.	26	1	7	8	4	18 ♉	11 ♈	28 ♈	20 ♈
MAY	25	0	6	12	0	10 ♊	11 ♉	5 ♊	22 ♉
JUNE ...	25	29 ♏	5	16	27 ♎	0 ♋	11 ♊	12 ♋	17 ♉
JULY ...	25	29	5	19	26	19	9 ♋	17 ♌	3 ♋
AUG. ...	26	28	6	22	28	9 ♌	9 ♌	23 ♍	2 ♍
SEPT. ...	26	28	8	23	3 ♏	29	9 ♍	25 ♎	28 ♍
OCT. ...	28	29	9	22	8	18 ♍	8 ♎	19 ♏	21 ♍
NOV. ...	29	0 ♐	11	20	15	8 ♎	9 ♏	23 ♏	12 ♏
DEC. ...	0 ♎	1	13	18	21	27	9 ♐	10 ♏	28 ♐

1971

MONTH	♇	♆	♅	♄	♃	♂	☉	♀	☿
JAN.	0 ♎	2 ♐	14 ♎	16 ♉	28 ♏	16 ♏	10 ♑	25 ♏	2 ♑
FEB.	29 ♍	3	14	16	3 ♐	6 ♐	12 ♒	26 ♐	21 ♑
MAR. ...	28	3	13	17	6	23	10 ♓	27 ♑	6 ♓
APR.	28	3	12	20	7	12 ♑	11 ♈	3 ♓	0 ♉
MAY	27	2	10	24	4	29	11 ♉	10 ♈	23 ♈
JUNE ...	27	1	10	28	1	14 ♒	10 ♊	17 ♉	20 ♉
JULY ...	27	1	10	2 ♊	28 ♏	21	9 ♋	23 ♊	21 ♋
AUG. ...	28	0	10	4	27	19	9 ♌	1 ♌	6 ♍
SEPT. ...	29	1	12	6	29	13	9 ♍	10 ♍	29 ♌
OCT. ...	0 ♎	1	14	6	3 ♐	15	8 ♎	17 ♎	2 ♎
NOV. ...	1	2	16	5	9	27	8 ♏	26 ♏	23 ♏
DEC. ...	2	3	17	3	16	14 ♓	9 ♐	3 ♑	28 ♐

1972

MONTH	♇	♆	♅	♄	♃	♂	☉	♀	☿
JAN.	2 ♎	4 ♐	18 ♎	0 ♊	23 ♐	4 ♈	10 ♑	11 ♒	18 ♐
FEB.	2	5	18	29 ♉	29	24	12 ♒	19 ♓	1 ♒
MAR. ...	2	5	18	0 ♊	4 ♑	13 ♉	11 ♓	24 ♈	23 ♓
APR.	1	5	17	3	8	4 ♊	12 ♈	28 ♉	10 ♈
MAY	0	5	15	6	8	23	11 ♉	25 ♊	15 ♈
JUNE ...	29 ♍	4	15	10	6	13 ♋	11 ♊	5 ♋	7 ♊
JULY ...	29	3	14	14	3	2 ♌	10 ♋	20 ♊	4 ♌
AUG. ...	0 ♎	3	15	17	29 ♐	21	9 ♌	27 ♊	20 ♌
SEPT. ...	1	3	16	19	28	11 ♍	9 ♍	24 ♋	23 ♌
OCT. ...	2	3	18	21	1 ♑	0 ♎	9 ♎	26 ♌	18 ♎
NOV. ...	3	4	20	20	5	20	9 ♏	2 ♎	2 ♐
DEC. ...	4	5	22	18	11	10 ♏	10 ♐	9 ♏	29 ♏

1973

MONTH	♇	♆	♅	♄	♃	♂	☉	♀	☿
JAN.	5 ♎	6 ♐	23 ♎	15 ♊	18 ♑	1 ♐	11 ♑	17 ♐	26 ♐
FEB.	4	7	23	14	25	23	13 ♒	26 ♑	15 ♒
MAR. ...	4	8	23	14	1 ♒	12 ♑	11 ♓	1 ♓	28 ♓
APR.	3	7	21	16	7	4 ♒	12 ♈	10 ♈	16 ♓
MAY	2	7	20	19	11	26	11 ♉	17 ♉	22 ♈
JUNE ...	1	6	19	22	12	17 ♓	11 ♊	25 ♊	25 ♊
JULY ...	1	5	19	26	11	7 ♈	10 ♋	1 ♌	2 ♌
AUG. ...	2	5	20	0 ♋	7	25	9 ♌	9 ♍	23 ♋
SEPT. ...	3	5	21	3	3	7 ♉	9 ♍	16 ♎	8 ♍
OCT. ...	4	5	22	5	2	8	8 ♎	21 ♏	28 ♎
NOV. ...	5	6	25	5	4	28 ♈	9 ♏	26 ♐	27 ♏
DEC. ...	6	7	26	3	8	25	9 ♐	25 ♑	20 ♏

1974

MONTH	♇	♆	♅	♄	♃	♂	☉	♀	☿
JAN.	7 ♎	8 ♐	27 ♎	1 ♋	14 ♒	1 ♉	11 ♑	11 ♒	6 ♑
FEB.	6	9	28	29 ♊	22	16	12 ♒	28 ♑	28 ♒
MAR. ...	6	10	28	28	28	2 ♊	11 ♓	1 ♒	1 ♓
APR.	5	9	26	29	6 ♓	19	11 ♈	25 ♒	15 ♓
MAY	5	9	25	1 ♋	12	7 ♋	11 ♉	26 ♓	7 ♉
JUNE ...	4	8	24	5	16	26	11 ♊	2 ♉	4 ♋
JULY ...	4	7	24	9	18	14 ♌	9 ♋	7 ♊	8 ♋
AUG. ...	4	7	24	13	17	3 ♍	9 ♌	14 ♋	23 ♋
SEPT. ...	5	7	25	16	13	23	9 ♍	22 ♌	22 ♍
OCT. ...	6	7	27	18	10	12 ♎	8 ♎	29 ♍	4 ♏
NOV. ...	7	8	29	19	8	3 ♏	9 ♏	7 ♏	26 ♎
DEC. ...	9	9	1 ♏	18	9	24	9 ♐	15 ♐	29 ♏

1975

MONTH	♇	♆	♅	♄	♃	♂	☉	♀	☿
JAN.	9 ♎	10 ♐	2 ♏	15 ♋	13 ♓	15 ♐	10 ♑	24 ♑	18 ♑
FEB.	9	11	3	14	19	8 ♑	12 ♒	3 ♓	26 ♒
MAR. ...	8	12	2	12	26	29	10 ♓	8 ♈	14 ♒
APR.	8	12	1	12	3 ♈	22 ♒	11 ♈	15 ♉	25 ♓
MAY	7	11	0	14	11	15 ♓	11 ♉	21 ♊	25 ♉
JUNE ...	6	10	29 ♎	17	17	8 ♈	10 ♊	25 ♋	23 ♊
JULY ...	6	10	28	21	22	0 ♉	9 ♋	24 ♌	18 ♊
AUG. ...	7	9	29	25	24	22	9 ♌	11 ♍	9 ♌
SEPT. ...	8	9	0 ♏	28	24	11 ♊	9 ♍	1 ♍	3 ♎
OCT. ...	9	10	1	1 ♌	21	25	8 ♎	29 ♌	23 ♎
NOV. ...	10	10	3	3	17	3 ♋	8 ♏	22 ♍	22 ♎
DEC. ...	11	11	5	3	15	28 ♊	9 ♐	24 ♎	10 ♐

APPENDIX IX

Teachers and Practitioners of Astrology
Members of the American Federation of Astrologers

ARIZONA

MARTIN CUTLER, 8320 E. Edward Ave., Scottsdale, Ariz. 85251
Subjects taught: All phases–esoteric, personal, class, private. Practitioner.

NOLA ELMO (Mrs.), 2215 North 9th St., Phoenix, Ariz. 85006
Subjects taught: Natal, prenatal in medical. Personal instruction. Practitioner.

ARKANSAS

DEAN FOSTER, P. O. Box 306, Lake Hamilton, Ark. 71951
Subject taught: Natal astrology. Class instruction.

CARYL HOLMES (Miss), 1116 Stage Coach Road, Little Rock, Ark. 72204
Practitioner.

GUSSIE H. MOORE (Mrs.), 1305 Greenwood Ave., Hot Springs, Ark. 71901
Subject taught: Natal. Personal instruction. Practitioner.

CALIFORNIA

LUCILLE L. ADAMS (Mrs.), 2919 Keats St., San Diego, Calif. 92106
Subjects taught: Natal, horary. Practitioner.

JOHN LAWSON AHERN, 717 Market St., San Francisco, Calif. 94103
Practitioner.

FRITZI ARMSTRONG (Mrs.), 435 Powell St., San Francisco, Calif. 94102
Subjects taught: All branches. Practitioner.

BETTY ATWATER (Mrs.), 9162 Oasis Ave., Westminster, Calif. 92683
Subjects taught: Natal, horary, class or private instruction. Practitioner.

NORMA BEALL (Mrs.), 1385 Lincoln Ave., Apt. 4, San Jose, Calif. 95125

Subject taught: Natal astrology.

NELL BOTTERILL (Mrs.), Route 3, Box 443, Escondido, Calif. 92025

Subjects taught: Natal, horary, mundane. Personal instruction. Practitioner.

FRANCES M. CONYERS (Mrs.), 8 Lanai St., Santa Ana, Calif. 92704

Subject taught: Natal astrology.

REV. PATRICIA G. CROSSLEY (Mrs.), 2702 Alden Place, Anaheim, Calif. 92806

Subject taught: Natal. Class and private instruction. Practitioner.

LYNN DALTON (Mrs.), 1243-1/2 N. Berenda St., Los Angeles, Calif. 90029

Personal instruction. Practitioner.

DORIS CHASE DOANE (Mrs.), 2337 Coral St., Los Angeles, Calif. 90031

Subjects taught: All branches. Courses by class, private, or mail.

ZIPPORAH DOBYNS (Mrs.), 18046 Pacific Coast Highway, Malibu, Calif. 90265

DARIEN GAILE DUNSHEE (Miss), 3175 Cauby St., Apt. 211, San Diego, Calif. 92110

Subjects taught: Natal, horary. Personal, class, mail instruction. Practitioner.

DAISY M. DUVALL (Miss), 1290 Wynn Road, Pasadena, Calif. 91107

Subjects taught: Natal, horary, rectification. Personal, class instruction.

CECILIA DVORAK (Miss), 1550 N. Genesee Ave., Hollywood, Calif. 90046

Subjects taught: Natal, horary, herbal. Personal, class, mail instruction. Practitioner.

ALYSE FOREY (Miss), 16114 Marlinton Drive, Whittier, Calif. 90604

Subjects taught: All branches. Personal, class instruction. Practitioner.

PATRICIA FRANKLIN (Mrs.), 480 Larch Lane, Santa Cruz, Calif. 95062

Subjects taught: Natal, horary. Personal, class instruction. Practitioner.

ANGELA LOUISE GALLO (Miss), 4805 Supulveda Blvd., #7, Sherman Oaks, Calif. 91403

Subjects taught: Natal, horary, locality. Personal, class instruction. Practitioner.

M. K. GANDHI, c/o Atkinson, 9000 Sunset Blvd., Hollywood, Calif. 90046

NORMA HAMMOND (Mrs.), 4767 Reinhardt Drive, Oakland, Calif. 94619

Subjects taught: All branches. Personal, class instruction. Practitioner.

IVY M. JACOBSON (Mrs.), 6374 N. Encinita Ave., Temple City, Calif. 91780

Subjects taught: Natal, horary, Johndro locality. Personal, class, correspondence course. Practitioner.

MILDRED JOHNSON (Mrs.), 1947 S. Bedford St., Los Angeles, Calif. 90034

Subject taught: Natal. Class, personal instruction. Practitioner.

PAULINE JORDAN (Mrs.), 5132 Lincoln Ave., Los Angeles, Calif. 90042

Practitioner.

LOTA KEMPSTER (Mrs.), 807-A E. Pedregosa St., Santa Barbara, Calif. 93103

Subjects taught: Natal, horary, mundane. Personal, class instruction. Practitioner.

MAYNE KENNY (Mrs.), 511 N. Kenmore Ave., Los Angeles, Calif. 90004

Subjects taught: Natal, Johndro locality. Personal instruction. Practitioner.

ELSIE MARGARET KNAPP (Mrs.), 247 Moreton Bay Lane, Goleta, Calif. 93017

Subjects taught: Horary, natal, mundane. Personal instruction. Practitioner.

MILO KOVAR, 1200 Fulton St., San Francisco, Calif. 94117

Subject taught: Natal. Personal, class instruction. Practitioner.

ELLEN B. LAGERWERFF (Mrs.), 2345 Cornell, Palo Alto, Calif. 94306

Subject taught: Natal. Personal, class instruction. Practitioner.

MARGARET LATVALA (Mrs.), 4437 Alpha St., Los Angeles, Calif. 90032

Subject taught: Natal. Personal and class instruction.

CHRIS LAU (Mrs.), 3585 Trieste Drive, Carlsbad, Calif. 92008

Subject taught: Natal. Personal, class instruction. Practitioner.

VIVIAN LONG (Miss), 456 S. Serrano Ave., Los Angeles, Calif. 90005

MABEL LYTTON (Mrs.), 2511 Kent St., Los Angeles, Calif. 90026

Subject taught: Natal. Personal instruction.

JIM MACPHERSON, 1936 Whitley Ave., Los Angeles, Calif. 90028

Practitioner.

ELAYNE J. MANAGO (Mrs.), 6225 MacArthur Way, Buena Park, Calif. 90620

Subjects taught: Natal, horary. Personal, class instruction. Practitioner.

MICHAEL M. McCARY, 1478 Excelsior Ave., Oakland, Calif. 94602

Subject taught: Natal. Personal instruction. Practitioner.

FRANKA MOORE (Miss), 8254 Oakdale, Canoga Park, Calif. 91306

Subjects taught: Natal, horary. Practitioner.

BURTON W. MORSE, 2141 Seville St., Balboa, Calif. 92661

Subjects taught: Natal, horary. Class instruction. Practitioner.

LOIS C. NAVARRE (Mrs.), 1127 Harding St., Long Beach, Calif. 90805

Practitioner.

D. MILTON NELSON, 403 Jewell St., San Rafael, Calif. 94901

Subjects taught: Natal, sidereal & tropical zodiac. Private instruction. Practitioner.

ANTOINETTE PAUL (Mrs.), 547 Newport Ave., Grover City, Calif. 93433

CAROL PEEL, Twelve Signs Inc., 7948 W. 3rd, Los Angeles, Calif. 90048

Subject taught: Natal. Private, class, mail instruction. Practitioner.

DALE RICHARDSON, 4664 Lilycrest Ave., Los Angeles, Calif. 90029

Practitioner.

MARTIN R. SHAW, 1655 N. Cherokee Ave., Rm. 318, Los Angeles, Calif. 90028

ELEANOR SIMMONS (Mrs.), 96 Gladys Ave., Mt. View, Calif. 94040

PHYLLIS E. STANICK (Mrs.), 748 Orange Ave., Long Beach, Calif. 90813

Subjects taught: Natal, horary.

EDWIN STEINBRECHER, 10604 W. Pico Blvd., Los Angeles, Calif. 90064

Subjects taught: Natal, electional. Private instruction. Practitioner.

W. O. SUCHER, Route 1, Box 1282, Meadow Vista, Calif. 95722

Subjects taught: Heliocentric. Combination of heliocentric and geocentric.

DR. HARLEY ARVIS TALLEY, 1060 Minnesota Ave., San Jose, Calif. 95125

Subjects taught: Natal, horary, lunar & solar returns. Class instruction. Practitioner.

IAN TJADER, 760 Cambridge Ave., Menlo Park, Calif. 94025

Practitioner.

FLORA URQUHART (Mrs.), 1425 Harrison St., Oakland, Calif. 94612

Subject taught: Natal. Personal, class instruction. Practitioner.

OSKAR ZENTARRA, 2928 Ventura Drive, Santa Barbara, Calif. 93105

Subjects taught: Natal, vocational. Personal, class, mail instruction. Practitioner.

COLORADO

DONALD R. OBLAND, 721 S. Corona St., Denver, Colo. 80209

Subjects taught: Natal, medical. Personal, class instruction. Practitioner.

DR. HOWARD W. POLK, D.C., 30 West Nevada Place, Denver, Colo. 80223

Subjects taught: Natal, horary, medical. Personal instruction.

MURIEL THOMAS (Miss), P. O. Box 1080, Pueblo, Colo. 81002

Subject taught: Natal. Class instruction.

WILL C. VORPAGEL, 165 S. Downing St., Denver, Colo. 80209

Subject taught: Natal. Personal, class instruction. Practitioner.

CONNECTICUT

RUTH GERRY (Mrs.), R. F. D. #1, Box 183, North Windham, Conn. 06256

Subjects taught: Natal, horary. Personal, class instruction. Practitioner.

DISTRICT OF COLUMBIA

SVETLANA GODILLO (Mrs.), 1421 Massachusetts Ave. N. W., Wash., D. C. 20005

Practitioner.

CATHARINE T. GRANT (Mrs.), 631 E. Capitol St., Washington, D. C. 20003

Subject taught: Natal. Mail instruction. Practitioner.

BARBARA H. WATTERS (Mrs.), 1331-21st St. N. W., Washington, D. C. 20036

Subject taught: Natal. Personal instruction. Practitioner.

FLORIDA

IRENE T. BEALE (Mrs.), Route 2, Box 350, Winter Haven, Fla. 33882

Subject taught: Natal. Personal, class instruction.

OLGA CHALAIRE (Mrs.), 5841 Coral Way, Miami, Fla. 33155

Subject taught: Natal. Personal, class instruction. Practitioner.

SARA E. COOPER (Mrs.), 7841 1st Ave. South, St. Petersburg, Fla. 33707

Subject taught: Natal. Personal, class instruction.

SYLVIA DELONG (Miss), P. O. Box 125, Cassadaga, Fla. 32706

Subjects taught: Natal, horary. Personal, class instruction. Practitioner.

DORIS HENSEL (Mrs.), 4616 Lumb Avenue, Tampa, Fla. 33609

Subject taught: Natal. Personal, class instruction. Practitioner.

GRACE C. JARRETT (Mrs.), 1624 N.E. 3rd Ave., Fort Lauderdale, Fla. 33305

Subject taught: Natal. Personal, class instruction. Practitioner.

MRS. VERN W. LEE, 2230 Nursery Rd., Apt. 32C, Clearwater, Fla. 33516

Subject taught: Mundane. Personal, class instruction. Practitioner.

M. DEAN SCHUMAKER, 331 Shore Dr., Ellenton, Fla. 33532

Subject taught: Natal. Personal instruction. Vocational, marriage guidance.

GWEN STEIFBOLD (Mrs.), P.O. Box 37, Marco Island, Fla. 33937

Subjects taught: All branches. Practitioner.

GEORGIA WARD (Mrs.), Box 15821, West Palm Beach, Fla. 33406

Practitioner.

GEORGIA

LOUISE C. BROMLEY (Mrs.), 3036 Margaret Mitchell Ct., N.W., Atlanta, Ga. 30327

Subject taught: Natal. Personal, class instruction.

ILLINOIS

NORMAN N. ARENS, 300 N. State St., Apt. 4934, Chicago, Ill. 60610

Subject taught: Natal. Personal instruction. Practitioner.

THELMA PATRICK DAVIS (Mrs.), 227 E. High Point Rd., Peoria, Ill. 61614

Subject taught: Natal. Personal, class instruction. Practitioner.

CHARLES E. GOLDSMITH, Box 7383, Main Post Office, Chicago, Ill. 60680

Practitioner.

LILY IRELAND (Miss), 505 N. Lake Shore Dr., Apt. 5301, Chicago, Ill. 60611

Subject taught: Natal. Personal, class instruction.

BEATA URBAN KNIES (Mrs.), 2940 N. Harlem Ave., Elmwood Park, Ill. 60635

Subjects taught: Natal, horary. Personal, class, mail instruction. Practitioner.

MARY SEWARD (Mrs.), 637 Groveland Park, Chicago, Ill. 60616

Subjects taught: Natal, horary. Personal instruction. Practitioner.

INDIANA

GEORGE EDWARD HARDY, 719 W. 9th, Anderson, Ind. 46016
Subject taught. Natal. Practitioner.

CAROL V. WILSON (Mrs.), 3042 Lake Shore Dr., Indianapolis, Ind. 46205
Subjects taught: Natal, horary, uranian, radix system, esoteric. Class and private instruction. Practitioner.

KANSAS

MILDRED SCHULER (Miss), 650 N. Dellrose, Wichita, Kansas 67208
Subjects taught: Mundane, horary, natal. Class instruction.

LOUISIANA

EVNA EDMUNDSON (Mrs.), 1021 Royal St., New Orleans, La. 70116
Subject taught: Natal, as a philosophy. Class and private instruction.

EDNA G. ROWLAND (Mrs.), 2150 Beech St., Baton Rouge, La. 70805
Practitioner.

MASSACHUSETTS

FREDERICK P. CHURCH, 220 Summer St., Malden, Mass. 02148
Subject taught. Natal. Personal class instruction.

CLARA V. COTTA (Mrs.), 30 Canterbury Road, Newton Highlands, Mass. 02161
Subject taught: Natal. Personal instruction. Practitioner.

HARRY F. DARLING, M.D., Box L, Buzzards Bay, Mass. 02532
Subjects taught: Advanced psychiatric, sociological, criminological. Personal, mail instruction. Practitioner.

JOAN HARMON (Mrs.), Lakeside Park, East Falmouth, Mass. 02536
Subjects taught: Natal, rectification, horary, comparisons, astrodiagnosis. Practitioner.

ISABEL M. HICKEY (Mrs.), 95 St. Botolph St., 2nd fl., Boston, Mass. 02116

Subjects taught: Natal, esoteric. Class, personal instruction. Practitioner.

MURIEL D. JAY (Mrs.), 17 Brattle St., Apt. 9, Arlington, Mass. 02174

Subjects taught: Natal, horary, mundane. Personal, class instruction. Practitioner.

MILDRED E. KETTELL (Mrs.), 97 Centre St., Brookline, Mass. 02146

Practitioner.

LEONORA K. LUXTON (Mrs.), 19 Old Stage Road, Chelmsford, Mass. 01824

Subjects taught: Natal, mundane. Personal, class instruction. Practitioner.

DOROTHEA LYNDE (Mrs.), 51 Belle Ave., West Roxbury, Mass. 02132

Subject taught: Natal. Private, class instruction. Practitioner.

FRANCES SAKOIAN (Mrs.), 1 Monadnock Road, Arlington, Mass. 02174

Subject taught: Natal. Personal, class instruction. Practitioner.

LYNNE L. SCANNELL (Mrs.), Box 1336, Norton, Mass. 02766

Practitioner.

OSCAR WEBER, 58 Birchcroft Road, Canton, Mass. 02021

Subjects taught: Natal, horary, potentialities. Practitioner.

MICHIGAN

VELMA S. BENHAM (Mrs.), 5237 Commonwealth, Detroit, Mich. 48208

Subjects taught: All branches. Personal, class instruction. Practitioner.

JAMES HARRIS, 5356 Linsdale Ave., Detroit, Mich. 48204

Subjects taught: Natal, horary. Personal, class, mail instruction. Practitioner.

H. DOUGLAS MILLER, 2414 Liddesdale, Detroit, Mich. 48217

Subject taught: Natal. Personal, class instruction. Practitioner.

JEANNETTE R. SNYDER (Mrs.), 416 W. Hillsdale St., Lansing, Mich. 48933

Subjects taught: Natal, mundane. Personal, class instruction. Practitioner.

MINNESOTA

GARY DUNCAN, 375 Sharon Lane, White Bear Lake, Minn. 55110

Subjects taught: Natal; solar, lunar returns; sidereal techniques. Personal, mail instruction. Practitioner.

MISSOURI

MARJORIE J. GROSSMAN (Mrs.), 9 Quailways Dr., Creve Coeur, Mo. 63141

Subject taught: Psychological. Class instruction.

PAULINE S. JOHNSON (Mrs.), 2239 E. 70th St., Kansas City, Mo. 64132

Subjects taught: Natal, horary. Class, private instruction. Practitioner.

FAYE KERSHAW (Mrs.), 4970 Eichelberger, St. Louis, Mo. 63109

Subjects taught: Natal, prenatal epoch, key cycle. Practitioner.

NEBRASKA

ELIZABETH MARIE GLACKIN (Mrs.), 2218 S. 43rd St., Omaha, Neb. 68105

Practitioner.

NEW HAMPSHIRE

MRS. JEROLD D. BAMFORD, Middle Hancock Road, Peterborough, N. H. 03458

Subjects taught: Natal, horary. Personal, class, mail instruction. Practitioner.

NEW JERSEY

TERISA GOULART (Mrs.), 370 S. Orange Ave., Newark, N. J. 07103

Subjects taught: Natal, horary. Personal instruction. Practitioner.

GEORGE J. McCORMACK, 39-25 Wenonah Drive, Fair Lawn, N. J. 07410

Subject taught: Astro-Meteorology *only,* a specialization.

EUGENE A. MOORE, 220 Swedesboro Road, Gibbstown, N. J. 08027

Subject taught: Natal. Class instruction. Practitioner.

SYLVIA SHERMAN (Mrs.), 21 Mellon Ave., West Orange, N. J. 07052

Subject taught: Natal. Personal, class instruction. Practitioner.

JULIENNE STURM (Mrs.), International Society for Astrological Research, Montclair, N. J.

Subjects taught: Natal, horary, esoteric. Personal, class instruction. Practitioner.

STELLA VOORHEES (Mrs.), 26 Woodcrest Ave., Short Hills, N. J. 07078

Subjects taught: Astro-psychology, philosophy. Personal, class instruction.

NEW MEXICO

STEPHEN H. FIELD, 504 San Clemente, N. W., Albuquerque, N. M. 87107

Subject taught: Natal. Personal instruction. Practitioner.

NEW YORK

VIRGINIA ANDERSON (Mrs.), 166 Hawthorne Ave., Yonkers, N. Y. 10705

Subjects taught: Natal, horary. Personal, class instruction. Practitioner.

CELESTINE M. BIDDLE (Mrs.), 6925 Maple Dr., North Tonawanda, N. Y. 14120

Subjects taught: Natal, horary, Bible. Private, class instruction. Practitioner.

CLIFFORD W. CHEASLEY, 107 W. Centennial Ave., Long Island, N. Y. 11575

Subjects taught: Natal, Astro-numerology. Personal, class, mail instruction. Practitioner.

KEITH CLAYTON, 16 West 46th St., Rm. 1208, New York, N. Y. 10036

Subjects taught: All branches. Personal, class instruction. Practitioner.

LLOYD COPE, 325 East 80th St., Apt. 3G, New York, N. Y. 10021

Subject taught: Natal. Personal, class instruction. Practitioner.

LIONEL E. I. DAY, 206 Smith Ave., Holbrook, N. Y. 11741

Subjects taught: Natal, mundane. Personal, class instruction. Practitioner.

FREDA FLOOD (Mrs.), 2698 Bailey Ave., Bronx, New York 10463

Subject taught: Natal. Personal, class instruction. Practitioner.

DORIS KAYE MACALDUFF (Miss), 22 East 38th St., New York, N. Y. 10016

Subject taught: Natal. Class instruction. Practitioner.

CAROLINE MASTANDREA (Mrs.), 58-03 211th St., Bayside, N. Y. 11364

Practitioner.

STACIA MASZE (Mrs.), 141-17 79th Ave., Flushing, N. Y. 11367

Subjects taught: Natal, horary. Personal, class instruction. Practitioner.

LYNNE PALMER (Miss), 500 E. 77th St., Apt. 2723, New York, N. Y. 10021

Subject taught: Natal. Class instruction. Practitioner.

OLIVE ADELE PRYOR (Miss), 33-44 149th Place, Flushing, N. Y. 11354

Subject taught: Natal. Personal and class instruction.

ELIZABETH A. SACHS (Mrs.), 91-60 193rd St., Apt. 3L, Hollis, N. Y. 11423

Subject taught: Natal. Practitioner.

OHIO

CLARA M. DARR (Mrs.), 2527 Broadway, Toledo, Ohio 43609

Subjects taught: All branches. Class, personal instruction. Practitioner.

PAULINE H. EVANS (Mrs.), 2801 Erie Ave., Cincinnati, Ohio 45208

Subject taught: Natal. Personal, class instruction. Practitioner.

MARGARET W. FISHER (Mrs.), Box 15684, Civic Center Sta., Columbus, Ohio 43215

Subjects taught: All branches. Class instruction. Practitioner.

CATHERINE G. HILL (Mrs.), 442 Liberty St., Painesville, Ohio 44077

Subject taught: Natal. Personal, class instruction.

DR. REGINA E. LORR, D.C., 14940 Euclid Ave., East Cleveland, Ohio 44112
Subject taught: Natal. Personal, class instruction. Practitioner.
ROBERT A. WONDER, Route #3, Box 93, Tiffin, Ohio 44883
Subject taught: Natal. Class instruction.

OKLAHOMA

LURENE GRIFFITH (Mrs.), 3603 East 36th, Tulsa, Okla. 74135
Subject taught: Natal. Personal, class instruction. Practitioner.
DAVID LEE GRISHAM, 131 N. Louisville, Tulsa, Okla. 74115
Subjects taught: Natal, horary. Personal, class instruction. Practitioner.
IDA K. JOHNSTON (Mrs.), 712 West 71st St., Tulsa, Okla. 74132
Subject taught: Natal. Personal, class instruction. Practitioner.

OREGON

HELEN H. McFARLAND (Mrs.), 405 Fine Arts Bldg., 1017 S. W. Morrison St., Portland, Ore. 97205
Subject taught: Natal. Personal instruction. Practitioner.

PENNSYLVANIA

WILMA H. BAIRD (Mrs.), 1824-72nd Ave., Philadelphia, Pa. 19126
Subjects taught: Natal, horary. Class, personal instruction.
AGNES V. BREYER (Mrs.), 2710 Holme Ave., Philadelphia, Pa. 19152
Practitioner.
ELEANOR DE VORE (Mrs.), 1221 Wagner Ave., Philadelphia, Pa. 19141
Subject taught: Natal. Personal, class instruction. Practitioner.
HARRIET W. FRIEDLANDER (Mrs.), P. O. Box 8241, Pittsburgh, Pa. 15217
Subject taught: Natal. Personal, class instruction. Practitioner.
RUTH L. SAMPTER (Mrs.), 1030 E. Lancaster Ave., The Chatwynd Apts., #910, Rosemont, Pa. 19010
Practitioner.

TEXAS

MELBA BURROUGHS (Mrs.), 3122 Pecan Lane, Garland (Dallas), Tex. 75040

Subject taught: Natal. Personal, class instruction. Practitioner.

RAUL DAVILA, JR., 110 Howerton Drive, San Antonio, Tex. 78223

Subject taught: Natal. Personal, mail instruction. Practitioner.

DAN R. FRY, 1204 South Brighton, Dallas, Tex. 75208

Subject taught: Natal. Personal, class instruction. Practitioner.

BETTY SUE GREEN (Mrs.), 6131 Belcrest, Houston, Tex. 77033

Practitioner. Rectification.

BEATRICE J. JAMESON (Miss), P. O. Box 595, San Antonio, Tex. 78206

Subject taught: Natal. Private, class, mail instruction. Practitioner.

WANDA J. SCHENCK (Mrs.), 2615 Abrams Road, Dallas, Tex. 75214

Subject taught: Natal. Personal, class instruction. Practitioner.

A. LEROI SIMMONS, P. O. Box 18623, Dallas, Tex. 75218

Subject taught: Natal. Personal, class instruction. Practitioner.

VIRGINIA

ROBERTA MUELLER (Mrs.), P. O. Box 891, Virginia Beach, Va. 23451

Practitioner.

WASHINGTON

HELENE S. BIRONDO (Miss), P. O. Box 82, Anacortes, Wash. 98221

Subject taught: Natal. Personal, mail instruction. Practitioner.

AMY PAULINE BOHN (Mrs.), 13111 42nd Ave. S., Seattle, Wash. 98168

Subject taught: Natal. Personal, class instruction. Practitioner.

JACQUELINE GRAY GOULD (Mrs.), 1218 Terry Ave., Seattle, Wash. 98101

Subject taught: Natal. Personal, class instruction.

EDNA KUMMER HEACOCK (Mrs.), 8633 31st Ave. S. W., Seattle, Wash. 98126
Subject taught: Private instruction.

WISCONSIN

LOUISE S. IVEY (Miss), 2315 N. Grant Blvd., Milwaukee, Wis. 53210
Subject taught: Natal. Personal, class instruction.

FLORENCE F. LYNN (Mrs.), 1611 College Ave., Racine, Wis. 53403
Subjects taught: Natal, esoteric. Personal, class instruction. Practitioner.

AUSTRALIA

DORIS GREAVES (Mrs.), P. O. Box 32, Chadstone 3148, Melbourne, Victoria
Subjects taught: Natal, mundane. Personal, class instruction. Practitioner.

IVON HYDE, 31 Croydon Road, Surrey Hills, Victoria 3127
Practitioner.

ALLAN L. JOHNSON, Box 2184 G.P.O., Sydney, N.S.W.
Subject taught: Natal. Personal, class instruction. Practitioner.

CANADA

T. BLAIR BIRMINGHAM, 129 Kenilworth Ave., Toronto 8, Ontario
Subjects taught: Natal, horary, mundane. Personal instruction. Practitioner.

FLORENCE L. FRASER (Mrs.), 4987 Earles St., Vancouver 16, B. C.
Subjects taught: Natal, horary. Private, class, mail instruction. Practitioner.

H. S. D. STARNAMAN (Mrs.), 337 Bain Ave., Toronto 6, Ontario
Subjects taught: All branches. Personal, class, mail instruction.

PARIS–BRUSSELS–SWITZERLAND

GERMAINE HOLLEY (Mme.), 127 Rue du Ranelagh, Paris 16, France

Subject taught: Natal. Personal and class instruction. Conducts classes in Paris: Centre d'Etudes d'Astrologie Experimentale (above address), and in Brussels and Switzerland.

WEST GERMANY

ALEX WISE, c/o European Life, 64 Hauptstrasse, Heidelberg, West Germany

Subjects taught: Natal, horary, mundane. Personal instruction. Practitioner.

JOCHEN VICK, 6531 Laubenheim, 37 Hauptstrasse, West Germany

Subjects taught: Natal, mundane. Personal and class instruction.

INDIA

G. SRI RAMA MURTHI, Director Bharet Astrology Institute, Srikakulam P. O., Andhra Pradesh

Subjects taught: Hindu, horary, predictive astrology; Parasara, Jaimini, and Tajick systems. Class, private, mail instruction. Practitioner.

JAPAN

YOUKO SHIOJIMA, 400 Hiyoshicho, Kohoku-Ku, Yokohama

Subjects taught: Natal, mundane, horary. Personal, mail instruction. Practitioner.

MEMBERS OF PROFESSIONAL ASTROLOGERS, INCORPORATED

John Lawson Ahern
717 Market St., Rm. 504
San Francisco, Calif. 94103

Rita Anton
P.O. Box 3145
Ventura, Calif. 93003

Sara Braun
5909 Monte Vista St.
Los Angeles, Calif. 90042

Herr Alan Brown
805 Freising
Rotkreuz Str. 38, Germany

Earnest W. Bullock
1434 W. "B" St.
Ontario, Calif. 91762

Patricia Cernuska
13802 McNab Ave.
Bellflower, Calif. 90706

Marguerite W. Cole
P.O. Box 544
Cambria, Calif. 93428

John E. Daniel
6217 Westbrook Dr.
Citrus Heights, Calif. 95610

Doris Chase Doane
P.O. Box 60903
Los Angeles, Calif. 90660

Mrs. Cecilia Dvorak
1550 N. Genesee Ave.
Los Angeles, Calif. 90046

Peggy Fatemi
14920 Genoa St.
San Fernando, Calif. 91342

Angela L. Gallo
4805 Sepulveda Blvd. #7
Sherman Oaks, Calif. 91403

Jeannette Y. Glenn
850 W. Center St.
#4 Villa Fino Apts.
Costa Mesa, Calif. 92626

Rosalao L. Hall
2756 E. Sierra Dr.
Westlake Village Ct., Calif. 91361

Barbara Harkins
5847 McDonie Ave.
Woodland Hills, Calif. 91364

Wanda Heller
8770 Shoreham Dr.
Los Angeles, Calif. 90069

Patricia M. Humphreys
13181 W. Lampson Ave. #111
Orange, Calif. 92668

Ellen B. Lagerwerff
2345 Cornell
Palo Alto, Calif. 94306

Tish LeRoy
417 N. Avon St.
Burbank, Calif. 91505

Mrs. Ursula Lewis
13350 Reedley St.
Van Nuys, Calif. 91402

Dr. Vivian Long
456 S. Serrano
Los Angeles, Calif. 90005

Elayne J. Manago
6225 MacArthur Way
Buena Park, Calif. 90620

Floyd F. Matthieson
P.O. Box 1023D
Glendale, Calif. 91209

Clinton Miller
1271 4th Ave.
San Francisco, Calif. 94122

Garet Rogers Miller
2569 Creston Dr. #23
Hollywood, Calif. 90028

Sabrinah Millstein
1124 Douglass Dr.
Pomona, Calif. 91766

Vicky Monbarren
14033 Sherman Way, Apt. 12
Van Nuys, Calif. 91406

Robert C. Mulkins
P.O. Box 1119
Atascadero, Calif. 93422

Angela Oddone
10254 Roscoe Blvd.
Sun Valley, Calif. 91352

Lynne Palmer
500 E. 77th St., Apt. 2723
New York, N.Y. 10021

Susan Peters
3071 Quail Run Road
Los Alamitos, Calif. 90720

Peggy Pfening
4700 Katherine Ave.
Sherman Oaks, Calif. 91403

Mrs. Alice Reichard
13059 Dickens St.
North Hollywood, Calif. 91604

Eileen Rinker
12015 King St.
North Hollywood, Calif. 91607

Lois M. Rodden
250 S. St. Andrews Pl.
Los Angeles, Calif. 90004

Mary Sample
3416 Manning Ave.
Los Angeles, Calif. 90064

Margaret Shrode
3649 Emerald St., #209
Torrance, Calif. 90503

Eleanor Simmons
96 Gladys Ave.
Mt. View, Calif. 94040

Phyllis E. Stanick
748 Orange Ave.
Long Beach, Calif. 90813

Mrs. Jeanne Stanton
27028 Silver Moon Lane
Palos Verdes Penn, Calif. 90274

Ralph Sterling
P.O. Box 85328
Los Angeles, Calif. 90072

Myra V. Terry
15303 Valley Vista, Apt. B
Sherman Oaks, Calif. 91403

Charles V. Tirone
14600 Saticoy St.
Van Nuys, Calif. 91405

Mrs. Michele Urban
5393 Fairview Blvd.
Los Angeles, Calif. 90056

Katalin B. Williams
328 Calle Mayor
Redondo Beach, Calif. 90277

Alice Zessin
2825 La Cuesta Dr.
Los Angeles, Calif. 90046

APPENDIX X

Glossary of Common Astrological Terms

Affliction–An adverse aspect (usually a square or opposition, sometimes a conjunction) between planets or planets and house cusps.

Angular–The angular first, fourth, seventh, tenth houses; planets have stronger influence in these houses.

Ascendant–The rising sign on the cusp of the first house, together with its degree; reflects the personality or outward approach of the individual.

Aspect–Angled degrees between planets and/or house cusps, which form some meaningful combination.

Benefics–Positive planets, Jupiter and Venus, sometimes Mercury, Mars and Uranus, which are ambivalent.

Cadent Houses–Normally weaker houses–the third, sixth, ninth, and twelfth, where planets have less influence than in the angular houses, or the succedent houses of the chart–second, fifth, eighth and eleventh–which immediately precede the cadent houses.

Cardinal Signs–The signs of the changing seasons, Aries, Cancer, Libra and Capricorn; they reflect considerable activity, with recognition.

Chart–The 12-sign, 360-degree zodiac, the individual's horoscope.

Common–or Mutable–signs–Gemini, Virgo, Sagittarius, Pisces. Versatile, adaptable, they blend and bend.

Conjunction–When planets occupy the same sign, or are in close orb or degree with each other or a house cusp.

Cusp–The beginning of a house position in the chart. Planets near the cusp have greater influence, and with the planet ruling the sign on the cusp, are considered rulers of that house.

Degree–There are 360 degrees in each chart, and each degree consists of 60 minutes, and each minute 60 seconds of zodiacal longitude. The closer the degree between planets, such as a precise 180-degree opposition or 90-degree square, the stronger the aspect.

Descendant–The seventh house cusp, opposing the ascendant.

Detriment–In the sign opposite the one it rules, as Mars in Libra, a planet is in its worst position, in its detriment.

Earthy triplicity—Taurus, Virgo, Capricorn, the down-to-earth signs, favorably trined.

Ecliptic—The apparent path of the Sun around the earth's orbit, reflected in its cycle through the twelve signs of the zodiac each year.

Elevated—A planet is said to be elevated near the Midheaven of the chart, in the tenth house, having its greatest influence there, especially when rising in the chart.

Exalted—By tradition, planets are considered at their best, or exalted, in certain signs—Moon in Taurus, Mars in Capricorn, and Venus in Pisces, for instance. A planet is doubly exalted in some cases, where, as Uranus in Aquarius, it also is the ruler of the sign.

Ephemeris—A book or almanac listing the planets' places for any year.

Fall—A planet is in its fall—not at its best—in the sign opposite its exalted sign.

Fiery triplicity—Aries, Leo, Sagittarius, the fiery, up-and-at-'em trio.

Fixed Signs—Taurus, Leo, Scorpio, Aquarius; determined, unyielding, they get there in the end.

Fixed Stars—Such as Caput Algol; they do not cross the ecliptic as the planets do, but are supposedly most influential or prominent when positioned near the ecliptic.

Grand Trine—A highly favorable aspect, in which three planets are 120 degrees from each other, forming a grand triangle.

Horary—A chart, set up at the time a question is asked, in which the question becomes the newborn infant and the time of the question its birth hour.

Houses—The twelve 30-degree segments of the astrological chart, which have their own qualities and influences (as given elsewhere in Appendix).

Lunar Low—The point in the horoscope where the transiting moon is opposed at 180 degrees to the natal sun. A low point emotionally for the individual.

Lunar return—The transiting Moon's return to its own place in the natal chart, triggering events in accordance with the aspects it forms in the chart.

Malefics—The bad guys in the zodiac—Mars, Saturn and Uranus, which, like Pluto and Neptune, can also be good guys when well-aspected or their challenge met by the individual.

Masculine signs–Aries, Gemini, Leo, Libra, Sagittarius, Aquarius; (feminine: Taurus, Cancer, Virgo, Scorpio, Capricorn, Pisces).

Midheaven–Important as the barometer of activity in a chart, the tenth house cusp, the meridian, noon point, or Medium Coeli (M.C.).

Natal Chart–The horoscope, drawn from the moment of birth, with planets distributed through the chart as they were at birth.

North Node–Generally, the ascending node of the Moon, at a point where it crosses from south latitude into north latitude; usually a good or bountiful influence, when favorably aspected; the South Node, descending, is usually considered ominous in aspect, indicating loss, but this is not necessarily so.

Opposition–An adverse aspect, when planets are in opposing houses, some 180 degrees apart (as given elsewhere in Appendix).

Orb–The distance in degrees within which a planetary aspect is effective; in progressed charts only one-degree orbs are considered effective; in natal charts the Sun may operate within an orb of thirteen, even sixteen degrees, if it is in aspect with another powerful planet, such as Uranus or Jupiter.

Part of Fortune–A calculated point in the zodiac, which is located by adding the Sign, degree and minute of the Moon to that of the Ascendant, and then subtracting the Sign, degree and minute of the Sun. Aries has the sign value of 0, Taurus 1, Gemini 2, etc. This Arabian part enhances the house in which it is located at birth. Symbolized by ⊕.

Planets–Eight planets, together with the two lights, the Sun and Moon, which are considered as planets, form the aspects which the chart is all about. The planets (discussed elsewhere in Appendix) are: Jupiter, Saturn, Uranus, Neptune, Pluto, Mars, Venus, Mercury.

Precession–The precession of the equinoxes, which takes the constellations analogous to the 12 signs through a complete cycle of the zodiac about every 26,000 years. In its apparent backward motion through the zodiac, it traverses each sign or constellation point every 2,160 years, passing at about this time from Pisces to Aquarius, and commencing the Aquarian Age.

Progression–Astrologers use the formula of a day for a year to advance the natal chart into the future, and make deductions from the new positions of the planets in the progressed chart (Marilyn Monroe's chart progressed elsewhere in Appendix).

Prominent–A planet is prominent in a strong angular house (first, fourth, seventh or tenth) or when strongly aspected to other planets, the ascendant, or the Midheaven.

Rectification–Correcting the given birth time, which may be erroneous, by correlating certain striking events, such as the death of the father or a first marriage, with planetary aspects that should govern these events.

Retrograde–An apparent backward motion of the planets, which gives them a negative influence in a chart. Only the Sun and Moon are never retrograde.

Rising Sign–The Ascendant.

Ruler–Planets are said to rule certain signs, such as the Sun ruling Leo, and Venus ruling Taurus, with the ruler having increased influence in its own sign.

Sextile–A favorable 60-degree aspect between planets or a planet, ascendant, Midheaven or house cusp; signifies benefit or opportunity.

Solar Chart–When the exact hour of birth is not available, but the date is known, the ascendant becomes the degree the day is into the Sun sign, and the Sun sign becomes the first house.

Square–A 90-degree aspect, which unlike the sextile contributes an adverse influence, can be a stumbling block or obstacle, or a lesson-learner through challenging stimulation.

Succedent–Those houses between the angular and the cadent–the second, fifth, eighth and eleventh–relate to the fixed signs in quality.

Table of Houses–Tables showing the signs and degrees to be placed on house cusps when mapping a chart, taking in the place of birth and so-called true or sidereal time.

Transit–The actual passage of a planet by position through the individual horoscope, having a special impact as it aspects natal house cusps and planets, and often triggering events.

Trine–Perhaps the most favorable aspect: planets or house cusps at, or close to, a 120-degree angle.

T-Square–A double square in the chart, taking the shape of a T, involving three rather than two aspects, with top lateral portion of the T bisecting the 360-degree circle. If Aries is on the left point of the horizontal line, Libra would be the opposite point, and Cancer, squaring both, would be at the bottom of the T, also squaring whatever planets were in Aries and Libra. It is a doubly difficult aspect, but does compel the native–the subject of the chart–to get up a good head of steam in his fight to overcome this aspect. An energizer. A grand square has two T-squares backed up on one another, and forces the individual to great efforts to survive. Many great men have had this aspect, achieving out of adversity.

Watery Triplicity–Cancer, Scorpio, Pisces–psychic, impressionable, moody, sometimes spiritual.

Zodiac–The twelve signs of the horoscope, as they form a 360-degree circle, with twelve equal houses of 30 degrees each.